Quest for Performance

The Evolution of Modern Aircraft

NASA SP–468

Quest for Performance

The Evolution of Modern Aircraft

Laurence K. Loftin, Jr.

NASA Scientific and Technical Information Branch   1985
National Aeronautics and Space Administration
Washington, DC

On the cover (left to right): British Sopwith F.1 Camel fighter (photo by William T. Larkins, courtesy of American Aviation Historical Society); North American P-51D fighter (photo by Peter C. Boisseau); North American XB-70A supersonic bomber (photo courtesy of North American Aviation)

Loftin, Laurence K.
    Quest for performance.
    (NASA SP ; 468)
    Includes bibliographies and index.
    1. Airplanes—History. I. United States. National Aeronautics and Space Administration. II. Title. III. Series.
    TL670.3 L63   1985   629.133'34'09   83–17262

For sale by the Superintendent of Documents, U.S. Government Printing Office
Washington, D.C. 20402

Contents

Preface

More than 75 years have passed since the Wright brothers' historic first flight of a powered, heavier-than-air aircraft at Kitty Hawk, North Carolina, on December 17, 1903. During this relatively brief period, the airplane has developed from a useless freak to a highly significant force in modern society. The transformation of the airplane during this period must be ranked as one of the great engineering accomplishments of all time. The magnitude of the achievement is emphasized by the nature of the vehicle and the rigorous requirements for precise design of every element. In no other type of machine, with the possible exception of space vehicles, do the often conflicting requirements of performance, safety, reliability, and economic viability place such a high premium on detailed design optimization, based on quantitative data and analysis.

The evolution of the airplane since 1903 rests on technological advances in such fields as aerodynamics, stability and control, propulsion systems, structures, materials, internal systems, and manufacturing technology. Advancements in all these areas have been made possible by millions of man-hours spent by highly motivated people. Private individuals, research laboratories operated by civil and military elements of the government, and universities—as well as industrial design, research, engineering, and manufacturing teams—have all contributed to the development of the airplane. The evolution of the modern airplane has been characterized by a series of technological levels, or plateaus, that extend over a period of years. Each level has been exemplified by an aircraft configuration type that is gradually improved by a series of relatively small refinements, without any major conceptual change. Under the stimulus of some form of competition, new technology in a number of disciplines has occasionally been combined synergistically in a new design to produce an aircraft of a new and higher level of technology. The Douglas DC–3 transport is a good example of this type of advancement. In a few rare instances, a revolutionary breakthrough or new concept has dramatically altered the course of aeronautical development and established a new and higher technical plateau. The advent of the jet engine and the concept of the swept wing for high-speed flight fall into this category.

Although some further refinement was possible, the technology of the propeller-driven airplane equipped with a reciprocating engine was, at the end of World War II, on a plateau with little expectation of major improvement. In the face of this depressing prospect, aircraft equipped with a new and revolutionary type of propulsion system, the jet engine, appeared on the scene in the closing months of the war. This innovative propulsion system introduced an entirely new level of technology in aircraft design. The subsequent advances in aircraft performance and capability made possible by the turbine engine have perhaps been even more spectacular than those characterized by the first 40 years of powered flight. The initial applications of jet propulsion were to military aircraft of various types. Indeed, the military airplane and the concepts of its various missions went through a complete metamorphosis as a result of this new type of propulsion system. The first jet-powered transport entered commercial operations in 1952. This event heralded the beginning of a revolution in domestic and international air transportation that has accompanied the development and refinement of this type of transport. The entire concept of common-carrier transportation has been radically altered by the jet transport.

This volume traces the technical development of the airplane from a curiosity at the beginning of World War I to the highly useful machine of today. Included are significant aircraft that incorporated important technical innovations and served to shape the future course of aeronautical development, as well as aircraft that represented the state of the art of aeronautical technology in a particular time frame or that were very popular and produced in great numbers. In order to reduce the scope of material under consideration, primary emphasis has been placed on aircraft originating in the United States (except in chapter 2). No adverse reflection on the quality of the many fine foreign designs developed over the years is intended by their exclusion. The aircraft described certainly do not include all the significant types designed in the time period 1914–80, but they do illustrate the primary features of the technical evolution of the airplane. If the reader's favorite aircraft is not included, the reference lists at the end of this volume include publications that catalog data and photographs for a wide variety of aircraft.

The discussion is related primarily to aircraft configuration evolution and associated aerodynamic characteristics and, to a lesser extent, to developments in aircraft construction and propulsion. The book is divided into two parts. Part I deals with the development of propeller-driven aircraft, and part II is devoted to subsonic jet-powered aircraft designed for civil and military use. Some of the jet aircraft described are capable of brief excursions into the realm of supersonic flight; however, long-range supersonic-cruising aircraft are an entirely different class of vehicle and are not discussed in the present volume.

The material is presented in a manner designed to appeal to the nontechnical reader who is interested in the evolution of the airplane, as well as to students of aeronautical engineering or others with an aeronautical background. The use of engineering terminology has been kept at a minimum, consistent with accuracy and the intent of the text; where unavoidable, suitable physical explanations have been included.

Acknowledgments

The author wishes to express his appreciation for the assistance provided by many present and former staff members of the NASA Langley Research Center in the preparation of this publication. In particular, the helpful comments and suggestions of Mr. Thomas A. Toll, who reviewed the entire manuscript, are gratefully acknowledged. Others who reviewed individual chapters and offered useful comments are Dr. John E. Duberg and Mr. Mark R. Nichols. Thanks are extended to the various sources for the photographs used in this book; credits are listed in the figure captions. Mr. Peter C. Boisseau and Mr. Martin Copp were particularly generous in providing photographs from their extensive collections. Finally, thanks are gratefully extended to Ms. Dorothy E. Coleman, who so expertly edited the manuscript.

Part I

THE AGE OF PROPELLERS

Chapter 1
Introduction

The first flight of a powered, heavier-than-air aircraft was, of course, made by Orville Wright on December 17, 1903. In the decade following this historic event, aircraft development was characterized by a proliferation of types, conceived primarily by inventors of varying degrees of competence. A few of these aircraft flew moderately well, some poorly, and some not at all. There was little scientific and engineering foundation for aircraft design, and many aircraft built during this period were constructed by nontechnical people as amateur, backyard-type projects. Most of these aircraft were designed for no other mission than to fly, and most were employed for exhibition purposes, races, or other spectacular types of events. No definitive aircraft configuration types had emerged by 1914, the beginning of World War I, and flying was regarded by most intelligent people—if at all—as a sort of curiosity not unlike tightrope walking at the circus. These viewpoints were utterly changed by the tactical and strategic uses of aircraft in the First World War. The demands of combat aviation, together with the opposing powers constantly vying for air superiority, resulted in the development of the airplane from a curiosity in 1914 to a highly useful and versatile vehicle, designed to fulfill specific roles, by the end of the war in November 1918.

The evolution of propeller-driven airplanes from 1914 to the present falls into five distinct, identifiable time periods that provide the framework for chapters 2 through 6. Significant design trends, as evidenced by changes in aircraft physical and performance characteristics, are discussed in chapter 7. Chapters 2 to 7 are restricted to a discussion of aircraft designed to operate from land-based fields and airports. Consequently, the flying boat, once an important class of aircraft but now almost extinct, is not included in these chapters; however, a brief description of the evolution of this unique and picturesque type of aircraft is contained in chapter 8.

3

As indicated in the preface, the discussion is restricted primarily to aircraft types developed in the United States. Chapter 2 on World War I aircraft is an exception; European aircraft form the basis for the material presented in this chapter since the United States developed no significant combat aircraft during the war years 1914–18.

The aircraft discussed in the following chapters, together with some of their physical and performance characteristics, are listed in tables I to IV in appendix A. The quantities tabulated are defined in the list of symbols contained in appendix B, and generally require no further elaboration. However, three of the aircraft aerodynamic characteristics presented deserve some further discussion. These are the zero-lift drag coefficient $C_{D,0}$, the drag area f, and the value of the maximum lift-drag ratio $(L/D)_{max}$.

The zero-lift drag coefficient $C_{D,0}$ is a nondimensional number that relates the zero-lift drag of the aircraft, in pounds, to its size and the speed and altitude at which it is flying. Generally speaking, the smaller the value of this number, the more aerodynamically clean the aircraft. For example, the value of $C_{D,0}$ for the North American P–51 "Mustang" fighter of World War II fame is about 0.0161 (table III) as compared with about 0.0771 for the Fokker E–III fighter of World War I (table I). Accordingly, the P–51 is a much cleaner aircraft than the Fokker E–III.

The drag area f is the product of the zero-lift drag coefficient and the wing area. The resulting number is of interest because it represents, approximately, the area of a square flat plate, or disc, held normal to the direction of flight, which has the same drag in pounds as the aircraft at a given speed and altitude. (The relationship is exact for a flat-plate drag coefficient of 1.0. According to reference 72, the actual drag coefficient of such a plate is 1.171.) For example, the drag area of the P–51 fighter is 3.57 square feet as compared with 12.61 square feet for the much smaller Fokker E–III of World War I. The improvement in aerodynamic efficiency over the 25-year period separating the two aircraft is obvious. Comparisons of the drag area of aircraft of different periods designed for the same missions can thus provide some indication of comparative aerodynamic cleanness or streamlining. Furthermore, the maximum speed is approximately proportional to the cube root of the ratio of the power to the drag area (ref. 90). The larger this ratio, the higher the top speed.

The value of the maximum lift-drag ratio $(L/D)_{max}$ is a measure of the aerodynamic cruising efficiency of the aircraft. In essence, it is inversely related to the amount of thrust required to sustain a given

4

weight in the air and is proportional to the miles of flight per pound of fuel for a given propulsion system efficiency and aircraft weight. The higher the value of $(L/D)_{max}$, the higher the cruising efficiency of the aircraft. The value of the maximum lift-drag ratio is a function of the zero-lift drag coefficient and the drag associated with the generation of lift. The drag-due-to-lift is, in turn, related to the wing aspect ratio (basically, the ratio of span to average chord) and becomes smaller as the aspect ratio is increased. The value of the aspect ratio A is given for each of the aircraft listed in the tables. Values of $(L/D)_{max}$ for propeller-driven aircraft vary from about 6.4 for early World War I fighters to about 16 for transports such as the Lockheed 1049G of the 1950's. The values of $C_{D,0}$ and $(L/D)_{max}$ given in the tables were estimated from published aircraft performance data according to the methods described in appendix C.

The references used in obtaining the characteristics of the aircraft are listed in tables I–IV or are specifically cited in the text. *Jane's All the World's Aircraft* (refs. 1–16) has been used extensively in compiling the characteristics of the aircraft presented in the tables. This definitive series of books has been published each year since 1909 and forms an invaluable source for anyone interested in aircraft development. A few references that provide useful background material, but which are not specifically cited in the the text, are offered for additional reading on the subject of aircraft development. For convenience, references 17 to 124 are listed alphabetically.

Chapter 2
Design Exploration, 1914–18

Background

A multitude of aircraft types were tested in combat in the war period 1914–18, and literally hundreds of prototypes were built and flown. These numbers become believable when one considers that the prototype of a fighter aircraft could be designed, constructed, and test flown within a period of a few weeks. In contrast to the essentially job-shop approach to aircraft construction that prevailed prior to 1914, an aircraft industry was developing, nurtured by large expenditures of money by the belligerent governments. The engineering principles of aircraft design were also beginning to take shape. Government laboratories, such as the Royal Aeronautical Establishment in England, contributed greatly to the foundations of aeronautical engineering. Scientific and engineering laboratories also existed in France, Italy, and Germany; and the National Advisory Committee for Aeronautics (NACA) was established in the United States by act of Congress in 1915. The results of NACA research, however, did not begin to have a significant impact on aircraft design until the mid- to late 1920's. In contrast to the European powers, the United States had essentially no air force and no real aircraft industry when war was declared on Germany in April 1917. Accordingly, the United States relied almost entirely on tried and proven European aircraft designs. Many of these aircraft were produced by European companies for use by the American Expeditionary Force, while others were manufactured under license in the United States.

Aircraft types of amazing variety were built in the continual quest for better fighting machines. Monoplanes, biplanes, and triplanes were employed in military operations at various stages of the war, and several quadruplanes were tested in prototype form. The wings of most of these aircraft were supported externally by a combination of wires and struts, although several designers developed aircraft with internally braced cantilever wings. Perhaps the most notable was the Dutch designer Anthony H. G. Fokker, who supplied many cantilever-wing fighter aircraft to the German air force. Both pusher- and tractor-type engine installations were employed, and multiengine bombers frequently utilized a combination of pusher and tractor powerplant installations. The pusher-type configuration was used extensively as a fighter, particularly by the British, in the early stages of the war. The internal structure of most of the aircraft consisted of a wooden framework braced with wire and covered externally with cloth. Some aircraft employed a mixture of metal and wood in their construction, and experiments were conducted with all-metal aircraft whose wings were internally braced. Dornier and Junkers in Germany were among the pioneers in all-metal aircraft construction. The types of alloys available at the time, however, did not lend themselves to the light weight required in aircraft design, and the concepts of light, stressed-skin metal construction lay in the future. All-metal aircraft did not play an important role in World War I. The use of plywood as an external covering, together with a minimum of internal structure, particularly in fuselage design, was also employed by several manufacturers. This type of construction, called monocoque, is described in more detail later.

Two vastly different engine types were employed in World War I aircraft: the stationary engine, usually water cooled, and the rotary engine. Water-cooled engines of 4, 6, 8, and 12 cylinders were extensively utilized. In concept, these engines were not unlike the present-day automobile engine; a few of the in-line engines were air cooled. The rotary engine had cylinders arranged radially around a crankshaft; but unlike the modern radial engine, the crankshaft was fixed to the aircraft, and the cylinders and crankcase, with propeller attached, rotated around it. This engine type was relatively light and was cooled easily by engine rotation, advantages that accounted for its extensive use. The rotary engine, perfected in France, had a primitive control system and introduced undesirable gyroscopic moments in the aircraft that adversely affected flying characteristics. The rotary engine is a curiosity that rapidly vanished from the scene following the close of World War I.

The design of a successful aircraft, even today, is not an exact science. It involves a combination of proven scientific principles, engineering intuition, detailed market or mission requirements, and perhaps a bit of inventiveness and daring. Aircraft design during World War I was more inventive, intuitive, and daring than anything else. Prototypes were frequently constructed from full-size chalk drawings laid out on the factory floor. The principles of aerodynamics that form so important a part of aircraft design today were relatively little understood by aircraft designers during the war. An indication of the state of the art in this area is given in the textbooks by Barnwell and Sayers published in 1917 (ref. 27) and by Klemin in 1918 (ref. 79). Structural design was haphazard, and stress analysis did not become an accepted part of the design process in many companies until midway through the World War. In an area of engineering in which structural strength, light weight, and aerodynamic efficiency are so important, it is indeed surprising that a number of relatively good aircraft were produced.

The evolution of the airplane during the turbulent years of World War I is described briefly in the following sections of this chapter. Fighter aircraft, which usually reflected the latest in design refinements, are considered first, after which consideration is given to heavy bombers and army cooperation aircraft.

Fighter Aircraft

A primary purpose of fighter aircraft is to destroy other aircraft, either in offensive or defensive modes of operation, or to pose such a compelling threat that enemy air operations are effectively curtailed. Enemy fighters, bombers, patrol and reconnaissance aircraft, as well as ground-support and transport aircraft, are the prey of the fighter. To perform its intended function, the fighter must be able to reach a favorable position for inflicting crippling damage on the enemy. This means that the fighter pilot must first be able to detect the enemy aircraft; the methods of detection employed in the First World War were primarily visual. Thus, the aircraft and pilot's position in it must be designed to provide the widest possible field of view. Detection means little, however, unless the aircraft possesses the performance and maneuverability necessary to achieve a favorable attack position and provides a steady gun platform together with sufficiently powerful armament to destroy the enemy once a favorable position has been achieved. Some of the performance and maneuverability characteristics of importance are speed in various flight conditions, rate of climb and ceiling, roll rate, turning radius and climb capability while in a turn, and range and endurance.

Sufficient strength must be provided for the aircraft to survive the loads imposed by high g maneuvers at high speed without structural failure. The ability to sustain a certain amount of enemy fire without

9

catastrophic damage is another important attribute of the successful fighter aircraft. Adding to the design challenge is the necessity for maintaining structural weight at a minimum, while at the same time providing the required strength and durability.

Another important ingredient inherent in a successful fighter aircraft is the manner in which it handles. The flying and handling characteristics of aircraft have been under study for over 60 years and continue to be the subject of investigation as new aircraft configurations evolve and new operating ranges of speed and altitude are encountered. Broadly speaking, an aircraft with good handling characteristics must obey the pilot's control inputs precisely, rapidly, and predictably without unwanted excursions or uncontrollable behavior and without excessive physical effort on the part of the pilot. Preferably, the aircraft should possess these desirable characteristics throughout its performance envelope. Further discussion of handling characteristics is contained in chapter 5.

The discussion above outlines in broad terms some of the more important characteristics of the successful fighter aircraft. These desirable characteristics have not changed very much over the years, although they have been more precisely defined. Also, the operating ranges of speed and altitude have changed, as have the weapons and the methods of detection. No aircraft has ever achieved perfection in all areas in terms of the state of the art available in a given time period. Aircraft design involves a compromise between many conflicting requirements. The successful fighter aircraft incorporates the proper blend of compromises that provides the characteristics necessary to counteract the enemy threat in a particular time period and combat environment. The evolution of this rather specialized type of aircraft in the hectic 4-year period of World War I is briefly described next. Discussed and illustrated are 11 fighters that operated over the Western front during this pioneer period of combat aircraft development.

Pioneer Fighters

The first true fighters to appear in World War I were the Fokker Eindecker series of monoplanes that caused a revolution in the concepts of the way in which a fighting airplane could be employed. The Eindecker was not particularly fast or maneuverable, but it was the first aircraft to effectively employ a fixed, forward-firing machine gun that was synchronized with the engine so that the bullets passed between the blades of the revolving propeller. The gun was aimed by aiming the entire airplane. This new flying weapon entered combat service in the summer of 1915. Credit for the invention of the synchronized machine gun is a matter of debate among aviation historians, but there is no doubt that the Fokker Eindeckers were the first aircraft to employ this concept in an effective operational sense. Anthony Fokker's version of the invention of the synchronized machine gun and its early use are contained in his autobiography (ref. 50).

The results achieved with the Fokkers were spectacular, and the months during which these aircraft reigned supreme are often referred to as the era of the "Fokker Scourge"; Allied aircraft were sometimes called "Fokker Fodder." German pilots Oswald Boelcke and Max Immelmann became famous for flying this type of aircraft; Immelmann was killed in one as the result of structural failure in the air. It has never been established whether this failure was caused by enemy gunfire or a design defect.

The Eindecker series of aircraft appeared in four versions, E-I to E-IV, with the E-III type produced in the greatest numbers. They were similar in appearance and were equipped with one machine gun, except for the E-IV, which was larger, more powerful, and had two guns. Between 450 and 475 Eindeckers were manufactured.

Some of the characteristics of the E-III are given in table I (appendix A), and a photograph of a type E-IV is presented in figure 2.1. The photograph depicts a fragile-looking midwing monoplane, with the wings braced by an array of wires extending from a pylon mounted atop the fuselage to the wing and then down to a complex arrangement of struts that formed the landing gear. The wing itself was quite thin, a common engineering practice through most of the war years. Thick wings were thought, quite incorrectly, to produce prohibitively high drag. It is not known whether this mistaken notion arose because of results obtained from the very low Reynolds number wind tunnels available at that time; or because of poor airfoil design; or perhaps, because birds' wings were thin, designers therefore considered that shape to be the best. In any case, airfoil thickness ratios of 4 to 6 percent (ratio of airfoil thickness to wing chord) were the norm, and only the Germans successfully applied thick airfoils to wing design later in the war.

The control system employed on the Eindeckers was archaic even by 1914 standards. Lateral control was achieved by wing warping in a manner similar to that employed by the Wright brothers in 1903, and the vertical and horizontal tail units consisted of one-piece free-floating

11

Figure 2.1 — German Fokker E–IV Eindecker fighter; 1916. [ukn via Martin Copp]

surfaces. The stability and control characteristics of the aircraft were, of course, related to the floating angles of these surfaces as the angles of attack and sideslip of the aircraft varied. The characteristics of the aircraft and the effectiveness of the control system can be judged by the comments of a modern pilot who has flown a replica of the E-III. The late Frank Tallman in his book *Flying the Old Planes* (ref. 110) says ". . . the major flight characteristic ever present is the feeling that if you took your hands off the stick or your feet off of the rudders, the Eindecker would turn itself inside out or literally swap ends." He also indicates that the all-moving surfaces continually hunted back and forth with an attendant feedback into the pilot's hands and feet. These characteristics describe an aircraft that by modern standards would be considered unpleasant to fly, would be unlicensable, and certainly would inspire little confidence in the mind of the pilot.

The Eindecker was of conventional frame construction covered with fabric "doped" with glue to stretch it tight and to provide weatherproofing. The wing structure was of wood, whereas the fuselage frame departed from common practice in that it was constructed of welded steel tubing with wire bracing.

The E-III was powered with the 100-horsepower Oberursel rotary engine. One of these interesting and unique rotary-type engines is shown in figure 2.2. In order to limit centrifugal stresses, rotary engines developed maximum power at relatively low rotational speeds, in the range of 1200 to 1400 revolutions per minute. The large diameter propeller on the Fokker E-IV shown in figure 2.1 was dictated by the low rotational speed of the engine. By modern standards, the engines of most World War I aircraft developed rated power at low rotational speed and utilized large diameter propellers. The propulsive efficiency was accordingly high at low speeds, which gave aircraft of that period good takeoff and climb characteristics.

A glance at the data in table I for the Fokker E-III indicates a rather light aircraft of 1342 pounds gross weight with a maximum speed of 87 miles per hour, a high zero-lift drag coefficient of 0.0771, and a low maximum lift-drag ratio of 6.4. Certainly these data do not suggest an aircraft of very impressive performance. Yet, the presence of an effective fixed, forward-firing, synchronized machine gun, which the Allied powers did not have, made the Eindecker the terror of the skies over the Western front in 1915 and secured for it an important place in the annals of World War I aviation history.

The German hold on air superiority was broken in the spring of 1916 by the appearance of several new British and French fighters that outclassed the Fokker Eindeckers. The British, who did not possess a satisfactory gun synchronizing gear, solved the problem of a forward-firing gun by a pragmatic, short-term configuration concept; the engine

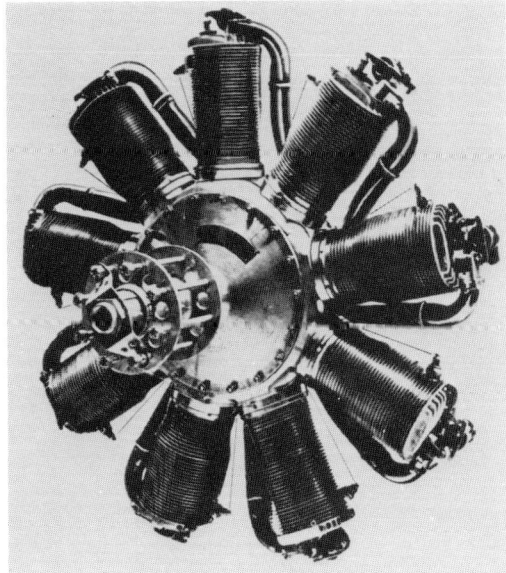

Figure 2.2—Nine-cylinder LeRhône rotary engine of 110 hp. [ukn]

13

and propeller were simply mounted behind the pilot, which allowed an unobstructed forward field of fire. Several pusher-type aircraft were developed. Typical of this design concept was the DeHavilland DH–2 shown in figure 2.3, designed by Geoffery DeHavilland for the Aircraft Manufacturing Company (AIRCO). The photograph depicts a strut-and-wire-braced, double-bay biplane employing thin, untapered wings. (A brief description of biplane terminology is contained in appendix D.) A small nacelle situated on the bottom wing contained the pilot's cockpit and gun in the forward portion and the 100-horsepower Gnome Monosoupape rotary engine in the pusher position in the rear. The horizontal and vertical tail surfaces were mounted behind the engine on an arrangement of four strut-and-wire-braced outriggers, or booms, which extended rearward from the wings. Cutouts in the trailing edges of the upper and lower wings provided clearance for the rotating propeller, which had four blades to minimize the extent of the cutouts and reduce the required spacing of the outriggers. The smaller diameter four-blade propeller, as compared with a two-blade propeller capable of absorbing the same power, also reduced the length of the landing gear.

Figure 2.3 — British DeHavilland DH–2 fighter; 1916. [National Archives via Martin Copp]

The pusher configuration arrangement of the DH–2 offered excellent visibility forward, upward, and downward to both sides, but a somewhat restricted view to the rear. Armament first consisted of a flexible, forward-firing gun or guns, but this was later replaced by a single fixed gun.

The biplane configuration employed on the DH–2, with detail design variations, was the most frequently used wing arrangements on World War I aircraft designs. The biplane design formula offered the best compromise between structural strength, light weight, and aerodynamic efficiency consistent with the state of the art. The British, as a matter of policy, were not interested in monoplanes because they had a reputation, perhaps undeserved, for structural weakness.

The DH–2 was of wooden frame construction covered with fabric, except for the top and forward parts of the nacelle, which were covered with plywood. Lateral control was provided by ailerons located on both the upper and lower wings, and the tail surfaces had both fixed and movable elements. According to reference 82, the aircraft was sensitive on the controls with a tendency to spin easily. Once they mastered it, however, pilots found the aircraft to be strong, maneuverable, and easy to fly.

A comparison of the data given in table I shows that the DH–2 was somewhat faster than the Fokker, was of greater aerodynamic efficiency, and had a significantly lower wing loading. The climbing capability of a fighter aircraft is a very important performance parameter, not shown by the data in table I. Curves showing the time required to climb to various altitudes, based on data given in reference 82, are presented in figure 2.18 for all the fighter aircraft discussed. The climb curves also give the DH–2 an edge over the Fokker. These advantages of the DH–2, together with control characteristics that were no doubt far superior to those of the Fokker, were responsible for the success of the "little pusher."

Major Leone G. Hawker, one of the early British aces, commanded the first Royal Flying Corps squadron equipped with the DH–2. While flying one of these aircraft, he was shot down by the German ace Baron von Richthofen flying an Albatros fighter. The DH–2 was a great success when introduced in the spring of 1916 but was outclassed by far superior German fighters by the time of Hawker's death in the late fall of 1916. The aircraft was belatedly withdrawn from combat in the summer of 1917. About 400 DH–2's were built.

One of the truly great fighter aircraft of the early war years was introduced to combat by the French in March 1916. The Nieuport 17, illustrated in figure 2.4, was a development of earlier Nieuport fighters and was extensively used not only by the French but by the British, Belgians, Italians, and Russians. After entering the war, the United States also employed the aircraft as a trainer. Many well-known Allied aces flew the Nieuport 17: Albert Ball and William Avery Bishop of the British Royal Flying Corps and René Fonck and Charles Nungesser of France exemplify aces who earned at least part of their reputation while flying the Nieuport 17. At the time the aircraft was introduced into combat, a satisfactory gun synchronizing gear was not available, but the deficiency was overcome by mounting a machine gun, which fired over the propeller arc, on the top of the upper wing. This arrangement is employed on the Nieuport 17 replica shown in figure 2.5. Subsequent versions of the aircraft employed the overwing gun in combination with a single synchronized gun firing between the propeller blades, or by a single synchronized gun alone. This later configuration is employed on the aircraft shown in figure 2.4.

Figure 2.4 — French Nieuport 17 fighter; 1916. [National Archives via Martin Copp]

The Nieuport 17 was a very neat, clean-looking, strut-and-wire-braced biplane powered by the 110-horsepower LeRhône 9J rotary engine. More properly, the configuration of the aircraft should be described as a sesquiplane since the lower wing is of much smaller chord than the upper one. The single-spar lower wing was connected to the upper wing of this single-bay biplane by V-type interplane struts. The small chord of the lower wing provided the pilot with excellent downward visibility, which is the most probable reason for the sesquiplane layout. In earlier Nieuport fighters, the small, single-spar lower wing had shown a tendency toward structural weakness; this deficiency was apparently corrected in the model 17. Lateral control was provided by ailerons on the upper wing only. The tail assembly consisted of an all-moving vertical surface, together with a fixed horizontal stabilizer equipped with a movable elevator. Construction was conventional wood framework covered with fabric, except for the tail which had a steel tube frame.

The data in table I indicate the Nieuport 17 to have been a light aircraft with a good weight-power ratio, low drag area, and high maxi-

Figure 2.5 — French Nieuport 17 with wing-mounted gun; 1916. [Peter C. Boisseau]

17

mum lift-drag ratio. The maximum speed was 107 miles per hour at 6500 feet. Comparing these characteristics, as well as the climb curves in figure 2.18, with those of the Fokker E–III and the DeHavilland DH–2 leaves little doubt of the superior qualities of the Nieuport 17. According to reference 23, this fighter was so well liked by the Allies that 317 of them were still in front-line service in August 1917—a long operational life for a combat aircraft in an era in which new aircraft were being developed in a matter of months.

The Two-Gun Fighter

High on the list of great fighter aircraft of the first world war is the name Albatros. Beginning with the introduction to combat of the model D–I in August 1916, Albatros fighters served in the German Air Force until the armistice in November 1918. Introduced in January 1917, the D–III and its refined variants the D–V and the D–Va were the best of the Albatros fighters and were produced in the greatest numbers. In November 1917, 446 D–III's and 556 D–V's and D–Va's were in service in combat squadrons with the German Air Force. Air superiority was again in Germany's hands from the late fall of 1916 until mid-summer of 1917. So great was the carnage inflicted on Allied aircraft by German pilots flying Albatros fighters that April 1917 is still referred to by aviation historians as "Bloody April." Among the famous German aces who flew Albatros fighters were Manfred von Richthofen, Ernst Udet, Bruno Loerzer, and Werner Voss. Although the name of Richthofen is usually associated with the Fokker triplane, he scored most of his 80 victories flying Albatros fighters (ref. 96).

Two views of the Albatros D–III are shown in figures 2.6 and 2.7, and the characteristics of this version of the Albatros are given in table I. The D–III was a streamlined strut-and-wire-braced biplane that had V-type interplane struts connecting the small-chord lower wing to the upper wing. According to some sources, this arrangement was copied, at the insistence of the German Air Force, from the very successful Nieuport 17. Power was provided by a water-cooled, six-cylinder Mercedes engine of 160 horsepower. Not evident in the photographs is the airfoil-shaped cooling radiator located in the upper wing. Water feed and return pipes connecting the engine to the radiator can, however, be seen. Also not visible in the photographs are the two fixed, forward-facing machine guns synchronized to fire between the revolving blades of the propeller. The Albatros fighters were among the first biplanes to be armed in this way and may be thought of as setting a trend in fighter design which was to last for the next two decades. For example,

Figure 2.6 — German Albatros D–III fighter; 1917. [ukn via Martin Copp]

Figure 2.7 — Side view of prototype Albatros D–III fighter. [Peter M. Bowers via AAHS]

the U.S. Navy purchased its last biplane fighter with two forward-firing, synchronized guns in 1938.

The Albatros had several structural features worthy of mention. Of particular interest is the fuselage, which was of semimonocoque construction. The term "monocoque" comes from France and means single shell. Thus, the true monocoque fuselage consists of an outside shell, usually formed of plywood, which is held in shape by a number of transverse bulkheads contained within the shell. Louis Bechereau, a French designer, first employed plywood monocoque construction in the fuselage of the 1911 Deperdussion racing monoplane. A semi-monocoque fuselage has, in addition to the transverse bulkheads, several longitudinal members to enhance the stability, stiffness, and strength of the structure. This type of construction was strong, rigid, fairly light in weight, and provided a smooth, streamlined shape. In addition, for a given outside diameter, a large usable internal fuselage diameter was available. The smooth, rounded shape of the fuselage of the D–III can be seen in figures 2.6 and 2.7. Interesting details of the semimonocoque type of construction, including many photographs, are given in reference 91. A number of other German aircraft manufacturers utilized this type of fuselage construction during the war years, and it will appear again on some of the racing aircraft of the 1920's (chapter 3) and on the high-performance Lockheed aircraft of the late twenties and early thirties (chapter 4).

The wings of the Albatros D–III were of conventional wood-frame construction covered with fabric. As in the Nieuport 17, the lower wing had only a single spar to which the V-type interplane struts were attached. The struts themselves were streamlined steel tubes. Throughout the life of the D–III, D–V, and D–Va designs, despite several modifications, the single-spar lower wing showed an inherent structural weakness that somewhat limited the performance of the aircraft. An examination of drawings of the lower wing (given in reference 91) shows that the single spar was located well behind the quarter-chord point (the approximate location of the aerodynamic center in the chordwise direction). This spar location suggests that the tendency of the wing to fail in high-speed dives was probably the result of aeroelastic divergence, a phenomenon apparently not understood at the time the Albatros fighters were developed. An increase in torsional stiffness or a relocation of the wing elastic axis, or a combination of both, is the usual cure for divergence. A brief description of aeroelastic divergence is given in the discussion of swept wings in chapter 10.

Control of the Albatros D–III was provided by ailerons on the upper wings and by an aerodynamically balanced rudder and elevator on the tail surfaces. The fixed portion of the vertical tail was covered with plywood and had elements above and below the fuselage. The tail skid formed an extension of the lower, or ventral, part of the fin. The fixed portion of the horizontal tail, like most aircraft of the period, was not adjustable and thus could not be used to trim the aircraft longitudinally while in flight. Accordingly, a constant push or pull on the control stick was necessary to maintain level flight at a constant speed and altitude. A rudimentary form of longitudinal "trim" system, consisting of a sliding collar on the control stick connected by a hinged link to the cockpit floor, was provided on the Albatros. A thumb-actuated set screw in the collar could be tightened, and the stick was then held in a fixed position; for brief periods, the pilot was then free to use both hands for other activities such as attempting to clear a jammed machine gun. The system is described and illustrated in reference 91. Information on the handling characteristics of the Albatros is limited, but what has been found indicates that it was easy to fly, with no dangerous characteristics.

A comparison of the data given in table I for the Albatros D–III and the Nieuport 17 leads to some interesting speculation. Although the D–III was heavier and had more wing area and a more powerful engine than the Nieuport, the values of the wing loading and the power loading for the two aircraft are not greatly different. Furthermore, the values of the zero-lift drag coefficient and the maximum lift-drag ratio are about the same. These two aircraft can therefore be considered to have about equal aerodynamic efficiency and, accordingly, to exhibit about the same performance characteristics. In fact, the maximum speeds given in table I are about the same although the altitudes at which the speeds were measured are somewhat different. Since, for small altitude variations, the decrease in drag that accompanies the reduction in air density is about offset by the reduction in power with altitude, the speed comparison of the two aircraft in the table is valid. Values of the time required to climb to various altitudes are also about the same for the two aircraft at the lower altitudes, as shown by the data in figure 2.18; however, the climbing capability of the Albatros is clearly superior to that of the Nieuport above 10 000 feet. This plus the heavier armament of the Albatros are no doubt responsible for the generally accepted opinion that it was a more effective fighter than the Nieuport 17.

The Triplane Phenomenon

Mention of World War I aviation evokes in the minds of many a vision of a brightly painted red triplane handled with consummate skill by the "Red Baron" as he closes for the kill of another Allied airplane. The triplane was, of course, the Fokker model Dr.–1, and the pilot was the great German ace Rittmeister Manfred Freiher von Richthofen. The Fokker Dr.–1 was a manifestation of a design phenomenon that swept the aircraft industry in the period 1917–18. During that time, no less than 34 triplane prototypes were constructed and test-flown in Germany (ref. 69). Other triplane prototypes were designed and tested by countries of the Allied Powers.

In today's terminology, all this triplane activity may be classified as an overreaction to the introduction in early 1917 of the British Sopwith triplane. This aircraft, in the hands of a few excellent pilots of the British Royal Naval Air Service, quickly made an enviable reputation as a formidable fighter. Raymond Collishaw was perhaps the best-known British pilot to fly the Sopwith triplane. Less than 75 of these aircraft were employed in combat operations; but so favorable were the reports of German pilots who had fought against the aircraft, as well as those of a few pilots including von Richthofen who had flown captured examples of the triplane, that the German government issued an invitation to industry for the submission of triplane prototypes for evaluation and indicated that production contracts would be forthcoming for deserving designs. Hence, the great triplane fad in Germany. Out of all this activity, the Fokker model Dr.–1 triplane was the only type produced in quantity; approximately 320 were ordered in the summer of 1917. The type was used in combat operations for about 1 year but was employed by a relatively few elite squadrons of the German Air Force.

A Fokker triplane replica is pictured in figure 2.8. The two wheels visible beneath the tail skid are not part of the aircraft but are attached to a dolly used for towing the aircraft on the ground. The Dr.–1 was a small, light machine equipped with a 110-horsepower rotary engine and, as indicated by the data in table I, had a gross weight of only 1290 pounds and a small upper wing of 23.7-foot span.

Although inspired by the Sopwith triplane, the Fokker Dr.–1 bore it no resemblance except for the three wings. The Sopwith employed a conventional strut-and-wire-braced wing arrangement, whereas the Fokker had no wire bracing between the wings and only a single strut connecting the lifting surfaces near the tips. These struts were intended to reduce wing vibration and flexing at high speed and did not materially contribute to the static strength of the structure. Interestingly,

Figure 2.8 — German Fokker Dr.–1 triplane fighter; 1917. [author's collection]

the first Fokker triplane flew without any interplane struts at all. The wings themselves were cantilever; that is, they obtained their strength entirely from internal bracing.

The radical departure of the Fokker Dr.–1 structure from contemporary aircraft design concepts was made possible by the use of wing airfoil sections much thicker than usual at the time. The mistaken notion that low wing drag could only be obtained with thin airfoil sections has been mentioned previously. The Fokker triplane and subsequent Fokker designs proved the incorrectness of the thin wing concept. The Göttingen 298 airfoil section of 13-percent thickness ratio, employed on the Dr.–1, is shown in figure 2.9 in comparison with three thin airfoils of the World War I period. These sections were of 4- to 5-percent thickness ratio.

The wing structure of the Fokker Dr.–1 consisted of two closely spaced box spars connected at the top and bottom with plywood sheets; the resulting torque box provided great strength and stiffness. The ribs were made of plywood with lightening holes and shear braces, and the leading edges were partially covered with plywood back to the front spar. The entire wing, including the plywood leading edge, was covered with fabric. In common with many World War I aircraft, the trailing edge of the wing was formed from wire and usually assumed a

23

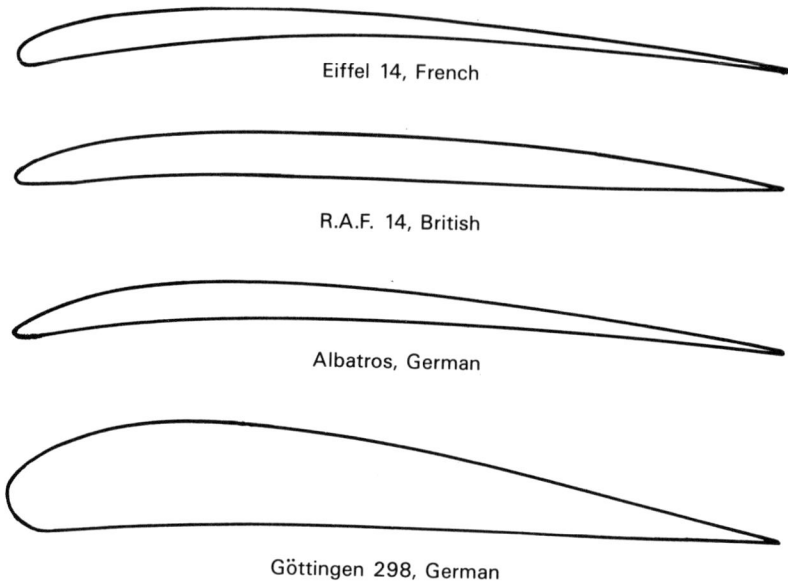

Eiffel 14, French

R.A.F. 14, British

Albatros, German

Göttingen 298, German

Figure 2.9 — Four examples of airfoil sections employed in wings of World War I airplanes.

scalloped appearance after the fabric had been tightened with dope. Following standard Fokker practice, the fuselage, tail surfaces, and ailerons were constructed of welded steel tubing. Illustrative drawings of the structural details of the Dr.–1 are given in reference 69.

Large horn-balanced ailerons were employed only on the upper wing of the Fokker Dr.–1. The planform of this wing, including the ailerons, is shown in figure 2.10 in comparison with upper wing planform shapes of several of the other aircraft discussed here. The horn balance on the Dr.–1 wing is that portion of the aileron that extends outboard of the wing tip and forward of the aileron hinge line. The purpose of the balances, sometimes informally referred to as "elephant ears," was to reduce the aileron hinge moments, and thus the force that the pilot had to exert on the control stick to roll the aircraft. According to reference 72, the "raked" tips of the other planforms shown in the figure might be expected to have a small beneficial effect on the drag associated with the production of lift.

The horizontal tail of the Fokker Dr.–1 consisted of a fixed stabilizer with large horn-balanced elevators. The vertical tail was an all-moving unit, without a fixed fin, and was similar in design to that of the Fokker E-III. Other features to note in figure 2.8 are the skids

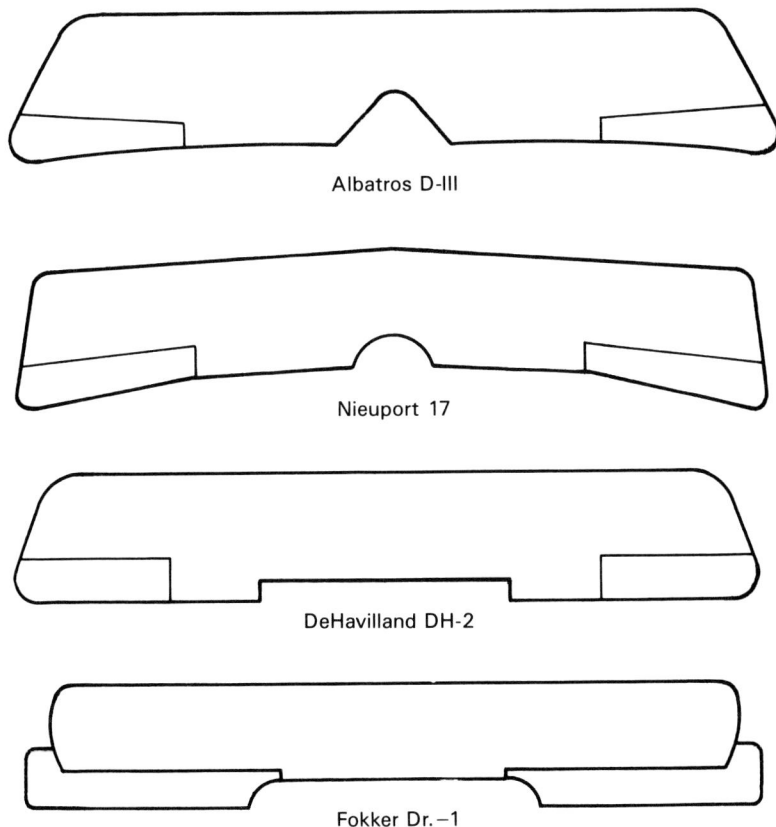

Figure 2.10 — Wing-planform shapes of four World War I fighter airplanes.

under the tips of the lower wings and the small winglike fairing that enclosed the axle between the wheels of the landing gear. This fairing became something of a trademark on many later Fokker aircraft.

The zero-lift drag coefficient of 0.0323 given in table I for the Fokker Dr.–1 was among the lowest of any of the World War I fighter aircraft analyzed, as was the drag area of 6.69 square feet. The maximum lift-drag ratio was a correspondingly high 8.0. The low zero-lift drag coefficient of the Fokker triplane was no doubt due in part to the relatively small surface area of the fuselage in relation to that of the wings. Another important ingredient contributing to the low drag of the aircraft was the absence of the multitude of bracing wires found between the wings on most other aircraft of that period. These wires, or cables, were often of round cross-sectional shape. On the basis of the drag coefficients given in reference 72, the drag in pounds of a smooth, 0.25-inch-diameter wire at the speeds of World War I aircraft is the same as that of a strut of the same length having a 25-inch chord and an airfoil section of 10- or 12-percent thickness ratio. The wires, intended to take only loads in tension, were, of course, lighter than struts designed for the same purpose. The gain in efficiency associated with a design from which the wires are eliminated is obvious. A good description of the interplane bracing cables employed on the Albatros D–Va is given in reference 91.

The speed of 103 miles per hour at 13 120 feet was not particularly high (table I); most discussions of the Fokker Dr.-1 in the literature indicate that the aircraft was slow but was highly maneuverable and had an outstandingly high rate of climb. The time-to-climb curves in figure 2.18 indicate a climb performance for the Dr.–1 that was far superior to that of the Albatros D–III and the Nieuport 17; in fact, it had a better rate of climb (indicated by the slope of the curve) than any of the other aircraft up to an altitude of between 8000 and 10 000 feet. Unfortunately, these data, taken from reference 82, cannot be considered conclusive since data from other sources, for example reference 119, show much higher times to climb than indicated in figure 2.18. Two sets of climb data are given in reference 69; one set is in essential agreement with the data of figure 2.18, whereas the other is similar to that in reference 119. In an attempt to resolve this discrepancy, the sea-level rates of climb for the Dr.–1 were estimated for several different weights with the use of the methods given in chapter 6 of reference 90. The calculations showed that the climb data in figure 2.18 might have been achievable with a light fuel load, but not with full fuel tanks. The aircraft weight for which the climb data of reference 82 apply is not known for any of the aircraft. The superior climbing capability of the Dr.–1 must be attributed to the thick airfoil sections that allowed operation at the high lift coefficients required for optimum climbing performance, not to the use of three wings instead of two.

The triplane fighter of World War I must be considered as something of an aberration in the course of aeronautical development. The design trade-offs and reasoning underlying the concept of such an aircraft are nowhere adequately explained in any of the reference documents. However, one might speculate along the following lines: For a given wing span and area, the effective aspect ratio (related to the drag associated with the production of lift) of a triplane is higher than that of a biplane or monoplane (ref. 103). Or, for a given aspect ratio, the span of a triplane can be less than that of a biplane or monoplane of the same wing area. Thus, the rolling inertia of the triplane can be less than that of a biplane or monoplane. Greater maneuverability might, therefore, be obtainable with a triplane configuration. Further, the triplane allows the wing area to be divided among three relatively narrow-chord wings, which may be arranged relative to the aircraft center of gravity in such a way as to provide the pilot with better visibility than could be achieved with a comparable biplane. Finally, for a given level of longitudinal stability, the physical distance between the wings and the tail may be reduced on a triplane as compared with a biplane.

The quantitative theoretical relationships between the drag-due-to-lift of monoplanes, biplanes, and triplanes were not available in 1916; however, as indicated by references 27 and 79, empirical design data together with qualitative theoretical ideas were available in the literature. The possible and perhaps nebulous advantages of the triplane, however, could not prevail against the increased complication and cost of constructing three wings instead of two and later, when monoplanes were better understood, one.

In any event, the Fokker triplane will remain an integral part of World War I aviation lore and will be discussed as long as that era is of interest. And inextricably interwoven with the Fokker triplane story is the name of the highest scoring ace of World War I — the legendary Baron von Richthofen.

Fighters in 1918

Discussed next are four fighter aircraft that served with distinction in front-line combat operations until the termination of hostilities in November 1918. Three of these aircraft, the French SPAD XIII and the British Sopwith Camel and Dolphin, were strut-and-wire-braced biplanes that had a conventional wood-frame structure covered with fabric. The fourth, the German Fokker D–VII biplane, had internally braced cantilever wings like the Fokker triplane, together with a typical Fokker welded steel tube fuselage.

Sopwith Camel

The Sopwith Camel evolved from the earlier Sopwith Pup and, as can be seen in figure 2.11, was an awkward-looking single-bay biplane powered with a rotary engine. It was the first British fighter with two forward-firing, synchronized machine guns. A small metal fairing cov-

Figure 2.11 — British Sopwith F.1 Camel fighter; 1917. [William T. Larkins via AAHS]

ered a portion of the guns, which gave the fuselage a humped appearance when viewed from the side. This hump coupled with the large dihedral angle of the lower wing and the flat upper wing are allegedly responsible for the name "Camel." The aircraft first began combat operations in July 1917 and was a front-line combat aircraft until the armistice in November 1918. Camels accounted for the destruction of more enemy aircraft than any other Allied fighter of the war — a total of 1294. Production of the Camel amounted to 5490 aircraft.

The flat upper wing of the Camel was dictated by a desire for production simplicity. The original intention was to construct the wing in one piece, although in production it was made in three pieces. The dihedral of the lower wing was accordingly made sufficiently large to compensate for the flat upper wing. The Camel utilized a relatively new innovation in wing-bracing wires. From a study of references 100 and 110 and an examination of detailed drawings of the Sopwith Dolphin, streamline wires were used for bracing on both the Camel and the Dolphin. (Streamline wires have a cross-sectional shape much like a symmetrical airfoil section.) Such wires were developed by the Royal Aircraft Factory at Farnborough, England and were first flown experimentally on the SE–4 in 1914 (ref. 39). The Sopwith Pup and triplane, both of which entered service in 1916, also had streamline bracing wires. The advantage in drag reduction of using this type of wire rather than the usual round wire is great; there is a factor of about 10 between the drag coefficients of the two types of wire. Yet, no significant use was made of this improved type of wire during the war except by British aircraft manufacturers. Because streamline wire was first developed at Farnborough, it was known as Rafwire.

The Camel was produced with a number of different power plants of varying horsepower; the greatest number of aircraft, however, had the Clerget 9B nine-cylinder rotary engine of 130 horsepower. Characteristics of the Sopwith F.1 Camel equipped with this engine are given in table I.

The Camel was a small, relatively light aircraft with a gross weight of only 1482 pounds. Its maximum speed of 105 miles per hour at 10 000 feet was not particularly fast, and its zero-lift drag coefficient and maximum lift-drag ratio do not suggest a very outstanding aircraft. The climb data given in figure 2.18 show that the Camel performed better than the Albatros D–III, but not so well as some of the other aircraft for which data are shown.

All the reference literature, however, credit the Camel with having superb maneuverability. Some of the agility displayed by the Camel is usually attributed to the Sopwith practice of locating the concentrated weights in the aircraft—pilot, engine, guns, and fuel—in close proximity to each other. Thus in the Camel the pilot's feet were beneath the rear components of the engine, the guns were over his legs, and the fuel tank was immediately behind his back in the fuselage. Some idea of the bunching together of these elements around the pilot is suggested by figure 2.12, where a present-day pilot is shown sitting in the cockpit of a Sopwith Camel replica. Certainly, the pilot was not seated in a very favorable position to withstand the effects of a serious crash.

In the hands of a skillful pilot, the Camel was a formidable weapon. Unfortunately, the flying careers of many mediocre or student pilots were ended abruptly and fatally as a result of the bizarre handling characteristics of the aircraft. In combination with the aerodynamic characteristics of the aircraft itself, the torque and gyroscopic moments associated with the heavy rotating engine gave an incredibly fast turning capability but, at the same time, were responsible for the peculiar handling characteristics of the aircraft. The confusing way in which the controls had to be manipulated in left- and right-hand turns

Figure 2.12—Pilot in cockpit of a replica Sopwith Camel. [Flt. Intl.]

provides an example of these characteristics. Based on the information contained in appendix II of reference 100 for the later Sopwith Snipe, the gyroscopic action of the engine caused a nose-up moment in a left turn and a nose-down moment in a right turn. Accordingly, left stick, a large amount of left rudder, and moderate back stick were required in a steep left turn; too much back stick caused the aircraft to stall and spin. Right stick, a moderate amount of *left* rudder, and full back stick were required in a steep right turn. There seems little doubt that these odd control techniques could cause confusion and indecision on the part of an inexperienced pilot.

The Sopwith Camel has been called the most loved and the most hated aircraft of World War I, loved by those who mastered it and exploited its peculiarities and hated by those who did not. The outstanding dogfighting capability of the Camel together with the record number of German aircraft it destroyed give it an honored place in the World War I aircraft hall of fame. If this were not enough, one version of von Richthofen's last fight has a relatively obscure Canadian ace, Captain A. Roy Brown, shooting down the famous baron while flying . . . a Sopwith Camel.

SPAD XIII

SPAD was the acronym of the French aircraft company Societé pour Aviation et les Derieves, headed by famed aviation pioneer Louis Bleriot, which produced a line of highly successful fighter aircraft in World War I. The SPAD model XIII C.1 is the subject of the following discussion.

The SPAD XIII descended from the earlier model VII which first entered combat in the fall of 1916. In contrast to the earlier aircraft, the model XIII was somewhat larger, had a more powerful engine, and was equipped with two synchronized machine guns rather than one. It entered combat in the fall of 1917 and served with the air forces of most of the Allied Nations, including the United States. Many famous aces flew the SPAD, but to Americans the best known was Captain Edward V. Rickenbacker, the top scoring U.S. ace of the First World War. A SPAD XIII in the markings of the 94th Pursuit Squadron of the American Expeditionary Force is shown in figure 2.13; the officer shown is Captain Rickenbacker.

Figure 2.13 — French SPAD XIII C.1 fighter; 1917. Captain Edward V. Rickenbacker is in front of the airplane. [USAF]

31

Figure 2.13 depicts a stubby but graceful-looking biplane with wings of equal chord and span, configured with no stagger and relatively small gap. The small gap in combination with the center cutout of the upper wing gave the pilot excellent visibility over the top of the wing. The design appears to be that of a double-bay biplane; however, the inner struts served only to stabilize the rather long wing-bracing wires and prevent their flapping and chaffing (ref. 22). The wires themselves consisted of round cables. The cockpit was close behind the engine with the pilot's feet and part of his legs located in aluminum tunnels beneath the engine (ref. 110). The landing gear was positioned well forward, ahead of the center of gravity, to minimize the risk of a nose-over on landing. Ailerons were on the upper wing only, and, as with the other aircraft described, no means of longitudinal trim was provided.

The SPAD XIII was powered with the Hispano-Suiza 8BA engine of 220 horsepower. The engine had eight water-cooled cylinders in two banks of four arranged in a V-type configuration, much like that of many modern automobile engines. The distinctive round radiator, equipped with manually operated (from the cockpit) shutters for controlling the cooling airflow, may be seen in figure 2.13. Long exhaust pipes ran on either side of the fuselage and terminated behind the pilot's cockpit. This arrangement resulted in a relatively quiet environment for the pilot (ref. 110). In an interesting survey of aircraft piston engine development, Taylor (ref. 111) credits the Hispano-Suiza with being one of the best and most advanced engines of World War I, as well as one that served as a sort of progenitor for a long line of Curtiss and Rolls-Royce liquid-cooled engines that culminated in the Rolls-Royce Merlin of World War II.

The data in table I indicate that the SPAD XIII had the most favorable power loading of any of the aircraft considered and a high (for its day) wing loading. These characteristics coupled with a relatively low zero-lift drag coefficient and low drag area gave the SPAD the highest speed of any of the aircraft listed in the table. As shown by the data in figure 2.18, the climb characteristics of the SPAD were bettered only by three of the Fokker aircraft.

The reference literature suggests that the SPAD XIII was not as maneuverable as some of the other fighters, but its high performance, great strength, and multigun armament made it a highly effective weapon. Its ability to dive steeply for prolonged periods of time without fear of structural failure is emphasized in all the reference material.

Piloting the aircraft required care, particularly at low speeds, and the use of moderate amounts of power was recommended in landing.

Although the SPAD XIII incorporated no new technical innovations, it synergistically combined an airframe of relatively high aerodynamic efficiency and great structural strength with an excellent engine to produce an outstanding aircraft. It may be regarded as representative of the top of the state of the art of a 1918 fighter aircraft equipped with thin, strut-and-wire-braced wings. The SPAD was so highly regarded that a number of countries maintained the aircraft as part of their active air force inventory for several years following the war. A total of 8472 SPAD XIII aircraft were manufactured.

Fokker D–VII

In the early 1970's, the U.S. Air Force announced with much fanfare a flyoff competition between prototypes of a new lightweight fighter aircraft. The resulting competition involved several years of research, engineering, and detailed flight evaluation before a winner was announced, the General Dynamics F–16. There was no novelty about the Air Force's prototype competition; it is a time-honored method of selecting military aircraft. The date of the first such competition is unknown, but one of the most renowned of German World War I fighters, the Fokker D–VII, was selected for full-scale production after being chosen the winner from about 30 competing prototypes. The time was late January 1918, and the place was Aldershof Airfield near Berlin.

As an indication of the speed with which prototype fighter aircraft could be developed at that time, Fokker alone entered no less than nine different types. Each of the competing aircraft was demonstrated by the manufacturer and then evaluated by well-known front-line pilots. The Fokker D–VII was the unanimous winner of the competition and first entered combat in April 1918 — an indication of the rapidity with which the unsophisticated aircraft of that era could be developed from prototype to combat readiness. Over 800 model D–VII aircraft were in front-line operations by mid-August 1918.

The Fokker D–VII is illustrated in figure 2.14 and, as can be seen, was a squarish-looking biplane equipped with an in-line engine and an automobile-type radiator located in the nose. The most advanced feature of the aircraft was the use of internally braced cantilever wings that had thick airfoil sections and a wooden structure similar to that previously described for the Fokker triplane. The thick wings were re-

Figure 2.14 — German Fokker D–VII fighter; 1918. [Merle Omstead via Martin Copp]

sponsible for many of the fine characteristics of the aircraft. The ailerons, located on the upper wing only, as well as the elevator and rudder had horn balances to reduce control forces. The winglike fairing between the wheels is also evident in figure 2.14; one experimental version of the D–VII had a fuel tank located in this fairing to reduce the fire hazard. The production aircraft was powered with either a Mercedes 160-horsepower engine or a BMW 185-horsepower engine. Both engines were six-cylinder, in-line, water-cooled types. The BMW was the preferred engine, however, as the aircraft proved to be somewhat underpowered when equipped with the Mercedes (ref. 112).

The Fokker D–VII was the heaviest of the fighters considered here and had wing loading and power loading values greater than those of the SPAD XIII. The power loading was in fact no lower than that of the Sopwith Camel, and the wing loading was higher. On the basis of these comparisons, the climb performance of the D–VII might be expected, according to the relationships given in chapter 6 of reference

90, to be inferior to that of both the SPAD XIII and the Sopwith Camel. On the contrary, the data in figure 2.18 show the D–VII to have much better climb performance then either of the other two aircraft. Brief calculations of the sea-level rate of climb by the methods in reference 90 indicate that the climb data for the Fokker D–VII are reasonable but that the SPAD should have had much better climb performance than indicated in figure 2.18. The explanation can no doubt be attributed, as mentioned for the triplane, to the thicker airfoil sections employed in the wings of the D–VII. The climb analysis showed that the maximum rate of climb could be achieved at lift coefficients of about 1.1 and 1.0 for the Fokker and the SPAD, respectively. The thick-wing D–VII could probably be flown with comfort at the required lift coefficient for maximum rate of climb, whereas the SPAD most likely could not. In fact, a lift coefficient of 1.0 might have been beyond the maximum value achievable by the SPAD XIII with its thin wings.

In other respects, the performance of the Fokker D–VII was good but not outstanding. The maximum speed of 124 miles per hour was not as high as that of the SPAD. This would be expected since the ratio of power-to-drag area was lower for the Fokker. The value of the maximum lift-drag ratio of the D–VII, however, was about 10 percent higher than that of the SPAD, which can be attributed to the higher aspect ratio of the Fokker wing configuration.

Not expressed by the data in table I were the superb handling characteristics that all the reference documents attribute to the Fokker D–VII. The aircraft was highly responsive, with light control forces; yet, unlike the Camel, it had no vices or contrary tendencies, and it could be flown with confidence throughout its flight envelope. Hence, the aircraft could be handled competently and safely by relatively inexperienced pilots and superbly by experienced ones. Frank Tallman clearly regarded the D–VII as the most outstanding of the World War I fighter aircraft he had the opportunity to fly (ref. 110).

Perhaps the greatest tribute to the D–VII can be found in article IV of the armistice agreement, which lists war material to be handed over to the Allies and specifically mentions all aircraft of the D–VII type — the only aircraft to be specifically cited in the armistice agreement. Certainly, this was a strong endorsement of the capabilities of the young Dutch designer, test pilot, and entrepreneur Anthony Herman Gerard Fokker, who provided the German Air Force with so many excellent aircraft . . . after being told by the Allied Powers that his services were not wanted (ref. 50).

35

Sopwith Dolphin

Unlike the SPAD XIII and the Fokker D–VII, the Sopwith Dolphin cannot be regarded as one of the great fighter aircraft of World War I, but it is included here as an illustration of one of the many unusual designs developed during that turbulent era. The aircraft is shown in figure 2.15. At first glance, the Dolphin appears to be a conventional double-bay biplane equipped with an in-line engine. A closer look, however, discloses that the wings are configured in an unorthodox fashion, with the lower wing located ahead of the upper wing. An aircraft with this wing arrangement is described as having negative stagger. The earlier DeHavilland DH–5 (a limited success) had this wing arrangement, as did the well-known Beech model 17 which appeared about 15 years after the Dolphin. (See chapter 4.)

The wing arrangement of the Dolphin was dictated solely by a desire to give the pilot improved visibility in the forward, upward, and rearward directions. Following the usual Sopwith practice of locating the concentrated masses in close proximity to each other, the pilot was positioned immediately behind the eight-cylinder Hispano-Suiza engine, with his feet actually resting on the rudder bar beneath the rear part of the crankcase. As in the Camel, the fuel tank was in the fuselage immediately behind the cockpit. To overcome the poor visibility of the Camel, the top wing of the Dolphin was located close to the fuselage so that the pilot's head protruded through a large cutout in the wing near the leading edge; this cutout can be seen in figure 2.15. Positioning the aerodynamic center in the proper relation to the aircraft center of gravity made it necessary to place the lower wing ahead of the upper wing, which was located relatively far back from the nose. The negative stagger configuration was the result.

The wing configuration of the Dolphin undoubtedly gave the pilot excellent visibility but held certain undesirable pitfalls as well. Should the aircraft turn onto its back in an accident, the entire weight of the aircraft might come to rest on the top of his head. Should he be able to duck his head in time to avoid this unpleasant possibility, the proximity of the upper wing to the fuselage, together with the cabane struts and wires on either side of the cockpit, effectively trapped him in the aircraft between a large engine in front and a fuel tank in back. As if this were not enough, the butts of the two forward-firing, synchronized machine guns protruded into the cockpit and, in addition, one or two semiflexible guns were usually mounted on the leading edge of the wing and fired at angles of 45° or more over the propeller. These guns also

Figure 2.15 — British Sopwith 5F.1 Dolphin fighter; 1918. [ukn via Martin Copp]

protruded into the cockpit. (The flexible guns are not mounted on the aircraft shown in figure 2.15.) Understandably, pilots were not entirely happy when posted to squadrons equipped with the Dolphin. Various methods of protecting the pilot in case of an accident, including "roll bars," were investigated, but no such device was universally incorporated on production aircraft.

The first prototype Dolphin had a radiator located in front of the engine, automobile style, but this installation greatly restricted visibility in landing. The single nose radiator was then replaced with two small radiators located on either side of the fuselage, just to the rear of the cockpit. These radiators can be seen in figure 2.15. The pipes connecting the radiators to the engine passed through the cockpit on each side. One Dolphin pilot described how the pipes were used as "hand warmers" during flight at high altitudes. While the control stick was held with one hand, the other glove-encased hand grasped the water pipe until it was warm, after which the pilot flew the aircraft with the warm hand while holding the pipe on the opposite side of the cockpit with his other hand (so said the late Charles E. Walton, formerly of No. 23 Squadron of the Royal Air Force, in conversation with the author). Such a story becomes believable in view of the temperatures of 0° F and below encountered at altitudes of 15 000 feet and above, even on a warm summer day.

According to the data given in table I, the Dolphin was a large, heavy fighter with a gross weight of 1911 pounds and a wing area of 263 square feet. The maximum speed was a very credible 128 miles per hour at 10 000 feet but was somewhat less that that of the SPAD. The climb results in figure 2.18 show a performance improvement of the Dolphin at the higher altitudes, as compared with the Camel, but the Dolphin was inferior at all altitudes to the SPAD XIII and the Fokker D–VII. Most references to the Dolphin allude to its excellent high-altitude capability, but the results shown do not support this contention. Data in reference 31, however, show a much improved climb capability when later versions of the aircraft were equipped with a more powerful 300-horsepower engine. The flying qualities of the aircraft apparently had no treacherous tendencies but were characterized by fairly heavy control forces and relatively slow response.

The Dolphin first flew in June 1917 and entered combat in squadron strength in January 1918. A total of 2150 Dolphins were ordered, but only 1532 were delivered by the end of the war. Not many combat squadrons were equipped with the aircraft. That the Dolphin was thought well of is indicated by the expressed intention of the French to build under license a 300-horsepower version of the aircraft for use by their air force.

Reappearance of the Monoplane Fighter

The German Air Force sponsored another flyoff fighter competition at Aldershof in June 1918. Twelve companies entered 25 prototypes; of these, 5 were Fokker monoplanes. The Fokker D–VIII monoplane was the overall winner, and a production order was placed for 400 of them. A second aircraft, the Junkers D–I, also received a limited production contract. Both of these aircraft arrived on the scene too late to make any sort of reputation in combat, but both are included in the present discussion because of their technical significance. The Fokker D–VIII and the Junkers D–I are shown in figures 2.16 and 2.17, respectively.

The configuration of the Fokker D–VIII is known as a parasol monoplane. This type is characterized by a single wing supported above the fuselage by an arrangement of cabane struts and has the advantage of giving the pilot good downward visibility, as compared with a midwing or low-wing design, but has the disadvantage of the drag-producing cabane struts. Like the wings of the Fokker D–VII and the Fokker triplane, the thick wing of the D–VIII was internally braced and

Figure 2.16 — German Fokker D–VIII fighter; 1918. [USAF via Martin Copp]

Figure 2.17—German Junkers D–I all-metal fighter; 1918. [ukn via Martin Copp]

full cantilever. Unlike the earlier aircraft, however, the D–VIII wing was covered entirely with plywood, which gave it great strength and rigidity. Also, it was one of the few wings of the World War I period to be tapered in both planform and thickness ratio. Wing taper not only increases aerodynamic efficiency but also structural efficiency, especially for a cantilever wing, since taper reduces the wing weight and root-bending stress for a given wing area. Wing damping in roll is also reduced by wing taper; this means a higher rate of roll for a given aileron-supplied rolling moment. The D–VIII wing, scaled to various sizes, was used on Fokker aircraft for many years (ref. 38).

The fuselage and tail structure were of typical Fokker design and consisted of welded steel frames covered with fabric. Power was supplied by an Oberursel rotary engine of 110 horsepower, which was the same engine that powered the earlier Fokker triplane. At 1238 pounds, the gross weight of the D–VIII was slightly less than that of the triplane and about the same as that of the Nieuport 17.

The maximum speed of the D–VIII was a modest 114 miles per hour at 6500 feet, but the climbing capability of the aircraft, shown by the data in figure 2.18, was outstanding. As discussed in connection with the triplane and the D–VII, the superb climbing performance of the D–VIII was due in large measure to the thick airfoil sections utilized in the wing. The small wing area with respect to the fuselage and tail area is partly responsible for the high zero-lift drag coefficient of 0.0552. Other important contributors to the high drag coefficient are the complex arrangement of cabane struts, fixed landing gear with large unstreamlined wheels, and open cockpit. Truly low drag coefficients can only be achieved when, in addition to cantilever wings, all these other drag-producing elements are eliminated and very careful attention is given to detailed design and refinement. This synergistic combination was finally achieved in the time period between 1930 and 1940. (See chapter 4.) To put the drag coefficient of the D–VIII in perspective, the value of this coefficient for a modern general aviation aircraft, the Beech Bonanza, is 0.0192.

Although the Fokker D–VIII is of technical interest because of its wing design, the data do not seem to indicate that the aircraft represented any significant improvement over the D–VII. The 145-horsepower Oberursel rotary engine was intended as a replacement for the 110-horsepower unit but was not manufactured in sufficient quantity to allow its use on production aircraft. Flight tests of an experimental model of the D–VIII equipped with the larger engine showed much better performance than indicated by the data in table I.

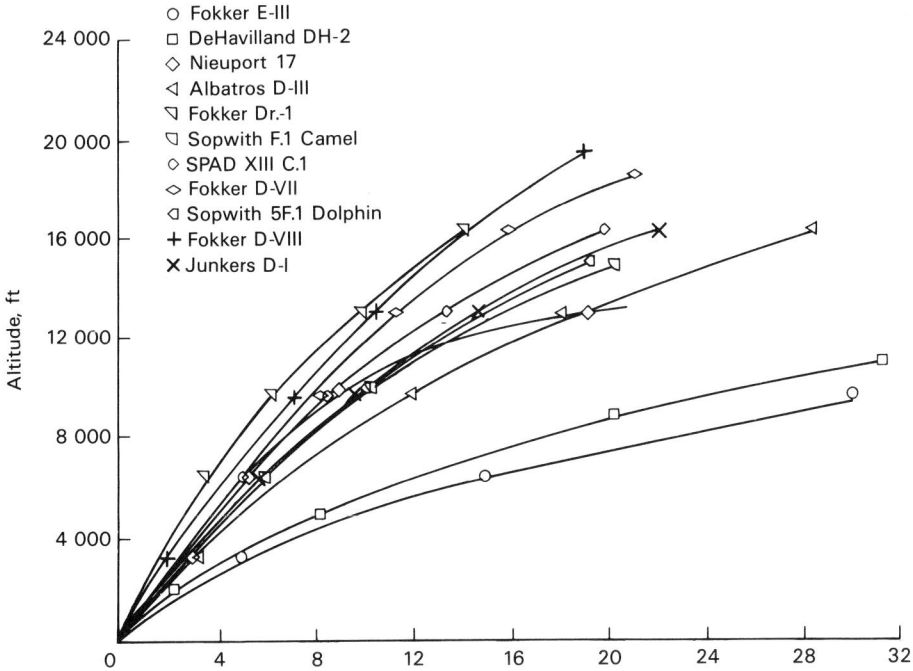

Figure 2.18 — Time required to climb to various altitudes for 11 World War I fighters.
[data from ref. 82]

No discussion of the Fokker D–VIII would be complete without mention of the structural problem encountered with the wing. Some 20 aircraft were delivered in late July 1918, but in a fairly short time, several were lost in flight as a result of structural failure of the wings. Although some disagreement as to the cause of these failures can be found in the literature, the account given by Fokker in his autobiography (ref. 50) seems reasonable. According to his account, the technical department of the German Air Force required that the rear wing spar of the production aircraft be strengthened to conform with design rules established for aircraft with conventional strut-and-wire-braced wings. In modern terminology, the elastic axis of the cantilever wing (the chordwise location of the axis about which the wing twists) was moved rearward, with the result that the wing diverged, or twisted off, at a certain critical speed that varied with altitude. (See chapter 10.) Once the wing design reverted to the original rear spar size, the elastic axis

41

was moved forward and no further difficulty was encountered. Wing divergence and flutter are well understood today but were something of a mystery for many years. An understanding of these phenomena is particularly important in the design of structurally sound cantilever wings. Such wings were regarded with grave suspicion for a long time because of problems such as those encountered with the D–VIII and other aircraft having cantilever wings. The Fokker D–VIII returned to combat operations in October 1918, and 85 were in use at the time of the armistice. A total of 381 examples of the aircraft, known informally as the Flying Razor, were delivered.

The configuration of the Junkers D–I monoplane fighter (fig. 2.17) was modern in appearance and featured a thick, full cantilever wing mounted in the low position at the bottom of the fuselage. Although not apparent in the photograph, the wing tapered in thickness ratio from approximately 17 percent at the root to about 12 percent at the tip, but was untapered in planform. The airfoil thickness ratio at the root was greater than that of any of the airfoil sections employed on the Fokker fighters. Other features to note on the aircraft are the 185-horsepower BMW engine with nose-mounted radiator, the all-moving vertical tail, and the roll bar located behind the cockpit to protect the pilot's head if the aircraft nosed over onto its back.

The most interesting aspect of the D–I was its all-metal structure. Professor Hugo Junkers was an early advocate of all-metal aircraft structures; the D–I was one of his early successful monoplane designs. The internal structure was made up of riveted aluminum alloy tubing that was covered with corrugated sheets of the same material. Most of the strength resided in the internal structure, with the corrugations in the covering providing local panel stiffness; the torsional stiffness of the wings was also enhanced by the metal covering. The type of construction employed in the D–I was relatively heavy but had great durability and was used in the design of many Junkers aircraft until well into the 1930's. In the United States, the famous Ford trimotor employed the Junkers type of structural design. (See chapter 4.)

The durability of the all-metal structure was one of its most attractive attributes. The types of cloth with dope finishes used on most World War I aircraft deteriorated rapidly, apparently a result of light of certain wave lengths in the Sun's spectrum. A great deal of study was given to finding means for protecting aircraft covering. Certain types of dope or paint were found to offer more protection from the Sun than others (ref. 39). Wooden wings, such as employed on the D–VIII and later Fokker designs, were subject to delamination, rot, and deterioration of glue joints. All these factors highlighted the advantages of all-metal construction, although the strut-and-wire-braced biplane covered with fabric continued, at that time, to give the lightest weight for a given strength.

The Junkers D–I had a relatively high zero-lift drag coefficient of 0.0612, due in part to reasons similar to those outlined for the Fokker D–VIII. In addition, the corrugations in the covering increased the wetted area (the surface area exposed to the airstream) by 20 to 40 percent (ref. 72); this increase is not accounted for in the conventional method of defining the drag coefficient. The maximum lift-drag ratio was a poor 7.0, which compares quite unfavorably with the value of 8.1 for the Fokker models D–VII and D–VIII, and 9.2 for the Sopwith Dolphin. The maximum speed quoted for the D–I varies from 115 to 149 miles per hour depending upon the reference consulted. A value of 119 miles per hour is listed here and is thought to be close to the maximum speed achieved. The climbing performance of the aircraft was about the same as that of the Sopwith Dolphin. The advantages of the thick wing apparently could not overcome the disadvantages of the high wing loading, high power loading, and the high zero-lift drag coefficient.

Forty-one Junkers D–I fighters were built, but apparently none saw combat service.

Fighter Progress, 1914–18

By the end of World War I, the fighter airplane had progressed from a flimsy, low-performance, and clumsy vehicle to a highly effective aircraft. Many configuration types were tried in combat, but the strut-and-wire-braced biplane equipped with two synchronized machine guns firing between the rotating propeller blades set a pattern in fighter design that lasted until the mid-1930's. Although the thick cantilever wing was successfully employed by Fokker, the concept was not widely used until the monoplane fighter became the standard configuration type just prior to World War II.

Engine power and reliability increased during the World War I period, as did aircraft structural strength and reliability. Detailed aircraft stress analysis, unusual in 1914, had become common design practice by 1918, and a fairly comprehensive body of aerodynamic data was available to the designer. Aircraft control and handling characteristics, though largely a matter of cut-and-try experimentation, also greatly improved during the 4-year period.

Aircraft performance improvements can easily be shown in a quantitative way by graphical means. The large improvements in climbing performance have already been discussed with the use of the time-to-climb curves given in figure 2.18. A more favorable relationship between the wing loading and power loading together with higher aerodynamic efficiency were responsible for much of the improved climb performance realized from 1914 to 1918. The importance of the thick airfoil sections employed by Fokker and Junkers in allowing the aircraft to climb at its optimum lift coefficient has also been indicated.

The trend in speed capability is shown in figure 2.19, in which the maximum speed V_{max} is plotted against the power parameter $\overline{H}$, which is the cube root of the ratio of engine power to drag area (ref. 90). Since the speeds in table I are not all specified at the same altitude, the parameter $\overline{H}$ contains an adjustment for the effect of altitude on drag and maximum available power as follows:

$$\overline{H} = \sqrt[3]{\frac{P_0}{f} \left(\frac{\gamma}{\sigma}\right)}$$

where P_0 is the maximum power available at sea level, f is the drag area, σ is the atmospheric density ratio for the given altitude, and γ is the percentage of maximum sea-level power available at that altitude. The values of both σ and γ were obtained from reference 90.

The method of presenting the speed data assumes that the drag due to lift is a small fraction of the total drag for the maximum-speed flight condition and that the propeller efficiency is about the same for the different aircraft. The near linear correlation of the data in figure 2.19 shows these to be good assumptions in most cases. In the 4-year period of World War I, the maximum speed of fighter aircraft increased from 87 to 134 miles per hour — or expressed another way, the maximum speed increased by 54 percent. This increase in achievable maximum speed resulted from a reduction in drag area, that is, more efficient aerodynamic design, and from increased engine power.

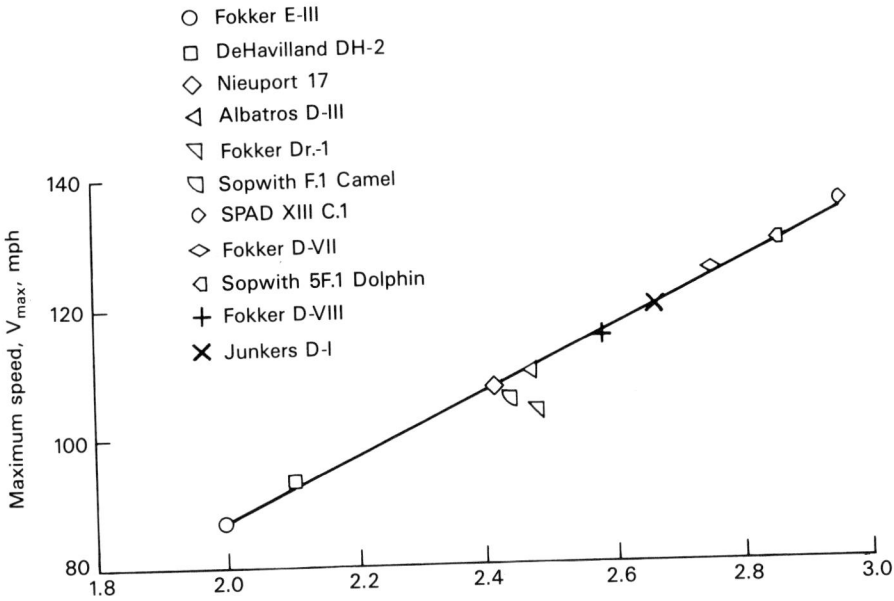

Figure 2.19 — Variation of maximum speed with power parameter H.

For example, numerical values for the Fokker E–III and the SPAD XIII, based on data from table I, illustrate the point as follows:

Aircraft	P_0	f	$\overline{H}^a$
Fokker E–III	100	12.61	1 99
SPAD XIII C.1	220	8.33	2.98

a For sea-level conditions.

In comparing the values of the two aircraft, the SPAD has over twice the power but only 65 percent of the drag area of the Fokker. The quest for high performance has always been exemplified by vigorous efforts to increase both aerodynamic efficiency and power. For example, the drag area and power of the World War II North American P–51 fighter (chapter 5) were 3.75 square feet and 1490 horsepower, respectively. The corresponding value of $\overline{H}$ was 7.35. Compare these numbers with those for the Fokker and the SPAD!

45

Aircraft structural efficiency is also of great interest and can be thought of in terms of the minimum weight structure needed to meet required strength and stiffness criteria. Simple methods of adequately illustrating trends in structural efficiency are difficult to define. One fairly simple but relatively crude approach was presented by Wilson in reference 122 and was later used in reference 90. Correlations in reference 122, augmented by the present writer with a great deal of new data, show that the sum of the weights of the payload, fuel, and propulsion system tends to be nearly a constant fraction of the gross weight in well-designed aircraft regardless of the method of construction or era in which the aircraft was designed. Put another way, the useful load fraction $1-(W_e/W_g)$ should correlate closely with the engine weight fraction W_t/W_g, where W_g is the gross weight, W_e is the empty weight, and W_t is the propulsion-system weight.

The useful load fraction is plotted as a function of the engine weight fraction in figure 2.20 for the 11 fighter aircraft discussed in this chapter. The empty and gross weights are given in table I; the engine weights are based on data contained in reference 24. The dry engine weights given in reference 24 for the water-cooled engines were

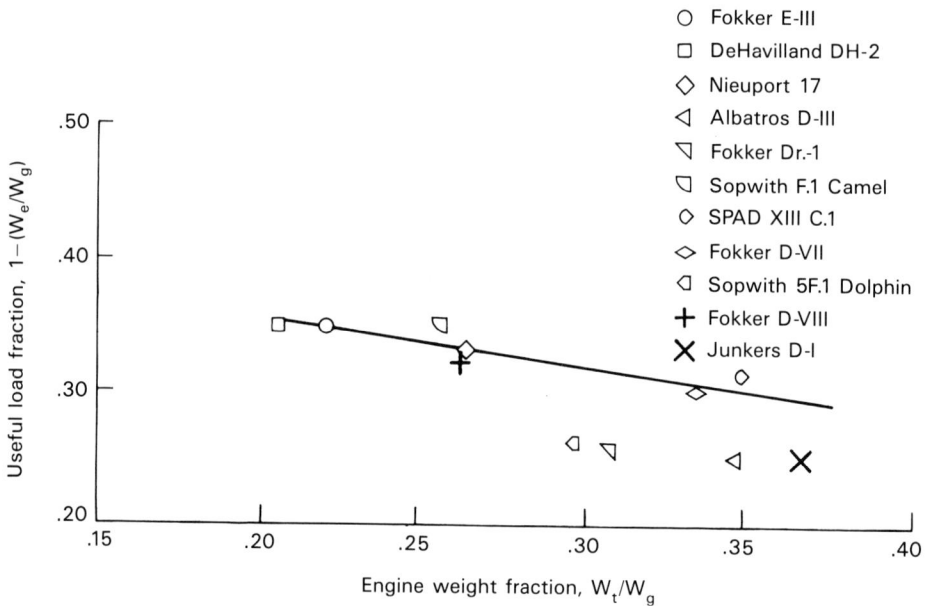

Figure 2.20 — Aircraft useful load fraction as function of engine weight fraction.

increased by 10 percent to account for the weight of the radiator and associated plumbing system and the cooling water.

Seven of the aircraft show a close correlation between the useful load and engine weight fractions. A relatively consistent level of structural efficiency is accordingly suggested. Four of the aircraft, however, show values of the useful load fraction significantly below the straight-line fairing through the data for the other aircraft. The four aircraft with reduced structural efficiency were the all-metal Junkers D-1, the Albatros D-III with its semimonocoque wooden fuselage, the Fokker Dr.-1 with its three wings, and the Sopwith Dolphin. The reduced values of useful load fraction are perhaps explainable by unique features incorporated in three of these aircraft, but there seems to be no clear reasons for the high empty weight of the Sopwith Dolphin.

This discussion of design and performance trends concludes the section on World War I fighter aircraft. Attention is now focused on multiengine bombers of that era.

Heavy Bombers

Most types of World War I aircraft, including fighters, were used at one time or another for tactical or ground-support bombing operations. The heavy bombers discussed in this section are what would be called strategic bombers in present-day terminology. They were used for bombing such targets as docks and harbor installations, rail yards, factories, and cities. The mission of these aircraft required them to have sufficient radius of action and payload capability to deliver a significant bomb load on a variety of targets and to carry enough defensive armament to offer a reasonable probability of mission success and safe return to base. Heavy bombers were used singly and in formations of several aircraft, on both day and night missions. Speed, maneuverability, and rate of climb were of secondary importance although a high ceiling was considered desirable.

The mission requirements for heavy bombers led to large, heavy (for that time period) multiengine aircraft just as they do today. Gross weights varied widely but usually fell in the range from 8000 to 16 000 pounds, and some of the German special-purpose R-planes weighed over 30 000 pounds (ref. 68). Two engines were used on most designs, although examples can be found of aircraft with three, four, and five engines. Most of the aircraft were multibay strut-and-wire-braced biplanes; however, several triplanes appeared, one of which is described herein. At war's end, there were several German designs for highly advanced monoplane bombers that incorporated thick, cantilever wings (ref. 68). Construction of most heavy bombers consisted of a conventional wood framework covered with fabric.

The first of the large, heavy bombers was the Sikorsky Ilya Muromets, which first flew in February 1914. Caproni, Gotha, Friedrichshafen, A.E.G., Handley Page, and Vickers are a few other names that will be forever linked with the large, heavy bombers of the World War I era. Three heavy bombers, the German Gotha G.IV, the British Handley Page 0/400, and the Italian Caproni CA.42 are discussed here to give a glimpse of the size and characteristics of this class of aircraft.

Gotha G.IV

The name Gotha still evokes in the minds of some people the terrifying image of a group of large aircraft dropping bombs on the helpless citizens of a great metropolitan area. The Gotha gained this dubious distinction because of its use in the bombing raids on London in 1917 and 1918. Twenty-seven Gotha attacks were made in the course of about a year. Not a large application of strategic air power by World War II standards but enough to cause great consternation in an era when the English Channel was still mistakenly thought to ensure protection of the British Isles against a foreign invader. The Gotha raids, conducted first in daylight and later at night, actually caused little physical damage, but the psychological impact was such that badly needed British squadrons were recalled from the front to protect Britain against the German invader. Actually, several types of German aircraft participated in the bombing of London, but the name Gotha has for some reasons become synonymous with the bombing of helpless cities.

The Gotha model G.IV depicted in figure 2.21 was a triple-bay biplane equipped with two pusher-type engines mounted between the upper and lower wings, one on either side of the fuselage. The thin wings incorporated a small amount of sweepback to position the aerodynamic center in proper relation to the aircraft center of gravity. Horn balances were employed on the ailerons and rudder to reduce the control forces required to maneuver this very large aircraft. The landing gear had four main wheels; two were positioned below the bottom wing at the location of each engine nacelle.

The Gotha G.IV was manned by a crew of three: a single pilot and two gunners. The front gunner armed with a flexible machine gun was

Figure 2.21 — German Gotha G.IV twin-engine bomber; 1917. [ukn via Martin Copp]

located in an open cockpit at the nose of the aircraft; this man also served as the bombardier. Behind the front gunner and just ahead of the upper wing was the pilot's cockpit. His flight controls consisted of the usual rudder bar and stick, but a "steering wheel," like that in an automobile, was mounted at the top of the stick and was used for deflecting the ailerons. The use of a full wheel, rather than a yoke as in modern aircraft, suggests that several revolutions of the wheel were required to move the ailerons through their full range of deflection. Aircraft response to control inputs must have been sluggish, and the piloting job must have seemed something like a wrestling match. The third crew member was another gunner located in an open cockpit behind the upper wing. His flexible machine gun could be utilized effectively in various quadrants above and to the sides of the aircraft and could also be fired downward and rearward through a sort of inclined tunnel that passed through the inside of the fuselage and opened on the bottom. The rear gunner could accordingly fire, through a limited angular range, at an aircraft attacking from below and to the rear. This feature proved to be a startling and unwelcome discovery to a number of unsuspecting Allied pilots.

The performance of the 8558-pound gross weight Gotha was not spectacular, as can be seen from the data in table I for the slightly improved Gotha G.V. The maximum speed was only 87 miles per hour, which suggests a cruising speed at 75-percent power of about 78 miles per hour. This cruising speed, coupled with an estimated stalling speed of 56 miles per hour gave the pilot a very narrow speed corridor in which to fly and maneuver the aircraft. The maximum lift-drag ratio of 7.7 seems reasonably high for an aircraft festooned with so many struts, wires, wheels, and other protuberances. The usual load of the Gotha on a London raid consisted of six 110-pound bombs carried externally.

The reference sources indicate that more Gothas were lost in flying accidents than in combat with the enemy. Sluggish response to control inputs together with its narrow speed corridor may have contributed to the high accident rate. Many accidents occurred in landing. The fuselage was reportedly weak, probably because of the gun tunnel, and frequently broke in half on a hard landing.

All in all, the Gotha does not seem to have been the superb aircraft that its fearsome reputation would suggest. The reality, as with so many other aircraft, does not live up to the legend.

Handley Page 0/400

Like the Gotha G.IV, the Handley Page 0/400 illustrated in figure 2.22 was a multibay biplane equipped with two engines mounted between the wings and with a four-wheel main landing gear; two wheels were mounted below the lower wing at the location of each of the engine nacelles. The appearance of the British Handley Page bomber, however, was startlingly different from that of the German Gotha. The large gap between the wings, marked wing dihedral angle, and large span of the upper wing as compared with the lower are distinctive features in the appearance of the aircraft. Also in marked contrast to the pusher engine arrangement of the Gotha, the 0/400 employed a tractor configuration. Another distinctive feature, not evident in the photograph, is the tail assembly, which consisted of two horizontal surfaces arranged in a biplane configuration. A single fixed fin, centrally located between the two horizontal surfaces, and two all-moving rudders, also located between the horizontal surfaces but positioned near the tips, comprised the vertical tail surfaces. Horn-balanced ailerons and elevators were utilized to reduce control forces.

The wings folded rearward, just outboard of the engines, to a position parallel to the fuselage. This complication was dictated by a requirement that the aircraft fit into a standard-size Royal Air Force

Figure 2.22 — British Handley Page 0/400 twin-engine bomber; 1916–17. [USAF via Martin Copp]

hangar. Apparently, the authorities responsible for aircraft procurement thought it more cost effective to complicate and perhaps compromise the aircraft than to build new hangars.

The crew of the Handley Page 0/400 usually consisted of four men. A gunner-bombardier, located in the nose of the aircraft, had two flexible machine guns. The two pilots were in an open cockpit behind the front gunner and just ahead of the upper wing; each pilot had a complete set of flight controls. The necessity for two pilots is suggested by the 9-hour flight maximum duration of the aircraft. The second gunner was located in a cockpit behind the upper wing and, as in the case of the front gunner, was provided with two flexible machine guns. In addition, a single flexible machine gun was mounted on the floor inside the fuselage and could be fired downward and rearward through a small trap door in the bottom of the fuselage. Apparently, the single rear gunner was expected to alternate between this gun and the two top-mounted guns, depending upon the position of the attacker. The frustration the single rear gunner must have felt in the event of a simultaneous attack from above and below can readily be imagined.

Surely, a second rear gunner must have been carried on missions in which aggressive attack by many enemy aircraft was anticipated.

The gross weight of the Handley Page was 14 425 pounds (table I), nearly 6000 pounds heavier than the Gotha, and the wing area was 1655 square feet as compared with 963 square feet for the German bomber. The maximum lift-drag ratio of the 0/400 was a very impressive 9.7, which was a full 26 percent higher than that of the Gotha. The Handley Page also had the higher top speed of the two aircraft. The 0/400 was large enough and had sufficient fuel capacity to deliver a 2000-pound bomb load on a target located 300 miles from home base and return safely. The bombs themselves were carried inside the fuselage in a vertical position ready for release. The Handley Page 0/400 seems to have been an outstanding aircraft for its time and, in most respects, superior to the Gotha except for its service ceiling of 8500 feet, which was less than half that attributed to the Gotha.

The size and certain other characteristics of the Handley Page 0/400 can be put in perspective by comparison with more modern aircraft. The wing loading and power loading of 8.7 and 20.5 are fairly close to the corresponding values of 6.9 and 18 for the famous Piper J-3 Cub (chapter 4), and the values of the maximum lift-drag ratio of the two aircraft are nearly the same. Thus, in a sense, the 0/400 can be likened to a 14 000-pound Cub, although the response to control inputs and the control forces required of the pilot must be considered as utterly different for the two aircraft. Cecil Lewis in reference 85 suggests the handling characteristics of the aircraft in the following quotation: "True, it was like a lorry in the air. When you decided to turn left, you pushed over the controls, went and had a cup of tea and came back to find the turn just starting."

Another interesting comparison of the Handley Page can be made with the modern-day Boeing 727-200 jet airliner (chapter 13). The wing areas of the two aircraft are almost the same, but the 727 is nearly 15 times as heavy as the Handley Page, is about 7 times as fast, and has a value of the maximum lift-drag ratio more than twice that of the 0/400. All these changes occurred in a time span of a little less than 50 years.

The first Handley Page bomber was flown in 1915, and the 0/400 version appeared in 1916. About 800 Handley Page bombers of all types were built during the war. The model 0/400 continued in military service for several years after the war, and several were converted for use as civil transports. The 0/400 was scheduled for large-scale production in the United States for use by the American Expeditionary

Force in France. By the time hostilities ceased in November 1918, only 107 examples had been completed and all production contracts were soon terminated.

The principal legacy of the Gotha and Handley Page heavy bombers was the twin-engine, strut-and-wire-braced, open-cockpit biplane configuration that dominated bomber development for many years following the end of World War I. Various models of the Keystone bomber were employed by the U.S. Army Air Corps until the mid-1930's. These aircraft incorporated the same configuration concepts as the Gotha and Handley Page, with fewer struts and wires, more powerful engines, better structures, and marginally better performance.

Caproni CA.42

The name Caproni is an honored one in the annals of World War I aviation. The Italian firm bearing that name, along with Sikorsky in Russia, first flew heavy multiengine bombers in the year 1913, and Caproni bombers were used throughout World War I, not only by Italy but by England and France as well. Production of one version of a Caproni bomber was also planned in the United States but had not materialized at war's end.

All Caproni bombers had three engines. Two of these were mounted in a tractor arrangement, with one engine at the nose of each of two fuselagelike booms that connected the wings and tail assembly. The third engine was a pusher installed in the rear of a nacelle situated between the wings. Pilot and gunner-bombardier were in cockpits ahead of the pusher engine. The rear gunner(s) was located in several different positions in the various Caproni bomber designs. Both biplane and triplane bombers were built by Caproni, with the number of biplanes produced far outnumbering the triplanes. About 200 Caproni bombers of all types were manufactured, of which about 30 were triplanes. In Italian service, these aircraft were extensively used for bombing targets in the Austro-Hungarian empire. Such raids originated in Italy and required round-trip flights across the Alps. Good high-altitude performance was accordingly an important design requirement.

Although production of Caproni biplanes far outnumbered the triplanes, the model CA.42 triplane bomber was selected for inclusion here because it represents an interesting application of the triplane formula to a very large aircraft. Some of the reasons for selecting a triplane configuration were given in the previous section describing the

Fokker Dr.–1 triplane fighter. For a very large airplane in which the physical dimensions are limited, perhaps by hanger size or tiedown area on the airfield, the triplane arrangement offers a higher effective aspect ratio for a given wing span and area than does a biplane. The triplane arrangement of the CA.42 probably derives from this argument since the aircraft had a very large wing area.

The Caproni CA.42 may be seen in figure 2.23 and offers a unique, if somewhat grotesque, appearance. The three wings were connected and braced by a veritable forest of struts and wires. A front view of the aircraft shows that the interplane struts were configured in a five-bay arrangement. The center nacelle containing the pusher engine, pilot, and forward gunner was attached to the undersurface of the center wing. The tips of the pusher propeller can be seen above and below the left fuselage-boom. A rear gunner was positioned in each fuselage-boom immediately behind the center wing. The boxlike pod on the lower wing housed the bombs. The main landing gear consisted of

Figure 2.23 — Italian Caproni CA.42 three-engine triplane bomber; 1917. [Stephen J. Hudek via Martin Copp]

eight wheels in two clusters of four each, skids were located under each wing tip, and rather tall tail skids were at the rear. The large number of wheels was intended to distribute the weight of the aircraft on the ground and thus prevent the aircraft from becoming mired in the relatively soft turf airfields in use at that time. Three rudders were mounted on a single horizontal tail; a later version of the aircraft had a biplane horizontal-tail configuration. Ailerons were employed on all three wings.

A number of sources were consulted in assembling the data given in table I. Although the various sources were in essential agreement on the dimensions of the CA.42, discrepancies were found in the weight and performance data. Engines of different power were employed on a number of the production aircraft and may account for the confusion in the data. The specifications in table I were taken from reference 1 and are for the aircraft equipped with U.S.-built Liberty engines of 400 horsepower each. At 17 700 pounds gross weight, the CA.42 is the heaviest of the aircraft considered, and the maximum speed of 98 miles per hour is higher than that of either the Gotha or the Handley Page 0/400. The lower wing loading and more favorable ratio of power to weight, as compared with the other two bombers, probably gave it a good high-altitude capability for transalpine flying. One reference gives a flight duration of 7 hours and a maximum bomb load of 3200 pounds. Assuming a cruising speed of 89 miles per hour at 75-percent power, the CA.42 had an estimated range of about 600 miles, or the ability to deliver its bombs on a target 300 miles from home base and return safely.

The Caproni CA.42 seems to have had a very creditable performance when equipped with Liberty engines; with lower power engines, the performance was not nearly so good. Perhaps the appearance of the Liberty engine relatively late in the war contributed to the small number of aircraft built. In one reference the aircraft was stated to be difficult to fly, but no specific details are given.

At least three CA.42 triplane bombers were sent to the United States for evaluation. One of these was to have been tested at Langley Field, Virginia, but was completely destroyed in a crash at Langley on its maiden flight in December 1917.

With this brief glimpse of the heavy bomber in World War I, attention is now focused on the two-seat army cooperation and light bomber types that constituted the workhorse aircraft of that era.

Army Cooperation Aircraft

The unglamorous two-seat aircraft, working in cooperation with army ground forces, formed the backbone of aerial activity in World War I and undoubtedly contributed more to military successes than any other class of aircraft. One of the primary functions of the much-heralded single-seat fighters was the protection of their own two-seaters and the destruction of those belonging to the enemy. Army cooperation aircraft performed a variety of diverse duties including photoreconnaissance, artillery spotting, observation of enemy troop movements, ground strafing, and daylight tactical bombing. Duties such as photoreconnaissance required steady and precise flying at a given altitude and along prescribed flight tracks if the photographs necessary for accurate mapmaking were to be obtained. All the while, the crews had to be constantly on the lookout for enemy air attack, and the steady flight path over enemy territory offered the antiaircraft gunners excellent opportunities for target practice. Certainly the men who flew these aircraft are among the unsung heroes of the First Great War.

The two-seater, as it evolved during the war, had the pilot in the front cockpit with one or two fixed, synchronized machine guns firing between the propeller blades; the observer was in the rear cockpit with one or two flexibly mounted machine guns in addition to the camera, wireless, or other special equipment. A steady platform was required for photoreconnaissance and bomb aiming, which meant that the two-seater had to be relatively stable; yet a certain amount of speed and maneuverability were required to avoid destruction by the enemy. Good high-altitude performance was another desirable characteristic. The correct mix of these sometimes conflicting requirements and the technical means for accomplishing that mix presented difficult design problems. In the early years of the war, two-seaters were often considered to be easy prey for fighter aircraft; but as designs improved, they gave an increasingly good account of themselves in combat operations.

The development of the two-seater presents little of technical interest beyond what has already been discussed in the preceding sections on fighters and bombers. A large number of two-seat types were developed during the war, and a number of configuration concepts, including monoplanes, biplanes, triplanes, and quadruplanes were investigated. As in the case of the fighters and bombers, however, the biplane emerged as the best compromise, consistent with the existing state of technology, between the various conflicting requirements. Three two-seat biplanes, the British B.E.2c, the German Junkers J–I, and the British DeHavilland DH–4 are described next.

56

B.E.2c

It would be difficult to conceive of an aircraft so poorly adapted to the rigors of aerial combat as the long-lived series of British B.E.2 two-seaters designed by the government-controlled Royal Aircraft Factory. The prototype first flew in 1912, and a B.E.2a was the first British aircraft to land in France, on August 13, 1914, after the beginning of the war. The B.E.2c and other models of the B.E. series remained in production until July 1917. More than 3500 B.E.2-type aircraft were constructed, and, unbelievably, a single-seat fighter version, the B.E.12, was also produced. The British ace Albert Ball referred to this machine in the following succinct terms, ". . . a bloody awful aeroplane."

The B.E.2 was developed on the premise that inherent stability in an aircraft was a highly desirable characteristic that would contribute to flying ease and flight safety. Further, the military thinking in 1914 envisioned the use of the airplane in warfare solely as an instrument for supporting the army ground troops. Again, inherent stability seemed a desirable characteristic for such duties as reconnaissance and artillery spotting. Unfortunately, experience early in the war showed that a two-seater required speed, maneuverability, and a good rate of climb to survive. The B.E.2c had none of these characteristics, yet production of the aircraft continued; it was callously referred to as "cold meat" by German fighter pilots.

As shown in figure 2.24, the B.E.2c was a strut-and-wire-braced, double-bay biplane equipped with an in-line engine swinging a four-blade propeller. The 90-horsepower R.A.F. la engine itself was somewhat unusual in that it was air cooled. Ailerons were incorporated in both upper and lower wings, and the horizontal and vertical tail units had both fixed and movable surfaces. The large dihedral angle evident in the wings was dictated by the requirement for inherent lateral-directional stability. Unlike most two-seaters, the pilot sat in the rear cockpit and the gunner was in the front cockpit. Although the B.E.2c was equipped with a single machine gun, the field of fire between the wings and over the pilot's head and vertical tail limited the gunner's effectiveness. Because of the position of the lower wing relative to the gunner, the pilot had to operate the camera on photoreconnaissance missions in addition to flying the aircraft.

The data in table I show the 2142-pound gross weight of the B.E.2c to have had a disastrously low maximum speed of 72 miles per hour at 6500 feet. Not shown in the table is the climb-performance data that indicate that 45 minutes were required to climb to the low service ceiling of 10 000 feet. The zero-lift drag coefficient, drag area,

Figure 2.24 — British B.E.2c army cooperation aircraft; 1914. [ukn via Martin Copp]

and maximum lift-drag ratio were comparable to many contemporary aircraft of the time; however, the ratios of power to weight and power to drag area were so low that only mediocre performance could be expected. In addition to its performance limitations, all reference sources indicate that the aircraft lacked maneuverability.

The shortcomings of the B.E.2c in armament, performance, and maneuverability resulted in a very poor front-line aircraft that was almost defenseless against determined enemy air attack. Untold numbers of British airmen perished in this monument to bureaucratic inertia and ignorance. The B.E.2c is presented here, not as an example of a good aircraft or one having significant technical innovations, but as an illustration of how an ineffective aircraft can be produced and fostered on the user long after it is obsolete. Similar examples can be found in the course of aeronautical history.

Junkers J-1

A bewildering variety of two-seat army cooperation aircraft were designed, developed, and operated by the Germans in World War I. Albatros, AEG, Roland, DFW, Halberstadt, AGO, Aviatik, LVG, Junkers, and Rumpler are only a few of the companies that produced army cooperation aircraft during the conflict. Some of these aircraft were designed for general-purpose reconnaissance duties, others for night bombing, and still others for the ground attack role in close co-operation with friendly ground troops. An interesting aircraft in this latter category, the Junkers J-I, is described here and is shown in figure 2.25.

The J-I biplane had a rather unusual appearance with thick, cantilever wings that were tapered in both planform and thickness ratio. Three-view drawings show that the aircraft was really a sesquiplane, with the bottom wing much smaller in span and chord than the upper wing. The small-chord lower wing, together with its position below the lower surface of the fuselage, afforded good downward visibility for the pilot in the front cockpit and the observer in the rear. The wings were connected to each other and to the fuselage by a rather complex cabane-strut arrangement. No interplane struts were used between the wings. Like all Junkers aircraft, the J-I incorporated an all-metal structure. The wing was composed of 0.08-inch corrugated aluminum alloy skin riveted to an internal framework of aluminum alloy tubing. The engine and crew were encased in an armored shell formed from 0.2-

Figure 2.25 — German Junkers J-I all-metal army cooperation aircraft; 1918. [Peter M. Bowers via AAHS]

inch sheet steel. The aft portion of the fuselage consisted of a metal alloy frame covered with fabric in early models but with sheet metal in later versions. Power was provided by a six-cylinder, water-cooled, Benz Bz.IV engine of 200 horsepower. The aircraft was usually armed with two fixed, synchronized machine guns firing between the propeller blades and with a single flexible gun for use by the observer. Two downward-firing guns were sometimes installed for the observer, but the difficulty of aiming these guns from a low, fast-flying aircraft rendered them ineffective, and they were quickly removed. A radio link connecting the aircraft with friendly ground troops in the forward area was also generally provided.

The physical and performance data given in table I indicate that the J–I was a remarkable aircraft in many respects. The gross weight of 4748 pounds seems large for an aircraft of only 200 horsepower, and the useful load fraction of 0.19 is very low compared with the values of 0.30 to 0.35 shown in figure 2.20 for fighter aircraft. A low structural efficiency is accordingly suggested; however, the 0.20-inch steel shell of armor alone weighted 1036 pounds, according to reference 119, and no doubt contributed in large measure to the low apparent structural efficiency. The power loading of 23.9 pounds per horsepower is about the same as that of the B.E.2c and suggests a powered glider more than a fighting aircraft. The J–I, however, had a maximum speed of 96 miles per hour, could climb to 6560 feet in 30 minutes, and had an endurance of 2 hours, a very creditable performance for an aircraft of relatively low power. The good performance of the aircraft was due in large part to the low value of the zero-lift drag coefficient of 0.0335 and the high value of the maximum lift-drag ratio of 10.3. The J–I was among the most aerodynamically efficient of the World War I aircraft analyzed here.

The J–I proved in action to be a very effective weapon in the ground-attack role for which it was designed. The prototype first flew in January 1917, but due to production difficulties the aircraft was not deployed in action until February 1918. Total production run was 227 aircraft. The Junkers J–I incorporated many advanced engineering features and was a truly remarkable aircraft. It has not received proper recognition in the literature of World War I aviation.

DeHavilland DH-4

Although the DeHavilland DH–4 was an ordinary looking, strut- and-wire-braced, double-bay biplane, it occupies a unique niche in aviation history as the only aircraft manufactured in the United States to serve in combat on the Western front in World War I. A total of 4846 DH–4 aircraft were built (under license) in the United States, and about 1600 of these reached France. They were all powered with the U.S.-designed and built 12-cylinder Liberty engine of 400 horsepower. The interesting story of the development of this outstanding engine is described in reference 45.

Two views of the DH–4 are shown in figures 2.26 and 2.27. The legend on the side of the aircraft pictured in figure 2.26 indicates that it was number 1000 off the United States production line and that it would leave (by ship) at 4:30 p.m., July 31, 1918. The DH–4 shown in figure 2.27 was the "pattern aircraft" sent from England to the United States in the summer of 1917 for use in developing production drawings for use by U.S. manufacturers.[1] The photograph was made in the

Figure 2.26 — American-built (British-designed) DeHavilland DH–4 army cooperation aircraft; 1918. [Warren Bodie via AAHS]

---

[1] According to a recent publication, this aircraft has been identified by personnel of the National Air and Space Museum as the first DH–4 manufactured in the United States and is not, as was previously thought, a British-built pattern aircraft. See Boyne, Walter J.: *The Aircraft Treasures of Silver Hill* (New York: Rawson Associates).

Figure 2.27 — National Air and Space Museum DH–4 on loan to the NASA Langley Research Center in 1967. Dr. Floyd L. Thompson, former Langley director, is shown with the aircraft. [NASA]

fall of 1967 when this historic aircraft, on loan from the National Air and Space Museum, was exhibited at the Langley Research Center of the National Aeronautics and Space Administration on the occasion of its 50th anniversary. The gentleman in the photograph is Dr. Floyd L. Thompson, former director and longtime research leader at the Langley center.

The DH–4 was designed as a day bomber and general-purpose reconnaissance aircraft by Geoffery DeHavilland for the Aircraft Manufacturing Company (AIRCO). It first flew in August 1916, was deployed in March 1917, and subsequently served on all British fronts. DH–4's built in Britain were powered with a variety of engines, including the well-known Rolls-Royce Eagle powerplants of 250 horsepower. Only 1440 DH–4 aircraft were built in England.

Figures 2.26 and 2.27 depict a very conventional-appearing biplane. Both photographs clearly show the maze of wires required to support the typically thin wings against flight and ground loads and to hold the wings in proper alignment. The aircraft had a conventional wood-frame structure covered with fabric, except for the forward part of the fuselage which was sheathed in plywood. An unusual feature of the aircraft was the large distance separating the pilot and the observer. The internal volume between the two cockpits was occupied by a large fuel tank. Communication between the pilot located under the top wing and the aft-placed observer was difficult, and the tank between the crew members was rumored to have a propensity for catching fire in an accident or when hit by enemy gunfire. As a consequence, the aircraft was sometimes unflatteringly referred to by crew members as the "Flaming Coffin."

The flight controls, which included ailerons on both upper and lower wings, were entirely conventional with the exception of the fixed portion of the horizontal tail, which could be adjusted in flight with a trim wheel located in the cockpit. The aircraft could accordingly be trimmed for zero longitudinal stick force as speed, weight, and altitude varied during the course of a flight. All modern aircraft have pitch trim capability, but this highly desirable feature was seldom found in World War I aircraft. Another unusual feature in the DH-4 was the tail skid that could be steered with the rudder bar; ground maneuverability was much enhanced by this feature. According to reference 28, the aircraft had light control forces and adequate stability and was easy to fly and land. Armament varied but usually consisted of two fixed, forward-firing machine guns operated by the pilot and two flexible guns for use by the observer. On daylight bombing raids, 10 small bombs were mounted beneath the lower wing, 5 on either side of the fuselage; these bombs are visible in figure 2.27.

The data in table I for the DH-4 are for the Liberty-powered, American-built version of the aircraft. It was a relatively heavy machine with a gross weight of 4595 pounds, but the 400-horsepower engine gave it ratios of power to weight and power to drag area that were nearly the same as those for the Fokker D-VII fighter; the values of the maximum lift-drag ratio of the two aircraft were also nearly the same. Fighterlike performance might therefore be expected of the DH-4, and the maximum speed of 124 miles per hour certainly confirms this expectation. The rather high, for its day, stalling speed resulted from the 10.4-pound-per-square-foot wing loading in combination with the low maximum lift coefficient of the thin wings. The aircraft had a service ceiling of 19 600 feet and could climb to 10 000 feet in 14 minutes.

Termination of hostilities in November 1918 resulted in cancellation of contracts in the United States for an additional 5160 aircraft. The end of the war, however, did not spell the end of the career of the DH–4 in the United States, as is seen in chapter 3.

The Heritage of World War I

Out of the profusion of different configuration types, structural concepts, and propulsion systems explored during the hectic days of World War I, there emerged the strut-and-wire-braced biplane, constructed of wood frame and covered with fabric, as the best overall compromise between structural strength, weight, and aerodynamic efficiency consistent with the existing state of technology. This "standard airplane" formula, with various improvements, was applied to all manner of single and multiengine civil and military aircraft for many years following the end of the war. In fact, one of the most extensively used training aircraft in the United States during World War II was the well-known Stearman PT–17 biplane. Even today, biplanes are flown for sport, aerobatic competition, and crop spraying.

Although a number of biplanes have been described above, a review of some of the salient features of the "standard airplane," the airplane design formula with which most countries entered the decade of the 1920's, may be of interest. By the end of the war, the rotary engine was obsolete, and the in-line, water-cooled type was predominant. Values of the ratio of dry weight to power had been reduced from between 3.5 and 4.0 for early Curtiss and Mercedes engines to 2.5 for the 220-horsepower Hispano-Suiza and 2.0 for the 400-horsepower Liberty. These values were lower than the typical value of 2.7 for the rotaries; however, the values given for the water-cooled engines do not include the weight of the radiator, associated plumbing, or cooling water. The propellers that transformed engine power to propulsive thrust were of fixed pitch design and laminated wooden construction. The limited speed range through which aircraft operated in that era did not warrant the use of any type of variable pitch arrangement. Large diameter propellers, consistent with the low rotational speed of most engines, were used and gave excellent takeoff and climb performance for a given amount of power. Engines were usually started by the simple expedient of having a mechanic swing the propeller by hand.

The callout of "off" and "contact" between the pilot operating the ignition switch in the cockpit and the mechanic turning the propeller was a familiar litany around airports for many years.

The wing loadings of aircraft in those early years were low, usually below 10 pounds per square foot, to allow operation from small fields. Most aircraft could take off and land in a few hundred feet. The typical fixed landing gear had large wheels for operation from soft unsurfaced fields and had no form of streamlining. No brakes were incorporated in the landing gear, and the tail skid was usually a fixed nonsteerable device. The action of the propeller slipstream on the rudder provided the only means of maneuvering the aircraft on the ground; accordingly, mechanics walking at the wing tips were frequently used to assist in ground handling. The tail skid served as a sort of brake on landing rollout as the aircraft moved across the soft unpaved field; it also assisted in keeping the aircraft headed in a given direction. Crosswind operations were rarely undertaken, and most airports were roughly square or circular in shape so that the pilot was always able to take off and land directly into the wind.

The control surfaces of the "standard airplane" were directly connected to the rudder bar and control stick by wires or cables; at least parts of these control lines were usually exposed to the airstream on the outside of the aircraft. Incredibly, the aileron control cables of the DH–4 ran along the leading edges of the wings. Most aircraft had no longitudinal trim system, and means for adjusting lateral and directional trim were unheard of. The relationship between the size of the control surfaces, the desired response characteristics of the aircraft, and the control forces required of the pilot were little understood in 1918. As a consequence, the flying and handling characteristics of aircraft of that day generally varied from poor to terrible as judged by modern-day standards. A fine-handling aircraft, of which there were a few, was more a matter of luck than anything else.

Typically, the crew rode in an open, drafty cockpit exposed to the elements. In fact, pilots of that day and for many years thereafter felt that "feeling the wind in their faces" was necessary in order to fly an aircraft with skill and safety. The cockpits were, of course, unheated with no supply of supplementary oxygen, even though altitudes as high as 20 000 feet could be reached by many aircraft. The extreme discomfort experienced by the flight crews at these high altitudes can readily be imagined. The well-equipped pilot's instrument panel usually consisted of oil temperature and pressure gages, water temperature gage, and tachometer. These instruments, together with some sort of fuel gage, served to indicate the health of the propulsion system. In the way of flight instruments, an altimeter, airspeed indicator, and compass usually completed the instrument panel although a crude type of inclinometer was sometimes included. Radios for navigational purposes were largely unknown. Radios used for communication with ground troops were sometimes carried, and these were powered by a wind-driven generator.

Such were some of the design features of the "standard airplane" that emerged from World War I. Post-World War I aircraft development, discussed in the following chapters, began on a foundation provided by the technology and concepts of the 1918 "standard airplane."

Chapter 3
The Lean Years, 1918–26

Background

The pace of aircraft development and production was extremely slow during the time period from the armistice in November 1918 until about 1926. World War I was thought to be the war "to end all wars," the war "to make the world safe for democracy." Postwar military appropriations, including funds for new aircraft, were accordingly small. The primary financial base underlying the development and production of new aircraft and advanced technology had dried up. The military made use of leftover and modified aircraft from World War I, of which the DeHavilland DH–4, previously described, was a prime example. In fact, the DH–4 continued to serve in various capacities in the Army Air Corps of the United States until the early 1930's. There was, of course, some development activity sponsored by both the Army and the Navy, and a number of prototypes of new aircraft were produced. These prototypes, however, usually followed the familiar biplane formula that emerged from World War I. Some small production contracts, generally no more than 15 or 20 aircraft, were placed with the existing manufacturers for some of these prototypes. Hence, the industry did not entirely collapse.

The requirements of civil aviation during this time period presented little incentive for advanced aircraft developments. No airlines devoted to the transportation of passengers existed in the United States; however, the Government operated a primitive airmail service that linked various cities in the United States, and the first coast-to-coast airmail service was established in 1921. The aircraft employed for carrying the mails consisted mostly of surplus World War I aircraft, with the ubiquitous DH–4 as the mainstay of the operation. Many modifications were made to the DH to make it more suitable for airmail service, and the aircraft was so utilized until at least 1927 or 1928.

General aviation as we know it today existed only in the form of barnstormers. These gypsy pilots roamed the country from town to town offering 5- to 10-minute rides for sums of around $5.00. The aircraft that served as the workhorse for the gypsy pilot was the Curtiss JN-4 or Jenny. This aircraft was a trainer that served during World War I to introduce thousands of neophytes to the mysteries of flying. In the decade following World War I, many young people, children and teenagers alike, were introduced to the wonderful world of flight by the sight of a Jenny gracefully gliding to a landing in a pasture close to the family homestead. Once seen and heard, the sight and sound of this ancient biplane with its slow-turning engine and the whistling noise of the wind through the bracing wires made an indelible impression on many young people in the 1920's and served as a springboard for their later entry into some aspect of aviation. The Jenny was similar in configuration and construction to the DH-4 shown in figures 2.26 and 2.27 (chapter 2), but, instead of having an engine of 400 horsepower, it was equipped with the 90-horsepower Curtiss OX-5 or the 150-horsepower Wright-Hispano. Most models of the Jenny used by barnstormers had the 90-horsepower engine and were designated JN-4D. The aircraft was quite slow and had a cruising speed that did not differ very much from the stalling speed. By today's standards, the handling characteristics of the Jenny would be considered unacceptable (shown by the data in ref. 101). The Curtiss Jennys, however, were available in large numbers following the end of World War I and could be purchased for as little as a few hundred dollars. Obviously, no new aircraft suited to the demands of the barnstormers could be developed and produced for any such ridiculously low price. Thus, the private sector provided no market for the development and production of new aircraft.

A Curtiss JN-4H with the Wright-Hispano engine is shown in figure 3.1, and the characteristics of this version of the Jenny are given in table II (appendix A).

Transport Developments in Europe

In contrast to the slow development of airline aviation in the United States, European air transport began almost immediately after the cessation of hostilities in 1918. The major capitals of Europe were soon connected by primitive passenger-carrying airlines. The aircraft types utilized for carrying passengers were at first hastily converted

Figure 3.1 — Curtiss JN-4H Jenny trainer; 1918. [NASA]

military bomber and observation types. Later, new aircraft were constructed for the infant airlines; however, these aircraft usually followed the standard biplane formula developed during World War I. Typical of these transport aircraft is the Handley Page trimotor shown in figure 3.2. The aircraft was a multibay biplane, similar in configuration to the bomber types of the war, but employed an enclosed cabin capable of carrying 10 passengers. The two pilots were accommodated in an open cockpit just forward of the leading edge of the upper wing, as can be seen in figure 3.2. Note the four-blade propellers and the multiple wheels of the landing gear. The use of the four-wheel gear was no doubt a concession to the relatively soft sod or mud landing fields of the period. A glance at the characteristics of the aircraft given in table II indicates a relatively heavy machine of 13 000-pound gross weight, but with only 840 horsepower as the combined output of the three engines. The wing loading was a very low 8.9 pounds per square foot in order that the aircraft could operate out of the small fields that existed at the time. The cruising speed was a modest 85 miles per hour; the drag coefficient at zero lift was 0.0549, which was larger than that of the DH-4. Although the use of multiple engines is usually thought to increase safety and reliability, that was not the case with the Handley

69

Figure 3.2 — Handley Page model W8F 12-passenger trimotor transport; 1924. [Flt. Intl.]

Page trimotor. The aircraft could not maintain level flight following the loss of one engine according to the information given in reference 75. The Handley Page trimotor was put into operation by the British Imperial Airways and the Belgium Sabena Airways Systems in about 1924 and continued in operation, at least to some limited extent, until about 1931. In fact, very large multiengine biplanes were utilized on some European airlines right up to the beginning of World War II.

Aircraft employing the monoplane configuration had been built since the early days of aviation. The first nonstop flight across the English Channel was made in 1909 by Bleriot flying a wire-braced monoplane, and many early World War I fighters were also monoplanes (chapter 2). Most early monoplanes employed a multitude of wires and struts in order to provide strength and rigidity to the wings. As a consequence, the drag characteristics of these aircraft showed little if any improvement compared with contemporary biplane drag characteristics. Furthermore, there seemed to be a lack of confidence in the structural integrity of the monoplane configuration. There were also experiments with internally braced, cantilever monoplanes. As indicated in chapter 2, the German designer Junkers built cantilever monoplanes constructed of metal. The materials and design methods available during World War I, however, did not lend themselves to the construction of light, all-metal cantilever designs. Another early proponent of the cantilever monoplane was the Dutch designer Anthony H. G. Fokker. Fokker designed and built fighter aircraft for the German Air Force during World War I. His first cantilever monoplane fighter was the model D–VIII, which featured an internally braced wing mounted on struts above the fuselage. (See figure 2.16.)

In 1920 and 1921, Fokker developed a single-engine transport employing an internally braced wing similar in concept to that of the D–VIII fighter. This aircraft, known as the Fokker F–2, is depicted in figure 3.3. The aircraft seated three or four passengers in an enclosed cabin, and a single pilot was located in an open cockpit just under the leading edge of the wing. The absence of external struts and wires to support the wing is obvious from the photograph. The relative aerodynamic cleanliness of the design would be expected to produce a correspondingly low value of the zero-lift drag coefficient. The data in table II, however, suggest that the value of $C_{D,0}$ is not much better for the Fokker than for the DH–4. The open cockpit together with a poor engine installation and consequent high cooling drag suggest themselves as possible reasons for the relatively high zero-lift drag coefficient. The wooden cantilever wing and steel-tube, fabric-covered fuselage formed the basis for a long line of Fokker aircraft built right up to World War II. An improved and larger version of the Fokker F–2, known as the T–2, was the first aircraft to fly nonstop across the United

Figure 3.3 — Fokker F–2 four-passenger transport; 1920. [Flt. Intl.]

States. This flight was made by the U.S. Army Air Service in 1923 (ref. 38). The famous Fokker trimotor was very similar in configuration to the F–2 but employed three modern engines, had a fully enclosed cabin and cockpit, and was much larger than the F–2. The first of the Fokker trimotors was employed by Richard E. Byrd and Floyd Bennett in their historic first flight over the North Pole in 1926.

High-Speed Racing Aircraft

The national and international air races helped stimulate and maintain public interest and support for aviation during the years immediately following World War I. The races also provided a focus for the development of new, high-performance aircraft. Many of these special aircraft were government sponsored. The Army and the Navy sponsored such developments in the United States, as did the air forces of France, Great Britain, and Italy in Europe. The most successful of these aircraft were highly developed forms of the biplane configuration. Typical of such aircraft is the 1923 Curtiss R2C–1 racer shown in figure 3.4. Standing beside the aircraft is Navy Lieutenant Alford J. Williams who flew it to first place in the 1923 Pulitzer race. The aircraft is seen to be extremely clean aerodynamically and had a phenomenally low zero-lift drag coefficient of 0.0206 (table II). The aircraft achieved a maximum speed of 267 miles per hour with a liquid-

Figure 3.4 — Curtiss R2C–1 racer; 1923. [NASM]

cooled engine of about 500 horsepower. Some of the features that accounted for the low drag coefficient and consequent high speed are the minimization of the number of wires and struts to support the wings, the smooth, highly streamlined semimonocoque wooden construction of the fuselage (this type of construction is briefly described in chapter 2 in connection with the Albatros D–III fighter), the all-metal Curtiss Reed propeller, and the very interesting skin-type radiators that were used to provide heat exchange surface for the water-cooled engine. The external surfaces of these radiators, which formed a part of the surface of the wing, were of corrugated skin with the corrugations aligned with the direction of air flow. The remainder of the wing surface was covered with plywood. The Curtiss PW–8 fighter, of which about 30 were produced in the mid-1920's, also employed the skin-type surface radiator. Although the skin radiators contributed significantly to obtaining a low drag coefficient, and hence to improving performance, they were not practical for use on operational combat aircraft. In addition to being prone to leak as a result of flexing of the wings, they were extremely vulnerable to battle damage, which was probably the deciding factor in their elimination from future combat aircraft.

A number of racing aircraft were developed that employed the monoplane configuration. Some of these aircraft had cantilever wings; others employed strut-braced wings; such advanced concepts as retractable landing gear were sometimes seen. For one reason or another, however, none of these monoplane racers was particularly successful. The Dayton Wright RB racer developed for the 1920 Gordon Bennett race was perhaps one of the most advanced concepts developed during the entire period. The aircraft is illustrated in figure 3.5, and some of its characteristics are given in table II. The pilot was entirely enclosed in the fuselage, which was of wooden semimonocoque construction. The cantilever wing was constructed entirely of wood and employed leading- and trailing-edge flaps. These flaps in effect provided variable camber so that the airfoil section could be adjusted to its optimum shape for both high-speed and low-speed flight. This extremely advanced feature did not appear on production aircraft until the development of the jet transport in the 1950's. The landing gear on the Dayton Wright racer retracted into the fuselage in very much the same way as that used in later Grumman fighters of the thirties and forties. The drag coefficient at zero lift of the Dayton Wright racer was 0.0316 (table II), which is considerably higher than the value of 0.0206 for the Curtiss R2C-1 but very much lower than the value of 0.0496 given in table I for the DH–4. Although highly advanced for its time, the

Figure 3.5 — Dayton Wright RB–1 racer; 1920. [NASM]

Dayton Wright racer was not successful in the 1920 Gordon Bennett race. The aircraft was somewhat underpowered and during the race had to withdraw because of a broken rudder cable. Unfortunately, the type was not further developed.

Another highly advanced monoplane racer, developed by the British for the 1925 Schneider trophy race, was the Supermarine S–4. The Schneider race was an international event for seaplanes. Shown in figure 3.6, the S–4 is a beautiful, highly streamlined, cantilever monoplane mounted on twin floats. The wing, constructed of a wooden framework covered with plywood, employed flush radiators that, unlike the previously described Curtiss racer, were not of the skin type. The wings had landing flaps that could be geared to the ailerons. The rear of the fuselage was of wooden semimonocoque construction, and the forward portion containing the engine was of metal. The engine had 12 cylinders arranged in 3 banks of 4. A front view of the engine gave the appearance of the letter "W"; accordingly, this cylinder arrangement was referred to as a W-type engine. A glance at the characteristics of the aircraft contained in table II indicates a drag coefficient of 0.0274, which must be considered quite low in view of the large amount of surface area of the exposed twin floats. The wing loading of about 23 pounds per square foot was high for the period and accounts for the use of the wing trailing-edge flaps. Another important factor that allowed the use of such a high wing loading was the relatively long take-

Figure 3.6 — Supermarine S-4 seaplane racer; 1925. [NASM]

off and landing runs possible with the use of rivers and harbors, as compared with the confined land airfields of the day. The aircraft was destroyed by wing flutter before the 1925 Schneider trophy race (ref. 117). According to reference 114, the ailerons on the S-4 were unbalanced, which no doubt contributed to the onsct of wing flutter at the high speeds of which the aircraft was capable. Flutter and divergence of cantilever monoplane wings were not understood at that period in the development of aeronautical technology. Later Supermarine racers, which were quite successful in subsequent Schneider trophy competitions, employed the more predictable wire-braced monoplane wings. The designer of the Supermarine S-4, R. J. Mitchell, later designed the famous Spitfire fighter of World War II. For those familiar with the Spitfire, some resemblance between the S-4 and the famous fighter can be seen in figure 3.6. The national and international air races and the aircraft of the early 1920's are described in comprehensive detail by Foxworth in reference 51.

Chapter 4
Design Revolution, 1926–39

Background

The pace of aircraft development began to accelerate by the middle 1920's. Policies were established within the United States that assured consistent, although somewhat small, yearly appropriations for the procurement and development of new military aircraft. In an attempt to improve the poor aviation safety record and thus enhance the image of aviation as a serious means of transportation, laws were enacted that required the licensing of civil aircraft and pilots. Airworthiness standards were developed for the aircraft, and proficiency requirements were established for the licensing of pilots. The aircraft airworthiness requirements opened a market for the development of new types of general aviation aircraft. War surplus aircraft, such as the Jenny, either could not meet the new requirements or their certification would have proved economically unfeasible. The airmail that had been carried by Government aircraft for many years reverted to private contractors. Thus began the airline industry, albeit in a small way. Under the stimulus of these influences, the aircraft industry began to grow.

The pace at which advanced aircraft can be developed is closely coupled to the generation of new and advanced technology. The results of research investigations by the Langley Memorial Aeronautical Laboratory of the National Advisory Committee for Aeronautics (NACA) began to play an increasingly important part in providing the new technology necessary for the development of advanced aircraft. Investigations in aerodynamics, stability and control, propulsion, loads, dynamics, and structures formed the research program of NACA. Wind tunnels, laboratories, flight research, and analytical studies were the means by which new technology was developed. The results of NACA's research investigations were made available to the industry in the form of technical reports. Bound volumes of these reports, covering the

77

entire lifespan of NACA from 1915 to 1958, are a part of most good technical libraries. Indexes such as those cited in reference 74 give a complete bibliography of research publications by NACA. Years subsequent to 1949 are covered in additional indexes. Brief accounts of the significant research activities of NACA are contained in references 49, 56, and 73.

The universities played an important role in educating young aeronautical engineers and in various aspects of aeronautical research. Schools of aeronautical engineering sponsored by the Guggenheim Foundation were particularly important. These schools existed at the Massachusetts Institute of Technology, the California Institute of Technology, New York University, the University of Michigan, the Georgia Institute of Technology, Stanford University, and the University of Akron. The contributions of the Guggenheim Foundation to the development of aeronautics in the United States are described in reference 70.

The military services played an extremely important role not only in the generation of new technology but in sponsoring the application of that technology in the development of new and useful operating systems. Thus, the development and operation of new military equipment provided a highly significant foundation of proven components, such as engines, for use in new civil aircraft. A summary of the contributions of military aeronautical research and development to the development of advanced commercial aircraft throughout the thirties, forties, and fifties is contained in reference 104. A close relationship can frequently be found between the development of advanced military aircraft and new commercial aircraft that employed not only many of the design features of military aircraft but also hardware and concepts that had been proved in military aviation.

Record Flights

Another important factor in the formula for accelerated development and production of new aircraft were the many record-breaking flights of the time. They were extremely popular with the general public and played an important role in popularizing aviation and its potential as a serious means of transportation. The nonstop solo flight of Charles A. Lindbergh from New York to Paris in May 1927 had the most profound and lasting influence of any of the record-breaking flights. His magnificent flight thrilled and captured the imagination of people all over the world and stimulated an interest and enthusiasm for aviation that had an incalculable effect on future aeronautical developments. As a result of his flight, a multitude of small companies dedicated to the manufacture of aircraft appeared throughout the United States. Most of these companies flourished for a few years and then quietly passed into bankruptcy as the country entered the Great Depression of the 1930's. Airline operations were given a tremendous boost by the enthusiasm engendered by the Lindbergh flight.

The Ryan monoplane employed by Lindbergh on his historic flight, illustrated in figure 4.1, was of the strut-braced, high-wing type equipped with a fixed landing gear. The fuselage consisted of a welded steel-tube frame, and the wings were of wooden frame construction. The entire aircraft was covered with cloth fabric. The pilot had no forward vision since the space immediately ahead of him was occupied by a large 360-gallon fuel tank. The wheels incorporated no brakes, and the tail skid was of the fixed type. The aircraft utilized the relatively new Wright Whirlwind engine. This engine had nine cylinders radially disposed about the crankcase and crankshaft. In contrast to the rotary engine described earlier, however, the cylinders and crankcase of the radial engine were fixed, and the crankshaft rotated with the propeller attached. The engine developed 220 horsepower and, for its day, was considered to be light and highly reliable. The air-cooled feature re-

Figure 4.1 — Ryan NYP Spirit of St. Louis; *1927.* [Ryan Aeronautical Library via David A. Anderton]

sulted in the deletion of the radiator and associated plumbing that was always a source of maintenance and reliability problems on liquid-cooled engines. The maximum gross weight of the aircraft was 5135 pounds, and the zero-fuel weight was 2150 pounds. Thus, the fuel in the aircraft represented more than half of the gross weight and gave the *Spirit of St. Louis* airplane a zero-wind range of about 4200 statute miles. The cruising speed of the aircraft was about 95 miles per hour, and the maximum speed, 120 miles per hour. The zero-lift drag coefficient $C_{D,0}$, given in table II (appendix A), was 0.0379. This coefficient represents a considerable reduction over the value of 0.0496 given for the DeHavilland DH–4 but still indicates that the fixed landing gear and multiple wing struts were serious drag-producing elements. The maximum lift-drag ratio of the aircraft was 10.1, which compares favorably with the value of 7.7 given for the DeHavilland 4. The higher effective aspect ratio of the monoplane, compared with the biplane, is in large measure responsible for the increased lift-drag ratio of the *Spirit of St. Louis* compared with the DH–4 and other typical contemporary biplane configurations. A complete description of the *Spirit of St. Louis* giving design and performance data is contained in the appendix of reference 86.

Record-breaking flights continued for many years to play an important role in the development of aviation, particularly as a means of focusing public attention on the possibilities of the aircraft as a safe and reliable means for travel. Long-distance flights, flights around the world, flights of exploration, and, of course, all sorts of air races formed part of the aeronautical scene in the late twenties and thirties. For example, Richard E. Byrd was in command of the first flight over the South Pole in 1929, and Wiley Post circled the globe alone in 7½ days in 1933. The world's absolute speed record was increased to 440 miles per hour in 1934 by an Italian seaplane. The aircraft was equipped with pontoons similar to those shown on the Supermarine S–4 in figure 3.6 and employed wire-braced monoplane wings and a 24-cylinder engine driving two counter-rotating propellers. The absolute speed record was raised to 467 miles per hour in 1938 by the Messerschmitt 209V1 racer. The list of record flights could go on endlessly but will not be continued here. The following paragraphs deal with some of the advanced aircraft that were developed from 1926 to 1939. This era may be characterized as one in which concepts of aircraft design underwent radical change and rapid advances were made in performance.

Monoplanes and Biplanes

The Ryan monoplane *Spirit of St. Louis* pictured in figure 4.1 popularized the monoplane configuration in America and marked the beginning of the decline of the biplane. Another immortal high-wing monoplane, the Ford trimotor, formed the mainstay of the infant U.S. airline industry in the late 1920's and early 1930's. The aircraft, pictured in figure 4.2, featured an internally braced wing, fixed landing gear, and three engines. The basic configuration was similar to the Fokker trimotor referred to earlier; however, the methods of construction employed in the two aircraft were totally different. The Fokker structure consisted of a mixture of wood, metal, and fabric; the Ford was of all-metal construction. The internal structure of the aircraft was entirely of metal, and the skin was a corrugated aluminum alloy. The corrugations provided stiffness in the skin panels and were aligned with the direction of air flow in order to minimize the drag. This type of construction was pioneered by Hugo Junkers in Germany.

The aircraft was produced in two versions: the model 4–AT and the model 5–AT. The aircraft were similar in appearance, but the model 5–AT was slightly larger and employed somewhat more powerful engines than the model 4–AT. Figure 4.2 depicts a model 4–AT, and the specifications given in table II are for the model 5–AT. The model 5–AT carried from 13 to 15 passengers in an enclosed cabin, had a gross weight of 13 500 pounds, and was equipped with three 420-horsepower Pratt & Whitney Wasp radial engines. By this time, the

Figure 4.2 — Ford 4–AT 12-passenger trimotor transport; 1928. [NASA]

two pilots were seated in an enclosed cockpit located ahead of the wing. Ground-handling characteristics were enhanced by the provision of differential braking on the main landing gear wheels and a swiveling tail wheel. Cockpit instrumentation was primitive by modern standards, and some of the instruments for the outboard engines were actually located on the engine nacelles, which required the pilots to look out the side windows to read them. The large, powerful engines were equipped with an inertia starter; this type of starter was often used for large engines beginning in the mid-1920's. A flywheel of large moment of inertia was brought to a high rotational speed through the use of either a geared handcrank or an electrical power source. When the proper speed had been reached, a clutch was engaged and the angular momentum of the flywheel caused the engine to rotate and start.

The Ford trimotor was especially designed to maintain flight after the loss of one engine. Under full gross weight conditions, however, the aircraft was not able to climb after takeoff following the loss of an engine, probably because of the excessive drag resulting from the windmilling propeller. Full-feathering propellers had not been developed at that time. The top speed of 150 miles per hour listed in table II for the Ford trimotor may be excessive; cruising speeds somewhat less than 100 miles per hour are indicated in reference 110 for a model 4–AT that is still flying today. The drag coefficient $C_{D,0}$ for the Ford is seen to be relatively high, as compared with that for the Ryan *Spirit of St. Louis*. The drag of the two outboard engines and the nacelles no doubt contributed significantly to the total drag of the trimotor and, to some extent, nullified the advantages of the cantilever wing. Furthermore, according to reference 72, the wetted area of an aircraft may be increased by as much as 20 to 40 percent by corrugations in the metal covering. No account was taken of this increment in calculating the drag coefficient given in table II.

The prototype of the Ford trimotor flew in 1926, and the last production aircraft rolled off the line in 1933. A total of 116 models of the 5–AT and 84 models of the 4–AT were constructed. Some of these aircraft are still flying today, and one was flying in scheduled airline service with the remarkable Island Airlines at Port Clinton, Ohio, into the 1970's. The longevity of these aircraft attests to their rugged construction and basic design soundness.

The Lockheed Vega shown in figure 4.3 was a very high-performance monoplane that first flew in 1927. The aircraft shown in the photograph is a fully developed model 5C version. Both the internal structure and the outer covering of the aircraft were wood. The wing was of

Figure 4.3 — Lockheed Vega 5C mail and passenger plane; 1929. [Peter C. Boisseau]

the internally braced, cantilever type, and the fuselage was of semimonocoque construction. A new feature, which appeared on this aircraft, was a circular cowling surrounding the 450-horsepower Pratt & Whitney Wasp air-cooled engine. This cowling concept was one of NACA's early contributions and provided substantial increases in the speed of aircraft employing radial engines, but, at the same time, directed the cooling air through the engine in such a way as to provide adequate cooling. The maximum speed of the Lockheed Vega was increased from 165 miles per hour to 190 miles per hour by the addition of the NACA cowling. Fairings, called pants, around the wheels of the landing gear also reduced the drag and resulted in an increase in the speed of the aircraft. The Lockheed Vega had a very low zero-lift drag coefficient of 0.0278, as shown by the data in table II. The low zero-lift drag coefficient was obtained through careful attention to detailed aerodynamic design of the aircraft and by the absence of drag-producing struts, wires, and other external drag-producing elements. The fixed landing gear, however, remained as a significant drag-producing feature of the airplane. The maximum lift-drag ratio of the Vega was 11.4, which was unusually high for that time period. The Lockheed Vega was used in airline service (six passengers) and was also employed in many record-breaking flights. The aircraft shown in figure 4.3 is painted to represent the famous *Winnie Mae*, which Wiley Post flew solo around

83

the world in about 7½ days in the summer of 1933. The actual aircraft Post flew on this remarkable flight is in the National Air and Space Museum in Washington, D.C. The Lockheed Vega was a highly advanced and refined design for its day, and, even now, the performance is very good for an aircraft with fixed landing gear.

The demise of the Jenny and its contemporaries opened the way for a new generation of general aviation aircraft for fixed-base operators and barnstormers. Most of these new aircraft employed a welded steel-tube fuselage and wooden wing structure and incorporated a fabric covering over the entire structure. The aircraft depicted in figures 4.4 and 4.5 are typical of the classes of aircraft produced during the latter part of the 1920's. The Curtiss Robin shown in figure 4.4 was designed along the lines of the strut-braced monoplane formula popularized by Lindbergh's *Spirit of St. Louis*. The aircraft was ruggedly built with a view toward operation from poorly prepared airfields or pastures. The enclosed cabin provided seating for a pilot in the front and two passengers in the rear seat. The aircraft was usually equipped with either a Curtiss Challenger six-cylinder radial engine or a Wright J6–5 five-cylinder radial engine. The specifications given in table II are for the Challenger-powered Robin, which had 185 horsepower and was capable of a maximum speed of 115 miles per hour. The aircraft was fitted with wheel brakes and a steerable tail wheel or skid. The drag coefficient of the Robin was a very high 0.0585, which probably resulted from the very large cylinders of the exposed radial engine, the many sharp corners of the forward-facing windshield, and the relatively unfaired junctures between the multitude of struts supporting the wings

Figure 4.4 — Curtiss Robin three-place-cabin monoplane; 1929. [Peter C. Boisseau]

Figure 4.5 — Travelair 4000 three-place open-cockpit biplane; 1928. [Peter C. Boisseau]

and landing gear. The zero-lift drag coefficient of the Robin is seen to be more than 0.020 greater than that of the Ryan *Spirit of St. Louis.*

The biplane type was still popular and is illustrated by the Travelair 4000 of 1928 shown in figure 4.5. The aircraft was typical of a large number of three-place open biplanes in which the pilot sat alone in the rear cockpit and two passengers were placed forward under the wing near the center of gravity in an open front cockpit. The aircraft is seen to employ struts and wires for bracing the wings, but they are far fewer in number than those used on the typical World War I biplane represented by the DH-4 pictured in figures 2.26 and 2.27. Many different power plants were used in the various open cockpit biplanes produced in the late 1920's. The venerable Curtiss OX-5 water cooled engine of World War I fame was still available in large numbers and formed a cheap source of power plants for new aircraft. Engines of higher power and greater reliability, such as the Wright Whirlwind, were also available, but these engines were considerably more costly than the surplus World War I engines. The Travelair 4000 shown in figure 4.5 has the Wright Whirlwind nine-cylinder radial engine. The large horn-balanced ailerons and rudder on the Travelair are particularly noteworthy. Balanced controls of this type were used on the World War I German Fokker D-7, figure 2.14, and formed a distinctive identifying feature of the aircraft. For this reason, the Travelair 4000, which was manufactured in Wichita, Kansas, is often referred to as the Wichita Fokker. Aircraft of the vintage of the Curtiss Robin and the Travelair 4000 are highly prized antiques today and are the subject of painstaking restoration. The Robin was used in the 1920's and 1930's in several record-breaking endurance flights, and in the late 1930's it was flown nonstop across the Atlantic by Douglas Corrigan.

Meanwhile, the military services remained wedded to the biplane concept for their fighters, observation planes, bombers, and other classes of aircraft. One of the last biplane fighters developed for the U.S. Army Air Corps, and one of distinctly elegant design, was the Curtiss Hawk P-6E shown in figure 4.6. This aircraft traces its lineage back to the Curtiss Hawk P-1 of 1925, which in turn was derived, at least in part, from the Curtiss racing aircraft of that period. The P-6E was the last of the biplane line of Hawk fighters built for the U.S. Army Air Corps. Various versions of the Hawk were also procured by the U.S. Navy and a number of foreign countries. The entire Hawk series employed tapered wings, and the model P-6E featured a low drag, single-strut landing gear together with a carefully streamlined installation of

Figure 4.6 — Curtiss Hawk P-6E fighter; 1931. [Peter C. Boisseau]

the 650-horsepower Curtiss conquerer engine. The construction of the aircraft was conventional; the fuselage was of the welded steel-tube type, and the wings were constructed of a wood framework. The entire aircraft except for the engine cowling, wing leading edges, and other special portions was covered with fabric. The P–6E was one of the first fighters to employ a droppable auxiliary fuel tank mounted under the fuselage and was equipped with wheel brakes and onboard oxygen equipment. The engine was liquid cooled and employed a chemical known as ethylene glycol rather than water as the coolant. This chemical is essentially the same as the antifreeze used in modern automobile engines. The drag coefficient of the Hawk was a relatively low 0.0371. A comparison of this coefficient with the corresponding value for the Ryan *Spirit of St. Louis* indicates that a well-designed biplane could be as efficient from the point of view of friction drag as a multistrutted monoplane. The lower effective aspect ratio of the biplane wing cell, however, gives a substantially lower maximum lift-drag ratio for the Hawk than for the *Spirit of St. Louis*.

The Hawk model P–6E made its first flight in 1931. A transitional monoplane fighter designed by Boeing was first flown in 1932. This aircraft, known as the P–26 or Pea Shooter, is shown in figure 4.7. The aircraft was a wire-braced monoplane design that incorporated a fixed landing gear and open cockpit but was of all-metal construction, including the skin. The cowling around the engine, known as a Townend ring, reduced the drag of the radial engine but was not as effective as

Figure 4.7 — Boeing P–26A fighter; 1932. [NASA]

the full NACA type of cowling discussed in connection with the Lock-heed Vega. The aircraft in its original form had a relatively high land-ing speed; consequently, all production versions were equipped with simple trailing-edge flaps to reduce the landing speed. This was the first fighter aircraft developed in the United States to employ landing flaps. Thus, the P–26 represented a strange collection of the old and the new in airplane design and was an anachronism when it went into production in 1934. The zero-lift drag coefficient of the Boeing P–26A given in table II is seen to be higher than that of the Curtiss Hawk bi-plane; however, the drag area of the P–26 is only about 60 percent of that of the Hawk. The P–26 was a transitional type of fighter and had a relatively short service life. Most of the P–26's had been recalled from first-line service by the beginning of World War II, although at least one P–26 flown by a Philippine pilot is thought to have engaged a Japanese fighter in the early days of World War II.

Synergistic Developments

The Lockheed Vega, illustrated in figure 4.3, represented the high-est level of aerodynamic efficiency achieved by a high-wing monoplane with fixed landing gear by the year 1930. Reduction in drag and subse-quent improvements in the performance of a monoplane such as the Lockheed Vega could obviously be achieved by retracting the landing gear. Retraction of the landing gear on a high-drag aircraft, such as the DH–4, would result in very little improvement in performance since the drag contribution of the landing gear was a relatively small percentage of the total drag coefficient. On an aircraft such as the Lockheed Vega, however, which was characterized by cantilever wings, highly stream-lined fuselage, and efficiently cowled engine, the drag of the landing gear would be expected to be a significant portion of the total drag; hence, retraction of the gear would be expected to give a large incre-ment in performance.

The Lockheed Orion, shown in figure 4.8, took this next step in improving aerodynamic efficiency. The Orion was a six-passenger, low-wing monoplane, with the pilot located in an enclosed cockpit forward of the wing. The method of construction employed in the Orion was the same as that utilized in the Vega. The low-wing configuration was particularly adaptable for the use of a retractable landing gear. The gear could be kept short and thus light, and the wing provided an ideal stowage space for the gear in the retracted position. The steerable tail wheel was also retractable in order to provide further increases in aero-

Figure 4.8 — Lockheed Orion 9D mail and passenger plane; 1931. [mfr]

dynamic efficiency. The engine on this aircraft, as on the Vega, employed a single-speed, geared blower to provide improved engine power output at the cruise altitudes of the aircraft. The data in table II indicate that the Orion had a maximum speed of 226 miles per hour at sea level and a cruising speed of 200 miles per hour. The corresponding value of the zero-lift drag coefficient $C_{D,0}$ is 0.0210. The value of this coefficient is seen to be remarkably low, even when compared with values for present-day aircraft; and a comparison with corresponding values for the Lockheed Vega gives a good indication of the magnitude of the improvement in aerodynamic efficiency realized by retracting the landing gear. The retractable landing gear had been thought for many years to be too heavy for practical use in aircraft design; however, the spectacular reductions in drag associated with its use on an aerodynamically clean aircraft were found to far outweigh the relatively small increases in weight. The Orion first flew in mid-1931 and was produced in only limited quantities, perhaps because it was not really large enough for an airline transport; then too, there was a growing feeling that airline aircraft should be equipped with multiengines. Later in the 1930's Government regulations disallowed the use of single-engine aircraft for scheduled passenger-carrying operations.

The configuration and design details of the Lockheed Orion represented an extremely high level of aerodynamic efficiency, a level that has seldom been exceeded in the years since 1931. Yet, the Orion lacked several features that later became an integral part of the propeller-driven aircraft in its final definitive form. An aircraft with as broad a speed range as the Lockheed Orion requires some sort of variable pitch propeller in order that the desired amount of power may be efficiently extracted from the engine over a wide range of flight conditions. The full aerodynamic potential of a low-drag high-performance aircraft cannot be realized without the use of a controllable-pitch propeller. Such propellers became generally available and were in common use on high-performance aircraft by the mid-1930's. Another feature the Orion lacked was an effective high-lift flap system for increasing the maximum lift coefficient and reducing the stalling speed. The aircraft had a rudimentary trailing-edge flap; but like most early flap systems, this was used primarily for increasing the drag in the approach and landing maneuver rather than increasing the maximum lift coefficient. Again, the use of effective high-lift flaps became standard practice on high-performance configurations later in the decade. Finally, the use of wood as a primary material for construction had many disadvantages, and some form of light, stiff, all-metal monocoque or semimonocoque structure was desired.

One of the first aircraft developed in the United States to employ an all-metal stressed-skin semimonocoque type of structure was the Northrop Alpha, illustrated in figure 4.9. In this type of structure, the metal skin is smooth, not corrugated, and contributes significantly to the stiffness and load-carrying capability of the structure. The stability of the thin metal skin is usually enhanced by numerous internal string-

Figure 4.9 — Northrop Alpha mail and passenger plane; 1931. [Peter C. Boisseau]

ers attached to the skin. The Alpha employed a low wing of cantilever construction and a full NACA-type cowling around the radial engine, but incorporated an anachronistic fixed landing gear together with an open cockpit for the pilot. The zero-lift drag coefficient for the aircraft is seen from table II to be about the same as that for the Lockheed Vega discussed earlier. The aircraft was used in limited numbers for mail and passenger operation, and the particular version shown here was employed for transportation of high-ranking military officers. Various forms of stressed-skin metal construction were destined to become the norm for propeller-driven aircraft in the years ahead.

The first aircraft that assembled most of the desirable features discussed above in a single configuration was the Boeing 247 shown in figures 4.10 and 4.11. The first flight of the aircraft was in February 1933, and airline operations were begun later that year. The enclosed cabin accommodated 10 passengers, 2 pilots, and 1 steward. Two 525-horsepower Pratt & Whitney Wasp engines were employed, and the aircraft could maintain an altitude of 6000 feet on one engine at full gross weight. The earlier models of the aircraft, such as the one shown in figure 4.10, had Townend rings on the engines and employed fixed-pitch propellers. The definitive version of the aircraft, the model 247D (fig. 4.11), had both controllable-pitch propellers and full NACA-type engine cowlings. All aircraft were later converted or retrofitted to the model 247D configuration. The synergistic design features of this aircraft are as follows:

(1) Cantilever wings
(2) Retractable landing gear
(3) Efficiently cowled, light radial engine
(4) Controllable-pitch propellers
(5) Single-speed geared supercharger
(6) All metal, stressed-skin construction

The Boeing 247D did not employ wing flaps and had a relatively low wing loading of 16.3 pounds per square foot. A contemporary and very similar aircraft, the Douglas DC–2, employed all the features mentioned for the Boeing machine and, in addition, had a higher wing loading and split-type landing flaps. The model 247D was one of the first transport aircraft to employ rubber deicer boots and a significant amount of instrumentation for blind flying. The aircraft is seen from table II to have a low zero-lift drag coefficient and a value of the maximum lift-drag ratio of 13.5, which compares favorably with the values

91

Figure 4.10 — Early version of Boeing 247 10-passenger twin-engine transport; 1933.
[Peter C. Boisseau]

Figure 4.11 — Fully developed Boeing 247D. [mfr]

of this parameter for the previously discussed aircraft. About 75 Boeing 247's were built but the type was not developed further, perhaps because of Boeing's preoccupation with bomber aircraft development during that period of time.

The Douglas DC-3 was developed from the DC-2 and is, by any measure, one of the best-known aircraft ever produced anywhere in the world. The aircraft first flew in December 1935 and was in airline operation by the summer of 1936. It incorporated all the advanced technical features of the Boeing 247 and the Douglas DC-2 but, in addition, was sufficiently large to carry 21 passengers. With this number of passengers and a cruising speed at 10 000 feet of 185 miles per hour, the airlines for the first time had an aircraft with operating costs sufficiently low so that money could be made from carrying passengers without complete dependence on revenue from airmail contracts.

A DC-3 in flight is shown in figure 4.12. A distinctive identification feature of the aircraft is the sweptback wing, which was inherited from the DC-2 and was used to position the aerodynamic center of the aircraft in the proper relationship to the center of gravity. The design of the DC-2 wing did not initially employ sweepback but had a highly tapered straight wing. As the design of the aircraft progressed, however, it became evident that the center of gravity was farther aft than had been anticipated. Mounting the outer panels with sweepback offered a simple means for moving the aerodynamic center into the correct position. The Douglas DC-3 was powered either with two Wright Cyclone radial air-cooled engines of 1000 horsepower each or two Pratt & Whitney R-1830 engines of 1200 horsepower each. Both the Wright and Pratt & Whitney engines had 14 cylinders arranged in 2

Figure 4.12 — Douglas DC-3 21-passenger twin-engine transport; 1935. [mfr]

rows of 7, one behind the other. The double-row radial engine was extensively used throughout the subsequent development of large high-performance piston-engine aircraft. A comparison of the aerodynamic parameters for the Douglas DC–3 and the Boeing 247D, given in table II, indicates that the zero-lift drag coefficient of the DC–3 is about 17 percent higher than that of the Boeing aircraft; the larger zero-lift drag coefficient of the DC–3 results from the larger ratio of wetted area to wing area caused by the larger fuselage of the DC–3, which was designed to accommodate three-abreast seating as compared with two abreast for the Boeing aircraft. The value of the maximum lift-drag ratio for the Douglas DC–3, however, is 14.7 as compared with 13.5 for the Boeing machine; the higher aspect ratio of the DC–3 is responsible for the larger value of maximum lift-drag ratio. The wing loading of 25 pounds per square foot for the DC–3, as compared with the 16 pounds per square foot for the Boeing 247, reflects the use of split trailing-edge flaps on the DC–3 aircraft.

A total of 10 926 DC–3-type aircraft were built in the United States between 1936 and 1945. Of this total, about 10 000 aircraft were procured by the military services for their use, and many of these were later converted for various commercial activities following the end of World War II; today, over 45 years after its first flight, there are still many hundreds of DC–3 aircraft in service throughout the world. The DC–3 has been used for every conceivable purpose to which an airplane can be put and surely must be considered as one of the truly outstanding aircraft developments of all time.

The Boeing B–17 bomber was a highly significant military aircraft that first flew in prototype form during July 1935. A fully developed version of the aircraft, a Boeing B–17G utilized during World War II, is illustrated in figure 4.13. The aircraft incorporated the same significant structural and aerodynamic design features discussed in connection with the Boeing 247D and the Douglas DC–3 but was equipped with four engines instead of two. The aircraft had a gross weight of 55 000 pounds, which was considered very heavy at the time of its introduction. The four engines developed 1200 horsepower each and were equipped with turbosuperchargers. In contrast to the gear-driven, single-speed supercharger previously discussed, the turbosupercharger makes use of the energy in the exhaust gases from the engine. The supercharger blower is connected to a turbine that is driven by the exhaust gases. The fraction of the total exhaust gas that passes through the turbine can be varied by a valve in accordance with the altitude at which the aircraft is flying. Thus, the maximum rated power of the

94

Figure 4.13 — Boeing B–17G World War II four-engine heavy bomber; prototype first flown in 1935. [Peter C. Boisseau]

engine can be maintained up to an altitude at which all the exhaust gases pass through the turbine; at higher altitudes, the power drops off with altitude in very much the same way as an unsupercharged engine at low altitude. The critical altitude for the engines on the B–17, that is, the maximum altitude at which rated power could be maintained, was 25 000 feet. Experiments with turbosuperchargers had been under-way for many years, but the B–17 was the first aircraft in large-scale production to employ such a device. The turbosupercharged engines together with the relatively good aerodynamic parameters shown in table II for the B–17 gave the aircraft outstanding speed and range capability. The B–17 was used by the U.S. Army Air Forces throughout World War II as a heavy bomber. Nearly 13 000 of these aircraft were constructed, and a number of them are still employed today for various purposes.

The transformation of the military fighter aircraft into a thoroughly modern form had also taken place by 1936. The Seversky XP–35 shown in figure 4.14 was typical of the modern fighter aircraft developed in the middle to late 1930's. The XP–35 was a low-wing cantilever monoplane with a retractable landing gear, a fully cowled radial engine equipped with a geared single-speed supercharger, and a controllable-pitch propeller; the enclosed cockpit was, at that time, quite an innovation in fighter design. The aircraft was of stressed-skin metal construction and employed trailing-edge landing flaps. Wheel brakes

95

Figure 4.14 — Seversky XP–35 fighter; 1937. [NASA]

and a tail wheel were also fitted. In 1939, the Seversky Aircraft Company changed its name to Republic Aviation Incorporated; thus, the XP–35 may be considered the progenitor of the famous P–47 Thunderbolt fighter of World War II. Only about 75 P–35 fighters were built, between July 1937 and August 1938, at which time the aircraft was probably obsolete or obsolescent because of its relatively low horsepower. Refinements in fighter aircraft development were taking place at a rapid pace during this time, although the basic configuration concept of the propeller-driven fighter aircraft changed very little from that of the P–35.

The Douglas DC–3, the Boeing B–17, and the Seversky XP–35 are representative of the definitive and final configuration of the propeller-driven aircraft concept as applied to transport aircraft, bombers, and fighters. Many aerodynamic and structural refinements lay in the future, and both radial and in-line engines of ever-increasing horsepower were employed, but the basic configuration of these aircraft may be thought of as something of an upper plateau in propeller-driven aircraft design.

General Aviation at End of Decade

As the 1930's drew to a close, the general aviation manufacturers offered the private owner and fixed-base operator a variety of high-priced, luxurious aircraft, as well as a number of inexpensive, more austere models. Among the latter, the Piper J–3 Cub is without question the outstanding example. The prototype of the Cub, first flown in 1931 during the early days of the Great Depression, fostered the development of a number of light, low-powered, and, above all, inexpensive aircraft. The aircraft was initially produced by the Taylor Aircraft Company, which was subsequently acquired by William T. Piper and became the Piper Aircraft Corporation. The original Cub was refined and improved through the years and appeared in the definitive model J–3 form in 1937. The aircraft is illustrated in figure 4.15 and is seen to be a conventional, strut-braced, high-wing monoplane equipped with a fixed landing gear. The Cub carried two people seated one behind the other in a small enclosed cabin, one side of which could be opened to provide cooling in warm weather. The aircraft was equipped with brakes and had a steerable tail wheel; but most J–3's had no electrical system, hence, no starter, and, of course, no radio.

Power was supplied by a variety of engines ranging from 40 horsepower to 65 horsepower, with the 65-horsepower version being the most numerous. All the engines were four-cylinder air-cooled types with the cylinders arranged so that two cylinders were oriented at 180° to the other two. This cylinder arrangement, known as a flat engine, is used almost exclusively today on modern general aviation aircraft equipped with reciprocating engines. The cylinders of the engines on

Figure 4.15 — Piper J–3 Cub two-place training aircraft; 1938. [Peter C. Boisseau]

97

the J-3 Cub protruded into the airstream to provide the necessary cooling.

An adjustable stabilizer was provided for trimming the aircraft in flight. The Cub had no landing flaps, nor were any needed; the low wing loading of 6.8 pounds per square foot together with the thick, high-lift airfoil section in the wing gave a stalling speed of just over 40 miles per hour. The large air wheels on the landing gear allowed the aircraft to be safely operated from soft muddy fields. The internal structure of the aircraft was conventional and consisted of a welded steel-tube fuselage, together with wings that incorporated metal spars and ribs (at least in the later models). The entire aircraft was covered with fabric. Most aircraft left the factory painted a distinctive yellow, which became almost a trademark for the Cub.

The first cost of the Cub was modest, the operating expenses were low, and maintenance was minimal. A glance at the specifications contained in table II shows that the performance was not spectacular, but the aircraft was completely viceless with respect to its flying and handling qualities. All these factors made the Cub an ideal primary trainer. Thousands of pilots received their first dual instruction and made their first solo flight in the Cub during the explosive expansion of the U.S. Army and Navy Air Forces during World War II. In addition to training, the Cub was extensively used for liaison, observation, and other military duties during the war. About 20 000 of the J-3-type Cubs were produced, and a modernized, higher powered version known as the Piper PA-18 Super Cub is still in production at this time. Today, the aircraft is used for crop spraying, glider towing, fish spotting, and various other utility tasks. Many thousands of Super Cubs have also been built. Surely, the Cub and its descendants have had one of the longest production runs of any aircraft in history.

The larger, higher performance monoplane for the private owner and fixed-based operator was typified by the Stinson Reliant SR-8B illustrated in figure 4.16. The Reliant represents the culmination of much experience accumulated by Stinson in the development of a long line of cabin monoplanes. The Stinson Reliant was a well-streamlined high-wing monoplane with a single strut supporting each wing, and a single strut type of landing gear with the wheels enclosed by pants. The radial engine was enclosed by a full NACA cowling and transmitted power to the air by means of a controllable-pitch propeller. The luxuriously appointed cabin accommodated five people and included roll-down windows such as those used in automobiles. The aircraft had

Figure 4.16 — Stinson Reliant SR–8B five-place-cabin monoplane; 1937. [Peter C. Boisseau]

dual controls and a self-starter and was equipped with brakes, flaps, and all the latest flight instrumentation. The aircraft could be purchased with one of a number of different engines that varied in power from 245 to 450 horsepower. The aircraft illustrated in figure 4.16 and described in table II was equipped with the Lycoming nine-cylinder radial engine of 245 horsepower. With this engine, the aircraft had a gross weight of 3650 pounds and a cruising speed of 140 miles per hour at 8000 feet. The performance of the Reliant is not particularly outstanding when compared with comparable general aviation aircraft today. However, the cabin of the Reliant was roomier and allowed elbow and leg room to a degree not usually available in modern single-engine general aviation aircraft. The entire structure of the aircraft was metal, with the exception of the skin which was the familiar doped fabric. During World War II, a version of the Reliant was built as a trainer for the Canadian government. Many of these aircraft reverted to civilian status following the end of World War II. Production of the beautiful Reliant did not resume following the close of the war, and, today, examples of this aircraft are highly prized by collectors of antique aircraft.

Many biplanes manufactured during the late twenties and thirties were still in use in 1939, and several types were in production. Of these, two were high-performance, high-priced cabin aircraft. The most distinctive, and the one that represented the highest level of technology ever achieved in a biplane design, was the Beechcraft D–17. The prototype of the D–17 was first flown in 1932, and the type was continually refined and developed for many years. Production of the D–17 ended in 1948 after 784 models had been produced. The aircraft is illustrated in figure 4.17 and is seen to be a highly streamlined biplane equipped with retractable landing gear, full NACA cowling around its radial engine, and only a single I-type of interplane strut between the two wings on either side of the fuselage. A minimum of wire bracing was employed between the wings. A distinctive feature of the aircraft is the negative stagger; that is, the upper wing was mounted behind the lower wing. This particular arrangement was not unique with the Beech but had been employed on such aircraft as the DeHavilland 5 and Sopwith Dolphin in World War I. (See chapter 2.) However, the arrangement has been rarely used and is responsible for the term "Stagger Wing Beech" by which the D–17 is almost universally identified today. The term is not definitive, however, since most biplanes have the wings staggered, with the upper wing usually being forward of the lower wing; this arrangement is referred to as positive stagger. One may speculate on the reasons why the negative stagger wing arrangement was used in the design of the Beech. If the landing gear is to be re-

Figure 4.17 — Beech D–17S four-place-cabin biplane; 1939. [Peter C. Boisseau]

tracted into the lower wing, a most desirable feature, then the wing must be placed sufficiently far forward so that the landing gear is well ahead of the center of gravity of the aircraft; this location is necessary for ground stability. (The prototype and the first few aircraft produced had a short, highly streamlined, fixed gear attached to the lower wing.) To place the aerodynamic center of the aircraft in the proper relationship to the center of gravity, the upper wing must then be mounted behind the lower wing.

The Beech D–17 could be purchased with any one of a number of engines, ranging from about 200 to 450 horsepower. The particular version shown in figure 4.17 is the model D17S of about 1939 and was equipped with the 450-horsepower Pratt & Whitney Wasp Jr. engine. The aircraft was fully equipped with all the latest innovations, including controllable-pitch propeller, self-starter, full instrument panel, and, of course, brakes. Plain flaps were also employed on the upper wing. Four passengers were accommodated in the luxuriously appointed cabin. The fuselage of the aircraft was constructed of welded steel tubing and employed wooden formers and stringers to provide the necessary streamlined shape. The wings were constructed of wood, and the entire aircraft was covered with fabric. According to table II, the cruising speed of the aircraft was 202 miles per hour at 9700 feet, and the stalling speed was a relatively low 50 miles per hour. The zero-lift drag coefficient was a very low 0.0182. The Beech D–17 can truly be said to represent the ultimate in biplane development.

Chapter 5
Design Refinement, 1939–45

Background

The years of World War II saw extensive manufacturing, engineering, and research and development activity in the aviation industry. A similar explosive growth in aeronautical activity occurred during World War I; yet, there was a difference. World War I, as discussed in chapter 2, was characterized by experimentation of all types; different configurations, different materials and types of construction, and radically different types of engines were investigated and tested under actual combat conditions.

The definitive form of the propeller-driven aircraft had crystallized by the beginning of World War II, as discussed in chapter 4. All high-performance military aircraft used in World War II were designed to the same basic formula: internally braced, all-metal monoplane, equipped with retractable landing gear, wing flaps, controllable-pitch propeller, and enclosed compartment for the crew. This design concept was successfully applied to fighters, bombers, observation aircraft, and various other types of aircraft utilized during the war. The emphasis on research, development, and engineering was on achieving higher performance with this standard design formula. The quest was for higher speeds and altitudes, more maneuverability, longer range, better handling characteristics, and means for maintaining the landing speed within acceptable limits. These demands called for lighter weight, stronger structures, higher powered engines, and detailed aerodynamic refinement. The following section briefly describes a few representative areas of aerodynamic refinement.

Aerodynamic Problems and Refinements

A vast amount of aerodynamic research was conducted in the United States, Great Britain, Germany, and Italy during the years of

World War II. No attempt will be made to give a complete summary or abstract of this work; however, a few examples taken from NACA research may serve to indicate the flavor of the activity. More detailed accounts of the research in aerodynamics may be found in references 49, 56, and 104.

Airfoils and High-Lift Devices

The low drag coefficients achieved by internally braced monoplanes equipped with retractable landing gears suggested that any further large reductions in drag could only be achieved through the maintenance of extensive laminar flow over the surfaces of the aircraft. The boundary-layer flow of contemporary aircraft was essentially all turbulent; and since the skin friction coefficients for turbulent flow are much higher than those for laminar flow, the achievement of laminar flow on the surface of the aircraft would be expected to yield large reductions in drag. For example, the skin friction coefficient on a flat plate is reduced by a factor of almost 2 as the point of transition from laminar to turbulent flow is moved from the leading edge to the 50-percent-chord location. In the late 1930's, NACA's Langley Memorial Aeronautical Laboratory undertook the development of special airfoils designed to achieve extensive regions of laminar flow. The problem involved extensive theoretical and experimental investigations and the development of an entirely new low-turbulence wind tunnel. The early work on laminar-flow airfoils is described by Jacobs in reference 76, which was originally published in June 1939. The development of laminar-flow airfoils continued throughout the years of World War II and for several years thereafter. Over 100 different airfoils were derived. The characteristics of these airfoils were published in summary form in reference 18, and a complete exposition of airfoil theory and presentation of airfoil aerodynamic characteristics are given in reference 17.

The profile shapes of two NACA low-drag airfoil sections compared with a conventional airfoil are shown in figure 5.1. The airfoils designated as NACA 66_1–212 and NACA 63_1–412 are the laminar-flow, or low-drag, sections; and the airfoil designated as NACA 23012 is a conventional airfoil designed during the 1930's. The 66_1–212 airfoil was designed to maintain laminar flow to the 60-percent-chord point, and the 63_1–412 was designed to maintain laminar flow to the 30-percent-chord point. The designation system used for these airfoils, as well as older conventional NACA airfoil sections, is described in reference 17. As compared with the conventional section, the laminar-flow sections are seen to have the point of maximum thickness located far-

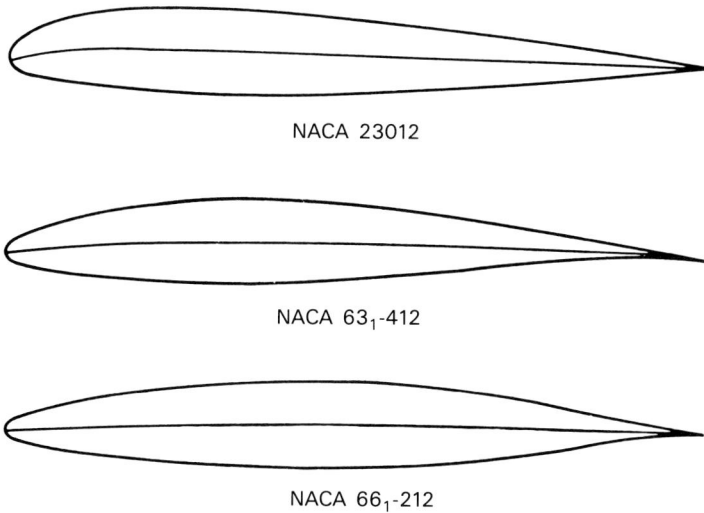

NACA 23012

NACA 63₁-412

NACA 66₁-212

Figure 5.1 — Shapes of two NACA low-drag airfoil sections compared with NACA 23012 airfoil section.

ther aft along the chord of the airfoil. The aft location of the maximum thickness point is associated with the need to achieve a particular type of airfoil-surface pressure distribution and is also desirable from the point of view of structural design. A comparison of the section drag characteristics of the NACA 63_1–412 airfoil and the NACA 23012 airfoil is shown in figure 5.2, in which the drag coefficient is plotted as a function of the lift coefficient for the two airfoils in both the smooth and rough condition.

The bucket in the drag curve for the 63_1–412 airfoil corresponds to the lift coefficient range in which laminar flow is achieved. In the rough condition, the drag characteristics of the conventional and laminar-flow airfoils are very similar. The roughness employed in the test was a sandlike material that was intended to fix transition near the leading edge in a manner corresponding to a rough and poorly maintained airplane wing. The North American XP–51, which flew in prototype form in 1940, was the first aircraft to employ a laminar-flow-type airfoil section, and most subsequent high-performance aircraft designs utilized these airfoils. One of the essential requirements for achieving laminar flow is that the surface of the wings be manufactured and maintained in an extremely smooth and fair condition. (The term "fair" means that the wing surfaces must be essentially free from waves, that is, ripples, and must conform very closely to the specified

105

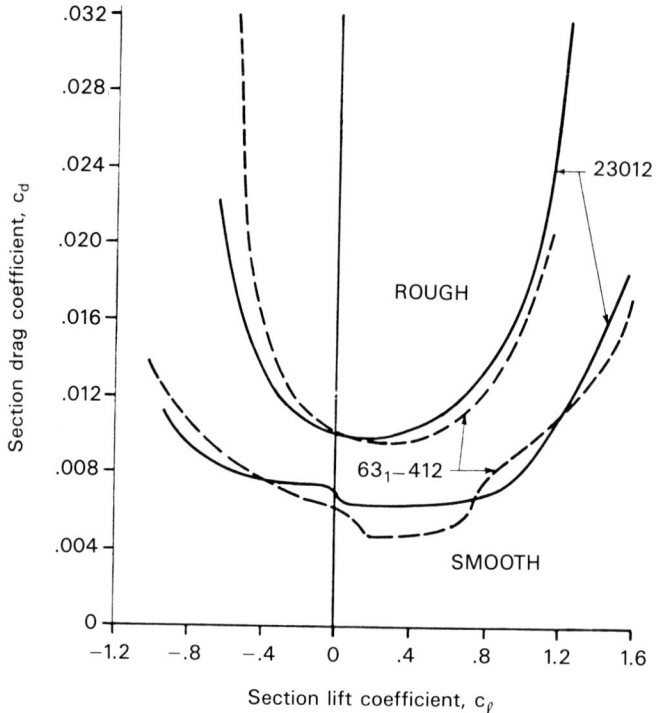

Figure 5.2 — Drag characteristics of NACA low-drag and conventional airfoil sections with both smooth and rough leading edges.

contour shape.) This requirement could be met with highly accurate wind-tunnel models. Unfortunately, methods of aircraft manufacture and maintenance during World War II, and even today, were such that only very small regions of laminar flow located near the leading edge of the wing could be achieved on practical operational aircraft. As a consequence, the use of NACA laminar-flow airfoil sections has never resulted in any significant reduction in the drag as a result of the achievement of laminar flow. A practical means for achieving extensive regions of laminar flow under everyday operating conditions remains a problem today and is still one of the great unsolved challenges in aeronautical research. The NACA low-drag airfoils have seen extensive use and continue to be used on high-performance aircraft because they have better characteristics at high subsonic Mach numbers than conventional airfoil sections. The effectiveness of the NACA laminar-flow airfoils as a means for delaying the adverse effects of compressibility at high subsonic Mach numbers is a classic example of a new technical concept developed to solve one problem but proving highly useful in the practical solution of an entirely different one. Figures 5.1, 5.2, and 5.3 were taken from the unpublished proceedings of a NACA conference held in September 1946 for the purpose of providing representatives of the general aviation industry with the results of previously classified technical data generated during the World War II years.

As the wing loadings of high-performance military aircraft steadily increased, the desirability of maintaining the stalling speed within acceptable limits dictated the need for extensive work on high-lift devices to increase the maximum lift coefficients of aircraft. The types of trailing-edge flaps used in the mid- to late 1930's were usually of the simple plain or split type. For example, the Douglas DC–3 employed simple split-type flaps. Extensive wind-tunnel studies, however, were made of more complex high-lift devices both before and during World

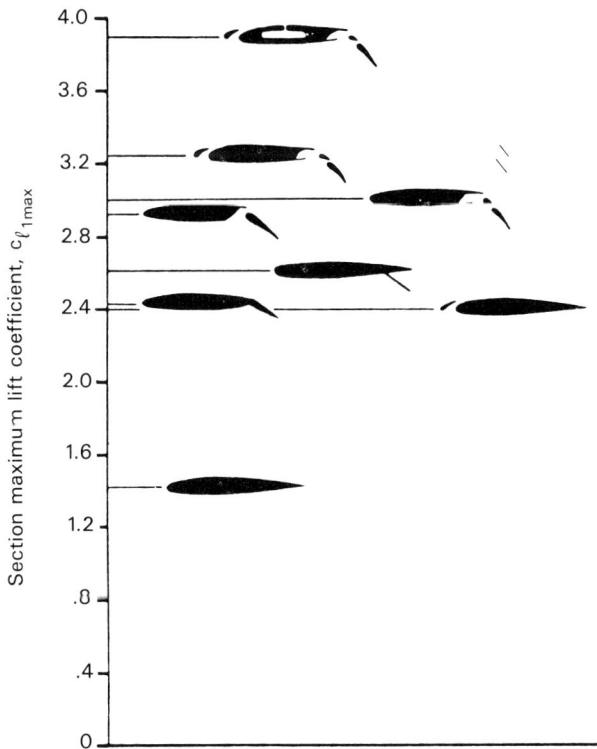

Figure 5.3 — Effect of various types of high-lift devices on airfoil section maximum lift coefficient.

War II. A summary of the state of the art of high-lift device design at the end of World War II is indicated in figure 5.3, in which the maximum lift capabilities of airfoils equipped with various types of leading- and trailing-edge high-lift devices are shown. The maximum lift coefficient of an airfoil equipped with a plain flap, split flap, single-slotted flap, double-slotted flap, and double-slotted flap in combination with a leading-edge slat are shown in figure 5.3. The use of a double-slotted flap and leading-edge slat increases the maximum lift coefficient from about 1.4 for the plain airfoil to a value slightly over 3.2. The Douglas A–26 was the first aircraft to employ a double-slotted flap, and the combination of double-slotted flap and slat was not used to any great extent until well after World War II. Many of today's jet transports employ double-slotted flaps or even triple-slotted flaps in combination with leading-edge slats and flaps. The leading-edge flap is not shown in figure 5.3 since it was a German development and was not known in this country until German data became available following the end of World War II. Many general aviation aircraft of today employ either plain flaps or single-slotted flaps. The airfoil with double-slotted flaps and slats shown at the top of figure 5.3 with a maximum lift coefficient of about 3.8 employed boundary-layer suction through a single mid-chord slot to delay separation of the boundary layer and thus increase the maximum lift coefficient. This concept was the subject of numerous experiments in wind tunnels but has never been utilized on a production aircraft. Various types of boundary-layer blowing have been employed for improving the maximum lift coefficient. This type of boundary-layer control became practical, however, only after the development of the turbine engine. The values of maximum lift coefficient given in figure 5.3 are for a two-dimensional airfoil section and are higher than would be obtained on a three-dimensional airplane wing equipped with partial span flaps.

Drag Cleanup

The internally braced monoplane with retractable landing gear, typified by the Douglas DC–3 shown in figure 4.12, would ideally be expected to have a zero-lift drag coefficient only slightly in excess of that which would be calculated with the use of the total wetted area of the airplane and a skin friction coefficient corresponding to a turbulent boundary layer. Such an ideal drag coefficient, however, is never achieved in actual service aircraft. The German Messerschmitt 109 fighter, for example, is shown in reference 72 to have a zero-lift drag coefficient about twice the value corresponding to the ideal based on wetted area and a turbulent skin friction coefficient. The increases in drag above the ideal value result from one or more of the following:

(1) Projection of various items outside of the smooth basic contour of the aircraft
(2) Roughness or unevenness in the aircraft surface
(3) Unintentional leakage of air through the aircraft structure
(4) The use of large quantities of excess air for various cooling functions
(5) Areas of local flow separation

Experience gained during the 1930's from the investigation of full-scale aircraft in the Langley full-scale (30- by 60-foot) wind tunnel had given an indication of the importance of detailed design in the achievement of low drag coefficients on actual full-scale aircraft. Thus, during World War II, some 23 military aircraft were the subject of drag cleanup investigations in the Langley full-scale tunnel. Individual reports were issued following the investigation of each aircraft, and two separate summary reports covering the drag cleanup work were issued by the close of World War II. Recently, the data obtained during these various investigations have been summarized again and issued as a NASA publication, reference 42. The data obtained in the drag cleanup tests during World War II have been reissued in a modern report in order that they may be more available to the designers of modern general aviation aircraft.

A full-size aircraft installed in the Langley full-scale tunnel for a drag cleanup investigation is shown in figure 5.4. In this case, the aircraft is a Curtiss SB2C–4 Navy dive bomber popularly known as the Helldiver. The aircraft is mounted on three struts, two of which are located near the longitudinal center of gravity on either side of the aircraft center line and the third is located near the tail of the aircraft. These struts are attached to scales from which the lift, drag, and pitching moment can be measured. The two large four-bladed fans visible in the background of the photograph are connected to 4000-horsepower electric motors that provide the power necessary to drive the tunnel. The top speed of the tunnel is about 100 miles per hour. An indication of the size of the tunnel is shown by the man standing on the lip of the exit bell of the open throat test section of the tunnel. The Langley full-scale tunnel was first put into operation in 1931, has been continually used through the years since then, and is still in use at this time.

Figure 5.4 — Curtiss SB2C-4 mounted in Langley full-scale tunnel for drag cleanup investigation. [NASA]

Drag cleanup investigations are still performed even today. A modern twin-engine general aviation aircraft is the most recent example of such an investigation. The procedure followed in a wartime drag cleanup study consisted of the following steps: First, the aircraft was examined in detail, those features suspected of causing unnecessary drag were identified, and necessary changes to eliminate the suspected unnecessary drag were planned. The airplane was then put in a faired and sealed condition in which all protrusions were either removed or carefully faired, all openings were closed, and all external leaks were sealed. The airplane was then returned to its service condition, item by item, and the drag was evaluated for each step. The procedure is illustrated by the results contained in figure 5.5 taken from reference 42, which shows the sources of drag for the Seversky XP–41 aircraft. The XP–41 airplane was very similar in appearance to the Seversky XP–35 shown in figure 4.14. Figure 5.5 shows that the aircraft drag was evaluated for 18 different conditions, which are indicated by sketches on the left-hand side of the figure and described on the right-hand side of the figure. The drag coefficient of the clean airplane was 0.0166, as com-

Condition number	Description	C_D (C_L = 0.15)	ΔC_D	ΔC_D, percent[a]
1	Completely faired condition, long nose fairing	0.0166		
2	Completely faired condition, blunt nose fairing	.0169		
3	Original cowling added, no airflow through cowling	.0186	0.0020	12.0
4	Landing-gear seals and fairing removed	.0188	.0002	1.2
5	Oil cooler installed	.0205	.0017	10.2
6	Canopy fairing removed	.0203	–.0002	–1.2
7	Carburetor air scoop added	.0209	.0006	3.6
8	Sanded walkway added	.0216	.0007	4.2
9	Ejector chute added	.0219	.0003	1.8
10	Exhaust stacks added	.0225	.0006	3.6
11	Intercooler added	.0236	.0011	6.6
12	Cowling exit opened	.0247	.0011	6.6
13	Accessory exit opened	.0252	.0005	3.0
14	Cowling fairing and seals removed	.0261	.0009	5.4
15	Cockpit ventilator opened	.0262	.0001	.6
16	Cowling venturi installed	.0264	.0002	1.2
17	Blast tubes added	.0267	.0003	1.8
18	Antenna installed	.0275	.0008	4.8
	Total		0.0109	

[a]Percentages based on completely faired condition with long nose fairing.

Airplane Condition

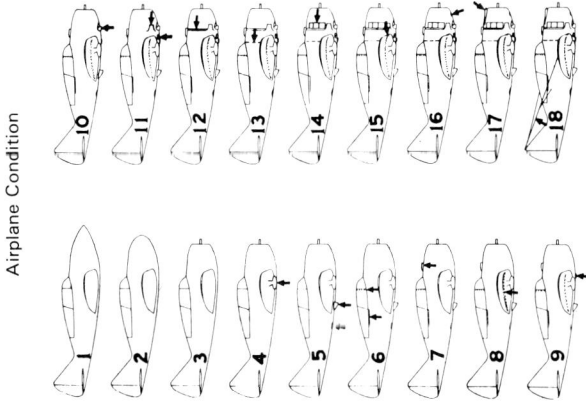

Figure 5.5 — Experimental study of drag sources on Seversky XP–41. [from ref. 42]

111

pared with 0.0275 for the aircraft in the service condition. In order to convert the clean configuration into a useful practical aircraft, the drag was increased by about 65 percent of the value obtained for the clean aircraft. All the additional drag, however, was found to be unnecessary. Further tests and analyses showed that the additional drag could be reduced by more than one-half through careful tailoring of various aspects of the design. The drag coefficient of a practical service aircraft of the XP–41 type was accordingly reduced from 0.0275 to 0.0226. The data in figure 5.5 indicate that the increments in drag coefficient corresponding to the 18 steps of the cleanup process are generally rather small and, in many cases, only a few percent of the total drag coefficient. Yet, taken all together, these increments add up to an impressive total. Important performance improvements resulted from the drag cleanup of the 23 military aircraft in the Langley full-scale tunnel. In many cases, the gains associated with care and attention to detailed design were found to be greater than the differences in drag between airplanes of different configurations. The drag cleanup work made an important contribution to the refinement of high-performance propeller-driven aircraft during World War II, and the gains resulting from the program often spelled the difference in performance between victory and defeat in the air.

Compressibility Effects

Until the late 1930's, aircraft were designed on the assumption that the air flowing over the wings and other surfaces was essentially incompressible, like water. As speeds and altitudes increased, however, the effects of compressibility on the flow over the aircraft began to assume increased importance. The ratio of the aircraft speed to the speed of sound provides a useful index for gaging the speed at which significant compressibility effects begin to manifest themselves on a particular aircraft. This ratio is called the Mach number, in honor of the famous Austrian physicist Ernst Mach. The critical Mach number is defined as the aircraft flight Mach number at which the local Mach number over some portion of the aircraft, such as the upper surface of the wing for example, equals unity; that is, the flow at this point has reached sonic velocity.

Large changes in the pressures, forces, and moments acting on a wing or body occur at Mach numbers somewhat in excess of the critical value. These changes in aerodynamic characteristics result from the formation of shock waves and attendant flow separation behind the shock wave. An example of the effects of compressibility on the lift and drag characteristics of a 15-percent-thick airfoil section is shown in figure 5.6 (from ref. 48). The section lift coefficient and the section drag coefficient are shown as a function of Mach number in figure 5.6(a) and (b), respectively. Precipitous reductions in lift coefficient occur with increases in Mach number beyond the critical value. The Mach number at which the lift begins to show a sharp decrease becomes smaller as the angle of attack is increased since the critical Mach number decreases with increasing angle of attack. Apparent also is the large reduction in lift-curve slope at the higher Mach numbers. For example, at a Mach number of 0.4, the lift coefficient increases from 0.2 to about 0.72 as the angle of attack varies from 0° to 5°; whereas, at a Mach number of 0.8, increasing the angle of attack from 0° to 5° results in an increment in lift coefficient of only about 0.2. The drag coefficient shows a large increase with Mach number as the Mach number is increased beyond the critical value. For example, at an angle of attack of $-1°$, the drag coefficient increases from about 0.015 at a Mach number of 0.65 to 0.13 at a Mach number of 0.9.

Engine cowlings, canopies, propellers, fuselages, and other aircraft components were also found to be subject to large compressibility effects. Although not shown by the data in figure 5.6, large Mach number effects were found in the pitching-moment characteristic of the airfoil and in the effectiveness of various types of trailing-edge control surfaces. The effect on the airplane of these various changes in aerodynamic coefficients manifested itself in the form of a limiting speed, large changes in stability and trim characteristics of the aircraft, important reductions in the control power of the control surfaces, buffeting, loss in propulsive efficiency and various types of aircraft oscillation, and unintended maneuvers. In some cases, aircraft flown deep into the compressible regime became completely uncontrollable and could not be recovered. Loss of the aircraft and pilot frequently occurred under these circumstances. The state of understanding of compressibility effects in 1941 is outlined in reference 105, which was initially issued as a confidential report; a broader survey of knowledge in the field of compressibility aerodynamics is given in the Wright brothers lecture for 1944, which is cited as reference 106.

Extensive investigations were undertaken in the United States and Europe in an effort to better understand compressibility phenomena and, in particular, to devise design methods for increasing the value of the critical Mach number and reducing the adverse effects of compressibility that occur beyond this Mach number. These efforts were ham-

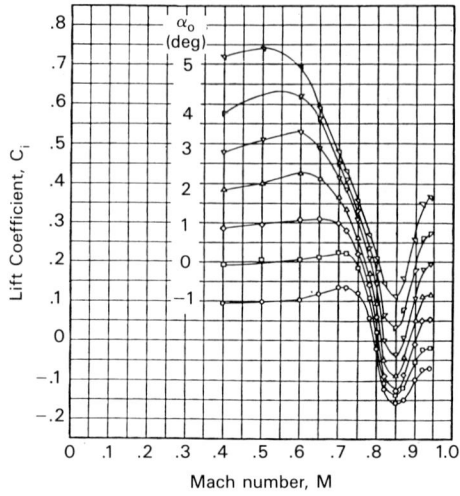

(a) Section lift coefficient.

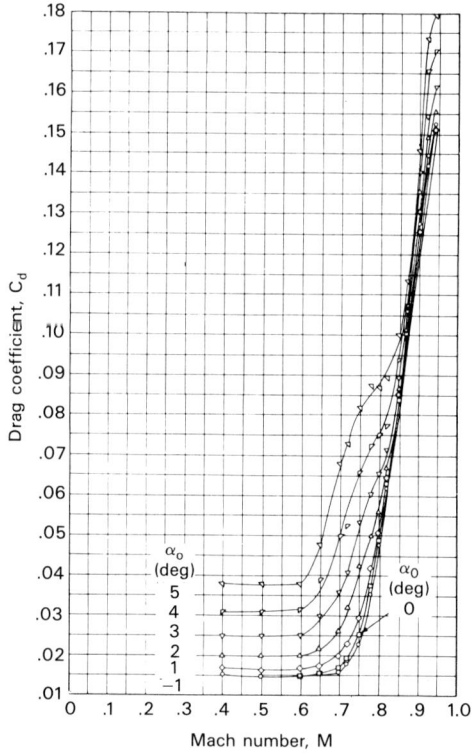

(b) Section drag coefficient.

Figure 5.6 — Lift and drag characteristics of NACA 2315 airfoil section as function of Mach number for several angles of attack. [data from ref. 48]

pered by fundamental difficulties in both theoretical and experimental methods of investigation. The governing equations for flows near Mach number 1.0 proved intractable to closed-form solution. Adequate solutions to these nonlinear equations were not possible until the advent of the large-capacity, high-speed digital computer in the late 1960's and 1970's. Practical theoretical approaches to the compressibility problem during the war years usually involved the application of relatively simple correction factors to results obtained under the assumption of incompressible flow. These correction factors worked fairly well up to Mach numbers relatively close to the critical value but broke down completely at higher Mach numbers. The wind tunnel which had proved so useful in past aerodynamic investigations also became of questionable value at Mach numbers somewhat in excess of the critical value. At some Mach number, not too much higher than the critical value for the airfoil or body, the tunnel "choked," which meant that no higher freestream Mach numbers could be obtained. A Mach number range between the subsonic choking value and some supersonic value, such as 1.2 or 1.3, was not available for wind-tunnel investigations. Supersonic tunnels operating beyond a Mach number of 1.2 or 1.3 were possible but were of little practical interest during the World War II time period. The solution to the problem of wind-tunnel choking was not found until the advent of the slotted and perforated-throat wind tunnel in the early 1950's.

In spite of these experimental and theoretical difficulties, a good deal of progress was made in devising improved configuration concepts for high-speed flight. The laminar-flow airfoil sections described previously did not achieve the desired objective of extensive laminar flow in flight; however, the pressure distributions of these airfoil shapes resulted in critical Mach numbers that were significantly higher for these sections than for other airfoil sections having the same thickness ratios. Most aircraft designed in the United States after 1940 employed the NACA laminar-flow airfoil sections or some modification of these sections, primarily because of the advantages they offered as a means for increasing the critical Mach number. The original NACA cowling, which was developed before aircraft speeds reached high enough values for compressibility effects to be important, had a critical speed of only about 300 miles per hour at 25 000 feet. New cowling shapes were developed that ultimately raised the critical speed to almost 600 miles per hour. Studies of various wing-body combinations led to configuration concepts that resulted in reduced interference effects and, hence, higher critical Mach numbers.

115

Propellers usually encounter the adverse effects of compressibility at flight Mach numbers below that at which the aircraft configuration itself penetrates the critical region because portions of the blades of the propeller, particularly near the tip, are traveling at a higher speed relative to the air than the aircraft itself. Compressibility problems on aircraft propellers were first encountered during the 1930's, and research studies were made in those years in an effort to improve propeller design. This work continued on through World War II. One major investigation that gives an indication of the type of research undertaken in the development of improved propellers is described in reference 108. New planform shapes, new twist distributions, and new airfoil sections designed especially for propellers all combined to result in significant increases in the stream Mach number at which the propeller showed serious losses in efficiency. It seemed clear, however, that the propeller was likely to constitute the ultimate limitation on the speeds that could be reached with aircraft employing this means of propulsion.

The basic principles underlying the proper design of aircraft configurations intended for flight at high subsonic and transonic Mach numbers were fairly clear by the end of World War II. The need for small thickness ratios on wings and tail surfaces and high fineness ratios on bodies became increasingly evident by 1945. The P-51D airplane, one of the best of the United States fighter aircraft of World War II, employed a wing of about 15-percent thickness ratio; by contrast, the wings of transonic and supersonic aircraft of today are more likely to be of the order of 4 to 5 percent in thickness ratio. The use of wing sweepback as a means for increasing the critical Mach number and reducing the adverse effects of compressibility beyond the critical Mach number was first proposed in the United States in 1945. (See ref. 77.) The advantages of sweepback had been recognized in Germany at an earlier date, and the Messerschmidt ME-163 tailless rocket fighter employed a sweptback wing. This aircraft saw limited operational use toward the end of World War II but was not particularly effective as a fighter because of the capricious nature of its rocket propulsion system. The use of wing sweepback, together with small thickness ratios and high fineness ratios, and later combined with the transonic area rule, provided the basic configuration elements needed for successful aircraft of high subsonic and transonic speed. The loss in propulsion efficiency at high subsonic Mach number remained the stumbling block to the development of successful aircraft for use at high subsonic and transonic speeds. The advent of jet propulsion solved this problem and, in addition, was capable of producing the large powers required for flight at these high speeds with a simple and light type of propulsion system. The large power-producing characteristic of the turbine engine is related directly to the large air-handling capability of this engine as compared with the reciprocating engine. The jet engine then became the basis for all high-performance aircraft developed after about 1945. When used in combination with the configuration concepts just discussed, this propulsion system resulted in the high-performance subsonic and supersonic aircraft in operation today. Jet aircraft form the subject of part II of this book.

Flying and Handling Qualities

The flying and handling qualities of an aircraft have been of great interest since the earliest days of aviation. As pointed out in chapter 2, an aircraft with good handling characteristics must obey the pilot's inputs precisely, rapidly, and predictably without unwanted excursions or uncontrollable behavior and, finally, without excessive physical effort on the part of the pilot. Preferably, the aircraft should possess these desirable characteristics throughout its performance envelope. A well-known NACA test pilot of World War II and earlier years, Melvin N. Gough, put it in a slightly different form when he stated that "the flying qualities of an aircraft may be defined as the stability and control characteristics that have an important bearing on the safety of flight and on the pilot's impressions of the ease and precision with which the aircraft may be flown and maneuvered." For many years, there was considerable speculation as to what flying characteristics were desired in an airplane, and the entire subject was discussed in terms of the qualitative opinions of various pilots. Several years prior to World War II, a flight research program was undertaken in which the response characteristics of the aircraft following known control inputs were measured and correlated with pilots' opinions of the behavior of the aircraft, and, finally, related to the engineering parameters employed in the design of the aircraft. NACA continued the investigation of flying and handling qualities of various aircraft and, by the beginning of World War II, had assembled complete qualitative information on 12 different aircraft. From the fund of information accumulated in these tests, it was possible, in 1941, for NACA to prepare a set of requirements (ref. 53) for satisfactory flying qualities in terms of quantities that had been measured in flight and could be estimated by engineers during the design of a new aircraft.

117

Flying qualities requirements may be listed under the broad headings of longitudinal stability and control characteristics, lateral stability and control characteristics, and stalling characteristics. The scope of flying qualities specification at that time is indicated in the following list of categories in which criteria were developed:

A. Requirements for longitudinal stability and control:
(1) Elevator control and takeoff
(2) Elevator control in steady flight
(3) Longitudinal trimming device
(4) Elevator control in accelerated flight
(5) Uncontrolled longitudinal motion
(6) Limits of trim due to power and flaps
(7) Elevator control and landing

B. Requirements for lateral stability and control:
(1) Aileron control characteristics
(2) Yaw due to ailerons
(3) Rudder and aileron trim devices
(4) Limits of rolling moment due to sideslip
(5) Rudder control characteristics
(6) Yawing moment due to sideslip
(7) Crosswind force characteristics
(8) Pitching moment due to sideslip
(9) Uncontrolled lateral and directional motion

C. Stalling characteristics:
(1) Pitching-moment characteristics
(2) Rolling- and yawing-moment characteristics
(3) Control forces
(4) Recovery

These various categories are not discussed in detail here and are only given to indicate the extent of design criteria available at that time. Most of the control criteria involved specification of the control power, that is, the ability of the control to cause the aircraft to respond in the desired manner, and control force and control-force gradients that relate to the physical effort the pilot must exert in order to actuate the controls by an amount needed to give the desired response. For example, the elevator control in accelerated flight is expressed in terms of the pounds of force that the pilot must exert on the control column in order to produce an acceleration of 1 g.

The U.S. Army and Navy revised the general NACA flying qualities specifications to their immediate specific requirements and looked to NACA to continue its investigations and refinement of existing and new military aircraft. By the end of World War II, the total number of airplanes studied in flight by NACA increased from 12 to 60. A good discussion of the state of understanding of aircraft stability and flying qualities at the close of World War II is given in reference 102. The study and refinement of aircraft flying and handling qualities have continued through the years as aircraft speed, size, and configuration have changed and today form a highly sophisticated branch of aeronautical engineering.

Although not a specific part of the flying qualities requirements as defined in reference 53, aircraft spinning and spin recovery might be briefly mentioned under category C above, designated as stalling characteristics. In 1936, NACA put into operation at the Langley Memorial Aeronautical Laboratory the world's first vertical free-spinning wind tunnel. This tunnel was developed for the purpose of studying the control motions required to permit rapid and desirable recovery of an aircraft once it was in a spin, and for developing stability and control criteria for aircraft design so that the aircraft would have desirable spin recovery characteristics. During the war years, spin investigations were conducted in the free-spinning tunnel on approximately 150 different military airplane designs to determine recovery characteristics from developed spins. From the results of these investigations, criteria were developed for selection during the design process of proper design parameters so as to ensure good spin recovery.

Summary Comments

The preceding paragraphs describe four aspects of aerodynamic technology that were the subject of intensive research and refinement during World War II. These are intended to serve only as typical examples of the type of detailed research and refinement that took place in all technical areas involved in aeronautical engineering. Many other aspects of the science of aeronautics were under intensive investigation. Structures and materials technologies were advanced and methods of mass production were developed that resulted in the output of over 95 000 airplanes in the United States during one year of World War II. Propulsion technology, including engines, superchargers, fuels, and so forth, was the subject of intensive research and development. As an example, the magnificent Rolls-Royce Merlin engine developed about 970

119

horsepower as installed in the original prototype of the Hurricane fighter; by the end of World War II, some versions of the Merlin engine developed 1600 to 1700 horsepower. The appearance of military aircraft changed very little in the time period between 1935 and 1945; however, the combat aircraft that existed in 1945 was far superior to its 1935 progenitor because of intensive work aimed at detailed refinement of all aspects of aeronautical design.

Examples of World War II Aircraft

Aircraft employed in World War II were usually designed to fill mission requirements in one or more of the following broad categories:

(1) Heavy bombers
(2) Attack and light bombers
(3) Fighters and interceptors
(4) Patrol and reconnaissance
(5) Transport and utility
(6) Training

Many aircraft specifically designed for use in one of these categories were later found to be useful in other categories with only minor modifications. There is no feasible way of describing all the outstanding World War II aircraft in such a short account as this one. A number of the books listed in the references at the end of this volume contain excellent detailed descriptions of the various aircraft used by the different warring powers during World War II. For those particularly interested in United States combat aircraft, reference 118 is highly recommended. Fighters and bombers of World War II are described in great detail in references 58 to 63. Combat aircraft of all the nations that saw operational service are described in reference 112.

A few examples of much-used United States bomber and fighter aircraft are illustrated and described below. These aircraft are representative of a vast array of very good aircraft produced by both Allied and Axis countries during World War II. The aircraft of no one country held a clear and continuing technical advantage over those of another country for very long. United States, British, and German aircraft were usually of about the same state of the art from a technological viewpoint. Detailed refinements discussed in the preceding paragraphs frequently spelled the difference between success and failure in combat operations. Essentially, all combat aircraft utilized in the World War II period were, as previously described, designed to the same cantilever monoplane formula with retractable landing gear, variable-pitch propeller, and metal construction.

Bomber Aircraft

The bomber aircraft discussed here fall into the following categories: heavy, very heavy, and medium multiengine bombers, and single-engine Navy scout bombers. Discussed first are the heavy bombers.

Two outstanding heavy bombers that served with the U.S. Army Air Force were the Boeing B-17 and the Consolidated B-24. The two types are best remembered as the aircraft that carried out the United States strategic bombing offensive against Germany. The Boeing B-17 Flying Fortress, which first flew in prototype form in 1935, is described in chapter 4 and illustrated in figure 4.13. The B-24 Liberator, designed several years later than the B-17, was first flown as a prototype in December 1939, and the first production aircraft was delivered in 1941. The B-24, a four-engine, 56 000-pound bomber, had roughly the same gross weight and was designed for the same mission as the B-17 but differed radically in design concept and appearance from the Boeing aircraft. The B-24 bomber is illustrated in figure 5.7, and the characteristics of a B-24J are given in table III (appendix A). The most distinguishing features of the B-24 as contrasted with the B-17 were the high-aspect-ratio wing mounted atop the fuselage, the tricycle landing gear, and the two fins and rudders. The wing of the B-24 had a very high aspect ratio of 11.55 and employed the much-publicized Davis airfoil section that, according to the popular aviation literature of the day, was supposed to provide the aircraft with unusually efficient aerodynamic characteristics. Later, wind-tunnel tests showed that while the Davis airfoil had reasonably good aerodynamic characteristics it offered no marked superiority over contemporary airfoils of that time period. The high-wing position employed on the B-24 offered the distinct advantage of allowing the bomb bay, including bomb-bay doors, to be housed directly beneath the wing, thus permitting the bomb load to be located in the optimum position with respect to the aircraft center of gravity. The high wing, however, had the disadvantage of requiring the use of relatively long, heavy landing-gear struts. An examination of the data given in tables II and III shows that the zero-lift drag coefficient of the B-24 was 0.0406 (table III) as compared with 0.0302 (table II) for the B-17. Because of its high-aspect-ratio wing, however, the maximum lift-drag ratio of the B-24 was about the same

Figure 5.7 — Consolidated B-24 heavy bomber. [NASA]

as that of the B-17. The B-24 had a maximum speed of 290 miles per hour and, on a typical mission, could carry a 5000-pound bomb load for a distance (one way) of 1700 miles. The B-24 was equipped with four 14-cylinder Pratt & Whitney engines of 1200 horsepower each. These engines employed turbosuperchargers, just as did the Wright Cyclone engines used on the B-17, and had a critical altitude of about 30 000 feet.

Both the B-17 and the B-24 were designed for high-altitude precision bombing in daylight without protection from fighter escort. In concept, the aircraft were to fly in close formation and protect themselves and each other with concentrated machine-gun fire. In accordance with this doctrine, the B-17G carried no less than 13 .50-caliber machine guns and the B-24J had 10 such guns. In spite of this formidable armament, however, combat experience showed an unacceptable loss rate from enemy air attack until fighter escort was provided for the bombers.

Another aspect of the United States strategic bombing offensive against Germany that deserves mention was the effect of the hostile high-altitude environment on the air crews. Neither the B-17 nor the B-24 was pressurized or heated. Temperatures in the range from $-30°$ F to $-50°$ F were encountered at altitudes of 25 000 feet and above; and although crew members wore electrically heated flying suits, severe cases of frostbite were not uncommon. Later-generation bombers intended for high altitude operations were both pressurized and heated.

Somewhat over 18 000 B-24's were produced—more than any other American combat aircraft; furthermore, it was used as a bomber

Figure 5.8 — Boeing B–29 very heavy bomber. [NASA]

in every theater of operation. Among the B–24 types produced was a cargo version known as the C–87 and a Navy patrol aircraft designated the PB4Y. The B–24 was a true workhorse and was used for many purposes other than its design role as a bomber.

Let us turn now to another and later class of bomber, the Boeing B–29. The B–29 was designated as a very heavy bomber by the U.S. Army Air Forces and, with a gross weight of 120 000 pounds (later to increase to more than 140 000 pounds), was the heaviest combat aircraft to be produced in quantity by any country during World War II. It grew from a requirement for an aircraft capable of carrying a significantly greater load for a longer range than was possible with either the B–17 or the B–24. The first test flight was made on September 21, 1942, and the first operational sortie was made on June 5, 1944 in a mission against Bangkok that originated in India. Truly, a phenomenally short development time for such an advanced aircraft. A major instrument in the defeat of Japan, the B–29 was used with great effectiveness in night raids against Japanese industry during the latter part of 1944 and in 1945. The aircraft also had the distinction, some may think a dubious one, of carrying the only atomic bombs ever dropped in war.

A B–29 is shown in figure 5.8, and characteristics of one version of the aircraft are given in table III. An examination of the photograph and accompanying data shows that the very-high-aspect-ratio wing (11.50) was mounted vertically in the midposition on the long, slim fuselage. In contrast with the earlier Boeing B–17, the B–29 had a tricycle landing gear with each leg having a two-wheel bogie and with the main gear retracting into the inboard engine nacelles. Each of the four

123

18-cylinder Wright 3350 twin-row radial engines had two General Electric turbosuperchargers that gave the 2200-horsepower engines a critical altitude of about 30 000 feet. Air induction to the turbosuperchargers was provided by ducts beneath the engine and gave the cowlings a distinctive oval shape. Engine power was transmitted to the air by means of four-blade controllable-pitch propellers. A notable design feature of the aircraft was the apparent lack of an identifiable windshield in front of the pilots' compartment. Actually, to reduce the drag associated with the usual type of windshield, the nose of the aircraft was transparent and provided visibility for both the pilots and the bombardier. Equipment innovations on the B–29 were pressurization and heating of the crew compartments and remotely controlled, power-operated gun turrets equipped with .50-caliber machine guns. Two of these turrets were on top and two were on the bottom of the fuselage. In addition, the tail gunner had two such machine guns as well as a 20-mm cannon.

In addition to its great weight, another indication of the size of the B–29 was provided by the wing span of 141.3 feet. By comparison, the wing span of a modern Boeing 727 jet transport is 108 feet. Other parameters of the B–29 included a maximum speed of 357 miles per hour at 25 000 feet and a zero-lift drag coefficient of 0.0241. This drag coefficient was substantially lower than the corresponding value of 0.0302 for the B–17G, and the maximum value of the lift-drag ratio of the B–29 was 16.8 as compared with 12.7 for the earlier bomber (tables II and III). Even with Fowler-type wing flaps, somewhat similar to the flap shown fourth from the top in figure 5.3, the stalling speed was 105 miles per hour. Such a stalling speed was considered quite high for so large an aircraft when the B–29 was introduced. For a ferry flight the aircraft had a range of about 5000 miles. A maximum payload of 20 000 pounds could be carried for 2800 miles; on a typical operational mission, 12 000 pounds of bombs could be carried for a distance (one way) of 3700 miles. The characteristics of the B–29 indicate that it represented a substantial advancement in design refinement as compared with earlier bombers.

The B–29 and its look-alike successor the B–50 continued in service with the United States Air Force for many years following the close of World War II. A number of these outstanding aircraft served their final years as tankers for air refueling of more modern, high-performance aircraft. The last of the B–50 tankers was retired in 1968.

In addition to strategic bombers, medium bombers and attack aircraft comprised another class of vehicle that usually had two engines and were considerably lighter than the heavy, strategic type of aircraft. They were employed for short-range bombing missions and various types of ground support activities. The United States used a number of aircraft types in short-range bombing and ground support missions. Perhaps the best known of these aircraft were the North American B-25, known as the Mitchell, and the Martin B-26, known as the Marauder. The Martin B-26 is illustrated in figure 5.9, and some of the important characteristics of the aircraft are given in table III. The twin-engine B-26 follows the same high-wing monoplane formula as the Consolidated B-24 and had the same type of tricycle landing gear. Both the B-25 and the B-26 had the tricycle gear, and these aircraft, together with the B-24, set a precedent for landing gear design in future Air Force bomber aircraft. The B-26 was equipped with two of the new 18-cylinder Pratt & Whitney twin-row radial engines of 2000 horsepower each. Since the aircraft was intended to operate at medium to low altitudes, these engines were only mildly supercharged and developed 1490 horsepower each at 14 300 feet. The aircraft weighed 37 000 pounds fully loaded and had, for that day (1940) the exceedingly high wing loading of 56.2 pounds per square foot. By comparison, the B-17 had a wing loading of 38.7 pounds per square foot, and the Seversky P-35 fighter had a wing loading of 25.5 pounds per square foot. As a result of the high wing loading and relatively ineffective flaps, the stalling speed of the B-26 was a very high 122 miles per hour. The high stalling speed together with certain other characteristics made the B-26 a demanding airplane for the pilot, and many accidents occurred in training with this aircraft. As a result, the B-26 was fre-

Figure 5.9 — Martin B-26F medium bomber. [Peter C. Boisseau]

quently referred to by such unflattering names as "widow maker" and "the flying prostitute" (i.e., no visible means of support). The zero-lift drag coefficient of the B-26 was 0.0314, which was considerably lower than the 0.0406 of the B-24 and about the same as the value of 0.0302 for the B-17. Other characteristics of the B-26 included a maximum speed of 274 miles per hour at 15 000 feet and the ability to carry a 4000-pound bomb load for a distance of 1100 miles. Armament consisted of 11 .50-caliber machine guns capable of being fired in various directions; several fixed, forward-firing guns were provided for ground attack use.

The Martin B-26 was ordered into production directly from the drawing board in September 1940, and a total of 5157 were built. The aircraft was used in both the European and Pacific theaters of operation but was little used in the peacetime Air Force following the cessation of hostilities in 1945. The North American B-25, counterpart of the B-26, was produced in greater numbers than the B-26 and is perhaps better known today because it was the aircraft used by James H. Doolittle in the famous Tokyo raid of April 1942. About 9800 models of the B-25 were constructed, and they served with the Air Force following World War II in a variety of training and support roles. In other countries, they remained as a primary bomber aircraft until comparatively recent years.

Multiengine bombers, such as those just discussed, usually dropped their bombs from a level flight attitude or, in the case of medium bombers in the ground attack mode, from a shallow dive. In contrast, an entirely different technique known as dive bombing was pioneered by the U.S. Navy during the decade preceding World War II. In this method of operation, the aircraft was put into a vertical or near-vertical dive at an altitude 15 000 to 20 000 feet and aimed directly at the target. Bomb release usually took place at about 3000 feet, after which the aircraft made a high-g dive recovery to a level flight attitude. Dive bombing was found to be especially suited for use against small, slow-moving targets such as tanks and ships and was employed with devastating effectiveness against Japanese naval forces during World War II.

Dive bombers were usually single-engine aircraft with a crew of two: a pilot and a rear-facing gunner situated behind the pilot. The most widely used U.S. Navy dive bomber during World War II was the Curtiss SB2C Helldiver series of which an SB2C-1 is illustrated in figure 5.10. The name "Helldiver" traced its origin to an earlier Curtiss dive bomber of biplane configuration that appeared in the 1930's.

With a wing span of nearly 50 feet and a normal gross weight of 14 730 pounds, the SB2C–1 was a large single-engine aircraft. Equipped with a 1750-horsepower twin-row radial engine, the aircraft had a maximum speed of 281 miles per hour at 12 400 feet; a stalling speed of 79 miles per hour facilitated operation of the SB2C–1 from the short deck of an aircraft carrier. Internal storage was provided in the fuselage for a 1000-pound bomb. Typically, the aircraft could carry this bomb load for a distance of 1100 miles. Armament varied with different models of the aircraft. In one arrangement, four .50-caliber machine guns were fitted in the wings and the observer had two .30-caliber guns.

Figure 5.10 shows the configuration of the SB2C–1 to have been entirely conventional for its time. A feature of the aircraft not evident in the photograph was the dive brakes used for limiting the speed of the aircraft while in its steep dive to the target. Trailing-edge split flaps that opened in a symmetrical configuration from the top and bottom surfaces of the wing were employed for this purpose; the symmetrical arrangement minimized the effect of flap deployment on longitudinal stability and trim. To reduce tail buffeting, the flaps were perforated with a large number of holes in the order of 3 inches in diameter (the exact size is not known). For landing, only the lower surface flaps were deflected. The need for dive brakes can be explained as follows: First, the normal acceleration, or g-load experienced by an aircraft during dive recovery, varies inversely as the radius of the pullout maneuver and directly as the square of the velocity; second, the accuracy with which the bomb can be dropped increases as the altitude of bomb release is reduced. Since 9 g's is about the maximum normal acceleration that a person can withstand and remain effective, the structural design

Figure 5.10 — Curtiss SB2C–1 carrier-based scout bomber. [NASA]

of the Helldiver was based on this loading. Hence, the dive speed had to be limited to stay within design load limits and, at the same time, permit bomb release at the desired altitude. Most modern jet fighters, of course, employ some form of speed brake, but the use of such devices was not common practice on World War II aircraft except for aircraft designed for dive bombing.

First flight of the Helldiver took place in December 1940, and it first entered combat in November 1943. Including Canadian production, a total of over 7000 Helldivers were manufactured. The type was withdrawn from service in the U.S. Navy in 1949 after a long and useful career.

Fighter Aircraft

Each of the major Allied and Axis powers developed a series of effective fighter aircraft. The British Hawker Hurricane and Supermarine Spitfire will long be remembered, particularly as being responsible for the air victory in the critical Battle of Britain in 1940. The famous German Messerschmitt 109 was the principal antagonist of the Spitfire and Hurricane during the Battle of Britain, and together with the Focke-Wulf 190, formed the mainstay of the Luftwaffe fighter forces until the end of World War II. The Japanese Mitsubishi Zero probably is the best-remembered Japanese fighter in this country because of the role it played in the attack on Pearl Harbor in December 1941. The North American P-51 Mustang, the Republic P 47 Thunderbolt, and the Lockheed P-38 Lightning are the best known of the U.S. Army Air Force fighters employed in World War II; the Grumman F6F Hellcat and the Vought F4U Corsair are equally well remembered for the outstanding role they played as Navy fighters during the fierce conflicts in the Pacific area. A brief description of the North American P-51 and the Grumman F6F follows. These aircraft are considered typical of World War II land- and carrier-based fighter aircraft as employed by the United States armed forces. Because of its unusual configuration and interesting technical features, the Lockheed P-38 Lightning is also discussed.

The North American P-51 Mustang is considered by many to represent the highest level of technical refinement ever achieved in a propeller-driven fighter aircraft. The P-51 was originally designed to a British specification for use by the Royal Air Force (RAF) and was later adopted by the U.S. Army Air Forces. The aircraft was ordered by a British purchasing commission during the hectic days of April 1940, with the understanding that the prototype was to be completed within 120 days. The prototype was completed on schedule; however, first flight was delayed until October 1940. The aircraft first saw combat service with the RAF in July 1942. At first, the aircraft was equipped with a 12-cylinder Allison in-line engine of about 1200 horsepower. With this engine, the aircraft was intended as a low-altitude fighter and ground-attack machine. Later, the North American airframe was mated with the British Rolls-Royce Merlin engine, and this combination resulted in one of the outstanding fighter aircraft of World War II. The Merlin was a liquid-cooled engine that employed 12 cylinders arranged in a V-configuration and was equipped with a two-speed two-stage gear-driven supercharger. The engine developed 1490 horsepower at takeoff and was capable of producing 1505 horsepower under war emergency conditions at the critical altitude of 19 300 feet. The Merlin engine was produced under license in the United States by the Packard Motor Car Company.

The P–51 Mustang was produced in many variants, of which the most numerous and best known was the P–51D illustrated in figure 5.11. Specifications for the aircraft are given in table III. Figure 5.11 shows the aircraft was equipped with a low wing, which was a highly

Figure 5.11 — North American P–51D fighter. [Peter C. Boisseau]

favored wing position for fighter aircraft during World War II. The use of the in-line engine of low frontal area resulted in a fuselage of relatively low total wetted area and gave the aircraft a lean, streamlined appearance. The low frontal area of the in-line engine was one of the chief advantages cited for this type of power plant; the disadvantage was the vulnerability of the cooling system to enemy fire. The aft location of the cooling radiator and its associated inlet and internal flow system is of interest. The system was designed with the objective of obtaining a net thrust from the cooling air as a result of heat addition from the engine coolant. This feature no doubt contributed to the very low drag coefficient of the aircraft. The P–51 was also the first aircraft to utilize the NACA laminar-flow airfoil sections, discussed earlier. Although it is doubtful that any significant laminar flow was achieved on production versions of the Mustang, the low-drag airfoils did provide improved characteristics at high subsonic Mach numbers.

A typical value of maximum gross weight for the P–51D was 10 100 pounds, although this value varied to some extent depending upon the external armament and fuel load. The wing loading corresponding to the 10 100-pound gross weight was 43 pounds per square foot, and the power loading was 6.8 pounds per horsepower. A typical maximum speed was 437 miles per hour at 25 000 feet, and the stalling speed was 100 miles per hour. The zero-lift drag coefficient of 0.0163 was the lowest of any of the aircraft analyzed herein, and the corresponding value of the maximum lift-drag ratio was 14.6. The Mustang was therefore an extremely clean airplane. The aerodynamic cleanness of the aircraft was due, in large measure, to careful attention to detailed design and continued refinement of the aircraft during its production lifetime.

The Mustang was utilized in various types of fighter operations, including high-altitude air-to-air combat as well as ground-support and interdiction missions. It had a service ceiling of 40 900 feet and could climb to 20 000 feet in 7.3 minutes. Armament varied but usually consisted of six .50-caliber machine guns, three in each wing, and it could carry two 1000-pound bombs or six 5-inch rockets. Equipped with drop tanks, the P–51D had a range of 1650 miles at a speed of 358 miles per hour and an altitude of 25 000 feet. In contrast to the short range of contemporary British and German fighters, the range capability of the Mustang, as well as the P–47 and P–38, allowed it to be used with great effectiveness in escorting formations of B–17 and B–24 bombers on long-range missions. The P–51 was the only fighter to fly over three enemy capitals — Berlin, Rome, and Tokyo.

A total of 14 490 aircraft of the P–51 series were constructed. The aircraft was used in all theaters of operation during World War II, was called into use by the U.S. Air Force again during the Korean War, and was used by a number of foreign air forces for many·years. Many P–51 aircraft are flying in the United States today as unlimited racing aircraft and even for executive transport use. A turboprop version of the Mustang has recently been proposed as a cheap, close-air-support aircraft for use by small, undeveloped countries in various parts of the world. An interesting history of the P–51 aircraft is given in reference 66.

Entirely different in configuration from the conventional single-engine fighter of World War II, the twin-engine Lockheed P–38 Lightning is depicted in early form in figure 5.12. In this unusual but highly practical arrangement, the pilot and armament were housed in the center pod, and the liquid-cooled engines together with cooling-air intakes, radiators, and turbosuperchargers were located in the twin booms that also supported the tail. The P–38 was the first fighter designed in the United States to be equipped with a tricycle landing gear: the nose gear retracted into the center pod; and the main gear, into the booms. It was also the first United States aircraft of any type to employ external surfaces composed of butt-joined metal skins with flush rivets. Other innovations employed in later versions of the aircraft included hydraulically boosted ailerons and provisions for use of partial deflec-

Figure 5.12 — Lockheed YP–38 twin-engine fighter. [Rudy Arnold via ukn]

131

tion (8°) of the trailing-edge Fowler flaps. Both of these modifications were intended to enhance maneuverability in combat. Powered controls and, to a lesser extent, maneuvering flaps are used on most modern jet fighters.

The P–38, intended as an interceptor with the mission of destroying enemy bombers at high altitude, was designed according to specifications issued in 1937 that called for speeds of 360 to 400 miles per hour (sources differ on the exact value) at 20 000 feet and the capability of reaching that altitude in 6 minutes. The specification also contained demanding requirements for range, endurance, and landing and takeoff field length. A single-engine aircraft could not meet the mission requirements with any engine available at that time. Hence, the P–38 employed two engines. First flight of the prototype XP–38 was in January 1939, and the aircraft was first deployed in Europe by the United States Army Air Force (USAAF) in the fall of 1942.

At a normal gross weight of 17 500 pounds and with a wing span of 52 feet, the P–38L, for which data are given in table III, was for its day a large fighter. All versions of the aircraft were equipped with Allison V–12 liquid-cooled engines; those on the P–38L developed 1470 horsepower each. Maximum speed was 414 miles per hour at 25 000 feet; stalling speed was 105 miles per hour. The P–38 could climb to 20 000 feet in 7 minutes and had a service ceiling of 44 000 feet. With internal fuel only, the aircraft had a range of 475 miles at 339 miles per hour, or 1175 miles at 195 miles per hour; with drop tanks, the range was 2260 miles.

Indeed, the P–38 was a high-performance aircraft. Even the prototype exceeded 400 miles per hour in 1939. Although its high speed was one of the great virtues of the P–38, this desirable characteristic was responsible for a serious problem encountered in the development of the aircraft. Little was known at that time about the problems associated with penetrating the Mach number regime characterized by large effects of compressibility (see discussion of fig. 5.6), and even less was known of means for alleviating such problems. A combination of the high speed reached in steep dives, together with a less than optimum high Mach number airfoil section, caused the P–38 to suffer severe compressibility problems. These problems manifested themselves in the form of buffeting, loss of control, difficulty in recovering from dives, and—in some cases—complete destruction of the aircraft. Many different modifications were tried before a successful solution to the problem was found. In the spring of 1942, NACA in conjunction with Lockheed devised a simple fix that came to be known as the dive-recovery flap (not to be confused with the dive brake used on the SB2C). A short-span flap was located at the 30-percent-chord position behind the leading edge of the lower surface of the wing, just outboard of the booms. Deflection of these flaps in a high-speed dive increased the lift on the wings so that successful dive recovery was possible. Such flaps appeared on production aircraft beginning with the P–38J version. Among other aircraft employing this very effective device were the P–47 Thunderbolt and the P–59 and P–80 jet fighters. (See chapter 11.)

Although never designed as a fighter for air-to-air combat with other fighter aircraft, the Lightning was widely used and highly effective in this role, particularly in the Pacific theater of operations. More Japanese aircraft were destroyed by the P–38 than by any other aircraft, and the two highest scoring American aces of World War II, Majors Richard I. Bong and Thomas B. McGuire, Jr., both flew the Lightning. It was used in all theaters in which the USAAF operated. As a fighter, several different combinations of armament were employed. Most aircraft had four .50-caliber machine guns and a 20–mm cannon located in the nose ahead of the pilot. Also, it could carry bombs weighing up to as much as 3200 pounds or 10 5-inch rockets. In addition to duties as a fighter, a photoreconnaissance version of the aircraft, designated F–5, saw extensive service. Many other types of military duty such as bombing and ground attack were performed by the P–38.

Nearly 10 000 P–38's, including all models, were produced. Several of these are still flying today in the hands of dedicated antique aircraft collectors, and they were used for many years after World War II in aerial survey work. German pilots in North Africa paid the P–38 a tribute of sorts when they dubbed it "Der gabelschwanz teufel" (the fork-tailed devil).

Navy fighter aircraft are intended primarily for operations from the short decks of aircraft carriers. Operation from an aircraft carrier poses certain constraints during the design of the aircraft. For example, the relatively short length of the flight deck (about 700 feet for the larger carriers employed during World War II) imposed restrictions on the stalling speed of the aircraft and thus required that Navy fighters have somewhat lower wing loadings than their counterparts in the USAAF. A tail hook must be provided to give rapid deceleration of the aircraft on touchdown, and this in turn required special strengthening of the rear portion of the fuselage. Furthermore, a carrier-based aircraft must be designed for higher landing sink rates than normally encountered in land-based aircraft; this higher sink rate requires a heavier landing gear and attachment structure. Since storage space both on the flight and hanger decks is at a premium on an aircraft carrier, provision must also be made for folding the wings so that the required parking space is reduced. A number of aircraft companies specialized in the design and production of fighters for use on aircraft carriers. The Grumman Aircraft Engineering Company was one of the leading producers of Navy fighter aircraft during the 1930's (as it still is today), and the Navy entered World War II with the Grumman F4F Wildcat as its first-line fighter.

Early in 1941, Grumman began the design of a new fighter as a replacement for the Wildcat. Much combat experience had been obtained in the European conflict and was utilized in the design of the new aircraft. Following entry of the United States in World War II in December 1941, the Wildcat saw extensive service in combat against the Japanese. Although the Wildcat was a good aircraft, it was not really competitive with the Japanese Zero shipboard fighter. The lessons learned in action with the Zero were also incorporated in the design of the new Grumman fighter. The prototype of this aircraft, known as the F6F Hellcat, first flew in June 1942, and deliveries of combat aircraft were made to the Navy in early 1943. The first operational use of the Hellcat was in the attack on Marcus Island from the carrier USS Yorktown in August 1943. It is indeed remarkable that the aircraft could be developed from a prototype to combat status in little more than a year.

The Hellcat is illustrated in figure 5.13, and some of its characteristics are listed in table III. The aircraft was a rather bulky looking low-wing monoplane equipped with an 18-cylinder Pratt & Whitney twin-row radial engine of 2000 horsepower. The engine was equipped with a geared supercharger and gave 1970 horsepower at 16 900 feet. Although the USAAF deployed highly successful fighters with both air-cooled radial and liquid-cooled in-line engines, the U.S. Navy had employed air-cooled radial engines exclusively since the mid-1920's. Apparently, the Navy felt that the advantages of simplicity and reduced vulnerability to gunfire offered by the radial engine more than offset the disadvantages of increased frontal area. Although not evident in figure 5.13, the landing gear of the F6F retracted rearward and was enclosed within the wing root stubs. Outboard of the landing gear the wing could be rotated and folded aft so as to lie essentially flush along the sides of the fuselage to minimize the deck area required for the aircraft's storage.

The Grumman F6F was, for its day, a relatively large aircraft with a fully loaded weight of 12 441 pounds. The wing loading, however, was

Figure 5.13 — Grumman F6F–3 carrier-based fighter. [Peter C. Boisseau]

only 37.3 pounds per square foot, which gave a relatively modest stalling speed of 84 miles per hour. The aircraft had a maximum speed of 375 miles per hour at 17 300 feet. In spite of its bulky appearance, the Hellcat was a clean aircraft having a zero-lift drag coefficient of only 0.0211. Range of the Hellcat was 1090 miles on internal fuel only, and with drop tanks it was 1590 miles. It had a service ceiling of 38 400 feet and an initial rate of climb of 3500 feet per minute. Its armament consisted of six .50-caliber machine guns, three in each wing, and two 1000-pound bombs or six 5-inch rockets.

The Grumman F6F Hellcat, of which 12 274 were produced, is considered by many to be the outstanding shipboard fighter of World War II. It was the standard carrier-based fighter employed by the U.S. Navy from mid-1943 until the end of World War II and accounted for the destruction of nearly 5000 enemy aircraft in air-to-air combat. The British Royal Navy took delivery of over 1100 Hellcats, which were used in operations from their carriers. The Hellcat was unusual, as compared with other combat aircraft employed in World War II, in that very few modifications were made to the aircraft during its service life. The F6F served for several years in the U.S. Navy following the close of the war.

Afterword

The propeller-driven combat aircraft powered with reciprocating engines played a decisive role in World War II and reached a high level of perfection during that conflict. The revolutionary jet engine shaped the course of development of high-performance military aircraft in the post-World War II period. The propeller continued, of course, to be employed on various types of utility, transport, and patrol aircraft; but the development of the jet engine spelled the end for the high-performance propeller-driven fighter, bomber, and attack aircraft. The postwar development of propeller-driven aircraft has been primarily concerned with commercial and general aviation operations and is considered in the next chapter.

Chapter 6
Design Maturity, 1945–80

Background

In the years since the end of World War II, turbojet- and turbofan-powered aircraft have come to dominate an increasingly large segment of aeronautical activity. The propeller-driven aircraft, however, remains an important part of aviation, both in this country and in various other parts of the world. The new propeller-driven aircraft that have appeared since 1945 differ little in configuration from those seen in the years immediately before and during World War II, nor has the level of aerodynamic refinement exceeded that of the earlier aircraft. The turboprop propulsion system is probably the most significant technical advancement to be incorporated in propeller-driven aircraft. In the realm of reciprocating engines, the supercharger has come into widespread use, both in commercial transport aircraft and in contemporary general aviation aircraft. The supercharger, together with the advent of cabin pressurization, has resulted in highly efficient cruising flight at high altitudes. High-altitude operation also offers the passengers freedom from the discomfort of rough air to a degree that was not possible in unpressurized aircraft.

A few examples of propeller-driven transports of the post-World War II period are described and discussed here, as are a number of contemporary general aviation aircraft.

Transport Aircraft

Two families of large, long-range, propeller-driven transports dominated U.S. airlines, as well as many foreign airlines, until the jet transport began to appear in significant numbers toward the end of the 1950's. These families of aircraft, which served on both long-range domestic and international routes, were the Douglas DC–6 and DC–7 series and the Lockheed Constellation series. Both were derived from aircraft developed during World War II; they had four supercharged

137

engines and pressurized cabins, and both series underwent large increases in size, power, and weight during their development history.

Representative of the long-range, four-engine transport is the Lockheed L. 1049G Super Constellation illustrated in figure 6.1; characteristics of the aircraft are given in table III (appendix A). The prototype Constellation, known by its USAAF designation of C–69, first flew on January 9, 1943, and the model L.1049G first flew on December 12, 1954. The total number of all models of the Constellation constructed was 856.

The Lockheed L.1049G was powered by four Wright turbocompound engines of about 3250 horsepower each. The Wright 3350 turbocompound engine employed a two-speed gear-driven supercharger and, in addition, was equipped with three exhaust-driven turbines. The three turbines were geared to a single shaft that in turn was hydraulically coupled to the engine crankshaft. Each turbine was driven by the exhaust of six cylinders. About 15 percent of the total power of the engine was obtained from reclamation of exhaust gas energy. The specific fuel consumption was probably the lowest ever achieved in a reciprocating aircraft engine.

The gross weight of the aircraft was 133 000 pounds, which was more than twice that of the Boeing B–17 "heavy" bomber of World War II fame. The wing loading was 80.6 pounds per square foot, and

Figure 6.1 — Lockheed 1049G Super Constellation 91-passenger four-engine airliner; 1954. [mfr]

the corresponding stalling speed was 100 miles per hour. The wings employed very powerful Fowler-type extensible slotted flaps to maintain the landing speed within acceptable limits. The landing gear was of the tricycle type that was standard on most post-World War II transports. The maximum speed of the aircraft was 352 miles per hour, and the normal cruising speed was 331 miles per hour at 23 000 feet. The pressurized cabin was capable of seating 71 first-class passengers or 91 coach passengers. Some versions of the aircraft were capable of carrying an acceptable payload nonstop from the east coast of the United States to the west coast. The zero-lift drag coefficient of 0.0211 and the maximum lift-drag ratio of 16 indicate a highly refined and efficient aerodynamic design.

Today, many Constellations and their Douglas counterparts are in operation in nonscheduled activities in different parts of the world. The use of these aircraft in long-range scheduled operations, however, terminated in this country during the 1960's following the introduction of the high-performance jet-powered transport.

The turbopropeller, or turboprop engine, is basically derived by gearing a conventional propeller to the shaft of a gas generator composed of a compressor, burner, and turbine. The turboprop engine may therefore be thought of as a turbojet engine that transmits power to the air by means of a propeller rather than through the jet exhaust. The turboprop engine is light and relatively simple as compared with the large high-power reciprocating engines. For example, a modern turboprop engine may develop between 2 and 3 horsepower per pound of weight, as compared with a maximum of about 1 horsepower per pound for a reciprocating engine, and has been made in sizes of up to 15 000 horsepower. The specific fuel consumption of the turboprop engine, however, is somewhat higher than that of the best reciprocating engines. The turboprop engine has been used in a number of highly successful transport aircraft and is still in fairly widespread use, particularly for short-haul, commuter-type transports.

The first civil airliner to be equipped with turboprop engines was the Vickers Viscount depicted in figure 6.2. The specifications of the Viscount 700 series are given in table III. The aircraft employed four Rolls-Royce Dart engines of 1600 horsepower each and had a gross weight of about 60 000 pounds. Depending upon the configuration, 40 to 59 passengers could be carried in the pressurized cabin. The cruising speed of the Viscount was 334 miles per hour at 25 000 feet. The aircraft employed double-slotted flaps and was equipped with a tricycle landing gear. The Viscount made its first flight in July 1948 and subse-

139

Figure 6.2 — Vickers Viscount 810 40-passenger turboprop airliner; 1948. [Peter C. Boisseau]

quently was used by airlines all over the world. A total of 441 Viscounts were built and many are still in use.

Two turboprop aircraft of much larger size were constructed in the United Kingdom. These were the Vickers Vanguard, with a gross weight of 146 500 pounds, and the Bristol Britannia, with a gross weight of 185 000 pounds. Many types of turboprop transport aircraft have been designed and built in Russia, as well. The largest passenger-carrying turboprop ever built was the Tupolev Tu–114. This aircraft has a gross weight of 377 000 pounds and is equipped with four 14 795 equivalent shaft horsepower turboprop engines. Each of these engines drives two counterrotating propellers. The wings are sweptback, which is unusual for propeller-driven aircraft; the amount of sweep is 34°. The aircraft carries 220 passengers and cruises at a speed of 478 miles per hour at an altitude of 29 500 feet. The Tu–114 is no longer in airline use, but a version known as the Bear is employed by the Soviet military forces as a reconnaissance aircraft. The Lockheed Electra is the only large turboprop airliner to be developed in the United States. Although the Electra was an efficient high-performance aircraft, it was never produced in large numbers because it was introduced at about the same time as the Boeing 707 jet airliner and could not compete with this aircraft. A few Electras are still in service with the scheduled airlines, and a number are employed in nonscheduled activities. The naval version of the aircraft, known as the P–3 Orion, is employed by the U.S. Navy for antisubmarine patrol work.

A number of highly successful turboprop aircraft have been developed for use as cargo carriers. The largest of these aircraft is the Russian Antonov AN–22, which weighs over 550 000 pounds and is equipped with four 15 000-horsepower engines. The Lockheed C–130 is perhaps the best known of the turboprop-powered cargo aircraft and the one that has been produced in the greatest numbers. The C–130 is used by all branches of the United States military forces and by the military forces of over 20 foreign governments. A commercial cargo version of the aircraft is also available. The first production contract for the aircraft was placed in 1952; over 1500 models of the C–130 have been built, and the aircraft is still in production.

A Lockheed C–130 is shown in figure 6.3, and specifications are given in table III. Many variations of the C–130 have been produced, and engines of slightly different power ratings have been employed. The specifications in table III are for the C–130E. The aircraft has an unswept wing mounted in the high position at the top of the fuselage and is equipped with four Allison T–56 turboprop engines of 4910 equivalent shaft horsepower each at takeoff. In order to minimize weight and complexity, the landing gear is retracted into blisters located on either side of the fuselage, rather than into the wing or engine nacelles. The high wing position is advantageous for a cargo aircraft because it allows trucks and other types of equipment to move beneath

Figure 6.3 — Lockheed C–130 turboprop cargo transport; 1955. [mfr]

the wing, and the fuselage can be brought close to the ground without causing interference with the engines and propellers. A rear loading door may be deployed from the bottom of the upswept, aft portion of the underside of the fuselage. The proximity of the forward portion of the fuselage to the ground results in an aft-loading ramp with only a small inclination to the ground so that vehicles can be readily driven or pushed into the aircraft. The Lockheed C–130 has a gross weight of 155 000 pounds and cruises at a speed of 386 miles per hour at 20 000 feet. The wing loading is 88 pounds per square foot, and the landing speed is 115 miles per hour.

A great variety of twin-engine airliners has been developed both in the United States and abroad during the postwar years. These aircraft are smaller than the large, long-range, four-engine aircraft and are employed on short-haul types of operations. Twin-engine airliners have been developed with both reciprocating and turboprop engines. The twin-engine Martin 404 and Convair 440 aircraft and earlier versions of these machines were perhaps the most-used postwar twin-engine transports powered with reciprocating engines. These aircraft are similar in configuration to the Douglas DC–3 but are larger, faster, and are equipped with pressurized cabins; in addition, they both employ the tricycle type of landing gear. The Fairchild F–27 (a Dutch Fokker design built under license by Fairchild in this country) and the Japanese YS–11A are probably the best known turboprop twins in the United States. The British Hawker Siddeley 748 turboprop-powered twin-engine airliner is widely used in many countries of the world.

Although the long-range propeller-driven transport is essentially a thing of the past, smaller, short-range aircraft of this type are becoming more numerous. Since the advent of airline deregulation in the United States in the latter part of the 1970's, there has been a large growth in short-haul, commuter-type airline operations. Many aircraft employed in this type of service are foreign built, are of high-wing configuration, and are equipped with two turboprop engines. Passenger capacity varies between 20 and 30, and at least one four-engine aircraft of this type carries 50 passengers. Generally speaking, these aircraft have straight wings and employ no new configuration concepts. In fact, some of them have fixed landing gears and strut-braced wings. Since high speed is unimportant and low initial and maintenance costs are critical, these retrogressive technical features are justified on a cost-effectiveness basis. The final forms of the commuter-type transport, however, are yet to emerge.

General Aviation Aircraft

The term "general aviation" covers all types of flying except military and commercial airline operations. Only contemporary aircraft designed for business and pleasure are considered here. General aviation aircraft designed for business and pleasure are available in both single-engine and twin-engine models; most models are equipped with horizontally opposed reciprocating engines. However, several high-performance turboprop types are offered. Single-engine types may be had with high- or low-wing location, retractable or fixed landing gear, controllable-pitch or fixed-pitch propeller, and in sizes varying from two place to seven place. The twin-engine aircraft usually employ the low-wing location and have retractable landing gear and controllable-pitch propellers. The twins may be had with or without turbosupercharging, with or without pressurized cabins, and with varying seating capacities. The modern aircraft designed for business or pleasure is almost invariably of all-metal construction, as contrasted with the metal, wood, and fabric construction typical of the pre-World War II general aviation aircraft. Reliability of the internal systems employed in the aircraft and the precision of the radio and navigational equipment have greatly improved as compared with pre-World War II standards. The general aviation aircraft of today are almost universally equipped with an electrical system to power the radios and other types of equipment installed in the aircraft and to operate the self-starter. Hand starting of production aircraft is a thing of the past. The cabins of these aircraft are generally relatively comfortable, are equipped with heaters for wintertime and high-altitude use, and are sometimes equipped with air conditioning for use on the ground and at low altitudes in the summer. The open cockpit is a thing of the past in production aircraft, except for special sport and aerobatic aircraft. Many aircraft employ complete instrumentation and communication equipment for flight under IFR conditions. Most contemporary aircraft employ a tricycle gear that greatly eases the problem of aircraft handling on the ground. The basic aerodynamic configuration of contemporary general aviation aircraft, however, differs little from those in use in 1939.

Contemporary Types, 1970–80

General aviation aircraft are manufactured in a number of different countries; however, the majority of these aircraft are produced in the United States. The major U.S. producers are the Cessna Aircraft Company, the Piper Aircraft Corporation, and the Beech Aircraft Corpora-

143

tion. Each offers a wide variety of aircraft designed for various needs and markets. Six aircraft of different levels of performance, size, and price produced by these manufacturers for different segments of the market are briefly described here.

Two single-engine aircraft representative of the lower performance and price spectrum are shown in figures 6.4 and 6.5. The Piper Cherokee 180 shown in figure 6.4 is an all-metal aircraft with an internally braced, cantilever wing mounted in the low position. The aircraft shown has four seats and is equipped with a 180-horsepower, four-cylinder Lycoming engine of the opposed type. The engine drives a fixed-pitch propeller. The landing gear on the aircraft is fixed, and although not visible in the photograph, the horizontal tail employed on the Cherokee is of the all-moving type equipped with a geared tab. The Cherokee 180 has a maximum speed of 148 miles per hour at sea level and cruises at 141 miles per hour at 7000 feet. The stalling speed with the split flaps deflected is 61 miles per hour. The gross weight of the aircraft is indicated in table III to be 2450 pounds. The Cherokee 180 is representative of one of the lower cost members of a complete family of Piper aircraft that carry the Cherokee name. Some of these aircraft have six or seven seats and more powerful engines that drive controllable-pitch propellers. Other versions of the Cherokee employ a retractable landing gear. The flight of the first production aircraft was made in February 1961, and well over 25 000 Cherokees of all types have now been produced.

Figure 6.4 — Piper Cherokee 180 contemporary general aviation aircraft. [NASA]

Figure 6.5 — Cessna Skyhawk contemporary general aviation aircraft. [mfr]

The Cessna Skyhawk shown in figure 6.5 is one of the lower cost members of an entire series of Cessna aircraft of the same basic configuration. The Skyhawk, like the Cherokee 180, is equipped with a fixed tricycle landing gear and has a four-cylinder, horizontally opposed engine driving a fixed-pitch propeller. Unlike the Cherokee 180, however, the Cessna Skyhawk is a high-wing configuration with a single wing strut on either side of the fuselage to brace the wing. The Skyhawk has a maximum speed of 144 miles per hour and cruises at 138 miles per hour at 8000 feet. The stalling speed with the flaps deflected is 49 miles per hour. The gross weight of the Cessna Skyhawk is 2300 pounds, and the wing loading and power loading are 13.1 pounds per square foot and 15.3 pounds per horsepower, respectively. These values are in the same order as those shown in table III for the Piper Cherokee. The zero-lift drag coefficient of the Skyhawk is 0.0319 as compared with 0.0358 for the Cherokee, and the maximum lift-drag ratios for the two aircraft are 11.6 and 10.0, respectively.

Two representative high-performance single-engine general aviation aircraft are shown in figures 6.6 and 6.7. The Beech Bonanza V–35B shown in figure 6.6 is of all-metal construction, has an internally braced wing mounted in the low position, has single-slotted flaps, and is equipped with a fully retractable tricycle landing gear. The aircraft is equipped with a six-cylinder, horizontally opposed Continental engine of 285 horsepower that drives a controllable-pitch propeller. The air-

145

Figure 6.6 — Beech Bonanza V–35B contemporary general aviation aircraft. [mfr]

craft can be configured for four, five, or six seats. Data for the Bonanza are given in table III. The unique Butterfly tail combines the stability and control functions of both the conventional vertical and horizontal tails. The gross weight of the aircraft is 3400 pounds. The aircraft has a maximum speed of 210 miles per hour at sea level, cruises at 203 miles per hour at 6500 feet, and has a stalling speed of 63 miles per hour. The zero-lift drag coefficient is a very low 0.0192, and the corresponding maximum lift-drag ratio is 13.8. The prototype of the Bonanza first flew in December 1945, and the aircraft has been continuously in production since 1947. Approximately 10 000 Beech Bonanzas have been built.

The Cessna Cardinal RG II shown in figure 6.7 is a high-performance aircraft with an internally braced wing mounted in the high position. The aircraft is equipped with a fully retractable tricycle landing gear and is equipped with a four-cylinder, horizontally opposed, Lycoming engine of 200 horsepower that drives a controllable-pitch propeller. The Cardinal is of all-metal construction and is equipped with trailing-edge flaps and an all-moving horizontal tail employing a geared trim tab. The aircraft has a maximum speed of 180 miles per hour at sea level, cruises at 171 miles per hour at 7000 feet, and has a stalling speed of 57 miles per hour. The aircraft weighs 2800 pounds. The

Figure 6.7 — Cessna Cardinal RG II contemporary general aviation aircraft. [mfr]

zero-lift drag coefficient of the Cardinal is 0.0223, and the corresponding maximum lift-drag ratio is 14.2.

The first twin-engine aircraft designed specifically for business use was probably the Beech Model D-18, first produced in 1937. This aircraft was similar to the Douglas DC-3 in general appearance, although much smaller, and was in continuous production from 1937 until the early 1970's. A wide variety of twin-engine aircraft of various sizes and with different levels of performance are now offered for business use. Two contemporary twin-engine aircraft are shown in figures 6.8 and 6.9.

The Cessna 310 shown in figure 6.8 is representative of one of the smaller contemporary twin-engine aircraft offered for business use. The aircraft is a low-wing configuration with an engine mounted in each wing on either side of the fuselage. The aircraft can be had with both normally aspirated engines or with turbosuperchargers. The specifications and performance given in table III are for the aircraft without turbosupercharging. The engines are six-cylinder, horizontally opposed, Continental engines of 285 horsepower each that drive controllable-pitch, full-feathering propellers. The aircraft normally has a seating capacity of five but can be configured for six. Maximum speed is 238 miles per hour at sea level, and cruising speed is 223 miles per hour at 7500 feet. The wings are equipped with split flaps which with a wing loading of 30.7 pounds per square foot result in a stalling speed of 77 miles per hour. The gross weight of the aircraft is 5500 pounds. The

147

Figure 6.8 — Cessna 310 contemporary twin-engine general aviation aircraft. [mfr]

Cessna 310 has a zero-lift drag coefficient of 0.0267 and a maximum lift-drag ratio of 13. The Cessna 310 was first flown in January 1953 and has been in continuous production ever since. The aircraft is unpressurized and may be thought of as the smallest of a whole line of Cessna twins, both pressurized and unpressurized.

The Beech Super King Air 200 shown in figure 6.9 is an example of a new, relatively large, high-performance twin-engine business aircraft. Provision is provided for 2 pilots and 6 to 13 passengers, depending on the configuration. The cabin is pressurized to permit comfortable cruising flight at high altitudes. Power is provided by two Pratt & Whitney PT6A–41 turboprop engines of 850 shaft horsepower each. The engines drive controllable-pitch, full-feathering, reversible propellers. The low-wing configuration of the aircraft is conventional although the use of a T-tail on a straight-wing propeller-driven aircraft is somewhat unusual. The use of this tail arrangement is said to reduce both vibration resulting from the slipstream of the engines and trim changes with flap deflection. The aspect ratio of the wing is 9.8, which must be considered as relatively high for any aircraft. The King Air 200 has a maximum speed of 333 miles per hour at 15 000 feet and a maximum cruising speed of 320 miles per hour at 25 000 feet. The aircraft is equipped with single-slotted flaps that together with a wing loading

Figure 6.9 — Beech Super King Air 200 contemporary twin-engine turboprop general aviation aircraft. [mfr]

of 41.3 pounds per square foot give a stalling speed of 92 miles per hour. The gross weight of the aircraft is 12 500 pounds. The Beech Super King Air 200 was certified in December 1973 and is now in series production.

Other Types of General Aviation Aircraft

The six aircraft just described may be considered as representative of generic classes of aircraft designed for business and pleasure use. In order to gain a true appreciation of the wide variety of such aircraft offered today, the reader is referred to the current year's issue of *Jane's All The World's Aircraft.* Other types of aircraft of interest and not described here are specially designed agricultural aircraft intended for spraying and dusting crops. These aircraft will also be found in *Jane's,* as will many types of sport and aerobatic aircraft. Another segment of general aviation aircraft is made up of the so-called home builts. These aircraft, which are built by individuals or clubs at home, are gaining in popularity and are flown in relatively large numbers in this country. They are usually not certified under any of the pertinent federal air regulations but, rather, operate in an experimental category. Many of the more popular types of home-built designs are also described in *Jane's All The World's Aircraft.*

149

Chapter 7
Design Trends

Introduction

This chapter briefly summarizes the progress in design of propeller-driven aircraft since the end of World War I by showing how a number of important design and performance parameters varied over the years 1920 to 1980. The following parameters are discussed:

(1) Maximum speed, V_{max}

(2) Stalling speed, V_S

(3) Wing loading, W/S

(4) Maximum lift coefficient, $C_{L,max}$

(5) Power loading, W/P

(6) Zero-lift drag coefficient, $C_{D,0}$

(7) Skin friction parameter, $\bar{C}_F$

(8) Maximum lift-drag ratio, $(L/D)_{max}$

The values of each of these parameters, obtained from tables I, II, and III (appendix A) and reference 90, are plotted against the appropriate year in figures 7.2 to 7.9. All of the parameters could not be obtained for some of the aircraft; in particular, the zero-lift drag coefficient and the maximum lift-drag ratio could not be determined for a number of the aircraft because of insufficient performance data from which to make the desired calculations. The symbols identifying each aircraft are given in figure 7.1 and have been used throughout the subsequent figures. At the left side of each figure (figs. 7.2 to 7.9), bars have been drawn to indicate the spread of each parameter during World War I as obtained from the data in table I. The year for which the characteristics of a given aircraft are plotted is in some degree arbitrary. For example, most of the World War II aircraft characteristics are plotted for the year 1942. In other cases, aircraft that were used for a number of years are shown at a year corresponding to the first year of production, or

151

○ DeHavilland DH-4

□ Handley Page W8F

◇ Fokker F-2

◁ Boeing B-29

◹ Curtiss SB2C-1

▢ Lockheed P-38L

◨ Ryan NYP

○ Ford 5-AT

◇ Lockheed Vega 5C

◁ Curtiss Robin

△ Travelair 4000

▽ Curtiss Hawk P-6E

● Boeing P-26A

■ Lockheed Orion 9D

◆ Northrop Alpha

◀ Boeing 247D

◤ Douglas DC-3

◣ Boeing B-17G

◢ Seversky P-35

● Piper J-3 Cub

◆ Stinson SR-8B

◢ Beechcraft D17S

▼ Consolidated B-24J

▲ Martin B-26F

◑ North American P-51D

◈ Grumman F6F-3

◀ Lockheed L. 1049G

◥ Vickers Viscount

◩ Lockheed C-130

◧ Piper Cherokee

◐ Cessna Skyhawk

◆ Beech Bonanza V-35

◀ Cessna Cardinal RG II

▼ Cessna 310 II

▲ Beech Super King Air 200

Figure 7.1 — Symbols used in figures 7.2 to 7.9.

after the aircraft had achieved a fully developed status. The points for the different aircraft show a large spread in the different figures; hence, lines representing an upper and lower bound are shown on each figure. (The shape of these bound lines may be varied according to the manner in which the data are interpreted. The lines shown are only suggested fairings of the data points presented.) One of these bounds corresponds to aircraft developed with the highest technology available at a particular time, and the other is for aircraft of a relatively low and slow-changing level of technology. Neither of these bounds represents boundaries of maximum and minimum values but, rather, corresponds to higher and lower levels of technology for operational aircraft of a particular time period. No data for racing or special performance aircraft are given in the figures.

Maximum Speed

Trends in maximum speed of propeller-driven aircraft are shown as a function of time in figure 7.2. The maximum speeds of high-technology operational aircraft are seen to increase steadily from about 125 miles per hour in 1920 to nearly 450 miles per hour in the World War II years. The highest maximum speed shown is for the P–51D aircraft, which had a speed of 437 miles per hour at 25 000 feet. Late in the war, a Republic P–47J achieved a speed in level flight of 507 miles per hour at 34 000 feet. The upper bound through the years closely follows the advancement of fighter-type aircraft. The large increases in maxi-

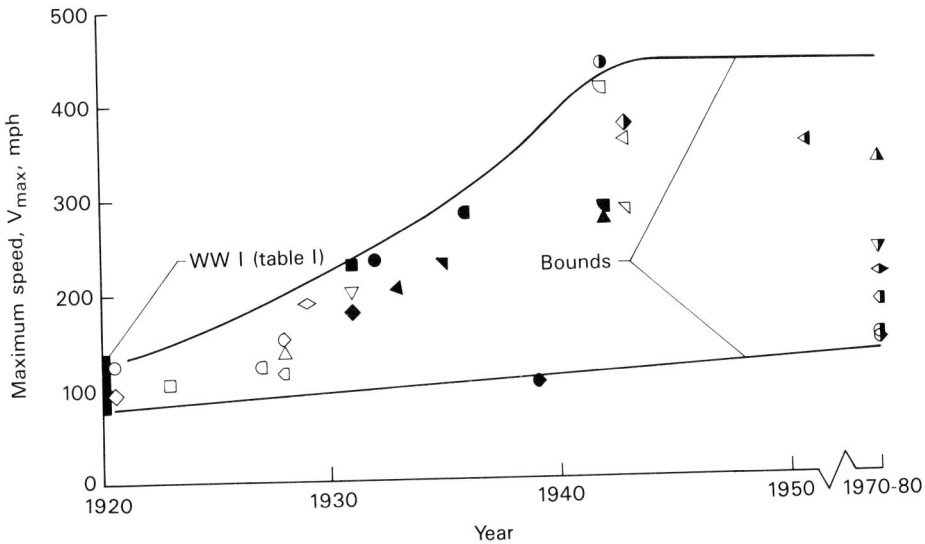

Figure 7.2 — Trends in maximum speed of propeller-driven aircraft.

mum speed that occurred between World War I and World War II resulted from increases in engine power and reductions in drag area through improved aerodynamic efficiency. For example, the 10 000-pound P–51 fighter of World War II had a drag area of only 3.8 square feet (this corresponds to a circular disc 2.20 feet in diameter) and was equipped with an engine of 1490 horsepower; by comparison, one of the highest performance fighters in use at the end of World War I, the 1807-pound SPAD XIII C.1 (chapter 2), had a drag area of 8.33 square feet (a circular disc 3.26 feet in diameter) and was powered with a 200 horsepower engine. The corresponding values of the ratio of power to drag area are 392.11 and 24.01, respectively. Also contributing significantly to the large increases in maximum speed were the development of the supercharger and controllable-pitch propeller, both of which permitted efficient high-power flight in the low-density, high-altitude environment. No increases in the maximum speed of operational propeller-driven aircraft have been achieved since the end of World War II because of the inherent limitations imposed by the effects of compressibility on the efficiency of conventional propellers.

The lower bound in figure 7.2 shows an increase in maximum speed from about 80 miles per hour to about 130 miles per hour. This bound indicates a continued desire for low-performance aircraft

153

throughout the years. The general aviation aircraft of today are seen to encompass a range of maximum speed from about 130 miles per hour to almost 350 miles per hour, which indicates the wide range of technical sophistication in contemporary propeller-driven aircraft.

Although not shown in the data presented in figure 7.2, the performance of representative, specially built, propeller-driven racing aircraft through the years may be of some interest and is indicated as follows:

(1) 1913, absolute speed record of 126.64 miles per hour established by French Deperdussin landplane

(2) 1920, absolute speed record of 194.49 miles per hour established by French Nieuport 29V landplane

(3) 1923, absolute speed record of 267.16 miles per hour established by American Curtiss R2C–1 landplane

(4) 1927, absolute speed record of 297.83 miles per hour established by Italian Marcchi M–52 seaplane

(5) 1931, absolute speed record of 406.94 miles per hour established by British Supermarine S–6B seaplane

(6) 1934, absolute speed record of 440.60 miles per hour established by Italian Marcchi-Castoldi MC–72 seaplane (This record for propeller-driven seaplanes still stands and is unlikely to be surpassed in the near future.)

(7) 1938, absolute speed record of 469.22 miles per hour established by German Messerschmitt 209V1 landplane

(8) 1969, absolute speed record of 483.04 miles per hour established by highly modified American Grumman F8F landplane

The world speed records cited above are officially recognized by the Fédération Aéronautique Internationale and were established under sea-level flight conditions.

Stalling Speed, Wing Loading, and Maximum Lift Coefficient

The stalling speed, wing loading, and maximum lift coefficient are shown as a function of years for various aircraft in figures 7.3, 7.4, and 7.5. The short, unpaved fields that served as airports in the early 1920's, together with the relatively poor flying characteristics of aircraft of that period, dictated the necessity for low values of the stalling

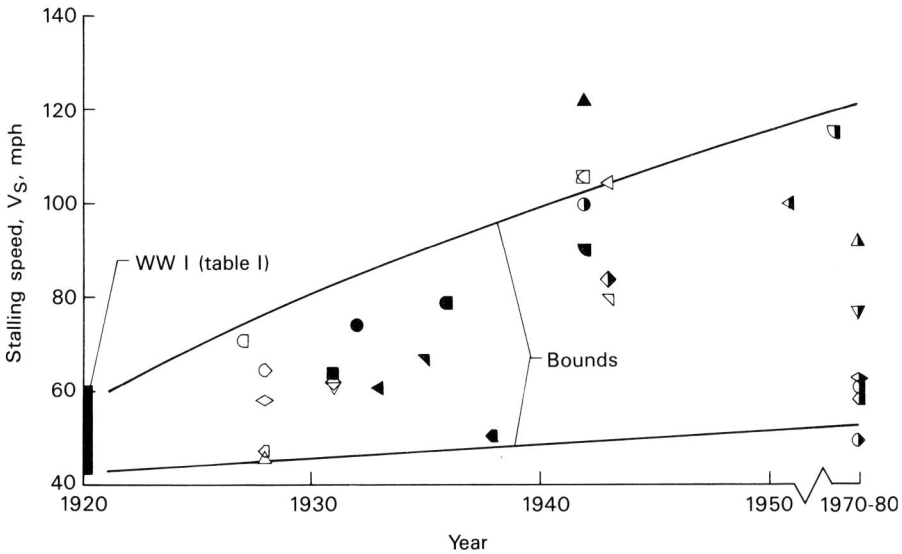

Figure 7.3 — Trends in stalling speed of propeller-driven aircraft.

speed. Values of the stalling speed of 40 to 50 miles per hour were not unusual, although precise data are not shown in figure 7.3 for the year 1920. High-lift devices were essentially unknown at that time; hence, the wing loadings needed to give the low values of the stalling speed were correspondingly low, as shown in figure 7.4. Values of the wing loading from 5 to 10 pounds per square foot were typical, and the 14-pound wing loading of the DH–4 was considered high in 1920. For a given atmospheric density, the wing loading is, of course, related to the square of the stalling speed by the value of the wing maximum lift co-efficient. Values of the maximum lift coefficient slightly in excess of a value of 1 were typical of unflapped aircraft with thin airfoil sections in 1920, as shown in figure 7.5. The demands for increased high-speed performance resulted in increases in wing loading and, hence, increases in the stalling speed. By the time of World War II, the stalling speeds of high-performance military aircraft were in the range of 80 to 100 miles per hour; wing loadings were in the range of 40 to 60 pounds per square foot. The development and the associated use of powerful high-lift devices, such as described in chapter 5, resulted in aircraft maximum lift coefficients of the order of 2.0 to 2.5 for high-perform-ance aircraft in the World War II period. These high-lift devices, and consequent high maximum lift coefficient, prevented the stalling speed

155

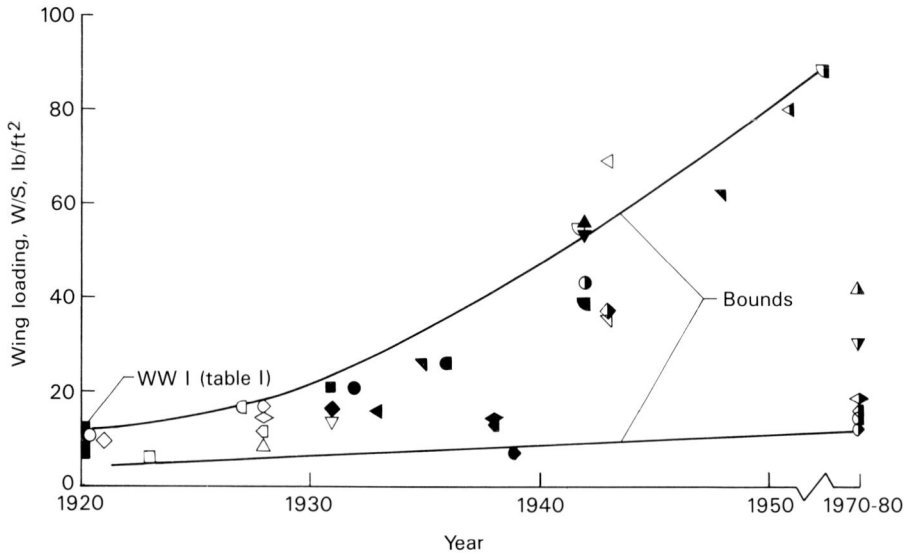

Figure 7.4 — Trends in wing loading of propeller-driven aircraft.

from increasing to an even greater extent than that shown in figure 7.3. Since World War II, the stalling speed of high-performance aircraft has continued to increase and is seen in figure 7.3 to be 115 miles per hour for the contemporary Lockheed C–130 cargo transport. The wing loading for this aircraft is about 90 pounds per square foot, as shown in figure 7.4, and the maximum lift coefficient is about 2.75. The high est maximum lift coefficient of any of the aircraft for which data are shown in figure 7.5 is about 3.0 and was obtained by the Lockheed Model 1049G Constellation. The corresponding wing loading for this aircraft is about 80 pounds per square foot. The high maximum lift co-efficient of the Constellation gave a relatively slow stalling speed of about 100 miles per hour.

The lower bounds in figures 7.3, 7.4, and 7.5 show modest in-creases in stalling speed, wing loading, and maximum lift coefficient for aircraft of relatively low performance. The data for current general aviation aircraft show a wide spread in level of technology, insofar as maximum lift coefficients are concerned, and a wide range of values of stalling speed and wing loading. Values of maximum lift coefficient for these aircraft vary from about 1.3 to about 2.2. The higher values of maximum lift coefficient achieved by current high-technology general aviation aircraft are about the same as those of military aircraft in

156

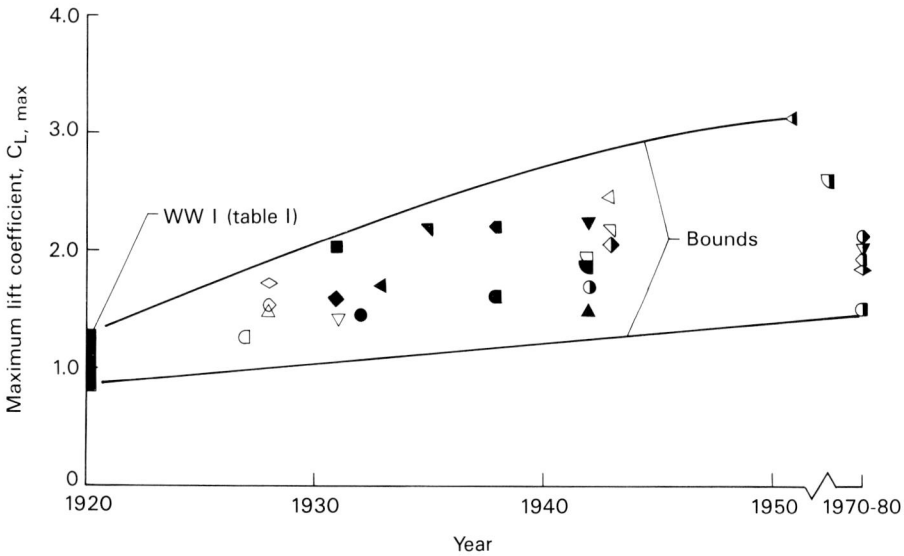

Figure 7.5 — Trends in maximum lift coefficient of propeller-driven aircraft.

World War II. The wing loading and stalling speeds of the high-performance general aviation aircraft of today are also seen to be in the same order as those of World War II military aircraft.

Power Loading

The power loading data shown in figure 7.6 appear to have nearly constant values for the upper and lower bounds. Within these bounds, the transport and bomber-type aircraft have power loadings that vary from about 12 pounds per horsepower in 1928 to 8 to 10 pounds per horsepower by the 1950's. Low-performance aircraft have a higher upper bound value of the power loading of about 16 pounds per horsepower although the venerable Piper Cub J–3 had a power loading value of about 19 pounds per horsepower. The lower bound of the power loading is formed by fighter aircraft, which tend to have power loadings in the range from 5 to 6 pounds per horsepower. These low values of power loadings have, through the years, been dictated by the rate of climb and maneuvering performance characteristics required in fighter-type aircraft. Present-day general aviation aircraft have power loadings that vary from nearly 16 pounds per horsepower for the very low-performance type of pleasure or training aircraft to about 8 pounds

157

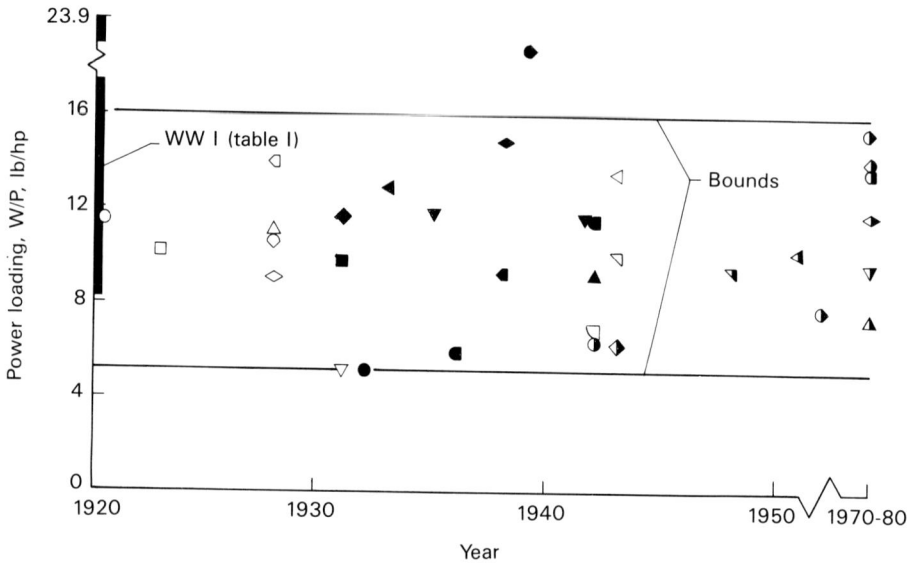

Figure 7.6 — Trends in power loading of propeller-driven aircraft.

per horsepower for the high-performance Beech King Air 200 (at low altitude).

Zero-Lift Drag Coefficient and Skin Friction Parameter

The value of the zero-lift drag coefficient $C_{D,0}$ is often used as an indicator of the aerodynamic cleanness or refinement of an aircraft. Values of $C_{D,0}$ calculated according to the methods of appendix C are shown as a function of years in figure 7.7. The lower bound of $C_{D,0}$ drops sharply from a value of about 0.040 in 1920 to a value of about 0.021 in the early 1930's. A smaller reduction in the lower bound values of $C_{D,0}$ took place in the years between the early 1930's and the years of World War II. The general aviation aircraft of today show a spread in the values of $C_{D,0}$ from near the upper bound to near the lower bound. The lower bound curve shows the dramatic reduction in $C_{D,0}$ that accompanied the basic change in airplane configuration from a strut-and-wire-braced biplane with a fixed landing gear to the highly streamlined, internally braced monoplane with retractable landing gear. As indicated in chapter 4, this transformation had largely taken place for high-performance operational aircraft by the early 1930's. Detailed aerodynamic refinements such as described in chapter 5 were responsi-

158

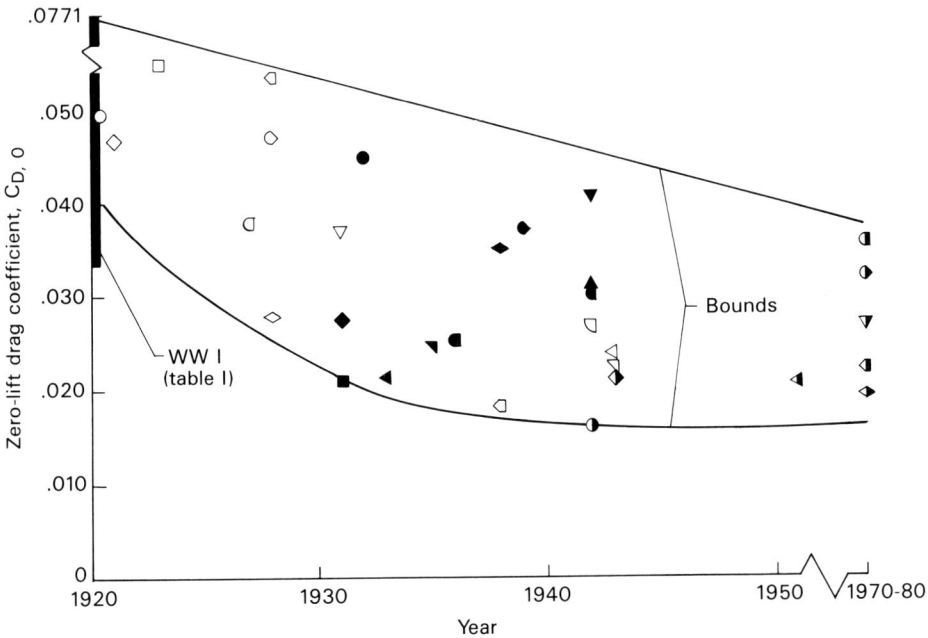

Figure 7.7 — Trends in zero-lift drag coefficient of propeller-driven aircraft.

ble for further improvements in aerodynamic efficiency as indicated by the lower bound curve.

The zero-lift drag coefficient, although useful as a measure of comparative aerodynamic refinement, has a basic limitation because the coefficient is based on wing area, and, for a given wing area, many different fuselage and tail sizes may be employed. Thus, differences in zero-lift drag coefficients may be interpreted as a difference in aerodynamic refinement when the difference may result from a significant difference in the ratio of wetted area to wing area.

In order to remove the effect of variations in the ratio of wetted area to wing area, a zero-lift drag coefficient based on total wetted area rather than wing area was estimated in reference 90 for most of the aircraft for which drag data are given in figure 7.7. The reference area for this coefficient, termed the skin friction parameter $\overline{C}_F$, consisted of the total surface area of the fuselage, wings, and tail surfaces. The parameter $\overline{C}_F$ was obtained from multiplication of $\overline{C}_{D,0}$ by the ratio of wing area to total wetted area. Values of $\overline{C}_F$ taken from reference 90 are shown as a function of years in figure 7.8. The upper and lower

159

bounds of the data show the same trends as do those for the zero-lift drag coefficient shown in figure 7.7. The lower bounds of the skin friction parameter indicate that essentially no progress has been made in reducing $\overline{C}_F$ since World War II, and little progress has been made since the early 1930's. The data for the current general aviation aircraft fall generally between the upper and lower bounds but do not reach as low a value as that of the lower bound curve. This suggests that these aircraft can be refined to a value at least as low as that achieved during World War II. There is little likelihood, however, that values of $\overline{C}_F$ significantly lower than the lower bound shown in figure 7.8 can be achieved unless some breakthrough is made that permits the achievement of a significant extent of laminar flow on the aircraft. Other than reductions in the value of the skin friction parameter, future reductions in the airplane zero-lift drag coefficient $\overline{C}_{D,0}$ can perhaps be achieved through configuration design aimed at reducing the ratio of wetted area to wing area. The pure flying wing represents the ultimate improvement by this means.

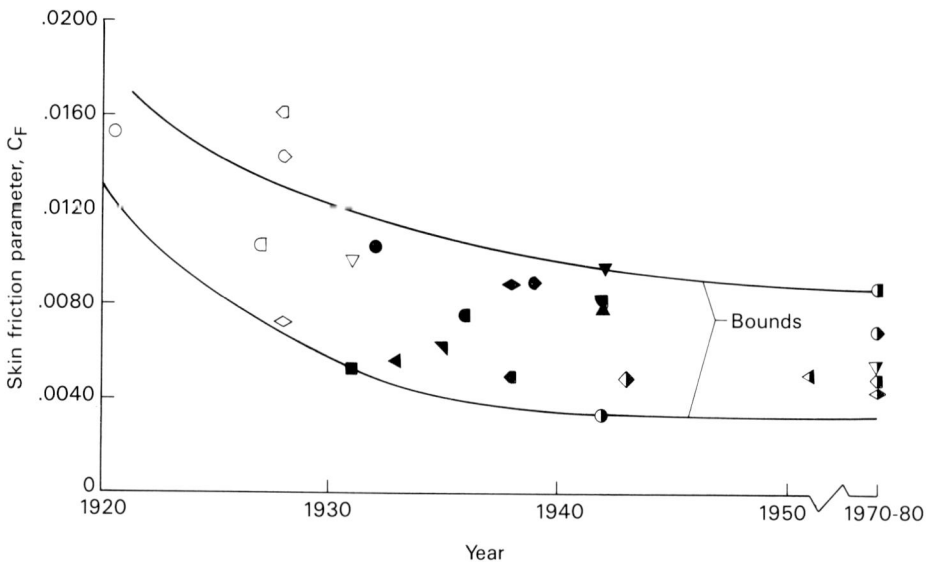

Figure 7.8 — Trends in skin friction parameter $\overline{C}_F$ of propeller-driven aircraft. [ref. 90]

Maximum Lift-Drag Ratio

The maximum lift-drag ratio of the various aircraft was calculated according to the methods described in appendix C and is shown as a function of years in figure 7.9. The value of the maximum lift-drag ratio $(L/D)_{max}$ is a measure of the aerodynamic cruising efficiency of the aircraft. The upper bound of $(L/D)_{max}$ varies from values of about 9 in 1920 to a value of 16.8 for the World War II Boeing B–29 and 16.0 for the Lockheed 1049G in 1952. The $(L/D)_{max}$ upper-bound curve shows a sharp rise between 1920 and the early 1930's, which corresponds to the reduction in zero-lift drag coefficient shown in figure 7.7 and to the emergence of the monoplane with its higher aspect ratio as compared with the biplane. Little change in maximum L/D has taken place since the end of World War II. Any further increases in maximum lift-drag ratio will require reductions in the value of the zero-lift drag coefficient and/or increases in wing aspect ratio that may be possible through the use of improved structural materials.

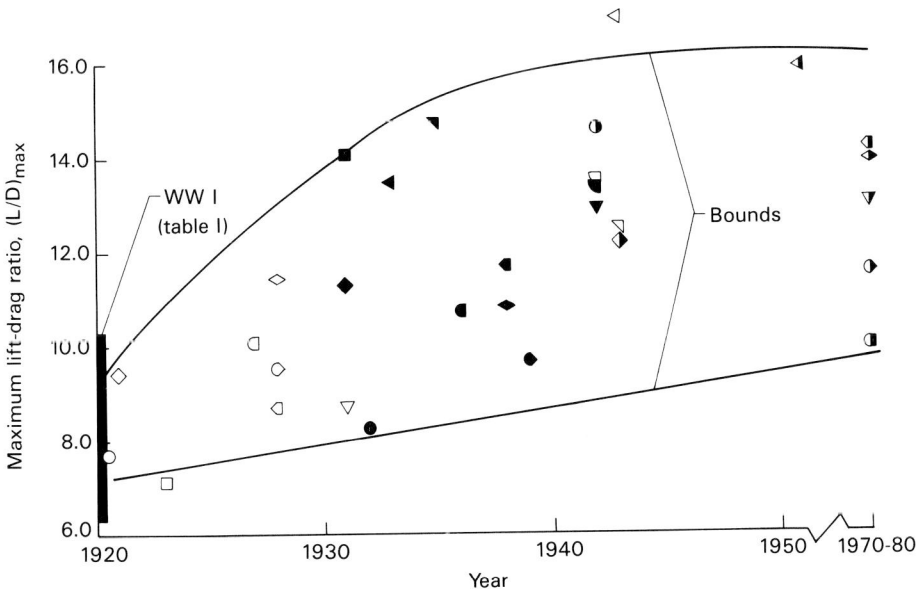

Figure 7.9 — Trends in maximum lift-drag ratio of propeller-driven aircraft.

Chapter 8
Boats in the Sky

Background

Seaplanes are aircraft designed to take off and land on the surface of the water. Aircraft of this type fall into two distinctly different categories. One category consists of conventional land planes that are mounted on floats, sometimes called pontoons, in place of a conventional landing gear with wheels. The other category consists of a basically different type of aircraft in which the lower part of the fuselage is shaped somewhat like a boat and which, at rest and low speed, floats on the surface just as a boat does — hence the term "flying boat."

From its inception and early demonstration by Glenn H. Curtiss in 1912 until a few years after the end of World War II, the flying boat was a key element of commercial and military aviation throughout the world. Large-scale commercial operations ceased 2 or 3 years after the war, but military use of the flying boat continued in the United States until the last squadron of these picturesque aircraft was decommissioned in 1967. No large flying boats have been built in the United States since 1960; however, both Japan and the Soviet Union produce such aircraft in limited numbers for military purposes, and a flying boat is still built in Canada for use as a water bomber in fighting forest fires.

The popularity and apparent demise of the flying boat as an important element of aviation can be traced to a combination of operational, performance, and economic characteristics. In the years prior to World War II, airports capable of handling large, long-range aircraft were few in number and nonexistent in most parts of the world, particularly in undeveloped nations. Most areas of the world that are of interest for trade and commerce, however, are located near bodies of water such as lakes, rivers, harbors, inlets, and other types of marine facilities. These natural resources, which require little if any development, provided an abundant and almost unlimited number of world-

163

wide facilities for the operation of large, long-range flying boats. Both military and commercial air operations made extensive use of these natural resources. Airlines operated both passenger and freight service with flying boats, and the military used these aircraft for reconnaissance, antisubmarine patrol, search and rescue, and other activities. In the absence of any permanent ground facilities, naval flying boats could operate for weeks in the most forbidding geographical areas while supported by a small ship called a seaplane tender. In addition, the flying boat seemed to offer on long over-water flights the prospect of a safe landing in the event of an engine failure, a very real possibility with the relatively unreliable engines available in the early days of aviation. The chances of a flying boat surviving a landing in rough seas on the open ocean were, of course, problematical; this advantage was perhaps more psychological than real. Yet, a number of cases have been recorded in which passengers and crew survived a landing in the open ocean after engine failure.

For all these reasons, the flying boat seemed for many years to have an important and permanent place in the aeronautical world. The flying boat, however, possessed certain disadvantages inherent in its dual capacity for operation on the water as well as in the air. The aerodynamic drag of the hull-fuselage was basically higher than that of the conventional fuselage of a landplane. Hence, the cruising speed tended to be lower than that of a comparable landplane, as was the aerodynamic cruising efficiency expressed by the maximum lift-drag ratio. The economic potential of the flying boat was accordingly limited in comparison with the landplane. Further, the ever-present danger of collision with submerged objects in the water and subsequent hull rupture and possible sinking, as well as difficulties in passenger handling to and from a moored flying boat, posed ever-present operational problems.

During World War II, many parts of the world saw the development of a large number of airports equipped with long, hard-surface runways. Large, fast, highly efficient landplanes suitable for carrying passengers and equipped with four reliable engines also emerged from the war. These two factors spelled the end of the flying boat as a viable means for the economical transportation of passengers and freight over long distances. Pan American Airlines, a pioneer in the use of flying boats on long over-water routes, terminated operation of this type of aircraft in April 1946, less than a year after the end of the war. Today, a few small flying boats built prior to World War II are still used in inter-island commuter-type operations. One small, four-place sport flying boat is still in limited production in the United States at the present time. For many years after the war, the U.S. Navy and Coast Guard continued to use flying boats for reconnaissance, antisubmarine patrol, and search-and-rescue missions. Long-duration turboprop land-planes and helicopters, however, gradually took over these duties and finally completely replaced the flying boat.

The technical evolution of the flying boat from 1914 to 1960 is briefly described below. Photographs of 21 representative flying boats are used to illustrate the development of this type of aircraft, and their physical and performance characteristics are presented in table IV (appendix A). The references used in compiling these characteristics are contained in the reference list at the end of this book, and the specific references employed for each aircraft are cited in the table. Some additional references dealing with flying boats not specifically cited in the tables are included in the reference list. Reference 80, for example, presents an interesting historical survey of the flying boat in the United States. As mentioned, primary emphasis in this book has been placed on aircraft originating in the United States. This has been done to limit the scope of material and is in no way intended as an adverse reflection on the many excellent flying boats developed in other countries.

Design Considerations

A flying boat must satisfy many of the same requirements for performance, efficiency, strength, and reliability as a landplane but, in addition, must possess some qualities of a boat in water and some qualities unique to the flying boat itself. It must be seaworthy, maneuverable, and stable on the water and have low water and air drag. The hull must be designed and the aircraft configured in such a way that the amount of spray passing through the propellers, striking the tail, and passing over the windshield is minimized. The hull must be designed with sufficient structural strength to withstand the various loads imposed by rough water in landing, taking off, and taxiing.

Some of the design features characteristic of a flying boat are illustrated by the Martin Mariner and Grumman Goose shown in figures 8.1 and 8.2, respectively. Both of these aircraft, which may be considered as relatively modern flying-boat designs, feature a high wing mounted atop a deep, voluminous hull, a high tail position, and wing-tip stabilizing floats. In both aircraft, the engines are mounted in the

165

Figure 8.1 — Design features of a World War II flying boat. [NASA]

Figure 8.2 — Design features of a flying boat. [NASA]

wings to minimize spray problems and reduce aerodynamic drag. The Mariner has a gull wing configuration with the engines mounted in the wing break to place them in a high position. The problem of spray ingestion by the engines and propellers is a basic design consideration in the configuration layout of a flying boat.

The tip, or stabilizing, floats are evident in both figures 8.1 and 8.2. These floats are necessary because the narrow beam hull coupled with a high center of gravity make the flying boat laterally unstable on the water. (In terms of naval architecture, it has a negative metacentric height.) The aircraft is usually designed so that it heels about 1° when one float touches the water. When laterally level as in takeoff from relatively smooth water, neither float touches the water. The floats are designed and mounted in such a way as to give a large dynamic lateral restoring moment when one float touches the water on takeoff or landing. Tip floats have historically been the most used form of lateral stabilization; however, a device called a sponson has sometimes been employed. This type of stabilizer is used on three of the aircraft described in this chapter.

The voluminous hull is usually designed with from 70- to 100-percent reserve buoyancy (ref. 46). When floating as a displacement boat, a 100-percent reserve buoyancy means that the hull will support twice the design weight of the aircraft without sinking. The reserve buoyancy is provided as a safety factor, particularly for operation in rough seas. The cross-sectional shape of the forward portion of the hull is usually in the form of a vee or modified vee. The outside angle of the vee is called the angle of deadrise. The larger this angle, the lower will be the impact loads imposed by operation in heavy seas. The friction drag on the forward part of the hull, however, increases with deadrise angle, as does the spray problem. The modified vee bottom of the Grumman Goose is clearly visible in figure 8.2. The intersections of the sides of the forward part of the hull with the vee bottom are called the chines and form a sharp angle. The design of the chines is important in determining the spray characteristics of the hull. To assist in controlling the spray, special spray strips are sometimes attached to the chines as shown by the experimental installation in figure 8.2.

The flying boat in figure 8.1 clearly shows the characteristic manner in which the hull bottom is separated by a transverse step into a forebody and afterbody. At low speeds the hull operates as a displacement boat with both the forebody and afterbody sharing the support of the aircraft in the water. Beyond a certain speed, called the hump speed (more about this later), the hull planes on the forebody

167

with the afterbody contributing little or nothing to the support of the aircraft. The step, acting somewhat like a spoiler on an airplane wing, causes the flow to break away from the afterbody and allows the boat to transition into the planing regime. The step is essential to the successful operation of the flying boat since lift-off from the water is normally not possible without it. This design feature was first introduced by aviation pioneer Glenn H. Curtiss. Two transverse steps have sometimes been employed in the design of flying-boat hulls, particularly on older boats. The more usual practice in later boats, however, is to taper (in planform) the afterbody to a point which effectively terminates the hull. The tail assembly is then carried on a fuselage extension above the hull. Some exceptions to this are pointed out later. The overall length-beam ratio of the hull as well as the value of this ratio for the forebody and afterbody individually are important design variables, as are the height and location of the step.

The design of the hull is important in determining the characteristics of the flying boat in all phases of its operation on the water. The importance of the hydrodynamic characteristics of the hull can be illustrated by considering the influence of hull water drag and aircraft weight on the takeoff distance and on the conditions under which the boat will not lift off at all. As is the case with a landplane, the seaplane must accelerate to a speed sufficiently high, determined by the wing loading and maximum lift coefficient, for the wings to support the weight of the aircraft in flight. The aerodynamic drag of the aircraft together with the rolling friction on the wheels on the runway constitute the resistance to acceleration of the landplane in its takeoff run. In addition to the aerodynamic drag, the flying boat must overcome the water drag associated with the hull. The manner in which this drag varies with speed makes the takeoff problem of a flying boat uniquely different from that of a landplane.

The variation of water drag with speed, along with the accompanying variation of engine thrust, is shown by the conceptual curves in figure 8.3 for a hypothetical flying boat. The water drag of the boat is separated into two distinct speed regimes. Below the hump speed, the speed for maximum drag, the aircraft is operating as a displacement boat with both the afterbody and the forebody assisting in providing the necessary buoyancy. Under these circumstances, the drag results primarily from the generation of water waves. At the hump speed, the boat may be thought of as climbing over its bow wave and beginning operation as a planing hull. In this latter regime, the weight of the boat is supported primarily by the dynamic reaction of the water against the

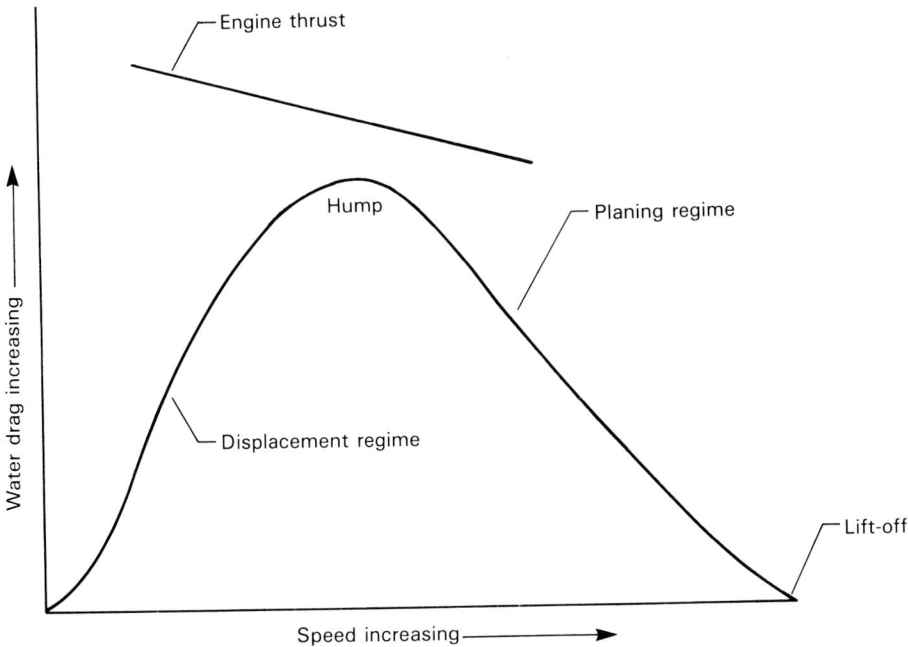

Figure 8.3 — Characteristic variation of water drag with speed for a hypothetical flying-boat hull.

forebody, and displacement buoyancy is relatively unimportant. The water drag in this speed range results primarily from skin friction between the water and the forebody. In addition to the support provided by the planing forebody, an increasing proportion of the aircraft weight is supported by the wings until, finally, the water drag becomes zero as the aircraft lifts off.

Also shown in figure 8.3 is the hypothetical variation of engine thrust with speed. At speeds well below and above the hump speed, a large margin exists between the drag and the thrust. The thrust margin at the hump speed, however, is a minimum, as is the acceleration. If the thrust is less than the drag at the hump speed, takeoff will not be possible. In actual performance calculations, the air drag must be added to the water drag to obtain the total drag as a function of speed.

The magnitude of the hump drag together with its corresponding speed are obviously critically important in determining takeoff performance. For a hull of given geometry, these quantities are approximately related to the length of the hull by the principles of Froude scaling (refs. 46 and 116). According to these principles, the speed V and the

169

length L of two geometrically similar hulls at and below the hump speed are related as follows:

$$\frac{V_1}{\sqrt{L_1}} = \frac{V_2}{\sqrt{L_2}}$$

or

$$\frac{V_1}{V_2} = \sqrt{\frac{L_1}{L_2}}$$

where the subscripts refer to the two different hull lengths. For a given value of the parameter $V/\sqrt{L}$, the wave drags of the two hulls D_1 and D_2 are also related to the length as follows:

$$\frac{D_1}{D_2} = \left(\frac{L_1}{L_2}\right)^3 = \frac{W_1}{W_2}$$

where W is the displacement of the hull in pounds and equals the weight of the aircraft when operating as a displacement boat. Thus, the values of speed and drag at and below the hump speed of one hull can be approximately translated to those of a similar hull of different length. The Froude relationships are of fundamental use in sizing the flying-boat hull and interpreting the results of hydrodynamic tests of model hulls. Clearly, the longer the hull, the higher will be both the hump speed and the corresponding wave drag.

In addition to the high drag associated with passage through the hump speed, a longitudinal pitching instability can occur. This instability is characterized by a pitch oscillation in which the boat rocks back and forth between the forebody and afterbody. A too-high or too-low pitch attitude can induce the onset of this instability. The range of stable pitch attitudes varies with speed and is a minimum in the vicinity of the hump speed. Thus, careful control of pitch attitude is required when traversing this critical speed range. The attitude at which the flying boat trims is influenced by both the aerodynamic and hydrodynamic design of the aircraft, the center-of-gravity position, and the pilot's manipulation of the elevator control.

The hydrodynamic characteristics of a flying boat, such as the variation of drag with speed just discussed, depend in a complex way on the detailed configuration of the hull and have been the subject of much study and research. An extensive literature exists on the subject, as can be seen from an examination of technical indexes such as reference 74.

The large body of experimental information available on the hydrodynamic design of flying-boat hulls has been accumulated with the use of a specialized type of experimental facility called a towing basin, or towing tank. Such a facility can be likened to a very long, narrow, indoor swimming pool. The test model is towed in the basin by means of a powered carriage, mounted on wheels, which is located above and across the channel of water. The model is connected to the carriage by struts that contain instrumentation for measuring the pressures, forces, and moments of interest, as well as attitude and position of the model.

Since the latter part of the 19th century, towing basins have been used in the design of surface ships. Although early hydrodynamic studies of flying boats were made with the use of such ship facilities, they were unsuited for that purpose because of the large differences in speed and size between surface ships and flying boats. In 1931, NACA put into operation at its Langley laboratory a towing basin especially designed for the study of the hydrodynamic characteristics of seaplane hulls (ref. 116). This unique facility was 2020 feet long, 24 feet wide, and 12 feet deep, and when filled contained 4 000 000 gallons of water. The test carriage was capable of attaining a speed of 60 miles per hour. (To keep pace with increases in seaplane performance, the capabilities of the basin were expanded in 1936; the length was increased to 2920 feet, and the carriage speed was increased to 80 miles per hour.) Another feature of the Langley basin was the provision of apparatus for producing artificial waves for use in the study of the rough-water characteristics of flying-boat hulls. The Langley towing basin was employed both for basic studies related to hull design and for tests of specific flying-boat designs. During its active life, no large flying boat was built in the United States without supporting tests in the Langley facility. The basin was operated by NACA/NASA from 1931 until the end of the era of large flying-boat development in about 1960.

So far, little has been said about the aerodynamic drag of the flying-boat hull. Yet, this characteristic is critically important in determining the speed and range of the aircraft. Obviously, the drag of the large, bulky hulls equipped with steps and sharp chines tended to be higher than that of the fuselage of a well-streamlined landplane of comparable capability. In recognition of the need to reduce hull aerodynamic drag, both hydrodynamic and aerodynamic studies were made

171

at Langley of hulls that were systematically varied in shape. From such studies, the hull for a given application that represented the best compromise between aerodynamic and hydrodynamic performance could be identified, or at least the direction to take in hull development was indicated. Much progress was made in the reduction of hull aerodynamic drag, while at the same time, acceptable hydrodynamic characteristics were maintained. The high length-beam ratio hulls developed late in the era of the flying boat (ref. 124) represented a large step in narrowing the gap between seaplane and landplane performance.

This has been a necessarily brief discussion of some of the elements of flying boat design. More complete discussions are contained in references 46, 55, 97, and 123, and a discussion of the special problems encountered in piloting a flying boat is contained in reference 81. In the next sections, attention is focused on the evolution of the flying boat in the United States.

Early Military Flying Boats, 1914–20

The years of World War I provided the stimulus and proving ground for the development of the flying boat into a useful and versatile class of aircraft. It was employed primarily for reconnaissance, patrol, and bombing operations. Each of the warring nations developed and operated military flying boats. Three pace-setting Curtiss patrol boats designed in the United States, or derived from Curtiss designs, are discussed in the next section, after which the first aircraft to cross the Atlantic Ocean is described.

Three Curtiss Patrol Boats

The world's first flying boat was designed, built, and flown by the American aviation pioneer Glenn H. Curtiss in 1912. The small single-engine biplane that was the centerpiece of this historic event was the progenitor of an entire family of single and multiengine flying boats that served with United States and British forces during World War I and made the name Curtiss almost synonymous with flying boat during that world conflict. Typical of the Curtiss flying boats developed during this period were the twin-engine H–16 and the HS–2L, a scaled-down single-engine version of the H–16. The two aircraft are shown in figures 8.4 and 8.5. After the American-developed Liberty engine (ref. 45) became available, both boats were equipped with this 400-horsepower power plant. A multibay, strut-and-wire-braced biplane configuration with the engine(s) mounted between the wings was employed for both aircraft. Whereas landplanes employing the biplane configuration usually had the lower wing attached near the bottom of the fuselage, the H–16 and the HS–2L had the entire wing assembly mounted atop the hull. The horizontal tail was mounted high on the vertical fin located at the rear of the fuselage extension above the hull. A single step together with a shallow vee bottom and wide beam characterized the hull itself. The lateral stabilizing floats can be clearly seen beneath the tips of the lower wing in figures 8.4 and 8.5. The finlike surfaces on top of the upper wing near the tips assisted in providing the necessary structural support for the large overhang of the wingtips. Barely visible in the photograph are the bracing wires that extended both inboard and outboard from the top of this surface to the wing. Wires also extended downward and inboard from near the upper wingtips to the juncture of the lower wing and the outboard interplane struts. A somewhat similar type of bracing arrangement was employed on the Handley Page 0/400 bomber shown in figure 2.22 and the Curtiss JN–4H Jenny shown in figure 3.1. The fabric covering was intended to reduce the drag of the struts projecting above the wing.

Figure 8.4 — Curtiss H–16 twin-engine flying boat; World War I era. [USN via Martin Copp]

Figure 8.5 — Curtiss HS–2L single-engine flying boat; World War I era. [mfr via Martin Copp]

The wings and tail surfaces of the H–16 and HS–2L were of conventional (for that time period) wood-frame construction covered with fabric. The hull construction consisted of a laminated wood-veneer covering attached to a wood frame. An undesirable characteristic of wooden-hull flying boats was a tendency to absorb a certain amount of water over a period of time. To some degree then, the aircraft empty weight was a variable and known only within approximate limits. Accordingly, conservatism had to be exercised in estimating allowable fuel and payload weights to avoid a risk of operating in an overweight condition.

The statement is frequently made that no United States-designed aircraft served in France in World War I (see chapter 2); this certainly applies to fighters, bombers, and army cooperation aircraft used in operations over the Western front. American naval forces, however, operated both the H–16 and the HS–2L over the coastal waters of France, with the first operational flight of the HS–2L occurring on June 13, 1918. After the cessation of hostilities, both of these long-lived aircraft continued in operation with the United States Navy until the late 1920's. Some of them, declared surplus by the Navy, were sold to civil

174

operators who employed them in short-lived airline operations. Some were also used as rum-runners during the prohibition era in the 1920's.

The British Royal Navy operated several types of Curtiss flying boats long before the United States entered the war but were not entirely satisfied with their hydrodynamic performance. New aircraft utilizing Curtiss-designed wings and tail surfaces, but incorporating an improved two-step hull that was more suited to the rough waters of the North Sea and gave a reduced takeoff distance, were accordingly developed. The work was carried out at the Felixstowe Naval Air Station, and the resulting flying boats were designated F-1 to F-5 depending on the Curtiss boat from which they were derived. These aircraft were highly successful, so much so that the United States Navy had over 200 of the F-5 version, derived from the H-16, built under contract in this country where they were given the designation F-5L. Those built here were equipped with the Liberty engine, which accounts for the "L" in the designation. Many of these aircraft were constructed by the Curtiss company and, since they had Curtiss-designed wings and tail, were usually referred to as Curtiss F-5L flying boats although that designation is not entirely accurate. The F-5L arrived on the scene too late to see action with United States forces during World War I, but in the postwar years it was a mainstay with Navy patrol squadrons until finally withdrawn from service in 1928.

The inflight photograph of an F-5L flying boat (fig. 8.6) clearly shows the configuration of this classic, triple-bay biplane aircraft. The two pilots sitting side by side, as well as the two men in the front gunners' cockpit, are clearly visible. The cockpit for the rear gunner, located behind the wings, is partially obscured in the photograph. A crew of three or four normally manned the aircraft. Armament consisted of several flexibly mounted machine guns together with a bomb load of up to four 230-pound bombs.

The wings of the F-5L are obviously similar to those of the H-16 shown in figure 8.4. In early versions of the F-5L the tail assembly was also the same as that of the H-16; but as shown in figure 8.6, an enlarged tail equipped with horn-balanced elevators and rudder was fitted to the F-5L. The modified tail was incorporated in all F-5L boats in the early 1920's. Noteworthy in figure 8.6 are the exposed cylinders and crankcases of the engines and the large automobile-type radiators positioned above the propellers. The flared sides of the broad-beamed hull are called sponsons (not to be confused with the winglike lateral stabilizing surfaces also called sponsons, which are discussed later).

175

Figure 8.6 — Curtiss F–5L twin-engine flying boat; World War I era. [USN via Martin Copp]

The physical and performance characteristics of the H–16, HS–2L, and the F–5L flying boats are given in table IV. That they were relatively large, heavy, and low-performance aircraft is indicated by the data presented. To put these characteristics in the proper context with respect to multiengine landplanes of that same time period, the following comparative data are given for the Curtiss F–5L flying boat and the Handley Page 0/400 twin-engine bomber (for which data are given in table I):

Aircraft	Wg	b	S	V_{max}	$C_{D,0}$	$(L/D)_{max}$
Handley Page 0/400	14 425	100.0	1655	94	0.0427	9.7
Curtiss F–5L	13 600	103.8	1397	90	0.0694	8.2

The data show the two aircraft are roughly the same size and weight, but the landplane is about 5 percent faster than the flying boat. In comparing the aerodynamic characteristics of the two aircraft, the zero-lift drag coefficient is about 60 percent higher and the maximum lift-

176

drag ratio is about 18 percent lower for the Curtiss F–5L flying boat than for the Handley Page 0/400 landplane. The large, low length-beam ratio, two-step hull of the flying boat no doubt contributed to its degraded aerodynamic performance, a price exacted for the operational versatility of the flying boat.

The configuration arrangement of the three Curtiss aircraft just described set a style in patrol-boat design that continued in the United States for many years.

The NC Boats, First Across the Atlantic

The NC boats are discussed here not so much for their advanced design features but rather because one of their number, the NC–4, was the first aircraft to fly across the Atlantic Ocean and thus secured for the type a permanent place in the annals of aviation history. The origins of the NC flying boat can be traced to a request issued by the British in 1917 for a long-range patrol aircraft for antisubmarine operations over the open ocean. In addition, it was desired that the aircraft be capable of flying from the United States to the British Isles, thus shortening delivery time and saving much-needed cargo space on available surface shipping. An aircraft designed to meet these specifications emerged from a collaboration between engineers of the United States Navy and the Curtiss company — hence the NC designation. The first of these flying boats, NC–1, was flown in the late fall of 1918, and the other three, NC–2, NC–3, and NC–4, were completed in the spring of 1919. These aircraft were built by the Curtiss company under the supervision of Glenn H. Curtiss himself; subsequently, six more NC boats were constructed by the Naval Aircraft Factory located in Philadelphia, Pennsylvania. Since World War I ended in November 1918, none of the NC boats were completed and tested in time to fill the wartime role for which they had been designed.

The United States Navy, however, organized a mission to fly across the Atlantic Ocean, a feat not yet accomplished, with the use of NC–1, NC–3, and NC–4. Bound for Plymouth, England, the three aircraft left Trepassy Bay, Newfoundland, on May 16, 1919, with intended refueling stops in the Azores and Portugal. The mission was under the overall command of Commander John H. Towers, who also served as commander of NC–3. The three aircraft soon became separated after leaving Newfoundland; and because of uncertainties as to their position and deteriorating weather conditions, NC–1 and NC–3 landed in the ocean, short of the Azores, with the hope of locating their position with radio equipment and subsequently continuing the flight. Although the crew was rescued, NC–1 capsized and sank because of heavy seas; NC–3, unable to take off again, taxied 200 miles to the Azores but was too badly damaged to continue the flight. Arriving at Plymouth, England, on May 31, 1919, NC–4 successfully completed the mission and thus became the first aircraft to fly across the Atlantic Ocean. The six-man crew for the flight was commanded by Lt. Albert C. Reed, who also served as navigator, and included two pilots, a radio operator, and two flight engineers. The chief pilot for the flight was Lt. (jg.) Walter Hinton. An interesting account of this historic flight is contained in reference 80.

The Navy-Curtiss NC–4 flying boat is shown in figure 8.7. The configuration of the aircraft featured a typical Curtiss three-bay, strut-and-wire-braced biplane wing arrangement mounted on top of a short, wide-beam, single-step hull designed by Navy engineers. The tail assembly was supported by wire-braced outriggers extending back from the top wing and the stern of the hull. This arrangement was chosen to minimize hull weight, as compared with designs like the F–5L, to place the tail high above the waves in rough seas, and to provide the rear gunner with a wide field of fire. The horizontal tail consisted of a biplane arrangement with three rudders mounted between the horizontal stabilizing surfaces. Fins were fixed ahead of the outboard rudders. Power was supplied by four of the ubiquitous, American-designed, 400-horsepower Liberty engines, located in three nacelles. One engine was carried in each of the outboard nacelles, and two engines in a tractor-

Figure 8.7 — Four-engine Navy-Curtiss NC–4 was first across the Atlantic Ocean; 1919. [ukn via Martin Copp]

pusher arrangement were mounted in the center one. The NC-1 was initially flown with only the three tractor engines but was found to be so underpowered that the fourth pusher engine was installed.

As described in connection with the H-16, the wings and tail surfaces of the NC boats were of wood-frame construction covered with fabric. The wooden frame of the short, broad-beam hull was covered on the sides and bottom with two layers of planking that were glued together with a sheet of canvas in between and had a three-ply wood-veneer turtle deck. The outriggers supporting the tail were of wooden box beam construction.

A glance at the physical characteristics of the NC-4 given in table IV shows that it was indeed a large aircraft. At a gross weight of 27 386 pounds, it was about twice as heavy as the F-5L and had a wing span of 126 feet as compared with 103.8 feet for the F-5L. The wing area of 2380 square feet was 70 percent greater than that of the F-5L and was only about 18 percent less than that of the modern Boeing 707 jet transport (chapter 13). The performance data show a maximum speed of only 85 miles per hour and estimated values of the cruising and stalling speeds of 77 and 67 miles per hour, respectively. Accordingly, the aircraft had to be carefully flown and maneuvered within the narrow speed range available to it. At 0.0899, the zero-lift drag coefficient of the NC-4 was the highest of any of the aircraft for which data are given in table IV, and the value of 7.0 was the lowest of any of the maximum lift-drag ratios shown. The maximum range of the aircraft is given in reference 109 as 1470 miles; with such a low value of maximum lift-drag ratio, this range could only be possible with a large aircraft having a relatively low empty weight as compared with gross weight. In spite of its shortcomings in aerodynamic efficiency, the NC-4 fulfilled these weight requirements and was able to make the Atlantic crossing for which it was designed.

Shortly after completion of its historic flight in 1919, the NC-4 was presented to the Smithsonian Institution, which completely restored the aircraft for the 50th anniversary of the famous flight in 1969. Today, the NC-4 may be seen at the United States Naval Air Museum located at the Naval Station in Pensacola, Florida.

Biplane Flying-Boat Developments, 1920-30

The slow pace of aeronautical development during the first half of the 1920's was briefly mentioned in chapter 3. If anything, technical advancements in flying-boat design during this period lagged behind those of contemporary landplanes and did not experience the rapid acceleration that characterized landplane developments in the latter half of the decade. The biplane configuration dominated flying-boat design, and most efforts were aimed toward military applications. In the following section, developments in Navy patrol boats are discussed, after which two significant amphibian aircraft developed in the 1920's are described.

The Refined Patrol Boat

According to reference 118, the United States Navy had an inventory of 1172 flying boats at the termination of hostilities in November 1918. By the middle of 1925, this number had shrunk to 117 aircraft consisting of outdated wartime H-16, HS-2L, and F-5L boats. Fortunately, the stagnation in military flying-boat development was relieved, to some extent, by the Naval Aircraft Factory, which continued design refinement of the biplane flying boat. The wartime F-5L, redesignated PN-5, formed the starting point of these activities, which resulted in a number of improved aircraft designs. Until 1928, prototypes of each of the improved designs were built in the limited facilities of the Naval Aircraft Factory, but lack of funds prevented placing production contracts with industry.

One prototype, the PN-9, was a much refined development of the PN-5 equipped with Packard engines and a hull of aluminum alloy construction. This aircraft achieved a dubious place in aviation history by its failed attempt to fly nonstop from San Francisco to Hawaii. With a crew of five under the command of Commander John Rodgers, the PN-9 left San Francisco on August 31, 1925, and came down at sea after flying 1841 miles, a new distance record, about 200 miles short of Maui, Hawaii. A higher-than-expected fuel consumption, coupled with the lack of anticipated tail winds, resulted in fuel exhaustion and the unanticipated landing at sea. Crude sails were fashioned from fabric torn from the lower wings, and the flying boat was literally sailed 450 miles to the Island of Kauai, which was sighted on the 10th of September. (Marginal steering capability prevented the aircraft from reaching the much nearer island of Maui.) Whatever may have been lacking in flight planning or in understanding of engine performance, the seaworthiness of the new all-metal hull and the seamanship of the crew were clearly demonstrated by this remarkable venture. Reference 80 is cited for a succinct description of the flight.

By 1928, the Navy had both a flying-boat design that it liked, the PN-12, and sufficient money to place production contracts with several aircraft manufacturers. Martin, Douglas, Keystone, and Hall Aluminum ultimately participated in the program, and aircraft produced by these companies were designated PM, PD, PK, and PH, respectively. The aircraft produced by each company were based on the Navy-designed PN–12, but they differed from this aircraft and from each other in a number of details that are not discussed here. Detailed descriptions of each of the aircraft can be found in references 109 and 118.

Typical of the patrol boats produced in this program was the Martin PM–1 illustrated in figure 8.8. The aircraft had the classic twin-engine biplane configuration, similar in concept to the F–5L, but was much cleaner than the earlier aircraft. The number of drag-producing interplane struts and wires had been reduced, and the tip-bracing arrangement on top of the upper wing had been eliminated. Neatly cowled nine-cylinder radial air-cooled engines on the PM–1 contrasted with the exposed in-line engines and clumsy radiators on the F–5L. The data in table IV show that the PM–1 had more power, was somewhat heavier, and had slightly less wing area than the F–5L it was designed to replace. The Martin, however, was nearly 30 miles per hour faster than the earlier aircraft and had a 31-percent lower zero-lift drag coefficient. The higher value of the lift-drag ratio of the F–5L resulted from the higher wing aspect ratio of this aircraft as compared with the PM–1. The lower aspect ratio of the Martin boat probably resulted from a design trade-off between aspect ratio and empty weight, in com-

Figure 8.8 — Martin PM–1 Navy patrol boat; 1929. [USN via Martin Copp]

bination with the effect on $C_{D,0}$ of more interplane bracing which would probably have been required for higher aspect ratio wings. The hull of the PM-1 was a refined version of the sponson-type, two-step hull employed on the F-5L and was of all-metal construction; the wings were of metal-frame structure covered with fabric and had thicker airfoil sections than those used on the F-5L.

Flying boats based on the PN-12 design, such as the PM-1, served the Navy until well into the 1930's. The U.S. Coast Guard also employed these aircraft and ordered several of those produced by the Hall Aluminum Company, the PH-3, as late as 1938.

The last and also the largest and highest performance biplane flying boat developed for the U.S. Navy was the Hall XP2H-1 shown in figure 8.9. (The largest biplane flying boat ever built was the Short Sarafand launched in England in 1932. It had a gross weight of 70 000 pounds, a wing span of 150 feet, and was equipped with six engines, mounted pusher-tractor style in three nacelles, totaling 5500 horsepower. The Sarafand, after service with the Royal Air Force, was scrapped in 1936.) The XP2H-1 was equipped with four in-line Curtiss V-12 engines of 600 horsepower each; the engines were configured in a

Figure 8.9 — Hall XP2H-1 four-engine Navy patrol boat; 1932. [USN via Martin Copp]

pusher-tractor arrangement in two streamlined nacelles mounted atop support pylons. The wings of the single-bay biplane were tapered, had a metal internal structure covered with metal sheet, and were braced with struts and wires. The single-step hull was of all-metal construction and had enclosed accommodations for the crew of six. Figure 8.9 shows a complex tail assembly featuring two fins and rudders mounted on top of a single horizontal surface, which in turn was attached to the hull by a single, low-aspect-ratio fin or pylon.

The data in table IV give a gross weight of 35 393 pounds for the XP2H–1 and a maximum speed of 139 miles per hour. The zero-lift drag coefficient of 0.0291 was about 40 percent lower than that of the Martin PM–1, and the maximum lift-drag ratio of 10.2 was about 30 percent higher than that of the Martin PM–1. At a much reduced speed, maximum endurance could be obtained by cruising on two engines, and the maximum range was estimated to be 4560 miles. Although the Hall XP2H–1 had very creditable performance, it arrived on the scene too late to compete effectively with the new monoplane flying boats that began to appear in the 1930's.

Ordered in 1930 and delivered to the Navy in the fall of 1932, the XP2H–1 was a one-of-a-kind aircraft. In 25 hours and 15 minutes, the aircraft made a notable nonstop flight from Norfolk, Virginia, to Panama in 1935. The pilot on this flight was Lt. John S. Thatch, who was destined for fame in World War II. The aircraft met an ignominious end later in 1935 when it sank during an open-sea landing attempt. The XP2H–1 represents the last in a long-lived line of United States-designed biplane flying boats.

Two Amphibian Developments

The amphibian flying boat is a unique type of aircraft equally at home operating from land or sea. Such aircraft trace their origins to early experiments by Glenn H. Curtiss, but the type did not gain popularity until the introduction of a highly innovative design produced in 1924 by the Loening Aeronautical Corporation. The Loening aircraft provided performance comparable to that of a landplane of similar size and performance, the DH–4, but offered the added capability of operation from either land or water. In an era of few airports, this versatility, coupled with high performance, was greatly appreciated. A photograph of a Loening OA–1C amphibian is presented in figure 8.10, and pertinent characteristics of the aircraft are given in table IV.

The Loening amphibian appears much as a conventional single-engine biplane but with the lower part of the fuselage configured as a single-step hull that extended forward of the engine and propeller. As can be seen in figure 8.10, the wheels could be retracted into cavities located on the sides of the hull for water operation. The entire configuration concept was made feasible by an inverted V–12 Liberty or Packard engine that placed the thrust line sufficiently high so that the propeller cleared the forward-projecting hull without, at the same time, causing a fuselage of excessive bulkiness. The two-bay biplane wing configuration was typical of the time period but was unique in utilizing the N-type interplane struts that eliminated much time-consuming effort in rigging the wings. The tip-mounted lateral stabilizing floats also incorporated skids to prevent damage in landplane operations.

The hull was of wood-frame construction covered with aluminum alloy sheets. Wooden spars and stamped aluminum alloy ribs comprised the wing structure, which was covered with fabric. Hand operation was required to retract the landing gear in early models, but actuation by an electric motor was provided in later versions. Open cockpits configured for two or three occupants were usually provided.

A comparison of the physical and performance characteristics of the OA–1C given in table IV with those of the DeHavilland DH–4 in table I indicates that the two aircraft are closely similar in size, power, weight, and performance. The added versatility of the Loening amphib-

Figure 8.10 — Loening OA–1C amphibian; 1924. [USAF via Martin Copp]

ian assured it of an important place in aeronautical activities in the 1920's and 1930's. Versions of the Loening amphibian were built not only by Loening but, after the demise of that company, by Keystone and even later by Grumman. The modernized version built by Grumman was in production well into the World War II years. These latter aircraft, designated Grumman JF and J2F were known as Ducks. All later versions of the aircraft employed radial air-cooled engines instead of the earlier water-cooled Liberty and Packard power plants. All three services of the United States—Army, Navy, and Coast Guard—as well as a number of civil operators utilized the aircraft. A civil version having a single cockpit and accommodations for four to six passengers in an enclosed cabin was available in addition to the military models. Loening amphibians participated in several record and exploratory flights that, together with descriptions of the aircraft and its development, are given in references 88 and 89.

Today, the name Igor Sikorsky is usually associated with the pioneer development of the helicopter; but in earlier years, he was known as the father of a number of multiengine aircraft, including several excellent flying boats and amphibians. One of these, the S–38 amphibian, first appeared in 1928 and established the great Russian designer in the United States. Serving in a number of pioneer airline operations, notably Pan American Airways, the aircraft was also used by various military services and in several exploratory operations.

A side view of the S–38 is shown in figure 8.11. In configuration concept, the aircraft was reminiscent of the NC boats described earlier and consisted of a short hull with the tail assembly attached to outriggers extending from the upper wing of the sesquiplane wing arrangement. Power was supplied by two Pratt & Whitney nine-cylinder radial air-cooled engines mounted side by side in nacelles located between the wings. A large number of struts integrated the hull, wings, tail assembly, and engines into a unified configuration. Lateral stabilizing floats were located beneath the tips of the lower wings, and the landing wheels retracted into the sides of the hull. A unique feature of the landing gear was the capability for lowering the wheels individually. One might question the advisability of such an action, but turning moments were produced by the water drag of one extended landing gear; thus steering capability, always a problem while maneuvering on the water at low speeds, was enhanced. Another interesting feature was incorporated in the vertical tail surfaces that were cambered and laterally spaced so that one surface was in the slipstream of each propeller. In the event of the failure of one engine, the cambered surface in the slip-

Figure 8.11 — Sikorsky S–38 10-passenger amphibian; 1928. [Joseph P. Juptner via AAHS]

stream of the other engine produced a yawing moment opposite in direction to that caused by the power loss. The relative magnitude of the two opposing yawing moments is not known.

Ten passengers and a crew of two could be accommodated in the short, single-step hull formed from a wooden frame covered with aluminum-alloy sheets. Before passage through the hump speed, large quantities of spray passed through the propellers and covered the windshield, effectively blinding the pilots. Although the aircraft was built for a number of years and various fixes were attempted, the spray problem on the S–38 was never effectively solved. Wings of the aircraft consisted of a metal structure covered with fabric.

According to the data in table IV, the S–38B had a gross weight of 10 480 pounds, a wing span of 71.7 feet, and a top speed of 125 miles per hour. Although the Sikorsky S–38 was somewhat smaller than the Martin PM–1, the performance of the two aircraft was nearly the same. The values of the zero-lift drag coefficient and the maximum lift-drag ratio were not those of an aircraft known for outstanding aerodynamic efficiency, but the ruggedness and operational flexibility of the S–38 made it well suited for many diverse roles.

186

About 120 examples of the S–38 were constructed, and its configuration served as a basis for the single-engine S–39 and the large four-engine S–40 flying boat operated by Pan American Airways. The S–41 was a further refinement of the twin-engine S–38, but the high-drag configuration of this series of aircraft was abandoned in favor of arrangements of higher aerodynamic efficiency in subsequent Sikorsky flying boats and amphibians.

Design Transformation, 1930–40

The 1930's saw a transformation in the American flying boat from a clumsy biplane of low aerodynamic efficiency, typified by the Martin PM–1, to the highly efficient monoplane types, like the Boeing 314, which appeared near the end of the decade. The impetus for this metamorphosis came from military requirements for increased performance as well as from the stimulus of commercial competition. As indicated in chapter 4, rapid advancements in aeronautical technology were being made in this time period that provided the basis for improved flying-boat design. In the following discussion, attention is first directed toward two early monoplane developments; after which three, large, long-range, passenger-carrying boats are described; and finally, three general-aviation-type flying boats are presented.

Early Monoplane Developments

Nonstop flights between the mainland of the United States and Panama, Alaska, and the Hawaiian Islands were major performance objectives for future Navy flying boats as the decade of the 1920's drew to a close. In response to the requirement for this mission capability, the prototype of a new breed of flying boat, the Consolidated XPY–1, appeared in January 1929. The aircraft, which represented a marked change in patrol-boat design, was a twin-engine strut-braced monoplane built to Navy plans and specifications. The prototype offered sufficiently improved performance so that bids were sought by the Navy for production of a number of similar boats. The Martin company was the winner of the production contract, and the resulting aircraft was designated the P3M–1. With this start, both Martin and Consolidated began a series of patrol-boat developments that extended into the 1950's.

Not to be outdone by the loss of the Navy contract, Consolidated offered a passenger-carrying version of their aircraft, which became known as the Commodore. A photograph of this flying boat, figure 8.12, depicts a parasol monoplane with the wing mounted well above the hull on a bridgelike arrangement of struts that also served to support the two engines located below the wing, as well as the lateral stabilizing floats. The entire layout suggests a high-drag aircraft; this is confirmed by the zero-lift drag coefficient of 0.0562, which is about 18 percent higher than that given for the Martin PM–1 biplane. The actual drag area of the two aircraft, however, is seen to be nearly the same. The high-aspect-ratio monoplane wing of the Commodore give it a maximum lift-drag ratio about 22 percent higher than that of the PM–1 and thus offered the potential for higher cruising efficiency and longer range than the older aircraft. On the other hand, values of both the zero-lift drag coefficient and the maximum lift-drag ratio of the Commodore compare unfavorably with those of the Hall XP2H–1 biplane. Going to a monoplane configuration was a step in the right direction, but the aerodynamic data for the Commodore indicate that the potential of the monoplane wing arrangement was not realized because of the many drag-producing elements, such as struts and uncowled engines, that were present in the design.

Other features of the Commodore were its single-step all-metal hull that could accommodate 32 passengers and a crew of 3. The full complement of passengers, located in three cabins, could only be car-

Figure 8.12 — Consolidated Commodore 32-passenger flying boat; 1931. [NASM]

ried on relatively short-route segments. For a 1000-mile flight, the boat probably could accommodate no more than 14 people including the crew (author's estimate). Wing and tail construction consisted of metal-frame structure covered with fabric except for metal-covered leading edges.

With a first flight in 1931, a total of 14 Commodore boats were built. They were used in airline service from the United States to South America where routes extended as far south as Buenos Aires, a distance of 9000 miles from Miami. They were out of service by 1935, having been superseded by more efficient aircraft such as the Sikorsky S-42. The Commodore may be considered as a first step in the United States along a road that was to lead to the highly efficient monoplane-type patrol and transport flying boats later in the 1930's. The XPY-1 and its civil counterpart the Commodore may be considered as progenitors in a series of flying-boat developments that led to the famous Consolidated PBY Catalina of World War II fame.

Although emphasis in the present volume is placed on aircraft developed in the United States, no discussion of the evolution of the monoplane flying boat would be complete without mention of the pioneering work of Dr. Claude Dornier, the German designer. As described in reference 68, he envisioned large, all-metal flying boats before the end of World War I, and such an aircraft was designed, but not built, before the end of that conflict.

In 1922, a twin-engine monoplane flying boat known as the Dornier Wal (whale), very similar to the earlier 1918 design, was first flown. This aircraft featured a single wing located a short distance above the hull with the two engines mounted in a single nacelle, tractor-pusher fashion, on top of the wing. This arrangement reduced the number and length of struts inherent in the Consolidated Commodore-type of arrangement in which the wing was high above the hull with the engines mounted below. So successful was the Dornier Wal that variants of the basic design remained in production until 1936, and Dornier flying boats of the same general configuration were used by the German Luftwaffe throughout the years of World War II. Even today proposals have been made for production of a refined version of a World War II Dornier flying boat equipped with turboprop engines.

The ultimate in the Wal configuration concept found expression in one of the most remarkable aircraft, either landplane or flying boat, ever built: the Dornier Do X, which first flew in 1929. This unique flying boat was the largest aircraft ever constructed up to that time and had a gross weight variously listed as 105 820 or 123 459 pounds. The lower value was probably the design gross weight; the higher, likely an allowable overweight condition for special long-range flights. In the United States, no aircraft exceeded the gross weight of the Do X until the one-of-a-kind experimental Douglas XB–19, at a gross weight of about 140 000 pounds, flew in 1941, and the Boeing B–29 bomber of World War II fame was the first production aircraft to have a higher gross weight. Incredibly, the Do X was powered by 12 engines. They were positioned in six nacelles, tractor-pusher style, strut-mounted on top of the wing. Tests were made with several different engines in the three Do X aircraft that were built. The data in table IV are for the version powered with 12-cylinder Curtiss V–1570 water-cooled engines of 640 horsepower each, a total of 7680 horsepower. Perhaps fortunately, no other aircraft has ever been equipped with so many engines. One can only guess at the difficulties encountered in keeping all of them operating simultaneously in an efficient manner.

A photograph of the Do X is presented in figure 8.13. As can be seen, the monoplane wing was mounted flush with the top of the hull-fuselage, and the six engine nacelles were located on struts above the wing. Instead of lateral stabilizing floats, short stub wings, called sponsons, projecting from the sides of the hull near the waterline provided lateral stability in the water. Each wing was braced by three struts extending upward and outward from near the tip of the sponsons. In turn, the sponsons were braced by three additional struts extending downward and outward from near the top of the hull to about the mid-

Figure 8.13 — German Dornier Do X flying boat with 12 engines; 1929. [NASM]

point of the sponsors. Two sets of horizontal tail surfaces of different size were configured in a sesquiplane arrangement, and directional stability and control were provided by a single fin and rudder. To reduce pilot control forces needed to maneuver so large an aircraft, small surfaces connected to the main control surface, called park-bench balances, were mounted above and ahead of the elevator and aileron hinge lines.

The all-metal hull had a modified vee bottom with a single transverse step and an afterbody that tapered to a sharp vertical stern post. To assist in maneuvering on the water, a small rudder was mounted at the stern post. Accommodations in the hull were divided among three decks. On the top deck were the pilots' compartment, navigation room, captain's cabin, and flight-engineers' compartment. Instruments and controls for operating the battery of 12 engines were located at the engineers' station. The passengers were carried on the second deck, which had several cabins with seats and sleeping accommodations as well as a bar and smoking and writing rooms. Cabins were spacious, and appointments included wood paneling, rugs, and other features of contemporary luxury liners of that day. Perhaps some of the weight of this equipment was more appropriate to a surface ship than an aircraft where lightness is an essential ingredient of efficient flight. But the 66 passengers for which the aircraft was configured no doubt traveled in a regal style unknown today. (On one occasion, 150 passengers, 10 crew, and 9 stowaways were carried on one short record flight.) Fuel and stores were carried on the lower deck.

The wing and tail surfaces consisted of a metal framework covered mostly with fabric. Having an area of 4844 square feet and a span of 157.5 feet, the large wing was sufficiently thick to incorporate walkways on which a person could pass through the inside of the wing. Access to the engines for maintenance was provided by hatches above the walkways at each engine nacelle position. Whether or not work on the engines was performed in flight is not known.

With a maximum speed of 134 miles per hour and an estimated cruising speed of 122 miles per hour at 75 percent power, the performance of the Do X appears, at first glance, to be very creditable (table IV). The zero-lift drag coefficient of 0.0472 was also as low or lower than most contemporary flying boats. Because of the low wing aspect ratio of 5.12, however, the maximum lift-drag ratio was a low 7.7, a full 22 percent lower than that of the Consolidated Commodore. In addition, the useful load fraction (ratio of payload weight plus fuel weight to gross weight) was only 27 percent for the 105 820-pound gross weight condition. By comparison, the useful load fraction for the Commodore was 35 percent and for the World War I vintage NC–4, 42 percent. The useful load fraction of modern jet transports varies between 45 and 55 percent, as can be seen from the data given in part II for transport aircraft. The combination of low maximum lift-drag ratio and small useful load fraction doomed the Do X as a commercial airplane capable of carrying an economically attractive payload on transoceanic routes. For example, estimates (by the author) suggest that at a gross takeoff weight of 105 820 pounds, including 66 passengers and a crew of 6, the maximum achievable range was between 600 and 650 miles at a cruising speed of 108 miles per hour at sea level.

A total of three Do X aircraft, including two for the Italian government, were constructed. None of these proved to be commercially viable. Yet the aircraft must be considered as an engineering achievement of considerable magnitude for the time; it showed that very large aircraft could be built and indicated some of the problems of such aircraft. Preserved for many years in a Berlin museum, the original Do X was destroyed in an Allied bombing raid during World War II.

The Flying Clipper Ships

Operated by Pan American Airways with substantial support from the U.S. Government, three types of large, four-engine flying boats pioneered long-range commercial flights across the Atlantic and Pacific Oceans in the latter half of the 1930's. In honor of the fast sailing ships that crossed the Pacific from China in the 19th century, these aircraft were collectively known as Clipper ships and each had a specific designation such as China Clipper or Dixie Clipper. Even today, Pan American applies the name Clipper to each of its jet transports.

The three legendary Clipper types of the 1930's were the Sikorsky S–42, the Martin 130, and the Boeing 314. These aircraft types are illustrated in figures 8.14, 8.15, and 8.16, respectively. Their appearance suggests a technical era far in advance of that of such earlier boats as the Martin PM–1 and the Consolidated Commodore. Indeed, as described in chapter 4, aeronautical technology had made significant advances by the mid-1930's; and just as the Boeing 247 and Douglas DC–3 represented a higher level of technology than the earlier Ford trimotor, so too were the Sikorsky, Martin, and Boeing flying boats the products of an advanced technological age.

Figure 8.14 — Sikorsky S–42 four-engine 32-passenger flying boat; 1934. [NASM]

Some of the significant design features of these flying boats were the following:

(1) All three aircraft were equipped with four radial air-cooled engines enclosed in drag-reducing NACA cowlings and were mounted, side by side, in the wing leading edge. This type of installation resulted in significant aerodynamic drag reductions as compared with strut-mounted engine nacelles located above or below the wing. In addition, the leading-edge engine installation allowed the wing to be mounted on or slightly above the top of the hull, thus reducing the length and drag of any supporting wing struts while, at the same time, keeping the propellers sufficiently high to avoid a major spray problem.

(2) Some form of variable pitch propeller was employed on all three boats. Their use resulted in an important increase in available power and efficiency over the speed-altitude operating envelope of the aircraft.

Figure 8.15 — Martin model 130 China Clipper class passenger-carrying flying boat; 1934. [mfr]

Figure 8.16 — Boeing model 314 four-engine passenger-carrying flying boat; 1938. [NASM]

(3)   Wing flaps were incorporated on all three aircraft. Flaps permitted the use of higher wing loadings for more efficient cruise flight, together with smaller and thus lighter wings, without increased stalling speeds.

(4)   All three aircraft were constructed of metal with certain small portions covered with fabric.

(5)   The Sikorsky S–42 had tip floats for lateral stabilization, whereas both the Martin and Boeing aircraft utilized sponsons for this purpose. These small surfaces were also used for fuel tanks and served as convenient ramps for embarking passengers.

(6)   While the Boeing 314 had full cantilever wings, the Sikorsky and Martin aircraft were characterized by a limited number of supporting wing struts.

(7)   The S–42 and Martin 130 had hulls with two transverse steps. The Boeing 314 had a single-step hull with an afterbody tapering to a sharp stern post.

The features cited above do indeed illustrate marked advances in flying-boat design as compared with aircraft discussed earlier. Some of the important quantitative characteristics of the three aircraft are compared in the following tabulation (other data are given in table IV):

Aircraft	W_g	V_{max}	$C_{D,0}$	$(L/D)_{max}$	$\overline{U}$	R_h
Sikorsky S–42	38 000	182	0.0362	12.2	0.37	2914
Martin 130	52 252	180	0.0303	11.9	0.53	4816
Boeing 314	84 000	201	0.0274	13.0	0.43	4059

where

W_g	gross weight
V_{max}	maximum speed
$C_{D,0}$	zero-lift drag coefficient
$(L/D)_{max}$	maximum lift-drag coefficient
$\overline{U}$	useful load fraction, $1 - (W_e/W_g)$, where W_e is empty weight
R_h	hypothetical range

The hypothetical range was estimated on the assumption of the weight of a four-member crew, with the remainder of the difference between gross and empty weights being taken up by fuel. The hypothetical range gives an indication of the range potential of the aircraft but corresponds to no real value because of restricted fuel-tank volume.

The tabulation shows that the Sikorsky S–42 was the lightest of the three aircraft, with a gross weight of 38 000 pounds. To lend perspective to this weight, the heaviest landplane transport in production in the United States at the time the S–42 first flew was the Douglas DC–2; it had a gross weight of 18 560 pounds. At a gross weight of 84 000 pounds, the Boeing 314 was by far the heaviest of the three boats. The maximum speed of the Boeing boat was also about 20 miles per hour faster than the 180 miles per hour of the other two aircraft.

Although the zero-lift drag coefficients varied significantly for the three aircraft, the corresponding values of the maximum lift-drag ratio showed a more modest variation, with the Boeing 314 having an improvement of about 8 percent as compared with the other aircraft. The useful load fraction of the Martin 130, however, was higher by 43 and 23 percent than for the S–42 and 314, respectively. As a consequence, the hypothetical range of the Martin 130 was the greatest of the three aircraft. Although the maximum lift-drag ratio of the Boeing 314 was somewhat higher than that of the Martin 130, the large useful load fraction of the Martin gave it a 757-mile, or 19-percent, advantage in hypothetical range over the Boeing. These comparisons of hypothetical range suggest the careful attention the designer must give to detail trade-off studies of weight and aerodynamic efficiency. An interesting indication of progress in flying-boat design during the 1930's is given by a comparison of the 4816-mile hypothetical range of the Martin 130 to the corresponding value of 1760 miles for the Consolidated Commodore, which first flew only a few years earlier.

The great flying clippers occupy a permanent place in the annals of transport aviation history. Present-day accounts by passengers who once flew on these aircraft speak of them with great affection and nostalgia. In spaciousness and comfort, they offered a means of air transportation as outmoded today as the luxury railway trains and steamships of the distant past.

First of the new-generation flying clippers was the Sikorsky S–42, which made its maiden flight on March 29, 1934, and began airline service between Miami and Rio de Janeiro on August 16 of that same year, an indication of the rapidity with which a transport aircraft could be flight tested and certified in that long-gone and technically simpler age. As the range-payload characteristics of the S–42 did not suit it for passenger service on the long overwater routes of the Pacific, the aircraft was used primarily on South American segments of the Pan American system. Equipped with extra fuel tanks, however, the S–42 made route-survey flights in the Pacific in 1935 and in the North Atlantic in

1937. For normal passenger operations, the aircraft was configured to carry 32 passengers, with 8 in each of 4 compartments, and a crew of 4 or 5. With this payload, the aircraft is estimated to have had a range of about 1200 miles. A total of 10 S–42 flying boats were built; 4 of these survived World War II and were broken up for salvage in 1946.

Chronologically, the second of the flying clippers, and the one most often associated with early trans-Pacific passenger-carrying operations, was the Martin 130, which made its first flight on December 30, 1934. Three of these aircraft were constructed and were christened China Clipper, Philippine Clipper, and Hawaiian Clipper. Generically, the type is referred to as the China Clipper. Proving flights were made in the Pacific during 1935 and the first part of 1936. Between November 22 and December 6, 1936, the China Clipper made the first commercial crossing of the Pacific Ocean from San Francisco to Manila. The 8210-mile flight was divided into five stages with intermediate stops in Hawaii, Midway, and Wake and Guam Islands. Five days and 60 flying hours were required for the flight. Later, the route was extended to Hong Kong.

The Martin 130 was configured to carry 41 passengers in 2 cabins with a spacious lounge in between. Actually, to allow for the weight of mail and light cargo, as well as a generous supply of reserve fuel, only 12 passengers were carried on trans-Pacific flights. A passenger on one of these flights once referred to rattling around in the spacious accommodations. The captain, first officer, radio operator, flight engineer, and steward comprised the usual crew of five.

Each of the Martin Clippers met a violent end. While on a flight from Guam to Manila in July 1938, the Hawaiian Clipper simply vanished. No trace of wreckage, no oil slick, nothing was ever found, and radio transmissions from the aircraft had given no hint of trouble. Even today, over 40 years later, speculation on the disaster continues, just as it does on the disappearance of Amelia Earhart in 1937. In January 1943, the Philippine Clipper was destroyed, along with everyone aboard, while on a flight from Hawaii to San Francisco. At the time of arrival in the San Francisco area, bad weather prevailed and the captain elected to fly a holding pattern until conditions improved. Unfortunately, a navigational error caused the aircraft to fly into a mountain east of San Francisco. According to some accounts, bits of the Philippine Clipper can still be found on the lonely mountainside where it crashed so many years ago. Finally, after flying millions of miles over a 10-year period, the famous China Clipper was lost while attempting a night landing at Trinidad in January 1945. All 25 persons aboard perished.

The last, the largest, and the most advanced of the flying clippers was the Boeing 314, which first flew in June 1938. Twelve of these flying boats were built, and they gave fast, comfortable, and reliable service for many years. Both Atlantic and Pacific routes were served by the Boeing 314. On June 28, 1939, the first regular, nonstop, trans-Atlantic service was inaugurated by the Dixie Clipper with a flight from New York City to Lisbon, Portugal. Several of the Boeing Clippers were transferred to the British Overseas Airways Corporation during the war, and one of these was used by British Prime Minister Winston Churchill on a round-trip flight from the British Isles to the United States in 1942. Photographs of the aircraft and of Churchill taking a turn at the controls were released after the flight, and the Boeing 314 became familiar to millions of people all over the world.

The interior of the Boeing Clipper was designed to accommodate 74 day passengers and a crew of 10. With this number of people aboard, the maximum range was estimated (by the author) to have been about 1900 miles. A range of 3685 miles is often found in specifications for the aircraft, but this range could only be achieved with a much-reduced passenger load. In an arrangement reminiscent of the Do X, crawlways in the wings connected the crew quarters in the hull to the engine nacelles, thus allowing simple engine repairs to be made in flight.

Because they were no longer competitive with high-performance, long-range landplanes, such as the Douglas DC-4, DC-6, and Lockheed Constellation, Pan American terminated operation of the Boeing 314 flying boats in 1946. Several of these aircraft were later used in nonscheduled operations. In forced landings at sea due to fuel starvation (poor flight planning), two of these aircraft demonstrated their seaworthiness when all passengers and crew members survived the open-sea landings unhurt and were later rescued by surface ships. All Boeing 314 operations ceased in 1950. So ended the colorful and pioneering era of the flying clippers.

The Flying Boat and General Aviation

Military and commercial operations are usually thought of as the principal arena of the flying boat. Yet almost from the beginning, flying boats have been operated by private individuals for sport, pleasure, and personal transportation and by small operators for short-range, commuter-type, passenger-carrying use. As early as 1913, versions of the Curtiss F boat were sold to private individuals, and in the early 1920's, the Loening air yacht was offered for both personal and commuter airline use. Later in the 1920's, a number of small flying boats and amphibians were produced. The single-engine Ireland amphibian and Eastman flying boat, both biplanes, as well as the civil version of the previously described Loening amphibian, appeared in this period. Described next are three general-aviation-type flying boats, actually amphibians, that appeared in the 1930's.

At a time when contemporary engineering practice called for a multitude of struts for support of flying-boat wings and engines, the Douglas Dolphin, shown in figure 8.17, clearly broke with tradition. This eight-place, twin-engine monoplane had a full cantilever wing located at the top of the hull, with the two radial engines strut mounted above the wing. Unlike the Loening amphibian, the landing gear did not retract into the hull for water operation but pivoted outward and upward at the juncture of the two lower struts with the side of the hull. A telescoping motion of the single long strut attached at the top of the hull permitted this action. The modified vee bottom hull had a single transverse step and a tapered afterbody that terminated in a sharp, vertical stern post. Structurally, the cantilever wing was of all-wood construction including the plywood covering, and the hull was all metal.

The aerodynamic cleanness of the Dolphin was somewhat marred by the strut-mounted engine installation and the exposed landing gear.

Figure 8.17 — Douglas Dolphin twin-engine utility amphibian; 1930. [mfr via Martin Copp]

Consequently, the $C_{D,0}$ and $(L/D)_{max}$ values of 0.0430 and 8.82, respectively, are somewhat disappointing. A maximum speed of 153 miles per hour, however, gave the 9387-pound amphibian an attractive performance, and the aircraft was certainly a long step ahead of contemporaneous flying boats such as the Martin PM-1. Although intended primarily for the civil market, most Dolphins were operated by the military services for various purposes. They continued to give good service as utility and search-and-rescue vehicles well into World War II. One Dolphin, in the hands of an antique airplane collector, is still flying today.

What must be regarded as one of the most long-lived flying boats ever produced was introduced by the Grumman Aircraft Engineering Corporation in 1937. Affectionately known as the Goose, the twin-engine Grumman G-21 is illustrated in figure 8.18. With the two cowled, 450-horsepower, radial, air-cooled engines mounted in the leading edge, the cantilever wing was located at the top of the hull. Lateral stabilization on the water was provided by tip-mounted floats, and the landing gear retracted neatly into the sides of the hull. Split trailing-edge flaps were incorporated in the wings, and power and efficiency were enhanced by controllable-pitch propellers. The aircraft was of all-metal construction except for the rear portion of the wing, which was covered with fabric. Depending on the interior arrangement, accommodations were provided in this 8000-pound aircraft for a crew of

Figure 8.18 — Grumman model G-21 Goose twin-engine utility amphibian; 1937.
[NASA]

two or three and four to seven passengers. The data in table IV indicate a maximum speed of approximately 200 miles per hour and values of $C_{D,0}$ and $(L/D)_{max}$ of 0.0325 and 10.5, respectively — a good performance even today for such a versatile aircraft.

The Goose has been used by private owners, airlines, charter operators, and the military services. Even today, 45 years after its introduction, at least two short-haul airlines utilizing water and land facilities employ the Grumman Goose in daily operation.

Serving as the first of a series of amphibian flying boats of similar configuration but different size, the Goose was followed in 1939 by the 4525-pound Widgeon, the 12 750-pound Mallard in 1946, and the 32 000-pound Albatros in 1947. Extensively used by the U.S. Navy, Coast Guard, and Air Force, the last Navy Albatros was retired in 1976 although the Coast Guard retained a few of these aircraft in active service for a while longer. Today, a completely remanufactured Albatros is being offered by Grumman for civil use by short-haul airlines employing water- and land-based facilities.

Intended strictly for the private owner, the four-place, single-engine Fleetwings F–5 Seabird amphibian is shown in figure 8.19. The monoplane wing was mounted on top of the hull and braced with wires that ran from the side of the hull to the wing and from the wing to the strut-mounted engine nacelle above the wing. For operation on the water, the landing gear was retracted in such a way that the wheels projected horizontally from the sides of the hull, well above the waterline, and all struts were buried either in the wing or sides of the hull. In the photograph, the tail wheel and water rudder are clearly visible behind the stern post of the single step hull. Lateral stabilizing floats were located near the wingtips.

The Fleetwings Seabird illustrates a basic problem that faces the designer of a single-engine flying boat. Most single-engine landplanes have the engine mounted in the nose. Obviously, this solution is not available to the flying-boat designer except for some restricted types of configuration such as the Loening amphibian. Many single-engine amphibians have employed pusher or tractor engine arrangements similar in concept to that of the Seabird. Struts and, sometimes, single streamlined pylons have been used to support the engine nacelle. In addition to considerations of center-of-gravity location, thrust line position, and spray avoidance, the engine must be located so that the rotating propeller poses no threat to persons leaving or entering the aircraft, or in case of blade failure, to persons sitting in the cabin. These various constraints frequently lead to a pusher configuration.

Figure 8.19 — Fleetwings model F–5 Seabird four-place single-engine amphibian; circa 1937. [Peter C. Boisseau]

To avoid the corrosion problem inherent in the operating environment of flying boats, extensive use was made of stainless steel in the structure of the Seabird. Both the internal structure and the covering of the hull of the aircraft were of stainless steel. The internal framework of the wings and tail surfaces were also formed of stainless steel, but these surfaces were covered with fabric. Wrinkles are evident in the skin of the hull (fig. 8.19), which indicates the extreme thinness of the metal covering. According to reference 81, the engine-turned pattern of the metal skin was intended to disguise the wrinkles.

With a 285 Jacobs radial air-cooled engine, the 3750-pound Seabird had a maximum speed of 150 miles per hour and a landing speed of 53 miles per hour. The aircraft thus offered good performance and operational flexibility for the private owner, without an alarmingly high landing speed and with a modest amount of power that promised relatively low hourly fuel consumption. The Seabird first flew sometime in the late 1930's. The total number built is not known, but at least one is still flying today in the hands of an antique airplane collector.

Boats at War, 1940–45

The primitive multistrut monoplane patrol boats produced by Consolidated and Martin in the late 1920's and early 1930's have been mentioned earlier. Fortunately, under the impetus of encouragement in the form of small contracts, both companies continued to develop improved forms of patrol boats during the period 1930–1940. Consequently, when war came to the United States in December 1941, the Navy had in hand two excellent twin-engine patrol boats as well as a new four-engine flying boat.

By any measure, the Consolidated PBY Catalina was the most successful patrol boat ever built. First flown in March 1935, 2398 Catalinas were built in this country, and a number were constructed under license in other countries, including Russia. In addition to the United States forces, British, Canadian, French, Australian, and Dutch forces used the PBY in World War II. After the war's end in 1945, the aircraft continued to be used by various military forces in different parts of the world, and a 22-passenger version was in use as an airliner in South America. Even today, a few Catalinas may be found employed in different activities. Certainly, the aircraft has been used, at one time or another, for every purpose for which a flying boat might be used — and perhaps a few never dreamed of by the designers.

The PBY was initially designed and produced as a pure flying boat; however, two later versions were amphibians. One of these, a PBY–5A, is depicted in figure 8.20. Although descended from the PY–1 and Commodore series of aircraft, the PBY family bore little resemblance to these earlier flying boats. As can be seen from the photograph, the semicantilever monoplane wing with engines mounted in the leading edge was positioned a short distance above the hull on a streamlined pylon. Two short struts on either side of the hull helped support the wing and engines. The hull itself had a single transverse step with an afterbody tapering to a sharp, vertical stern post. No means of lateral stabilization is evident in the photograph since the floats used for this purpose were retractable and formed part of the wingtip in the stowed position. They were, of course, extended only when the aircraft operated from the water. Controllable-pitch propellers were used, but the aircraft had no flaps, which accounted for the relatively high estimated stalling speed of 79 miles per hour.

Innovative is a word that might justifiably be used to describe the configuration of the PBY series of aircraft. The values of $C_{D,0}$ and $(L/D)_{max}$ of 0.0309 and 11.9 indicate a relatively aerodynamically clean flying boat for its time. The maximum and cruising speed of 179 and 117 miles per hour were not particularly fast but were satisfactory for a World War II patrol boat. The Catalina was of all-metal construction except for the trailing-edge portion of the wing and the control surfaces, which were covered with fabric.

Figure 8.20 — Consolidated PBY–5A Catalina twin-engine Navy patrol boat; World War II era. [NASA]

Accommodations in the Catalina provided for a gunner located in the nose, side-by-side seating for the pilot and copilot behind the nose gunner, a navigator/radio station behind the pilots, and a flight engineer's station located in the pylon supporting the wing. Figure 8.20 shows a small window in the pylon for use by the flight engineer. Located in the hull behind the wing were two gunners in transparent blisters on either side of the aircraft. Some aircraft also had a gun that could be fired downward and to the rear through an inclined tunnel that opened on the bottom behind the stern post of the hull. For offensive operations, the PBY–5A could carry either 2000 pounds of bombs, two torpedoes, or four 325-pound depth charges. The range of the aircraft, of course, varied with the payload. For purely patrol operations without any bombs, etc., the range given in reference 118 is 2545 miles. Surely, the Catalina must rank as one of the great flying boats of all time.

With the great clarity afforded by 20–20 hindsight, questions are sometimes raised as to whether a particular aircraft should have been developed at all, not necessarily because the aircraft considered as a flying machine was inferior but because of flaws in the operational concepts that engendered its development. Such questions surround the only four-engine patrol boat operated by the United States in World War II, the Consolidated PB2Y Coronado series of aircraft.

A 1936 Navy requirement for a long-range, four-engine patrol boat capable of carrying a greater payload than the PBY was responsible for the Coronado family of aircraft. The prototype first flew in December 1937; a later version of the aircraft, the PB2Y–2, is depicted in figure 8.21, and physical and performance characteristics of the PB2Y–3 may be found in table IV.

In configuration concept, the PB2Y was similar in many respects to the Boeing 314 (fig. 8.16) with the wing positioned on top of the deep, large-volume hull and the four radial air-cooled engines mounted in the wing leading edge, two on either side of the hull. In contrast to the sponsons used for lateral stabilization of the Boeing 314, however, the PB2Y had retractable wingtip floats similar to those on the Catalina. These floats and their supporting struts are clearly visible in figure 8.21, as are details of the bottom of the single transverse step hull. Although wheels are visible in the photograph, these were used only for beaching and ground handling. The aircraft was not an amphibian. The PB2Y was a thoroughly modern aircraft for its day and featured all-metal construction, trailing-edge flaps, controllable-pitch propellers, and engines equipped with two-stage superchargers for high-altitude operation.

The similarity between the configuration of the Boeing 314 and the Consolidated PB2Y has already been mentioned. A comparison of the data in table IV further highlights the similarities and differences between the two aircraft. The zero-lift drag coefficient and the maximum lift-drag ratio of the two aircraft were about the same. The

Figure 8.21 — Consolidated PB2Y–2 Coronado four-engine Navy patrol boat; World War II era. [Ray Wagner via AAHS]

Boeing, however, was 23 percent heavier, had more wing area and thus more drag area, and more power than the Consolidated boat. Both aircraft first flew with a single vertical fin and shared a common aerodynamic problem. In their initial form, both the 314 and the PB2Y had insufficient lateral-directional stability, no doubt caused by the large side area of the deep hull forward of the center of gravity. Boeing solved the problem by adding two additional fins, one on either side of the original center fin, near the tips of the horizontal stabilizer (fig. 8.16). The Consolidated solution consisted of eliminating the center fin and placing large vertical surfaces at the tip of each side of the horizontal tail and introducing a small amount of dihedral in the horizontal surfaces. Although great progress had been made during the 1930's in achieving an understanding of the science and art of aerodynamics, the lateral-directional problems of the Boeing and Consolidated boats clearly showed that more was yet to be learned.

As an instrument of war, the PB2Y could carry 12 000 pounds of bombs, had eight machine guns, six of them in pairs of two located in power-operated turrets, and was equipped with self-sealing fuel tanks and a certain amount of armour plate. It had a maximum ferry range of 3120 miles and could carry 8000 pounds of bombs for a distance of 1380 miles.

Although the Coronado seemed to have considerable potential as a patrol bomber, it saw little operational use in this role. The basic problem was one of cost effectiveness. A Coronado cost three times as much as a Catalina. Yet it is doubtful that a single Coronado could effectively patrol as large an ocean area as three Catalinas or whether the one large aircraft could attack a single surface target with as high a probability of success as three of the smaller boats. Questions such as these limited the operational use of the PB2Y as a weapon of war. As a consequence, most Coronados were used in freight or passenger/carrying roles and all were retired from the Navy by the end of 1945. Total production of all versions of the aircraft was only 217. The Coronado is an illustration of how a basically good aircraft was little used because of faulty assumptions in the formulation of the basic requirements for the aircraft.

In the years of World War II, a worthy stablemate of the workhorse Catalina was the Martin PBM Mariner series of patrol boats. The prototype made its initial flight in December 1939; before production ended 10 years later, 1360 examples of the Mariner, including many different versions, had been constructed. The last Mariner was retired from the U.S. Navy in 1958.

Figure 8.22 — Two versions of the Martin PBM Mariner twin-engine Navy patrol boat; World War II era. [mfr via Martin Copp]

Four different Mariners are depicted in figure 8.22, and a PBM–3D was used in figure 8.1 to illustrate certain general features of flying-boat design. Early versions of the PBM incorporated retractable tip floats similar in concept to those employed on the PBY and the PB2Y. Because of difficulties experienced with them, however, all versions of the Mariner beginning with the PBM–3 were equipped with fixed, tip-mounted floats. The two aircraft in the foreground of figure 8.22 had retractable floats, and those in the background were later versions of the aircraft with fixed floats.

Perhaps the most unusual feature of the PBM configuration was the gull shape of the full cantilever wing, with the engines located at the juncture of the wing break on either side of the hull. This particular wing-engine arrangement was intended to minimize spray passage through the propellers and, together with the relatively deep hull, served as an alternate to the shallow hull and pylon wing mounting of the PBY. Another distinctive feature of the Mariner configuration was the two vertical-tail surfaces mounted at the tips of the horizontal tail. And like the PB2Y, dihedral was incorporated in the horizontal surface. This particular empennage design probably gave improved directional control with one failed engine, as compared with a single fin configuration, and assisted in minimizing spray impingement on the tail. Of modern all-metal construction, the PBM also had trailing-edge flaps and controllable-pitch propellers. Although most versions of the Mariner were pure flying boats, a few were completed as amphibians in 1948 and 1949. A number of transport versions were also built.

A comparison of the data in table IV shows that the PBM–3D was a larger aircraft than the PBY–5A. For example, the Mariner was 52 percent heavier and had 58 percent more power than the Catalina, but the two aircraft had about the same wing and drag areas. As would be expected, both the maximum and cruising speeds of the Mariner were somewhat higher than those of the Catalina, as was the value of the maximum lift-drag ratio.

The PBM–3D had eight .50–caliber machine guns and 1058 pounds of defensive armament and could carry either bombs or depth charges housed behind the engines in lengthened nacelles in the PBM–3D and later versions of the Mariner. A total of eight 325-pound depth charges could be carried. The range potential of the aircraft varied with the payload. For example, the ferry range with no payload was 3000 miles, and with four 325-pound depth charges, the aircraft was capable of a range of 2580 miles.

Like all highly successful aircraft, the Mariner was produced in many versions, with different engines, different equipment, and different capabilities. The data in table IV are for only one version, the PBM–3D. Complete descriptions of the various versions of the Mariner, as well as the Catalina and the Coronado, may be found in references 64, 109, and 118.

Twilight of an Era, 1945–

Although the Boeing 314, last of the four-engine, commercial flying boats developed in the United States, was first flown in 1938 and scheduled commercial operations of these aircraft ended in 1946, limited flying-boat development continued for some years following the end of World War II. The Grumman Mallard, for private and short-haul use, and the Albatros, for military missions, have already been mentioned. An ambitious flying-boat project begun during the war, the Hughes H–4 Hercules, reached fruition in 1947. With a wing of 320-foot span and an area of 11 430 square feet (the Boeing 747 has a wing area of 5500 square feet), the H–4 was, and is, the largest (in terms of dimensional size) airplane ever built. Powered by eight Pratt & Whitney 28-cylinder radial air-cooled engines of 3000 horsepower each, the aircraft was unique in being constructed almost entirely of wood. This material was used to conserve strategically important aluminum alloys during World War II. One flight at an altitude of 70 feet and of about 1 mile in length was made by the aircraft at the hands of pilot Howard Hughes in November 1947. It never flew again but was preserved by the eccentric Mr. Hughes in an environmentally controlled hangar at Long Beach, California, for over 30 years. Today, the aircraft, an experiment that somehow failed, can be seen by the public, along with the ex-luxury liner *Queen Mary,* at Long Beach.

An interesting postwar experiment that received greater success than the Hughes H-4 was the turboprop-powered Convair R3Y Tradewind transport. Originally conceived as a patrol boat, this 123 500-pound aircraft was equipped with four 5100-shaft-horsepower Allison engines, each driving two three-blade contrarotating propellers. Ultimately used by the U.S. Navy as passenger and cargo transports in the 1956–58 time period, a total of 11 of these aircraft were built; some were used for experimental purposes, others were lost, and the remainder were retired in 1958 because of persistent propeller and gear-box problems.

During the postwar period, two large, new flying boats, both built by Martin, successfully served with the U.S. Navy. These were the JRM Mars cargo transport and the P5M Marlin patrol boat. Based on the earlier XPB2M-1 patrol bomber (later converted to a transport), 20 of the JRM transports were ordered in January 1945. Following the cessation of hostilities, however, the order was reduced to six aircraft. First flight took place in July 1945, and the last of the six flying boats had been delivered by the fall of 1947. The last one completed, designated JRM-2, was heavier and had more powerful engines than the JRM-1, for which data are given in table IV.

With its full cantilever wing mounted at the top of the hull and the four radial engines located in the leading edge of the wing, the JRM had a configuration that, by the 1940's, had become nearly standard for large flying boats. The JRM-1 Hawaiian Mars is shown taking off from the water in figure 8.23. With a wing span of 200 feet and a gross weight of 145 000 pounds (165 000 pounds for the JRM-2), the Mars was the largest operational flying boat ever developed in the United States. Equipped with four Wright R-3350-8 double-row, 18-cylinder engines of 2200 horsepower each at takeoff, the JRM-1 was capable of maximum and cruising speeds of 222 and 153 miles per hour. With split trailing-edge flaps and a wing loading of 39.4 pounds per square foot, the aircraft had an estimated stalling speed at gross weight of 88 miles per hour.

209

Figure 8.23 — The 145 000-pound Martin JRM-1 Mars cargo transport; 1945. [mfr
via Martin Copp]

A zero-lift drag coefficient of 0.0233 and a maximum lift-drag ratio
of 16.4 made the JRM the most aerodynamically efficient of any of the
flying boats for which data are given in table IV. An indication of the
range potential of the aircraft is given by its record 4375-mile flight
from Patuxent River, Maryland, to Natal, Brazil, while carrying a payload of 13 000 pounds. (The flight was made by the early patrol-
bomber version of the aircraft.)

Accommodations aboard the two-deck aircraft provided for duty
and reserve crews of four men each. Included were two shower baths,
one for officers and one for enlisted men. Special loading hatches, tiedown rings, and a hoist with a 5000-pound capability were part of the
equipment included for cargo handling. As an assault transport, the
JRM-1 could carry 132 fully equipped troops and 7 Jeeps; or as an am-
bulance aircraft, 84 stretcher cases and 25 medical attendants could be
accommodated.

Early in their operational life, two of the JRM-1 aircraft, the Mars
and the Marshall Mars, were destroyed; the remaining four served the
Navy until they were retired in 1956. In 1959, these aircraft were purchased by Canadian interests to be converted to water bombers for use
in controlling forest fires. In this configuration, the aircraft could carry
6000 gallons of water. The tanks could be replenished in flight by extending scoops and skimming along the surface of a lake or other body
of water. The Marianas Mars was lost in a flying accident, and the
Caroline Mars (JRM-2) was destroyed by a hurricane. The other two
aircraft, the Philippine Mars and the Hawaiian Mars, continue in use

today as water bombers — certainly an application never foreseen by its designers but nevertheless a useful occupation in retirement for a good aircraft whose design goes back more than 35 years.

No large, multiengine propeller-driven flying boat has been developed in the United States since the Martin P5M Marlin first flew in 1948. (The jet-powered Martin P6M Seamaster flying boat is described in part II.) With a gull wing of the same size as that used on the earlier PBM Mariner, the P5M was, however, a much heavier aircraft equipped with more powerful engines. Although bearing many configuration similarities to the PBM, the P5M had an entirely new, high length-beam ratio hull with a planing-tail afterbody. This new and greatly improved hull form had been extensively studied in both the towing tank and wind tunnels at the NACA Langley laboratory (refs. 36, 37, and 124, for example) and offered the possibility of reducing the unfavorable drag differences between flying boats and landplanes. It was found that by maintaining the product bl^2 constant and increasing the value of the length-beam ratio l/b, the water drag and spray characteristics of the hull were little altered and the aerodynamic drag was significantly reduced (l and b are the length and beam of the hull, respectively). The planing-tail afterbody ameliorated the stability problems of porpoising and skipping. As compared with more usual values of 5 to 6, the hull length-beam ratio of the P5M was 8.5, while some of the experimental data in reference 124 are for hulls of length-beam ratio as high as 15.

The P5M–2 version of the Marlin is depicted in figure 8.24 and clearly shows the new hull form. Although the P5M–2 differed from the P5M–1 in a number of respects, the high T-tail of the P5M–2, as compared with a low tail on the P5M–1, immediately identifies the later aircraft. The 76 595-pound gross weight Marlin was powered by two Wright R–3350–18 turbocompound, 18-cylinder, radial air cooled engines that drove controllable-pitch, fully reversible propellers. (Further details of this engine are given in chapter 6 describing the Lockheed 1049G Super Constellation.) These propellers, together with individually extendible flaplike surfaces below the waterline at the end of the hull, greatly enhanced the maneuverability of the Marlin on the water. Power-boosted controls and spoiler ailerons were other modern features of the aircraft. As compared with its look-alike wartime ancestor, the PBM, the Marlin had a 19-percent lower zero-lift drag coefficient and a 9-percent higher maximum lift-drag ratio. With the low specific fuel consumption of the Wright R–3350 engines, the hypothetical range of the Marlin was over 4800 miles as compared with 3500 miles for the Mariner. The maximum and cruising speeds of the Marlin were

Figure 8.24 — The Martin P5M–2 Marlin was the last Navy patrol boat; 1953.
[Robert L. Lawson via AAHS]

251 and 159 miles per hour as compared with 202 and 135 miles per hour for the Mariner. Clearly, the Marlin was a more capable aircraft than its well-known predecessor.

The Marlin was primarily an antisubmarine aircraft and, as such, was equipped with a variety of electronic detection equipment. Offensive armament consisted of various combinations of torpedoes, bombs, depth charges, and rockets. A number of these stores could be carried in the elongated engine nacelles. Several power-operated turrets were provided for defense. Like most large, long-range patrol aircraft, the P5M had a galley and provisions for crew rest on long flights.

Of a total of 259 P5M boats built, 145 were the P5M–2 version. The last new one was accepted by the Navy in 1960. After a long and useful career, the P5M was finally retired from Navy service in 1967.

Today, the four-place Lake amphibian flying boat for the private owner, equipped with a 200-horsepower engine, is the only new flying boat offered for sale in the United States. Is the proud era of the flying boat ended, or will new applications of this versatile type of aircraft be found? Perhaps the next few years will provide the answer.

Comparative Aerodynamic Efficiency

Because of the size and shape of the hull, the assertion has frequently been made that the aerodynamic efficiency of a flying boat, in any given time period, is inherently less than that of a landplane. To

212

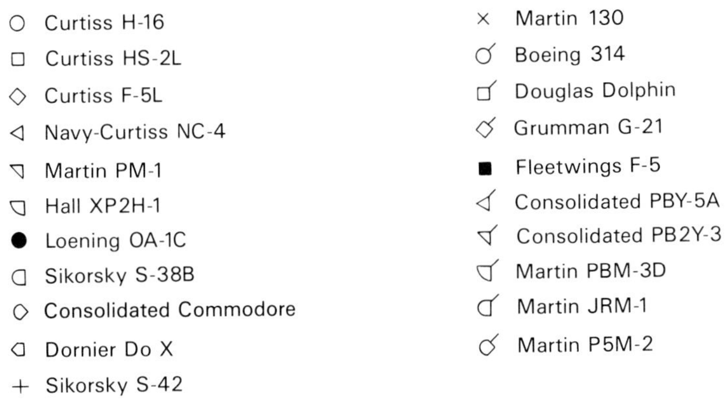

Curtiss H-16
Curtiss HS-2L
Curtiss F-5L
Navy-Curtiss NC-4
Martin PM-1
Hall XP2H-1
Loening OA-1C
Sikorsky S-38B
Consolidated Commodore
Dornier Do X
Sikorsky S-42
Martin 130
Boeing 314
Douglas Dolphin
Grumman G-21
Fleetwings F-5
Consolidated PBY-5A
Consolidated PB2Y-3
Martin PBM-3D
Martin JRM-1
Martin P5M-2

Figure 8.25 — Flying-boat symbols used in figures 8.26 and 8.27.

.08
.07
.06
.05
.04
.03
.02
.01
Zero-lift drag coefficient, C_D,0
Landplane
Boeing 247D
Douglas DC-3
Boeing B-17G
Lockheed 1049G
Bounds, flying boats
Lower bound, landplanes (chapter 7)
1920
1930
1940
1950
1960
Year

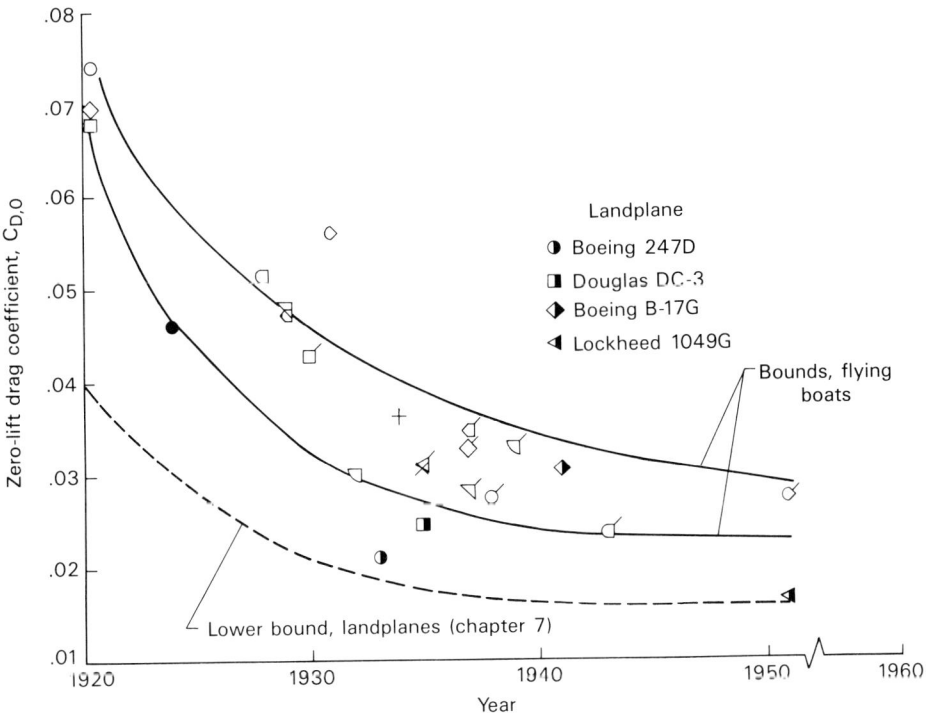

Figure 8.26 — Trends in zero-lift drag coefficient for propeller-driven flying boats.

provide some quantitative basis for the assessment of the comparative aerodynamic efficiencies of landplanes and flying boats, values of the zero-lift drag coefficient $C_{D,0}$ and maximum lift-drag ratio $(L/D)_{max}$ are

shown as a function of time in figures 8.26 and 8.27, respectively. The symbols used to identify the various flying boats in the figures are identified in figure 8.25. Values of $C_{D,0}$ and $(L/D)_{max}$ are plotted on the figures for all the flying boats listed in table IV. The bound lines for landplanes shown in the figures were taken from the trends shown in chapter 7 of this volume, as were the data shown for four specific multiengine landplanes.

As was the case with landplanes during the same time period, the data in figure 8.26 show that the value of $C_{D,0}$ for flying boats rapidly decreased in the years between 1930 and 1940. In comparison with the trend for landplanes, however, the lower bound of $C_{D,0}$ values for flying boats is significantly higher. For example, the lower bounds of drag coefficient are separated by about 40 percent in the period of the early 1940's. Since some of the data used to form the lower bound for landplanes were for high-performance single-engine aircraft, specific data for four multiengine landplanes are also shown in figures 8.26 and 8.27. Two of the $C_{D,0}$ points are seen to be close to the landplane lower bound, and two are near the flying-boat lower bound. In general,

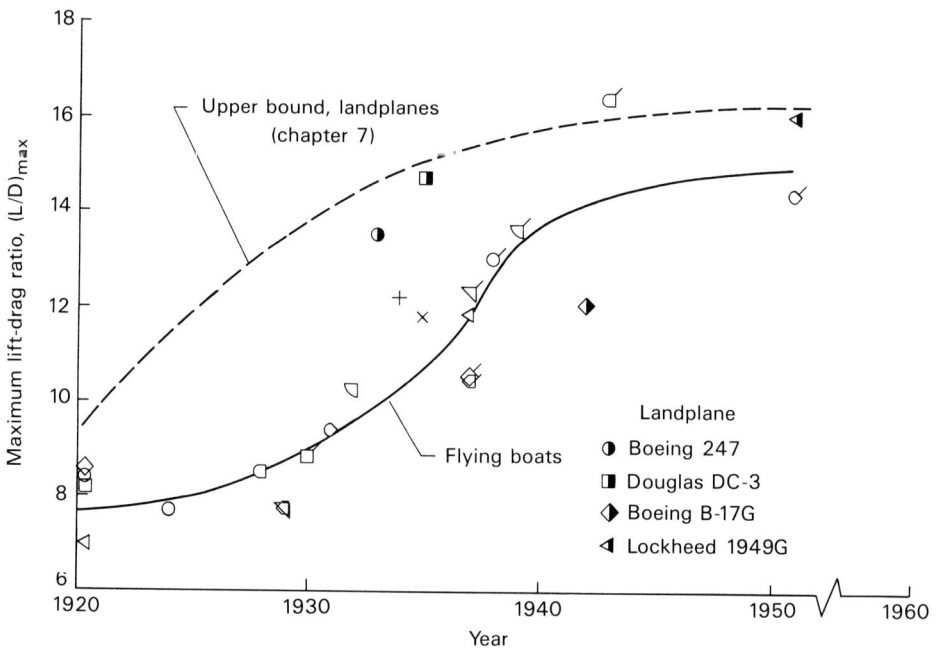

Figure 8.27 — Trends in maximum lift-drag ratio for propeller-driven flying boats.

the trends and data suggest that, in a given time period, zero-lift drag coefficients have been higher for flying boats than for landplanes.

In figure 8.27, the variation of the maximum lift-drag ratio with time shows a rapid increase, beginning in about 1930, followed by a leveling off in the 1940's. Again, the aerodynamic efficiency of the flying boat is seen to be lower than that of its landplane counterpart. Between 1930 and 1942, however, the difference between the two types of aircraft, in terms of $(L/D)_{max}$, was significantly reduced. For example, the upper-bound line for landplanes was about 40 percent higher in 1930 than the best values of $(L/D)_{max}$ for flying boats, but this difference had been lowered to about 14 percent by 1942. The high value of $(L/D)_{max}$ shown for the Martin JRM–1 resulted not only from its low value of $C_{D,0}$ but also from the high aspect ratio, nearly 11, of its wing.

If the large flying boat is ever revived, a major challenge will be to give it acceptable hydrodynamic characteristics while, at the same time, making its overall efficiency and cost effectiveness comparable to contemporary landplanes.

Part II

THE JET AGE

Chapter 9
Introduction

The development of the propeller-driven aircraft from a curiosity to a highly useful machine has been described in part I of this volume. As the first 40 years of powered flight drew to a close, aircraft equipped with reciprocating engines had about reached the end of their development in what must be ranked as one of the most spectacular engineering achievements in history. Although some further technical refinement was possible, the technology of that class of aircraft had reached a plateau with little prospect of major improvement in the future. In the closing months of World War II, however, there emerged a revolutionary new type of propulsion system: the jet engine. Although operationally introduced in somewhat primitive form, the subsequent development of this entirely new type of propulsion system resulted in advancements in aircraft design that have been almost as spectacular as those which characterized the first 40 years of powered flight.

Jet propulsion was initially applied to military aircraft of various types. Indeed, since the inception of jet fighters, the performance of these aircraft and their offensive and defensive weapons have resulted in a capability far exceeding anything imagined in World War II. Speed, rate of climb, maneuverability, range, and payload of military aircraft have increased spectacularly as a result of the turbine engine and associated radical changes in aircraft design concepts. Maximum speeds have exceeded Mach 3, and maximum sea-level rates of climb in excess of 50 000 feet per minute have been achieved with some modern fighter aircraft. Gross and payload weights of many modern fighter and attack aircraft are greater than those of heavy bombers of World War II vintage.

Perhaps the greatest impact of the jet engine on our modern way of life has been in the area of mass transportation. Introduction of the jet-powered transport in 1952 heralded the beginning of a revolution in domestic and international air transportation that has accompanied the development and refinement of the jet-powered transport. The modern jet transport with its high speed, safety, and economical appeal has altered peoples' concepts of the relative accessibility of various places in the United States and throughout the world. Methods of communication have accordingly changed, as have methods of conducting business operations. Whereas air travel was once regarded as the province of the adventurer and the affluent, all classes of people are now traveling by air both for business and pleasure. Americans are traveling today by air in unprecedented numbers, on schedules undreamed of 20 or 30 years ago, and are seeing and experiencing cultures in other parts of the country and the world to an extent that would have been incomprehensible to past generations.

Some indication of the size and scope of past, present, and projected future airline transport activity is given in the following tabulation (based on data from refs. 146, 156, and 181):

Year	Domestic flights, billions of RPM	International flights, billions of RPM	Total
1949	—	—	8.8
1959	25.4	7.1	32.5
1969	106.0	30.1	136.1
1976	147.0	41.5	188.5
1986 (projected)	267.5	79.0	346.5

The total number of revenue passenger miles (RPM) flown by scheduled United States carriers is seen to have increased from 8.8 billion in 1949 to 188.5 billion in 1976. The corresponding number in 1986 is forecast to be 346.5 billion. Thus, the number of revenue passenger miles has increased by a factor of more than 20 in the 27-year time period from 1949 to 1976. The introduction of the jet transport marked the beginning of the end of the ocean-going ship as a serious means of overseas travel. The statistics in the tabulation show that overseas travel by air comprised 7.1 billion revenue passenger miles in 1959, 41.5 billion in 1976, and is projected to increase to 79.0 billion by 1986. By way of comparison, in 1939 steamships of all nations are estimated to have operated about 3 billion revenue passenger miles between the United States and other countries of the world. Thus, the airplane has not only supplanted the steamship but has, in fact, generated a new and greatly enlarged market for overseas travel. Air travel today is accepted as a major component of the common-carrier transportation system, and the modern jet transport is largely responsible for the revolution that has made air travel for the masses what it is today.

The technology, development, and design features of various types of civil and military jet-powered aircraft are discussed in part II of this book. To limit the scope of the material, the discussion is restricted, as in part I, primarily to aircraft developed in the United States. No adverse reflection on the quality of the many fine foreign designs developed over the years is intended by their exclusion.

The aircraft discussed, together with some of their performance and physical characteristics, are listed in tables V to VIII in appendix A. The quantities tabulated are defined in the list of symbols contained in appendix B and generally require no further elaboration. Some of the quantities listed are discussed in more detail in the introduction to part I. The references used in obtaining the characteristics of the aircraft are listed in the tables or are specifically cited in the text. *Jane's All the World's Aircraft* (refs. 125 to 131) has been used extensively in compiling the characteristics of the aircraft presented in the tables, as have various directory issues of *Flight International Magazine* (for example, refs. 150, 167, 168, and 177) and other well-known reference works. A few references that provide useful background material but are not specifically cited are offered for additional reading on the subject of aircraft development. For convenience, references 132 to 210 are listed alphabetically.

Chapter 10
Technology of the Jet Airplane

Background

The highly developed technology of the propeller-driven aircraft formed the foundation from which the jet airplane evolved. Compared with its propeller-driven ancestors, however, the modern jet aircraft incorporates many refinements in such areas as structures, materials, aerodynamics, methods of construction, and onboard systems. A description of all these various improvements and innovations is beyond the scope of the present discussion. In order to exploit fully the performance potential of the jet engine, however, certain basic configuration changes in the form of the airplane were necessary. Wing design and wing-fuselage integration for high-speed flight are briefly discussed in the following paragraphs, as are certain characteristics of high-speed aircraft at large angles of attack. Included in the discussion is a description of some of the powerful high-lift devices employed on most modern, long-range jet aircraft. However, the jet engine itself and some of its variants and characteristics are considered first.

Jet Propulsion

The speed at which a conventional propeller-driven aircraft may fly efficiently is fundamentally limited by the loss in propeller efficiency that occurs as the tip speed approaches a Mach number of 1.0. (See chapter 5.) One of the important advantages of jet-type propulsion systems is that they overcome this fundamental limitation. The air intake and internal flow systems for jet engines are designed in such a way as to limit the velocity of the air at the first stage of compressor blading so that severe adverse Mach number effects are not encountered.

Another advantage found in jet propulsion systems is the small weight per unit power and the tremendous amount of power that can be packaged in a single unit. An interesting illustration of the power and weight features of jet propulsion can be obtained from the following comparison of some of the characteristics of the modern Boeing 747 jetliner and the earlier propeller-driven Lockheed 1049G Super Constellation. The Super Constellation is typical of the final generation of high-performance, piston-engine transports and is described in chapter 6. The total power, the power per engine, and the ratio of power to dry engine weight of the two aircraft are compared in the following tabulation:

Characteristic	Lockheed 1049G	Boeing 747
Weight, W, lb	112 000	700 000
Speed, V, mph	330	530
Altitude, ft	23 000	35 000
Lift-drag ratio, L/D	15	16
Number of engines	4	4
Total cruise power, hp	6 585	59 934
Power per engine, hp	1 646	14 984
Dry engine weight, lb	3 675	8 600
Power-to-weight ratio	0.45	1.74

In this case, the power is defined as the total amount of power usefully employed in propelling the aircraft at the assumed conditions of weight, speed, and lift-drag ratio. The power used in the tabulation may be thought of as being proportional to the total number of British thermal units supplied to the engine per unit time multiplied by the overall efficiency with which this energy is converted to useful work; that is,

$$P = \frac{WV}{(L/D)550}$$

where P is in horsepower and V is in feet per second. The given values of W, V, and L/D employed in the equation are only estimates that may not be entirely consistent but are thought to be sufficiently accurate for the present purpose.

The Boeing 747 cruising at 530 miles per hour at a weight of 700 000 pounds is seen to require 59 934 horsepower; the corresponding values for the Super Constellation are 330 miles per hour, 112 000 pounds, and 6585 horsepower. The power per engine for the two aircraft is seen to be 14 984 horsepower and 1646 horsepower for the 747 and Super Constellation, respectively. The Wright 3350 turbocompound engines that powered the Lockheed aircraft are among the most powerful reciprocating engines ever developed for aircraft use. These engines developed a maximum of 3250 horsepower at takeoff; the value given in the table is for a normal cruise power setting. The enormous amount of power generated by the Pratt & Whitney turbofan engines of the 747 as compared with the reciprocating engines that propelled the Super Constellation is obvious. The values of power-to-weight ratio for the two types of propulsion systems are also of great interest. The weights used in this ratio are the dry, uninstalled engine weights as given in reference 205. The turbine engines in the Boeing aircraft develop nearly four times as much power for each pound of engine weight as do the reciprocating engines that power the Lockheed aircraft.

The jet propulsion system avoids the compressibility problem that limits the speed at which the propeller may be efficiently employed, is light in weight for a given amount of power as compared with a reciprocating engine, and can be successfully produced in single units capable of generating very large amounts of power. Jet propulsion systems also require much less maintenance than do reciprocating engines and may be operated for many thousands of hours without major overhaul. Engine failures are also relatively rare with jet propulsion systems.

Turbojet and Turbofan Systems

Turbojet and turbofan propulsion systems are employed extensively in jet-powered aircraft. Schematic drawings of the two propulsion systems, taken from reference 133, are given in figure 10.1. The turbojet shown at the top of the figure consists of high- and low-pressure compressors, combustor, and high- and low-pressure turbines. In the turbojet, all the inlet air passes through each element of the engine. The compressors raise the pressure of the inlet air; the pressure ratio varies for different engines but may approach 30 to 1. The high-pressure air enters the combustor where fuel is injected. The fuel-air mixture is ignited and the resulting hot gases pass through the turbines that, in turn, drive the compressors. The exhaust from the turbines provides the thrust that propels the aircraft.

The turbojet shown in figure 10.1(a) is called a twin-spool engine. The low-pressure compressor is driven by the low-pressure turbine,

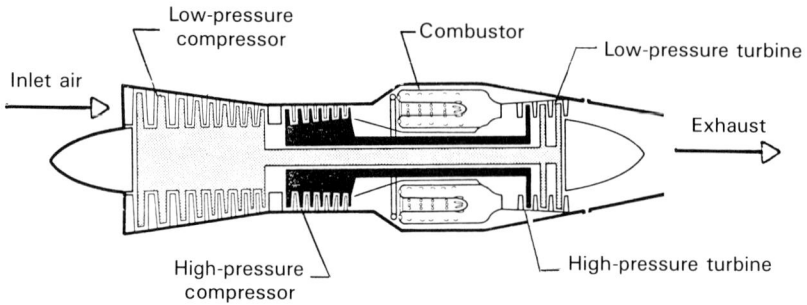

(a) Turbojet

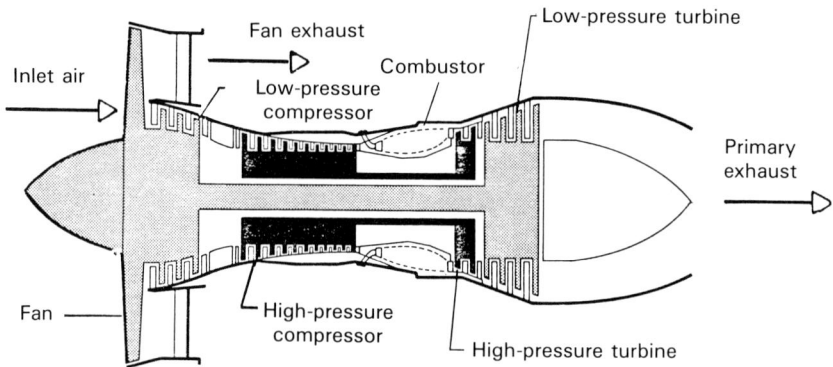

(b) High-bypass-ratio turbofan

Figure 10.1 — Two types of jet propulsion systems.

and the high-pressure compressor is driven by the high-pressure turbine. These two units rotate at different speeds in order to maintain
high efficiency in all stages of compression. The engine shown in figure
10.1(a) has nine stages and seven stages in the low-pressure and high-
pressure compressors, respectively, and the low-pressure and high-
pressure turbines contain two stages and one stage.

A schematic drawing of a turbofan engine is shown in figure
10.1(b). The turbofan engine contains all the elements of the turbojet
shown in figure 10.1(a), but in addition, some of the energy in the hot
jet exhaust is extracted by a turbine that drives a fan. A portion of the
inlet air that enters the fan is bypassed around the engine; the fan,
then, is somewhat like a propeller being driven by the turbomachinery.

Unlike the propeller, however, a single fan stage may contain from 20 to 50 blades, is surrounded by a shroud, and is more like a single-stage compressor than a propeller. For example, the pressure ratio across a single fan stage is usually in the range of 1.4 to 1.6; whereas the pressure ratio across the propeller discs of the Lockheed Super Constellation in cruising flight is somewhat less than 1.02.

The bypass ratio of a turbofan engine is defined as the ratio of the mass of air that passes through the fan, but not the gas generator, to that which does pass through the gas generator. Bypass ratios between 1 and 2 are typical of the first turbofan engines introduced in the early 1960's. The more modern turbofan engines for transport aircraft have bypass ratios that usually fall between 4 and 6, and the engine employed on the Lockheed C-5A has a bypass ratio of 8. The larger the bypass ratio, the greater the amount of energy extracted from the hot exhaust of the gas generator; as much as 75 percent of the total thrust of a turbofan engine may be attributed to the fan.

The single-stage front fan shown on the engine in figure 10.1(b) is integral with the low-pressure compressor, and a four-stage turbine drives both the fan and the compressor. Some turbofan engines are of the three-spool type. The hot gas generator employs two spools, like the turbojet shown in figure 10.1(a), and a third spool that is independent of the other two contains the fan and its own turbines. Fans of more than one stage have also been used, as have aft-mounted fans. The aft-fan design is one in which the fan blades form an extension of an independently mounted turbine situated in the hot exhaust of the gas generator.

Most modern civil and military aircraft are powered by some form of turbofan engine because such engines consume less fuel to produce a given amount of useful power than do comparable turbojet engines. The higher efficiency of the turbofan engine can be explained with the use of Newton's second law of motion. From this well-known law, it may be deduced that a given level of thrust can be produced at a given flight velocity, either by the addition of a small increment of velocity to a large mass flow of air or by the addition of a large increment of velocity to a small mass flow of air. The required energy addition (fuel), however, is less for the first than for the second case. (A simplified analytical proof of this statement is contained in appendix E.) The improved efficiency of the turbofan as compared with the turbojet is, therefore, directly related to the larger air-flow capacity of the fan engine at a given thrust level.

To give quantitative definition to the preceding discussion, the overall propulsion system efficiency at different speeds is compared in figure 10.2 for several propulsion systems. The overall propulsion system efficiency η is the efficiency with which the energy in the fuel is usefully employed in propelling the aircraft and consists of the product of the cycle efficiency η_c and the propulsive efficiency η_p as follows:

$$\eta = \eta_c \eta_p$$

The cycle efficiency is expressed as the percentage of the heat energy in the fuel that is converted to mechanical energy in the engine, and

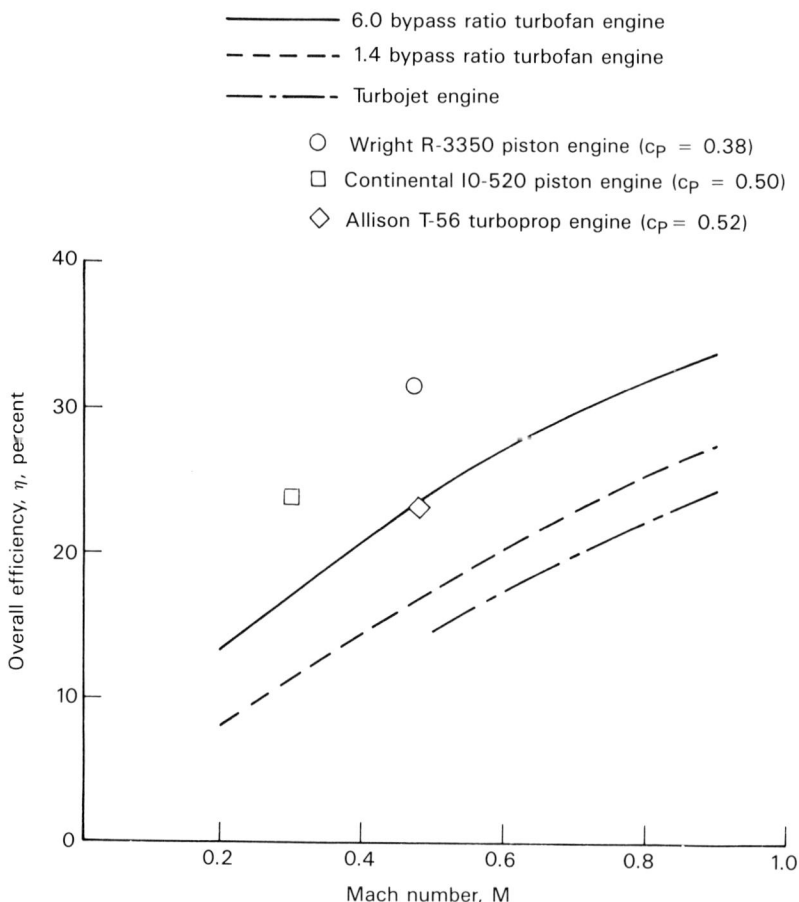

Figure 10.2 — Overall efficiency ($\eta = \eta_c \eta_p$) of several types of aircraft propulsion systems. (c_p is defined in appendix F.)

the propulsive efficiency is expressed as the percentage of this mechanical energy that is usefully employed in propelling the aircraft. The methods used in calculating the values of efficiency given in figure 10.2 are described in appendix F.

The curves in figure 10.2 show the overall propulsion-system efficiency as a function of Mach number for a turbojet and two turbofan engines. The turbojet engine and the turbofan engine of bypass ratio 1.4 have the same gas generator. Both engines show a large increase in efficiency as the Mach number increases. For example, the efficiency of the turbofan with a bypass ratio of 1.4 increases from 8 percent to 27.5 percent as the Mach number is increased from 0.2 to 0.9. The 13-percent improvement in efficiency of the fan engine as compared with the pure jet (at a Mach number of 0.8) results entirely from the addition of the fan. The large increase in efficiency that accompanies an increase in the bypass ratio from 1.4 to 6.0, however, is only partly attributable to the increase in bypass ratio. The overall compressor compression ratio of the engine with bypass ratio of 6.0 is about 25, whereas the corresponding ratio for the other fan engine is about 14. Part of the increase in efficiency shown by the engine of higher bypass ratio is accordingly due to an increase in cycle efficiency.

Also shown in figure 10.2 are points for two reciprocating engines and a turboprop engine. The Wright R–3350 turbocompound engine employed on the Lockheed Super Constellation (see chapter 6) was probably the most efficient reciprocating engine ever designed for aircraft use. The overall efficiency of this engine is shown plotted at the cruising speed of the Constellation. Comparison of the point with the curve for the high bypass ratio turbofan engine indicates that the efficiency of the fan engine is as high as that of the Wright engine at a Mach number twice that at which the Constellation cruised. Thus, the overall propulsion efficiency of the 747 flying at its normal cruising speed is about the same as that of the Constellation at its normal cruising speed. The overall efficiency of the engine with a bypass ratio of 1.4, however, is about 20 percent lower than that of the reciprocating engine even at the normal cruise Mach number of the fan engine of about 0.8. The value of the overall efficiency of the 747 is about 32 percent at a Mach number of 0.8. The trends in figure 10.2 clearly show that, with respect to overall propulsion efficiency, the bypass ratio should increase as the cruising speed decreases, and at some speed the propeller or low-solidity fan becomes the most efficient type of propulsion system. The selection of the optimum bypass ratio for a particular aircraft, however, involves trade studies of many factors, such as the details of the performance requirements of the aircraft in different flight regimes, the efficiencies of the various components of the engine, and the weight and size of the fan and its installation. Also of importance in the selection of the bypass ratio, particularly for an engine intended for application on a civil aircraft, are the noise characteristics of the engine. Engine noise has not been mentioned so far but is briefly discussed in a later section of this chapter.

The point indicated by a square symbol in figure 10.2 is for a modern six-cylinder, horizontally opposed, reciprocating engine of the type employed in present-day general aviation aircraft. The value of the efficiency of this engine at a Mach number of 0.3 is about 24 percent as compared with about 17 percent for the turbofan at the same Mach number. The point indicated by a diamond symbol in figure 10.2 is for a contemporary turboprop engine employed in a widely used cargo aircraft. The efficiency of this propulsion system is about the same as that of the turbofan at a Mach number of 0.49. The turboprop engine for which the point is shown in figure 10.2 is an old engine that has a compressor compression ratio of only about 10. An engine of more advanced design would be expected to have a higher value of overall propulsion efficiency. The values of the specific fuel consumption c_p for the reciprocating and turboprop engines were obtained from reference 205.

The preceding paragraphs indicate that the turbofan engine, as compared with the reciprocating engine driving a conventional propeller, offers the following advantages:

(1) The turbofan avoids the compressibility losses that limit the speed at which a propeller-driven aircraft may efficiently cruise.

(2) The weight of the turbofan engine per unit power is significantly less than that of the reciprocating engine.

(3) The turbofan engine is capable of developing a very large amount of power in a single unit without prohibitive mechanical complication.

(4) The overall efficiency of the turbofan propulsion system is about the same as that of the most efficient reciprocating engines ever designed for aircraft use. The turbofan engine attains this efficiency at a higher speed than that which is appropriate for reciprocating engines.

(5) The turbofan engine is more reliable than the reciprocating engine and can be operated many thousands of hours without major maintenance work.

These five basic reasons explain why the turbojet and turbofan propulsion systems have caused a revolution in aircraft design and in our concepts of the way in which aircraft may be effectively used.

Afterburning Engines

Many military aircraft have need for a large, short-time increase in thrust to be used in such operations as takeoff, climb, acceleration, and combat maneuvers. The afterburning engine provides the answer to this need. In this engine, additional fuel is injected directly into the engine exhaust and burned in the tail pipe. Thrust increases of 50 to 80 percent are achievable by this means in modern engines, but at a large increase in fuel consumption. Afterburner operation is feasible because a jet engine operates at a "lean" fuel-to-air ratio to limit temperatures in the hot, rotating parts of the engine to values consistent with the high-temperature limitations of the materials with which these parts are constructed. Thus, the turbine exhaust contains the excess oxygen necessary for afterburner operation.

Shown in figure 10.3 are sketches (based on ref. 133) of hypothetical turbojet and turbofan engines equipped with afterburners. The rotating elements of these engines are not unlike those of the nonafterburning types shown in figure 10.1. The long afterburner duct, fuel spray bars, flame holders, and adjustable nozzle distinguish the afterburning engine from its nonafterburning counterpart. Fuel is injected into the exhaust of the rotating part of the engine by the fuel spray bars, and the flame holders stabilize the flame and prevent it from being blown out the end of the tailpipe. To obtain maximum thrust from the engine in both afterburning and nonafterburning operation, an adjustable exhaust nozzle is necessary. A nozzle of continuously varying size and shape would be desirable to maximize performance at all flight and engine-operating conditions. In actual practice, however, a two- or three-position nozzle is usually employed to reduce mechanical complication.

In the turbofan engine shown in figure 10.3(b), afterburning takes place in a mixture of the primary exhaust air and the fan bypass air. In a variation of this design, called the duct-burning turbofan, the spray

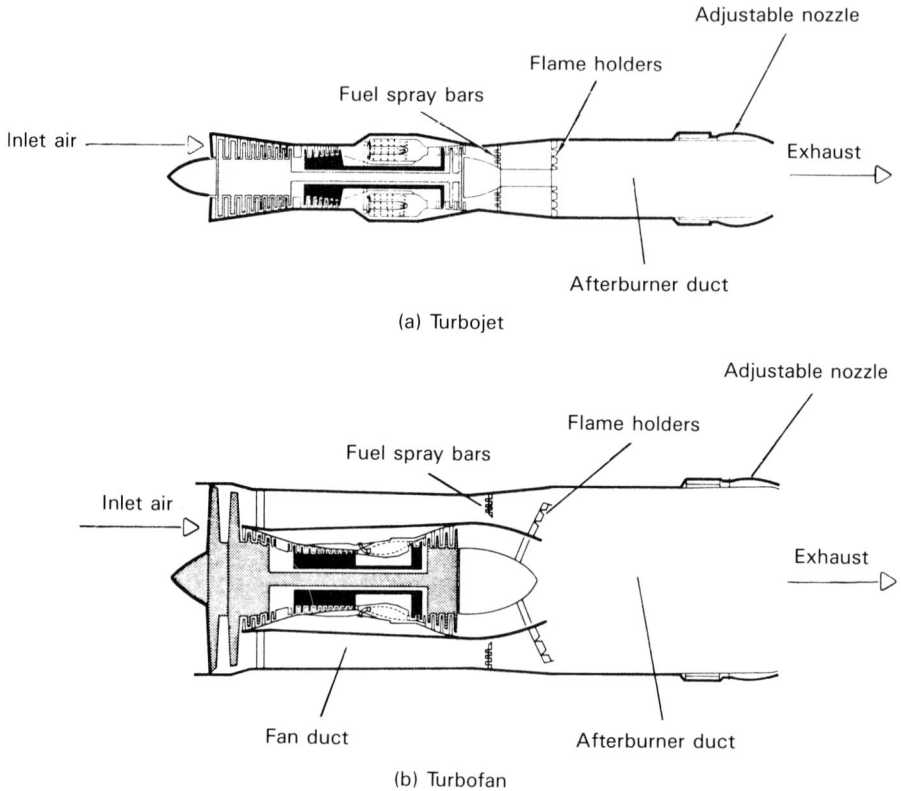

Figure 10.3 — Two types of afterburning jet propulsion system.

bars and flame holders are located in the fan duct, and all the after-burning takes place in the bypass air. The bypass ratios employed on afterburning fan engines are usually in the order of 2, much less than is common practice on modern nonafterburning engines for transport air-craft, because afterburning fans are usually found on military aircraft designed to penetrate the transonic and low-supersonic speed ranges. When performance requirements encompass these speed ranges, as well as subsonic flight under various conditions, a low bypass ratio be-comes the best compromise.

The afterburner provides a light and mechanically simple means for achieving a large boost in thrust. Fuel consumption with afterburn-ing is large, however, as is engine noise. This latter characteristic is particularly troublesome when afterburning is used for takeoff and ini-tial climb. Afterburning is generally not used in cruising flight except for aircraft and engines specifically designed for long-range supersonic flight. The Anglo-French Concord supersonic transport and the American Lockheed SR–71 supersonic reconnaissance aircraft fall into this latter category.

Thrust Reversers

The amount of force required to stop an aircraft in a given distance after touchdown increases with the gross weight of the aircraft and the square of the landing speed. The size of modern transport aircraft and the speed at which they land makes the use of wheel brakes alone unsatisfactory for routine operations. Most propeller-driven transports produced since World War II employ reversible-pitch propellers to assist in stopping the aircraft on the landing rollout.

The advent of the turbojet and turbofan types of propulsion system required the development of new concepts for augmenting the stopping power provided by the brakes. Some military aircraft deploy one or more parachutes after touchdown as shown in figure 10.4. The aerodynamic drag of the parachutes provides the additional stopping force to augment the brakes. Following each landing, the parachutes must be detached from the aircraft and repacked. The use of these devices for deceleration is not an attractive alternative for any type of routine operations and, by Western standards, is completely unacceptable for commercial airline operations. In contrast, a number of Soviet transport aircraft, including early versions of the Tupelov Tu–134 twin-jet transport, were equipped with braking parachutes. Another drag-producing method of assisting aircraft deceleration consists of deploy-

Figure 10.4 — North American XB–70 with three drag chutes deployed. [mfr via Martin Copp]

233

ing wing spoilers after the aircraft is on the runway. This technique is routinely used on many jet-powered transports. (See the section on high-lift systems at the end of this chapter.)

To augment the wheel brakes and aerodynamic drag in decelerating the aircraft, the engines of turbojet- and turbofan-powered transport aircraft are equipped with some form of diverter that, when activated, reverses the thrust and thus provides a powerful stopping force. A schematic drawing of a possible thrust reverser for a high-bypass-ratio turbofan engine is shown in figure 10.5. (See ref. 133.) Both the fan exhaust and the hot exhaust from the gas generator are reversed in the design shown. The elements of the reverser are cascades and clam

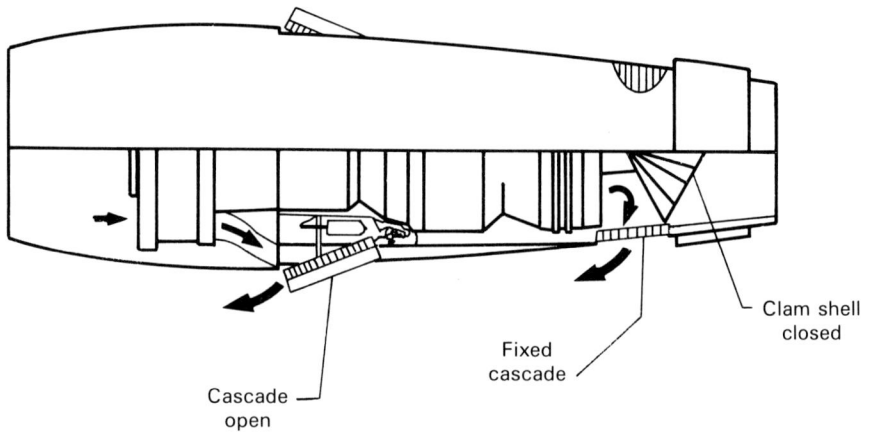

(a) Reverse thrust configuration

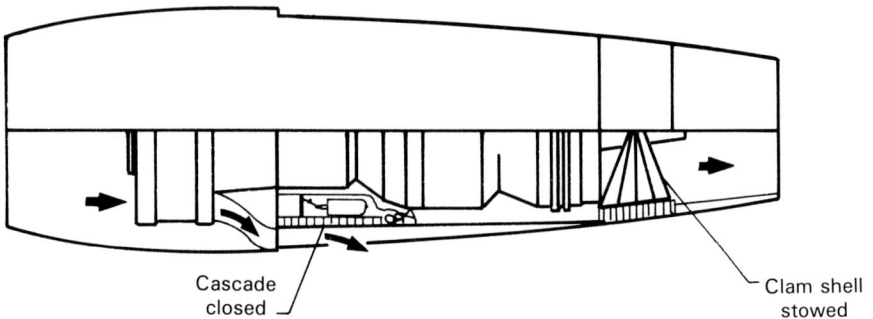

(b) Forward thrust configuration

Figure 10.5 — Thrust reverser for turbofan engine.

shells. A cascade is an array of closely spaced, highly cambered airfoils and is used for changing the direction of airflow; it may also be thought of like the blades of a compressor of constant chord laid out parallel to each other rather than radially about a single axis. The clam shell closes the exhaust nozzle and diverts the gas flow outward and forward.

The engine is shown in the reverse and forward thrust configurations in figures 10.5(a) and 10.5(b), respectively. The fan exhaust is reversed by opening the forward cascade so that the impinging exhaust is turned by the blades in the cascade into the forward direction. In the reverse configuration, the exhaust from the hot gas generator strikes the closed clam shell doors and is diverted forward and outward through circumferential openings in the engine nacelle. Fixed cascades are installed in these openings and aid in turning the exhaust gas forward. In the forward thrust configuration, the stowed clam shell closes the cascade and thus prevents leakage of exhaust gases. The front cascade in the forward thrust configuration is closed on the inside so that the fan exhaust cannot pass through it.

Most thrust reversers employ either or both cascades and clam shells in various configurations depending upon the design of the engine, the bypass ratio, and the type of nacelle in which the engine is mounted. In order to prevent ingestion of hot gases or debris into the engine inlet, the thrust reversers are usually not operated below some minimum speed. This minimum speed depends on the design of the aircraft and engine and their integration; 70 miles per hour is a typical value of the minimum speed for operation of the thrust reverser. Although the primary use of the thrust reverser is to shorten the landing distance, reverse thrust is also employed in flight on some aircraft. In this application, reverse thrust is used when a very rapid, steep descent is required to follow a desired flight profile.

Engine Noise

The preceding paragraphs outline the many advantages of jet propulsion systems. A major disadvantage is the noise problem encountered with these types of propulsion systems applied to commercial transport aircraft. The high noise levels of the propulsion system must be considered in relation to the design of the cabin of the aircraft and to the environment external to the aircraft in the vicinity of the airport. The use of light, effective soundproofing material in the cabin has resulted in interior noise levels that are acceptably low without excessive weight penalty.

235

The primary impact of the high noise levels associated with jet propulsion systems has been felt by people living in communities surrounding airports from which jet-powered transport aircraft operate. Not only were the early jet transports noisier than contemporary aircraft powered with reciprocating engines, but the increased airline traffic that resulted from the widespread adoption of the jet transport resulted in an increased frequency of aircraft operations at most major airports.

The noise problem became so severe and the associated pressure on the U.S. Congress so great that part 36 of the Federal Air Regulations was formulated and became law on December 1, 1969. These regulations specify certain noise levels that must not be exceeded by new aircraft certified after that date. The regulation further states that all aircraft operated in the United States must comply with the regulations after January 1, 1985.

The present certification process for transport aircraft involves experimental measurements of aircraft noise under controlled conditions. The noise level is measured at specified positions under the approach and climb paths of the aircraft and at a specified position to the side of the runway. The allowable noise levels vary to some extent with the gross weight of the aircraft and thus reflect what is technically possible and realistic. Lower allowable noise levels will no doubt be specified at some future time to reflect advancements in the state of the art.

Aircraft noise reduction has been the subject of intensive research and development for the past two decades. The aircraft and engine manufacturing companies as well as various government research and regulatory organizations have been involved in this work. As a result, much has been learned about methods of noise reduction, and considerable literature exists on the subject.

Four approaches have been followed in the various studies aimed toward reducing aircraft noise. First, much work has been directed toward obtaining an understanding of the basic noise generation and propagation process. Second, new concepts in engine design have been developed to reduce the amount of noise generated at the source. Third, methods for suppressing and absorbing a portion of the noise emanating from the engine have been found. Fourth, aircraft operational techniques have been devised for minimizing noise impact on communities surrounding the airport.

The early jet transports were powered with turbojet-type engines. The hot, high-velocity exhaust is the primary source of noise in this type of propulsion system. The amount of energy in the exhaust that is transformed into noise varies as approximately the eighth power of the exhaust velocity, and the noise-frequency spectrum is related to the circumference of the exhaust jet. The relative amount of noise energy in the lower frequencies increases as the circumference of the jet increases. Many of the early noise suppressors employed on turbojet propulsion systems were based on the concept of effectively breaking the large exhaust jet into a number of small jets so that the relative amount of noise at the lower frequencies is reduced. The amount of attenuation that accompanies transmission of the noise through the atmosphere increases as the noise frequencies increase. Thus, by breaking up a large jet into a number of small jets, the amount of energy transmitted as noise over a given distance is reduced. The noise suppressors shown in figures 10.6(a) and (b) are based on the principle just described.

Another type of noise suppressor proposed for the early turbojet-powered transports is shown in figure 10.6(c). The ejector-type suppressor entrains free-stream air, which is then mixed with the high-velocity exhaust. The velocity of the resulting mixed exhaust is therefore lower than that of the free exhaust of the engine alone, and the noise is accordingly reduced at the source.

A great deal of information has accumulated on the manner in which the various components of the engine should be designed so as to reduce the noise generated by the engine. The turbofan engine and the beneficial effects of increasing the bypass ratio on the propulsive efficiency have been discussed earlier. The advent of the turbofan type of propulsion system had an important effect on the nature of the aircraft noise problem. The extraction of energy from the gas generator for the purpose of driving a fan in a high-bypass-ratio engine would be expected to reduce the noise of the fan engine as compared with a turbojet for the same thrust level. The fan itself, however, was found to constitute a new and highly disturbing source of noise. Studies of the relatively low-bypass-ratio, first-generation fan engines showed that the noise that was propagated from the inlet and the fan discharge ducts was greater than that associated with the high-velocity exhaust from the gas generator.

The noise associated with the fan can be greatly reduced by proper detail design of the fan and by the use of acoustic treatment in certain key areas of the inlet and fan discharge ducts. Acoustic treatment consists in the application of sound absorbing material to the interior passages of the nacelle, as shown in figures 10.7(a) and (b) for short and

(a) Corrugated-perimeter-type
noise suppressor

(b) Multiple-tube-type noise
suppressor

(c) Ejector-type noise
suppressor

Figure 10.6 — Three types of jet noise suppressor.

long fan duct installations. (Figure 10.7 was taken from reference 185, which contains a comprehensive summary of basic information dealing with acoustic treatment for noise suppression.) An experimental application of acoustic treatment to the nacelle of a first-generation, low-bypass-ratio turbofan engine is shown in figure 10.8. Most modern high-bypass-ratio engines employ some form of acoustic treatment. The splitter rings shown in figure 10.7 have not been used in any production installations for a number of practical operational reasons, such as possible difficulties in deicing and the possibility of the rings

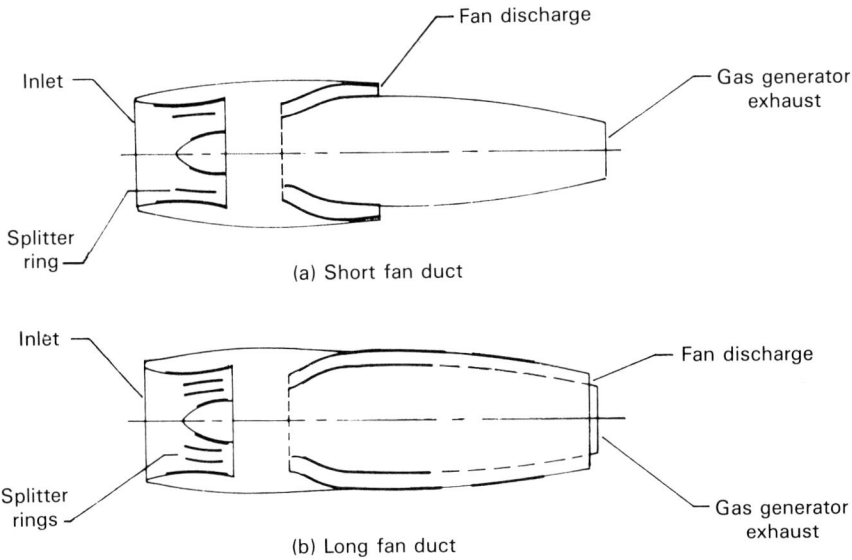

Figure 10.7 — Examples of acoustic treatment to short and long fan duct nacelles. (Heavy lines indicate acoustic treatment.)

being broken by foreign object ingestion with subsequent damage to the rotating parts of the engine.

The development of operational techniques for noise abatement will not be dealt with here other than to indicate that these techniques usually involve (1) selected routing into and out of the airport in order to avoid flight over certain heavily populated areas and (2) the use of power reductions and reduced climb angles on certain segments of the climb following takeoff.

Air Inlets

The tremendous amount of power that can be extracted from a single, modern turbopropulsion system has already been discussed. To generate this power with maximum efficiency, the large quantities of propulsion-system air must be delivered to the engine face with minimum aerodynamic loss, turbulence, and flow distortion. High efficiency must be maintained for different engine-operating conditions, different aircraft speeds and altitudes, and for a wide spectrum of angles of attack and sideslip. As one example, a jet transport must inhale air efficiently in the near static condition at the beginning of takeoff roll, in

239

the relatively low-speed, high-power climb condition, and in high-speed, high-altitude cruise flight. At all flight conditions, the propulsion-system air must be decelerated to a low-speed, high-pressure state at the engine compressor face. The detail design of the air intake and internal flow system determines the efficiency with which the air is delivered to the propulsion system. In this case, the efficiency is defined as the ratio, expressed in percent, of the average total pressure of the air entering the engine to that of the free-stream air. The total pressure is the sum of the static, or ambient, pressure of the air and the impact pressure associated with its motion. Modern jet transports may cruise with values of the pressure recovery, that is efficiency, of 97 to 98 percent. Supersonic aircraft with well-designed, practical inlet and internal flow systems may have pressure recoveries of 85 percent or more for Mach numbers in the 2.0 to 2.5 range.

The demanding requirements for high inlet and internal-flow-system efficiency stimulated a large amount of research, development, and engineering effort in the years following the end of World War II. Fortunately, this effort could be based on a solid foundation of earlier work on such things as cowlings and radiator scoops for piston engines. Inlet activity intensified as aircraft penetrated the transonic and supersonic speed ranges, and the field of inlet and internal flow system design soon became a well-recognized engineering specialty. Especially in modern fighters that may have thrust-to-weight ratios in the order of 1, the inlet and its integration with the airframe exert a powerful influence on the overall aircraft design. The aim in engine airframe integration is to minimize airplane drag, weight, and complexity and to maximize propulsion-system efficiency while, at the same time, ensuring that the aircraft mission requirements have not been compromised. A detailed discussion of the many facets of inlet design is beyond the scope of the present discussion; however, a few examples of inlets that have been used on civil and military aircraft are illustrated and described in the following paragraphs.

Already shown in the discussion of aircraft noise is an inlet typical of those currently employed on modern subsonic transport and strategic bomber aircraft. The splitter rings in the inlet shown in figure 10.8 are part of an experimental installation, which, as mentioned, are not used on production aircraft. The open nose inlet shown is simple, is light in weight, and when used with a pod-mounted engine, has a short, low-loss duct connecting the engine to the inlet. High-pressure recoveries that are relatively insensitive to normal variations in angle of attack and sideslip are possible with this type of inlet.

Figure 10.8 — NASA experimental treated nacelle mounted on McDonnell Douglas DC–8 airplane. [NASA]

In contrast to the pod-type mounting found on so many multiengine transport aircraft, most fighters have one or, at the most, two engines situated inside the fuselage. A variety of inlet locations and designs have been employed to supply air to the propulsion system on these aircraft. Each of these arrangements have both advantages and disadvantages. Four typical installations employed on fighter aircraft are illustrated in figure 10.9. These do not by any means constitute all the successful configurations that have been employed on such aircraft over the years. Most installations, however, are variants of those shown.

The simple nose inlet employed on the North American F–86 fighter is illustrated in figure 10.9(a). As indicated previously, this type of installation enjoys good characteristics through a wide range of angle of attack and sideslip and, when located in the front of the fuselage as contrasted with a pod, is free from aerodynamic interference effects—such as flow separation—from other parts of the aircraft. The long internal duct leading from the inlet to the engine, however, tends to have relatively high pressure losses. In addition, interference between the duct and the pilot's cockpit may be encountered. In some designs, the duct passes under the cockpit; in others, it is split and passes around the cockpit on either side of the pilot. Perhaps the largest drawback of the nose inlet, however, is that neither guns nor radar can be mounted in the front of the fuselage. A nose inlet has not been used on a new fighter in the United States since the early 1950's.

The chin inlet employed on the F-8 airplane shown in figure 10.9(b) has many of the advantages of the simple nose inlet but leaves space in the front of the fuselage for radar or guns and has a somewhat shorter internal duct. Care should be taken in such a design to ensure that at no important flight condition does separated or unsteady flow enter the inlet from the nose of the aircraft. The proximity of the inlet to the ground introduces a possible risk of foreign object ingestion, and, obviously, the nose wheel must be located behind the inlet. The chin inlet, however, is a good choice for some applications and is employed on one new contemporary aircraft (the General Dynamics F-16).

Shown in figure 10.9(c) is the wing-root inlet installation employed on the McDonnell F-101 fighter. Inlets located in this manner offer several advantages. Among these are short, light, internal flow ducts, avoidance of fuselage boundary-layer air ingestion, and freedom to mount guns and radar in the nose of the aircraft. Further, no interference between the cockpit and internal ducting is encountered in this arrangement. The short, curved internal ducts, however, require careful design to avoid flow separation and associated losses, and the inlet-wing integration must be accomplished in such a way that neither the function of the wing nor the inlet is compromised. Wing-root inlets were used on a number of aircraft in the first decade of the jet fighter, but such inlets are not suitable for modern fighters of high thrust-to-weight ratio because of the large-size inlets required by these aircraft and the difficulty of integrating them with the wing.

Side-mounted inlets as used on the Grumman F11F are illustrated in figure 10.9(d). Used on both single- and twin-engine fighters, the side-mounted inlet arrangement probably offers the best compromise of all the conflicting aerodynamic, structural, weight, and space requirements, and it is used on many modern combat aircraft. Great flexibility in inlet size, shape, vertical position, and fore and aft location is offered by the side-mounted installation. Although the F11F is a design of the 1950's, side-mounted inlets are used on many fighters of the 1970's and 1980's, as described in chapter 11. Before leaving the discussion of figure 10.9(d), it should be noted that the boundary-layer diverter plates are located so as to prevent ingestion by the inlets of the fuselage boundary-layer air. Such boundary-layer diverters are a feature, really a complication, of all fuselage-mounted inlets.

The inlets just described are of the fixed-geometry type; that is, they do not change shape or size as the aircraft speed varies. Fixed-geometry inlets are suitable for aircraft designed to operate at subsonic

(a)

(b)

(c)

(d)

Figure 10.9 — Four inlet locations used on jet-powered fighter aircraft. [NASA]

243

and low supersonic speeds. For flight at Mach numbers much beyond 1.6, however, variable-geometry features must be incorporated in the inlet if acceptably high inlet pressure recoveries together with low external drag are to be achieved. This complication is dictated by the physical laws governing the flow of air at supersonic speeds. The nature of supersonic flows is not discussed here, but two variable-geometry inlets are illustrated in figure 10.10. Shown at the top in figure 10.10(a) is the D-type side inlet used on the McDonnell Douglas F–4 fighter. Evident in the photograph are the large fixed diverter plates that also serve to begin compression of the entering flow. The adjustable ramps provide further compression along with the desired variation of throat area with Mach number. The angle of the ramps varies automatically in a prescribed manner as the Mach number changes.

The quarter-round inlet equipped with a translating centerbody or spike, as used on the General Dynamics F–111 airplane, is illustrated in figure 10.10(b). The inlet is seen to be bounded on the top by the wing and on one side by the fuselage. An installation of this type is often referred to as an "armpit" inlet. The spike automatically translates fore and aft as the Mach number changes. Although not evident in the photograph, the throat area of the inlet also varies with Mach number. This is accomplished by expansion and contraction of the rear part of the spike. The diverter for bypassing the fuselage boundary air is also shown in the photograph. The cover over the inlet is to prevent foreign objects from entering the propulsion system while the aircraft is parked on the ground, and, of course, is removed before flight.

The design of inlet systems for supersonic aircraft is a highly complex matter involving engineering trade-offs between efficiency, complexity, weight, and cost. Some of the factors involved in supersonic inlet design are discussed in references 157 and 179, and the problems of engine-airframe integration on supersonic aircraft are summarized well in reference 180. The highly important problem of selecting and integrating the variable-geometry nozzle of afterburning engines is beyond the scope of the present discussion but is also included in the material presented in reference 180.

Historical Note

This discussion of turbojet and turbofan engines concludes with a few comments on the origins of the propulsion systems. Although rotating turbines and compressors had been in use for various purposes for many years, the idea of coupling the two components, with burners

(a)

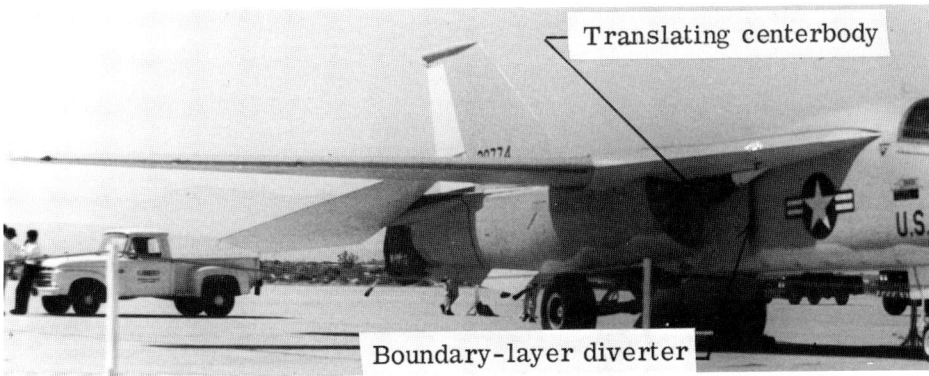

(b)

Figure 10.10 — Two types of variable-geometry inlet. [(a) Arthur L. Shoeni via AAHS; (b) George E. Gillburg via AAHS]

in between, and utilizing the resultant turbine efflux to propel an aircraft was uniquely that of two men working independently with no knowledge of the other's work. These men were Frank Whittle in England and Hans Joachim Pabst von Ohain in Germany.

Simple as the basic idea was, translation of the turbojet concept into a useful aircraft propulsion system presented formidable problems that required technical innovation and engineering of the highest

245

order. Among the many problems were the design of turbines and compressors of sufficiently high efficiency and the proper matching of these components. If the efficiency of these units was not sufficiently high, the turbine would drive the compressor but have a low velocity exhaust incapable of producing useful thrust. Compressor and turbine efficiencies higher than those of other applications of these components were necessary to produce a usable jet engine.

Any aircraft engine of merit must be light in weight. Satisfaction of this requirement with materials of sufficient strength to withstand, for a protracted length of time, the high-temperature, high-stress environment of the hot rotating parts of the engine was a major problem in early jet engines — and remains with us today as engine temperatures continue to rise in the never-ending quest for increased efficiency. Finally, there remained the myriad detail design problems, such as bearings, lubrication, clearances, methods of fabrication and joining, and so on, that must be solved in any new type of machine. Yet, all these problems were overcome in a rudimentary way in the late 1930's and early 1940's, and useful turbojet engines were first produced in this time period. An exhaustive history of turbojet development, beginning with the water wheel, is given in reference 151. Interesting accounts of the early gestation of the turbojet engine are presented in separate papers by Whittle and von Ohain in reference 140.

Air Commodore Sir Frank Whittle (ret.) is often regarded as the father of modern jet propulsion systems. As a young officer in the British Royal Air Force, he became interested in advanced forms of aircraft propulsion. He tried without success to obtain official support for study and development of his ideas but persisted on his own initiative and received his first patent on jet propulsion in January 1930. With private financial support, he began construction of his first engine in 1935. This engine, which had a single-stage centrifugal compressor coupled to a single-stage turbine, was successfully bench tested in April 1937; it was only a laboratory test rig, never intended for use in an aircraft, but it did demonstrate the feasibility of the turbojet concept.

The firm of Power Jets Ltd., with which Whittle was associated, received its first official support in 1938. It received a contract for a Whittle engine, known as the W1, on July 7, 1939. This engine was intended to power a small experimental aircraft. In February 1940, the Gloster Aircraft Company was chosen to develop the aircraft to be powered by the W1 engine. The vehicle, which would be known today as a research aircraft, was covered by specification E28/39 and is frequently referred to by this designation. It was also known as the Pioneer.

The aircraft that emerged from the Gloster factory in 1941 was a small, single-place, low-wing monoplane equipped with a retractable tricycle landing gear. Air for the engine was supplied by a bifurcated nose inlet that passed the intake air around the pilot in separate ducts to the engine located in the rear of the fuselage. The E28/39, which was designed by George Carter of the Gloster Company, weighed 3440 pounds, had a wing span of 29 feet, and was capable of a speed of about 340 miles per hour. The W1 engine installed in the aircraft developed 860 pounds of thrust.

The historic first flight of the Pioneer took place on May 15, 1941, with Flight Lieutenant P. E. G. Sayer as pilot. The aircraft was used for a number of years in the exploration of the problems of flight with jet propulsion and was finally placed in the Science Museum in London in 1946. A brief but interesting account of the development of the E28/39 and its Whittle W1 engine, together with a detailed discussion of the first British operational fighter, is given in reference 188.

Great Britain was not the only European nation to show an interest in jet propulsion prior to 1940. The German aircraft manufacturer Ernst Heinkel was searching for new concepts in aircraft propulsion in the mid-1930's. His interest was stimulated when he heard that a young scientist at Goettingen University, Hans Joachim Pabst von Ohain, was investigating a new type of aircraft engine that did not require a propeller. Ohain joined Heinkel in 1936 and continued with the development of his concepts of jet propulsion (ref. 165). A successful bench test of one of his engines was accomplished in September 1937. To avoid the combustor development problems associated with the use of liquid fuel, gaseous hydrogen was employed in this early test demonstration. Later engines used liquid petroleum fuels.

A small aircraft was designed and constructed by Ernst Heinkel to serve as a test bed for the new type of propulsion system. The aircraft, designated the He178, was a shoulder-wing monoplane in which the pilot's enclosed cockpit was placed ahead of the wing and the conventional landing gear (tail-wheel-type) retracted into the side of the fuselage. The air for the 1000-pound thrust engine was supplied by an inlet located in the nose of the fuselage. The fuselage was constructed of metal, and the internally braced wing was made of wood. The wing span of the aircraft was 26 feet, 3 inches; the length was 24 feet, 6 inches; and the area of the wing was 85 square feet. The aircraft weighed about 4000 pounds; and although the maximum speed achieved with the aircraft is not known, the anticipated maximum speed was 527 miles per hour according to reference 201.

The Heinkel He178 flew for the first time on August 27, 1939, almost 2 years before the first flight of the British Gloster E28/39. The pilot on this historic first flight of a jet-powered airplane was Flight Captain Erich Warsitz. Little official interest was shown at this time by the German Government in the new form of propulsion system demonstrated by the He178, and the aircraft was actually flown only a few times before being retired to the Berlin Air Museum. The aircraft was destroyed during an Allied air raid in 1943. Later jet aircraft developments in Germany during World War II are described in references 160 and 201.

Wings and Configurations for High-Speed Flight

The revolutionary new jet propulsion systems that had their beginnings in the 1940's are briefly described above. The potential for high speed offered by these systems, however, could in no way be realized by typical aircraft designs of the World War II era. High-speed aircraft of this period were usually characterized by straight wings having thickness ratios in the range from 14 to 18 percent. (The wing thickness ratio, expressed in percent, is defined as the thickness of the wing divided by its chord.) The aerodynamic design of such aircraft could, to a first approximation, be thought of in terms of the linear addition of various elements of the aircraft. For example, the drag of the wing, fuselage, and tail, measured separately, could be added together with only minimum consideration of interference effects to obtain the drag of the entire aircraft. As jet propulsion opened the prospects of flight in the high-subsonic, transonic, and supersonic flight regimes, however, these and other time-honored tenets of airplane design were to undergo radical change. The classic shape of the airplane of the 1940's had to be fundamentally altered to permit efficient and safe operation in these new speed ranges. Some of the new configuration concepts for high-speed flight are discussed below.

Swept Wings

The critical Mach number of a wing is the flight Mach number of the aircraft at which the local Mach number at some point of the wing becomes 1.0. At a Mach number slightly in excess of this critical value, shock waves form on the wing, and further increases in speed cause large changes in the forces, moments, and pressures on the wing. The effects on the lift and drag characteristics of increasing the Mach number beyond the critical value are briefly discussed and illustrated in chapter 5. Subsonic aircraft usually do not cruise at Mach numbers much beyond the critical value. For supersonic flight, however, the aircraft must have sufficient power to overcome the high drag in the transonic speed range and be capable of controlled flight through this capricious Mach number range.

For many years, reducing the airfoil thickness ratio was the only known method of increasing the wing critical Mach number by any significant amount (ref. 139). Then in 1945, Robert T. Jones of NACA offered a fundamental breakthrough when he proposed the use of wing sweep as a means for increasing the critical Mach number (ref. 172). The use of wing sweep to increase the efficiency of aircraft intended for flight at supersonic speed was first suggested by Busemann in 1935 (ref. 142); the effectiveness of wing sweep as a means for increasing the critical Mach number had been recognized in Germany before 1945 (ref. 143), but this work was unknown in the United States until after World War II.

The way in which sweepback increases the critical Mach number is illustrated in figure 10.11. If the swept wing is of infinite aspect ratio, the critical Mach number is related to that of the corresponding unswept wing as follows:

$$\frac{M_{cr,\Lambda}}{M_{cr,\Lambda=0}} = \frac{1}{\cos \Lambda}$$

where Λ is the wing sweep angle, $M_{cr,\Lambda=0}$ is the critical Mach number of the unswept wing, $M_{cr,\Lambda}$ is the critical Mach number of the swept wing, and the airfoil thickness ratio normal to the leading edge, or other appropriate spanwise element, remains constant as the wing is rotated to different angles of sweepback. This relationship is based on the assumption that the critical Mach number of the wing is controlled only by the flow normal to the leading edge and is independent of the Mach number parallel to the leading edge. Thus, the free-stream Mach number, that is, the flight Mach number of the aircraft, is resolved into components normal and parallel to the leading edge of the wing. The assumption of independence of the two components of the stream Mach number is strictly true only for invisid flow, but the assumption works reasonably well in predicting the effect of sweep on the critical Mach number of wings operating in real flows with viscosity.

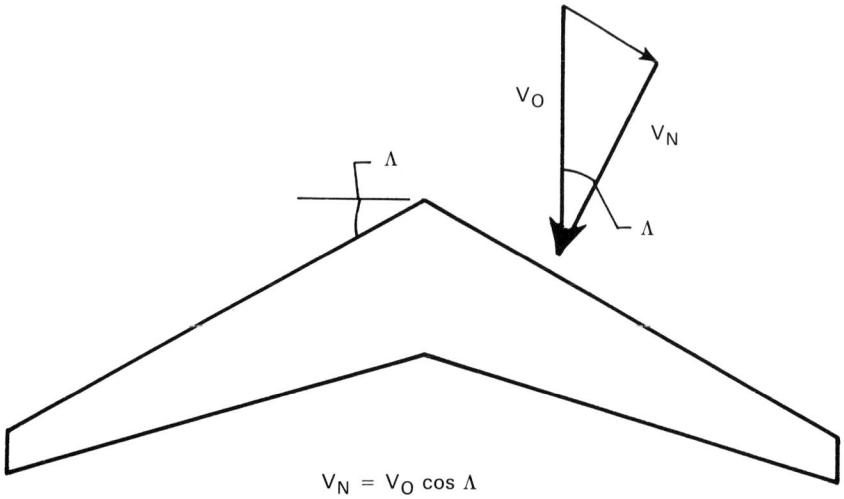

$$V_N = V_O \cos \Lambda$$

Figure 10.11 — Sweptback wing showing resolution of stream velocity into components normal and parallel to leading edge.

The effect of sweepback on the critical Mach number of finite wings is usually analyzed in terms of a wing of given aspect ratio and airfoil thickness ratio in the free-stream direction. The airfoil thickness ratio normal to the leading edge varies, in this case, as the wing sweepback angle is changed. For this reason, and because the flow at the wing root and tip cannot conform to the simple resolution of components normal and parallel to the leading edge, the simple cosine relationship overestimates the magnitude of the effect of sweepback on the critical Mach number. The swept wing, however, must be regarded as a cornerstone of the aerodynamic design of modern high-subsonic-speed jet airplanes. As compared with a straight wing, the swept wing offers significant increases in cruising Mach number and, at the same time, permits the use of wings of sufficient thickness to allow aspect ratios high enough for good values of the maximum lift-drag ratio. The aspect ratio, sweep angle, airfoil thickness ratio, and wing weight necessary for adequate wing strength and stiffness are all related and require a complex series of trade-off studies to arrive at an optimum design for a given set of requirements. The internal volume required for fuel storage and landing-gear retraction also forms an important part of these trade-off studies.

Early jet fighters capable of flight at high-subsonic Mach numbers profited greatly from the use of wing sweepback. A number of such aircraft were developed in the late 1940's and early 1950's. Perhaps the best known of these was the North American F–86 Sabre (described in chapter 11). Only a few years after the end of World War II, however, competitive pressures underlined the need for fighter aircraft capable of flight at transonic and low-supersonic speeds. Efficient flight at these speeds required the use of afterburning jet engines, new configuration concepts, and much reliable aerodynamic design data.

The difficulties encountered in the use of conventional wind tunnels for aerodynamic tests near a Mach number of 1.0 are briefly described in chapter 5. To overcome these difficulties, several alternatives to the wind tunnel were utilized for aerodynamic studies in the last half of the 1940's. These alternative techniques included the free fall, or drop body, and the rocket-model methods. In the free-fall technique, test wings were mounted on a heavily weighted, streamlined body that was dropped from an airplane at altitudes as high as 40 000 feet. With radio transmission of measurements made with internal balances and ground tracking by radar, the forces and moments acting on the wing could be deduced as the test body passed through the transonic speed range. A variation on this technique that offered the potential for higher speeds and longer test times was the rocket-boosted model launched from the ground.

Two other techniques, entirely different from those just described, were used for aerodynamic studies at transonic speeds. In one of these, called the wing-flow technique, a small wing model was mounted perpendicular to the top surface of the wing of a high-speed fighter aircraft. As the aircraft Mach number approached its critical value, transonic speeds developed on top of the wing to which the model was mounted. Forces and moments as measured by a small balance in the airplane wing were then recorded. In a variation of this technique, known as the transonic bump, the small test model was attached normal to a streamlined bump mounted on the floor of a conventional high-subsonic-speed wind tunnel. The high induced velocities over the top of the bump, as on an airplane wing, provided the desired transonic test environment. Several of these techniques are discussed in reference 159.

Although useful as temporary measures, the wind-tunnel alternatives just discussed were time consuming, lacked test flexibility and controllability, and, in some cases, provided results of doubtful quantitative validity. The slotted-throat transonic wind tunnel developed at the NACA's Langley laboratory provided a new dimension in transonic testing. The 8-foot tunnel at Langley was modified with slots and put into operation in 1950 (ref. 138). In this facility, controlled study of large-size models could be made under a variety of test conditions and at Mach numbers that could be varied continuously through the transonic speed range. With the use of facilities such as the 8-foot tunnel, new ideas and the supporting engineering data needed for the development of transonic aircraft began to emerge.

The effectiveness of wing sweep as a means for increasing the critical Mach number of subsonic aircraft has already been discussed. Data obtained from the new facilities showed that wing sweep and airfoil thickness ratio also played a key role in establishing the drag level at transonic speeds. These effects are clearly shown in figure 10.12, which is based on information contained in reference 154. Figure 10.12(a) shows the minimum drag coefficient for a wing with 47° sweepback plotted as a function of Mach number for airfoil thickness ratios of 9, 6, and 4 percent. The dramatic reduction in drag coefficient at Mach numbers in excess of 1.0 as the airfoil thickness ratio is reduced from 9 to 4 percent is obvious. The variation of minimum drag coefficient is shown in figure 10.12(b) for a 4-percent-thick wing having sweepback angles of 11°, 35°, and 47°. Increasing the sweep angle for a wing of given thickness ratio also reduces significantly the drag level at speeds above Mach 1.0. Clearly, the message portrayed in figure 10.12 is that the wings of aircraft designed to penetrate into the low-supersonic speed range should be thin and swept. These purely aerodynamic considerations for choosing a wing of low drag do not necessarily result in an optimum wing for a given airplane. Again, as in the case of subsonic aircraft, detailed trade-off studies between the various wing geometric/aerodynamic characteristics and wing strength, weight, and stiffness must be made. Because of the requirements for very thin airfoil sections, these trade-offs almost inevitably lead to wings of low aspect ratio on fighter aircraft designed to penetrate the transonic and low-supersonic speed regimes. As compared with aspect ratios of 7 to 8 commonly found on subsonic jet transports, values as low as 2 to 3 are not unusual on fighter aircraft.

The wings illustrated in figures 10.11 and 10.12 are swept back, as are most of the wings seen on operational aircraft. But, according to the simple theory in which the streamwise velocity is resolved into components normal and parallel to the leading edge of the wing, the wing could just as well be swept forward. The experimental Junkers Ju 287-1, built in Germany during World War II and described in reference 201, had sweptforward wings, and one of the business jet transports described in chapter 14 also incorporates wings with forward sweep.

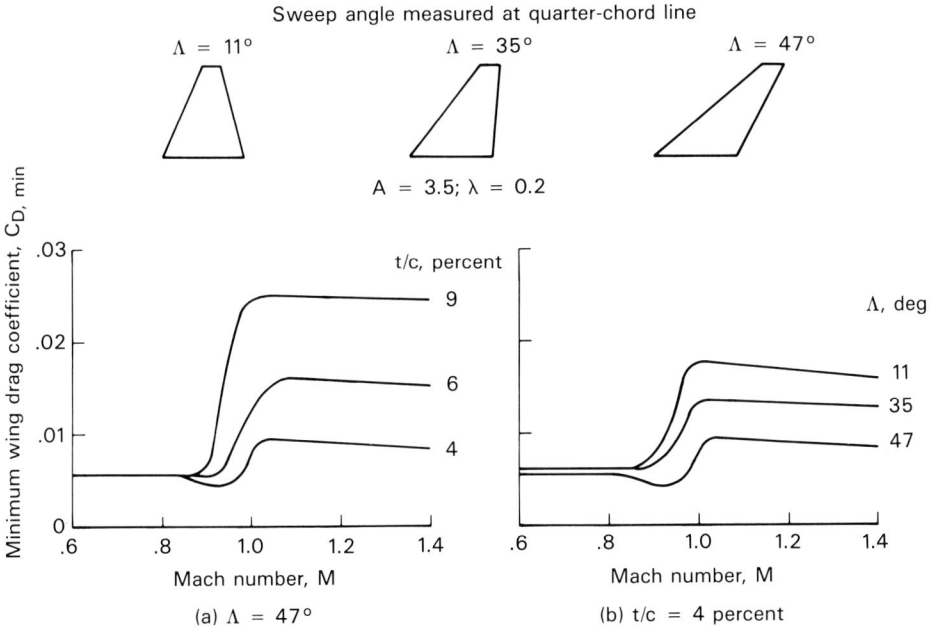

Figure 10.12 — Conceptual effect of wing sweepback angle and airfoil-section thickness ratio on variation of wing drag coefficient with Mach number.

Sweptforward wings, however, have a fundamental aeroelastic problem that has mitigated against their use. Simply stated, an increase in load on the wing twists the outer portions of the sweptforward wing to higher angles of attack. When the dynamic pressure reaches a critical value, the increment in aerodynamic twisting moment associated with an incremental change in angle of attack is equal to the corresponding incremental change in torsional resisting moment provided by the structure. Any further increase in dynamic pressure will result in the wing twisting off the aircraft. The critical condition at which this catastrophic failure occurs is termed the divergence speed, or divergence dynamic pressure. Structural studies of wings constructed of conventional metal alloys have shown that a sweptforward wing of a given aspect ratio will be heavier than a sweptback wing of the same aspect ratio and sweep angle. The additional weight results from the increased torsional stiffness required to prevent divergence within the flight envelope of the aircraft. The advent of composite materials, however, seems to offer the possibility of constructing sweptforward wings with little or no weight penalty (ref. 166). A number of studies of the possible advantages of such wings on fighter aircraft have been made, and a research-type fighter with sweptforward wings is now (1982) under development.

Delta Wings

A variation on the swept wing theme is the delta wing first proposed by the German aerodynamicist Alexander Lippisch in the years prior to World War II (ref. 175). This wing derives its name from the Greek letter Δ, which describes the planform shape. Sweep of the leading edge varies with the application but usually falls in the range between 70° and 40°. Shown in figure 10.13(a) is a simple 45° delta wing; three variations of the simple delta planform are shown in figures 10.13 (b), (c), and (d). Many other variants are possible. In fact, the wings of some modern fighter aircraft defy classification as simple delta

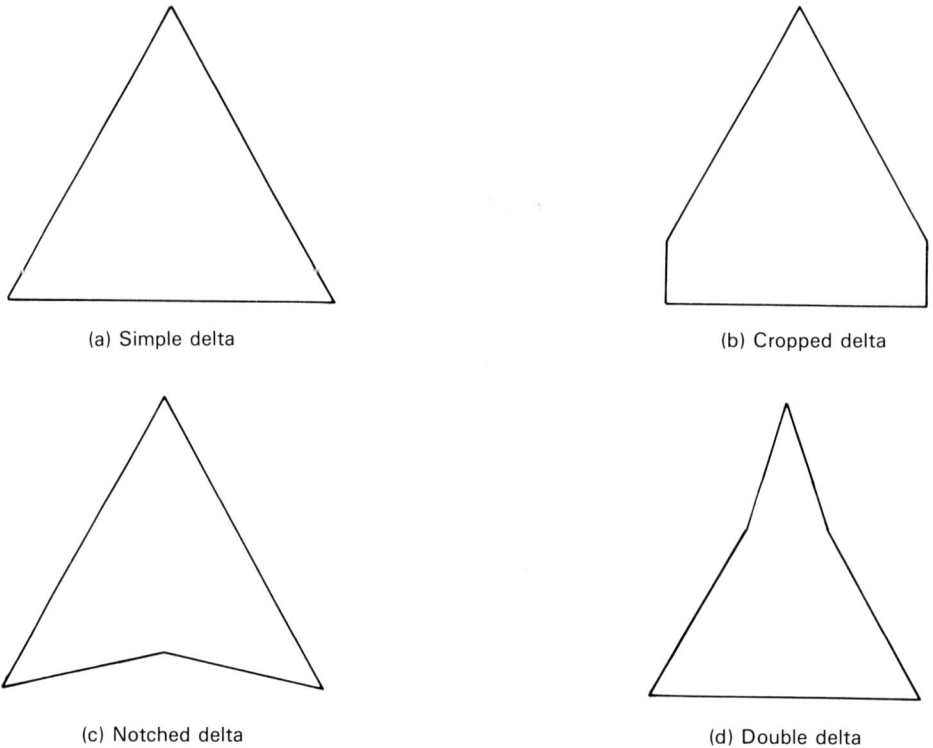

(a) Simple delta

(b) Cropped delta

(c) Notched delta

(d) Double delta

Figure 10.13 — Four delta-wing planforms.

or swept wings since they have some of the geometric characteristics of both. Typical wing-planform shapes of fighter aircraft are illustrated in chapter 11.

The delta wing is particularly well suited to tailless, all-wing configurations since the flap-type longitudinal controls can be located on the wing trailing edge, far behind the aircraft center of gravity. Other advantages of the delta wing as compared with the swept wing are its large internal storage volume, relatively good characteristics at high angles of attack, and lessened susceptibility to aeroelastic problems. On tailless applications, however, trailing-edge high-lift devices cannot be used because of the large pitching moments generated by these devices. Further, the high drag due to lift inherent in the low-aspect-ratio delta wing must be carefully evaluated in relation to such aircraft characteristics as wing loading, as well as cruise speed and altitude. Again, as mentioned previously, the choice between swept, delta, straight, or some hybrid wing planform must rest on the results of trade-off studies for a given application. A good discussion of such studies is presented in several of the papers contained in reference 155.

Variable-Sweep Wings

Thin swept wings of low aspect ratio are part of the aerodynamic ingredients of a low-drag supersonic aircraft but, at the same time, yield an aircaft with a relatively low maximum lift-drag ratio at subsonic speeds, as well as certain undesirable handling characteristics in the low-speed, high-angle-of-attack regime. (Even so, the poor subsonic maximum lift-drag ratio is higher than that at supersonic speeds; flight in the low-supersonic speed range is not very efficient.) There are several types of mission, however, in which a supersonic capability coupled with high subsonic efficiency is highly desirable. For example, an attack mission may be comprised of a long-range, high-efficiency subsonic segment followed by a supersonic dash over enemy territory to the target, after which subsonic cruise is used for the return trip home. Many military-mission profiles combining efficient subsonic cruise with a supersonic capability have been postulated. In the civil arena, the supersonic transport not only requires good supersonic cruising efficiency but must also be able to fly efficiently at subsonic speeds for route segments over land (such aircraft are forbidden to fly at supersonic speeds over land because of the sonic boom) and for holding in the terminal area.

These multimission requirements suggest a wing whose sweepback angle, and thus aspect ratio, can be mechanically adjusted in flight to the optimum position for each speed regime. A model of a conceptual variable-sweep aircraft with its wings set in three different sweep positions is shown in figure 10.14. The increase in wing span, and thus aspect ratio, that accompanies movement of the wing to lower sweep angles is obvious. The maximum lift-drag ratio at subsonic speeds increases, of course, with the aspect ratio, as quantitatively shown in ap-

Figure 10.14 — Model of a conceptual variable-sweep aircraft with the wing in three different sweep positions. [NASA]

pendix C. The near-zero sweep angle with accompanying high aspect ratio would be appropriate for landing, takeoff, and climb; whereas the intermediate sweep could be used for normal cruise at subsonic speeds. Flight at high-subsonic and supersonic speeds would call for the wing to be swept fully back.

Aircraft with variable sweep wings have been discussed since the concept of wing sweep was first introduced. Some of the aerodynamic problems introduced by the variable sweep concept together with possible solutions, based on material contained in reference 184, are illustrated in figure 10.15. Figure 10.15(a) shows a wing that changes its sweep angle by rotating about a single inboard pivot located on the fuselage center line. At the bottom of the figure the rearward movement of the wing center of lift with increasing sweep angle is shown for both subsonic and supersonic speeds. The slight rearward shift of the aircraft center of gravity is caused by the rearward shift of the wing weight. Indicated by the cross-hatching is the distance between the center of gravity and the center of lift. This distance is a measure of the longitudinal stability of the aircraft and greatly increases as the sweep angle increases. A small amount of longitudinal stability is highly desirable, but the large increases with sweep angle shown in figure 10.15(a) cause reductions in aircraft maneuverability and large increases in trim drag. (Trim drag is associated with the large negative lift load that must be carried by the tail to balance the pitching moment induced by the distance between the centers of gravity and lift.) A single pivot wing of the type shown in figure 10.15(a) is accordingly unacceptable, and no aircraft utilizing this concept has ever been built.

A solution to the problem highlighted in figure 10.15(a) is illustrated in figure 10.15(b). Here, the wing translates forward as the sweep angle increases so that the stability remains essentially the same at all sweep angles. The increase in stability at supersonic speeds is not related to variable sweep but is characteristic of all wings as they pass from subsonic to supersonic speeds. The rotating and translating variable-sweep wing has been explored on two experimental aircraft. First was the Bell X–5 research airplane, which made its initial flight in 1951. The sweep angle on this aircraft could be varied from 20° to 60°, as shown by figure 10.16. No problems were encountered with the variable-sweep mechanism on the X–5, and flight characteristics of the aircraft were fairly good at all sweep angles. At a somewhat later date, the Grumman XF10F variable-sweep fighter entered flight testing. Like the X–5, the Grumman fighter had a wing that combined rotation and translation to control the relationship between the centers of lift and gravity. Because of problems entirely unrelated to the variable-sweep feature, the XF10F was not a success and was never put into production. Both the X-5 and the XF10F were subsonic aircraft in which the variable-sweep feature was intended to increase, as compared with a fixed-wing aircraft, the critical Mach number at high-subsonic speeds and reduce the landing speed at the other end of the scale. These goals were accomplished in both aircraft. The translating and rotating variable-sweep wing, however, is heavy and leads to undesirable mechanical complications.

Shown in figure 10.15(c) is the basic solution to the variable-sweep stability problem employed in the design of all operational variable-sweep aircraft in use today. The wing pivot is located outboard of the fuselage with a highly swept cuff extending from the pivot to the side of the fuselage. In this concept, developed at the NASA Langley Research Center, the fixed and movable components of the wing are configured so that the wing span-load distribution varies with sweep angle in a manner to minimize the rearward shift in the center of lift. As illustrated in figure 10.15(c), the distance between the centers of lift and gravity are the same at subsonic speeds for two sweep angles — one low and one high.

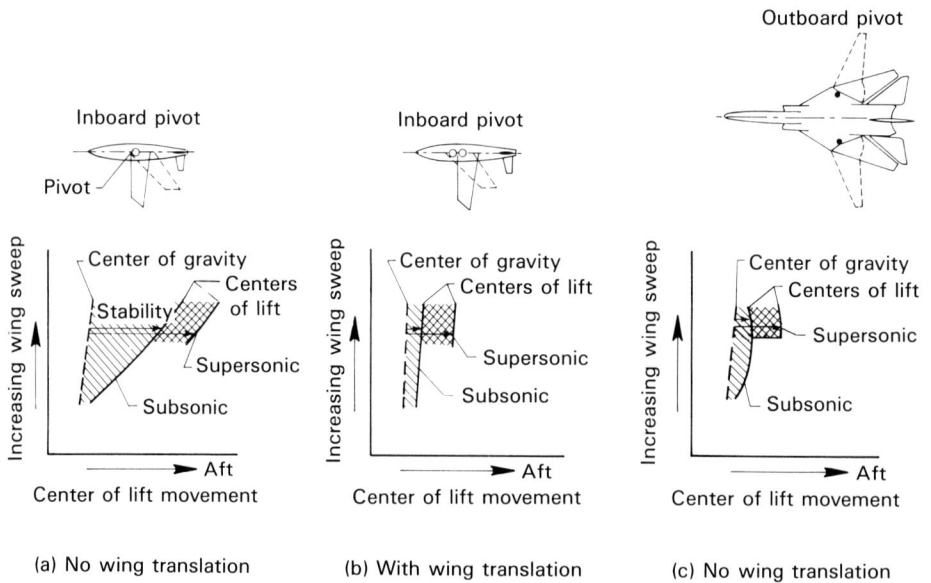

Figure 10.15 — Aft movement of center of lift with increasing sweep angle for three variable-sweep concepts.

Figure 10.16 — Bell X-5 research aircraft equipped with variable sweep wings. [NASA]

Three variable-sweep aircraft employing the outboard pivot concept are in operational use or under development in the United States
today. These are described in chapters 11 and 12. Several variable-
sweep aircraft are also in operational use in Europe. Interesting accounts of the development of variable-sweep concepts and aircraft are
contained in references 155 and 184.

The Area Rule

The large increment in drag that accompanies an increase in Mach number from subsonic to supersonic values is clearly indicated by the curves in figure 10.12 for wings of different sweep angle and thickness ratio. The formation of shock waves on the wing and body as the aircraft passes through the transonic speed range is responsible for this large increase in drag. Both aerodynamic theory for this speed range and early experimental results obtained from tests in the slotted-throat transonic wind tunnel indicated that the wave drag of a wing-fuselage combination would be significantly higher than the sum of the drag of these two elements measured separately.

In the early 1950's, Richard T. Whitcomb of the NACA Langley Memorial Aeronautical Laboratory first experimentally demonstrated an aerodynamic principle that has had a profound and far-reaching effect on the entire process of airplane configuration synthesis. Known as the transonic area rule (ref. 202), this principle is illustrated in figure 10.17(a). According to Donlan, from whose 1954 paper (ref. 153) the sketch in figure 10.17(a) was taken, "the basic tenet of the area rule . . . states that the wave drag of an airplane configuration depends primarily on the longitudinal distribution of the total cross-sectional area. This concept results in the proposition that the wave drag of a simple equivalent body of revolution (that is, a body having the same longitudinal distribution of total cross-sectional area) would be the same as that of the more complex wing-body arrangement." As shown in figure 10.17(a), the cross-sectional area distribution is determined from planes passed through the configuration perpendicular to the longitudinal axis of the body. This procedure is correct only for a Mach number of 1.0, but with a relatively simple modification it can be applied at supersonic speeds (ref. 203).

Figure 10.17(b) shows the variation of drag coefficient with Mach number for a smooth body and the same body having a bump corresponding to the cross-sectional area of a wing. The dramatic increase in drag associated with the addition of a bump to the body is apparent. An obvious conclusion to be reached is that the cross-sectional area distribution of a low-drag wing-body combination should be the same as that of a smooth body of optimum shape. Thus, at transonic speeds, the time-honored principle that the drag of the individual elements of an airplane could be added in a linear manner to give the approximate drag of the entire configuration was forever ended, and the era of the "wasp waist" or "Coke bottle" airplane with indented fuselage began.

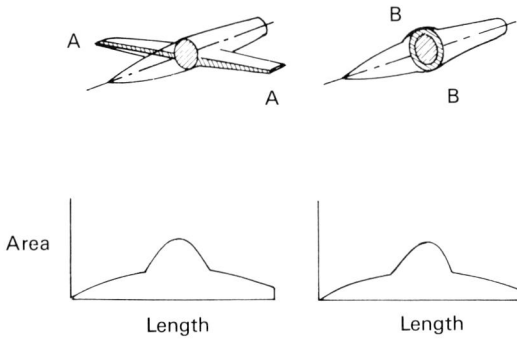

(a) Equivalent body concept

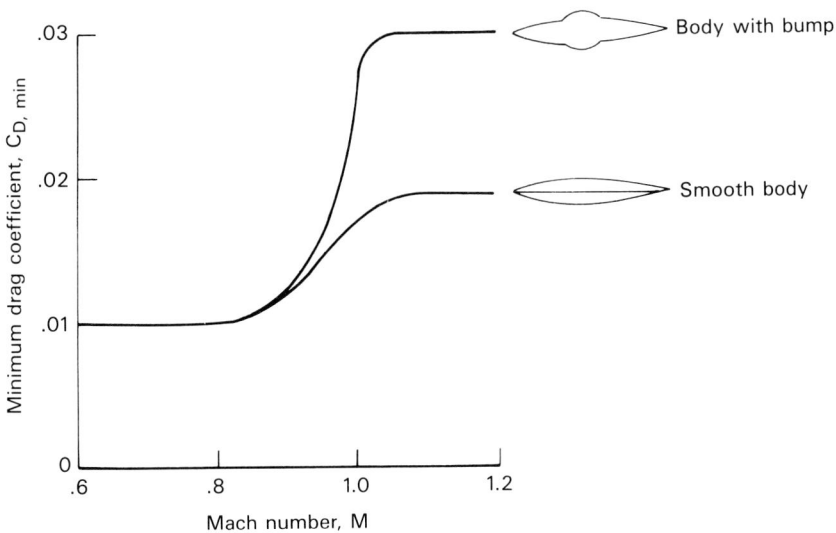

(b) Variation of drag coefficient for two bodies

Figure 10.17 — The transonic area rule.

The first aircraft to which the area-rule principle was applied was the Convair F–102 delta-wing fighter. With its relatively low-thrust engine, the prototype of this supposed supersonic fighter was unable to pass through Mach 1.0. At the top of figure 10.18 is the total cross-sectional area distribution of the aircraft, together with that of the vari-

261

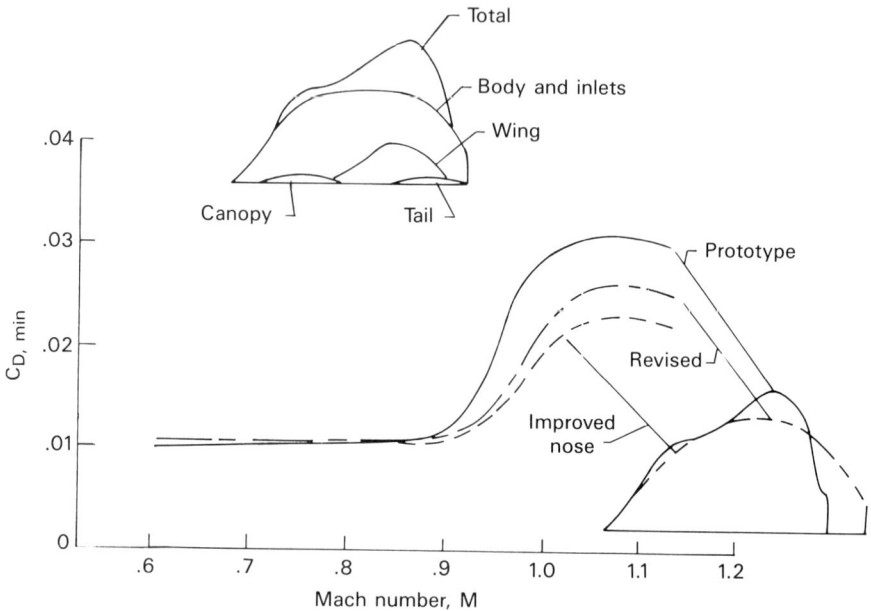

Figure 10.18 — Effect of area-rule modifications on drag of Convair F–102 delta-wing fighter.

ous components that make up the complete area distribution. At the bottom of the figure is the variation of drag coefficient with Mach number for the original configuration and for the aircraft with modifications made in accordance with the transonic area rule. The modified aircraft easily passed through Mach 1.0 and entered the supersonic speed regime. The way in which the appearance of the F–102 aircraft was altered by application of the area rule is illustrated in figure 10.19. At the upper left is the experimental Convair XF–92A delta-wing research aircraft. At the upper right is the prototype F–102 delta-wing fighter that was unable to penetrate the supersonic speed range. Incorporating area-rule principles, the F–102A is shown at the lower left with its obvious fuselage indentation. The definitive form of the Convair delta-wing fighter, the F–106, is shown at the lower right and clearly displays the application of the area-rule concept. The reason for the appellation "wasp waist" or "Coke bottle" for aircraft designed according to area-rule concepts is obvious from figure 10.19.

The area-rule principle is now an accepted part of aircraft configuration synthesis and must be regarded as one of the cornerstones of

Figure 10.19 — Convair delta-wing aircraft with and without area-rule design. [mfr via Donald D. Baals]

transonic and supersonic aircraft design. It clearly differentiates these aircraft from their subsonic ancestors.

Stalling of Swept Wings

The advantages of wing sweep for aircraft designed to fly at high-subsonic, transonic, and supersonic speeds have been discussed above. Along with such advantages, however, these wings can pose serious sta-

263

Figure 10.20 — Bell L–39 research aircraft intended to explore the problems of low-speed flight with swept wings. [NASA]

bility, control, and handling problems at high angles of attack in the stalled flight condition; such problems can occur at both high and low speeds. An early NACA flight study of the handling characteristics of an aircraft with swept wings was carried out in 1947 with a modified Bell P–63 propeller-driven fighter. This aircraft, fitted with wings of 35° sweepback, was redesignated the L–39 and is shown in figure 10.20. Note the wool tufts that are attached to the wing surfaces to indicate areas of unsteady or stalled flow. Extensive wind-tunnel studies of the high-angle-of-attack behavior of swept wings and of aircraft configurations equipped with such wings were also made in the years following World War II.

The nature of the problem is illustrated in figure 10.21, in which the variation with spanwise position of the wing aerodynamic load is shown for wings of aspect ratio 4.0 and different sweepback angle and

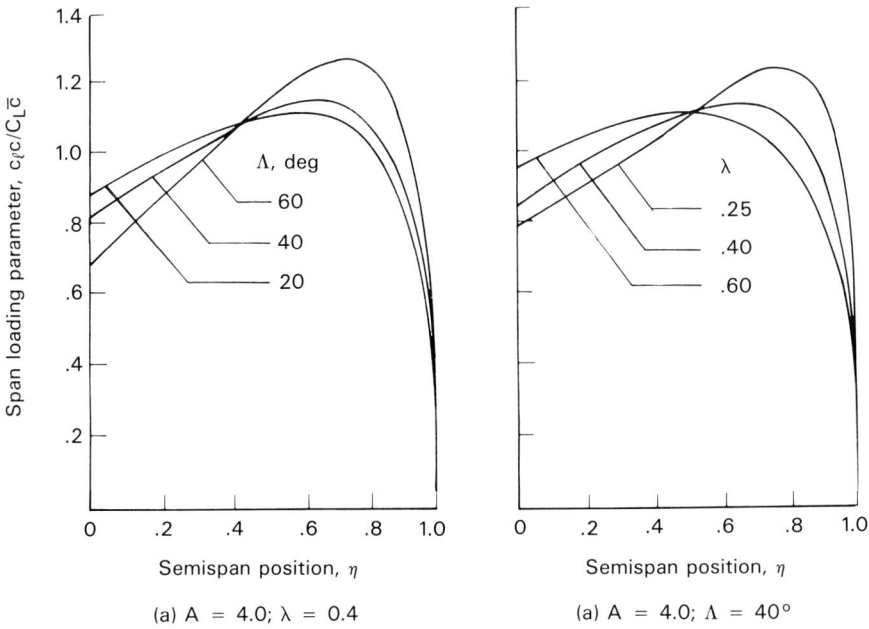

Figure 10.21 — Effect of wing-planform shape on span load distribution.

taper ratio. The relative amount of aerodynamic load at each spanwise station is expressed by the span loading parameter $c_i c / \overline{C}_L c$, which is the product of the local section lift coefficient at a particular spanwise station and the wing chord at that position, divided by the product of the wing lift coefficient and the mean aerodynamic chord. The curves in figure 10.21(a) indicate that an increase in sweepback angle from 20° to 60° results in a large increase in the value of the loading parameter near the tip relative to that at the root for wings of aspect ratio 4.0 and taper ratio 0.4. Reducing the taper ratio from 0.6 to 0.25 on wings of aspect ratio 4.0 and 40° of sweepback causes a corresponding increase in the relative amount of load carried near the wingtip, as shown by figure 10.21(b). Variations in the aspect ratio for a given sweepback angle and taper ratio also have an important influence on the shape of the span loading curve.

An increase in the value of the span loading parameter from root to tip indicates that the amount of load carried by each section of the wing increases as the tip is approached. If the wing is tapered, the section lift coefficients increase at a greater rate than the loading parameter. Thus, for untwisted wings equipped with airfoil sections having the same maximum lift coefficients, the initial wing stall would be expected to occur near the wingtip at the spanwise location at which the loading parameter is a maximum. Further increases in angle of attack would cause an inward progression of the stall. A loss in load near the wingtip may, depending on the sweep angle, taper ratio, and aspect ratio, cause a forward shift in the wing aerodynamic center of sufficient magnitude to cause the aircraft to become unstable and pitch up to a higher angle of attack and further into the stalled and poorly controlled flight regime. This behavior is in contrast with that of a straight-wing aircraft that has inherent stability at the stall and pitches down to a lower angle of attack and into an unstalled and fully controllable flight condition. Pitch-up at the stall is considered to be a highly undesirable flight characteristic. In the development of a new aircraft, much attention is given to wing design and configuration arrangement to avoid pitch-up. Electromechanical devices (described later) must be used in some cases to provide acceptable flight characteristics at high angles of attack.

The approximate boundary shown on the left side of figure 10.22 delineates the combinations of wing sweep and aspect ratio that show reduced stability, or pitch-up, at the stall from those combinations that show increased stability at the stall. Combinations of aspect ratio and sweep angle that give reduced stability at the stall are in region II to the right of the boundary. The types of pitching-moment curves that might be expected in region II are indicated at the top right side of figure 10.22. Combinations of sweep and aspect ratio that are characterized by positive stability at the stall are in region I to the left of the boundary, and the corresponding shape of the pitching-moment curves is shown at the lower right side of the figure. If positive stability at the stall is desired, the curve in figure 10.22 indicates that the aspect ratio must decrease as the sweep angle is increased.

The stability boundary given in figure 10.22 was taken from reference 183 and is for untwisted wings with a taper ratio of 0.5. The results given in reference 189 indicate that increasing the taper ratio from 0.5 to 0 raises the stability boundary; that is, the limiting aspect ratio for stability at the stall is increased for a given sweep angle. Highly swept and tapered delta wings as used on many fighter aircraft generally do not have a pitch-up characteristic, which is one of the attractive features of this planform. Twisting the wing so that the geometric angle of attack of the tip is less than that of the root (termed "washout") may be used to reduce the tendency toward tip stall, as can various types of leading-edge high-lift devices. Some of these devices are briefly discussed in the next section. The spanwise flow along the

I Increased stability at the stall
II Reduced stability at the stall

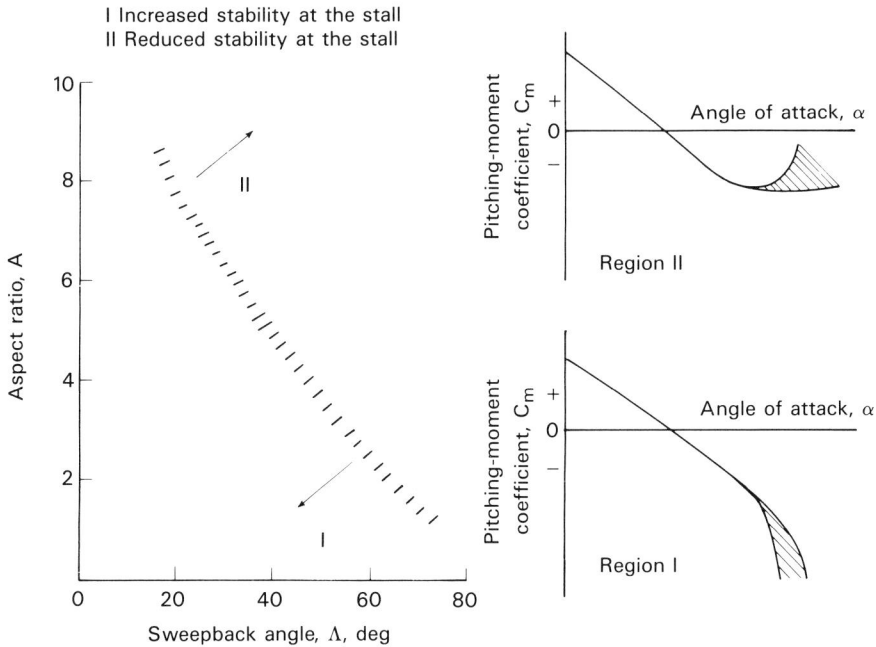

Figure 10.22 — Effect of wing-planform shape on static longitudinal stability at the stall. Tail off; taper ratio of 0.5.

wing that results from the sweepback causes the boundary layer on the outboard sections of the wing to thicken, as compared with an unswept wing. The thicker boundary layer near the tip of the wing causes the maximum lift capability of these sections to be reduced, as compared with the two-dimensional value. The fences seen on the upper surface of many swept wings are intended to limit the spanwise boundary-layer flow and thus increase the maximum lift capability of the outboard sections; at the same time, the boundary layer builds up inboard of the fences and reduces the maximum lift coefficent of that part of the wing. Both these effects of the fence reduce the tendency toward pitch-up.

The discussion so far has dealt only with wing-alone stalling behavior. The stalling and subsequent pitching characteristics of the aircraft, however, are highly dependent upon the details of the aircraft configuration. The longitudinal and vertical position of the horizontal tail with respect to the wing is particularly important. A detailed development of the relationships involved is beyond the scope of the present discussion but may be found in references 189 and 195.

Some indication of the flow phenomena involved in the wing-tail relationship, however, may be gained from figure 10.23. At the top left side of the figure is an aircraft configuration on which the horizontal tail is slightly above or below the chord plane of the wing. At position 1 the wing is just beginning to stall and the tail is immersed in the wake. The hypothetical pitching-moment curve in the lower portion of figure 10.23 shows that a reduction in stability is beginning at point 1. At position 2 the aircraft is at a higher angle of attack, and the wake from the wing passes above the chord plane of the tail. The contribution of the tail to the positive stability of the aircraft is therefore increased at point 2, as compared with point 1, because the tail is operating in a flow field characterized by smaller downwash angles and higher dynamic pressure. The pitching-moment curve shown at the bottom of figure 10.23(a) shows the higher stability of the aircraft at position 2 and indicates that there is no real pitch-up, although a small reduction in stability occurs at the stall. The pitching-moment curve for the aircraft configuration with the tail mounted in the low position would be considered acceptable, although not as desirable as that of a design that showed no reduction in stability at the stall.

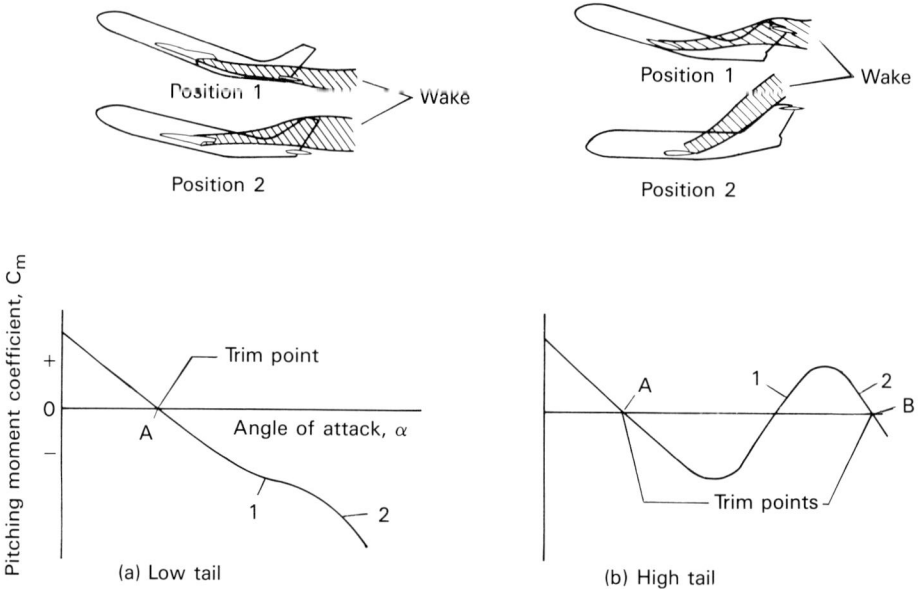

Figure 10.23 — Effect of horizontal-tail position on static longitudinal stability.

An aircraft configuration in which the horizontal tail is mounted high above the chord plane of the wing is shown in figure 10.23(b). A greater portion of the wing is stalled on this type of configuration, as compared with the design with the low tail, before the tail encounters the stalled wake. The wake is therefore broader in width and of a lower dynamic pressure for the high tail position. Position 1 in the upper part of figure 10.23(b) shows the high tail immersed in the wide, low-energy wake. The hypothetical pitching-moment curve at the bottom of the figure indicates the large reduction in stability that accompanies an increase in angle of attack as the tail passes through the wake. Following emergence of the tail from the wake, the aircraft again becomes stable and with further increases in angle of attack reaches a second trim point as indicated by point B on the pitching-moment curve. If the longitudinal control surfaces are in the full nose-down position and the pitching-moment curve appears as depicted in figure 10.23(b), no recovery is possible if the aircraft is allowed to reach the second trim point B.

Although fighter aircraft have in the past been configured with a high tail position, the requirement for fighter-type aircraft to engage in high-g maneuvers at high-subsonic and transonic speeds makes the use of a low tail position very desirable to avoid the possibility of pitch-up into an uncontrolled flight condition. The consequences of such an uncontrolled maneuver in a combat situation can well be imagined. The low tail position as employed on the Grumman F11F fighter, introduced in the mid-1950's, is shown in figure 10.24. The good handling characteristics of this aircraft are evident from its use for many years by the U.S. Navy Blue Angels demonstration team.

Since high-g maneuvers are not required on large transport aircraft, acceptable pitching-moment characteristics can usually be obtained with a high tail position by careful tailoring of the wing and tail designs and their relationships to each other. For configurations that employ engines mounted on the aft portion of the fuselage, careful attention must be given to exact placement of these engines since the wake from the engine nacelles at high angles of attack may combine with that of the wing and contribute to the loss in effectiveness of the horizontal tail. In some cases, acceptable pitching-moment characteristics cannot be achieved by aerodynamic refinements alone. In these cases, mechanical devices such as stick shakers or stick pushers, sometimes both, are employed to prevent the aircraft from entering a potentially dangerous angle-of-attack region. A stick shaker is a mechanical device that causes the control column to vibrate violently as the aircraft

Figure 10.24 — Grumman F11F with all-moving horizontal tail mounted in the low position. [NASA]

approaches a restricted angle-of-attack range. The vibration is intended to alert the pilot to an approaching stall and to make him take corrective action to reduce the angle of attack. A stick pusher causes the control column to be pushed forward mechanically with a considerable force, perhaps 100 pounds, as the critical angle-of-attack range is approached. Sometimes the devices are employed together, in which case, the stick shaker is first activated, and if the pilot ignores the warning and permits the aircraft to continue pitching to a higher angle of attack, the stick pusher comes into action. Both the stick pusher and the stick shaker are activated by signals from instruments that sense parameters such as angle of attack, rate of change of angle of attack, attitude and its rate of change, or some combination of these parameters.

The preceding discussion deals with the major aerodynamic problem of the swept wing. Other aerodynamic problems of a less fundamental nature are also associated with the use of the swept wing. There are also problems in the areas of structures and aeroelasticity. While these problems are beyond the scope of the present discussion, an indication of the nature of the structures and aeroelastic problems is suggested in figure 10.21(a) by the wings with an aspect ratio of 4 and sweepback angles of 20°, 40° and 60°. Increasing the sweepback angle for a given aspect ratio results in an increased length of the wing panel. The length-to-width ratio of the panel, sometimes referred to as the panel aspect ratio, is increased by the factor $1/\cos \Lambda$ for a given aerodynamic aspect ratio. For a given aerodynamic aspect ratio and airfoil thickness ratio, increasing the sweepback angle increases the wing length and causes a reduction in wing bending and torsional stiffness. As a consequence, the problems of aeroelasticity, flutter, and dynamic loads can be intensified by the use of sweepback.

High-Lift Systems

Increases in the capability of high-lift devices have always accompanied the use of higher wing loadings. This trend has been particularly evident in the evolution of the modern jet transport aircraft. Data given in chapter 3 of reference 176 show that airplane maximum lift coefficients of about 3 are being obtained in flight on modern operational jet transport aircraft. The corresponding two-dimensional airfoil maximum section lift coefficients for the flapped sections are probably somewhat in excess of 4. By comparison, the data in figure 7.5 show that airplane maximum lift coefficients slightly in excess of 2 were being achieved by the end of World War II. The technology for achieving two-dimensional maximum lift coefficients, without boundary-layer control, of about 3.2 existed at the end of World War II, as shown by the comparative data in figure 5.3.

The high-lift system employed on modern jet transport aircraft consists of an assortment of various types of leading- and trailing-edge devices. A number of these devices and the manner in which they are mechanically actuated are described in reference 197. Although the detail design and relative effectiveness of the different devices vary, the basic means by which they increase the maximum lift coefficient remain the same. Trailing-edge devices are designed to increase the effective angle through which the flow is turned and thus increase the lifting capability. Leading-edge devices are basically designed to assist the flow in negotiating the sharp turn from the lower surface, around the leading edge, and back for a short distance on the upper surface, without separating. Modern high-lift devices as used on large transport aircraft form the subject of the next few paragraphs.

Two typical high-lift configurations are shown in figure 10.25. A wing section equipped with a leading-edge slat and a triple-slotted trailing-edge flap is shown in figure 10.25(a). The trailing-edge flap deploys rearward and downward and separates into three components. The slots in the flap allow flow from the lower surface to the upper surface. The flow through the slots energizes the boundary-layer flow on the top surface, which is negotiating a positive pressure gradient, and prevents separation and subsequent loss of lift. The detail design of the slot contours is very critical and must be carefully worked out in wind-tunnel studies. Both the leading- and trailing-edge devices are completely retracted in cruising flight and are only deployed for landing and takeoff.

A wing section equipped with a leading-edge Krueger flap and a trailing-edge double-slotted flap is shown in figure 10.25(b). The Krueger flap is somewhat less effective than the slat but is probably simpler in mechanical design. Some aircraft employ slats on the outboard portion of the leading edge, where more powerful flow control is required, and Krueger flaps on the inboard portion of the leading edge. The double-slotted trailing-edge flap is not as powerful as the triple-slotted flap but is mechanically simpler and easier to implement than the triple-slotted flap. The simple single-slotted flap is often used as a trailing-edge device. This flap consists of a single unsegmented

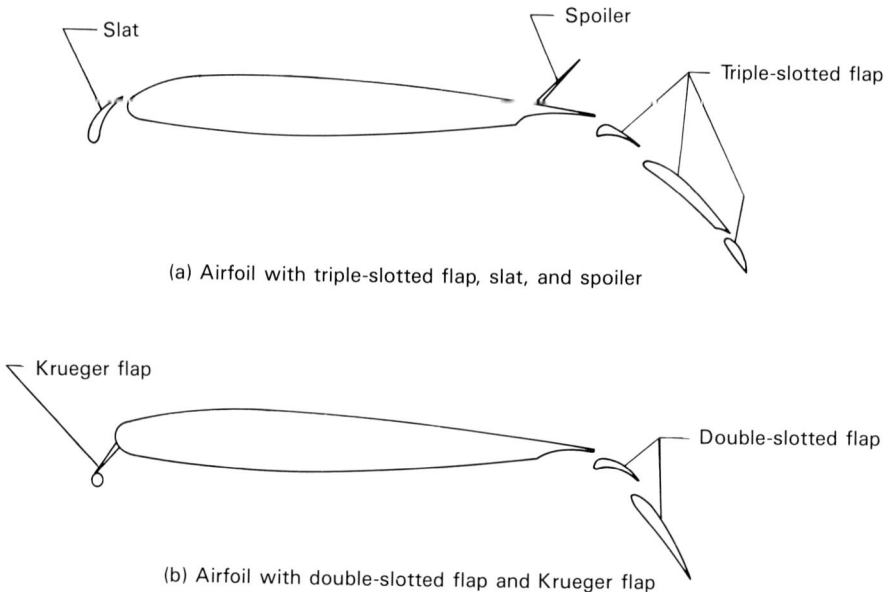

(a) Airfoil with triple-slotted flap, slat, and spoiler

(b) Airfoil with double-slotted flap and Krueger flap

Figure 10.25 — Typical flap systems employed on jet-powered aircraft.

element that is deployed by moving rearward and downward. Although less effective than either of the other two types of trailing-edge devices described, it is by far the most mechanically simple of the three, and the aerodynamic design is the simplest. Many other types and combinations of high-lift devices may be used on jet transport aircraft. The types shown in figure 10.25 are only intended to be representative of typical installations.

Also shown on the upper surface of the wing in figure 10.25(a) is a spoiler in the deployed position. The spoiler is flush with the wing surface when retracted. The action of the spoiler in the deployed position is to "spoil" or separate the flow downstream. The lift of the wing is therefore reduced and the drag increased. These two aerodynamic effects are utilized in several ways. When deployed on only one wing of an aircraft, they cause that wing to drop and thus serve as a lateral-control device. The wings of many jet transport aircraft employ several spoiler elements on each wing. These elements may act simultaneously or in reduced number, depending on the flight condition and the function they are intended to fulfill. Some elements of the spoilers are frequently used in combination with conventional ailerons to assist in lateral control. The mix between ailerons and spoilers varies with the flight conditions under which the aircraft is operating. For example, the dynamic pressure corresponding to cruising flight at 35000 feet and a Mach number of 0.8 is 223 pounds per square foot, whereas that for an approach speed of 135 knots at sea level is 60 pounds per square foot. The need for additional lateral-control devices for flight at low speeds, as compared with cruising flight at high Mach numbers, is clearly shown by the difference in the dynamic pressure for the two flight conditions.

The spoilers are also used to reduce lift and increase drag when deployed symmetrically, that is, in the same manner on each wing. The spoilers are usually deployed in this way immediately after touchdown on landing to assist in stopping the aircraft. The increased aerodynamic drag serves as a braking function for the aircraft, and the reduction in lift increases the percentage of the aircraft weight on the runway and thus increases the effectiveness of the wheel brakes. Many aircraft also utilize symmetrical deployment of the spoilers in flight to increase the rate of descent, for example, to comply with air-traffic-control requirements during the transition from high-altitude cruising flight to flight in the terminal area.

Figure 10.26 — Lower-surface view of triple-slotted flap on Boeing 737 airplane. [NASA]

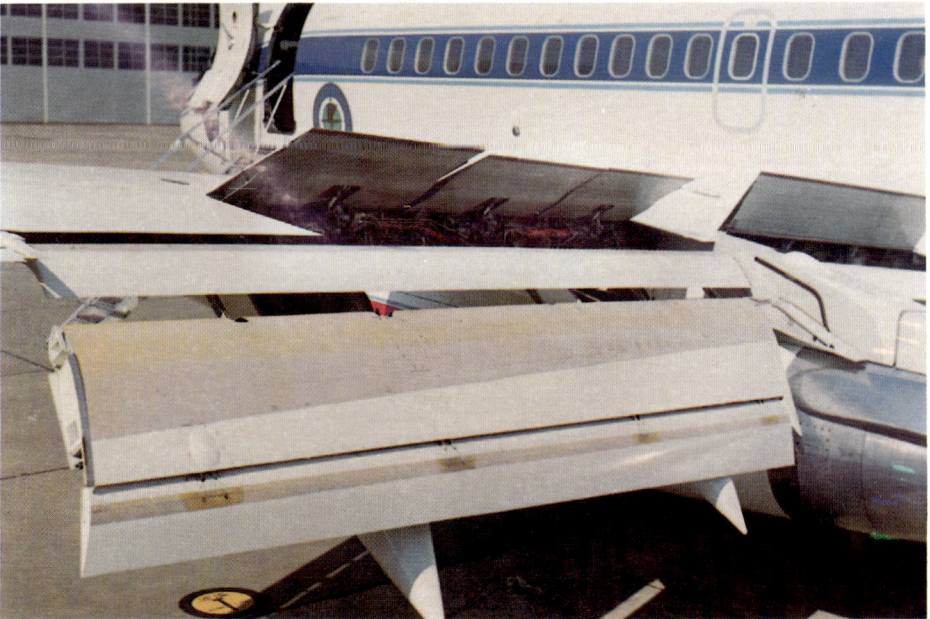

Figure 10.27 — Upper-surface view showing triple-slotted flap and spoilers on Boeing 737 airplane. [NASA]

Two views of a triple-slotted flap installed on a Boeing 737 aircraft are shown in figures 10.26 and 10.27. The large fairing shown on the lower side of the wing and flap in figure 10.26 houses the mechanism for deploying the flap. The four segments of the spoiler system employed on each wing are shown in the deflected position in figure 10.27. The leading-edge slat is shown in the deployed position in figure 10.28.

Figure 10.28 — Lower-surface veiw of leading-edge slat on Boeing 737 airplane.
[NASA]

Chapter 11
Early Jet Fighters

Background

A little more than a quarter of a century separated the endings of World Wars I and II. During this time, the maximum speed of propeller-driven fighter aircraft increased from 134 miles per hour for the SPAD XIII to 437 miles per hour for the North American P–51D. Integration of the jet engine with an airframe incorporating selected design innovations such as discussed in chapter 10 resulted in a quantum increase in the capability and performance of fighter aircraft in the decade following the end of World War II. For example, maximum speeds had reached about 1500 miles per hour by 1955. Further increases in the capability of jet fighters and their engines have continued to the present, albeit at a slower pace than that which characterized the first 10 years following the end of World War II.

The missions of fighter aircraft have also changed drastically since they first appeared in World War I. In that conflict, the role of the fighter was described in chapter 2 as follows: "The primary purpose of fighter-type aircraft is to destroy other aircraft, either in offensive or defensive modes of operation, or to pose such a compelling threat that enemy air operations are effectively curtailed." In the 60-plus years since that great conflict, the role of the fighter has so expanded that today this class of aircraft might be described as an all-purpose combat machine. In addition to the air-superiority and interception roles defined above for the World War I time period, the modern fighter may be employed for ground-attack operations, long-range interdiction missions, and photoreconnaissance duties. Indeed, some modern fighter aircraft can carry a greater bomb load than the World War II Boeing B–17 Flying Fortress four-engine bomber. The fighter may be designed and equipped for daylight, clear-weather operations or for night, all-weather missions. Frequently, a fighter optimized for one particular type of mission is adapted for other types of operations through changes in design and alterations of armament and mission-oriented electronic gear; thus, for example, an aircraft initially intended as an air-superiority fighter may later be modified for ground-attack missions, and with other alterations, for interceptor use.

The fighter aircraft incorporating jet propulsion form the subject of the present chapter. Beginning in March 1942 with the first flight of the Messerschmitt Me 262 twin-engine jet fighter, the technical evolution of this class of aircraft is traced to the modern fighters of the early eighties. Described and illustrated are 19 jet fighters that show the progression of the state of the art for this type of aircraft over the past 35-plus years. As with most successful aircraft, many versions of most of these fighters were developed and used over a period of years. Only one version of each aircraft is described. Works such as reference 200 give the characteristics of most versions of a particular aircraft. Finally, some design trends are discussed in the concluding section.

A number of the physical and performance characteristics of the 19 aircraft described are presented in table V in appendix A. The quantities given in the table are defined in the list of symbols given in appendix B and, in most cases, require no further explanation. Some further clarification of certain of the characteristics, however, seems desirable. Empty weight, normal gross weight, and maximum gross weight are given for many of the aircraft. The normal, or design, gross weight of the aircraft is the maximum weight at which the aircraft can be maneuvered to its design load factor. The maximum gross weight is limited by some design or performance characteristic other than the maximum design load factor. So many range-payload combinations are possible on modern fighter aircraft that no attempt has been made to delineate them in the table. The unrefueled ferry range, however, is given to provide some idea of the capability of the aircraft in this respect. Values of the subsonic minimum drag coefficient and maximum lift-drag ratio given in table V for some of the aircraft are based on information taken from various industrial sources. Finally, the first-flight dates given are for the first prototype of the entire series of aircraft, not necessarily for the particular version for which data are given in the table.

Pioneer Jet Fighters

First of the pioneer jet fighters was the German Messerschmitt Me 262, which made its initial flight on March 25, 1942. In the following 4 years, a number of these pioneer, or first-generation, jet fighters were developed. In basic concept, these aircraft were small extrapolations of the technology of contemporary propeller-driven aircraft of that period. As compared with those which were to appear later, wings were basically straight, with relatively thick airfoil sections, and were not really suited for flight into the speed range above the critical Mach number. The systems for lateral, directional, and longitudinal control were usually manually operated with no power boost. The jet engines used were of low thrust by present-day standards.

The performance characteristics of early jet fighters exhibited certain peculiarities as compared with those of contemporary propeller-driven aircraft equipped with reciprocating engines; these differences were related to the manner in which the thrust and power of turbojet engines vary with speed. A reciprocating engine generates the same amount of power at takeoff as at high speeds, whereas the turbojet at the same altitude has nearly the same thrust at both high and low speeds.

To give meaning to the different operating characteristics of the two types of engines, a simple example is offered as follows: A 10 000-pound propeller-driven fighter is powered by a 1600-horsepower engine and is capable of a maximum speed at sea level of 410 miles per hour. Near the beginning of the takeoff roll, the thrust at 25 miles per hour is estimated to be about 7500 pounds. Since the power is constant and proportional to the thrust times the velocity, the thrust at 410 miles per hour is about 1168 pounds. (Propeller efficiencies of 30 and 80 percent were assumed for the low-speed and high-speed conditions, respectively.) Accordingly, the thrust-to-weight ratio for the two conditions varies from 0.75 at 25 miles per hour to 0.12 at high speed. A jet fighter with the same 10 000-pound gross weight and having an engine of 2500-pounds thrust has a takeoff thrust-to-weight ratio of 0.25 — and at 410 miles per hour still retains this thrust-to-weight ratio because of the nearly constant thrust characteristic of the engine. The power usefully employed in propelling the jet aircraft varies from 167 to 2740 horsepower as the speed increases from 25 to 410 miles per hour. These results are summarized in the following tabulation:

Characteristic	Propeller	Jet
P_{25}	1600	167
P_{410}	1600	2740
T_{25}	7200	2500
T_{410}	1168	2500
$(T/W)_{25}$	0.75	0.25
$(T/W)_{410}$	0.12	0.25

where the subscripts 25 and 410 refer to speeds of 25 and 410 miles per hour, respectively.

The results in the tabulation indicate the following two conclusions:

(1) The thrust-to-weight ratio T/W of the jet aircraft is small compared with that of its propeller-driven counterpart at low speeds. Thus, the acceleration of the jet aircraft on take-off will be low; and the takeoff distance, correspondingly long.

(2) The maintenance of a nearly constant thrust-to-weight ratio through the speed range, however, gives the jet aircraft an important advantage at the high-speed end of the flight spectrum. Assuming that both hypothetical fighters considered have approximately the same drag area, the jet-powered machine would be expected to be much faster than the 410 miles per hour given for the propeller-driven aircraft. (Actually, level flight speeds as much as 100 miles per hour faster than those of contemporary propeller-driven fighters could be achieved by several of the early jet fighters.)

Because of the high-speed capabilities of the early jet fighters, deep penetrations into the Mach number range characterized by severe compressibility effects were possible. In addition to high drag, a variety of stability, control, and maneuverability problems were encountered. Typical of these was "tuck-under," a condition in which a rapid loss of lift on the wing, together with a change in tail load, caused the aircraft to nose over abruptly. Rapid recovery was frequently hindered by a loss of effectiveness and change in hinge-moment characteristics of the elevator control. Buffeting was a violent shaking of the aircraft caused by unstable separated flow behind the positions at which shock waves were located on the wings and other parts of the aircraft. Most of these problems had been encountered previously on high-performance propeller-driven fighters when flown in steep dives at high altitudes. The new jet fighters, however, had sufficient thrust at high speed to enter the Mach number range characterized by these difficulties in level flight, or slight dives, over a broad range of altitudes. Resolution of these difficulties came in later generations of jet fighters with thin wings and tails, usually with some sweepback, together with other improvements including powered controls. In the following, five pioneer jet fighters that appeared prior to 1947 are briefly described.

Three Jet Fighters of 1942–43

Two jet fighters that saw limited operational service in World War II were the German Messerschmitt Me 262 and the British Gloster Meteor. Because of the limited thrust capability of jet engines available at that time, both aircraft were necessarily of twin-engine design to meet desired mission and performance objectives. The Me 262 and the Meteor are illustrated in figures 11.1 and 11.2. Configuration of the two aircraft was similar in that both had engines mounted on the wing outboard of the fuselage and both had a tricycle landing gear that was to become standard on all jet fighters. (The first Me 262 had a conventional landing gear that was abandoned for several reasons, one of which was the runway damage caused by impingement of the hot engine exhaust.) Significant improvements in visibility and ease of ground handling are offered by the tricycle landing-gear arrangement. In the United States, this type of landing gear had already been standard practice on multiengine, propeller-driven aircraft for a number of years; however, some design difficulties are presented by a retractable, tricycle arrangement on a single-engine propeller-driven fighter. Placement of the jet engines in the wings or in the fuselage behind the pilot obviated these difficulties.

The axial-flow Junkers Jumo turbojet engines were mounted below the wing of the Me 262. The innovative Junkers engine employing an axial-flow compressor may be considered as the precursor of all large, modern axial-flow engines. An interesting account of the development of this milestone engine is contained in a paper by its designer included in reference 140.

The wing of the Messerschmitt has a relatively high aspect ratio of 7.23, a taper ratio of 0.5, and, for that time, relatively thin airfoil sec-

Figure 11.1 — Messerschmitt Me 262 Schwabe twin-engine jet fighter. [NASM]

Figure 11.2 — Gloster Meteor twin-engine jet fighter. [Flt. Intl.]

tions that tapered from a thickness ratio of 11 percent at the engine nacelle to 9 percent at the tip. According to reference 141, the wing was swept back slightly to position the wing aerodynamic center in the correct relation to the airplane center of gravity. (See discussion of Douglas DC–3 transport in chapter 5.) Some increase in critical Mach number, however, probably resulted from the 18.5° leading-edge sweepback. Fowler-type high-lift flaps were provided at the trailing edge of the wing, and full-span slats were incorporated in the leading edges. The slats were actuated automatically by surface pressures at the leading edge when the angle of attack exceeded a prescribed value. The use of these devices gave the aircraft acceptable landing and take-off performance with a wing loading of about 60 pounds per square foot. (Within limits, the higher the wing loading, the smaller the wing area and drag area; thus for a given thrust level, the higher the maximum speed.) In addition to improving takeoff and landing performance, the slats improved the high-g turning capability in maneuvering flight. Such leading-edge slats were also a feature of the famous Messerschmitt Me 109 propeller-driven fighter employed by the German Air Force throughout World War II.

The stabilizer angle could be varied with an electric motor activated by the pilot to provide rapid changes in trim with speed. This highly desirable feature was used on many later jet fighters. A deficiency in the aircraft was the lack of a speed brake, which is important for speed control in high-performance aircraft.

The data in table V show a high performance for the 14 000-pound Me 262, particularly in view of the low thrust-to-weight ratio. The speed of 540 miles per hour at 19 685 feet was about 100 miles per hour faster than that of the North American P–51, one of the best of the propeller-driven fighters of the war. The Me 262 seems to have been a carefully designed aircraft in which great attention was given to the details of aerodynamic design. Such attention frequently spells the difference between a great aircraft and a mediocre one.

The Me 262 was employed as both a day and night fighter, as well as for ground-attack and reconnaissance operations. Depending upon the mission, it appeared in both single- and two-seat versions. As a fighter, named the Schwabe, it was armed with four 30-mm cannons located in the nose. First encounter with an enemy aircraft was on July 25, 1944. About 1400 Messerschmitt Me 262 aircraft, including all versions, were constructed. Fortunately for the Allies, only a small percentage of these saw action, and effective tactics designed to exploit the performance of the aircraft were not developed in a systematic and consistent way in the various operating squadrons. Follow-on Messerschmitt fighter aircraft, including one with about 40° of wing sweep, were being studied when termination of hostilities put an end to all German aircraft development.

Although bearing a number of configuration similarities to the Messerschmitt Me 262, the Gloster Meteor differed in a number of significant respects from the German fighter. The Rolls-Royce Derwent centrifugal-flow turbojet engines of 3500 pounds thrust each were mounted in the chord plane of the wing rather than below it. The front spar actually passed through the inlet, and the rear spar was split and formed hoops around the top and bottom of the engine. The data in table V show that the wing was of low aspect ratio and had no sweep-back. Airfoil-section thickness ratio varied from 12 percent at the root to 10.4 percent at the tip. Simple split flaps for lift augmentation were located on the wing lower surface between the fuselage sides and engine nacelles. These relatively small, ineffective, high-lift devices dictated the relatively low wing loading of 43 pounds per square foot, a value about 63 percent lower than that of the Me 262. As compared with the German fighter, the Meteor was characterized by both higher wing area and drag area. Highly desirable dive brakes were provided on the upper and lower surfaces of the wing between the nacelles and the sides of the fuselage. To clear the jet exhaust, the horizontal tail was mounted high on the vertical tail. Longitudinal trim changes could be made with an elevator tab. An innovation at that time was the pressurized cockpit, which maintained the cabin pressure at a value corresponding to 20 000 feet when the actual altitude was 40 000 feet.

Performance characteristics shown in table I give a maximum speed for the Gloster Meteor F. Mk. 4 of 570 miles per hour, or a Mach number of 0.81, at 20 000 feet. One source (ref. 162) indicates that at high speeds the Meteor experienced large trim changes, high aileron stick forces, and a tendency toward snaking. Snaking may be described as a self sustained yawing oscillation; it plagued many of the earlier jet fighters. According to reference 188, numerous modifications were tried in an effort to cure the problem on the Meteor — none of them were entirely successful. (Later research indicated that the problem was probably related to incipient flow separation from the relatively thick airfoil sections used in the tail.) Climb performance of the aircraft was outstanding. The sea-level rate of climb was 7500 feet per minute, and an altitude of 30 000 feet could be reached in 5 minutes. Clearly, the performance of the Meteor F. Mk. 4 was much superior to the performance of the Messerschmitt Me 262A for which data are given in table V. To put this comparison in proper perspective, however, the Meteor F. Mk. 4 did not fly until after the end of World War II and had a thrust-to-weight ratio of 0.47 as compared with 0.28 for the earlier German aircraft. The author's analysis of the physical and performance characteristics of the two aircraft suggests that the superior performance of the Meteor was due to the higher thrust of its engines and not to any inherent superiority in aerodynamic design.

The first flight of the Gloster Meteor took place in March 1943, and development and refinement of the type continued for a number of years following World War II. Over 3500 Meteors were built, including versions intended to perform almost every role a fighter might be called upon to fill. For many years, it was used by the Royal Air Force, as well as by the armed forces of 15 other nations. It was the only jet-powered aircraft fielded by the Allies to see action in World War II. In July 1944, a Meteor shot down a V-1 Buzz bomb; and in the spring of 1945, it served the Allies in the ground-attack role. It saw further combat in the Korean war.

Although a strictly subsonic aircraft, the Meteor did have high performance for a straight-wing fighter; it was rugged, versatile, and capable of being readily adapted to various missions. An interesting account of the development and operational history of the Meteor may be found in reference 188.

The first jet fighter to be developed in the United States was the Bell P-59 Airacomet; its maiden flight took place on October 1, 1942, about 5 months earlier than the date on which the British Gloster Meteor first flew. Unfortunately, the P-59's performance showed no advantage over that of advanced propeller-driven fighters in use toward the end of the war. Hence, the aircraft was never to fill its intended role as a fighter but served instead as a transition trainer to introduce American pilots to some of the peculiarities encountered in flying jet-powered aircraft. About 60 P-59 aircraft were built.

The Bell P-59 is depicted in figure 11.3 flying alongside its ancestor, the Bell P-63 propeller-driven fighter. The P-59 was powered by two General Electric J31-GE-5 turbojet engines (derived from the British Whittle engine) of 2000 pounds thrust each. The engines were contained in pods that blended into the sides of the fuselage, with the exhaust nozzles below and behind the wing trailing edge. The unswept wing was mounted in the shoulder position and had a constant airfoil thickness ratio of 14 percent, which was significantly greater than that used on the wings of the Me 262 and the Meteor.

Although having about the same total thrust as the Me 262, along with a thrust-to-weight ratio over 30 percent greater than that of the German aircraft, the P-59A was slower by about 130 miles per hour. Analysis shows that the 65-percent-greater wing area and consequent greater drag area of the P-59A was responsible for much but not all of the difference in performance of the two aircraft. Perhaps the thick airfoil sections of the P-59A or some other sources of added drag con-

Figure 11.3 — Bell P–59A Airacomet twin-engine jet fighter. (Propeller-driven P–63 flying alongside.) [USAF]

tributed to its poor performance, or perhaps the engines did not perform as anticipated. An obvious question concerns the choice of so large a wing area for the aircraft. In comparison with the 60-pound-per-square-foot wing loading of the Me 262, the corresponding value for the Airacomet was 28 pounds per square foot. The use of sophisticated leading-edge and trailing-edge high-lift devices on the Me 262 gave acceptable takeoff, landing, and maneuver characteristics with a small wing area and high wing loading on this aircraft. Only small, simple, inboard trailing-edge flaps were used on the P–59A, and the resultant low maximum lift coefficient no doubt played a large part in dictating the choice of a low wing loading and associated large wing area.

In any event, the poor performance of the P–59A precluded its adoption as a production fighter for the U.S. Armed Forces. The P–59 is included here only because of its historic interest as the first jet aircraft developed in the United States.

First Operational United States Jet Fighters

"Frantic" best describes the pace of some aircraft development programs during World War II. Surely falling into this category was the Lockheed P–80 Shooting Star program. By the summer of 1943, the poor performance of the Bell Airacomet spelled the need for the development of a new U.S. jet fighter. Lockheed had been making design studies of such an aircraft and in June 1943 was awarded a prototype development contract with the stipulation that the aircraft be ready for flight in 180 days. Completion of the aircraft actually required only 150 days, but first flight was delayed by engine problems until January 1944.

Illustrated in figure 11.4 is a Lockheed P–80B Shooting Star. Conventional in basic configuration, the P–80 featured an unswept wing of 13-percent thickness mounted in the low position and, unlike the twin-engine Meteor and the Me 262, had a single engine located in the fuselage behind the pilot. Air was delivered to the engine by side inlets located on the fuselage just ahead of the wing root, and the jet exhaust nozzle was at the extreme end of the fuselage. Adjacent to the fuselage side may be seen the bleed slots that removed the fuselage boundary layer from the engine intake air and thus prevented flow separation inside the inlet. No such slots were provided on the prototype, and intermittent separation did occur in the inlets. "Duct rumble" was the term used to describe this phenomenon because of the alarming noise heard by the pilot. Evident in the photograph is the deployed speed brake located on the bottom of the fuselage. Like the P–38 described in

Figure 11.4 — Lockheed P–80B Shooting Star single-engine jet fighter. [mfr via Martin Copp]

287

chapter 5, the P–80 had a small dive-recovery flap near the leading edge of the lower surface of the wing. Again like later versions of the P–38, the P–80 had power-operated ailerons. The other controls were manually operated. Split trailing-edge flaps provided lift augmentation at low speeds.

The cockpit of production models of the Shooting Star was pressurized and air-conditioned. In the prototype, no air-conditioning was provided so that the temperature resulting from a combination of the high temperatures of the California desert and sustained high Mach number flight at low altitude caused the interior surfaces of the cockpit and controls to become uncomfortably hot. For example, with an ambient temperature of 90° some parts of the aircraft would reach a temperature of 150° in prolonged flight at a Mach number of 0.73. Another advance in cockpit equipment was the ejection seat incorporated in the P–80C model of the Shooting Star. (The first successful manned test of an ejection seat took place in July 1946.)

Although the P–80 was conventional in appearance, the aircraft was the result of a careful synthesis of weight, size, and thrust parameters, as well as close attention to aerodynamic refinement. As a consequence, it had performance far superior to that of the P–59A although the thrust-to-weight ratio of the earlier aircraft was actually about 12 percent greater than that of the P–80A. For example, the maximum sea-level speed of 558 miles per hour was 145 miles per hour greater than that of the maximum speed of the P–59A, which occurred at 30 000 feet. As seen in table V, the climbing performance of the P–80A was also far superior to that of the earlier aircraft; the much smaller wing and resultant drag area of the P–80A no doubt played a significant role in ensuring the higher performance of the Shooting Star. In comparison with the drag area of the famous World War II Mustang, the drag area of 3.2 square feet of the P–80A was about 15 percent lower than that of the earlier propeller-driven aircraft. (Compare data in table III and table V.)

The P–80 came too late for operational service in World War II, but the F–80C did see action in the Korean conflict of the early 1950's. (Note that in 1948 the designation "P" was changed to "F" on all Air Force fighters.) Designed as an air-superiority fighter, the F–80 could not compete in that role with the Soviet-built MiG–15 supplied to the opposing forces by the Soviet Union. It was, however, extensively employed in the ground-attack mode. Armament consisted of six .50-caliber machine guns in the nose and externally mounted bombs and rockets.

The F–80 was withdrawn from first-line United States Air Force (USAF) service in 1954; production of the aircraft consisted of about 1700 units. But, this is not quite the end of the F–80 story. A two-seat trainer version of the aircraft appeared in 1948. Known in the USAF as the T–33 and in the Navy as the T2V, over 5000 of these trainers were built; a number of them are still in service and can be seen frequently at air bases in different parts of the country. Certainly a long and useful life for an airplane developed in the closing years of World War II! An account of the development and use of the P–80 and its derivatives is given in reference 206.

The advent of the jet engine with its promise of greatly improved high-speed performance placed the U.S. Navy in something of a dilemma. As discussed, the early jet engines not only promised increased maximum speeds but also appallingly long takeoff distances. Thus, a jet-powered aircraft seemed incompatible with the short takeoff runs necessary for successful operations from the deck of an aircraft carrier. To be competitive with land-based fighters, however, the Navy needed the high-speed capability of the jet-powered airplane. Proposed as a solution to the problem was a hybrid-type aircraft propelled by a reciprocating engine driving a propeller in addition to a jet engine. Takeoff would be shortened by the high thrust of the reciprocating engine at low speed, and high speed would be ensured by the jet engine.

The only hybrid or composite to be produced in any quantity was the Ryan FR–1 Fireball shown in figure 11.5. Except for the tricycle landing gear, the FR–1 looked like a conventional propeller-driven fighter of the World War II time period. A small 1600-pound-thrust jet engine was mounted in the fuselage behind the pilot and was fed by air inlets in the wing leading edge. High-speed performance of the aircraft was similar to that of the P–59A but was in no way competitive with the Lockheed P–80. Takeoff performance was, of course, much improved by the propeller with its reciprocating engine. Fortunately, catapult launching of jet-powered aircraft from the deck of an aircraft carrier provided the solution, still in use, to the Navy dilemma of operating high-performance jet aircraft from carriers. As a consequence, the hybrid concept exemplified by the FR–1 quietly passed into oblivion after production of only 66 aircraft.

The first U.S. Navy jet fighter designed for carrier operation with catapult launch appeared in 1945; it was produced by a new aircraft company whose name has been closely associated with fighter developments from that time until the present. Illustrated in figure 11.6 is the McDonnell FH–1 Phantom, which made its first flight on January 26,

Figure 11.5 — Ryan FR-1 Fireball composite jet fighter. [mfr via Martin Copp]

1945, was first operated from a carrier in the summer of 1946, and entered squadron service in 1948. The aircraft was conventional in design and employed an unswept wing with simple high-lift devices; manual flight controls were provided about all three axes. Mounted in the wing roots were the two 1560-pound-thrust Westinghouse axial-flow jet engines. Although not visible in the photograph, the inlets were located in the leading edge of the wing roots. As can be seen, the exhaust nozzles protruded from the wing trailing edge close to the side of the fuselage.

Although the thrust-to-weight ratio of the McDonnell FH-1 was less than that of the Bell P-59, the data in table V show the performance of the Phantom to be much improved over the earlier aircraft but not nearly so good as for the P-80. The low wing loading of 36.4 pounds per square foot was dictated by the necessity for a landing speed compatible with operation from an aircraft carrier deck.

Because newer aircraft had much superior performance, the short service life of the FH-1 ended in 1950. With much the same configuration, a much improved McDonnell fighter, the F2H Banshee, first flew in 1947. This heavier, more powerful aircraft with higher performance remained in Navy service until the mid-1960's. Total Banshee production consisted of 364 units.

Figure 11.6 — McDonnell FH–1 Phantom twin-engine jet fighter. [ukn via AAHS]

The P–80 Shooting Star and the FH–1 Phantom were the first operational jet fighters employed by the armed services of the United States. Both aircraft had unswept wings. A number of other straight-wing jet fighters for both Air Force and Navy use appeared after World War II. None of these aircraft showed any major new technical advancement or innovation and hence they are not discussed. Descriptions of these various aircraft may be found in reference 200.

The Swept Wing Emerges

Described in chapter 10 are the advantages of wing sweepback as applied to aircraft designed for flight at high-subsonic or supersonic Mach numbers. At subsonic speeds, increasing sweepback angle increases the wing critical Mach number, that is, the Mach number at which the adverse effects of compressibility first begin to appear. The effect of sweepback on the critical Mach number was first pointed out in the United States by Robert T. Jones of NACA in 1945. German engineers under the leadership of A. Busemann were aware of the importance of wing sweep in high-speed-aircraft design at an earlier date; and, following the end of World War II, much experimental information that had accumulated in Germany became available in the United

291

States. Together with data obtained in NACA's wind tunnels, this information served as the basis for the first swept-wing fighters designed in this country. The early swept-wing fighters were strictly subsonic aircraft. Discussed in the following paragraphs are the first USAF and Navy fighters to incorporate wing sweepback. Both aircraft had long and distinguished careers, and both will find an important place in any account of the development of jet fighters.

First of the swept-wing subsonic jet fighters to serve in the USAF was the North American F–86 Sabre, which made its first flight on October 1, 1947. Before production ended, nearly 10 000 Sabres had been produced in 20 different variants (including the Navy FJ series known as the Fury), with five different engines. During its long service life, the F–86 formed a part of the air forces of 24 different countries. As late as 1980, eight Third World nations still included a number of F–86 fighters in their inventories (ref. 177). Production lines were established in four foreign countries, with the last aircraft coming from the Japanese line in 1961. The Sabre saw extensive service with the USAF during the Korean war, in which it achieved an outstanding exchange ratio of nearly 14 to 1 in combat with the Soviet-built MiG–15. Surely the F–86 must be ranked, along with its illustrious World War II ancestor the P–51 Mustang, as one of the great fighter aircraft of all time.

Originally designed as a fair-weather air-superiority fighter, the F–86 later appeared in all-weather interceptor and ground-attack versions. Some of these variants had major design differences; consequently, the F–86 must be considered as a whole family of related aircraft. Included here is a brief description of the F–86E air-superiority version of the aircraft. Data for this version are given in table V, and an F–86F in flight is shown in figure 11.7.

Identifying features of the F–86 are the graceful sweptback wing and the nose inlet located in the fuselage. According to the comprehensive paper by Blair contained in reference 155, the 4.78-aspect-ratio wing of 35° sweepback was derived from captured German data for the advanced Messerschmitt fighter under design study at the time hostilities ended. Streamwise airfoil-section thickness ratios varied from 9.5 percent at the root to 8.5 percent at the tip. (These thickness ratios are based on data contained in the paper by Blair in ref. 155; other sources, e.g., ref. 126, give larger values for the thickness ratios. The apparent discrepancy is largely resolved, however, if the higher thickness ratios cited in ref. 126 are assumed to be based on a wing chord length measured in a direction perpendicular to the quarter-chord line

Figure 11.7 — North American F–86F Sabre single-engine jet fighter. [mfr via Martin Copp]

rather than in the streamwise direction.) Pitch-up was prevented on many versions of the aircraft by full-span leading-edge slats. As on the Messerschmitt Me 262, deployment of the slats was automatically initi-ated at the correct angle of attack by aerodynamic loads acting at the leading edge of the wings. On some versions of the aircraft, the slats were replaced by a sharp, extended-chord, cambered leading edge. Single-slotted high-lift flaps and outboard ailerons were incorporated **in the trailing-edge portions of the wing. The ailerons were hydrau-lically actuated, as were the horizontal-tail surfaces, which, on the F–86E,** consisted of a movable stabilizer with linked elevator. Some versions of the F–86 had an all-moving, slab-type horizontal tail with no elevator. Greater control effectiveness is possible at high-subsonic and super-sonic Mach numbers with the all-moving horizontal tail, and this arrange-ment was to become standard on future transonic/supersonic fighters. The hydraulically actuated controls of the F–86E were of the fully pow-ered, irreversible type with artificial control feel provided for the pilot. Fully powered, irreversible controls aid in eliminating such instabilities as aileron and rudder buzz, in addition to permitting maximum deflec-tion of the control surfaces without requiring excess physical effort on the part of the pilot. These controls differ from the hydraulically boost-

293

ed controls used on some early versions of the F–86, as well as on other aircraft. In a boosted control system, the pilot is still directly linked to the aerodynamic control surfaces, but his strength is augmented by a hydraulic booster. Dive brakes were mounted on either side of the fuselage behind the wing.

As mentioned, another identifying feature of many versions of the F–86 was the fuselage nose-inlet installation. Inlet air was ducted under the cockpit and delivered to the turbojet engine located behind the pilot; the exhaust nozzle was at the rear end of the fuselage. To minimize the depth of the fuselage in the cockpit area, the shape of the duct leading from the inlet to the engine was changed from a circular to an elliptical shape with the long axis being in the horizontal plane. In the all-weather interceptor versions of the aircraft, notably the F–86D, K, and L models, the distinctive nose inlet was replaced by a chin installation to provide space in the nose for the necessary radar gear. In contrast to other F–86 variants, the all-weather interceptor models were equipped with afterburning engines to provide the high rates of climb and high-altitude capability necessary to execute interception missions.

Armament of the fighter versions of the aircraft consisted of 3 .50-caliber machine guns buried in each side of the fuselage near the nose and provisions for carrying 2 1000-pound bombs or 16 5-inch rockets on the wings. Interceptor versions of the aircraft carried 24 2.75-inch rockets mounted on a retractable tray contained in the bottom of the fuselage. The tray extended only long enough to launch the rockets. Environmental control in the cockpit consisted of air-conditioning, heating, and pressurization; in addition, the pilot was equipped with an ejection seat.

The data in table V show that the thrust-to-weight ratio of the F–86E was about the same as that of the P–59A. Yet, as compared with the earlier aircraft, the Sabre showed a speed advantage of nearly 300 miles per hour at sea level. A smaller wing area, wing sweepback, and thinner airfoil sections, together with careful attention to aerodynamic design, were responsible for the large increment in maximum speed between the two types. Also, improved engine performance, not reflected in the values of static thrust given in the table, no doubt played a role in the superior performance of the F–86. Drag area was a little greater for the F–86 than for the P–80 by an amount that corresponds closely to the difference in wing area of the two aircraft. As would be expected, the zero-lift drag coefficients were about the same for both aircraft. Comparison of values of the maximum lift-drag ratio shows the

P–80 to have had the advantage by about 17 percent; this difference is primarily due to the lower wing aspect ratio of the F–86. Although the Sabre was strictly a subsonic aircraft, low-supersonic speeds could be achieved in a shallow dive. Flight through Mach 1.0 first took place on April 26, 1948.

Sea-level rate of climb was 7250 feet per minute, and 6.3 minutes were required to reach an altitude of 30 000 feet; service ceiling was 47 200 feet. For the afterburning F–86D interceptor, the sea-level rate of climb was 12 000 feet a minute, and 6.9 minutes were required to reach 40 000 feet; service ceiling was 49 750 feet. Ferry range for the F–86E is given in table V as 1022 miles. According to reference 162, the combat radius of action with internal fuel was only 321 miles; with drop tanks the radius of action was increased to 424 miles.

Surpassed in performance in the early 1950's by the Century Series fighters, the F–86 has long been retired from the USAF operational inventory. A number are still in use as target drones and for various flight-test purposes, and at least one manufacturer uses an F–86 as a chase plane.

While recognizing the high-speed performance advantages of the swept wing, there was skepticism within the Navy regarding the carrier compatibility of a swept-wing fighter. Low maximum lift coefficients, poor stability and control characteristics at low speeds, and high angles of attack during the landing approach were cited as serious deficiencies that mitigated against the use of sweepback on Navy fighters. Nevertheless, swept-wing Navy fighters were under development in the late 1940's; and one of these, the tailless Vought F7U Cutlass, made its maiden flight in 1948. Because of engine and/or airframe problems, however, neither the Cutlass nor any of the new Navy fighters were in operational use when the Korean war began in June 1950. During the early months of the conflict, however, an urgent need developed for a Navy fighter with a higher performance than then available with straight-wing Navy jet fighters.

The first operational swept-wing Navy fighter was a product of the urgent Korean war need and consisted of a hasty albeit skillful and highly successful modification of an existing straight-wing Navy fighter. Since its first flight in 1947, the Grumman F9F Panther straight-wing jet fighter had been developed into a highly capable aircraft that first entered operational service in 1949. In the incredibly short time period of about 6 months, the Panther was converted into an effective swept-wing fighter, which made its first flight on September 20, 1951. Named the Cougar, the new aircraft was designated the F9F–6; later versions were the F9F-7 and the F9F-8. Operational service of the Cougar began in November 1952, and so successful was the aircraft that over 1500 were built. The last of these, a trainer version, was finally withdrawn from service in 1974. During its active lifetime, it was employed as a fighter as well as for ground-attack and photoreconnaissance duties and, with an added second seat, as a trainer.

Three-quarter front and rear views of an F9F-7 are shown in figures 11.8 and 11.9, and the approximate shape of the wing planform of an F9F-8 is depicted in figure 11.10. This wing-planform sketch, as well as those presented later for several other aircraft, was based on information contained in references 162 and 171.

The Cougar was a midwing monoplane with leading-edge wing-root inlets feeding the single 7250-pound-thrust Pratt & Whitney turbojet engine located behind a large fuel tank immediately to the rear of the pilot. In a somewhat unusual arrangement, the vertical-tail surfaces extended beyond the end of the fuselage, which contained the engine exhaust nozzle. The horizontal tail was positioned part way between the top and bottom of the fixed portion of the vertical tail. Advantages offered by this configuration design are a reduction in tailpipe length and associated internal losses and external fuselage drag while providing at the same time a satisfactorily long tail moment arm.

Figure 11.10 shows the unusual planform shape of the 35° swept-back wing of the F9F-8. A distinctive feature of the wing is the large increase in wing chord between the inboard end of the flap and the

Figure 11.8 — Grumman F9F-7 Cougar single-engine jet fighter. [NASA]

Figure 11.9 — Rear view of Grumman F9F-7 Cougar single-engine jet fighter. [NASA]

side of the fuselage. An acceptable airfoil thickness chord ratio, while permitting the large physical thickness required to accommodate the inlet and internal flow duct, is the reason for the large increase in wing chord. Hydraulically actuated spoilers on the upper surface of the wing just forward of the flaps provided the sole source of roll control — no ailerons were used. Space was accordingly available for large trailing-edge flaps. On the F9F-6, the trailing-edge flaps operated in conjunction with full-span leading-edge slats to provide the high-lift capability needed for carrier operation. Later versions of the aircraft incorporated a wing of larger chord, without slats, to decrease the wing thickness ratio and thus increase the critical Mach number; the corresponding 12-percent increase in wing area also increased the lifting capability of the wing and no doubt compensated to some degree for the removal of the leading-edge slats. The relatively sharp wing leading edge together with the fence and leading-edge snag, or dogtooth, provided the necessary wing flow control to avoid serious pitch-up problems.

The longitudinal control system on the aircraft consisted of a fully powered stabilizer with a linked elevator; an interconnect between the flaps and the stabilizer provided automatic pitch-trim compensation with flap deflection. The rudder was operated manually since this control was little used in the high-speed regime where hinge moments are high. As mentioned, roll control was accomplished by wing spoilers. An ejection seat was provided for the pilot, and the cockpit was heated,

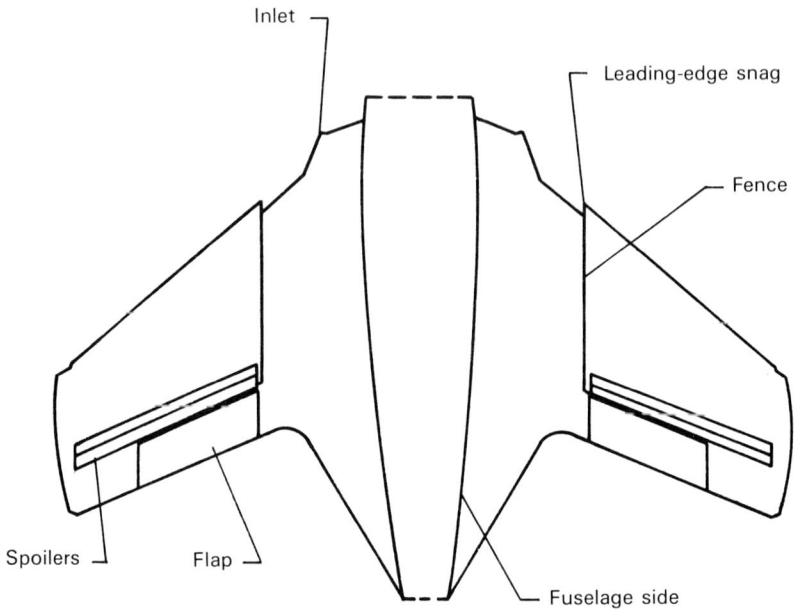

Figure 11.10 — Approximate wing-planform shape of Grumman F9F-8 carrier-based jet fighter.

air-conditioned, and pressurized. Armament on the fighter version of the F9F consisted of four 20-mm cannons and two Sidewinder missiles. For ground-attack missions, the aircraft could carry up to four 500-pound bombs.

A glance at the data in table V indicates that the maximum speed of the Cougar was nearly the same as that of the F–86 at an altitude of 35 000 feet; near sea level, the F–86 was about 30 miles per hour faster than the Cougar. Data in reference 200 show that the Cougar was 40-plus miles per hour faster than its straight-wing cousin the Panther. The higher performance of the swept-wing Cougar was achieved with about the same thrust as the straight-wing Panther in spite of a drag-producing increase of 35 percent in wing area. Together with the high-lift devices on the Cougar, the larger wing area resulted in a stall speed of about 140 miles per hour for both aircraft (ref. 200).

The North American Sabre and the Grumman Cougar, both good aircraft, have been described here as being the first swept-wing jet fighters operated by the USAF and the Navy. Both services operated other subsonic swept-wing fighters representative of the same level of technology as the two aircraft. Details of these various aircraft can be found in references 162, 163, and 200.

Through the Transonic Range

Many knowledgeable engineers once thought that reasonably safe and controllable flight past Mach 1.0 was highly unlikely, if not completely impossible. By the mid-1940's, much had been written in the popular press about the so-called "sonic barrier." That an aircraft could successfully fly past Mach 1.0, however, was convincingly demonstrated on October 14, 1947 by Captain Charles E. Yeager flying the rocket-propelled Bell X–1 research airplane. This historic event set the stage for an intensive research and development effort, which had as its objective the production of jet fighters capable of passing through Mach 1.0 and into the once forbidden supersonic speed range. During this stimulating time period, from the late 1940's to the mid-1950's, a number of supersonic fighter aircraft were developed that later served in the United States air forces as well as those of a number of other countries. Some of these aircraft types saw extensive action in the Vietnam conflict, and some are still in service.

To put the first-generation supersonic fighters in proper perspective, these aircraft should be thought of as basically high-performance subsonic machines with design features that allowed flight through Mach 1.0 and at supersonic speeds for very brief periods of time. In no sense were they designed for sustained cruising flight at supersonic speeds. The following considerations of drag, thrust, and specific fuel consumption readily show this to be so. As the supersonic fighter accelerated from high-subsonic speed to supersonic speed, the drag coefficient usually increased by a factor of 2 or more. The increase in actual drag force, however, was much larger than that of the coefficient. For example, the dynamic pressure at Mach 2.0 for a given altitude is about five times that at Mach 0.9 for the same altitude. Thus, the actual drag force and the thrust required to balance this force in steady flight increases by a factor of at least 10 as the Mach number increases from 0.9 to 2.0. Further, the specific fuel consumption (pounds of fuel per pound of thrust per unit time) of the afterburning turbojet at Mach 2.0 is two to three times the value of that for the nonafterburning engine at subsonic Mach numbers. At Mach 2.0 the actual fuel consumption per unit time may accordingly be 20 to 30 times that at Mach 0.9. To compound the problem further, the time required by the early supersonic jet fighters to accelerate from Mach 0.9 to Mach 2.0 was usually in the range from 3 to 10 minutes depending on the aircraft, engine, and altitude. The long acceleration times, which resulted from the relatively small margin between thrust and drag, when coupled with the high fuel consumption per unit time during acceleration, severely restricted the time available for cruising flight at maximum Mach number. The range available to fighter aircraft operating at supersonic speeds was accordingly quite limited. For these reasons, even modern supersonic fighters spend most of their flying lifetime at subsonic speeds. Most of the design features of the supersonic fighters, however, also increased the operational capability of these aircraft at high-subsonic speeds. Accordingly, these aircraft should really be thought of as highly effective subsonic fighters with a supersonic dash capability that is useful and important in certain military missions. For example, a short burst of supersonic speed might be necessary in overtaking or escaping from a hostile aircraft or in avoiding antiaircraft fire in a bombing run at low altitude.

The supersonic fighters developed in the 1950's shared a number of important technical features. All the aircraft had afterburning engines that provided a substantial boost in thrust as well as fuel consumption throughout the speed range. A large increase in thrust as the Mach number increased was also characteristic of the afterburning engines. Both fixed- and variable-geometry inlets were used. Power-operated control surfaces with artificial "feel" provided to the pilot were standard features; and, in some cases, rudimentary stability augmentation was incorporated to improve the inherent stability characteristics of the aircraft. The increased control effectiveness of the all-moving horizontal tail at supersonic and transonic speeds dictated its use rather than the more conventional elevator. Wing thickness ratios fell in the range from about 7 to 4 percent. By comparison, the thickness ratio of a typical World War II propeller-driven fighter was about 14 percent. Wing planforms were usually of the swept or delta type, although one fighter of this period had a straight wing.

By the end of 1956, prototypes of seven supersonic fighters for the USAF had been developed and flown. Six of these aircraft reached production status and operational service. In the same period, two supersonic fighters were developed for the Navy. To illustrate interesting design features of supersonic fighters developed during the 1950's, four USAF and one Navy aircraft, all capable of supersonic flight, are briefly discussed in the following paragraphs. Some of the physical and performance characteristics of these aircraft are given in table V. Where two values of engine thrust are given (16 000/10 000, for example), the first value indicates the sea-level static thrust with maximum afterburning and the second value indicates maximum thrust without afterburning. Also note that the values of zero-lift drag coefficient $C_{D,0}$, drag area f, and maximum lift-drag ratio $(L/D)_{max}$ are for subsonic speeds. As mentioned, the values of $C_{D,0}$ increased by a factor of 2 to 3 as the Mach number increased from subsonic to supersonic values. The maximum lift-drag ratio at supersonic speeds for the fighter aircraft discussed were usually in the range from 3 to 4.

A glance at the data in table V indicates that the weights, wing loadings, and thrust loadings of the supersonic fighters were usually greater than those of earlier subsonic machines. The afterburning supersonic fighters were designed to achieve both their maximum speed and corresponding Mach number at high altitudes. The maximum speed at low altitudes was usually restricted to values near Mach 1.0 by high drag was well as by airframe or engine limitations imposed by the high temperatures and dynamic pressures encountered in low-level flight at high speeds. At high altitudes, the maximum speeds of most of the aircraft approached or exceeded Mach 2.0.

The Century Series Fighters

Because the first of their number was designated the F–100, the USAF supersonic fighters developed in the 1950's were aptly christened with the appellation "Century Series." Design studies of an F–86 equipped with a thin 45° swept wing, known as the Sabre 45, marked the genesis of the F–100; but the aircraft that finally emerged with that designation was an entirely new machine.

First flight of the F–100, the world's first fighter capable of sustained supersonic speeds in level flight, took place on May 25, 1953. Views of the F–100, known as the Super Sabre, are shown in figures 11.11 and 11.12. The low-mounted wing had a sweepback angle of 45°, a taper ratio of 0.25, and an airfoil-section thickness ratio of about 7 percent. Like the wing of its ancestor the F–86, the leading edge was equipped with automatic slats for stall control and the trailing edge incorporated plain flaps. Location of the ailerons mounted a short distance inboard of the tip reduced adverse wing twisting due to aileron deflection. (Under conditions of high dynamic pressure, adverse wing twist due to aileron deflection can become so large that, on some air-

Figure 11.11 — North American F-100 Super Sabre single-engine jet fighter. [ukn via AAHS]

craft, roll takes place in a direction opposite to that intended. This condition is known as aileron reversal.)

The low-mounted horizontal tail of the F-100 is clearly shown in figure 11.12. As discussed in chapter 10, this tail position assists in preventing pitch-up. As a further assist to stall control, most models of the F-100 had wing fences. Also shown in figure 11.12 is the variable-area nozzle necessary for efficient operation of the afterburning engine; the nozzle is in the nonafterburning configuration in figure 11.12. The petals of the nozzle open to a larger diameter for afterburning. The boxlike structure on the vertical tail about one-third of the span from the tip, evident in figure 11.12, housed a radar warning antenna.

The oblong nose inlet shown in figure 11.11 provides an immediate recognition feature of the F-100 series of aircraft. As compared with a circular inlet, the oblong design provides better pilot visibility over the nose and, since the duct passes under the pilot's seat, the vertical dimension of the fuselage is reduced at this location. No area ruling was incorporated in the design of the F-100.

All new aircraft encounter problems of varying degrees of seriousness, particularly in new and largely unexplored regimes of flight or with new configuration concepts, and the F-100 was no exception. An unanticipated problem was encountered during flight tests of the F-100 that resulted in loss of the aircraft as well as its well-known North American test pilot. Compared with piston-engine fighters and earlier jets, aircraft such as the F-100 had much higher values of the ratio of

302

Figure 11.12 — Rear view of North American F-100 Super Sabre single-engine jet fighter. [USAF via Martin Copp]

lengthwise to spanwise mass. As a consequence, a gyroscopic couple that caused large yaw excursions occurred during dive pull-out maneuvers accompanied by large rolling velocities. During the performance of such maneuvers in an early model F-100, the angle of yaw became so large that the aerodynamic loads on the vertical tail exceeded its structural strength and the tail separated from the aircraft. A larger and stronger vertical tail solved the problem on the F-100. All new fighter aircraft under development at that time, however, were carefully scrutinized for possible "rolling pull-out" problems; this maneuver is now a standard one that must be analyzed on all new fighter designs.

Maximum speed of the F-100D was 927 miles per hour, or Mach 1.39, at 35 000 feet; at sea level, the maximum speed was just below the sonic value. Maximum sea-level rate of climb was 22 400 feet per minute, or about three times that of the F-86, and the service ceiling was 51 300 feet. With a lift-drag ratio of 13.9 at subsonic speeds, the F-100 had a ferry range of 1971 miles. According to reference 200, the combat radius was 599 miles with maximum external fuel load and 279 miles with only internal fuel and six Snakeye bombs.

Originally intended as an air-superiority fighter, the F-100 was used operationally as a fighter-bomber and saw extensive service in this

303

role with the USAF in the Vietnam war. As a fighter-bomber, armament consisted of four 20-mm cannons mounted in the bottom of the fuselage below the cockpit with provision made for up to 6000 pounds of external ordnance such as bombs and rocket pods.

Before production was terminated, a total of 2194 F–100 aircraft were manufactured. Although no longer a part of the USAF inventory, the type was still in service in 1980 with four foreign air forces (ref. 177).

Since the end of World War II, the primary mission of interceptor-type aircraft has been to prevent attacking enemy aircraft from reaching targets on United States territory. Several subsonic jet-powered interceptors, including the F–86D Sabre, filled the air-defense role until the supersonic Convair F–102A Delta Dagger entered the inventory in 1956. As described in chapter 10, the F–102, which first flew in 1953, was able to fly in the supersonic speed range only after being redesigned according to the precepts of the transonic area rule. Even with this modification, however, the F–102A was underpowered and could achieve a maximum Mach number of only about 1.2 at 35 000 feet.

First flight of a vastly improved Convair interceptor with the same general configuration layout as the F–102A took place on December 26, 1956. Known as the F–106 Delta Dart, this aircraft is pictured in figures 11.13 and 11.14 and is described by the physical and performance data given in table V.

Instant recognition features of the F–106 are the distinctive low-mounted delta wing, fuselage-mounted inlets just forward of the wing,

Figure 11.13 — In-flight view of Convair F–106A Delta Dart interceptor. [mfr via David A. Anderton]

Figure 11.14 — Convair F-106A Delta Dart interceptor. [USAF via Martin Copp]

and absence of a horizontal tail. The F-102A can be distinguished from the F-106 by its pointed vertical tail and by inlets located farther forward and lower down on the fuselage than on the F-106. (See fig. 10.19.) As with the F-102A, the F-106 was carefully area ruled to reduce the drag rise accompanying an increase in Mach number from subsonic to supersonic values. This careful attention to drag reduction, together with the large 24 000-pound-thrust (with afterburning) Pratt & Whitney J75 turbojet engine, gave the Delta Dart a maximum speed of 1525 miles per hour (M=2.31) at 40 000 feet and the capability of climbing to its combat ceiling of 51 800 feet in 6.9 minutes; service ceiling was 52 700 feet. Together with excellent handling qualities, the high maximum speed and good climb characteristics of the F-106 have made it an outstanding interceptor that first began to replace the F-102 in 1960. As a result, the F-106 is still in use today with many interceptor squadrons (ref. 177).

Roll and pitch control of the F-106 is provided by elevons, which are flaplike movable surfaces on the trailing edge of the wing. Working in phase in response to fore and aft motions of the control stick, these surfaces provide longitudinal control moments about the pitch axis; differential deflection of the surfaces in response to lateral movement of the stick gives roll control. The lack of a horizontal tail for pitch trim prevents the use of high-lift flaps on the wing. The landing speed of the 34 510-pound-gross-weight airplane is maintained at an acceptable value (173 mph according to ref. 200) by the large wing area of nearly 700 square feet, which gives a relatively low wing loading of 49.5

pounds per square foot. (Compare this wing loading with that of some of the other supersonic fighters.)

Primary armament of the F–106 consists of a Genie missile with nuclear warhead and four Falcon, radar-homing, infrared, heat-seeking missiles. Immediately after takeoff on an interception mission, control of the aircraft passes from the pilot to a ground controller who, by radio signals to the autopilot, directs the aircraft to the vicinity of the enemy intruder as displayed on a radar scope. Once within range of the enemy aircraft, the radar on board the Delta Dart locks onto the intruder, guides the interceptor to a favorable attack position, and initiates firing of the missiles. Then ground control again takes over and flies the aircraft back to its base where the pilot performs the landing. Throughout this automatic mission, the pilot can at any time assume manual control of the aircraft.

A total of 875 F–102A's had been completed, by April 1958, as well as 111 TF–102 two-place trainer versions of the aircraft. The last Delta Daggers were retired from the active Air Force inventory in 1973. Only 340 of the much more capable F–106's were built, the last of which came off the production line in 1961. The relatively few F–106's manufactured, as compared with the number of F–102A's, reflects the changing nature of the threat from enemy bombers to ballistic missiles that took place in the 1960's. Although still in use after more than 20 years, the F–106 is now being gradually replaced in the air-defense role by an interceptor version of the McDonnell Douglas F–15 Eagle. In contrast with most fighter aircraft adapted to a variety of missions, the F–102A and the F–106 were never employed for any role other than interception.

Based on lessons learned in the Korean war, the Lockheed F–104 Starfighter was originally intended as a lightweight interceptor with very high maximum speed and rate of climb. However, the aircraft saw only limited service in that role with the USAF, perhaps because it was too small to accommodate the sophisticated all-weather navigation and fire-control systems required by the Air Defense Command. A redesigned fighter-bomber version of the F–104 saw limited service with the USAF Tactical Air Command, including action in the Vietnam war, but enjoyed spectacular success in export sales to foreign governments. The aircraft has been in the inventory of 15 different countries and manufactured in 7 countries including the United States.

The North American F–100 and Convair F–102/106 just described are examples of supersonic aircraft configurations having sweptback and delta wings. Most supersonic aircraft have wings of one or the other of these shapes, or some hybrid form derived from a blending of the two types. In contrast, the Lockheed F–104 was designed in accordance with an entirely different configuration concept, which featured an almost vanishingly small straight wing and a horizontal tail mounted in the T-position at the top of the vertical tail. Different views of the F–104 are shown in figures 11.15 and 11.16, and physical and performance characteristics of the F–104G version of the aircraft are given in table V.

With an area of 196.1 square feet, the wing of the F–104 was about one-half as large as that of the F–100 and less than one-third as large as that of the F–106. From the side of the fuselage to the wingtip measured only 7 feet, 7 inches. The actual thickness of the wing varied from a maximum of 4.2 inches at the root to 1.96 inches at the tip. The corresponding airfoil thickness ratio was 3.4 percent. Sharp leading-edge airfoil sections (sharp enough to pose a safety hazard to ground personnel) were used to minimize the drag rise in passing through Mach 1.0. Even so, experimental data show that the transonic drag rise on this straight-wing aircraft with no area ruling was about 40 percent higher than that of the F–106 (in terms of drag coefficient). Both leading- and trailing-edge flaps were used to increase the lifting capability of the wing. Effectiveness of the simple trailing-edge flaps was augmented by boundary-layer control employing high-pressure bleed air from the engine. Ailerons were used for lateral control. Clearly shown

Figure 11.15 — Lockheed F–104G Starfighter single-engine jet fighter. [Denis Hughes via AAHS]

Figure 11.16 — Front view of Lockheed F–104 Starfighter. [Clyde Gerdes via AAHS]

in figure 11.16 is the pronounced wing anhedral angle (droop) that served to partially offset the rolling moment due to sideslip induced by the tail surfaces. During the flight test program, the aircraft was found to have a severe pitch-up problem at the stall. Immersion of the high-mounted horizontal tail in the wake from the stalled wing and long fuselage nose undoubtedly caused the problem. A stick shaker/pusher (see chapter 10) to limit the maximum attainable angle of attack eliminated the pitch-up problem.

The side-mounted inlets incorporated a fixed conical centerbody whose vertex angle and position were chosen so as to place the oblique shock from the nose of the centerbody on or just above the lip of the inlet at the maximum design Mach number. The conical centerbody inlet along with appropriate auxiliary inlet doors provided the proper engine airflow through the design Mach number range. Of lower performance than the production aircraft, the prototype XF–104 had normal shock inlets without the centerbody.

Photographs of this version of the aircraft are frequently seen in various references.

Armament carried on the F-104 consisted of one six-barrel 20-mm Vulcan rotary cannon. This weapon can be likened to the 19th-century Gatling gun but was, of course, power operated instead of hand cranked. Four thousand pounds of various types of external stores could also be carried. On a typical ground-attack mission, the aircraft was capable of delivering 2510 pounds of bombs at a combat radius of 620 miles. Both pylon and tip-mounted fuel tanks were dropped during the course of the mission, which was carried out at an average speed of 585 miles per hour. Cruise altitude varied from about 22 000 feet at the beginning of the mission to 34 000 feet at the return to home base. Weapons delivery took place at near sea-level altitude.

The data in table V show the F-104G to be significantly lighter than the other Century Series fighters and, with its small wing, to have the highest wing loading of the group. Maximum speed is Mach 2.0 at 35 000 feet and Mach 1.13 at sea level. Initial rate of climb at sea level is a spectacular 48 000 feet per mimute. In May 1958, a world speed record of 1404 miles per hour was set by an F-104, and a record zoom-climb to an altitude of 91 243 feet was made.

Before ending this discussion of the Lockheed Starfighter, some mention of its flying characteristics must be made. In many quarters, the F-104 has the unenviable reputation of being a difficult and dangerous aircraft to fly, an aircraft with unforgiving handling characteristics. Certainly, it has had an appallingly poor safety record in use with some air forces but a relatively good one in others. In fairness, the record seems to suggest that the aircraft can be flown with reasonable safety if the pilots are properly trained and the aircraft is maintained and flown strictly in accordance with the manufacturer's recommendations. Apparently, however, the aircraft can be terribly unforgiving of any departure from these recommended procedures. An interesting discussion of the F-104 and its safety record is contained in reference 186.

First flight of the F-104 prototype took place on February 7, 1954, and production aircraft first entered service with the USAF in January 1958. By the time the last Starfighter was built in Italy in 1978, a total of 2536 units had been constructed in this multinational program. A final question and observation on the somewhat controversial F-104: Why did the aircraft receive such wide acceptance by foreign air forces while, at the same time, it was essentially rejected by the USAF? Relatively light in weight, the aircraft offered a very high performance at a reasonable price. These were no doubt important ingredients in the formula that assured its widespread sale abroad, as was the highly aggressive and effective sales campaign mounted by the Lockheed organization. Limited payload and range, however, restricted the usefulness of the F-104 in service with the USAF — an organization that could and did pay for exactly what it wanted.

Designed from the outset as a fighter-bomber for long-range interdiction missions, the Republic F-105 Thunderchief was a large, heavy aircraft with Mach 2 performance. A unique feature for a fighter was the internal bomb bay intended to house a nuclear weapon. First flight of the Thunderchief took place on October 22, 1955. After winning a flyoff competition with the North American F-107 in 1956, the F-105 first entered squadron service in 1958. (As an interesting sidelight, the F-107 was the last of the Century Series of fighters to fly and the last fighter aircraft to bear the name "North American.") Two views of the F-105B are shown in figures 11.17 and 11.18, and physical and performance data for the F-105D, the most numerous variant of the aircraft, are given in table V. The configuration incorporated a shoulder-mounted 45° sweptback wing with airfoil thickness ratios varying from 5.5 percent at the root to 3.7 percent at the tip. Trailing-edge Fowler

Figure 11.17 — Republic F-105B Thunderchief single-engine jet fighter. [mfr via Martin Copp]

Figure 11.18 — Front view of Republic F–105B Thunderchief single-engine jet fighter.
[mfr via Martin Copp]

flaps together with leading-edge flaps were used to increase the maximum lift coefficient of the wing. Roll control was achieved by short-span outboard ailerons assisted by upper-surface spoilers. The all-moving horizontal tail was mounted in the low position to aid in preventing pitch-up. Careful fuselage area ruling reduced the magnitude of the drag rise as the Mach number increased from subsonic to supersonic values. A most unusual feature of the aircraft are the two-dimensional variable-area supersonic inlets mounted in the wing-root position. The speed brake was an unusual petal-type arrangement that surrounded the jet nozzle.

Already mentioned is the internal bomb bay designed to accommodate a nuclear weapon. Not long after the F–105 became operational, however, the concept of carrying a nuclear weapon in the aircraft was

311

discarded, and the bomb bay was used to house additional fuel. A six-barrel Vulcan 20-mm rotary cannon was carried in the aircraft, and there were provisions for 12 000 pounds of external armament including bombs, rockets, and missiles. Such a large load could be carried only on short-range missions, however, with a more normal load being 6000 pounds. Combat radius for this load varied from 600 to 800 miles depending on the amount of external fuel carried. The F–105 was provided with all the necessary electronic equipment for full all-weather capability.

Maximum Mach number of the F–105D was 2.08, or 1372 miles per hour, at an altitude of 36 090 feet; at sea level, the maximum Mach number was 1.1, or 836 miles per hour. Normal cruising speed was 584 miles per hour. Sea-level rate of climb was a spectacular 38 500 feet per minute; only 1.7 minutes were required to reach an altitude of 35 000 feet. Ferry range with no war load was 2207 miles. With a maximum gross weight of 52 838 pounds, the F–105D is by far the heaviest fighter so far considered, nearly as heavy as the 55 000-pound, four-engine B–17 bomber of World War II.

A total of 833 F–105 aircraft were manufactured before production ended in 1964. Extensively used in ground-attack operations in Vietnam, the Thunderchief continued to serve with the USAF for a number of years following the end of the conflict. Last of the F–105's was withdrawn from the Tactical Air Command in 1980, but a few are still in service with the Air National Guard.

The Navy Goes Supersonic

A number of Navy fighters developed during the 1950's were capable of flight at high-subsonic speeds, but only two production types could pass through Mach 1.0: the Grumman F11F Tiger and the Vought F8U Crusader. Capable of a maximum Mach number of about 1.1, the Tiger was just barely able to enter the supersonic flight regime. With a maximum Mach number of 1.75 at 35 000 feet and a Mach 1.0 capability at sea level, however, the Crusader had much the higher performance of the two aircraft and is discussed in the next few paragraphs.

Before discussing the F8U, however, a few words on the change in the method of military aircraft designation that took place in 1962 is in order. Up until this time, the Navy designation system indicated the purpose of the aircraft, the manufacturer, and details of the aircraft geneology. For example, the designation F8U-1 is explained as follows:

F indicates a fighter-type aircraft

U is the identifying letter assigned to the manufacturer, in this case Vought

8 indicates the 8th fighter-type aircraft developed by Vought

1 indicates the first model of the aircraft

The Navy system was useful for those who understood it and knew the letter of the alphabet assigned to the various manufacturers. For the uninitiated, however, the system was clumsy and obscure. Further, when the same basic aircraft was used by both the USAF and the Navy, two distinctly different designations were used. For example, the USAF North American F–86 Sabre became the Navy F4J Fury. Following the introduction in 1962 of a simplified designation system for both USAF and Navy aircraft, the F8U Crusader became simply the F–8A where the number "8" indicates the fighter type and the letter "A" signifies the first model. The designation F–1A was assigned to the oldest Navy fighter then in service; Air Force aircraft then in service retained their original designations. (See refs. 171 and 200 for further discussion of designation systems.)

Three-quarter front and rear views of the Vought F–8A Crusader are shown in figures 11.19 and 11.20, respectively, and physical and performance characteristics are given in table V for the F–8H version of the aircraft. Configuration features of the F–8 include a variable-inci-

Figure 11.19 — Vought F–8A Crusader single-engine jet fighter. [NASA]

313

Figure 11.20 — Rear view of Vought F–8A single-engine jet fighter. [NASA]

dence, 35° swept wing mounted at the top of the fuselage, an all-moving horizontal tail mounted below the extended chord plane of the wing, and a chin inlet to feed air to the single 16 600-pound-thrust Pratt & Whitney turbojet engine. Although not evident in the figures, the fuselage was carefully shaped in accordance with the transonic area rule.

The two-position variable incidence wing of the F–8 is a unique feature dictated by aircraft-carrier landing requirements. With the low-aspect-ratio swept wing of the F–8A, a high angle of attack was needed to reach the desired lift coefficient in the carrier approach and landing maneuver. To avoid tail scrape and possible damage at touchdown, the landing-gear configuration of the aircraft severely limited the maximum usable aircraft pitch angle. For this reason, and to provide the pilot with improved visibility during the approach, the required angle of attack was achieved by shifting the wing from the low to the high incidence position while, at the same time, maintaining the aircraft pitch angle within the desired range. Seven degrees was the amount by which the incidence changed as the wing was shifted from the low to the high position. In figures 11.19 and 11.20 the wing is in the high incidence position.

Other features of the approximately 6-percent-thick wing included a chord extension, sometimes called a snag or dogtooth, beginning at about the midsemispan position and extending to the wingtip. A vortex generated at the beginning of the snag helps alleviate pitch-up in much the same manner as a wing fence (discussed in chapter 10). High-lift devices consisted of inboard and outboard leading-edge flaps and plain trailing-edge flaps. To further increase the maximum lift coefficient, the capability of the trailing-edge flap was augmented by blowing boundary-layer control using bleed air from the engine. Small inboard ailerons were used for lateral control; these surfaces could also be deflected symmetrically to increase lift at low speeds.

The fixed-geometry inlet seems, at first glance, to be somewhat incongruous on an aircraft of such high performance as that of the Crusader. The nose of the aircraft protrudes forward of the chin inlet, however, and probably serves much the same purpose as the fixed conical bodies employed on the inlets of the Lockheed F–104. As compared with a nose-mounted normal-shock inlet, the chin inlet would accordingly be expected to have better pressure recovery at the supersonic speeds achieved by the F–8.

The Crusader was the first carrier-based aircraft to reach a speed of 1000 miles per hour. Not quite as high in maximum speed or rate of climb as the later-model Century Series fighters, the F–8H is nevertheless shown by the data in table V to be a high-performance supersonic aircraft. As a fighter, it was usually equipped with four 20-mm cannons and two or four Sidewinder missiles. Initially, a clear-weather air-superiority fighter, the Crusader was later modified to have limited all-weather capability.

First flight of the F–8 took place on March 25, 1955; and before production ended, 1261 Crusaders had been constructed. In addition to the U.S. Navy, the French Navy and the Philippine Armed Forces used various versions of the F–8. In the Vietnam conflict, the Crusader saw extensive service in photoreconnaissance, ground-attack, and fighter-escort roles. U.S. Navy fighter service for the Crusader ended in March 1976, but a few are still on duty as photoreconnaissance aircraft. According to reference 177, some F–8's are still in use with French and Philippine forces.

Fighters of the 1960's

A profusion of new aircraft types came upon the fighter scene in the 15 years between the end of World War II and 1960. Many of these did not progress beyond the prototype stage; others entered production and became part of the fighting inventory of the U.S. Armed Forces. As discussed, many new design innovations were explored in this seminal period of jet-fighter design. By the end of the 1950's, however, most of the new concepts had been explored, and the days of rapid design and construction of new prototypes were at an end. A major contributor to the demise of the multiple prototype approach was the great complexity and associated high development cost of any new fighter by the 1960's. Consequently, only three new fighters came into the USAF and Navy inventories in the 1960's. Of the three, the McDonnell F-4 and the Northrop F-5 series of fighters incorporated no really new design concepts but were carefully engineered combinations of proven design features aimed at achieving specified mission capabilities. The third aircraft of this group was the General Dynamics F-111; it enjoys the distinction of being the first production aircraft of any type in any country to have a variable-sweep wing. These three aircraft, which are still in service, are discussed below.

McDonnell F-4 Phantom II

If the number of aircraft produced is any measure of success, then surely the McDonnell F-4 aircraft must be considered the most successful supersonic fighter ever produced in the United States. From the time of its first flight on May 27, 1958 until the end of production in 1979, slightly over 5000 F-4's of approximately 15 variants were produced.

Originally developed as a carrier-based fleet-defense fighter for the Navy, the F-4 (F4H in the old Navy designation system) was designed to have higher performance and a larger and more versatile weapons load than the F-8, as well as complete all-weather capability. The F-4 Phantom II first entered Navy service in late 1960, and in 1962 the USAF began procurement of the F-4 for service in its fighter squadrons. Today, the aircraft serves in the air forces of 10 foreign countries, as well as with the USAF, Navy, and Marine Corps.

A three-quarter front view of an Air Force RF-4C (reconnaissance version of the aircraft) is shown in figure 11.21; a three-quarter rear view of a Navy F-4J fighter is presented in figure 11.22; and a sketch of the wing planform shape is given in figure 11.23. Details of the physical and performance characteristics of the USAF F-4E are given in table V.

316

Figure 11.21 — McDonnell Douglas RF–4C Phantom II twin-engine jet fighter. [Peter C. Boisseau]

Figure 11.22 — Rear view of McDonnell Douglas F-4J Phantom II twin-engine jet fighter. [Peter C. Boisseau]

A large anhedral angle (negative dihedral angle) of the horizontal tail in combination with a sharply defined positive dihedral in the outer wing panels are two conspicuous identifying features of the aircraft. These two features are related to the position of the exhaust nozzles located only a short distance behind the low-mounted wing. To avoid impingement problems with the hot jet exhaust, the tail surfaces are

317

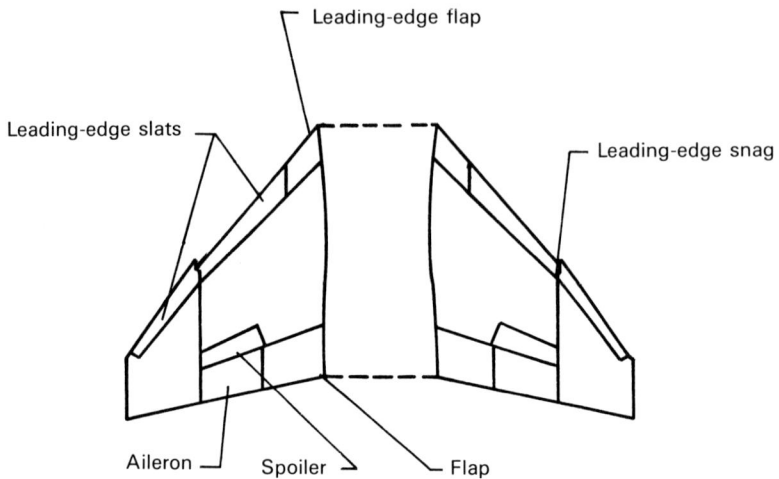

Figure 11.23 — Approximate wing-planform shape of McDonnell Douglas F-4 jet fighter.

mounted on an aft fuselage extension above the nozzles. As indicated by early wind-tunnel studies, the resultant high position of the horizontal tail in combination with the wing-shape parameters led to undesirable nonlinear pitching-moment characteristics at high angles of attack. The large anhedral angle, or droop, of the horizontal-tail surfaces greatly improved the pitching-moment characteristics, as well as increasing directional stability. To achieve the proper balance in dihedral effect for the integrated aircraft configuration, however, a large positive dihedral angle was incorporated in the outer panels of the wing. In addition, the wing dihedral elevated the wingtip vortexes relative to the horizontal tail and further improved the pitching-moment characteristics of the aircraft. Another identifying feature of the F-4 is the large vertical-ramp variable-geometry inlet located on each side of the fuselage. These inlets feed the two 17 900-pound-thrust afterburning General Electric turbojet engines.

Contained in reference 155 is an interesting paper by Bennett and Rousseau that describes seven different wing configurations used on the F-4; the reader should consult this paper for details of these various wings. The planform of the low-aspect-ratio 45° sweptback wing is depicted in figure 11.23. Different combinations of leading-edge flaps and slats, together with trailing-edge flaps, were used on various versions of the aircraft. As a result of combat experience in the Vietnam conflict, the leading-edge slats shown in figure 11.23 were incorporated

318

to improve manuevering capability in air-to-air engagements. Leading-edge and trailing-edge boundary-layer control using high-pressure engine bleed air was provided on Navy models of the aircraft (as well as some USAF versions) to give the desired low approach speeds so necessary in carrier operations. Lateral control was provided by a combination of upper-surface spoilers and midspan ailerons. Thickness ratio of the wing varied from 6.4 percent at the root to 4 percent at the tip.

Originally intended as a fleet-defense fighter, the F–4 had no guns but was equipped only with missiles. Four Sparrow missiles with a 10-mile range and four Sidewinders with a 2-mile range were semiburied on the lower side of the aircraft beneath the wings and fuselage. Navigation and target acquisition was handled in the all-weather aircraft by the radar intercept officer seated behind the pilot. All Phantom II aircraft were of two-seat configuration. As later used in the ground-attack mode, a wide variety of external stores could be carried. For example, two 370-gallon fuel tanks could be mounted on inboard wing pylons, together with a 600-gallon centerline tank. On a typical ground-attack mission, six 750-pound bombs could be delivered at a combat radius of 514 miles at an average speed of 566 miles per hour. Four air-to-air missiles were also carried, and about 42 percent of the total fuel load was accommodated in external tanks. As a result of Vietnam combat experience, a Vulcan six-barrel 20-mm cannon was added to the armament of the F–4 to increase its effectiveness in the air-superiority role.

A glance at the data in table V indicates that the F–4E was a large, heavy, twin-engine aircraft with Mach 2.25 supersonic performance coupled with a sea-level rate of climb of 54 200 feet per minute and service ceiling of 59 200 feet. As compared with earlier Century Series fighters, however, the F–4 had a relatively high zero-lift drag coefficient and low maximum lift-drag ratio. Once described in the press as a triumph of thrust over aerodynamics (with at least some degree of truth), the F–4 was nevertheless an astute ensemble of aircraft design parameters synthesized in such a way as to produce an outstanding fighter. Extensive service in Vietnam clearly showed that the aircraft could be employed effectively in a wide variety of roles encompassing most missions a fighter might be called upon to perform.

The high performance of the Phantom II coupled with its great versatility and twin-engine reliability have resulted in its wide acceptance throughout the world. It will be a familiar silhouette in the sky for many years to come. The various models of the aircraft as well as a summary of its war record may be found in reference 200.

Northrop F-5 Tiger

A fighter totally different in concept from the McDonnell F-4, but one that has received worldwide acceptance, is the Northrop F-5 family of fighters. Today, this versatile aircraft serves in the air force inventories of 27 countries. It is a lightweight, easy-to-fly, simple-to-maintain, and (relatively) cheap supersonic fighter that was selected in the early 1960's for use by underdeveloped countries as part of the U.S. Military Assistance Program (MAP). Its origins can be traced to design studies begun by Northrop in the mid-1950's; development proceeded along two lines. In response to a USAF requirement for a supersonic trainer, the two-place T-38 Talon was produced. First flight took place on April 10, 1959, and eventually 1189 of these aircraft were manufactured for use by the USAF, the Navy, NASA, and the Federal Republic of Germany. Most of these were delivered by the mid-1960's. In addition to its trainer and pilot proficiency roles, the T-38 was flown for a number of years by the USAF Thunderbird exhibition team.

In the meantime, first flight of the prototype of the fighter version of the aircraft, designated F-5, occurred in July 1959; in May 1962, it was selected by the United States for use in MAP. First known as the Freedom Fighter and later as the Tiger, initial deliveries of the F-5 were made to Iran in January 1965. Attracted by its performance, reliability, and low cost (in 1972, the cost of an F-5 was about one-third that of an F-4), other countries outside MAP soon began buying the F-5. To date, some 2225 F-5's have been manufactured, and production

Figure 11.24 — Northrop F-5A Tiger twin-engine jet fighter. [Denis Hughes via AAHS]

continues at this writing. An advanced version of the aircraft, known as the F–20 Tigershark, is now under development.

A three-quarter front view of a Northrop F–5A Tiger can be seen in figure 11.24, and an in-flight view of its close relative, the T–38 Talon supersonic trainer, is shown in figure 11.25. Physical and performance characteristics of the F–5E Tiger II are contained in table V.

In configuration the F–5 is a low-wing monoplane equipped with an all-moving horizontal tail mounted in the low position; the fuselage is carefully contoured in accordance with the transonic area rule. Small side-mounted inlets supply air for the two General Electric J85 afterburning turbojet engines. The 4.8-percent-thick wing has 24° sweepback at the quarter chord line. As can be seen by the T–38 in figure 11.25, the wing trailing edge is nearly straight, giving a trapezoidal shape to the planform. Lateral control is provided by small ailerons located near midsemispan; single-slotted high-lift flaps extend from the inboard end of the ailerons to the sides of the fuselage. Leading-edge flaps are used to improve maneuvering performance. (These flaps are not incorporated in the wings of the T–38.) As can be seen in figure 11.25, speed brakes are mounted on the bottom of the fuselage. Turning performance is enhanced by an aileron-rudder interconnect system, and handling characteristics are improved by artificial damping about the pitch and yaw axes. The F–5 is reported to have good handling characteristics and, in contrast with the F–4, does not have a propensity for entering unintentional spins.

Figure 11.25 — Northrop T–38 Talon trainer, a close relative of the F–5 Tiger. [mfr via Martin Copp]

A glance at the data in table V shows that the F-5E is indeed a small, light aircraft. Its design gross weight of 15 745 pounds is only about 30 percent of the 53 848-pound design gross weight of the F-4. In performance, the F-5 has a Mach 1.51 capability at about 36 000 feet and a sea-level rate of climb of 28 536 feet per minute — a good performance but not comparable with that of the F-4. Certainly, the load-carrying capability of the F-5 is much less than that of the larger aircraft.

The F-5 was originally designed as a daytime, air-to-air fighter, but it has also been extensively used as a ground-attack aircraft. Photoreconnaissance versions of the F-5 have also been produced. Armament for the air-to-air combat role consists of two 20-mm cannons and two Sidewinder missiles. Radius of a typical air combat mission with this armament and external fuel tanks is 375 miles, and average mission speed is 541 miles per hour. In the ground-attack mode, about 7000 pounds of external ordnance may be carried. Evaluated in Vietnam by the USAF, the F-5 was later used by Vietnamese forces. Never a part of the USAF tactical forces, it has been used as an aggressor aircraft to represent a hostile fighter in simulated combat with U.S. fighters. (Some of the characteristics of the F-5 resemble those of the Soviet-built MiG-21 in certain altitude ranges.)

Like the McDonnell F-4 Phantom II, the F-5 Tiger will be a familiar sight in many parts of the world for a long time to come. An interesting account of the development of the F-5 and T-38 is contained in reference 134.

General Dynamics F-111

In 1960 the USAF formulated requirements for a new all-weather fighter-bomber to replace the Republic F-105. An aircraft that combined transatlantic ferry capability, short-field landing and takeoff, and both subsonic and supersonic attack modes was desired. Such a great mission flexibility was made possible and feasible by the newly developed NASA single-pivot, variable-sweep wing concept described in chapter 10. At the same time, the Navy had a requirement for a new combat-air-patrol aircraft that could loiter for long periods of time at a distance from the fleet and have the capability of preventing any intrusion of hostile aircraft within a specified zone surrounding the fleet. In the summer of 1961, the new Secretary of Defense decided that, to reduce program costs, a single aircraft to satisfy both Air Force and Navy requirements was both possible and desirable. Competing for the contract to develop this entirely new type of aircraft were Boeing and General Dynamics, with Grumman as a subcontractor for the Navy version of the aircraft. General Dynamics was selected as the winner of the competition in December 1962. The source selection and subsequent development and early operational use of the F–111 were fraught with technical problems and political controversy. No discussion of these difficulties is offered here other than to note that the variable-sweep wing itself caused no problems.

First flight of the F–111A, the Air Force version of the aircraft, took place in December 1964, and the Navy version, the F111B, made its initial flight about 5 months later. Unfortunately, the decision to develop a single aircraft to satisfy both USAF and Navy requirements compromised both versions of the aircraft. To satisfy the low-level supersonic range requirement of the Air Force, a long slender aircraft of high fineness ratio was required to give the desired low level of supersonic wave drag. The length of the aircraft necessary to achieve the desired low wave drag, however, was incompatible with physical restrictions imposed by critical constraints of aircraft-carrier deck and elevator size. Consequently, the aircraft was shortened to meet Navy requirements. The consequent increase in drag resulted in increased fuel load and weight in order to accomplish even a much shorter than desired low-level supersonic range for the critical Air Force mission. Eventually, because of increased weight and degraded performance, the Navy withdrew from the program after the construction of only seven F–111B aircraft; the Grumman F–14, to be described later, was then developed to fill the role for which the F–111 was intended. The Air Force, however, continued with the program and, before production ended, took delivery of 563 aircraft including the FB–111 version for the Strategic Air Command.

A three-quarter front view of an F–111F is presented in figure 11.26, and an in-flight view of an F–111B with the wings in the low sweep position is shown in figure 11.27. Figure 11.28 shows a three-view drawing of the F–111A, which was part of the General Dynamics press release on the occasion of the first aircraft rollout in 1964. The F–111 is a high-wing monoplane with quarter-round variable-geometry supersonic inlets positioned at the intersection of the lower wing surfaces and the sides of the fuselage. The inlet design is shown in greater detail in figure 10.10(b). Inlet air is supplied to two bypass ratio 1.1 Pratt & Whitney TF30–P–9 afterburning turbofan engines of 20 840 pounds thrust each. Located approximately in the extended chord plane of the wing, the all-moving horizontal tail can be deflected differ-

Figure 11.26 — General Dynamics F–111F twin-engine tactical strike fighter. [James T. Brady via AAHS]

Figure 11.27 — General Dynamics F–111B twin-engine Navy strike fighter. [ukn via AAHS]

entially for roll control as well as symmetrically to control pitch. Wing spoilers are used to augment the roll-control power supplied by differential deflection of the horizontal tail.

Wing sweepback angle can be varied from 16° to 72.5°; the corresponding wing span varies from 63 to 32 feet. To assist in achieving short takeoff and landing (STOL) performance, the wing is fitted with leading-edge slats and trailing-edge double-slotted flaps. The very large wheels evident in figures 11.26 and 11.27 are to reduce footprint pressure and thus allow operation from semiprepared fields.

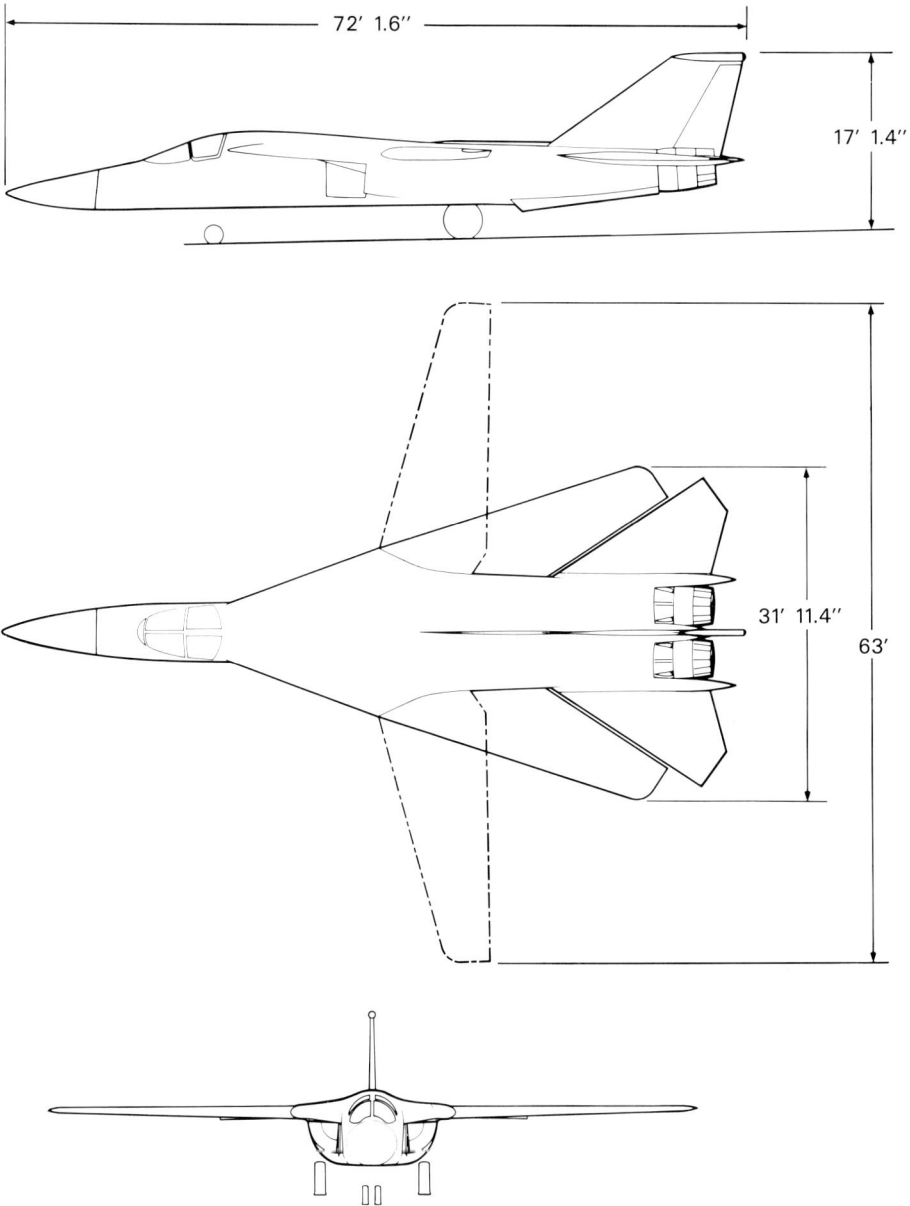

Figure 11.28 — Three-view drawing of General Dynamics F–111A twin-engine tactical strike fighter.

The two crew members are seated beside each other in an air-conditioned and pressurized cockpit that forms part of an escape module. In the event that evacuation of the aircraft is necessary, the entire module separates and is lowered to the ground by parachute.

As can be seen from table V, the F-111D is a large, heavy aircraft with a design gross weight of 82 819 pounds and a maximum gross weight of 98 850 pounds. The corresponding values of wing and thrust loading for the design gross weight are 157.8 and 0.50, respectively. To add perspective to these numbers, the World War II B-17 four-engine heavy bomber had a gross weight of 55 000 pounds and a wing loading of 38.5 pounds per square foot. (See chapter 4.)

A wide variety of weapons can be accommodated on the F-111. Included are an internal bomb bay for a nuclear device, a Vulcan six-barrel 20-mm cannon, and provisions for externally mounting up to 20 000 pounds of stores — both weapons and fuel tanks. On the variable-sweep wing panels, the store-mounting pylons swivel so that the stores remain aligned with the airstream as the sweepback angle is varied.

Precision all-weather attack capability is provided by a computerized radar coupled with an inertial navigation system. Terrain-following radar feeds signals into the autopilot so that the aircraft can fly up and down hills at very low altitude and thus minimize the risk of detection by enemy radar. In a typical low-altitude attack mission, a 2000-pound bomb can be delivered at a distance of 920 miles from home base. The trip to the target is made at sea level at a Mach number of about 0.5 with the last 44 miles being at a Mach number of 1.2. The return trip is accomplished at an altitude of approximately 34 000 feet and a Mach number of 0.75.

The performance figures in table V show the F-111D to have maximum Mach numbers of 2.2 at 50 100 feet and 1.2 at sea level; coupled with this is a 3298-mile unrefueled ferry range. How variable sweep is used to advantage in achieving this versatile performance is shown by the curves in figure 11.29, which were taken from reference 184. The wind-tunnel data shown were obtained with a research configuration, not with a model of the F-111; nevertheless, the trends shown are indicative of the way in which sweepback can be used to increase aircraft versatility. On the vertical scale is the lift-drag ratio, a measure of aerodynamic cruising efficiency, and on the horizontal scale is the wing sweepback angle. For sweepback angles over 90° the wing panels fold rearward until the tips nearly meet over the top of the fuselage. (This feature is not employed on any existing aircraft with variable-sweep

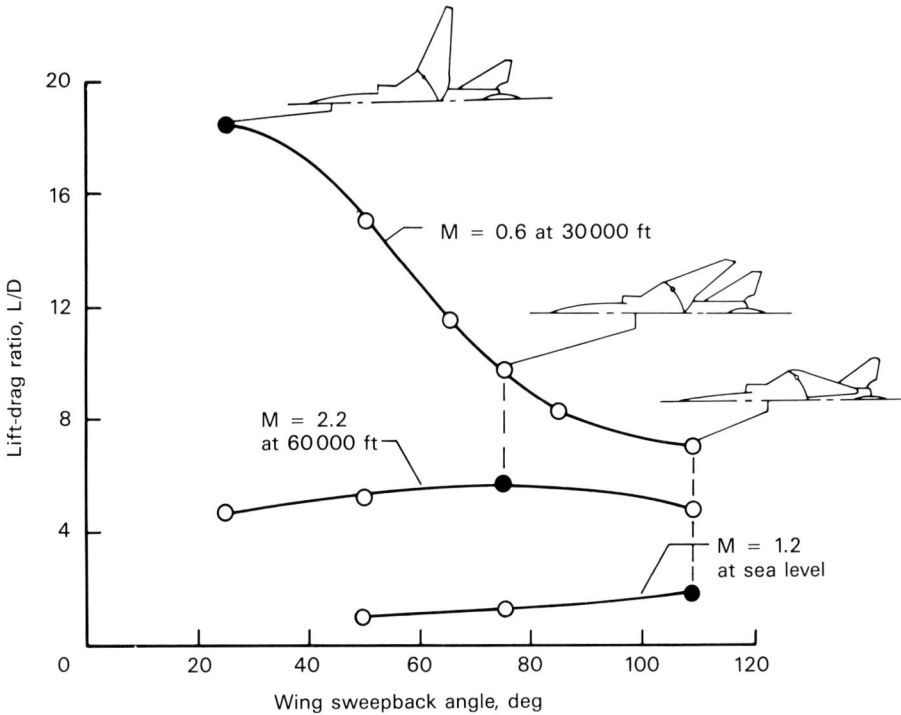

Figure 11.29 — Effect of wing sweep on aerodynamic efficiency. Weight, 60 000 pounds.
[ref. 184]

wings.) For the ferry mission at Mach 0.6 and altitude of 30 000 feet, a wing sweep of 20° is optimum, whereas a wing sweep of about 75° is best for Mach 2.0 flight at 60 000 feet. If the sweep angle was to be fixed at 75°, however, the subsonic lift-drag ratio and consequently the range in this speed regime would be cut in half. For Mach 1.2 at sea level, a sweep angle of about 110° appears best. Thus, by varying the sweepback angle, a single aircraft can be optimized for several widely different flight conditions.

In addition to the important effects on aircraft performance just described, variable sweep can be used to control, at least to some extent, the magnitude of the gust loads imposed on the aircraft. As anyone who has flown in a transport aircraft knows, rough air is usually encountered more frequently at low rather than high altitudes. Mach 1.2 flight at sea level constitutes a particularly severe gust-loads environment, not only because of the frequency of gust encounter but because the magnitude of the load imposed on the aircraft for a given

327

size gust increases with speed. Minimizing the magnitude of these loads reduces structural weight and pilot fatigue and increases the accuracy of weapons delivery. Fortunately, the large sweep angles needed to reduce drag at supersonic speeds also reduce the magnitude of the gust loads. Finally, the low sweep position is useful in obtaining the maximum lift coefficients needed for STOL field lengths. The field lengths listed in reference 162 for the F-111 are less than 3000 feet.

The F-111 first entered operational service in 1967 and saw action in the Vietnam conflict. This very versatile aircraft, though failing to meet some of its original performance objectives, is still an outstanding machine and is likely to remain in the USAF inventory for many years. An interesting account of the aerodynamic research that led to the F-111 concept is contained in reference 184.

Contemporary Fighters

The decade of the 1970's saw the introduction of four new fighters into the armed services of the United States. Entering the Navy was the Grumman F-14A Tomcat, while the McDonnell F-15 Eagle and the General Dynamics F-16 Fighting Falcon became part of the USAF inventory. Finally, the unique British Aerospace AV-8A Harrier vertical takeoff and landing (VTOL) fighter entered service with the U.S. Marine Corps. These aircraft are described below. Since these machines are currently first-line equipment in the United States inventory, only limited performance data are available for them in the open literature. Hence, performance and aerodynamic data in table V for these aircraft are limited.

Grumman F-14A Tomcat

In January 1969 the Grumman Aerospace Corporation was named the winner in a design competition for development of a Navy fighter to fill the role for which the F-111 was rejected. First flight of the new fighter, known as the F-14A Tomcat, took place on December 21, 1970, and the first operational squadrons were deployed on the *U.S.S. Enterprise* in September 1974. In addition to the previously described combat-air-patrol (CAP) mission, the F-14A was designed to fill several other roles including escort of carrier-launched strike forces, deck-launched interceptions, close-in air-to-air combat, and low-altitude strike missions. These varied missions spelled the need for an aircraft with a combination of high cruise efficiency at subsonic speeds, good maneuverability at high-subsonic/transonic speeds, and a supersonic capability extending to Mach 2.4. Finally, as in all Navy fighter aircraft, low approach speeds compatible with carrier operations were required. As a consequence, it came as no surprise that the F–14A turned out to be an aircraft featuring variable-sweep wings.

Photographs of the F–14A are presented in figures 11.30 and 11.31, and the wing-planform shape is shown in figure 11.32; physical and performance data for the aircraft are contained in table V. As compared with the variable-sweep F–111, the Tomcat has distinct differences in appearance. Among the distinguishing features of the F–14A are the large two-dimensional horizontal-ramp supersonic inlets. In accordance with the Mach number, the angle of the upper ramp, that is, the inside horizontal surface of the upper part of the inlet, varies automatically at supersonic speeds to maintain high inlet pressure recovery. Another identifying feature of the aircraft is the two vertical-tail units necessary for adequate directional stability and control at high angles of attack and high Mach numbers. The crew of the Tomcat is accommodated in a tandem arrangement, in contrast to the side-by-side seating in the F–111.

An examination of the physical data in table V shows that the F–14A is significantly lighter than the F–111 and has a lower wing loading, a higher thrust-to-weight ratio, and a much shorter length. All

Figure 11.30 — In-flight view of Grumman F-14A Tomcat twin-engine jet fighter.
[ukn]

Figure 11.31 — Grumman F-14A Tomcat twin-engine jet fighter. [author's collection]

these differences increase carrier compatibility. Two Pratt & Whitney TF30-P-412A afterburning turbofan engines power the F-14A; this is a version of the same engine used in the F-111. Repowering the aircraft with a more modern engine was originally planned; but so far, this has not taken place.

Wing sweepback angle of the Tomcat varies in flight from 20° to 68°; to decrease the space required for storage on the aircraft carrier, the wing span is further reduced by increasing the wing sweepback angle to 75°. Wing thickness ratio (in the streamwise direction) varies from 9 percent for the low sweep position to 5 percent for a sweep angle of 68°. An important difference in the wing geometry of the F-14 and F-111 is shown in figures 11.28 (F-111A) and 11.32 (F-14A). In terms of the wing semispan in the low sweep position, the pivot of the F-14A is 10 to 12 percent farther outboard than that of the F-111. According to the paper by Kress in reference 155, the more outboard pivot location results in a much reduced rearward movement of the center of lift with increasing sweep angle. As a consequence, trim drag is reduced and available pitch-control power is increased. The favorable effect of locating the pivot in the proper outboard position is, of course, in accordance with NASA basic research. (See chapter 10.) An interesting feature of the F-14A wing is the retractable vane located on the fixed portion of the wing; the vane is shown in figure 11.32 in both

330

the retracted (low wing-sweep) and extended (high wing-sweep) positions. The function of the vane is to reduce the rearward shift in the
center of lift that accompanies an increase in Mach number from subsonic to supersonic values. (See figure 10.15.)

Leading-edge slats and trailing-edge flaps are used to improve maneuverability at high subsonic speeds as well as to increase wing maximum lift coefficient at low speeds. The auxiliary flap shown in figure
11.32 is used only at low speeds to increase maximum lift. In normal
operation, the maneuvering flaps, wing-sweep angle, and vane position
are automatically controlled by a computer in accordance with a stored
program that utilizes inputs from several measured flight parameters
such as angle of attack, static and total pressures, and temperature.
Manual operation of the wing is also possible. Roll control of the aircraft is provided by a combination of wing spoilers and differential deflection of the horizontal-tail surfaces.

Although available performance information on the F-14A is
sketchy, the data in table V show maximum Mach numbers of 2.4 at

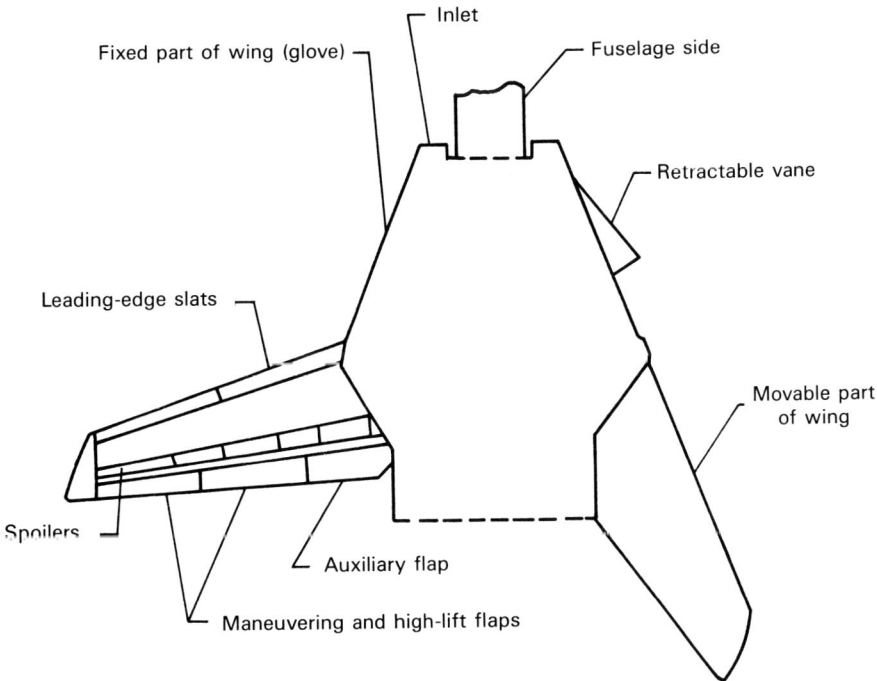

*Figure 11.32 — Approximate wing-planform shape of Grumman F-14A variable-sweep
jet fighter.*

331

49 000 feet and 1.2 at sea level and a time of only 2.1 minutes required to reach an altitude of 60 000 feet. According to the Kress paper in reference 155, the maximum subsonic lift-drag ratio is about 15, which is much higher than the value of 8.58 given in table V for the F–4.

The F–14 is armed with the Vulcan 20–mm rotary cannon for close-in combat and, depending on the mission, can carry a combination of Sidewinder, Sparrow, and Phoenix missiles. As many as six of the latter missiles can be carried on a combat-air-patrol mission. The attack radar is capable of tracking simultaneously 24 separate targets at ranges as great as 100 miles. (Drones have been hit at ranges of over 100 miles with the Phoenix missile in practice missions.) All six of the Phoenix missiles can be fired together, and each can be guided to a different target. With a range of only 2 miles, the Sidewinder is used in short-range air-to-air combat, while the Sparrow with a 10-mile range is employed for more distant engagements. All the missiles are carried externally, but none are attached to the movable portions of the wing; hence, the complication of swiveling store-mounting pylons, such as used on the F–111, is avoided.

The Tomcat appears to be a fighter with very high performance and great operational versatility. By the beginning of 1980, about 400 F–14 aircraft had been built. Included in this group were 80 units for Iran. The aircraft is still in production and is likely to remain so for a number of years.

McDonnell Douglas F–15 Eagle

Experience in the Vietnam conflict showed the F–4 Phantom II to have maneuvering performance inferior to that of the Soviet-built MiG–21. In response to this finding, the USAF developed a set of requirements for a dedicated air-superiority fighter with a maneuvering capability greater than any existing or foreseeable-future fighter aircraft. McDonnell Douglas, North American Rockwell, and Fairchild-Republic submitted proposals in the ensuing design competition. McDonnell Douglas was chosen as the winner in late 1969, and the F–15 Eagle made its first flight on July 27, 1972. By mid-1980, 941 of these aircraft had been built or were on order, including units for Israel, Japan, and Saudi Arabia as well as those for the USAF. In addition to United States production, the aircraft is also being manufactured under license in Japan.

To understand the design of the F–15 and its unique capabilities, some insight into the meaning of maneuverability and its relation to several aircraft design parameters is necessary.

Aircraft Maneuverability

The maneuvering capability of an aircraft has many facets, but one of the most important of these is its turning capability. In a combat situation between two opposing fighters flying at the same speed, the aircraft capable of turning with the shortest radius of turn without losing altitude usually has the advantage. This assumes equality of many other factors such as aircraft stability and control characteristics, armament, and, of course, pilot skill.

In steady, turning flight the lift developed by the wing must balance not only the weight of the aircraft but the centrifugal force generated by the turn. (The term "balance" is used here in a vector sense; that is, the lift vector must equal the sum of the weight and centrifugal force vectors.) The load factor is defined as the ratio of the lift in the turn to the weight of the aircraft and is usually expressed in g units, where g is the acceleration due to gravity. Thus, a 2-g turn is one in which the wing must develop a lift force twice the weight of the aircraft. The value of the load factor is uniquely defined by the aircraft angle of bank. For example, 2-g and 5-g turns require bank angles of 60° and 78.5°, respectively. Finally, for a given bank angle and thus load factor, the turning radius varies as the square of the speed; for example, doubling the speed of the aircraft increases the turning radius by a factor of 4. It would then appear that two different aircraft flying at the same speed would have the same turning radius; however, this conclusion is not necessarily correct. The maximum load factor and associated turning radius may be limited by wing stalling. For a given speed and altitude, stalling occurs as a function of the wing maximum lift coefficient and the wing loading in straight and level flight. Clearly then, the turning capability of different aircraft types may vary widely.

To give some physical significance to these qualitative ideas on turning performance, the variation with altitude of the maximum achievable load factor is shown in figure 11.33(a) for wing loadings of 50 and 100 pounds per square foot; the corresponding variation of turning radius with altitude is shown in figure 11.33(b) for the same two wing loadings. The curves were calculated for a Mach number of 0.85 and a limit maximum lift coefficient of 0.70. For a wing loading of

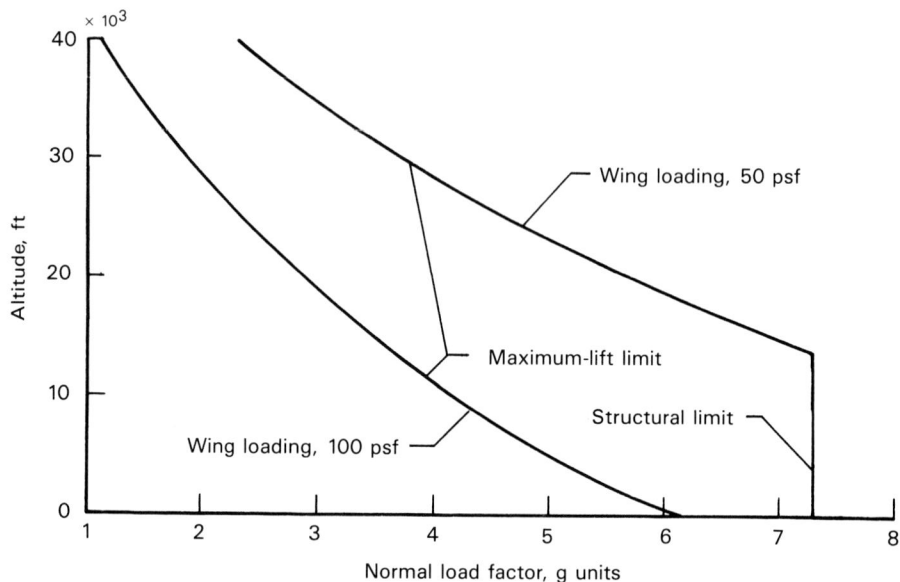

(a) Variation of normal load factor with wing loading and altitude

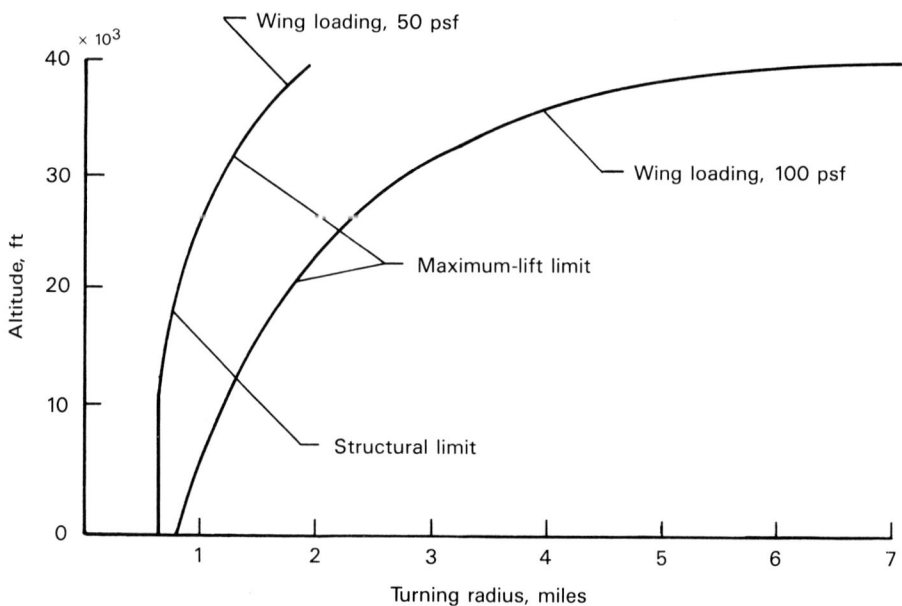

(b) Variation of turning radius with wing loading and altitude

Figure 11.33 — Effect of wing loading and altitude on turning performance of a fighter aircraft. $M = 0.85$, $C_L = 0.7$, *constant altitude.*

50 pounds per square foot, the structural design load limit of 7.33 g can be realized up to an altitude of nearly 15 000 feet; after which, the maximum lift capability of the wing limits the allowable load factor until only 2.3 g can be achieved at 40 000 feet. In comparison, the maximum lift capability limits the achievable load factor of the aircraft with a wing loading of 100 pounds per square foot at all altitudes, with straight and level flight at 1g being just barely possible at 40 000 feet. The corresponding effects of wing loading and altitude on turning radius are equally dramatic, as shown in figure 11.33(b).

The effect of wing maximum lift coefficient is inverse to that of wing loading; that is, increasing the maximum lift coefficient acts in the same way as reducing the wing loading. For example, increasing the maximum lift coefficient from 0.7 to 1.4 would shift the curve for a wing loading of 100 pounds per square foot to the exact position as that occupied by the curve for a wing loading of 50 pounds per square foot and a maximum lift coefficient of 0.7. At a given Mach number, the maximum lift coefficient depends upon the wing-planform shape, the airfoil section, and the type of maneuvering flaps used if any. To further complicate the picture, the maximum lift coefficient also varies with Mach number in a manner that again depends upon the wing design parameters. The message of figure 11.33, however, is quite clear: the turning performance improves as the wind loading decreases and the maximum lift coefficient increases.

Two other important aircraft physical parameters may also limit turning performance. First, at a given speed and altitude, the aircraft drag increases rapidly with lift coefficient; as a consequence, the available thrust may not be sufficient to balance the drag at some load factors that the wing can sustain. In this case the aircraft loses altitude in the turn, an undesirable situation in combat. As for maximum lift coefficient, the drag rise with increasing lift depends upon the wing design and Mach number, as well as upon the added drag required to trim the aircraft at high lift coefficients. Finally, the turning performance may be limited by the control power available in the horizontal tail for trimming the aircraft at the high maneuvering lift coefficients.

These ideas are embodied in a technique for describing and specifying fighter aircraft maneuverability. Known by the term "energy maneuverability," the technique involves the specification of desired aircraft climb and/or acceleration capability for various combinations of speed, altitude, and turning load factor. The quantity specified for each of these combinations is labeled "specific excess power" P_s and is simply the excess power available per unit aircraft weight as compared with the power required to maintain constant altitude in the turn. As an illustration, a value of P_s of 500 might be specified for a 6-g turn at Mach 0.6 at an altitude of 25 000 feet. This simply means that sufficient power is available in the aircraft to establish a steady rate of climb of 500 feet per minute while maintaining the specified turn. Alternatively, the excess power could be used to accelerate to a higher speed while in the turn.

For the first time, extensive use was made of the energy-maneuverability technique in establishing the requirements that led to the McDonnell Douglas F-15 Eagle air-superiority fighter. Values of P_s were specified for 13 combinations of speed, altitude, and g-loading at subsonic, transonic, and supersonic Mach numbers for the new fighter. In addition, maximum and cruise Mach numbers were specified, as well as landing, takeoff, and range requirements.

Aircraft Description

The McDonnell Douglas F-15 Eagle emerged from the complex and extensive set of requirements established by the USAF. Views of the all-weather single-place fighter are shown in figures 11.34 and 11.35, and a sketch of the wing-planform shape is given in figure 11.36. Configuration of the twin-engine aircraft is characterized by a high-mounted wing, twin vertical tails mounted at the rear of the short fuselage, and large, horizontal-ramp variable-geometry external-compression inlets located on the sides of the fuselage ahead of the wing. The horizontal-tail surfaces are mounted in the low position on fuselage extensions on either side of the exhaust nozzles.

The data in table V show that, based on the design maximum weight, the wing loading of the F-15 is significantly lower and the thrust loading much greater than corresponding values for earlier fighter aircraft. At the lower weights to be expected during combat, wing loadings as low as 55 pounds per square foot and static thrust-to-weight-ratios of as much as 1.35 might be expected. (As the Mach number increases at a given altitude, the thrust of the afterburning turbofan also increases. For example, the thrust of the F-15 engine at sea level and Mach 0.9 is nearly twice the sea-level static value.) The values of these parameters represent a significant departure from previous fighter design philosophy and resulted from the energy-maneuverability concepts employed in specifying the aircraft. Note that even at design takeoff weight, the aircraft is capable of sustained vertical flight. Maximum speeds are listed as Mach 2.54 and 1.21 at 40 000 feet and

Figure 11.34 — McDonnell Douglas F–15 Eagle twin-engine jet fighter. [mfr]

sea level, respectively. Service ceiling is 63 000 feet, and ferry range with maximum external fuel is 3570 miles. No other performance information is available, but the aircraft undoubtedly has outstanding performance and maneuvering capability.

The wing planform of the F–15, shown in figure 11.36, suggests a modified cropped delta shape with a leading-edge sweepback angle of 45°. Ailerons and a simple high-lift flap are located on the trailing edge. No leading-edge maneuvering flaps are utilized, although such flaps were extensively analyzed in the design of the wing. This complication was avoided, however, by the combination of low wing loading and fixed leading-edge camber that varies with spanwise position along the wing. Airfoil thickness ratios vary from 6 percent at the root to 3 percent at the tip. An interesting discussion of the wing design and the many trade-off studies involved in its finalization are contained in a paper by Niedling included in reference 155.

Propulsion of the F–15 is supplied by two Pratt & Whitney F100–PW–100 afterburning turbofan engines of 23 904/14 780 pounds thrust each. Developed especially for the F–15, these high-pressure-ratio engines are reported to have much improved efficiency over earlier engines for fighter aircraft.

Figure 11.35 — Front view of McDonnell Douglas F–15 Eagle twin-engine jet fighter.
[mfr]

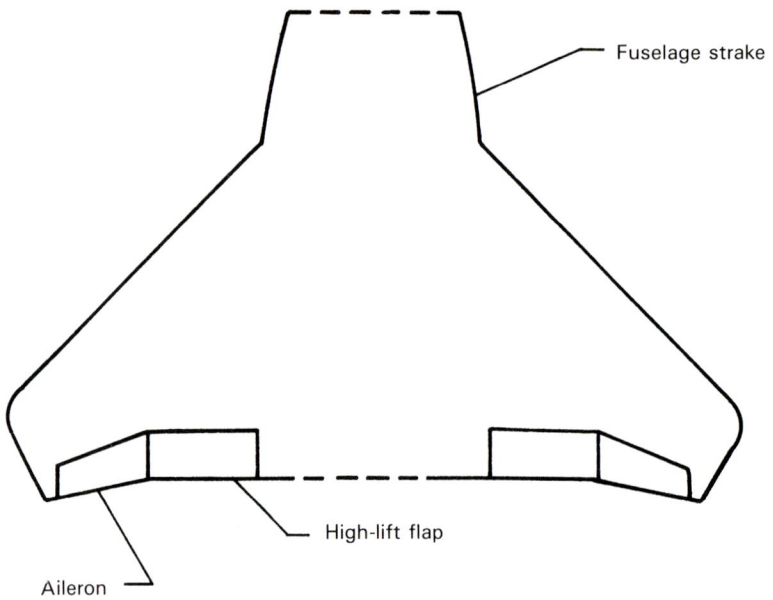

Figure 11.36 — Approximate wing-planform shape of McDonnell Douglas F–15 jet fighter.

When employed as an air-superiority fighter, armament of the F–15 consists of a Vulcan 20-mm rotary cannon together with four Sidewinder and four Sparrow missiles. Although originally billed as a dedicated air-superiority fighter, the F–15 is now replacing the Convair F–106 Delta Dart as an interceptor, and trials are being made of a ground-attack version of the aircraft known as the Strike Eagle. For this latter mission, some 16 000 pounds of external ordnance can be carried. Certainly, the McDonnell Douglas F–15 Eagle will be an important part of the USAF inventory for a long time to come.

General Dynamics F–16 Fighting Falcon

In February 1972, the USAF issued a request for proposal for an experimental, lightweight, low-cost, highly maneuverable day fighter with a Mach 2.0 capability. Although there was no assurance of a follow-on production contract, five companies submitted proposals; from these, General Dynamics and Northrop were selected to build prototypes to be used in a flyoff-type competition for selection of a final winner. The single-engine General Dynamics F–16 was eventually selected over the Northrop F–17; in January 1975, the USAF announced that the aircraft would be put into quantity production. (The twin-engine Northrop F–17 later became the basis for the Navy F–18 Hornet. Descriptions of the F–18 can be found in refs. 161, 163, and 200.) Seven other countries also selected the F–16 for their use, and production lines were established in both the Netherlands and Belgium. According to reference 177, about 1800 aircraft had been built or ordered by 1980. First flight of the F–16 took place in January 1974, and it first entered squadron service with the USAF in January 1979.

The F–16 Fighting Falcon is shown in figure 11.37, and a sketch of the wing-planform shape is given in figure 11.38. The aerodynamic configuration of the F–16 is a highly integrated synthesis of such components as wing, fuselage, and inlet, with the aim of achieving maximum favorable flow interaction with subsequent optimization of overall performance. Configuration features include a cropped delta wing mounted near the top of the fuselage with large strakes extending forward from the leading edge to the sides of the fuselage. A single vertical tail is utilized together with a small fixed ventral fin located on the bottom of the fuselage (fig. 11.37). The all-moving horizontal tail is mounted in the low position and incorporates a small amount of negative dihedral.

Figure 11.37 — General Dynamics F–16 Fighting Falcon single-engine jet fighter. [mfr]

A fixed-geometry, chin-mounted inlet supplies air to the single Pratt & Whitney F100–PW–200 turbofan engine, which is a variant of the same power plant utilized in the F–15. Since the forward portion of the fuselage provides some external flow compression, reasonable inlet efficiency is obtained even at a Mach number of 2.0. Good inlet efficiency through a wide range of angle of attack is ensured by the location of the inlet on the bottom side of the fuselage at a fore-and-aft location behind the forward intersection of the wing strakes with the side of the fuselage.

As shown by figure 11.38, the cropped delta wing blends into the fuselage sides with large strakes that extend forward from the wing leading edges. Vortexes generated by these strakes help prevent wing stall at high angles of attack and thus increase the lifting capability of the wing. Leading-edge sweepback angle is 45°, and the airfoil-section thickness ratio is 4 percent. Trailing-edge flaparons serve the double purpose of high-lift flaps and ailerons for lateral control. Leading-edge maneuvering flaps are deployed automatically as a function of Mach number and angle of attack.

In some respects, the control system of the F–16 represents a complete departure from previous fighter design practice. Although conventional-type aerodynamic control surfaces are employed, the control system utilizes a novel method of transmitting pilot commands to these surfaces. In previous fighter designs, some form of mechanical device linked the control stick and the rudder pedals to the hydraulic actuating system that moved the control surfaces. In contrast, the F–16 utilizes a fly-by-wire system in which movement of the pilot's controls ini-

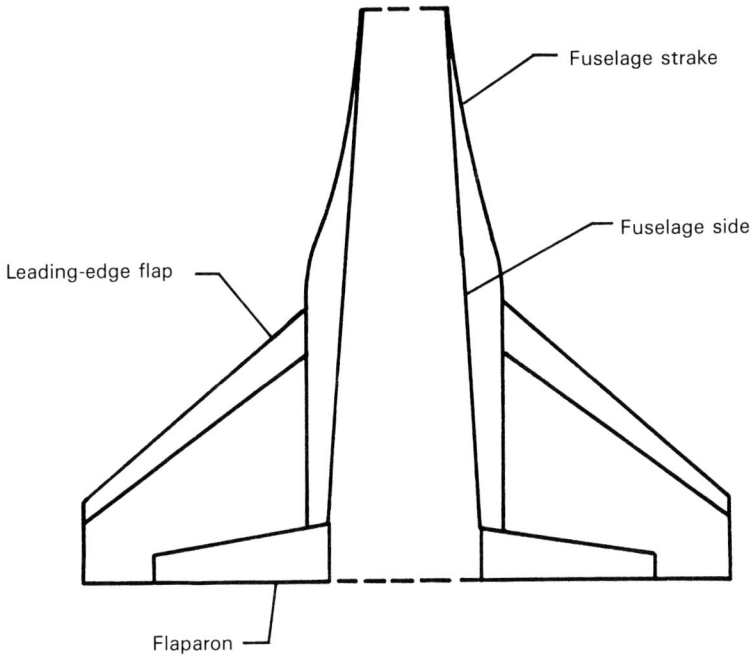

Figure 11.38 — Approximate wing-planform shape of General Dynamics F–16 jet fighter.

tiates electrical signals that activate the hydraulic systems and cause the control surfaces to be moved in a prescribed manner. The fly-by-wire system is lighter, simpler, and more precise than the older mechanical systems, but it does raise questions relating to electrical system reliability. In the F–16, redundancy is provided in the electrical generating and distribution equipment, and four dedicated sealed-cell batteries give transient electrical power protection for the fly-by-wire system. Two completely separate and independent hydraulic systems supply power for actuation of the aerodynamic control surfaces and other utility functions.

Another novel feature in the control system of the F–16 is the incorporation of "relaxed static stability." This means that the inherent longitudinal stability is reduced, to a level traditionally thought to be unacceptable, by moving the aircraft center of gravity to a point very near the aerodynamic center of the aircraft. Tail load and associated trim drag are reduced by this process. Compensation for the loss in inherent aerodynamic stability is provided by a combination electronic-hydraulic stability augmentation system that senses uncalled-for depar-

341

tures from the intended flight condition and injects corrective signals into the flight control system.

Finally, the arrangement of the pilot's control stick is a radical departure from standards that trace their origin to the early days of World War I. Traditionally, the fighter pilot's control stick used for actuation of the ailerons and elevators has consisted of a lever mounted on the floor of the cockpit between the pilot's legs. (There have, of course, been many variations in the detail design of the control stick.) On the F–16, the traditional control stick has been replaced by a short "side-arm controller" mounted on the right-hand console of the cockpit. The side-arm controller is a small-displacement pressure-sensitive handle that, together with the fly-by-wire system, gives the pilot the ability to exercise very precise control of the aircraft. To help prevent unwanted commands to the control handle, the pilot rests his right arm in a carefully designed support. In order to increase the pilot's tolerance to g forces, his seat is inclined 30° in the rearward direction with his legs in a raised position.

The data in table V show the design gross weight of the F–16A to be 23 357 pounds, or only about half that of the F–15C. However, wing loading and thrust-to-weight ratio of the two aircraft are nearly the same. Little performance information is available for the F–16A; the limited data in table V do show, however, a maximum Mach number of 2.02 at 40 000 feet and a ferry range of 2535 miles.

Originally conceived as a simple air-superiority day fighter, the aircraft was armed for that mission with a single six-barrel Vulcan 20-mm cannon and two Sidewinder missiles, one mounted at each wingtip. Over the years, however, the mission capability of the aircraft has been extended to include ground-attack and all-weather operations. With full internal fuel, the aircraft can carry up to 12 000 pounds of external stores including various types of ordnance as well as fuel tanks,

The F–16 Fighting Falcon is an advanced and innovative fighter that, like the F–14 and the F–15, will be a part of the fighter scene for many years.

British Aerospace AV–8A Harrier

Discussed next is a totally unique aircraft that has an operational versatility unmatched by any other fighter in the western world. The British Aerospace Harrier can take off and land vertically like a helicopter but, unlike the well-known rotary-wing machine, accomplishes this vertical-flight operation by means of a specially designed jet engine that is also able to propel the aircraft in forward flight at Mach numbers as high as 0.95 at an altitude of 1000 feet. An early prototype, known as the Hawker P–1127, flew in 1960 and was the basis of a more refined aircraft that appeared later. Known as the Kestrel, a number of these aircraft were employed during the mid-1960's in a joint military evaluation of the VTOL fighter concept conducted by the governments of the United States, the United Kingdom, and the German Federal Republic. In the 1970's, the aircraft now called the Harrier entered the active inventory of several air forces. Of the same basic design, the progression from P–1127 to Kestrel to Harrier was characterized by increased power, weight, and performance.

The Kestrel is shown in figures 11.39 and 11.40. This particular aircraft served in the joint United States, British, and German evaluation; it was later used in extensive flight studies at NASA's Langley Research Center. Today it may be seen in the National Air and Space Museum in Washington, D.C. A Harrier in service with the U.S. Marine Corps is shown in figure 11.41. The designation AV–8A is used to describe these aircraft.

The Rolls-Royce (Bristol division) Pegasus turbofan engine is the key to the great versatility of the Harrier. Unlike other jet engines with only one jet-exhaust nozzle, the Pegasus has four exhaust nozzles; two

Figure 11.39 — British Aerospace Kestrel single-engine VTOL jet fighter. [NASA]

Figure 11.40 — British Aerospace Kestrel in hovering flight. [NASA]

Figure 11.41 — British Aerospace Harrier single-engine VTOL jet fighter. [ukn]

are located on each side of the engine. The two front nozzles discharge unheated air compressed by the fan, and the rear nozzles discharge the hot jet exhaust. A rotating cascade of vanes is used in each nozzle to vector the thrust from a horizontal direction for high-speed flight to a vertical direction for hovering and vertical takeoff and landing. Intermediate positions are used for short takeoff and landing (STOL) and

344

for maneuvering in combat situations. (This latter technique is referred to as VIFF, vectoring in forward flight.) The use of VIFF to enhance aircraft maneuverability and hence combat effectiveness was pioneered in flight studies at the Langley Research Center in the late 1960's and early 1970's. For rapid deceleration, the nozzles can actually be rotated past the vertical position to about 98°. The thrust-vectoring nozzles can be seen in the side of the fuselage in figure 11.39.

Another key element in the Harrier concept is the method for controlling the aircraft. When operated as a conventional airplane, the usual ailerons, rudder, and horizontal tail are used to generate aerodynamic control moments about the roll, yaw, and pitch axes, respectively. In hovering flight and at low forward speeds, however, the aerodynamic controls are ineffective, and reaction jets are used to provide the necessary control moments. At intermediate speeds, both reaction jets and aerodynamic controls are used. As indicated in figure 11.39, pitch jets are located at the nose and tail of the fuselage, a roll jet is at each wingtip, and a yaw jet is located behind the tail. The reaction jets utilize compressed air from the high-pressure engine compressor and respond in a proportional fashion to conventional movements of the control stick and rudder pedals. The control jets come into operation automatically when the thrust-vectoring nozzles are rotated to any angle in excess of 20°. Control of the thrust-vectoring nozzles is exercised by a lever in the cockpit located alongside the throttle.

Although the engine and reaction control system are the key elements that give unique operational capability to the Harrier, the airframe itself exhibits several interesting features. With 12° anhedral (negative dihedral), the 34° sweptback wing is mounted on top of the fuselage; like the wing, the all-moving horizontal tail has a large anhedral angle (15°). The anhedral angles of the wing and horizontal tail are intended to minimize the aircraft rolling moments due to sideslip. Even so, at certain combinations of low speed and high angle of attack, aerodynamic rolling moments greater than the combined aerodynamic and reaction control power may occur if the angle of sideslip is allowed to exceed a prescribed value. To assist the pilot in maintaining the angle of sideslip within acceptable limits, a small yaw vane that provides a visual indication of sideslip angle is mounted on the fuselage just ahead of the windshield.

The unusual landing gear of the Harrier is designed to avoid interference with the engine and thrust-vectoring nozzles. A single two-wheel bogie is located in the fuselage behind the engine, and a single steerable nose-wheel is in front of the engine. Balancing outrigger wheels mounted at the wingtips retract into the reaction control fairings. (See fig. 11.41.) The wing anhedral angle minimizes the length of the outrigger landing-gear struts. Also evident in the figure are the large side-mounted subsonic inlets that supply air to the 21 500-pound-thrust engine.

The fighter version of the aircraft is manned by a single pilot; a two-seat trainer with the full military capability of the single seater is also available. As with so many modern jet fighters, the Harrier is equipped with zero-zero ejection seats; that is, crew escape is possible on the runway at zero altitude and zero speed.

The data in table V for the AV–8A version of the Harrier show a design gross weight of 18 000 pounds for VTOL operation and 26 000 pounds for STOL use. For the design gross weight as a VTOL aircraft, the thrust-to-weight ratio is 1.19 and the wing loading is 89.5 pounds per square foot. Maximum speed is listed as Mach 0.95 at an altitude of 1000 feet, and 2.38 minutes are required to reach 40 000 feet; service ceiling is 48 000 feet, and ferry range with maximum external fuel is 2070 miles.

Primary mission of the Harrier as employed by the Royal Air Force is that of a ground-attack fighter-bomber. In this role, a variety of external ordnance with maximum weight up to 5000 pounds may be carried, as well as two 30-mm cannons. The Royal Navy employs the aircraft in a fleet air-defense role; in this capacity, Sidewinder missiles are carried in addition to the cannon and various external stores. In naval use, the Harrier employs a short takeoff technique from a small carrier equipped with a ski-jump launching ramp; after its mission and at a much reduced weight, the aircraft makes a vertical landing on the carrier. This mode of operation is referred to as STOVL, short takeoff and vertical landing. Although generally available information is far from complete, the Harrier was apparently employed with great effectiveness in the Falkland Islands dispute between Great Britain and Argentina in 1982.

At the present time, the British Aerospace Harrier is used by the Royal Air Force and Royal Navy, the U.S. Marine Corps, and the navies of Spain and India. By mid-1980, about 304 aircraft had been produced or were on order; of this number, 110 were in service with the U.S. Marine Corps (ref. 177). An improved version of the Harrier, known as the AV–8B, is now being sought by the Marine Corps. If procured in production quantity, this aircraft will be manufactured in the United States by McDonnell Douglas under an agreement with the British Aerospace Corporation.

Design Trends

Described above are a few of the many jet-fighter aircraft developed in the past four decades. Major increases in performance and capability have taken place since the end of World War II. A quick overview of some of these changes is provided by the trends shown in figures 11.43 to 11.47. In these figures, several of the aircraft physical and performance characteristics tabulated in table V have been plotted as a function of years. The quantities shown are as follows:

(1) Maximum speed, figure 11.43
(2) Sea-level rate of climb, figure 11.44
(3) Wing loading, figure 11.45
(4) Thrust-to-weight ratio, figure 11.46
(5) Maximum subsonic lift-drag ratio, figure 11.47

An upper-bound, or envelope-type, curve enclosing all the data points is shown on each figure. As a reference mark, data are given on most of the figures for the North American P–51 propeller-driven fighter of World War II fame. The symbols used to identify the various aircraft are given in figure 11.42.

Maximum Speed and Sea-Level Rate of Climb

A major objective in fighter aircraft design over the years has been the achievement of ever higher maximum speeds. In figure 11.43, the upper-bound curve of maximum speed as a function of years clearly

○	Messerschmitt Me 262A	▽	Republic F-105D
☐	Gloster Meteor F. Mk. 4	◁	Convair F-106A
◇	Bell P-59A	▷	Vought F-8H
△	Lockheed P-80A	◇	McDonnell F-4E
◁	McDonnell FH-1	◠	Northrop F 5E
▽	North American F-86E	◇	General Dynamics F-111D
◸	Grumman F9F-6	▷	Grumman F-14A
▷	North American F-100D	◁	McDonnell Douglas F-15C
◹	Lockheed F-104G	+	General Dynamics F-16A

Figure 11.42 — Symbols used in figures 11.43 to 11.47.

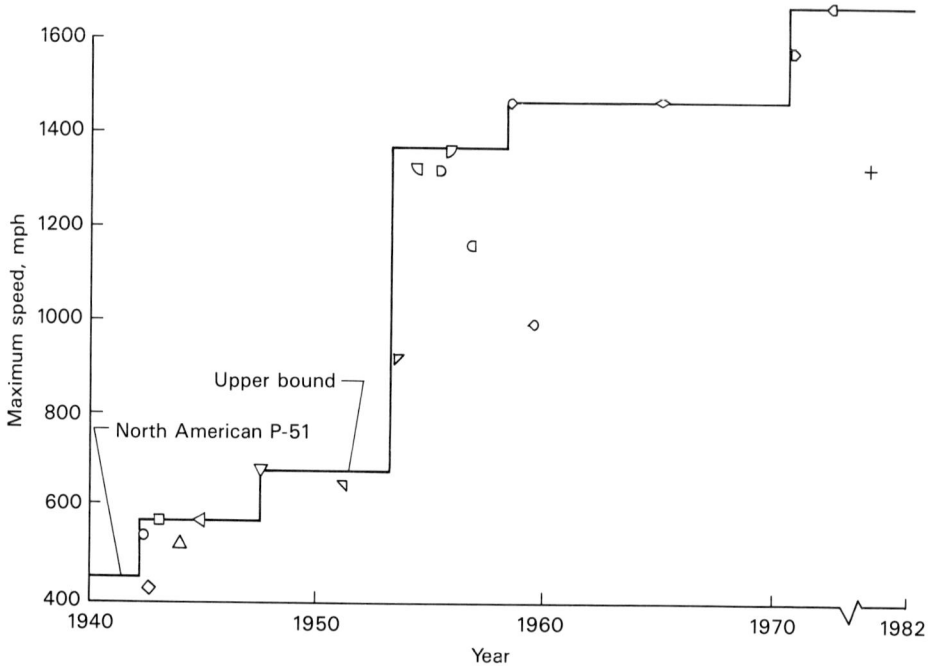

Figure 11.43 — Trends in maximum speed for jet fighter aircraft.

shows this trend and is characterized by a series of ever higher plateaus that correspond to different levels of technical capability. As compared with the North American P–51, the straight-wing fighter incorporating a jet engine raised the maximum speed plateau by about 100 miles per hour; the use of sweepback in a purely subsonic airframe raised the plateau by another 100 miles per hour. In the early 1950's, the upper-bound curve shows an increase in maximum speed of about 700 miles per hour, or a doubling of the speed achievable in an operational fighter aircraft. The afterburning engine together with the major aerodynamic innovations (discussed generally in chapter 10 and for individual aircraft in the present chapter) are responsible for this large increase in maximum-speed capability. Detailed airframe refinement and increased engine thrust are the ingredients in the upper-bound increments evident in 1958 and 1970.

Like the maximum-speed trend, the upper-bound curve for sea-level rate of climb shown in figure 11.44 is also characterized by increasing plateaus. In contrast with the maximum-speed trend, however, the introduction of sweepback in a subsonic airframe resulted in no in-

348

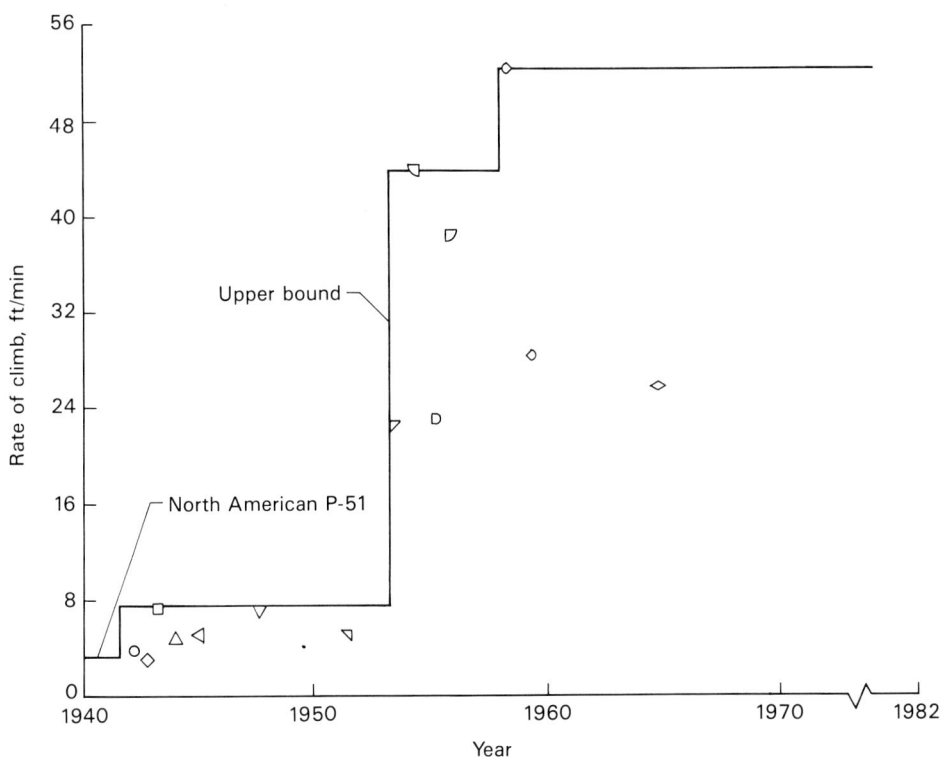

Figure 11.44 — Trends in sea-level rate of climb for jet fighter aircraft.

crease in rate of climb. Unfortunately, rate-of-climb data are not available for the newer fighters.

Wing Loading and Thrust-to-Weight Ratio

The quest for ever increasing maximum speeds was a primary driver in jet-fighter development for many years. If maximum speed were the only requirement, wing loading and thrust loading (thrust-to-weight ratio) might be expected to increase with time in a fashion closely related to the increase in maximum speed. In addition to maximum speed, however, both the wing and thrust loading of a new aircraft must be chosen to satisfy a number of other, often conflicting requirements. For example, landing and takeoff performance, range, subsonic cruising speed, rate of climb, and maneuverability all exert, in varying degrees, an influence on the final choice of wing and thrust

349

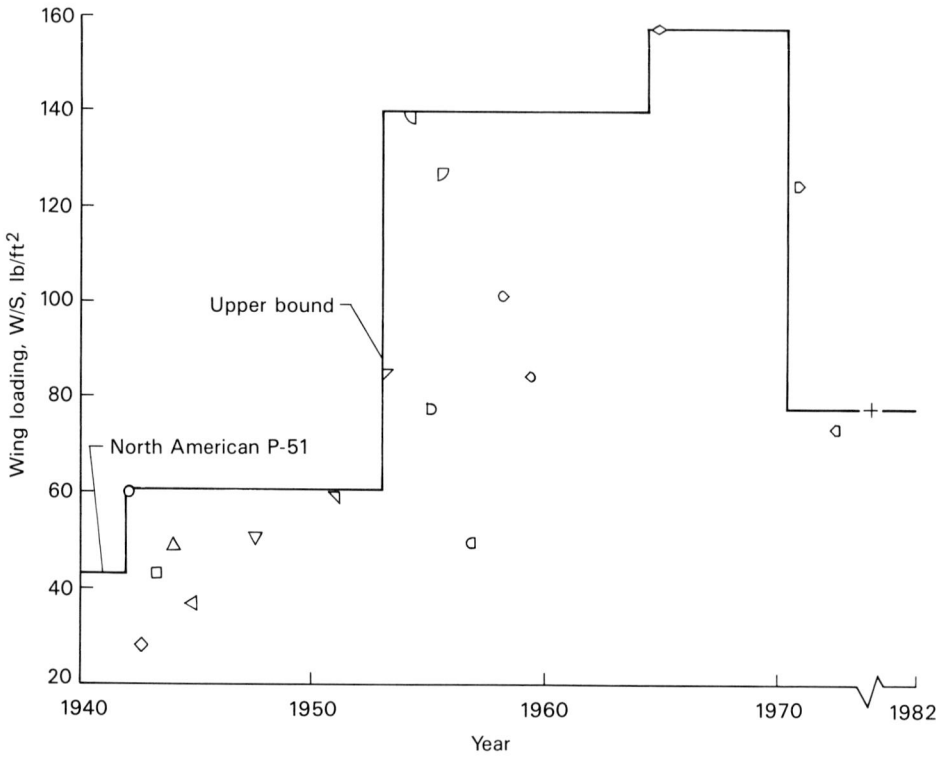

Figure 11.45 — Trends in wing loading for jet fighter aircraft.

loading. Hence, the data defining the trend with time of these quantities would be expected to show a good deal more scatter than is evident in the speed correlation shown in figure 11.43.

The expected increase in data dispersion is indeed shown in figures 11.45 and 11.46, which depict the variation in wing and thrust
loading with years. Nevertheless, successively increasing plateaus of
these quantities are shown to occur with the passage of time. As described previously regarding the McDonnell Douglas F–15 Eagle, increased aircraft maneuverability received great emphasis in the late
1960's. The corresponding reduction in wing loading and increase in
thrust loading are clearly shown by the trends in figures 11.45 and
11.46 and indicate how new requirements can change these two important aircraft design parameters.

As a matter of interest, the maximum wing loading shown in figure
11.45 is about 157 pounds per square foot; this value for the General

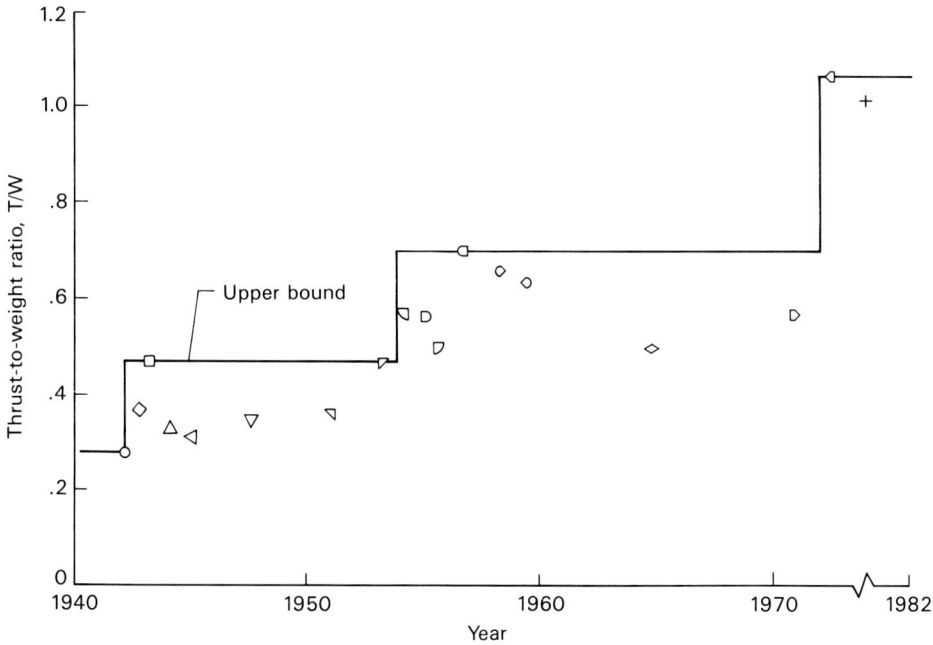

Figure 11.46 — Trends in thrust-to-weight ratio for jet fighter aircraft.

Dynamics F–111D compares with about 49.2 for America's first operational jet fighter, the Lockheed P–80 Shooting Star. The corresponding thrust loading for the P–80 was 0.33; by comparison, the thrust loading of the contemporary McDonnell Douglas F–15C is 1.07 at design gross weight. A much higher thrust loading is usually available under combat conditions at a reduced weight.

Maximum Subsonic Lift-Drag Ratio

Although aerodynamic data are not available for all the aircraft discussed in this chapter, a key aerodynamic indicator of subsonic cruising efficiency—the maximum lift-drag ratio—is shown in figure 11.47 as a function of years for the aircraft for which this parameter is given in table V.

For those aircraft designed solely for operation at subsonic speeds, the maximum lift-drag ratio is higher than that of the North American P–51. For example, the Lockheed P–80 has a value of $(L/D)_{max}$ of 17.6 as compared with 14.6 for the P–51; the swept-wing North American F–86 with its relatively low-aspect-ratio wing still has a maximum lift-drag

351

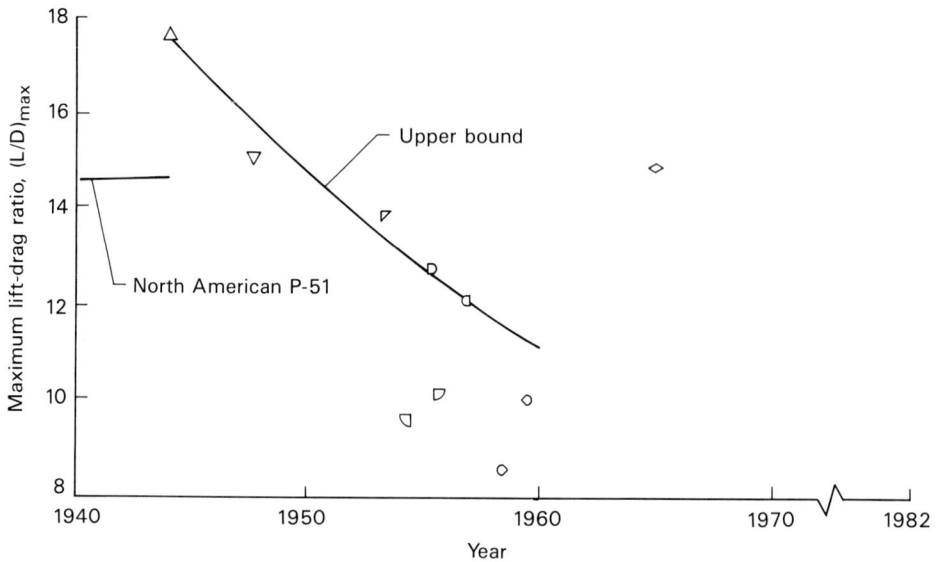

Figure 11.47 — Trends in maximum lift-drag ratio for jet fighter aircraft.

ratio of about the same magnitude as that of the P–51. The comparatively high efficiency of the subsonic jet fighters is certainly due in part to the absence of large cooling drag increments and adverse propeller interference effects that characterize propeller-driven fighters.

Once an aircraft incorporates the features necessary for even short-duration flight at supersonic Mach numbers, however, the maximum subsonic lift-drag ratio is significantly reduced, as shown by figure 11.47. The highly swept, thin, low-aspect-ratio wings characteristic of supersonic aircraft are largely responsible for the low values of maximum subsonic lift-drag ratio. Significantly, the General Dynamics F–111D with its variable-sweep wing shows a maximum lift-drag ratio higher than that of the P–51 although its maximum speed is in excess of Mach 2.0. At supersonic speeds, the values of $(L/D)_{max}$ of fighter aircraft are usually less than half of the subsonic values. The simultaneous achievement of satisfactorily high values of the maximum lift-drag ratio at both subsonic and supersonic speeds remains a major challenge in aircraft design.

Concluding Remark

Five important aircraft design parameters have been shown as a function of time in figures 11.43 to 11.47. Many significant fighter-aircraft improvements have been made in the past 40 years that are not so easily shown in trend figures. For example, fully powered controls together with sophisticated stability augmentation systems make the flying and handling qualities of the modern jet fighter much more tractable than those of its propeller-driven ancestors. Modern all-weather navigation and attack systems were unknown in 1945. The great power and light weight of the jet propulsion system combined with advanced airframe designs give the modern jet fighter a broad range of mission capability that embraces the spectrum from air-to-air interception to ground-attack operations. The list of improvements could be extended almost endlessly but will be terminated here with the following conclusion: The modern jet fighter is an outstanding example of the development and application of modern technology by the cooperative efforts of thousands of individuals in government, academia, and industry.

Chapter 12
Jet Bomber and Attack Aircraft

Background

Offensive military air operations against ground targets can be broadly divided into two major classes. First, strategic air power is employed to destroy the enemy's industrial base and necessary resources for conducting war, or for fear of reprisal, to deter military aggression by an unfriendly nation. Second, tactical air power is intended to provide broad support for military operations against specific targets in the battle area. The evolution of jet-powered aircraft optimized to fill these two vastly different military roles is discussed in this chapter.

The first tentative expression of the concepts of strategic air power can be found in the sporadic and relatively ineffectual German air raids against London in World War I. First Zeppelins and later the notorious multiengine Gotha bombers were used in these raids. (See chapter 2.) The ideas and methods of strategic air power were vigorously espoused, refined, and implemented during the period between the wars by the disciples of such visionary prophets of air power as Douhet, Trenchard, and Mitchell. During World War II, the concepts of strategic bombing were vigorously practiced by the air forces of the United States and Great Britain. The highly refined, four-engine propeller-driven bomber was the universal instrument employed for this purpose by both countries.

The ultimate long-range, strategic air weapon of World War II was the Boeing B–29 Superfortress (see chapter 5), which was used with such devastating effectiveness against the Japanese home islands during the last months of the war and which had the dubious distinction of dropping the first atomic bomb on Hiroshima in August 1945. Following the end of hostilities, this highly efficient, long-range aircraft became the backbone of the United States Strategic Air Command

355

(SAC). Equipped with atomic weapons, SAC served then and serves now as a nuclear deterrent to massive aggression in any part of the world. An improved version of the B–29, the Boeing B–50, entered SAC in 1948. Finally, the six-engine Convair B–36 (the six reciprocating engines were later augmented by four jet engines) became a mainstay in the SAC inventory in 1950.

As described for fighter aircraft in chaper 11, however, the advent of jet propulsion, together with advanced aerodynamic concepts, offered the promise of large increases in performance and operational capability of strategic bomber aircraft. These significant advances in technology sealed the fate of the large propeller-driven bomber and eventually banished it to total oblivion. Today, examples of this once ubiquitous class of military aircraft are primarily relegated to museums, with a few still being flown and demonstrated at air shows by enthusiastic (and well-financed) collectors of antique aircraft.

The German Arado 242 made its maiden flight in June 1943 and was the world's first jet-powered bomber; it saw limited action in the last year of World War II (ref. 201). The first operational jet bomber built in the United States entered service with SAC in 1948 and showed a speed advantage over the propeller-driven B–29 of more than 200 miles an hour. Phase-out of large propeller-driven bombers from first-line operational service, however, took place over a much longer period of time than was the case for the propeller-driven fighter; the last B–36 was retired from SAC in 1959, after which the United States heavy-bomber force was entirely jet powered.

In contrast to the diversity of jet-fighter types developed following the end of World War II, the evolution of the jet bomber in the United States has been characterized by the development and production of only a few types. Since the late 1950's, only two entirely new large bombers have been built in this country. Neither of these aircraft was put into production. Escalating costs, increased reliance on intercontinental ballistic missiles, doubts as to the ability of the manned bomber to penetrate enemy airspace and survive attack by increasingly effective surface-to-air missiles, all played an interrelated part in limiting development of new bombers. One body of opinion even suggested that the usefulness of the manned bomber had about reached an end. New aircraft concepts and operational techniques, new weapons, and new electronic capabilities now seem to assure the continued effectiveness of the manned bomber; production of at least one new aircraft type is now planned.

The technical development of the large jet bomber for the USAF is traced in this chapter. Also included are brief descriptions of a number of jet-powered attack aircraft. Attack aircraft are employed in tactical and interdiction-type operations against enemy ground targets and have formed an integral part of military air power since the days of World War I. The lineage of these aircraft is more related to fighters than to strategic bombers, but they usually have lower performance than fighters and are not optimized for air-to-air combat. They are included here to complete the picture of jet aircraft designed for offensive military operations against ground targets.

A number of the physical and performance characteristics of the 11 aircraft discussed are presented in table VI in appendix A. The quantities given are defined in the list of symbols provided in appendix B and, in most cases, require no further explanation. A further clarification of certain of the characteristics, however, seems desirable. A multitude of range-payload combinations are possible for all the aircraft. The value of the payload W_p given for each aircraft is for one specified type of mission with a radius R_D. The mission radius is the distance at which the payload (e.g., bombs) can be delivered with sufficient fuel remaining for a safe return to home base. The ferry range R_F is the total distance that the aircraft can fly with no disposable weapons payload and with maximum internal and external fuel load. Finally, the values of zero-lift drag coefficient and maximum lift-drag ratio given in table VI for some of the aircraft are based either on information obtained from industrial sources or on estimates by the author according to the methods given in chapter 3 of reference 176.

Early Jet Bombers

With an initial flight date of May 17, 1946, the Douglas XB–43 has the distinction of being the first jet-powered bomber to fly in the United States. Derived from the earlier propeller-driven XB–42, the XB–43 served as a useful test bed for several years but offered insufficient capability to warrant production. Prototypes of five, more capable, higher performance jet bombers were flown in 1947; two of these, the North American B–45 and the Boeing B–47, were selected for production. The two aircraft are described in the following paragraphs.

North American B–45 Tornado

With a first-flight date of March 17, 1947, the North American B–45 Tornado was the first jet-powered bomber to be put into production in the United States and the first to enter operational service with the USAF. Two views of a B–45A are shown in figures 12.1 and 12.2, and physical and performance data for the more capable B–45C are given in table VI. The C model differed from earlier models of the B–45 in several respects; the most obvious difference in the appearance of the C model was the 1200-gallon fuel tank mounted at each wingtip.

The configuration of the B–45 is reminiscent of a World War II bomber equipped with jet engines instead of propellers driven by reciprocating power plants. The unswept wing had an average airfoil thickness ratio of about 14 percent and was equipped with trailing-edge single-slotted flaps for lift augmentation in landing and takeoff. Lateral control was accomplished with the use of conventional ailerons.

All control surfaces were hydraulically boosted, and an electrically actuated tab on the elevator was used to maintain longitudinal trim. The aerodynamic power of the trim-tab-elevator combination was so great that, in the event of an inadvertent maximum tab deflection, the pilot's strength was insufficient to overcome the resulting large elevator hinge moments if the hydraulic boost system failed or was turned off. Total in-flight destruction of at least one B–45, the aircraft operated by

Figure 12.1 — North American B–45A jet bomber. [mfr via Martin Copp]

NACA and pictured in figure 12.2, was probably caused by this combination of circumstances that resulted in a normal load factor far greater than the design value. The technology of power-assisted controls was in its infancy at the time of development of the B–45, and much was yet to be learned about the effective and safe application of such control techniques.

In performing the landing maneuver, pilots found that speed and flight-path angle during the approach as well as touchdown point on the runway were difficult to control with precision because of the absence of speed brakes or some other means of increasing the drag of the aircraft. As a result of the low drag, only a small amount of engine thrust was required in the approach configuration. In this low thrust range, changes in thrust with throttle movement required a relatively long period of time and rendered control of flight path and speed difficult. At higher thrust levels, changes in thrust with time were more rapid. Hence, higher aircraft drag and consequently higher required thrust would have been desirable in the approach and landing configurations. As described in chapter 11, somewhat similar problems with speed control were experienced with the Messerschmitt Me 262, the first jet fighter to enter operational service. Again, experience taught

Figure 12.2 — North American B–45A Tornado jet bomber. [NASA]

important lessons applicable to the design of later jet-powered bomber aircraft.

Manned by a crew of four, the B–45 had two pilots seated in tandem under a transparent canopy, a bombardier located in the nose, and a tail gunner. Only the pilots were equipped with ejection seats. In an emergency, the bombardier, located in the nose of the aircraft, was expected to evacuate through a hatch located in the side of the fuselage. To minimize the hazards associated with the high-velocity airstream, a fuselage flap was deployed ahead of the hatch to deflect the airstream away from the exiting bombardier. An escape hatch with deflector flaps was also provided for the tail gunner. Environmental control for the crew included pressurization, heating, and cooling.

With a gross weight of 110 050 pounds, the B–45 was in the same weight class as the wartime Boeing B–29 (chapter 5) but had a maximum speed advantage over the B–29 of more than 200 miles per hour. A 10 000-pound weapon load could be delivered by the B–45 at a mission radius of 1008 miles. Ferry range of the aircraft was 2426 miles. The maximum lift-drag ratio of the B–45 was 16.3, about the same as that of the B–29, and its zero-lift drag coefficient was a much lower 0.0160 as compared with 0.0241 for the earlier aircraft.

The Tornado first entered service with the Strategic Air Command in November 1948, and final retirement of the type from operational service took place in 1958. Total production consisted of 139 units.

Boeing B–47 Stratojet

In concept, the Boeing B–47 was as revolutionary as the North American B–45 was conventional. The Stratojet was far ahead of any contemporary bomber in its performance and operational capability. A total of 2041 of these aircraft were manufactured, more than any other United States bomber built under peacetime conditions. As a key element in the Strategic Air Command, the B–47 served in operational squadrons until withdrawn from service in 1966. The aircraft was used for various types of special operations, however, for at least another 10 years.

A three-view drawing of the B–47E is shown in figure 12.3, and photographs of the aircraft are presented in figures 12.4, 12.5, and 12.6. Physical and performance data for the definitive version of the aircraft, the B–47E, are given in table VI.

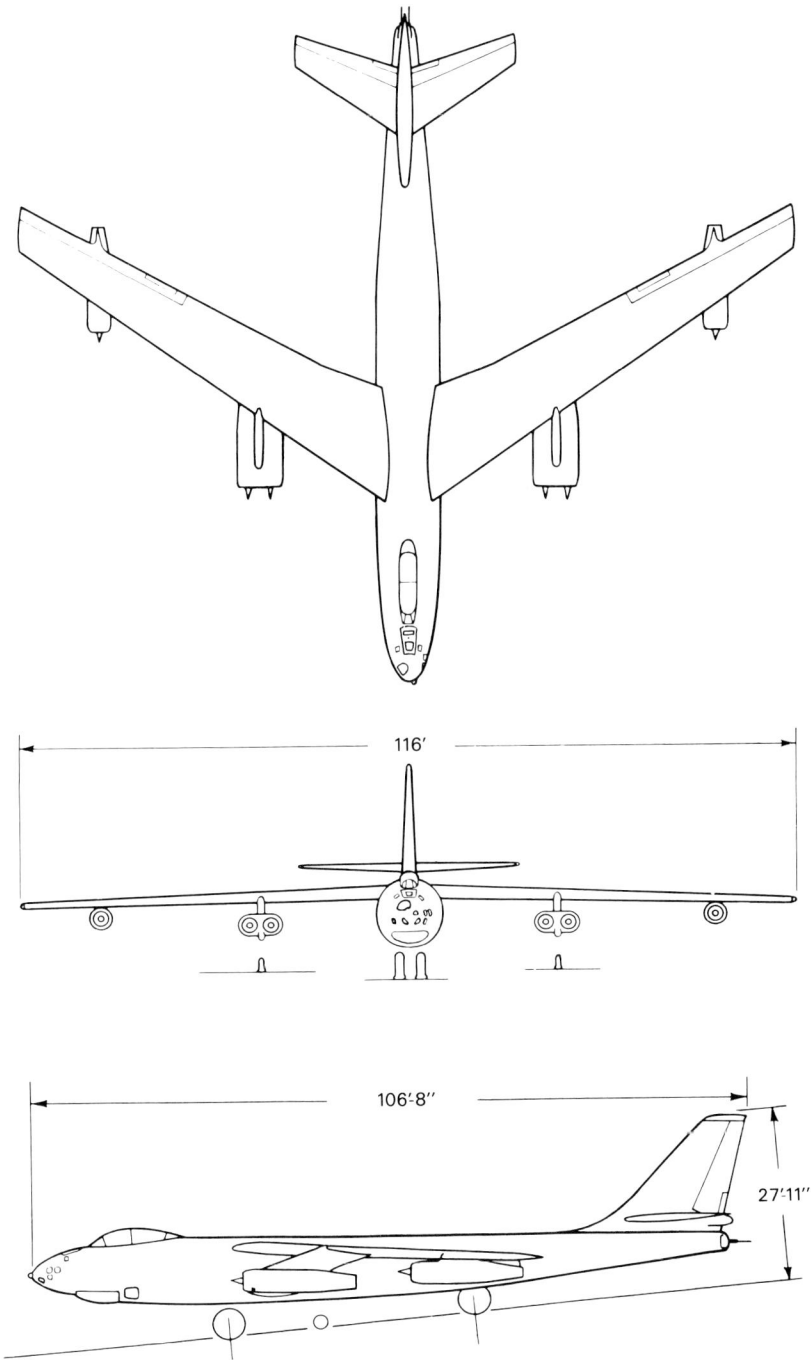

116'

106'-8"

27'11"

Figure 12.3 — Three-view drawing of Boeing B–47E Stratojet bomber. [mfr]

Figure 12.4 — Boeing B–47E Stratojet bomber. [mfr]

The configuration of the aircraft is characterized by (1) a thin, high-aspect-ratio sweptback wing mounted in the shoulder position near the top of the fuselage, (2) six jet engines mounted in pods beneath the wing, and (3) an unusual bicycle-type landing gear.

Design of the wing featured an average thickness ratio of about 12 percent, an aspect ratio of 9.42, and a sweepback angle of 35°. Single-slotted flaps located at the trailing edge provided high lift for landing, and conventional ailerons were used for lateral control. All control surfaces were hydraulically boosted. Location of the wing near the top of the fuselage allowed the bomb load to be carried in the fuselage, beneath the wing and near the center of gravity, and to be released through doors in the bottom of the fuselage without interference from the structure of the wing center section. Further, the shoulder position of the wing allowed adequate ground clearance for the engine nacelles.

Design of the landing gear posed a problem that led to a novel solution not seen before on a production airplane. Wing thickness was not large enough to house the gear and, in addition, the high position of the wing would have resulted in long, heavy landing-gear struts. The solution of the problem was found in an unusual bicycle arrangement in which a two-wheel bogie was located along the fuselage centerline in

362

Figure 12.5 — Boeing B-47 taking off with JATO (jet-assisted takeoff). [mfr]

front of and behind the bomb bay. Small, retractable outrigger wheels extended from the inboard nacelles to assist in providing lateral balance while the aircraft was on the ground. The front bogie was steerable to give ground maneuverability. Details of the landing gear can be seen in figure 12.6.

One of the most innovative features of the B-47 configuration, and one that was to have a marked influence on future civil and military aircraft of large size, was the engine mounting. The nacelles containing the engines were attached to pylons mounted to and extending below the wings. Two engines were mounted in each of two nacelles, one of which was attached through a pylon to each wing well outboard of the fuselage. The other two engines were mounted singly in nacelles nearly flush with the wing and located near the wingtips. A number of advantages may be cited for the engine arrangement pioneered by the B-47; namely:

(1) The engine nacelles are widely separated from each other and the fuselage. Thus, the danger to the aircraft and other engines that results from the disintegration of one engine is reduced. This advantage is somewhat nullified in the B-47 because two of the nacelles contain two engines.

363

Figure 12.6 — Landing-gear arrangement of Boeing B–47 Stratojet bomber. [mfr]

(2) The aircraft is easy to balance because the engines can be located near the aircraft center of gravity.

(3) The weight of the engines mounted outboard on the wing reduces the wing bending moments in flight.

(4) The engines are easy to maintain and can be readily removed because of their proximity to the ground.

(5) Since the engine inlets are usually outboard of the spray pattern from the nose and main landing gear, the outboard wing mounting offers good protection from FOD (foreign object damage) to the engines when the aircraft is operated on the ground.

A number of disadvantages may also be cited for the type of engine arrangement employed on the Boeing B–47, as follows:

(1) Failure of an engine, particularly during takeoff or climb, may produce large yawing moments that require immediate correction by the pilot. The magnitude of the corrective yawing moments required to counteract the unsymmetrical

thrust in the engine-out condition may determine the necessary size of the rudder.

(2) A small reduction in maximum lift coefficient may result from unfavorable interference effects in the nacelle-wing juncture and from the impingement of the nacelle wake on the wing at high lift coefficients. The wing-nacelle-pylon relationships must also be carefully tailored, usually in wind-tunnel studies, to eliminate or minimize any interference drag. A positive aerodynamic benefit, however, results from the pylons, which act somewhat like wing fences in alleviating the pitch-up problem so often found in aircraft with sweptback wings.

(3) The addition of concentrated weights, such as engines or stores, is usually thought to reduce the wing flutter speed. The relationship of the engine center of gravity to the wing elastic axis as well as the dynamic coupling between the engines and the wing strongly influence the effect of the engines on the wing flutter speed. These, as well as other relationships, must be carefully tailored by a detailed process involving mathematical analysis and wind-tunnel tests. By this means, a reduction in flutter speed can usually be avoided.

(4) The dynamic loads imposed on the wing structure during operations on the ground are usually intensified by the concentrated engine masses mounted on the wings.

The thin, high-aspect-ratio swept wing of the B-47 coupled with its long high-fineness-ratio fuselage contributed to the high aerodynamic efficiency of the aircraft. The maximum lift-drag ratio of about 20 is the highest of any aircraft yet considered in this book, and the zero-lift drag coefficient was a low 0.0148. Maximum speed is given in table VI as 607 miles per hour at 16 300 feet; the corresponding Mach number is 0.85, which is nearly 0.1 higher than that of the B-45.

The very features that contributed to the high performance of the B-47, however, also introduced some new problems that have been present in the development of all subsequent large jet-powered multi-engine aircraft.

Aeroelasticity, the interaction of aerodynamic, elastic, and inertial forces, has formed a branch of aeronautical engineering for many years. Because of the flexibility of the long, thin elements of the B-47, however, the need to consider aeroelastic effects in the basic aircraft design process assumed critical importance. For example, in static tests the total deflection of the B–47 wingtip was 17 feet from maximum positive to negative deflection. Areas in which aeroelasticity are important are stability, control, loads, and, of course, flutter.

Flutter is a phenomenon in which an aircraft or one of its components, such as a wing or control surface, extracts energy from the moving airstream and converts it to a harmonic oscillation of the structure that may grow in amplitude until total destruction occurs. Flutter analysis and prediction is an arcane science in which flutter prediction and design for its avoidance have historically been the subject of detailed mathematical analysis. Uncertainties as to the nature of oscillating air forces, however, as well as the complex participation of the entire aircraft in the various structural vibration modes made mandatory the development of new experimental wind-tunnel techniques for studying these phenomena during development of the B–47.

Flutter tests and analyses had usually been limited to individual components of the aircraft such as the wing plus aileron or horizontal and vertical tail surfaces. The aircraft as an entity was usually not considered in the determination of the critical flutter speed, nor was such consideration necessary. However, the concentration of large masses beneath the wings, together with the high degree of flexibility of the wings and other components of the aircraft, required that motions of the complete airplane be considered in determining the critical flutter speeds of the B–47. Both symmetrical and antisymmetrical flutter modes needed to be studied. In a symmetrical mode, each wing deforms in exactly the same way, and the motion of the wings is accompanied by a vertical, up-and-down, and pitching motion of the fuselage. In antisymmetrical flutter, the wings on either side of the fuselage deform in exactly opposite directions, and the wing motion is accompanied by a rolling and yawing of the fuselage.

The wind-tunnel technique devised by the Boeing Company to deal with this complex problem is shown schematically in figure 12.7, which shows the cross-section of the wind-tunnel test section. A ⅜-inch rod extended from the floor to the ceiling of the tunnel test section. The model was attached to a gimbal joint located at the center of gravity. The gimbal allowed freedom in pitch and yaw, and was itself attached to the vertical rod by an arrangement of rollers that allowed the model freedom in vertical translation. The snubber lines shown in figure 12.7 were used to arrest the vertical motion of the model if it became too large or uncontrollable. At each tunnel speed, the aircraft

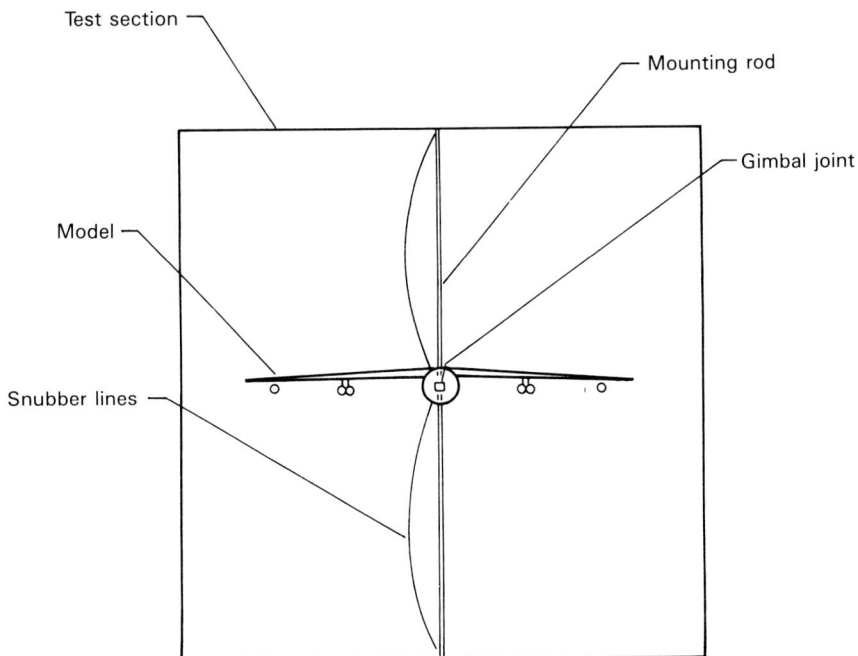

Figure 12.7 — Sketch of flutter model mounted in wind-tunnel test section.

model was trimmed so that the lift force balanced the weight of the model. Pitch trim was maintained as the tunnel speed varied by remote adjustment of a tab on the horizontal tail. Limited rolling freedom was provided by looseness in the gimbal joint and flexibility in the mounting rod. The model was constructed in such a way as to simulate the stiffness and mass properties of the aircraft and, accordingly, was quite complex and expensive to design and build.

The technique illustrated in figure 12.7 was successfully employed in the development of the B-47 as a means for identifying flutter-critical combinations of speed and altitude and development of design fixes for flutter avoidance. A detailed description of the technique is given in reference 173. The mounting rod limits the usefulness of the technique to fairly low subsonic speeds because of aerodynamic interference effects associated with the formation of shock waves on the rod at high subsonic Mach numbers. The complete model flutter tests made on the B-47 were carried out in a low-speed wind tunnel, and the results were then adjusted for estimated Mach number effects. Later techniques developed by NACA and NASA allow flutter tests of complete airplane

367

models to be made at high subsonic and transonic Mach numbers in a wind tunnel especially designed for high-speed flutter investigations.

Along with this rather general discussion of various engineering aspects of the B–47, a few more specific features of its design should be pointed out. The aircraft was manned by a crew of three. Two pilots sat in a tandem arrangement under a bubble-type canopy in a manner similar to that of a fighter; a bombardier-navigator sat in an enclosed compartment located in the nose of the aircraft. Upward-firing ejection seats were provided for the pilots, and the bombardier was equipped with a downward-firing ejection seat. Crew compartments were heated, ventilated, and pressurized. As fast or faster than most fighters, the Stratojet was equipped with only two 20-mm cannons situated in a remotely controlled turret located in the tail of the aircraft. Aiming and firing of these guns was the duty of the copilot whose seat could be rotated 180° to face rearward.

For assistance in the landing maneuver, the B–47 was equipped with a drag chute that was deployed during the approach. The added drag of the parachute aided in controlling the speed and the flight-path angle during this phase of the landing maneuver. Once on the runway, a large braking chute was deployed to assist in stopping the aircraft. An interesting insight into the airport performance of the B–47 is provided by a comparison of its stalling speed of 175 miles per hour with the cruising speed of 182 miles per hour given in chapter 4 for the World War II B–17G. Not surprisingly, the length of hard-surface runways at military air fields increased dramatically in the years following World War II.

Although the B–47 was equipped with six 7200-pound-thrust (with water injection) turbojet engines, the thrust-to-weight ratio at maximum gross weight was only 0.22, which, coupled with its high stalling speed, resulted in a long takeoff ground roll. To reduce the takeoff field length, the aircraft was initially equipped with 18 short-duration booster rockets. These units were an integral part of the aircraft and were known by the acronym JATO (jet-assisted takeoff). Nine JATO nozzles were located on each side of the fuselage; they may be seen in figure 12.4 just ahead of the national insignia. On some later versions of the aircraft, weight was saved by replacing the integral JATO units with a jettisonable external rack containing the rockets. In this installation, 33 rockets of 1000 pounds thrust each were provided. A B–47 taking off with a boost from the external JATO pack is shown in figure 12.5.

By post-World War II standards, the B–47 was classified as a medium bomber; but with a gross weight of 198 180 pounds, the B–47E was far heavier than any bomber flown in World War II (the gross weight of the B–29 was 120 000 pounds), and it ranked second only to the 357 500-pound B–36D as the heaviest aircraft operated by the USAF in the early 1950's. Designed as a strategic bomber, the B–47 also filled various other roles such as photoreconnaissance. In its design role as a strategic bomber, the B–47 could deliver a 10 845-pound weapons load at a mission radius of 2013 miles. Ferry range was 4035 miles (table VI). With air-to-air refueling, which became standard operating procedure following the close of World War II, both the mission radius and the ferry range were greatly increased, and targets in Eastern Europe could be reached from bases in the United States with sufficient range potential to allow safe return to friendly territory.

In the strategic bombing role for which the B–47 was designed, weapons delivery at the target was originally intended to take place from high altitudes. By the mid-1950's, however, the increasing effectiveness of methods for detecting aircraft at high altitudes, as well as the growing capability of surface-to-air missiles and fighter aircraft, required the development of new methods of weapons delivery. As a means of avoiding detection by radar, penetration of enemy airspace was to take place at high speed and at an altitude of only a few hundred feet. At the target, the aircraft was to execute an Immelmann turn with weapons delivery taking place in near vertical flight. (An Immelmann turn consists of a half loop followed by a half roll from inverted to normal flight attitude at the top of the loop. A change of 180° in direction coupled with a gain in altitude are accomplished during the maneuver.) This method of weapons delivery was known as LABS (low-altitude bombing system) and was intended to provide the aircraft a means for escaping destruction from the blast effects of its own weapon.

Constant practice of the LABS technique subjected the B–47 fleet to the severe gust-load environment of high-speed low-altitude flight, as well as the maneuver loads associated with weapons delivery. The aircraft was not designed for this type of service. As a consequence, structural fatigue problems were encountered, and several aircraft were lost as a result of structural failure. At one point, the entire B–47 fleet was grounded for inspection and incorporation of necessary design modifications.

Both the structural fatigue problem and the much greater capability of the Boeing B-52, which began entering the inventory in 1955, played a part in the retirement of the B-47 from first-line service. Its life with the Strategic Air Command began in 1951 and ended 15 years later in 1966.

The Boeing B-47 should be viewed as a landmark aircraft that established a new technical plateau for large, multiengine, jet-powered aircraft.

The Long-Lived Stratofortress

The origin of the Boeing B-52 Stratofortress can be traced to design studies of a replacement aircraft for the very large propeller-driven Convair B-36. Too complex to be traced here are the many interwoven facets of these studies. An interesting history of the Boeing B-52 may be found in a book by Walter J. Boyne entitled *Boeing B-52— A Documentary History* (published by Jane's Publishing Co., 1981). First flight of the prototype B-52 took place on April 15, 1952, and now after more than 30 years, the type still serves as a major element of this nation's nuclear deterrent force. No more impressive tribute to the basic soundness of an aircraft design could be found. After a total production run of 744 units, the last B-52 was delivered in October 1962. The aircraft first became operational in the Strategic Air Command in June 1955.

The B-52 was produced in models A through H. A three-view drawing of the B-52G is shown in figure 12.8; photographs of a B-52H are presented in figures 12.9 and 12.10. The landing-gear arrangement is illustrated in figures 12.11 and 12.12; refueling of a B-52 by a Boeing KC-135 is illustrated in figure 12.13. As with so many successful aircraft, the term B-52 encompasses a whole family of generically related types of similar appearance but with major and minor differences in systems, equipment, and performance. Physical and performance data are given in table VI for the last version of the aircraft, the B-52H.

As seen in figure 12.8, the basic configuration of the B-52 is similar in concept to that of the B-47. The shoulder location of the swept-back wing, wing-mounted engines, and bicycle landing gear are all reminiscent of the earlier aircraft. As shown in table VI, however, the B-52 is a much larger and heavier aircraft than its predecessor.

185'

11'-4"

148'-5"

157'-6.9"

40'8"

17'-5.2"

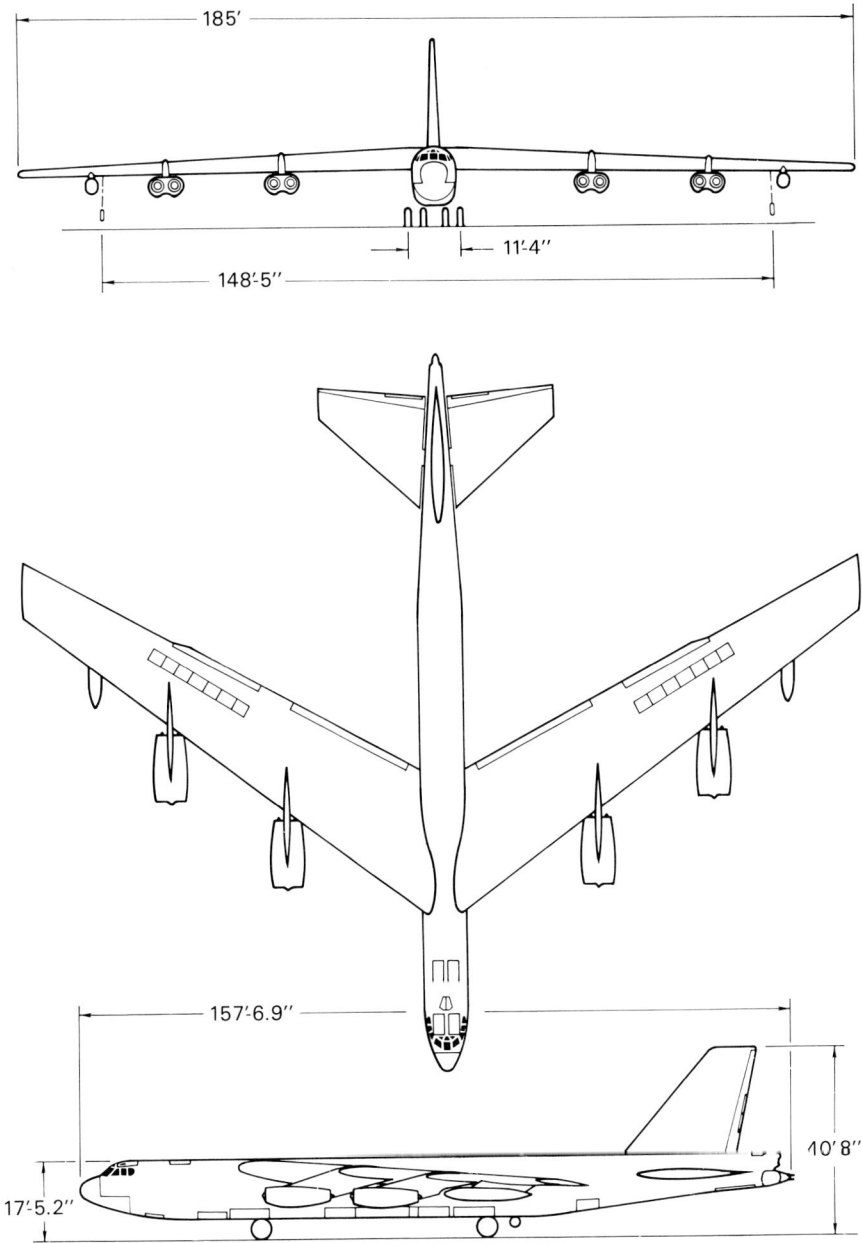

Figure 12.8 — Three-view drawing of Boeing B–52G Stratofortress bomber. [mfr]

Figure 12.9 — Boeing B-52H Stratofortress with Skybolt missiles. [mfr]

Figure 12.10 — Boeing B-52H Stratofortress with Hound Dog missiles. [mfr]

Figure 12.11 — Crosswind landing gear as seen on Boeing XB-52 Stratofortress. [mfr]

The wing of the B-52 has a sweepback angle at the quarter chord of 35°, an aspect ratio of 8.56, and airfoil thickness ratios that vary from 14 percent at the root to 8 percent at the tip (these thickness ratios are only approximate). Fowler-type single-slotted flaps for lift augmentation are located at the trailing edge of the wing. These large flaps may be seen in figure 12.11. Hydraulically actuated spoilers are used for lateral control and, in the symmetrically deployed configuration, assist in flight-path control during landing approach and braking during rollout. On the A through F models of the aircraft, lateral control was provided by the spoilers working in conjunction with conventional ailerons. Wing area of the B-52 is 4000 square feet, nearly three times larger than that of the B-47.

Elevators and rudder, both of small chord, are used for longitudinal and directional control. An aerodynamic servotab system actuates these surfaces in response to the pilot's control inputs. A hydraulically adjustable stabilizer is used for trimming the aircraft longitudinally. This surface has sufficient aerodynamic power to rotate the aircraft on takeoff; the B-47, which did not have an adjustable stabilizer, could not be rotated and was flown off the runway at the attitude angle imposed

Figure 12.12 — Front landing-gear units of Boeing B–52 Stratofortress. [mfr]

by the bicycle landing gear. The far forward position of the aircraft center of gravity relative to the rear bogie requires an aerodynamic moment for rotation much larger than could be provided by the small, manually actuated elevators.

The landing gear of the B–52 is of the same bicycle arrangement as employed on the B–47 but has four two-wheel bogies instead of the two bogies used on the earlier aircraft. Details of the landing gear are shown in figures 12.11 and 12.12. As compared with their location on the B–47, the outrigger wheels are positioned much nearer the wingtip on the B–52. (Compare photographs in figs. 12.11 and 12.6.) An interesting feature of the B–52 landing gear greatly eases the problems posed by crosswind landings. Both the front and rear bogies can be set at angles of as much as 20° to either side of the straight-ahead position. In a crosswind landing, consequently, the aircraft can be headed directly into the wind while rolling down a runway not aligned with the wind. In figure 12.11, the gear is shown set for a crosswind landing. Only the front bogies are used for steering on the ground. Although the wing spoilers obviate the need for an approach chute on the B–52, a 44-foot-diameter braking chute is provided for deployment in the landing rollout. The aircraft is not equipped with JATO units for use on takeoff.

Figure 12.13 — Boeing B-52G being refueled by Boeing KC-135 tanker. [mfr]

All production models of the B-52 have been powered by eight engines located in pairs of two in four nacelles. All four of the nacelles are attached to the wings by sweptforward pylons that extend below the lower surface of the wing. Except for the B-52H, all models of the aircraft have been equipped with a version of the Pratt & Whitney J-57 turbojet engine of about 13 750 pounds thrust. A fan version of the J-57, the TF-33 of 17 000 pounds thrust, powers the B-52H. This engine is essentially similar to the Pratt & Whitney JT3D turbofan that powers the Boeing 707 and Douglas DC-8 commercial airliners. Much improved performance, particularly range and takeoff field length, resulted from application of the turbofan engine to the B-52.

The B-52 is normally manned by a crew of six. Two pilots are seated side by side near the nose in a manner similar to a commercial transport. (The two prototype aircraft had the pilots seated in a tandem arrangement similar to that of the B-47. This cockpit configuration can be seen in the photograph of the XB-52 shown in fig. 12.11.) On a lower deck beneath the pilots' compartment are seated the navigator and radar navigator. Behind the pilots on the upper deck are seated the electronic warfare officer and, on the G and H models, the gunner who remotely controls the guns located in the tail. On earlier versions of the aircraft, the gunner was physically located in the tail end of the

375

fuselage. Movement of the gunner from the tail to a position behind the pilots removed this unfortunate individual from an isolated location that in turbulent air promised a ride similar to that of a high-speed roller coaster. Several types of tail guns have been employed on different versions of the aircraft. A 20-mm six-barrel rotary cannon is installed in the tail location on the G and H models of the B–52.

All crew stations are pressurized, heated, and air-conditioned. In the event of an emergency, means for crew escape is provided by upward ejection seats for those on the upper deck and downward ejection seats for those on the lower deck. For those versions of the aircraft in which the gunner was located in the tail, the entire tail capsule was separated in an emergency and the gunner was expected to fight his way clear of this unit and then complete his escape by a hand-operated parachute. Needless to say, the morale of the gunner was greatly increased when he was relocated to a position behind the pilots.

With a gross weight of 488 000 pounds, the B–52H is even today one of the heaviest offensive military aircraft operated by any nation in the world. Maximum speed of the B–52H is 639 miles per hour at 20 700 feet, or a Mach number of 0.91, and cruising speed is 525 miles per hour. According to table VI, mission radius is 4480 miles with a weapons load of 10 000 pounds. Many other combinations of payload and range are, of course, possible. Range is, of course, greatly increased by in-flight refueling. A B–52 being refueled by a Boeing KC–135 is shown in figure 12.13. External configuration of the KC–135 is closely similar to that of the Boeing 707 commercial transport, described in chapter 13.

As an indication of the capability of the B–52 with in-flight refueling, a nonstop flight of 24 325 miles was made around the world in January 1957. The flight required 45 hours and 19 minutes. The unrefueled range of the aircraft may be judged by the world-record nonstop flight of 12 532 miles made by a B–52H on January 10 and 11, 1962. Average speed for the flight was 575 miles per hour, and elapsed time was 22 hours and 9 minutes. This world-record flight certainly attests to the high maximum lift-drag ratio of the aircraft, the low specific fuel consumption of the engines, and the large fuel capacity of the aircraft that, in normal operations, can accommodate an astonishing 47 975 gallons of fuel. (An average American automobile could be driven 12 000 miles a year for about 80 years on this quantity of fuel.) Fuel tanks are located in both the wing and fuselage, and a 700-gallon external tank is carried under each wing as can be seen in figures 12.9 and 12.10.

The B–52 can carry a wide assortment of offensive weapons including conventional "iron bombs," nuclear bombs, and a variety of missiles such as the ALCM (air-launched cruise missile) and the SCRAM (short-range attack missile). Four Skybolt ballistic missiles are mounted on the wings of the B–52H pictured in figure 12.9; this missile was not put into production. Two Hound Dog missiles are mounted under the wings of the B–52H shown in figure 12.10. The Hound Dog is really a small jet-powered airplane with a range of up to 700 miles and a maximum speed of Mach 2.1. A more detailed discussion of the offensive-weapon capability of the B–52 is beyond the scope of the present discussion, as is a description of the vast array of exotic electronic gear carried aboard the aircraft.

Thankfully, the B–52 has never been called upon to deliver a nuclear weapon upon an enemy target. It served with distinction, however, during the Vietnam conflict. Operating from bases on the island of Guam, many thousands of tons of conventional bombs were dropped on targets in North Vietnam. From Guam to the area of conflict involved a round-trip flight of nearly 5000 miles. Total mission times were in the order of 16 to 18 hours. Surface-to-air missiles as well as combat with enemy aircraft were always a possibility in the target area. Certainly, these missions were a severe test for both men and machines.

The B–52 was originally designed for high-altitude weapons delivery over the target. Like the B–47, however, the increasing effectiveness of enemy antiaircraft defenses required the development of low-altitude high-speed penetration tactics for the B–52. Again like the B–47, the B–52 has suffered from its share of structural fatigue problems. To cure these problems, many modifications have been made to the aircraft during its long-lived career. But the B–52 lives on and is likely to form a major part of this nation's nuclear deterrent force for the foreseeable future.

Two Pioneering Explorations

Described next are two radically different aircraft, both of which were pioneer explorations into new realms of aeronautical technology. First discussed is the Convair B–58 Hustler. This aircraft was the first United States bomber to have a supersonic dash capability and required the development of much new technology. Although the B–58 was thought by many to be the harbinger of future generations of more advanced supersonic bombers, only about 115 of these unique aircraft were built, and they were quietly withdrawn from the SAC inventory after less than 10 years of service.

The second aircraft discussed, the Martin P6M Seamaster, was hailed as the precursor of a new era in naval aviation. When the program was terminated, however, only 12 aircraft had been produced and these never saw operational service. The Seamaster was the first and perhaps the last large jet-propelled flying boat to be developed in the United States. Perhaps the most advanced flying boat ever developed, the P6M had many advanced technical features worthy of examination.

Convair B-58 Hustler

Mission requirements for the Convair B-58 Hustler called for a subsonic cruise segment of several thousand miles followed by a supersonic dash (Mach 2.0) in the target zone of as much as 500 miles and, finally, a post-strike cruise segment. Diverse requirements such as these call for an aircraft of high aerodynamic efficiency at both subsonic and supersonic speeds, together with a versatile propulsion system capable of efficiently providing the required thrust in the different flight regimes. Today's response to the B-58 mission requirements would no doubt be a variable-sweep configuration employing afterburning turbofan engines. (See discussion of the F-111 in chapter 11 and of the B-1 in a later part of this chapter.) Unfortunately, the technology for a practical variable-sweep aircraft did not exist in the early 1950's when the B-58 was being designed — nor did afterburning turbofan engines. The only possible way in which the difficult mission objectives could be met in that time period was with the use of in-flight refueling.

As can be seen from figures 12.14 and 12.15, configuration of the B-58 was characterized by a delta wing and the absence of a horizontal tail. The wing had 60° sweepback at the leading edge, an aspect ratio of 2.09, and airfoil sections that varied in thickness ratio from 3.46 percent at the root to 4.08 percent at the tip. Conical camber was employed in the leading edge to reduce drag at lifting conditions and thus increase cruising efficiency. (A conically cambered wing is one which has a leading-edge camber shape formed from part of the surface of a cone whose apex is located at the longitudinal plane of symmetry of the wing. The amount of camber accordingly increases progressively

Figure 12.14 — Convair B-58 Hustler bomber without auxiliary pod. [NASA]

Figure 12.15 — Convair B-58 Hustler bomber with auxiliary pod installed. [mfr via David A. Anderton]

with spanwise distance from the fuselage.) Absence of a horizontal tail for trimming prevented the use of any trailing-edge high-lift devices. Elevons for pitch and roll control extended from the side of the fuselage to the outboard engine nacelles. All the controls were power operated.

The four General Electric J–79 turbojet engines were located in individual nacelles suspended below the wings on sweptforward pylons — an arrangement analogous to that employed on the B–47 and B–52. Area ruling was employed in the high-fineness-ratio fuselage with the single vertical fin and rudder mounted at the rear. Crew members consisting of pilot, bombardier-navigator, and defense-systems operator were housed in a tandem arrangement to aid in maintaining the desired long, narrow shape of the fuselage. Each crew station was an individual rocket-powered escape module capable of providing safe crew egress even at Mach 2.0. The entire crew compartment as well as the wheel wells and electronics bay were pressurized and air-conditioned. Cooling of the tires and electronic equipment was required because of the high temperatures generated by prolonged flight at Mach 2.0. Landing gear consisted of a tricycle design with each main gear having eight wheels arranged in two rows of four. The large number of wheels was used to maintain the landing-gear footprint pressure within acceptable limits while, at the same time, allowing the use of small diameter wheels capable of being stored in the thin wing with only small fairings bulging from the lower wing surfaces. The conventional nose gear had two wheels; a braking chute was provided to assist in stopping the aircraft on landing rollout.

A comparison of figures 12.14 and 12.15 shows a large streamlined pod under the fuselage of the aircraft in the latter but no such pod in the former. The pod served the dual purpose of housing a nuclear warhead (bomb) and several thousand gallons of fuel. Large amounts of fuel were also carried in the wings and fuselage. The pod was divided into two main parts: the portion containing empty fuel tanks was to be jettisoned on the outboard flight to the target, and the other component containing the warhead, as well as additional empty fuel tanks, was then to be dropped at the target. The B–58 might thus be considered as a sort of two-stage system. Armament on the aircraft consisted of a single six-barrel 20-mm rotary cannon controlled by the defense-systems operator.

To give a light, strong, stiff structure for the thin high-fineness-ratio elements of the aircraft, the B–58 made extensive use of aluminum honeycomb panels. Most of the outer covering of the aircraft consisted of such panels having outer and inner aluminum skins bonded to a honeycomb of aluminum and fiber glass. In addition to its light weight, this type of structure had a smooth exterior surface. In service, however, problems were encountered in ascertaining and maintaining the integrity of the bonded joints.

With a gross weight of 163 000 pounds and a maximum speed of 1321 miles per hour (Mach 2.0) at 63 150 feet altitude (table VI), the B–58 was an impressive aircraft by any standard. This performance was dramatically demonstrated in a number of record flights. Perhaps the most notable of these was the May 26, 1961, nonstop flight of 3 hours and 19 minutes from New York to Paris. Average speed for the 3669-mile flight was 1105 miles per hour; three in-flight refuelings by KC–135 aircraft were required. Interestingly, almost 34 years earlier on May 20 and 21, 1927, Charles A Lindbergh required 33.5 hours to make the first nonstop flight from New York to Paris — a remarkable advancement in aeronautical technology during a time period of just a little more than three decades.

In spite of the spectacular records set by the B–58, the data in table VI show that the aircraft was woefully deficient in range performance. Without in-flight refueling, the radius of action, including a 450-mile supersonic dash, was only 1500 miles. With no supersonic dash, the maximum radius increased to 2000 miles, thus indicating the relatively poor supersonic cruising efficiency of the aircraft. Ferry range at subsonic speeds was 4025 miles. With in-flight refueling, a target distance of 4300 miles, including a supersonic dash of 500 miles, was possible. After weapons delivery, the aircraft had a range of 1500 miles — hopefully enough to reach a friendly base but not enough to reach the point of departure. With in-flight refueling, ferry range was 6995 miles.

The limited range capability of the B–58 can be directly traced to the compromises required in its aerodynamic design. The Mach 2.0 dash requirement dictated the use of a delta wing with leading-edge sweep angle of 60° and a low aspect ratio of about 2. As a consequence, the value of the maximum subsonic lift-drag ratio, without the fuel and weapons pod, was only 11.3 (compare this with the value of 21.5 for the B–52G); an even lower value would be expected with the pod attached. The value of $(L/D)_{max}$ at Mach. 2.0 was slightly greater than 5. Thus, the aircraft was not capable of efficient cruising flight at either subsonic or supersonic speeds. Aircraft configuration design for highly efficient cruising flight at subsonic speeds is well understood, as demonstrated by the B–47 and B–52 as well as by the numerous highly efficient jet transports described in the following chapter. Unfortunate-

381

ly, the design of a highly efficient and practical supersonic cruising aircraft still remains somewhat elusive although much progress has been made since the design of the B–58. Still more elusive is a configuration concept that enjoys high cruising efficiency at both subsonic and supersonic speeds, such as required by a commercial supersonic transport. Variable sweep, however, now offers a means for achieving good subsonic cruising efficiency in combination with a reasonably efficient supersonic dash capability.

With the increased effectiveness of enemy detection and antiaircraft capability discussed previously, the high-altitude Mach 2 method of weapons delivery became increasingly less viable, and an on-the-deck method of attack became the preferred mode of operation. For this type of weapons delivery, however, the payload-range characteristics of the B–58 were much inferior to those of the B–52. For whatever reason, the last B–58 was withdrawn from service in January 1970 after about 10 years in the active inventory. First flight of the aircraft took place on November 11, 1956; approximately 115 units were built.

As a final comment, the B–58 represented a significant technical achievement in the 1950's time period, but the mission requirements called for innovations that far exceeded the technical state of the art then available.

Martin P6M Seamaster

The evolution of the propeller-driven flying boat in America is traced in chapter 8. Although the U.S. Navy continued to operate a few flying boats as late as the mid-1960's, the era during which this picturesque class of aircraft played an important role in civil and military aviation really ended with the close of World War II. As a last effort to prolong the usefulness of the military flying boat, the Navy sponsored development of a large, jet-powered boat for long-range, mine-laying, and reconnaissance duties. Operation from bodies of water in dispersed and remote locations, with minimum support facilities, was envisioned as a means of avoiding the inherent vulnerability of large numbers of aircraft situated at congested air bases. With first flight on July 14, 1955, the Martin P6M Seamaster was developed to fill the prescribed role.

The Martin Seamaster is shown in figures 12.16 and 12.17, and data for the YP6M–1 version of the aircraft are contained in table VI. Configuration of the aircraft featured a sweptback wing mounted near the top of a single-step, high-length-beam-ratio hull. Two afterburning jet engines were located side by side in each of two nacelles mounted on top of the wing immediately adjacent to either side of the fuselage. (The afterburners, an unusual feature for a large subsonic aircraft, were for use on takeoff.) Inlets swept back at nearly the same angle as the wing leading edge were found to be unsatisfactory and, as shown in figure 12.16, unswept inlets were finally adopted; exhaust nozzles were behind the trailing edge of the wing, as can be seen in both figures. The location of the engines was, of course, strongly influenced by the necessity of minimizing spray ingestion during operation on the water. The horizonal tail was positioned atop the vertical fin in a T arrangement and featured a pronounced positive dihedral angle. Impingement of both jet exhaust and spray was minimized by the tail configuration. Coupled with the large vertical tail, the positive dihedral of the horizontal surface working with the negative wing dihedral gave the proper dihedral effect for the integrated configuration. The negative wing dihedral allowed the lateral balancing floats to be mounted flush

Figure 12.16 — Martin YP6M-1 Seamaster flying boat moving at high speed on the water. [mfr via Lester Rose]

383

Figure 12.17 — In-flight view of Martin YP6M-1 Seamaster flying boat. [Ray Wagner via AAHS]

against the wingtips with neither drag-producing mounting struts or pylons.

The 40° sweptback wing had an aspect ratio of 5.53 and airfoil thickness ratios that varied from 11 percent at the root to 8 percent at the tip. Lift augmentation was achieved with trailing-edge flaps and with slats located over the outer portion of the leading edge; the slats can be seen in the deployed position in figure 12.16. Wing spoilers were used for roll control; elevators together with an adjustable stabilizer were used for pitch control; and a single rudder was provided for control about the yaw axis. Maneuvering on the water was enhanced by hydroflaps located on both sides of the hull afterbody. When opened individually, these flaps served as rudders for directional control while symmetrical deployment provided braking. The hydroflaps may be seen outlined in black in figure 12.17.

The Seamaster crew consisted of a pilot, copilot, navigator-minelayer, and radio armament-defense operator. All crew quarters were pressurized and each crew member was equipped with an ejection seat.

Armament consisted of two remotely operated 20-mm cannons located in the tail. The mine bay had a watertight rotary door, the outside of which served as part of the bottom of the hull. A rack for mounting mines or other types of stores was fastened to the inside of the door. Rotation of the door in flight provided the means for weapons delivery.

With a gross weight of 167 011 pounds, the YP6M-1 was a large aircraft capable of attaining a maximum speed of 646 miles per hour (Mach 0.86) at 5000 feet and cruised at a speed of 540 miles per hour. Even higher performance was shown by the P6M-2, which had engines of higher thrust than those on the YP6M-1. From the data given in reference 200, the mission radius of the aircraft as a minelayer seems to have been about 800 miles with a payload of 30 000 pounds and 1350 miles for the high-altitude reconnaissance role. Ferry range is estimated to have been about 3500 miles.

In spite of the promising characteristics of the P6M, the Navy terminated the program in August 1959 after 12 aircraft had been constructed, including 2 prototypes that had been lost. Shortage of funds coupled with demands of higher priority programs no doubt played a major part in the cancellation. The Seamaster was the last large flying boat developed in the United States, and many viewed its demise with regret and nostalgia.

Search for a New Strategic Bomber

Even before the first flight of the Boeing B-52, studies of its successor were underway. As a means for reducing both weapons delivery time and vulnerability to enemy defenses, increasing speeds into the supersonic range seemed to offer the most favorable approach to the development of a more effective, large bomber aircraft. Although not too successful, the B-58 was a first result of this type of thinking. Next to appear was the impressive XB-70 Valkyrie supersonic bomber developed by North American Aviation — the same company that had already developed so many highly effective aircraft types for the armed services of the United States. A contract for this 521 000-pound Mach 3.0 strategic bomber was signed on December 23, 1957. Discovery of new methods for configuring a supersonic aircraft so as to achieve favorable aerodynamic interference effects made supersonic cruising efficiency much superior to that of the B-58 seem possible.

A growing conviction that a Mach 3.0 aircraft cruising at 75 000 feet had little chance of successfully penetrating enemy defenses, however, resulted in cancellation of the program in 1961. Only two proto-types were constructed, and these were used for flight research studies of the problems of large supersonic cruising aircraft. Initial flight of the first XB–70 took place on September 21, 1964, and the second one that flew about a year later was destroyed in a mid-air collision in 1966. A joint NASA-USAF flight research program utilizing the remaining aircraft extended over a period of several years. Last flight of the unique XB–70 was on February 4, 1969, when it was delivered to the Air Force museum in Dayton, Ohio, where it is now on display. The first prototype XB–70 is shown in figure 12.18, and descriptive material on the aircraft may be found in references 127, 170, and 200.

Although cancellation of the XB–70 program was seen by some as signaling the end of the manned bomber as an important weapon, others continued to feel that a new and more capable bomber was es-sential for the defense of the United States. With due consideration of the state of existing and possible future technology in such areas as aeronautics, electronics, and weapons, detailed studies of the potential effectiveness of various types of aircraft and mission profiles were made. These studies extended over a period of several years and re-sulted in the issuance of new bomber requirements and a request for proposal. On June 5, 1970, Rockwell International, the conglomerate

Figure 12.18 — North American XB–70A supersonic bomber. [mfr]

that had absorbed North American Aviation, was awarded the contract for development of a new manned bomber to be known as the B–1A.

Requirements for the B–1A called for high-efficiency cruising flight at both subsonic speeds and at a supersonic Mach number of 2.2. In addition, a low-altitude penetration capability at near-sonic speeds was specified. To reduce vulnerability while on the ground, takeoff and landing field lengths short enough to permit operation from air fields other than large, established SAC bases were also called for. Not surprisingly, the configuration proposed by Rockwell incorporated variable-sweep wings; this feature really offered the only viable means for meeting the mission requirements of the aircraft. The manner in which variable sweep can be used to adjust the aircraft configuration to meet requirements of different flight regimes is illustrated in figure 11.29.

First flight of the prototype took place on December 23, 1974. By 1979, four prototypes had been constructed with the fourth vehicle representing a fully operational aircraft complete with electronic systems installed. In the meantime, the B–1A production program was cancelled in June 1977 during the first year of the Carter administration. High cost of the aircraft perhaps tempered with some lingering doubts regarding its ability to successfully penetrate enemy defenses were apparently reasons for the cancellation. During the first year of the Reagan administration, however, the B–1 program was revived, and production of a somewhat simplified and less costly version of the aircraft is now planned. In this version, known as the B–1B, the Mach 2.2 supersonic cruise requirement has been eliminated, and the maximum speed is limited to a Mach number of about 1.2 at high altitude. Because of a lack of definitive information on the B–1B, the following discussion is limited primarily to the B–1A version of the aircraft.

The B–1A is shown in figures 12.19 and 12.20 with the wings in the high and low sweep positions, respectively. Maximum and minimum sweepback angles are 67.5° and 15°, and the corresponding aspect ratios are 3.13 and 9.85. Maximum aspect ratio at the low sweep position is slightly higher than that of the B–52; the lower sweepback angle of 15° for the B–1A, as compared with 35° for the B–52, has a favorable effect on the drag due to lift. The outboard location of the wing pivots is in accordance with the NASA research findings discussed in chapter 10. The large-span single-slotted trailing-edge flaps as well as the full-span leading-edge slats are clearly visible in figure 12.20. The powerful leading- and trailing-edge high-lift devices together with the small minimum wing sweepback angle all contribute to the high-lift capability of the aircraft and the corresponding short landing and take-

Figure 12.19 — Rockwell International B–1A bomber with wings in the maximum sweep position. [mfr]

off field lengths. Not visible in the photographs are the wing spoilers that, together with differential deflection of the horizontal tail, are used for roll control. Symmetrical deflection of the spoilers is used to aid in deceleration on the landing rollout.

Location of the two rectangular-shaped engine nacelles on the bottom of the fixed portion of the wing is shown in figure 12.20. Each nacelle contains two General Electric afterburning turbofan engines with bypass ratio of 2.0 and overall compression ratio of 27. The variable-geometry inlets on the B–1A will be replaced by more simple and less costly fixed-geometry inlets on the B–1B. Position of the exhaust nozzles behind the trailing edge of the wing may be seen in figure 12.20. The landing-gear arrangement is conventional and consists of four-wheel bogies on each of two main-gear struts and a two-wheel nose gear.

Other features of interest include the small size of the fuselage, which is carefully area ruled and blends smoothly into the wings. A small fuselage wetted area is an important factor in achieving a high

Figure 12.20 — Rockwell International B–1A bomber with wings in the minimum sweep position. [mfr]

value of the maximum lift-drag ratio. One of the small vanes located on either side of the nose of the aircraft can be seen in figures 12.19 and 12.20 These vanes are part of a special "structural mode control system." In response to signals received from sensors located in the aircraft, the vanes are actuated to aerodynamically attenuate gust-induced normal accelerations in the cockpit. In a similar manner, yawing motions are suppressed by automatic actuation of the lower part of the three-piece rudder. Crew fatigue encountered in the rough air of low-altitude high-speed penetration missions is reduced, and accuracy of weapons delivery is increased by the structural mode control system.

Normal crew of the B–1A consists of pilot, copilot, offensive-systems operator, and defensive-systems operator. Contrary to conventional practice in large aircraft, the pilots are provided with fighter-type control sticks instead of the traditional control wheels. The power-actuated control system is tailored to give light control forces and rapid response characteristics. For the first three prototypes, the entire crew compartment was ejected and lowered by parachute in the event that crew escape was necessary. As a means of reducing aircraft costs, the fourth prototype had individual ejection seats; this type of escape equipment will be incorporated on all subsequent aircraft. No guns are carried on the B-1, but extensive gear for electronic warfare is provided. Various types of nuclear and conventional weapons can be carried in three internal bomb bays. Provision for mounting external weapons are also included. By careful attention to design, the radar signature of the B-1 is only about 5 percent of that of the B-52; hence the B-1 is much less visible to enemy radar than the earlier aircraft.

According to table VI, the gross weight of the B-1A is 389 000 pounds and the cruising speed is listed as 648 miles per hour (Mach 0.85) at 50 000 feet. Gross weight of the B-1B is indicated by some sources to be about 476 000 pounds. No definitive range-payload data are available for either the B-1A or the B-1B.

According to present plans, 100 B-1B bombers will be built, with the last aircraft to be delivered in 1988. Thus with the reactivation of the B-1 program, the strategic bomber that traces its origins to the cumbersome Gotha and Handley Page biplanes of World War I seems assured of an important role in the front line of United States military power until well into the 21st century.

An Air Force Night Intruder

Korean war experience revealed an urgent USAF need for a high-performance jet-powered night-intruder aircraft capable of precise nighttime and bad-weather weapons delivery on moving targets located hundreds of miles from home base. The need was considered so pressing that the time usually required for development of a new aircraft was deemed unacceptable. Hence, an existing "off the shelf" aircraft was sought to fill the mission requirements. From a number of candidate vehicles, including the previously discussed North American B-45 Tornado, the English Electric Canberra bomber was selected to fill the USAF night-intruder role. Contracts for its license production in the United States were given to the Martin Company.

The Canberra was originally developed in response to a British requirement issued in 1945 for a high-altitude bomber. First flight of the aircraft took place in May 1949. The first Martin-produced Canberra, known as the B-57 in USAF nomenclature, made its initial flight in July

1953; before production of the Martin-built B–57 ended, 403 examples of the type had been produced. In England, total production of the Canberra was 984 units. By the summer of 1980, about three decades after the first flight of the Canberra, the type was still in the active inventory of 12 countries. The aircraft is no longer in active service with combat units of either the USAF or the RAF although a few are still used by the United States Air National Guard. A number of B–57 aircraft also fill a variety of utility roles with different United States Government agencies. An interesting account of the various versions of the B–57 is contained in reference 135.

A Martin B–57A is shown in figure 12.21, and data for a B–57B are contained in table VI. As with so many of the early jet aircraft, configuration of the B–57 was similar in concept to contemporary twin-engine propeller-driven aircraft but with jet engines replacing the reciprocating units. The unswept wing had a relatively low aspect ratio of 4.27 and airfoil thickness ratios that varied from 12 percent at the root to 9 percent at the tip. With so low an aspect ratio, the maximum lift-drag ratio might be expected to be very low. On the contrary, the large

Figure 12.21 — Martin B–57A night intruder. [mfr via Martin Copp]

surface area of the wing relative to that of the fuselage and other elements of the aircraft gave a low zero-lift drag coefficient of 0.0119 and a maximum lift-drag ratio of 15.0. Power was provided by two nonafterburning Wright J65–W–5 turbojet engines of 7200 pounds thrust each. These Wright engines were an American-built version of the British Rolls-Royce Avon. The location of the engine nacelles is clearly shown in figure 12.21. Conventional rudders, ailerons, and elevators were used for control of the aircraft. Simple high-lift flaps were located in the wing trailing edge between the engine nacelles and the sides of the fuselage.

The two-man crew of the B–57 consisted of a pilot and navigator-bombardier-radar operator who were seated in a tandem arrangement. As compared with the B–57A shown in figure 12.21, later versions of the aircraft had an extended canopy to enhance visibility for both crew members. Pressurization, air-conditioning, and ejection seats were provided for the crew. Various types of weapons such as bombs and rockets could be carried externally as well as in an internal bomb bay located in the fuselage. A Martin innovation, not included on the British Canberra, was the unique rotary bomb door described in the section on the P6M flying boat. In the closed position, bombs were attached to the inner side of the door, and bomb release took place after the door was rotated through 180°. Armament consisted of eight .50-caliber machine guns.

The B–57 is usually considered to be a light bomber; however, this classification must be related to the time frame under discussion. With a gross weight of 53 721 pounds, the B–57B was only 2000 pounds lighter than the Boeing B–17G, one of the standard heavy bombers of World War II. Mission radius of the B–57B was 948 miles with a payload of 5240 pounds, and ferry range was 2722 miles. Maximum speed was 598 miles per hour (Mach 0.79) at 2500 feet and cruising speed was 476 miles per hour. Comparison of the data given in table VI for the B–57B and the B–45C shows that the performance characteristics of the two aircraft have many similarities. Being about twice as heavy as the B–57B, the B–45C carried nearly twice the payload for approximately the same mission distance.

The Canberra class of aircraft has seen action in many wars, including service with the USAF in Vietnam. More recently, it was used by the Argentine Air Force in the undeclared war with Britain in the Falkland Islands. Although the B–57 was originally procured by the USAF as a night intruder, it has been successfully used in many other roles, including photoreconnaissance and strategic bombing. No distinctive design innovations were incorporated in the purely subsonic B–57; however, its pertinent design parameters were chosen in such a way that the aircraft was readily adaptable to a variety of roles calling for diverse characteristics.

Although not a technically exciting aircraft, the B–57 has certainly proved its worth in many years of effective operation. Because of its wide range of capabilities and docile handling characteristics, the B–57 has sometimes been likened to a Goony Bird with jet engines. ("Goony Bird" is the nickname for the USAF version of the famous Douglas DC–3.) Could a more complimentary epithet be found for any aircraft!

Three Navy Attack Aircraft

Described next are three Navy attack aircraft (one is also used by the USAF) that appeared between 1954 and 1964. The three aircraft relied heavily on fighter technology of the 1950's, but in contrast with fighters of that period, none had a supersonic capability. Hence, none incorporated area ruling and none was equipped with afterburning engines. All three aircraft were equipped with power-operated controls and arresting hooks for carrier operation; all had pressurized cockpits and ejection seats for crew escape. Designed under the restraints imposed by aircraft-carrier operation, the three differed primarily in their range-payload characteristics and the conditions under which they were expected to operate. Yet, just as with the fighters of the mid-1940's, they differed markedly in appearance.

Douglas A–4 Skyhawk

Designed as a light naval attack aircraft capable of delivering a nuclear weapon, the Douglas A–4 Skyhawk (A4D in the old Navy nomenclature) made its initial flight on June 22, 1954. When the last aircraft of this type rolled off the production line in February 1979, a total of 2096 units had been produced in a remarkably long 25-year production history. These ubiquitous aircraft have been in the military inventories of nine different countries, one being the United States, and have seen action in numerous world trouble spots including Vietnam, the Middle East, and the Falkland Islands where they served with the Argentine forces. Although retired from United States Navy fleet use in 1976, the aircraft is still used extensively by various elements of the Navy and Marine Corps for training and utility purposes. The A–4 is also currently flown by the famous Navy Blue Angels exhibition team. Approximately 15 variants of the A-4 were produced during its long production life. Although primarily a single-place aircraft, the Skyhawk has also been produced in a two-place trainer version known as the TA-4.

Shown in figures 12.22 and 12.23 are two versions of the Skyhawk, and data for the A-4E are given in table VI. Configuration of the aircraft is characterized by a cropped delta wing of 33° sweepback mounted in the low position on a short, stubby fuselage with a large vertical tail and dorsal surface. The horizontal tail is mounted part way up the vertical fin just above the wing chord plane extended and consists of an electrically actuated stabilizer and hydraulically powered elevator. The hydraulically actuated rudder is of a unique design, consisting of a single central skin with external riblike stiffeners. (See figs. 12.22 and 12.23.) According to the interesting account of the development of the A-4 given in reference 164, this design feature was found to offer a solution to problems of rudder buffet or buzz.

Two inlets mounted high on the fuselage just ahead of the wing supply air to the single Pratt & Whitney turbojet engine of 8500

Figure 12.22 — Douglas A-4E Skyhawk attack aircraft. [Peter C. Boisseau]

Figure 12.23 — Douglas A-4 Skyhawk as used by the Navy Blue Angels aerobatic team.
[Peter C. Boisseau]

pounds thrust. Clearly shown in figure 12.23 are the boundary-layer diverters located just ahead of the inlets. The long landing-gear struts were dictated by clearance requirements for large stores carried beneath the wings on either side and between the main landing-gear legs. A braking chute was provided for use at shore-based landing facilities.

For simplicity, the wing of aspect ratio 2.91 was built as a single unit with continuous top and bottom skins. It was so small that no folding was necessary for storage and movement on the aircraft carrier, an unusual feature in a Navy aircraft. Automatic leading-edge slats and trailing-edge split flaps were provided for lift augmentation. Outwardly extending speed brakes were mounted on either side of the rear of the fuselage.

The Skyhawk is capable of carrying literally hundreds of combinations of external stores including fuel tanks, both conventional and nuclear bombs, rockets, and Sidewinder missiles. Armament consists of two 20-mm cannons, one of which is mounted in each wing root.

The data in table VI show that the Skyhawk has a remarkably low gross weight of 18 311 pounds but can deliver a weapons load of 2040 pounds at a mission radius of 680 miles with two 300-gallon external tanks; unrefueled ferry range is 2130 miles. Maximum speed of the aircraft is 673 miles per hour (Mach 0.88) at sea level, and cruising speed is 498 miles per hour. Ceiling is just over 40 000 feet. Certainly, the aircraft has an impressive performance for a lightweight attack aircraft.

The Skyhawk was designed at a time when the complexity, weight, and cost of combat aircraft were escalating at an alarming rate. Under the supervision of designer Edward H. Heinemann, an intensive effort was made during the design and development of the aircraft to keep it light and uncomplicated (ref. 164). The effort paid off so well that the first version of the Skyhawk had a gross weight of only about 15 000 pounds. Growth in capability resulted in the increase in gross weight to 18 311 pounds shown in table VI for the A–4E. The light weight of the aircraft caused it to have at least two appellations: "The Bantam Bomber" and "Heinemann's Hotrod." The long production life of the Skyhawk, together with its widespread use in a variety of roles, attests to the basic soundness of the original design and its potential for growth and adaption to differing requirements. The Skyhawk should continue to be a familiar sight for many years.

Grumman A–6 Intruder

The Grumman A–6 Intruder was designed in response to a Navy requirement for a true all-weather attack aircraft capable of precision weapons delivery at night under conditions of zero visibility. These difficult mission specifications dictated a relatively heavy, twin-engine aircraft manned by a crew of two, consisting of a pilot and a weapons-systems operator, and equipped with a complex array of electronic gear.

First flight of the A–6 (A2F–1 in the old Navy designation system) took place in April 1960, and the first squadron to use the aircraft was formed in early 1963. Operational sorties against North Vietnam were begun in 1965 from carriers located off the coast. The A–6 and its derivatives have been in continuous production since 1960 and are still rolling off the production line at this time. A close relative of the A–6 is the EA–6B Prowler electronic warfare aircraft, which first flew in May 1968. The Prowler differs from the Intruder mainly in the amount and type of equipment carried and in the use of a four-man instead of a two-man crew.

The A–6A is shown in figures 12.24 and 12.25, and physical and performance data are given in table VI for the more advanced A–6E.

Figure 12.24 — Grumman A–6A Intruder all-weather attack aircraft. [Arthur L. Schoeni via AAHS]

Configuration of the midwing subsonic aircraft features a 5.31-aspect-ratio wing of moderate sweepback (25°) and one turbojet engine nestled on either side of the fuselage in the intersection of the lower wing surface and the fuselage side. Exhaust nozzles are located just behind the wing trailing edge, and, as can be seen in the figures, side-mounted inlets are low and far forward on the fuselage. A side-by-side seating arrangement accommodates the crew in the A–6. Clearly seen in the photographs is the refueling probe located on top of the fuselage just ahead of the cockpit canopy. To provide the lift augmentation necessary for carrier operations, nearly full-span leading-edge and trailing-edge high-lift devices are installed. The deployed leading-edge slat can be clearly seen in figure 12.24. The trailing edge of each wingtip outboard of the fold line splits to form speed brakes that deflect above and below the wing when deployed. As seen in figure 12.25, the outer portion of the wing folds upward to facilitate carrier storage. Also evident in the figure is one of the two short flow-control fences located on each wing. Spoilers are used for lateral control, and the longitudinal control surface is an all-moving horizontal tail.

No guns of any kind are carried aboard the A–6, and the aircraft has no internal bomb bay. A wide variety of stores, however, can be

397

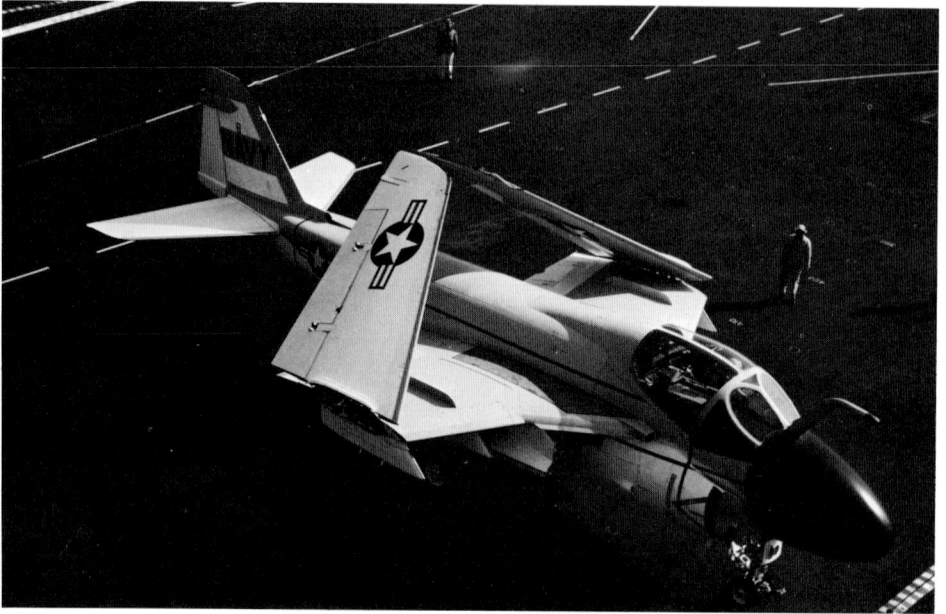

Figure 12.25 — Grumman A–6A Intruder with wings folded. [Arthur L. Schoeni via AAHS]

mounted externally; these include both conventional and nuclear bombs, fuel tanks, and an assortment of rockets and missiles. Two of the store-mounting stations are visible in figure 12.25.

As shown in table VI, the A–6E is capable of a maximum speed of 653 miles per hour (Mach 0.86) at sea level and a cruising speed of 390 miles per hour. Although the wing loading of the A–6E is over 40 percent higher than that of the A–4E, the stalling speeds of the two aircraft are nearly the same, which attests to the effectiveness of the high-lift devices on the A–6. The zero-lift drag coefficient of the A–6E is about 20 percent higher than that of the B–57B; however, the maximum lift-drag ratios of the two aircraft are about the same. The higher-aspect-ratio wing of the A–6E compensates for its higher zero-lift drag coefficient in determining the maximum lift-drag ratio.

As with all versatile attack aircraft, many combinations of payload and mission radius are available to the A–6E. For example, a weapons load of 2080 pounds consisting of a Mark 43 nuclear bomb can be delivered at a mission radius of 890 miles. For that mission, four 300-gallon external tanks are carried. Alternatively, 10 296 pounds can be delivered at a mission radius of 450 miles with two 300-gallon external tanks. Unrefueled ferry range is 3300 miles. Normal gross weight of the aircraft is 54 393 pounds, nearly three times that of the A–4E.

The subsonic A–6 has no spectacular performance or design features but is superbly suited to the particular attack role for which it was so carefully tailored. The A–6 Intruder and its close relative the EA–6 Prowler will no doubt continue in service with the U.S. Navy and Marine Corps for the foreseeable future.

Vought A–7 Corsair II

As applied to an aircraft, the name Corsair has its origins in a series of famous biplanes built for the Navy by the Vought Corporation between World Wars I and II. Later, the name was applied to the famous Vought F4U series of fighters flown by Navy and Marine pilots during World War II. Discussed next is the modern-day descendant of these historic aircraft — the Vought A–7 Corsair II.

The Corsair II was developed in response to a Navy requirement for a single-place, fair-weather subsonic attack aircraft capable of carrying a much heavier weapons load than the Douglas A–4 Skyhawk. First flight of the new aircraft (Vought A–7D) took place on September 27, 1965, and it has been in continuous production since then with a total of 1534 units produced by mid-1980. In addition to the Navy and Marine Corps, the USAF as well as air forces of two other nations operate the A–7. The definitive versions of the aircraft are the USAF A–7D and the closely related Navy A–7E. An in-flight view of an A–7D is shown in figure 12.26, and a close-up view of an A–7E is pictured in figure 12.27. Physical and performance data are given in table VI for the A–7D.

That the lineage of the A–7 can be traced directly to the Vought F–8 Crusader fighter is obvious from a comparison of figures 12.26 and 12.27 with figures 11.19 and 11.20. Like the F–8, the configuration of the A–7 is characterized by a high wing, low horizontal tail, chin inlet, and short landing-gear legs that retract into the fuselage. Since the A–7 is a subsonic aircraft, however, no area ruling is incorporated in the fuselage, which is also shorter and deeper than that of the supersonic F–8. Because of the larger mass flow of the turbofan engine employed in the A–7, the size of the chin inlet is somewhat larger than that of the turbojet-powered F–8. These differences make the A–7 appear shorter and more stubby than the earlier fighter. The A–7 is

Figure 12.26 — Vought A–7D USAF attack aircraft. [Arthur L. Schoeni via AAHS]

Figure 12.27 — Close-up view of Vought A–7E Navy attack aircraft. [Peter C. Boisseau]

sometimes unofficially called the SLUF (Short Little Ugly Fella) by USAF crews.

The wing of the A–7 is closely related in geometry and physical size to that of the F–8. (Compare data in tables V and VI.) Leading-edge flaps and single-slotted trailing-edge flaps are fitted to the wing, as are upper surface spoilers located ahead of the flaps. Not used on the A–7 is the unique variable-incidence feature of the F–8 wing. The shorter length of the fuselage together with the slight "upsweep" of the underside of the afterbody (fig. 12.27) allow the A–7 to be rotated to a significantly higher pitch angle on takeoff and landing, without tail scrape, than was possible for the F–8. The higher available ground pitch attitude, together with the good augmentation capability of the high-lift system, no doubt played a large part in obviating the need for a variable-incidence capability in the wing. Speed brakes are located on the bottom of the fuselage about midway between the nose and the tail. A braking chute is provided for use in shore-based operations.

Original power plant of the A–7 was a nonafterburning version of the Pratt & Whitney TF30 turbofan. This is the same engine that, equipped with an afterburner, powers both the F–111 and the F–14. Beginning with the A–7D, however, the more powerful Allison TF41–A–1 turbofan was installed. An American-made version of the British Rolls-Royce Spey, the TF41–A–1 has a bypass ratio of 0.7 and uses a five-stage fan.

A wide assortment of external stores can be accommodated on the A–7. Eight store-mounting positions are provided. There are three pylons under each wing, and a single mounting station is located on each side of the fuselage. Two of the underwing pylons and one of the fuselage mounting stations are visible in figure 12.27. A total of 15 000 pounds of stores can be carried. Table VI shows that 6560 pounds can be carried on a typical mission with a radius of 556 miles. A six-barrel 20-mm Vulcan cannon is located on the left side of the fuselage near the bottom of the aircraft. A portion of the muzzle of the gun is visible below the word "intake" in figure 12.27.

Although the A–7 was originally intended as a fair-weather aircraft, later versions (beginning with the A–7D) were equipped with extensive electronic gear for all-weather operations. The various modes in which this equipment may be utilized in attack operations, along with many other aspects of the A–7 story, are discussed in reference 136.

According to the data in table VI, the gross weight of the A–7D is a little more than twice that of the A–4E but is significantly less than that of the A–6E. Maximum speed of the A–7D is listed as 663 miles per hour (Mach 0.89) at an altitude of 7000 feet. Stalling speed at maximum gross weight is a very high 174 miles per hour. For landing on an aircraft carrier following a mission, however, a weight much less than the maximum value, along with a reduction in stalling speed, would normally be expected. For example, with a weight of 23 000 pounds, the stalling speed would be about 135 miles per hour.

The A-7 is one of those aircraft with a demonstrated capability of performing well in a wide variety of missions. Other aircraft are faster or have a greater range-payload capability or have a faster rate of climb; sometimes, certain of these characteristics is deemed so important that it dominates the entire design. What results is a "point-design" aircraft that can perform one mission extremely well but is relatively much less effective in any other mission. The design parameters of the A-7 were chosen so that the aircraft has great mission versatility. It was successfully employed in just about every conceivable attack role during the Vietnam conflict where it first saw action in 1967.

Close-Air-Support Aircraft

A need arose during the Vietnam conflict for a specialized aircraft capable of giving close air support to troops operating in the forward battle area. Needed was a heavily armed aircraft that could respond rapidly to a call for help and had the ability to destroy tanks, artillery batteries, and other types of enemy strongholds. Neither a fast aircraft nor one with long range was required; good maneuverability, extended loiter time in the battle area, and a lethal weapons load were needed. Low cost, easy maintenance with minimum turnaround time, and high survivability in the face of enemy ground fire were other characteristics desired. The aircraft was intended only for daytime operations in fair weather.

Detailed requirements for such a close-air-support aircraft were issued by the USAF in May 1970. Fairchild-Republic and Northrop were given contracts for the construction of prototypes to be used in a flyoff competition from which a winner would be selected for production. Fairchild-Republic with its A-10A was declared the winner in January 1973. First flight of the aircraft occurred in May 1972, and the first squadron to be equipped with the A-10A became operational in October 1977. The aircraft is still in production with a planned output of over 700 units.

The A–10A, dubbed the Thunderbolt II, is shown in figures 12.28 and 12.29. Configuration of the Thunderbolt II is like that of no other modern aircraft and, in some respects, seems to be a throwback to an earlier aeronautical age. The unswept wing is tapered only slightly and is mounted near the bottom of the flat-sided fuselage, about midway between the nose and the tail. Airfoil sections vary in thickness ratio from 16 percent at the root to 13 percent at the tip. An aft-loaded camber line is used in the airfoil sections to improve turning perform-ance at low speeds in the battle area. In effect, this camber line acts like a flap with a small permanent deflection. A single-slotted trailing-edge flap is provided, and ailerons are used for lateral control. For aer-odynamic braking, the upper and lower surfaces of the ailerons sepa-rate and deflect above and below the wing.

Two General Electric turbofan engines are contained in separate nacelles that are pylon mounted slightly above and to either side of the fuselage and behind the wing. The horizontal tail is below and to the rear of the engines; the vertical surfaces are at the tips of the horizontal tail outboard of the engines. Serious exhaust impingement on both the

Figure 12.28 — Fairchild-Republic A-10A close-air-support aircraft. [USAF via Martin Copp]

Figure 12.29 — In-flight view of Fairchild-Republic A–10A close-air-support aircraft.
[USAF via Martin Copp]

horizontal and vertical surfaces is avoided by this arrangement. Conventional elevators and rudders are provided for pitch and yaw control, respectively. Main-landing-gear units retract into fairings below the wing, and the single nose-wheel gear is offset to facilitate optimum location of the offensive cannon. The single pilot's cockpit is near the nose of the fuselage and is equipped with a zero-zero ejection seat. (A successful escape can be made at zero altitude and speed.) Protection of the cockpit area is provided by an armored "bathtub" constructed of titanium said to be able to withstand the impact of projectiles of up to 23 mm in size.

Primary armament of the A–10 is a large 30-mm seven-barrel rotary cannon. This impressive weapon can fire at a rate of either 2100 or 4200 rounds per minute. Equipped with 1950 rounds of ammunition, the gun weighs 4041 pounds; its empty weight is 1975 pounds. The gun is positioned in the nose so that the firing barrel is always located on the centerline of the aircraft. Muzzle of the cannon may be seen protruding from the nose in figures 12.28 and 12.29. In addition to the formidable 30-mm cannon, four store-mounting stations are provided under each wing and three are located beneath the fuselage. A wide assortment of different stores can be carried on the aircraft. With full internal fuel tanks, the maximum external load is a remarkable 14 341 pounds.

The data in table VI show a maximum gross weight of 40 269 pounds for the Thunderbolt II. With a payload of 9540 pounds, mission radius is 288 miles, including a 2-hour loiter period on station. Ferry range with no payload and maximum external fuel is 3510 miles. At a cruising speed of 329 miles per hour, time required for the single pilot to fly this distance is a little over 10 hours. Certainly a fatiguing flight, but not a remarkably long one for a single pilot. Maximum speeds for the A–10A given in table VI are comparable to those achievable by the fastest propeller-driven fighters of World War II.

Certainly the Thunderbolt II (sometimes irreverently referred to by crew members as the Warthog) will never reap any honors for ascetic appeal. Yet, given its unique mission requirements, a more practical design is difficult to envision. Its ultimate usefulness in a combat situation, however, has yet to be proven.

Conclusion

First discussed in this chapter were early jet-powered bombers that, from a technical point of view, were little more than World War II-type configurations powered with jet engines. Revolutionary new design concepts for long-range, high-speed subsonic aircraft were then pioneered by the large Boeing B–47 and, later, the B–52 jet-powered bombers. Because of continuing disagreement and debate over the relative effectiveness of manned bombers as contrasted with ballistic and cruise missiles, however, subsequent bomber development has been sporadic and has yielded no new advanced long-range subsonic aircraft. The further development and refinement of this class of aircraft has taken place in the field of civil transports. Evolution of this class of ve hicle, which has had such a profound effect on modern society, is discussed in chapter 13. Military explorations into supersonic bomber aircraft have been largely unproductive.

The attack aircraft discussed in this chapter do not represent any significant advancement in air-vehicle technology but have provided a useful capability to the armed services that far exceeds anything possible with propeller-driven aircraft.

Chapter 13
Jet Transports

Background

The development and design features of jet transport aircraft from the pioneering DeHavilland Comet of 1949 to the wide-body jets of today are briefly described in this chapter. The particular aircraft discussed were selected because of their significance in the evolution of the modern jet transport, or because they are representative of an important configuration type, or because they are particularly successful. No attempt is made to describe all the jet transport aircraft developed since the end of World War II.

Successful jet transports tend to have long operational careers and are usually produced in many versions. Engine changes and improvements, changes in wing area and high-lift systems, aerodynamic and structural refinements, and modernization of onboard systems may take place during the production life of a successful aircraft type. "Stretching" is another modification technique frequently employed. In this case, the fuselage is lengthened by the addition of "barrel sections" so that the passenger capacity of the aircraft is accordingly increased. A description of the sometimes numerous versions of a particular aircraft is beyond the scope of the present discussion. A representative version of a particular aircraft will be described here; information on the different versions may be obtained from the references contained at the end of this book.

The aircraft discussed are listed in table VII (appendix A), together with some of their important physical and performance characteristics. Although the terms used in table VII are defined in the list of symbols given in appendix B, clarifying remarks about several of these quantities are in order. The range-payload diagram is so fundamental to the understanding of transport aircraft performance that a brief description is provided at this point. A hypothetical range-payload diagram is given in figure 13.1 in which the range is plotted on the abscissa; and the payload, on the ordinate. Point B corresponds to maximum aircraft gross weight and maximum payload weight with all available seats and cargo space filled but with fuel tanks only partially filled. The gross weight of the aircraft remains the same along the line segment BC, but fuel weight is exchanged for payload weight; that is, payload is off-loaded and the fuel tanks are completely full at point C. Along the line segment D, increases in range are achieved by further reductions in payload although no additional fuel can be carried, and the gross weight is lower than the maximum value. The gross weight of the aircraft along line segment A is less than the maximum value, except at point B, and the fuel load is reduced as the range is reduced. No in-

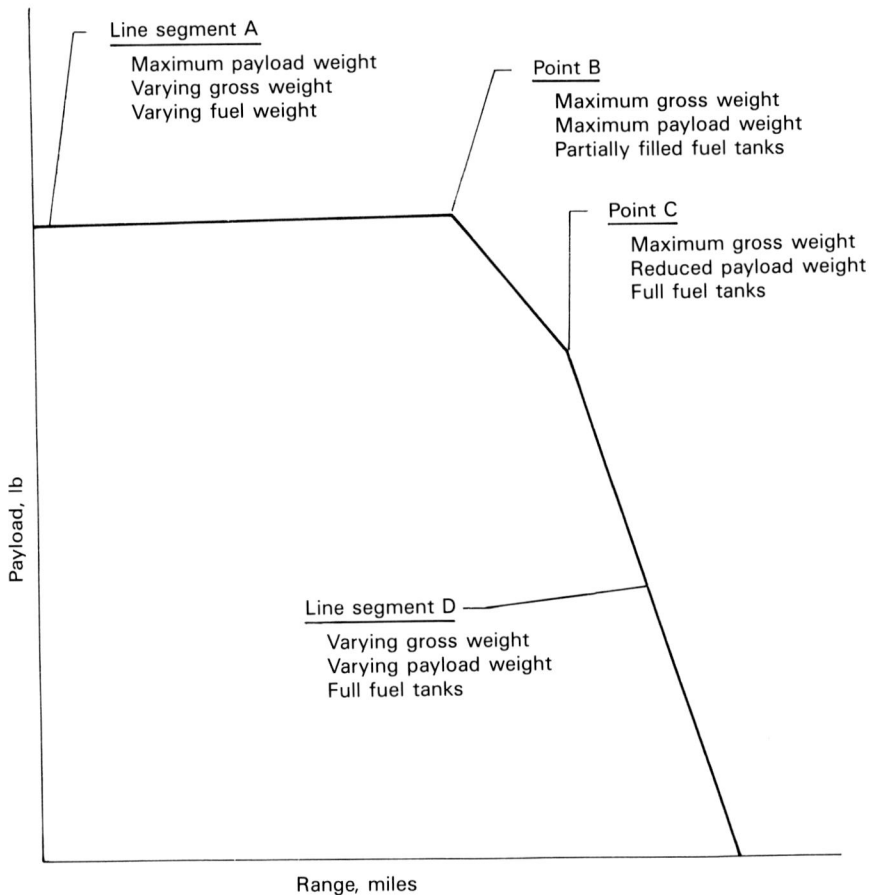

Figure 13.1 — Hypothetical range-payload diagram.

crease in payload is shown along line segment A because all payload space is filled. The range at maximum payload, point B, and the range and payload for full tanks, point C, are the two combinations of range and payload given in table VII. The range values given in the table are based on utilization of all fuel onboard the aircraft; thus no allowance is made for necessary reserve fuel to cover such contingencies as diversion to an alternate airport, a missed approach, or holding in the vicinity of an airport. All passenger-carrying airline flights are required to carry a specified amount of reserve fuel. One set of guidelines for determining the necessary amount of reserve fuel is briefly discussed in appendix G. Two cruising speeds are given in table VII. The maximum cruising speed is given by the symbol V_c; the cost-economical cruising speed is denoted by V_{ce} and is the speed for minimum cost per mile. The landing and takeoff field lengths given in the table are called FAR (Federal Air Regulations) field lengths and contain certain built-in safety margins. A simplified description of these field lengths is given in appendix H. Values of the zero-lift drag coefficient and maximum lift-drag ratio are not given for the aircraft listed in table VII. Such data are not generally available in the open literature because of the highly competitive nature of the modern-jet-transport business. Values of these quantities (estimated by the author according to the methods given in reference 176) are quoted in the text for several of the aircraft described, but these values should not be interpreted as necessarily being consistent with company estimates.

Pioneer Transports

The age of jet transportation began on May 5, 1952, with the inauguration of scheduled service from London to Johannesburg, South Africa. Later in the year, service was established from London to Ceylon and from London to Singapore. Then, in April 1953, scheduled flights were begun from London to Tokyo, a distance of 10 200 miles. The flying time was 36 hours, as compared with 85 hours for the propeller-driven aircraft then in use on the route. The pioneering jet transport that began commercial operations in 1952 was the DeHavilland Comet 1.

The design of the Comet airliner had its origins in the waning days of World War II, and the layout of the aircraft was completed in 1947. The first flight of the prototype took place on July 27, 1949, with John Cunningham as pilot. The performance and physical characteristics of the Comet 1A are given in table VII, and a three-view drawing of the aircraft is presented in figure 13.2. A photograph of a Comet 3, similar in appearance to the Comet 1A, is given in figure 13.3. The configuration of the Comet was not significantly different from that of contemporary long-range propeller-driven aircraft. A comparison of the characteristics of the Comet given in table VII with those of the Lockheed Constellation given in table III indicates that the Comet was a somewhat lighter aircraft, had a lower wing loading and a wing of lower aspect ratio but had a cruising speed of 490 miles per hour at 35 000 feet as compared with 331 miles per hour at 23 000 feet for the Constellation. The range with maximum payload of 44 passengers was 1750 miles. At a much reduced payload, a range of slightly over 4000 miles was possible. By present-day standards, the Comet 1A was a small, relatively low performance aircraft. By comparison with other aircraft of the early 1950's, however, it was extremely fast.

The Comet 1A was powered with four DeHavilland Ghost turbojet engines of 5000 pounds thrust each. The takeoff thrust-to-weight ratio was a very low 0.17. As a consequence of this low thrust-to-weight ratio, very precise control over the aircraft attitude was required during the takeoff roll to prevent overrotation and subsequent high drag and loss of acceleration. At least one aircraft was lost as a result of overrotation during takeoff. The four engines were mounted in the wing roots, two on each side of the fuselage. This engine arrangement has the advantages of placing the engines near the longitudinal center-of-gravity position and of minimizing the asymmetrical yawing moment that accompanies loss of an engine during takeoff; at the time, it was also thought to be a low-drag arrangement. The proximity of the engines to each other and to the passenger cabin, however, posed a possibly hazardous situation in the event one of the engines disintegrated. Engine disintegration was a very real concern in 1950. Engine maintenance was also complicated by the wing-root mounting arrangement.

The aerodynamic design of the wing was conventional except for the use of 20° of sweepback. The aspect ratio of 6.6 was low, as compared with contemporary long-range propeller-driven aircraft. The high-lift system consisted in a combination of simple plain and split trailing-edge flaps. Some aircraft employed fences on the wings. The aerodynamic controls were hydraulically boosted. The passenger cabin was pressurized to maintain a cabin altitude of 8000 feet at an aircraft altitude of 40 000 feet.

The Comet 1 was sold to British, French, and Canadian airlines, and it appeared that Great Britain had produced a truly outstanding new aircraft that would be sold in large numbers throughout the world.

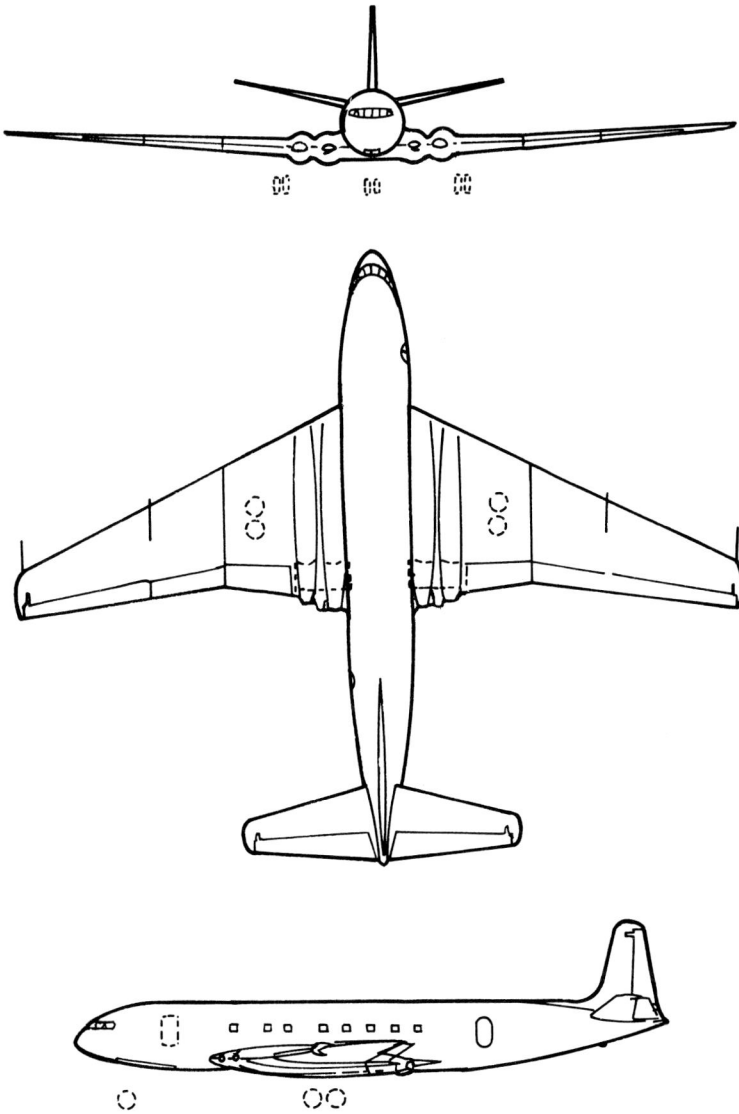

Figure 13.2 — DeHavilland Comet airliner prototype.

Prospects for the Comet dimmed, however, when three accidents occurred in which the aircraft disintegrated in flight. All Comet 1 aircraft,
over 20 in number, were withdrawn from service in 1954. Extensive
laboratory studies were undertaken in an effort to diagnose the problem. Fatigue failure and subsequent rupture of the pressurized fuselage
as a result of pressure recycling was finally identified as the cause of
the accidents. The Comet was completely reengineered and emerged as

411

Figure 13.3 — DeHavilland Comet 3 airliner. [David A. Anderton]

a much changed and improved aircraft in 1958. This version, identified as the Comet 4, was not really competitive with the new generation of jet transports coming into use at that time, and only 74 were built.

The commercial success of the Comet was limited, but it was the first jet transport and represented a large step forward in our concepts of air transportation and its utility. It is unfortunate that the pioneering work of the designers and builders of the Comet was not rewarded with greater success. The Comet, in highly modified form, survives today as a marine reconnaissance aircraft known as the Nimrod. An interesting account of the development of the various versions of the Comet is contained in reference 169.

The Tupolev Tu–104 is the second of the pioneer jet transports. This aircraft was first flown on June 17, 1955, and went into scheduled airline operations in 1956 on the Moscow-Omsk-Irkutsk route. In 1957, an improved version of the aircraft, the Tu–104A, captured a number of records for speed, altitude, distance, and load-carrying capability. The Tu–104 transport was developed from the "Badger" bomber and utilized the same wings, tail surfaces, engines and inlets, landing gear, and fuselage nose section as the earlier bomber aircraft. Figure 13.4 depicts a Tu–104B, and the data in table VII are for this version of the aircraft.

As can be seen in figure 13.4, the Tu–104B is a low-wing aircraft with a conventional tail arrangement and a wing incorporating pronounced sweepback. The transparent nose adopted from the bomber version of the aircraft is clearly visible in the photograph. The two engines that power the Tu–104 are located in nacelles that are faired into

412

the wing roots. This arrangement is somewhat similar to that employed on the Comet; however, the nacelles are larger and the circular inlets extend forward of the leading edge of the wing, as contrasted with the leading-edge inlets on the Comet. The two main landing-gear struts are fitted with four-wheel bogies and retract rearward into pods on the wing. The aircraft has a seating capacity of 100 passengers arranged in a 5-abreast configuration. The sweepback angle of the aspect ratio 6.5 wing is 40° from the root to about the midsemispan position and is 37.5° from there to the tip. Each wing has two large fences located in the streamwise position on the top surface of each wing. One of these is at the position where the sweep angle changes, and the other is farther outboard. As indicated in chapter 10, these fences help control the boundary layer and, hence, improve the stalling characteristics of the wing. Lateral control is provided by conventional ailerons that are operated manually; manual longitudinal control is also used. The rudder is actuated hydraulically. The wings are equipped with trailing-edge Fowler-type flaps and have no leading-edge devices. A Fowler flap is similar to the double-slotted flap shown in figure 10.25(b), but without the small segment between the wing and the main portion of the flap.

The Tu–104B is powered by two Mikulin turbojet engines of 21 385 pounds thrust each. The engines are equipped with thrust reversers, although some of the early models did not have this equipment. These early aircraft employed two braking parachutes to assist in stopping the aircraft on landing. Insofar as can be determined, no other commercial transport aircraft (except early versions of the Tupo-

Figure 13.4 — Tupolev Tu–104B airliner. [Flt. Intl.]

413

lev Tu–134) has utilized braking chutes as a routine operational procedure. The gross weight of the aircraft is 167 551 pounds, which is somewhat heavier than that of the piston-engine transports at the end of the era in which these aircraft dominated the world's airlines. With the large turbojet engines, the thrust-to-weight ratio of the aircraft, 0.26, is nearly as high as any of the large transports whose characteristics are given in table VII. The wing loading of 84.8 pounds per square foot is relatively low compared with more modern designs; however, comparison of the data given in table VII for different aircraft indicates that the combination of low wing loading and relatively simple high-lift devices on the Soviet aircraft give stalling speeds comparable to those of more modern high-performance jet transports.

The range of 1500 miles given in table VII for the Tu–104 aircraft with maximum payload places it in the short-range category. The cost-economical and maximum cruising speeds are 497 and 590 miles per hour, respectively; these speeds correspond to Mach numbers of 0.75 at 35 000 feet and 0.85 at 25 000 feet.

The Tu–104 was built in a number of versions, and some are still in use on domestic routes inside the Soviet Union. Production of the aircraft ended after 250 units were constructed. The development history of the Tu–104 series of aircraft is completely described in reference 190.

Both the DeHavilland Comet and the Tupolev Tu–104 were pioneers in a new and exciting concept of air transportation, and both have a well-deserved place in the history of aeronautical development. In many respects, however, the design of these aircraft reflected the philosophy of contemporary propeller-driven aircraft. For example, the low wing loadings, unsophisticated high-lift devices, and simple control systems are typical of high-performance propeller-driven transports. The need for high wing loadings and powerful high-lift devices in order to permit cruising at near maximum values of the lift-drag ratio, but at the same time retaining satisfactory stalling speeds, is discussed in chapter 3 of reference 176. The engine location on the Comet and the Tu–104 are no longer used on modern jet transports and must be considered obsolete for this type of aircraft. The advantages and disadvantages of mounting the engines in the wing roots are discussed above in the description of the Comet. This aircraft, as well as the Tu–104, employed turbojet engines of relatively small diameter. The beginnings of the high-bypass-ratio turbofan engine with its large diameter fan poses an additional problem with the wing-root engine location because of the difficulty of integrating the large engine into the wing root.

First-Generation Transports

In this section, three families of transports that were configured and sized to more fully exploit the unique capabilities of jet propulsion in commercial aircraft are discussed. These aircraft were responsible for the beginnings of the revolution in air transportation caused by the jet transport, and the configuration concepts of these designs have had a lasting influence on jet transport aircraft.

Boeing 707

The Boeing 707 transport was the first of the long-range and, for its day, high-passenger-capacity aircraft that marked the real beginning of the revolutionary jet age in air transportation. Even today, many people consider the terms 707 and jet transport to be synonymous. The prototype of this remarkable aircraft first flew in July 1954, and an early production version first entered airline service in the fall of 1958. Over 900 Boeing 707 commercial transports have been built, but by 1980 the 707 was no longer in production as a commercial transport. A tanker version of the aircraft, the KC–135, has been built in large numbers for the USAF; and the Airborne Warning and Control System aircraft (AWACS) now being delivered to the Air Force utilizes the basic 707 airplane.

The prototype of the 707 was known in the Boeing Company as the model 367–80, and within the company it has always been referred to as the Dash-Eighty. The aircraft served as a test vehicle for the exploration and development of new ideas for many years. Finally retired in 1972, it was presented to the Smithsonian Institution. The aircraft is shown in figure 13.5, and a few of its characteristics are given in table VII.

A fully developed Boeing 707–320B is shown in figure 13.6, and a three-view drawing of this version is given in figure 13.7 The 707–320B is the last version of the aircraft built solely for passenger use. The last variant produced was the 707–320C, which is similar in most respects to the B model but is fitted with a cargo door and strengthened floor structure; the aircraft may therefore be used for cargo or mixed cargo and passenger service. Data for the 707–320B are given in table VII. Specifications and performance data quoted below are for this version of the aircraft.

The wing of the Boeing 707 is mounted in the low position at the bottom of the fuselage; this wing location has been preferred on transports designed for passenger use since the Boeing 247 and Douglas

415

Figure 13.5 — Boeing model 367–80, prototype of Boeing 707 series transports. [mfr]

DC–2 of the early 1930's. The wing has an aspect ratio of 7.1 and employs a 35° sweepback angle. This wing geometry provides a combination of good cruising efficiency at high subsonic speeds, low structural weight, and large internal volume for fuel. The main landing gear consists of two struts to which are mounted four-wheel bogies. The landing gear is attached to the wing and is retracted inboard into the thickened juncture of the wing and fuselage. The nearly straight trailing edge of the wing near the fuselage is dictated by the required storage space for the landing gear in the retracted position. The two-wheel nose gear retracts forward into the fuselage.

The four engines are mounted similarly to the manner pioneered by the B–47 bomber described in chapter 12. Each engine is contained in a single nacelle that is attached to the bottom of the wing by a sweptforward pylon. According to reference 182, consideration was given to mounting two engines in each of two nacelles; such an arrangement was employed in mounting the four inboard engines of the B–47. This engine configuration was abandoned on the transport because of the possibility that disintegration of one engine might cause failure of an adjacent engine. This possibility was apparently not acceptable on a passenger-carrying transport. Early versions of the 707 were powered with turbojet engines. Several different engines were used, but most of these early aircraft employed the Pratt & Whitney JT3C engine, which is basically a civil version of the military J–57 turbojet used by such aircraft as the Boeing B–52 bomber and the North American F–100 fighter. Most 707 aircraft manufactured since the early

416

Figure 13.6 — Boeing 707–320B airliner. [mfr]

1960's, however, have been powered with a turbofan version of this engine. The Pratt & Whitney JT3D turbofan engine utilizes the same basic gas generator as the J–57 but has a front-mounted two-stage fan with a pressure ratio of about 1.8. The bypass ratio is 1.43, and the sea-level static thrust is about 19 000 pounds. The fan discharges through a short duct that appears somewhat similar to a NACA cowling of the type employed on many radial-type piston engines. The short duct can be seen in figure 13.6. Thrust reversers are employed to assist in stopping the aircraft on its landing rollout. Reverse thrust may also be used to increase the rate of descent. The aerodynamic efficiency of the 707–320B may be judged by the value of the maximum lift-drag ratio, which is estimated to be in the range from 19 to 19.5. This value of $(L/D)_{max}$ is just slightly lower than the value of 20.0 given for the B–47 in table VI, primarily because of the lower aspect ratio of the wing employed on the 707.

The 707–320B's wing loading is a relatively high 111.6 pounds per square foot; however, the stalling speed is maintained at an acceptably low 121 miles per hour by the use of trailing-edge slotted flaps and leading-edge flaps. The lateral control system of the aircraft consists of a combination of spoilers and ailerons that are mixed in their use according to the speed regime in which the aircraft is flying. (See the section on high-lift systems in chapter 10.) The spoilers are also used for reducing the stopping distance of the aircraft on landing and for rapid descents in flight. Descent rates of as high as 15 000 feet per minute can be achieved by deployment of the spoilers and the use of reverse engine thrust.

417

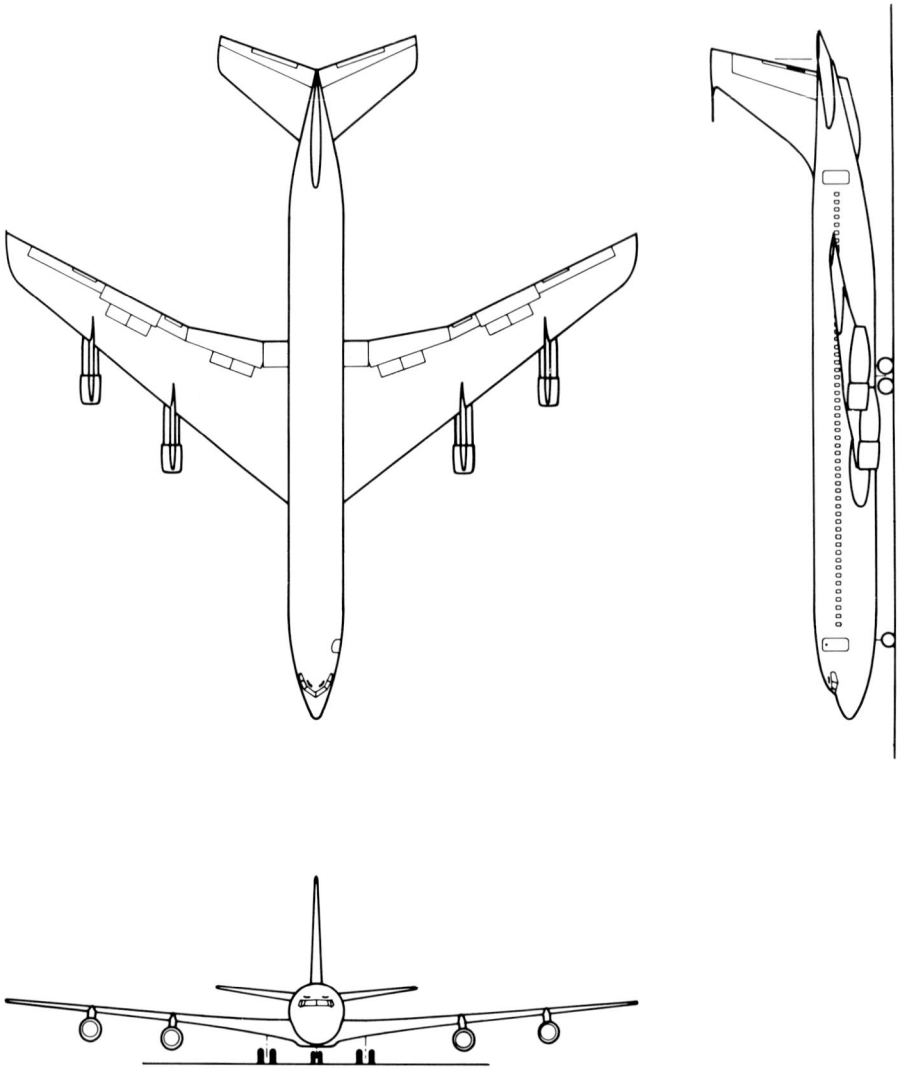

Figure 13.7 — Three-view drawing of Boeing 707–320B airliner. [mfr]

The elevators and ailerons are aerodynamically balanced and are manually operated by aerodynamic servotabs. In this type of control system, the pilot's primary flight controls deflect tabs on the main control surfaces. The hinge moment of the control surface is altered by deflection of the tab, and, consequently, the floating angle of the surface is altered. This change in angle of the main surface provides the necessary control moments for the aircraft. The spoilers and rudder on the 707 aircraft are operated hydraulically. Small changes in longitudinal trim are made with the use of trim tabs on the elevators. Large changes in trim, such as those caused by flap deflection, are balanced by adjusting the angle of the horizontal stabilizer. Movement of this surface is power actuated.

The gross weight of the Boeing 707-320B is 336 000 pounds, nearly three times the weight of the Comet 1A. The cabin can be configured to carry a mix of first-class and tourist-class passengers or an all-tourist arrangement. In the all-tourist configuration, 189 passengers can be accommodated. With a maximum payload of 53 900 pounds, the aircraft has a range, without reserves, of 6240 miles; with full fuel tanks and a payload of 33 350 pounds, the range is 7975 miles. With this range capability, the aircraft is capable of connecting many of the important population centers of the world. The aircraft has a maximum cruising speed of 593 miles per hour at 30 000 feet and a cost-economical cruising speed of 550 miles per hour at 35 000 feet; the corresponding cruising Mach numbers are 0.87 and 0.83, respectively. The takeoff field length on a standard day is a relatively long 10 000 feet, which can be directly related to the low thrust loading of 0.23 and the high wing loading of 111.6 pounds per square foot. (See chapter 3 of ref. 176.)

By any measure, the 707 series of aircraft must be ranked as one of the most successful transports ever produced. The present fleet of aircraft will no doubt fly on for many years in different parts of the world. Concluding this brief discussion of the Boeing 707 is the presentation in figure 13.8 of one of the Boeing 707 aircraft used by the President of the United States — perhaps one of the best-known aircraft in the world.

McDonnell Douglas DC-8 and Other Four-Engine Transports

The second long-range, high-passenger-capacity transport that, along with the Boeing 707, initiated the jet revolution in air transportation was the McDonnell Douglas DC-8 (originally the Douglas DC-8). This aircraft was ordered by Pan American World Airlines in 1955, and first flight was made in 1958. The aircraft entered airline service in August 1959. The DC-8 was built in many different versions; one of the principal modifications incorporated in the aircraft was a stretched fuselage to provide increased passenger capacity. Over 550 DC-8 aircraft were built before production was terminated in 1972.

In most essential respects, the basic configuration of the McDonnell Douglas DC-8 is the same as that of the Boeing 707. Early versions of the two aircraft were virtually indistinguishable except to

Figure 13.8 — Boeing 707 used by the President of the United States. [mfr]

someone very familiar with them. There were, of course, many differences in the detailed aerodynamic and structural design and in the systems employed on the aircraft. The McDonnell Douglas DC–8 Super 63 is shown in figures 13.9 and 13.10, and some of the characteristics of the aircraft are given in table VII. As compared with earlier versions of the DC–8, the fuselage of the Super 63 has been stretched by the addition of a 20-foot section ahead of the wing and a 17.8-foot section aft of the wing. Also, the wing span of the aircraft has been increased 6 feet over that of the original DC–8. The wing and engine locations are similar to those used on the 707; however, the aspect ratio and sweepback angle are slightly different. The main landing gear consists of two struts to which are mounted four-wheel bogies; the two rear wheels of each bogie can be put in a free swiveling mode to assist in making sharp turns on the ground. The main landing gear is mounted on the wing and retracts inward into the fuselage. The two-wheel nose gear retracts in a forward direction.

420

Figure 13.9 — McDonnell Douglas DC–8 Super 63 airliner. [mfr]

Figure 13.10 — Underneath view of McDonnell Douglas DC–8 Super 63 airliner. [mfr]

The aerodynamic efficiency of the DC–8 is indicated by the maximum value of the lift-drag ratio, which is estimated to be about 17.9. The value of $(L/D)_{max}$ is lower for the DC–8 Super 63 than for the 707 because of the DC–8's longer fuselage and consequently increased ratio of wetted area to wing area. The relationship between wetted area,

421

wing area, and $(L/D)_{max}$ is discussed in chapter 3 of reference 176. The loss in aerodynamic efficiency associated with the long fuselage is more than compensated by the increased passenger-carrying capacity and consequent reduction in direct operating costs per seat mile.

The wing is equipped with trailing-edge double-slotted flaps and slats over the inboard sections of the leading edge. These high-lift devices provide a lift coefficient that gives a stalling speed of 123 miles per hour at the maximum landing wing loading. The maximum landing wing loading is somewhat less than the value given in table VII, which is for maximum takeoff gross weight. The lateral control system consists of inboard and outboard ailerons that are connected by a torque tube that acts as a torsion spring. The inboard sections are power operated. The outboard sections only operate at the lower values of the dynamic pressure where they are needed. As the dynamic pressure increases, the aerodynamic resisting moment of the aileron becomes greater in relation to the torque that can be transmitted through the torsion bar; hence, the aileron deflection is reduced. The amount of deflection of the outboard aileron varies smoothly with variation in dynamic pressure and, therefore, provides the desired variation of aerodynamic control moment with speed and altitude. The rudder is also power operated. Both the rudder and the ailerons have a manual reversion mode in the form of aerodynamic servotabs. Elevator control is manual and makes use of an aerodynamic servotab. The variable-incidence horizontal tail is power operated and is used for longitudinal trim. Wing spoilers are automatically deployed on landing by nose-wheel contact with the runway.

The gross weight of the DC-8 Super 63 is 358 000 pounds; in an all-tourist configuration, the aircraft seats 259 passengers in a 6-abreast arrangement. With a maximum payload of 67 735 pounds, the range is 4882 miles; and with maximum fuel, a payload of 37 101 pounds can be carried for a distance of 6997 miles. As can be seen in table VII, the cruising speeds of the DC-8 are about the same as those of the 707.

Recently, a number of DC-8 aircraft have been retrofitted with modern CFM-56 high-bypass-ratio turbofan engines. Manufactured by GE Snecma, these engines have 22 000 pounds thrust and a bypass ratio of 6.0. The modified aircraft are designated DC-8-71, DC-8-72, and DC-8-73 depending upon the 60-series aircraft from which they were derived. Improved performance and economy together with reduced noise are advantages resulting from installation of the new engines. Characteristics of these modified aircraft may be found in reference 150. With retrofit of the new engines, the DC-8 has indeed received a new lease on life. Along with the 707, the DC-8 has been a workhorse of great productivity for many years; and although out of production, it will continue to be operated for a long time to come.

Two other aircraft of this first generation of large jet transports are nearly the same in configuration as the Boeing 707 and the McDonnell Douglas DC-8. In fact, when seen at the airport, the Convair 880 and 990 are often confused with one or the other of the more familiar 707 or DC-8 aircraft. The Convair 880 first flew in 1959, and the first flight of the more advanced Convair 990 was in 1961. The maximum cruising Mach number of the 990 is 0.89, which is the highest of any of the subsonic jet transports. The high cruising Mach number of the aircraft is due in part to the Whitcomb bumps on the trailing edge of the wing. The two pods mounted on each wing at the trailing edge make the aircraft readily identifiable and are used to increase the critical Mach number as well as to augment fuel volume.

Both the 880 and the 990 are somewhat smaller and lighter in weight than are the 707 and the DC-8. The gross weight of the 880 is 192 700 pounds and that of the 990 is 253 000 pounds. The range of neither aircraft is really intercontinental, and the payloads are lower than those of the Boeing and Douglas aircraft. For these reasons, perhaps, and because both aircraft became available to the airlines somewhat later than the 707 and the DC-8, only a relatively small number of Convair jet transports were built. Total production of the 880 was 65, and 37 examples of the 990 were built. At this time, neither type is used in scheduled airline service in the United States.

Sud-Aviation Caravelle

The French Sud-Aviation Caravelle was the first really successful short-range jet transport to be developed in the western world. First flight of the prototype took place in May 1955, and the aircraft entered airline service in Europe in April 1959. As with most successful jet transports, the Caravelle was produced in a number of versions; a total of 280 aircraft of all versions were produced before production was terminated in the early 1970's. Many are still in operation in various parts of the world. A Sud-Aviation Caravelle model V1 is depicted in figure 13.11. The aircraft shown carries the markings of United Airlines, which operated a fleet of 20 Caravelles for a number of years. Characteristics of the Caravelle V1-R are given in table VII.

The primary technical significance of the Caravelle was its pioneering use of an entirely new and innovative approach in the integration

Figure 13.11 — Sud-Aviation Caravelle short-range airliner. [United Air Lines]

of the engines and airframe. Figure 13.11 shows that one of the two engines is mounted on either side at the aft end of the fuselage. This engine arrangement set the pattern for many future jet transport aircraft of two , three , and four engine design. When the engine location proposed for the Caravelle was first made known, many engineers expressed doubts about the practicality of such an arrangement. For example, questions were raised about the operation of the engines in the wake of the wing as the aircraft approached a stalled condition, or the effect on engine operation of large angles of sideslip. The aft-engine location, however, has proved to be highly workable. Some advantages and disadvantages of this aft-engine arrangement are as follows:

(1) The short lateral distance between the engines results in relatively small yawing moments following the loss of an engine. The required vertical-tail size is accordingly reduced as compared with that of an aircraft with wing-mounted engines, such as the Boeing 707.

(2) The rear location of the engines results in a relatively low engine-noise level through most of the cabin.

(3) Removal of the engines from the wing results in a small in-

crease in the maximum lift coefficient and elimination of wing-pylon-nacelle interference drag. The integration of the engines at the aft end of the fuselage, however, requires careful design in order to minimize interference drag in this area.

(4) The location of the engines at the aft end of the fuselage, as compared with the underwing position, reduces the problem of interference between the engines and the ground, a problem that becomes particularly important as the size of the aircraft is reduced.

(5) Mounting the engines on either side of the aft portion of the fuselage prevents location of the horizontal tail in a low position. In the case of the Caravelle and a number of other aircraft, the tail is mounted at some location between the root and tip of the vertical-tail surface. Other aircraft utilize the T-tail position in which the horizontal tail is mounted at the tip of the vertical surface. The use of a high tail position offers several advantages: If the vertical tail is swept back, the horizontal-tail moment arm is increased as the tail is moved toward the tip of the vertical surface. The horizontal-tail size, and hence the weight of the tail, may therefore be reduced for a given level of static longitudinal stability. In the T-tail arrangement, the horizontal tail acts as an end plate and reduces the required size of the vertical surface for a given level of static directional stability. Again, a reduction in tail weight may be realized. Structural and aeroelastic problems may, however, cause some increases in weight of the vertical tail. Whether the overall empennage weight is reduced by the use of the T-tail arrangement, as compared with the more conventional low tail position, however, is debatable and depends on the detailed design requirements of the particular aircraft.

(6) The high tail position also has some disadvantages. A brief qualitative discussion of the influence of horizontal-tail position on the static longitudinal stability of swept-wing aircraft is given in chapter 10. As indicated there, certain inherent aerodynamic problems are encountered in the design of an aircraft with a high tail location. Careful attention to the detail design of such a configuration is required in order to achieve reasonably acceptable longitudinal aerodynamic characteristics. Lack of proper care in the design process can

425

result in an aircraft with highly undesirable longitudinal aerodynamic characteristics.

(7) The rear engine location results in large concentrated
weights that are a long distance behind the aircraft center of
gravity. This arrangement, therefore, causes some problems
in balancing the aircraft in certain loading configurations.
However, these balance problems have been overcome in a
large number of highly successful aircraft that employ the
aft-engine arrangement.

Other than the engine arrangement, the Caravelle's configuration
is conventional, with the 20° swept wing of aspect ratio 8 mounted in
the low position on the fuselage. Two large fences can be seen on each
wing in figure 13.11. These fences are intended to control the spanwise
flow of the boundary layer on the swept wing and thus improve the
stalling characteristics of the aircraft. The wing-pylon-engine arrangement on the 707-type configuration serves the same purpose. The
high-lift system consists of trailing-edge Fowler flaps. Large airbrakes
are mounted ahead of the flaps on the top and bottom surfaces of the
wing. All the flying controls are hydraulically actuated. The aircraft is
powered with two Rolls-Royce Avon turbojet engines of 12 000 pounds
of sea-level static thrust.

A study of the characteristics of the Caravelle given in table VII
indicates that the gross weight of the aircraft is a relatively light
114 640 pounds, even lighter than the Comet, and that it is capable of
a range of 1829 miles with a maximum payload of 16 800 pounds.
Eighty passengers can be accommodated in a five-abreast configuration. The cost-economical cruising speed of 488 miles per hour at
35 000 feet is somewhat lower than the 550 miles per hour given in the
table for the Boeing 707. The lower cruising speed of the Caravelle
would be expected in a short-range airplane and explains the low
sweepback angle of the wing. The relatively short landing and takeoff
field lengths indicate that it was designed to operate from the many
small airports appropriate to a short- or medium-range airliner. Again,
a wing of low sweepback angle is desirable. A highly successful short-
range jet transport, the Caravelle's place in the history of aeronautical
development is secure as a result of its pioneering use of the aft-fuselage-engine location.

Second-Generation Transports

The second-generation jet transports are considered to be those which first flew in prototype form in the 1960's. The following 11 aircraft constitute the second-generation jet transports:

Country	Manufacturer	Model	First flight [a]	Engines
United States	Boeing	727	1963	3
United States	McDonnell Douglas	DC–9	1965	2
United States	Boeing	737	1967	2
United Kingdom	British Aircraft Corporation	1–11	1963	2
United Kingdom	Hawker Siddley	Trident	1962	3
United Kingdom	British Aircraft Corporation	VC–10	1962	4
Netherlands	Fokker	F–28	1967	2
U.S.S.R.	Tupolev	Tu–134	1964	2
U.S.S.R.	Tupolev	Tu–154	1968	3
U.S.S.R.	Ilyushin	Il–62	1963	4
U.S.S.R.	Yakolev	Yak–40	1966	3

[a] First flight dates are for prototype of first version.

Most of the aircraft listed are representative of about the same level of technology and have no large state-of-the-art advances over the first-generation jet transports previously discussed. All the aircraft are equipped with turbofan engines of relatively low bypass ratio that are of about the same level of technical sophistication as the fan engines that powered the first-generation transports. Basically, with a few evolutionary refinements, the second-generation aircraft represent an application of the technology developed in the first-generation aircraft to transports specifically tailored to various types of airline route structures and payload requirements. All the aircraft, except the Boeing 737, employ aft-fuselage-mounted engines in either two- , three- , or four-engine configurations. Four of the aircraft are briefly described in the following paragraphs; they are the three-engine Boeing 727, the twin-engine McDonnell Douglas DC–9, the twin-engine Boeing 737, and the four-engine British Aircraft Corporation VC 10.

Boeing 727

By any standard, the three-engine Boeing 727 must be considered the most successful jet transport aircraft yet produced. The prototype first flew in 1963, and the type was introduced into service by Eastern Airlines in early 1964. Total orders to mid-1982 numbered 1825, with

427

the aircraft being produced at the rate of 2 per month.[1] The 727 is operated all over the world by some 85 airlines; it is rarely possible to visit a domestic airport served by a scheduled airline without seeing a Boeing 727 during the course of a day. The 727 is popular with the airlines primarily because it can be operated profitably over range segments of various lengths and passenger-load requirements, and its relatively short field capability permits operation from a large number of airports too small to accommodate 707 class aircraft. Many studies were made over the years in an effort to find a replacement for the ubiquitous Douglas DC-3; though with different range and payload characteristics, and with different field length and cruising speed capabilities, the 727 may be considered as the modern-day counterpart of the DC-3 that first appeared in 1935.

The aircraft was first produced as the 727-100, and a later stretched version designated the 727-200 was introduced. Of the 1825 aircraft so far ordered, over 1300 have been for the 727-200, which is the only version now in production. The aircraft is produced in both passenger and convertible cargo-passenger configurations. A 727-200 in American Airlines markings is shown in figure 13.12, and the characteristics of this version of the aircraft are given in table VII.

The choice of three engines for the 727 was dictated by a compromise between cost and airport performance. For operation on hot days from airports located at high altitudes, the three-engine arrangement

---

[1] The last Boeing 727, a cargo version, will be delivered in August 1984; the total number of 727 aircraft produced will be 1832.

Figure 13.12 — Boeing 727–200 medium-range airliner. [mfr]

428

offered significantly better takeoff and climb performance with one engine out than was practical for an efficient twin-engine design, but at a great deal lower cost than for a four-engine aircraft. An interesting discussion of this trade-off, as well as other aspects of the design and development of the 727, is contained in reference 145.

The most distinguishing recognition feature of the 727 is probably the mounting of the three engines, which are located at the aft end of the fuselage. The inlet for the center engine is on top of the fuselage ahead of the vertical tail. The engine itself, however, is located in the fuselage in the same horizontal plane as the two outboard engines and exhausts through the tail end of the fuselage. Placement of the three engines in this way simplifies maintenance and servicing and allows a high degree of commonality in ground-support equipment. This arrangement, however, necessitates the use of an S-shaped duct to deliver air from the upper-fuselage-mounted inlet to the front face of the center engine. The design of inlet and duct for the center engine requires careful attention if unacceptable internal aerodynamic losses are to be avoided. The advantages and disadvantages of the aft-fuselage-engine location have been discussed in connection with the twin-engine Caravelle and apply equally well to a three-engine design like the 727. Arrangement of nacelles and exhaust nozzles are shown in the rear vew of a 727–100 presented in figure 13.13. Also note the rear-loading stair. Flight tests of a rear-fuselage-mounted engine were made on the Boeing 367–80 to prove acceptable engine operation with the wing in a stalled condition. This test arrangement is shown in figure 13.14.

Power for the 727–200 is supplied by Pratt & Whitney JT8D–17 engines of 16 000 pounds thrust each. These engines, which have a bypass ratio of 1.06, have probably been used to power more jet transport aircraft than any other engine.

The 727–200 is seen from figure 13.12 to be a low-wing design; according to the data given in table VII, the wing planform geometry is similar to that of the 707. The engine arrangement results in a horizontal tail mounted at the tip of the vertical fin in a T-tail configuration. Some of the advantages and disadvantages of this arrangement are briefly discussed in chapter 10 as well as in this chapter in connection with the Sud-Aviation Caravelle. The lateral and longitudinal control surfaces are of the same type as those employed on the 707. In contrast to the 707, however, all the controls on the 727 are hydraulically actuated. In order to allow operation from airports of medium size, the 727 is equipped with very powerful high-lift devices. The trail-

Figure 13.13 — Rear view of Boeing 727 airliner. [mfr]

ing edge of the wing has triple-slotted flaps of the type shown schematically in figure 10.25(a) and illustrated in figures 10.26 and 10.27. The leading edge has a slat on the outboard two-thirds of the span and Krueger flaps on the inboard portion of the wing. With these high-lift devices, a stalling speed of 121 miles per hour is obtained at the maximum landing weight of 160 000 pounds. The main landing gear employs two-wheel bogies instead of the four-wheel type used on the 707. The gear retracts inward into the wing at the root. The leading- and trailing-edge high-lift devices are shown in the takeoff position in figure 13.15. Also note the large negative deflection of the horizontal tail and the flame trailing from the tail skid as it drags along the runway. The dramatic high-angle-of-attack takeoff illustrated in figure 13.15 was made for test purposes and is not typical of normal operating practice.

The Boeing 727–200 has a gross weight of 210 000 pounds and in full tourist configuration can accommodate 189 passengers in a 6-abreast arrangement. The upper fuselage diameter of the aircraft is the

Figure 13.14 — Fuselage-mounted engine under test on Boeing 367–80. [mfr]

Figure 13.15 — Takeoff test of a Boeing 727–100 at maximum rotation angle. [mfr]

same as that of the 707 and the shorter range Boeing 737. Thus, to the passenger, all three aircraft appear to have the same cabin size except for length. The 727–200 is capable of a maximum range of 3738 miles with full fuel tanks; with maximum payload, it has a range of 3335 miles. The cruising speeds of the aircraft are comparable to those of the 707 and the DC–8.

McDonnell Douglas DC-9

The twin-engine McDonnell Douglas DC-9, in its many versions, generally has a smaller passenger capacity, shorter range, and shorter field length capability than the Boeing 727. It has been produced in six major versions and is now in operation on airlines all over the world. The six versions now in operation vary in (1) passenger capacity from 90 to 172, (2) length from 104 to 147 feet, and (3) gross weight from 80 000 to 148 000 pounds. Perhaps more than any other aircraft type, the DC-9 represents an entire family of aircraft. The prototype of the DC-9 first flew in February 1965, and nearly 1100 examples have been produced to date. The type is still in production at the rate of four or five per month, and it seems destined to roll off the production lines for several more years to come.

The DC-9-30, one of the most numerous versions of the aircraft, is illustrated in figure 13.16 in the Royal Dutch Airlines livery, and some of the characteristics of this aircraft are presented in table VII. Basic configuration of the aircraft is similar to that of the Caravelle in that the two engines are mounted in the aft-fuselage position. The T-tail arrangement employed by the DC-9, however, is different from that of the Caravelle. The engines that power the aircraft are the same basic Pratt & Whitney JT8D turbofans as are employed on the Boeing 727. For this particular version of the DC-9-30, the two engines have 15 500 pounds of thrust each.

The sweptback wing of the DC-9 has a somewhat smaller sweep angle than that of the 727, and the cruising speeds given in table VII

Figure 13.16 — McDonnell Douglas DC-9 twin-engine short-range airliner. [mfr]

for the aircraft are correspondingly lower than those of the 727. As pointed out in the discussion of the Caravelle, the lower cruising speed of the DC-9 results from tailoring the characteristics of the aircraft to the relatively short range segments and small airports for which it was intended. The high-lift system on most versions of the DC-9 consists of trailing-edge double-slotted flaps and leading-edge slats (the DC-9-10 had no slats). The lateral control system utilizes inboard and outboard ailerons, with the outboard ailerons being used only at low speeds as in the DC-8. Speed brakes are mounted on the upper surface of the wing. With the exception of the elevators, all the control surfaces are hydraulically actuated. As in the DC-8, the elevators of the DC-9 are manually controlled through aerodynamic servotabs.

The gross weight of the DC-9-30 is 109 000 pounds, which is about half that of the 727-200, and the 115 tourist-class passengers are seated in a 5-abreast configuration. The higher thrust loading and lower wing loading of the DC-9, as compared with the 727, result in a much lower takeoff field length for the Douglas aircraft; the landing field lengths for the two aircraft, however, are about the same. The range at maximum payload for the DC-9-30 is 1812 miles, which is about half that of the Boeing 727. Clearly, the DC-9 and 727 are intended for different types of airline-route structures and passenger-load requirements. Both highly successful aircraft complement each other in airline operation, and both seem destined to fly on together for many years.

Boeing 737

The twin-engine Boeing 737 was developed as a direct competitor of the McDonnell Douglas DC-9 but did not fly until about 2 years after the latter's introduction. The 737 has been produced in two versions, the 737-100 and the 737-200. Except for 30 units, all the aircraft produced have been the 737-200 version, which is a stretched, higher capacity, and heavier aircraft than the 737-100. The total number of orders for the 737 was 978 by mid-1982, and the type is currently being manufactured at the rate of 8 per month (ref. 150).

A Boeing 737-200 in United Airlines' markings is shown in figure 13.17, and some of the characteristics of the aircraft are given in table VII. The two engines are mounted under the wings in a manner similar to that of the 707. The proximity of the engine nacelles to the under surface of the wing highlights the problem, previously mentioned, incurred by the underwing engine location as the size of the aircraft is reduced. The desire to avoid a high-mounted horizontal tail, and its

433

Figure 13.17 — Boeing 737–200 twin-engine short-range airliner showing underwing location of two engines. [mfr]

possible stability problems, apparently was largely responsible for the choice of this engine location instead of the aft-fuselage-mounted arrangement. As figure 13.17 shows, the horizontal tail is located on the fuselage below the root of the vertical tail. The 737 uses basically the same Pratt & Whitney engines as those employed on the Boeing 727 and the McDonnell Douglas DC–9.

The 737 fuselage appears short and stubby, due to its large upper-fuselage diameter, which is the same as for the 707 and the 727, and its short length, which is less than for the 707 or the 727. The higher fineness ratio fuselage and greater length of the DC–9 results from the use of a five-abreast seating arrangement and consequent smaller fuselage diameter. The short fuselage length of the 737 along with the wide lateral separation of the underwing-mounted engines result in the large vertical tail on the aircraft.

The geometry of the 737 wing is very similar to that of the DC–9 as is shown by the data in table VII. The high-lift and control systems of the 737 are like those described for the 727.

An examination of the data in table VII for the 737–200 and the DC–9–30 shows a close similarity in the size, weight, and performance of the two aircraft. This similarity would be expected since they were designed for similar operations. The major difference in performance of the two aircraft is the longer range of the 737 with full fuel tanks.

A major new derivative of the Boeing 737 is under development and scheduled for initial deliveries late in 1984. Designated the 737–300, the new aircraft will be a stretched, heavier variant of the 737–200 powered with the GE Snecma CFM turbofan engines of 20 000 pounds thrust and bypass ratio of 6.0. Lower seat-per-mile costs and reduced noise are among the advantages offered by the improved aircraft.

British Aircraft Corporation VC–10

Two long-range, four-engine, heavy jet transports were developed in the 1960's. These were the British VC–10 developed by Vickers Armstrongs, which later was absorbed into the British Aircraft Corporation, and the Soviet Ilyushin Il–62. The two aircraft closely resemble each other in configuration and employ an engine arrangement different from any existing four-engine jet transport. On each aircraft, the four engines are mounted at the aft end of the fuselage, two on either side, in a four-engine adaptation of the twin aft-engine configuration pioneered by the Caravelle. Both aircraft weigh over 300 000 pounds, and both were designed for long-range operation.

The VC–10 was developed in response to a requirement of the overseas division of British Airways, formerly the British Overseas Airways Corporation (BOAC), for use on its long-range routes to Africa, India, and Australia. First flight took place in June 1962, and the type entered service with BOAC in April 1964. Production of the aircraft was terminated in 1974 after 54 units were manufactured.

The VC–10 is shown in figure 13.18, and some of the characteristics of the aircraft are given in table VII. The four aft-mounted engines are, of course, the most distinctive feature of the configuration. The power is supplied by Rolls-Royce Conway turbofan engines of 21 000 pounds thrust each. These engines have a bypass ratio of 0.6 and employ a four-stage front-mounted fan.

Like all aircraft that employ the aft-mounted engine arrangement, the wing of the VC–10 appears quite clean and uncluttered. The sweepback angle is 32.5°, and the aspect ratio is 6.9. Although the sweep angle is slightly less than that of the Boeing 707, the wing-planform geometry employed on the two aircraft is nearly the same. The high-lift system consists of trailing-edge Fowler flaps, which are similar to the double-slotted flap shown in figure 10.25(b) with the small middle element removed, and leading-edge slats. Three leading-edge fences are employed on each wing, as can be seen in figure 13.18. Lateral control is provided by a combination of ailerons and spoilers. The

Figure 13.18 — British Aircraft Corporation VC–10 four-engine long-range airliner. (Note engine arrangement.) [Flt. lntl.]

spoilers are also used as air brakes and can be seen deployed as such in figure 13.18. All control surfaces are hydraulically actuated.

A comparison of the performance data of the VC–10 and the Boeing 707–320B given in table VII indicates that the maximum payload and corresponding range are significantly less than those of the Boeing 707–320B. The cost-economical cruising speeds of the two aircraft are also about the same; however, the maximum cruising speed of the 707 is somewhat higher than that of the VC–10. Many of the airports served by British Airways are located in tropical or subtropical areas characterized by high temperatures. Such temperatures increase the ground speed required for takeoff and reduce the maximum thrust produced by the engines. The VC–10 was accordingly designed to cope with these difficult takeoff conditions that, in some cases, were aggravated by airport elevations considerably above sea level. As a consequence, the takeoff field length for "standard day" conditions given in table VII is about 2000 feet shorter for the VC–10 than for the 707.

The VC–10 is no longer in airline service, but a few are in the Royal Air Force inventory. The economics of the aircraft apparently could not compete successfully with those of the Boeing 707 and the McDonnell Douglas DC–8; hence, the VC–10 enjoyed a relatively limited production run. The Soviet Il–62, counterpart of the VC–10, is still in production and is widely used on Aeroflot's long-range routes. According to reference 150, about 190 of these aircraft have been constructed.

Wide-Body Transports

Four families of aircraft make up the fleet of wide-body transports that began operation on airlines throughout the world in the 1970's. These aircraft are the Boeing 747, the McDonnell Douglas DC–10, and the Lockheed L–1011, which are manufactured in the United States, and the Airbus A–300, which is produced by a consortium of European countries. All aircraft are still in production,[2] and all are expected to continue in service for the foreseeable future. In addition to these aircraft, the Soviet Union has developed a large four-engine wide-body transport. This aircraft, the Ilyushin 86, first flew on December 22, 1976, and airline operations began in 1980.

The use of the term "wide body" in describing these aircraft is derived from the interior arrangement of the passenger cabin. Consider first the arrangement of the cabin of a "narrow-body" transport such as the 707 or 727, as shown in figure 13.19. The cabin is divided into a small first-class compartment with four-abreast seating and a large tourist-class cabin with six-abreast seating. A single aisle runs the entire length of the cabin with three seats located on either side. For an aircraft of large passenger capacity, the fuselage of the narrow-body type tends to become very long, which, in turn, may dictate a long, heavy landing gear in order to permit the desired rotation angle on takeoff without scraping the rear end of the fuselage on the runway. The long aisle also causes lengthy delays in passenger loading and difficulty for the cabin attendants in serving meals and refreshments.

A schematic drawing of the interior cabin arrangement of a conceptual wide-body transport is shown in figure 13.20. The first-class cabin consists of a small four-abreast compartment in the forward part of the fuselage and a large seven-abreast tourist cabin. The tourist cabin is divided by two longitudinal aisles that run the length of the cabin. In the particular arrangement shown, two seats are located on either side of the aircraft next to the windows, and three seats are disposed about the centerline of the cabin with an aisle on either side.

---

[2]Lockheed L–1011 production has now ended.

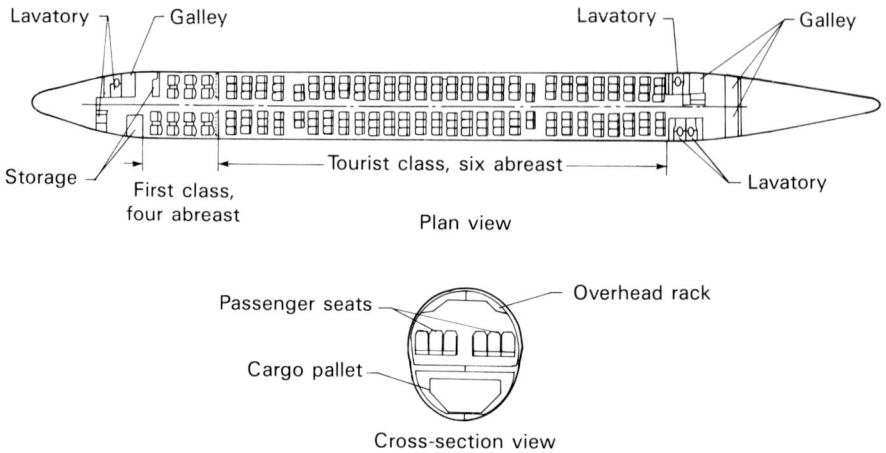

Figure 13.19 — Interior arrangement of narrow-body, single-aisle jet transport aircraft.

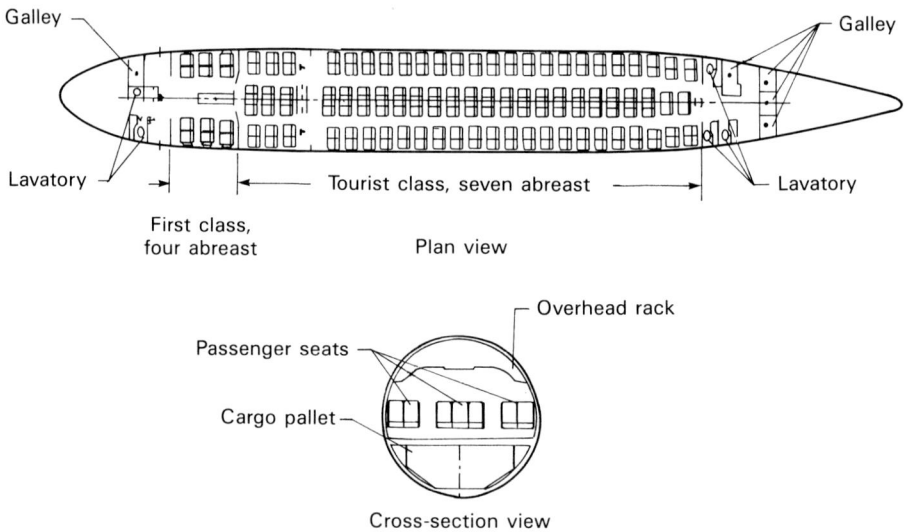

Figure 13.20 — Interior arrangement of wide-body, double-aisle jet transport aircraft.

Some wide-body aircraft are designed to accommodate as many as 10-abreast seats. Current high-density versions of the Boeing 747, for example, may seat as many as 550 passengers in a 10-abreast arrangement.

For large-capacity aircraft, the double-aisle arrangement offers easy passenger loading and simplifies the serving problem for the cabin attendents. The design may also offer the passenger somewhat wider seats and a feeling of greater spaciousness. The landing-gear problem previously referred to is alleviated by the relatively short fuselage offered by the wide-body design for a given passenger capacity.

The large-diameter fuselage of the wide-body aircraft is often cited as a source of increased skin friction drag. The bulky appearance of these aircraft is no doubt responsible for this viewpoint. Actually, the ratio of wetted area to wing area for wide- and narrow-body aircraft of the same passenger capacity and wing loading may not be greatly different because of the shorter length of the wide-body aircraft. The trade-offs between fuselage length and diameter can be assessed with the use of figure 3.11 in reference 176.

The wide-body jet transports introduced in the 1970's are characterized by two other distinguishing features. First, these aircraft are very large in comparison with earlier jet transports. For example, one version of the Boeing 747, the largest of the wide-body aircraft, is certified at a maximum takeoff gross weight in excess of 800 000 pounds. Although the wide-body concept was originally applied only to very large aircraft, new designs for use in the 1980's utilize the wide-body concept in aircraft of the 707 weight category.

A second distinguishing feature of the wide-body transports is the type of engines used to power them. All the aircraft are powered by very large engines of high bypass ratio. Because of the high bypass ratio and high compressor pressure ratio of these engines, the values of their cruise-specific fuel consumption are about 20 percent lower than earlier low-bypass-ratio engines such as the Pratt & Whitney JT3D. Another outstanding feature of these engines is their relatively low noise levels, as compared with earlier engines, even though the thrust produced by the new engines is significantly higher than values typical of the earlier ones. The low-noise-level characteristic of the high-bypass-ratio engines results from an improved understanding of the mechanism of noise generation, as influenced by engine design, and through the use of new sound-absorbing materials in various parts of the inlets and other flow passages. (See the section on engine noise in chapter 10.)

Three families of modern, large, high-bypass-ratio turbofan engines are the Pratt & Whitney JT9D, the General Electric CF6, and the Rolls-Royce RB.211. Each of these engines is produced in a number of variants with different capabilities. The maximum takeoff thrust of the various versions lies in the range from 45 000 to 55 000 pounds. The bypass ratios of the engines are 5:1 for the Pratt & Whitney JT9D, 5.9:1 and 4.4:1 for the General Electric CF6, and 4.4:1 for the Rolls-Royce RB.211. As indicated, the CF6 engine is available with two different bypass ratios. The compressor pressure ratios of the different engines fall in the range from 24:1 to 30:1. Detailed information on the various versions of the engines may be found in references 130 and 199.

In other respects, the wide-body aircraft, as compared with earlier jet transports, have only evolutionally technical refinements. The widespread use of sophisticated, high-speed computational equipment has resulted in more refined aerodynamic and structural design and in improved machine control in manufacturing. As a result of more sophisticated analysis techniques and new developments in transonic aerodynamics, some improvements may be found in wing and airfoil design. Basically, however, the aerodynamic design of the wide-body aircraft is similar to the preceding generation of aircraft. Again, in the area of structural design, no radical innovations are to be found. All the aircraft use fully powered flight control systems, and all employ sophisticated autopilots and other onboard systems.

The combination of large passenger capacity, more efficient and quieter engines, and more sophisticated detail design has resulted in transport aircraft that are safe, reliable, environmentally acceptable, and, from the airlines' viewpoint, profitable. From the passengers' viewpoint, the aircraft are fast, convenient, and relatively comfortable, and they offer reasonable fares.

As discussed, most jet transport aircraft actually consist of a series of aircraft of varying characteristics that evolve from a single basic design. Each variant of the series has characteristics that are intended to adapt the aircraft to a particular set of operating requirements. The wide-body transports also follow this trend, and the generic aircraft type of each manufacturer actually represents an entire family of aircraft. In the following, a brief description of a representative model of the Boeing 747, the McDonnell Douglas DC–10, and the Lockheed L–1011 is given. Descriptions of the various versions of the different aircraft may be found in references 129, 130, 150, and 161.

Boeing 747

The first of the wide-body turbofan-powered transports to enter airline service was the Boeing 747. Design work on the aircraft was initiated in the 1960's, and the first details were announced in April 1966. Simultaneously, Pan American World Airways announced orders for 25 of the new aircraft. First flight took place in February 1969, and certification was completed by December of that year. The first passengers were carried on a flight from New York to London on January 22, 1970. The 747 aircraft is utilized by 32 operators throughout the world. Over 595 units have been ordered by mid-1982, and the type will likely remain in production for the foreseeable future.

A side view of a Boeing 747 in the livery of Pan American World Airways is shown in figure 13.21, and a front view of the aircraft in the landing configuration may be seen in figure 13.22. Some indication of the size of the 747 can be determined from figure 13.23, which shows a young boy standing beneath the nose of the aircraft. Some of the characteristics of the Boeing 747–200B are given in table VII.

The appearance of the four-engine 747 is very similar to that of its well-known ancestor, the Boeing 707. In addition to its large size, however, the 747 has two distinguishing features. First, the passenger cabin extends all the way to the forward end of the fuselage. The flight deck, with a small cabin behind it, is mounted on a second level and is reached by a circular stairway from the main cabin. This interior arrangement results in a distinctive hump in the external appearance of the top, forward end of the fuselage. A second distinguishing feature of the 747 is the main landing gear, which is unique for a passenger-carrying aircraft. The main gear consists of four struts, or posts, to which are attached four-wheel bogies. The two rear struts are mounted on the fuselage near the trailing edge of the wing and retract forward into the fuselage. The other two struts are mounted in the wing, farther forward, and retract inward into the wing. The four-post main gear is re-

Figure 13.21 — Boeing 747 wide-body transport. [mfr]

quired in order to properly distribute the massive weight of the aircraft on the runway. The aircraft shown in the approach configuration in figure 13.22 clearly shows the extended four-strut main gear as well as the nose gear that retracts forward into the fuselage.

The engines first offered on the 747 were the Pratt & Whitney JT9D turbofans. In addition to these engines, the aircraft is now certified with the General Electric CF6 and the Rolls-Royce RB.211 turbofans. The 747–200B, for which data are given in table VII, is powered with four JT9D–7R4G2 engines of 54 750 pounds thrust each.

The aerodynamic configuration of the 747 is very similar to that of the 707. The 747 wing has slightly more sweepback than that of the 707 and is of about the same aspect ratio. An improved airfoil design is also incorporated in the wing of the 747. The maximum lift-drag ratio of the aircraft, $(L/D)_{max}$, is estimated to be about 18, as compared with a value somewhat over 19 for the 707. The lower value of $(L/D)_{max}$ results from a higher value of ratio of wetted area to wing area on the 747 than on the 707.

The high-lift system employed on the 747 is typical of Boeing practice and consists of trailing-edge triple-slotted flaps, similar to those employed on the 727, and leading-edge flaps. The large trailing-edge flaps are clearly visible in figure 13.22. The lateral control system utilizes a combination of spoilers together with inboard and outboard ailerons. The spoilers are also used for lift and drag control when de-

Figure 13.22 — Boeing 747 in landing configuration. (Note four-post main landing gear and large flaps.) [mfr]

ployed symmetrically. The horizontal tail is located in the conventional low position at the rear of the fuselage. Longitudinal control is provided by an elevator and adjustable stabilizer trim system. No trim tabs are employed. All controls are fully powered.

The very large size of the Boeing 747 is the most striking feature of the aircraft. The gross weight of the 747–200B is seen from table VII to be 836 000 pounds, more than that of any other aircraft ever built. The Lockheed C–5A military cargo transport discussed below is the next largest aircraft at a weight of 769 000 pounds. The 747–200B can carry a maximum payload of 144 520 pounds for a distance of 6854 miles and has a cost-economical cruising speed of 564 miles per hour (Mach number of 0.85) at an altitude of approximately 35 000 feet. With a maximum fuel load and a reduced payload of 87 800 pounds, the range is 8706 miles. In a maximum capacity configuration, the aircraft can carry 550 passengers with 10-abreast seating. In this arrangement, four seats are placed in the middle of the aircraft, between the two aisles, and three seats are located against either side of the cabin. Many other seating arrangements for a smaller passenger load are used in the aircraft. The particular seating arrangement utilized is dictated by the airline using the aircraft and is based on the passenger density anticipated on the various routes served by the aircraft.

The Boeing 747 is available in 10 versions adapted to various airline needs. One major variant of the 747 is the 747SP (Special Performance), which is shown in figure 13.24 along with a standard-size 747. The 747SP is lighter and has a smaller fuselage and lower passenger capacity but has a longer range than any other version of the aircraft. Latest version of the 747 to fly is the 747–300, which has an upper deck extended by nearly 24 feet. Sixty-nine passengers can be carried in a six-abreast configuration in the upper deck of this aircraft and total capacity is 624. Overall size and gross weight are not altered by the extended upper deck. New and larger capacity variants of the aircraft will no doubt appear in the future. Currently, the Boeing 747 is considered to be one of the world's outstanding commercial aircraft; certainly, it is by far the largest.

Lockheed L–1011 and McDonnell Douglas DC–10

The Lockheed L–1011 and the McDonnell Douglas DC–10 are wide-body transports in a weight class between that of the 707 and the very heavy 747. Both aircraft are powered by three high-bypass-ratio turbofan engines located in a new configuration arrangement; one engine is mounted under each wing, and the third engine is mounted

Figure 13.23 — View of Boeing 747 indicating size of aircraft. [mfr]

Figure 13.24 — View of Boeing 747 and 747SP. [mfr]

Figure 13.25 — Lockheed L–1011 TriStar three-engine, wide-body transport showing arrangement of three engines. [mfr]

at the rear of the aircraft. The L–1011 and the DC–10 were initially designed to an airline requirement for a high-capacity transport with transcontinental range, but growth versions of each are presently available with intercontinental capability.

445

Initial flights of both aircraft occurred in 1970. An early version of the DC–10 entered airline operation in 1971, and the L–1011 began service in 1972. Both aircraft are in wide use throughout the world.

The Lockheed L–1011, also known as the TriStar, is shown in figure 13.25, and the McDonnell Douglas DC–10 is depicted in figure 13.26. Some of the characteristics of the two aircraft are given in table VII. The three-engine configuration employed on both aircraft is clearly shown. This arrangement, in which two of the engines are located near the aircraft center of gravity, offers an advantage in aircraft balance over an arrangement in which all three engines are mounted at the rear of the fuselage (Boeing 727, for example). Placement of two of the engines under the wing also allows the horizontal tail to be mounted in the highly desirable low position, as contrasted with the T-tail arrangement. The large lateral distance between the wing-mounted engines, however, causes larger yawing moments following loss of power of one of these engines as compared with a similar power loss in the rear-mounted engine arrangement.

The method of mounting the rear engine is seen to be quite different on the L–1011 and the DC–10. The L–1011 utilizes a mounting arrangement similar to that of the Boeing 727. The center engine is mounted in the aft end of the fuselage and is connected through an S-shaped duct to the large inlet mounted on top of the fuselage. In contrast, the center engine of the DC–10, including inlet and exhaust

Figure 13.26 — McDonnell Douglas DC–10 three-engine, wide-body transport. [mfr]

nozzle, is integrated with the fin above the fuselage. The improved engine efficiency resulting from this straight inlet-engine-nozzle config- uration, as compared with the S-shaped duct arrangement, was thought to more than offset the structural complexity (and probable weight in- crease) of integrating the engine with the fin. The high performance of both aircraft, however, suggests that either method of engine installa- tion can be made to operate successfully.

The Lockheed L-1011-200 is powered with three Rolls-Royce RB.211-524 engines of 48 000 pounds thrust each. The McDonnell Douglas DC-10-30 is powered by three General Electric CF6-50C1 en- gines of 52 500 pounds thrust each but is also available with a version of the Pratt & Whitney JT9D engines.

The main landing gear of the L-1011 has two struts to which are attached four-wheel bogies. Early versions of the DC-10 employed a similar arrangement. The heavier DC-10-30, however, employs a third strut, equipped with a two-wheel bogie mounted on the fuselage cen- terline between the other two main landing-gear struts. This arrange- ment helps to distribute the weight of the aircraft on the runway and thus keeps the runway-bearing stress within acceptable limits.

The aerodynamic design of both of the three-engine jet transports is conventional. The wings of both aircraft have about 35° of sweep- back with aspect ratios in the range of 7.0 to 7.5 and feature transonic airfoils of advanced design. The wings have double-slotted trailing- edge flaps and leading-edge slats. Lateral control is provided by a com- bination of ailerons and spoilers. The spoilers are also used to control lift and drag when deployed symmetrically. Longitudinal control of the L-1011 is provided by a variable incidence stabilizer to which the ele- vator is mechanically linked. The DC-10 employs separately actuated elevators and stabilizers. Neither aircraft employs longitudinal trim tabs. The maximum lift-drag ratio of the two aircraft is estimated to lie in the range between 17.0 and 17.5.

The data in table VII indicate that the L-1011-200 and the DC- 10-30 are very large aircraft. For example, at a gross weight of 468 000 pounds and with a maximum payload of 74 200 pounds, the L-1011- 200 is capable of flying for a distance of 4884 miles. With a maximum fuel load and a reduced payload of 42 827 pounds, the range is 6204 miles. The aircraft is capable of carrying 400 economy-class passengers in a 10-abreast double-aisle configuration. An interesting feature of the interior design of the L-1011 is the location of the galleys below the passenger deck; food service is provided to the passenger cabin by means of elevators.

The economical cruising speed of the L–1011 is 567 miles per hour at 31 000 feet, which corresponds to a Mach number of 0.84. The takeoff field length of 8070 feet is relatively short compared with 10 370 feet for the DC–10–30 and 10 450 feet for the 747. According to the data in table VII, the values of gross weight, payload weight, and range of the DC–10–30 are significantly larger than the corresponding values for the L–1011–200. A comparison of the values of the wing loading and thrust loading of the two aircraft clearly shows why the takeoff distance of the DC–10–30 is greater than that of the L–1011–200. Methods for rapid estimation of the takeoff distance are discussed in chapter 3 of reference 176. The cost-economical cruising speeds of the two aircraft are comparable.

Total orders for the DC–10 number 382, and it remains in production at the rate of 1 aircraft per month. Included in these figures are a small number of tanker versions of the aircraft for the USAF. These carry the Air Force designation of KC–10. Lockheed, however, has announced termination of the TriStar program after completion of aircraft number 250 in the fall of 1983.

New Transports of the 1980's

The year 1982 saw the introduction into airline service of an entirely new American-built jet transport, and a second new aircraft by the same manufacturer began service in 1983. Neither aircraft is of the "jumbo-jet" size such as discussed above. Both are designed to supplement and ultimately replace current transports in use on medium- and short-range stage lengths. In the design of both aircraft, increased fuel costs led to great emphasis on improved flight efficiency and careful matching of range-payload capabilities to specific airline needs. A few details of the two new aircraft are given below.

Boeing 767–200

With a first flight date in September 1981, the Boeing 767–200 entered airline service in the late summer of 1982. The aircraft is shown in figures 13.27 and 13.28, and physical and performance data for one version of the aircraft are given in table VII.

The Boeing 767–200 is a 290-passenger, double-aisle, wide-body airliner designed to replace the aging Boeing 707 and McDonnell Douglas DC–8 transports now used on domestic and foreign medium-range route segments. Average stage lengths over which the aircraft will be operated are estimated by Boeing to lie between 850 and 1150

Figure 13.27 — Rollout of Boeing 767-200 wide-body, twin-engine airliner. [mfr]

miles. Maximum range is, of course, much greater and includes a non-stop United States coast-to-coast capability; the twin-engine 767–200 is not intended for long over-ocean flights.

As can be seen in figures 13.27 and 13.28, configuration of the Boeing 767–200 is conventional with the wing located in the low position at the bottom of the fuselage and with one of the two engines pylon mounted beneath each wing. Location of the engines under the wing, rather than to the rear of the fuselage, allows the horizontal tail to be mounted in the low position. As discussed in chapter 10, a low tail position is helpful in minimizing pitching-moment nonlinearities that are often characteristic of sweptback wings at angles of attack in the vicinity of the stall. The main landing gear consists of two struts, each with a four-wheel bogie, that retract inward into the wing root.

Although of conventional configuration, the detailed aerodynamic design of the 767–200 is highly refined, as might be expected by the nearly 25 000 hours of wind-tunnel time required in the development of the aircraft. To place this wind-tunnel effort in perspective, 14 000 and 4000 wind-tunnel hours were expended in developing the Boeing 747 and 727, respectively.

The Boeing 767–200 has been widely advertised as being much

449

Figure 13.28 — In-flight view of Boeing 767-200 airliner. [mfr]

more fuel efficient than earlier generations of jet transports. Although the careful aerodynamic design just mentioned contributes to the efficiency of the aircraft, the high-bypass-ratio turbofan engines employed on the 767–200 are primarily responsible for its high fuel efficiency. At present, the 767–200 is offered with two versions of both the Pratt & Whitney JT9D and the General Electric CF6 turbofan engines. Both of these engines are in the 48 000- to 50 000-pound thrust range and have bypass ratios between 4.5 and 5.0 and compressor pressure ratios between 25 and 30. Specific fuel consumption of these engines, expressed in pounds of fuel per pound of thrust per hour, is between 20 and 25 percent lower than that of the Pratt & Whitney JT3D engine that powers both the McDonnell Douglas DC–8 and the Boeing 707.

Comparison of certain characteristics of the 767–200 with those of the older Boeing 707–320B is of interest. Examination of the data in table VII shows that the wings of the two aircraft are nearly the same size, with only small differences in area and span. Sweepback angle and aspect ratio of the new 767–200 are 31.5° and 8.0, respectively, as compared with 35° and 7.1 for the 707–320B. These differences in wing geometry would be expected to increase aerodynamic efficiency by a small amount. Incorporated in the wing of the 767–200 is a new Boeing-developed supercritical-type airfoil section. The basic technology of the supercritical airfoil section was pioneered by Richard T. Whitcomb of the NASA Langley Research Center. Use of such sections allows increased wing thickness ratio without corresponding reductions

450

in the Mach number at which large adverse compressibility effects begin to occur. Reduced wing structural weight, increased aspect ratio, and reduced wing sweepback angle—or some combination of the three—are accordingly possible. Incorporation of this new type of airfoil section on the Boeing 767–200 contributes to high overall efficiency.

High-lift devices on the wing consist of full-span leading-edge slats and a combination of both single- and double-slotted flaps on the trailing edge, with the double-slotted flaps placed on the inboard part of the wing. Inboard and outboard ailerons in combination with spoilers are used for lateral control. When deployed symmetrically, the spoilers help decelerate the aircraft on the landing rollout and aid in making rapid in-flight descents. An elevator and adjustable stabilizer are used for longitudinal control, and a conventional rudder is provided for control about the yaw axis. All controls are of the fully powered, irreversible type.

New techniques for navigation and flight control are used on the 767–200. These techniques herald an entirely new relationship between the aircraft and the flight crew. An automatic flight control system coupled with a computer allows storage of an entire flight plan and gives automatic guidance and control of the aircraft from takeoff to landing. Included in the system are not only navigation functions but vertical flight-path control to minimize fuel consumption. To a large extent, the traditional electromechanical instrumentation has also been replaced by more simple cathode-ray-tube displays that provide different types of information at the command of the crew. A detailed description of this new equipment and its use are beyond the scope of the present discussion. Let it be noted, however, that aircraft such as the 767–200 may herald the end to most hands-on flying of transport aircraft and introduce an age in which the pilot is increasingly a button-pushing systems manager. Automatic flight management techniques such as those employed in the new Boeing transports will certainly result in more efficient fuel utilization in future airline operations.

All versions of the 767–200 can accommodate a maximum of 290 passengers seated in a 7–abreast double-aisle configuration. The aircraft is now offered in six variants, with gross weights falling in the range from 302 000 to 337 000 pounds. Listed in table VII are the characteristics of the 337 000-pound version of the aircraft, which is powered by two Pratt & Whitney JT9D-7R4E turbofans of 50 000 pounds thrust each. This particular variant of the aircraft, available in 1984, has nearly the same gross weight as the Boeing 707–320B but carries about 100 more passengers over a much shorter range. Maximum cruising speed of the 767–200 is about 40 miles per hour slower than that of the 707–320B, and takeoff and landing field lengths of the new aircraft are significantly shorter than those of the 707. These differences in speed and field length reflect the differing requirements of a long-range aircraft designed for international operations and one designed for medium-range domestic use. Aerodynamic efficiency of the 767–200 can be judged by the maximum lift-drag ratio, estimated to be about 18. The larger ratio of wetted area to wing area of the 767–200, as compared with that of the 707–320B, results in a value of $(L/D)_{max}$ somewhat lower than that of the older aircraft. The much larger passenger capacity and more efficient engines, however, make the new aircraft more efficient in terms of cost-per-seat-mile.

The Boeing 767–200 has just entered airline service, and although its characteristics seem highly promising, its ultimate place in the spectrum of successful transport aircraft has yet to be determined.

Boeing 757–200

The second new Boeing jetliner of the 1980's, designated the 757–200, made its initial flight in February 1982 and is scheduled to enter airline service in the spring of 1983. Intended as a fuel-efficient replacement for the long-lived Boeing 727 on short-range route segments, the 757–200 can accommodate as many as 239 passengers in a single-aisle six-abreast cabin arrangement. Average route segments are expected to be about 575 miles or less and to require less than 2 hours' flight time. A narrow six-abreast single-aisle configuration usually has slightly less wetted area, and thus less drag, than a six-abreast twin-aisle arrangement designed for the same number of passengers. Apparently, passengers are willing to accept the single-aisle layout for short flights but prefer the more spacious wide-body design for flight times greater than several hours.

The first 757–200, photographed on the occasion of its rollout in January 1982, is shown in figure 13.29, and data for one version of the aircraft are given in table VII. Configuration of this twin-engine aircraft is seen to be very similar to that of the 767–200 shown in figures 13.27 and 13.28; however, the data in table VII show that the 757–200 has a smaller wing of less sweepback angle and is much the lighter of the two aircraft.

Like the 767–200, the fuel efficiency of the 757–200 derives largely from the high-bypass-ratio turbofan engines employed on the aircraft.

Figure 13.29 — Rollout of Boeing 757–200 narrow-body, twin-engine airliner. [mfr]

Listed in reference 150 are the characteristics of three versions of the 757–200. The aircraft currently in production are powered by the Rolls-Royce RB211–535C engines of bypass ratio 4.36 and thrust of 37 400 pounds. By the end of 1984, the aircraft will also be available with the Rolls-Royce RB211–535E4 engine of 40 000 pounds thrust, or with the all-new Pratt & Whitney 2037 turbofan of 40 000 pounds thrust. All three of these engine types offer a 20- to 25-percent reduction in cruise-specific fuel consumption as compared with the various versions of the Pratt & Whitney JT8D engine that powers the 727.

Many of the design features of the 767–200 described above are incorporated in the 757–200. The same supercritical airfoil section is employed in the wings of both aircraft. The high-lift and lateral control systems of the two aircraft are nearly the same, although some differences are evident in the trailing-edge flaps and ailerons. In contrast with the 767–200, the trailing-edge high-lift system of the 757–200 consists almost entirely of double-slotted flaps, and no inboard ailerons are used. Cockpit layout and automatic flight control and navigation systems are essentially identical on the two aircraft.

Gross weight of the version of the 757–200 now in production is 221 000 pounds. With the more advanced Rolls-Royce and Pratt &

Whitney engines, gross weight will be 241 000 pounds. The data in table VII are for the heavier version of the aircraft powered with Pratt & Whitney 2037 engines. As compared with the 727–200 it has been designed to replace, the 757–200 is shown by the data in table VII to be larger and heavier and to have a larger passenger capacity. Wing sweepback angle of the new aircraft is 7° less than that of the 727–200, and the maximum cruising speed is 49 miles per hour lower than that of the older aircraft. This speed differential is relatively unimportant on the short-range segments for which the aircraft is intended; also, it reduces fuel consumption.

As with the larger 767–200, only time and experience will measure the success of the 757–200 in airline operation and in the domestic and international marketplace.

Dedicated Cargo Transports

The jet transport has so far been discussed only in the context of a passenger-carrying aircraft, and those described have indeed been configured with passenger transport as a primary design consideration. Most modern jet airliners, however, have some type of cargo-carrying capability. Even those aircraft configured primarily for passengers usually carry a limited amount of cargo, along with baggage, in the hold below the passenger deck. This cargo space is illustrated by the fuselage cross-section views in figures 13.19 and 13.20. Many jet transports are also available in convertible form and may be changed quickly from a passenger to an all-cargo configuration. In this case, the passenger seats are removed and cargo is carried in the space usually occupied by the passengers as well as in the hold. The floor of the passenger cabin is usually strengthened to allow for the higher unit floor loadings likely to be encountered with cargo. A large cargo door is also provided on convertible passenger-cargo aircraft.

Some jet transports are available in dedicated cargo versions. In addition to special cargo doors and strengthened floors, these aircraft have no facilities for attending to passenger needs and may even be constructed with no cabin windows. A crew rest compartment is sometimes located immediately behind the flight deck. An in-flight view of a dedicated Boeing 747 jet freighter is shown in figure 13.30. (Note the absence of passenger windows.) The visor-type loading door located in the nose of a 747 freighter is shown in figure 13.31, and the large rear cargo door is pictured in figure 13.32.

Another class of cargo aircraft, designed to meet the special needs of certain types of military operations, has evolved since the end of World War II. These aircraft are used to transport various types of military cargo such as trucks, tanks, jeeps, and artillery pieces, as well as troops. The size and shape of the fuselage is dictated by the number and type of vehicles to be carried, and some important aspects of the overall configuration are strongly influenced by the requirements for cargo handling and loading. One of the best-known military cargo aircraft is the turboprop-powered Lockheed C–130 shown in figure 6.3. This aircraft is in use by the military services of over 20 countries throughout the world. The Soviet military services also operate turboprop-powered cargo aircraft of the same configuration concept as the C–130. One of these, the Antonov An–22, is very large with a gross weight of about 550 000 pounds.

Two jet-powered cargo aircraft that employ many of the configuration features embodied in the C–130 design have been developed in the United States. These are the Lockheed C–141 StarLifter and the Lockheed C–5A Galaxy. The C–141 has a gross weight of about 317 000 pounds, which places it in the same size class as the Boeing 707–320B, and first flew in December 1963. The very large C–5A has a gross weight of 769 000 pounds, in the same weight class as the Boeing 747, and first flew in 1968. The C–141 and the C–5A are similar in appearance, but the difference in size is very obvious when the aircraft are seen side by side. The Soviet Ilyushin Il–76 military transport is similar in appearance to the two Lockheed aircraft and has a gross

Figure 13.30 — Boeing 747 freighter showing absence of passenger windows. [mfr]

Figure 13.31 — Cargo being loaded through nose-door of Boeing 747 freighter. [mfr]

weight of 350 000 pounds. First flight of the Il–76 took place in 1971. As representative of dedicated, jet-powered, military cargo transports, the Lockheed C–5A is briefly described below.

In the early 1960's, several aircraft companies began design studies of a heavy logistic jet transport intended to replace and augment the capabilities of the aging Douglas C–133 and complement the existing fleet of C–141 jet-powered transports. The aircraft was intended to deliver payloads in the range of 100 000 to 200 000 pounds over intercontinental distances and be able to operate from semiprepared runways. Following a design competition, Boeing, Douglas, and Lockheed were given contracts for further development of their designs. Concurrently, General Electric and Pratt & Whitney were given design contracts for high-bypass-ratio turbofan engines to power the new aircraft.

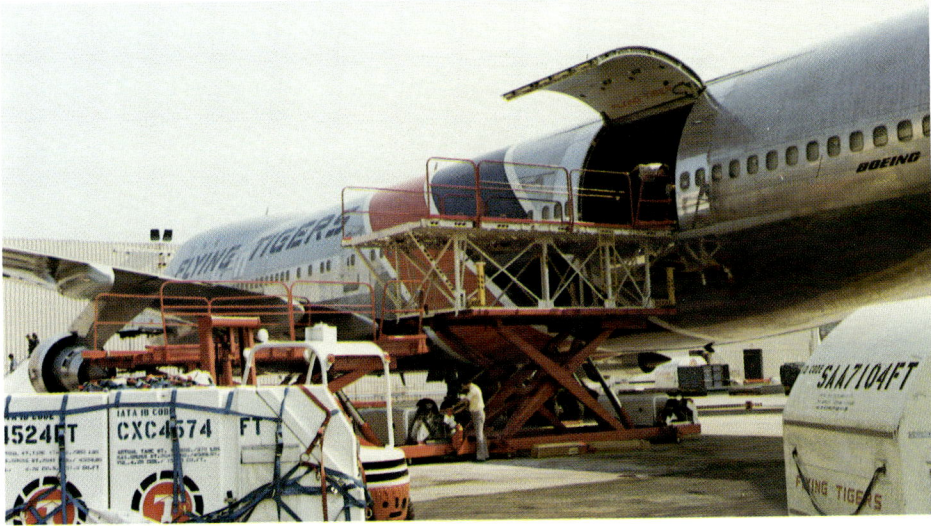

Figure 13.32 — Rear-loading cargo door of Boeing 747 freighter. [mfr]

The weight of the aircraft was expected to be in the 700 000-pound class, and the thrust level required of the new engines was about 40 000 pounds. The selection of the General Electric Company to develop the engine was announced in August 1965, and in October of that same year, the Lockheed Aircraft Corporation was selected to develop the aircraft. First flight of the C–5A took place on June 30, 1968, and the last of a fleet of 81 aircraft was delivered to the USAF in May 1973. An interesting account of the engineering development of the C–5A is given in reference 158. Several views of the aircraft are shown in figures 13.33 to 13.36.

The C–5A is a high-wing monoplane with the wing mounted at the top of the fuselage. The aircraft is equipped with four engines mounted in pods that are attached to the lower surface of the wings in much the same fashion as that employed on the 707 and DC–8 aircraft. The General Electric TF–39 engines that power the aircraft develop a take-off thrust of 41 000 pounds each and have a bypass ratio of 8.0. The gas generator of this engine serves as the basis of the General Electric CF6 commercial engine discussed previously.

In order to minimize weight and complexity, the landing gear is retracted into blisters located on either side of the fuselage rather than into the high-mounted wing. The aspect ratio 8.0 wing is swept 25° at the quarter chord and is equipped with Fowler-type single-slotted flaps and leading-edge slats. Lateral control is provided through a combina-

457

Figure 13.33 — Lockheed C–5A military freighter. [mfr]

Figure 13.34 — Lockheed C–5A in approach configuration showing 28-wheel landing gear and large Fowler flaps. [mfr]

Figure 13.35 — View showing fore and aft loading capability of Lockheed C–5A. [mfr]

Figure 13.36 — Photograph of man standing on horizontal tail is indicative of large size of Lockheed C–5A. [mfr]

tion of ailerons and spoilers. The ailerons are also used to reduce wing bending moments when the aircraft undergoes normal acceleration as a result of maneuvers or gusts. In this technique, called active load distribution control system (ALDCS), the ailerons are symmetrically deflected in response to signals received from accelerometers located in various parts of the aircraft. For a positive acceleration, the ailerons are deflected upward whereby the load is shifted inboard and thus the wing-root bending moments are reduced. This technique is expected to find application in many new aircraft designs.

The empennage consists of a horizontal tail mounted in the T-position at the top of the swept vertical fin. According to reference 158, this arrangement, rather than a low-tail arrangement, results in a weight savings. The horizontal tail consists of elevators and an adjustable stabilizer. No trim tabs are provided.

The high-wing position employed on the C–5A is advantageous for a cargo aircraft because it allows trucks and other types of equipment to move beneath the wing, and the bottom of the fuselage can be brought close to the ground for easy cargo loading without causing interference with the engines. A rear door, which serves as a loading ramp when lowered, is deployed from the bottom of the upswept aft portion of the fuselage. The proximity of the bottom of the fuselage to the ground results in a ramp with only a small inclination to the ground; thus, vehicles can be readily driven or pushed into the aircraft. The rear door is also used for aerial deployment of vehicles and equipment by parachute. The fuselage is provided with a forward loading door in the nose of the aircraft. The door is like a visor and lifts up and over the flight deck (somewhat like that shown in fig. 13.31 for the Boeing 747 freighter). The entire cross-section of the cargo compartment is exposed when the nose visor is raised. Figure 13.35 shows a rear view of the C–5A with both forward and aft doors open and with various types of equipment ready for loading.

The length of the C–5A cargo deck, excluding the loading ramps, is about 121 feet, and the maximum width is 19 feet. The height of the cargo compartment is 13.5 feet. In addition to the lower cargo compartment, the fuselage also has an upper deck divided into three sections. The forward section contains the flight deck and is followed by a rest area for 15 people that is usually occupied by relief crews. The flight crew of five persons consists of the pilot, copilot, flight engineer, navigator, and load master. Behind the rest area is a passenger compartment that will accommodate 75 fully equipped troops. The lower cargo compartment may also be utilized for troop transport; for this

460

purpose, the aircraft can carry 270 soldiers. Both the lower cargo compartment and the upper deck are fully pressurized.

The capability for operation from semiprepared runways was one of the specified design requirements of the C–5A cargo transport. The achievement of a relatively low unit loading on the runway surface was therefore necessary. In order to meet this design requirement, the main landing gear is equipped with 24 wheels, and the nose gear has 4 wheels. The main gear consists of four struts to which are attached six-wheel bogies. Each bogie has a two-wheel truck forward of the strut and two two-wheel trucks located side by side behind the strut. In order to provide further flexibility in rapidly adapting the aircraft to various runway-bearing capabilities, the pressure in the tires can either be increased or decreased while the aircraft is in flight. The landing-gear bogies may be set at an angle of as much as $\pm 20°$ from the centerline of the aircraft to simplify takeoff and landing operations in various crosswind conditions. Ground maneuverability is enhanced by allowing the front two bogies to castor freely while the aircraft is being taxied. The landing gear is also provided with a kneeling capability to lower the floor of the main deck for ease of transferring cargo from a truck to the aircraft. With the landing gear in the kneeling position, the lower deck is just over 4 feet from the ground at the front loading door and just over 5 feet from the ground at the rear door. The highly versatile landing gear may be seen in figures 13.33 and 13.34.

With a gross weight of 769 000 pounds, the C–5A is a very large aircraft by any standard. The data in table VII show that the C–5A, in comparison with the 747–200B, has a larger wing span and area and a greater fuselage length. The 747 is, however, somewhat heavier than the C–5A. An indication of the large size of the aircraft can be obtained from figure 13.36, which shows a man standing on the horizontal tail. The aircraft is capable of performing missions with various combinations of range and payload. Two mission profiles given in table VII indicate a range of 3744 miles with a payload of 220 967 pounds and 6521 miles with a payload of 112 600 pounds. The aircraft has a maximum cruising speed of 541 miles per hour at an altitude of 25 000 feet. This corresponds to a Mach number of 0.78. The stalling speed at maximum landing weight is 120 miles per hour.

As indicated previously, the final C–5A was delivered to the USAF in May 1973. A recent decision has been made, however, to put the type back in production to augment the United States' heavy air-lift capability. The new aircraft will be designated the C–5B, of which the total number to be procured has not been finally determined.

Conclusion

The introduction of the first jet transport over a quarter of a century ago marked the beginning of a transportation revolution. The modern jet transport has altered forever the travel concepts and habits of people all over the world.

An account of the technical development of the jet transport has been presented from the pioneering DeHavilland Comet of the early 1950's to the highly efficient, safe, reliable, and economical transport aircraft of today. Many of the transport aircraft currently in production will continue to be produced for many years. Improvements, modifications, and adaptations to new routes and markets will be made to current aircraft as time and circumstances change and as new technologies evolve.

Several entirely new aircraft will probably be developed in the next two decades. These new aircraft will no doubt utilize emerging new technologies in aerodynamics, structures, guidance and control, and propulsion. Improved aerodynamic design, composite structures, active controls, and engines of improved efficiency and reduced noise are only a few of the new technical developments that suggest themselves. The increased cost of fuel will place a great emphasis on energy-efficient aircraft. Accordingly, aerodynamic and propulsion-system efficiency and light structural weight will be of greater importance than ever before.

Chapter 14
Business Jet Aircraft

Background

The venerable Curtiss Jenny may have been the first aircraft to be used for business purposes. In the late 1920's and early 1930's, higher performance aircraft were adapted to business use. Although several Ford trimotor airliners were converted for corporate operations, most business aircraft of this period had a single engine and an open cockpit or small cabin. The long-lived twin-engine Beech model 18, first flown in 1936, was probably the first multiengine aircraft designed specifically for business use. Following World War II, the Douglas DC–3 was extensively involved in corporate flying, and in the 1950's a number of smaller aircraft equipped with two reciprocating engines were offered for this purpose. A large number and variety of such aircraft are still on the market today. (See chapter 6.)

The first jet-powered aircraft designed especially for business use began to appear in the late 1950's and early 1960's. Presently, no fewer than 9 companies in 6 different countries are offering 18 various models of jet-powered business aircraft. The world fleet of such aircraft now totals more than 2900 (ref. 144). Some of the design features and characteristics of business jet aircraft are discussed in the next section, after which eight representative aircraft types are illustrated and described. Physical and performance characteristics of these aircraft are given in table VIII (appendix A), which contains the same quantities presented in table VII for jet transport aircraft. Note, however, that the values of range given in table VIII are based on a reserve-fuel allowance sufficient for 45 minutes of flying after the destination airport is reached. This standard has been adopted by the National Business Aircraft Association and is different from the rules described in appendix G for transport aircraft.

463

Configuration Features

Most business jet aircraft are of low-wing design and have engines mounted at the aft end of the fuselage. Except for one three-engine and one four-engine design, all are powered with two engines. Both pure jets and turbofan engines are used. Most of the modern aircraft produced today have turbofan engines; some of these are repowered versions of aircraft that originally appeared with turbojet engines. The wings of most of the aircraft have a modest amount of sweepback, although one business jet described below has a sweptforward wing.

Like any aircraft, the size and performance of business jets vary with the function for which the aircraft has been designed. Aircraft are available that vary in gross weight from about 11 000 to 65 000 pounds. Cruising speeds lie in the range from 0.7 to 0.85 Mach number. Ranges vary from intercontinental values to as low as 1150 miles. Many of the new aircraft being produced have at least nonstop transcontinental capability. The number of passengers that can be accommodated, even on aircraft of the same design, varies widely depending on the interior cabin arrangements. Aircraft can be found with the capability of carrying from 5 to 19 passengers.

Most corporate aircraft are expected to operate from a wide variety of airports. The landing and takeoff field lengths they require are accordingly shorter than those for the larger transport aircraft. The desired landing and takeoff field lengths of business jets, as compared with transports, are usually obtained through a combination of low wing loading and high thrust-to-weight ratio, together with a relatively simple high-lift system. A simple slotted trailing-edge flap frequently constitutes the entire high-lift system.

The small size of many business jets imposes certain design constraints not encountered in large transport aircraft. One dimension that cannot be scaled as the size of an aircraft is reduced is the size of the human body that occupies the cabin. This essentially invariant dimension is usually a predominant factor in determining the fuselage diameter. A small fuselage diameter is desirable in order to reduce weight and to maintain as low a value of the ratio of wetted area to wing area as possible. Accordingly, only the very large business jets have a cabin diameter sufficiently large to accommodate a person standing in an upright position. Figure 14.1 shows the cabin size of three business aircraft relative to a 6-foot-tall person. Some of the smaller aircraft are essentially sit-down vehicles in much the same sense as an automobile. Some feature a cabin diameter that permits limited mobility in a

JetStar   Falcon   Learjet

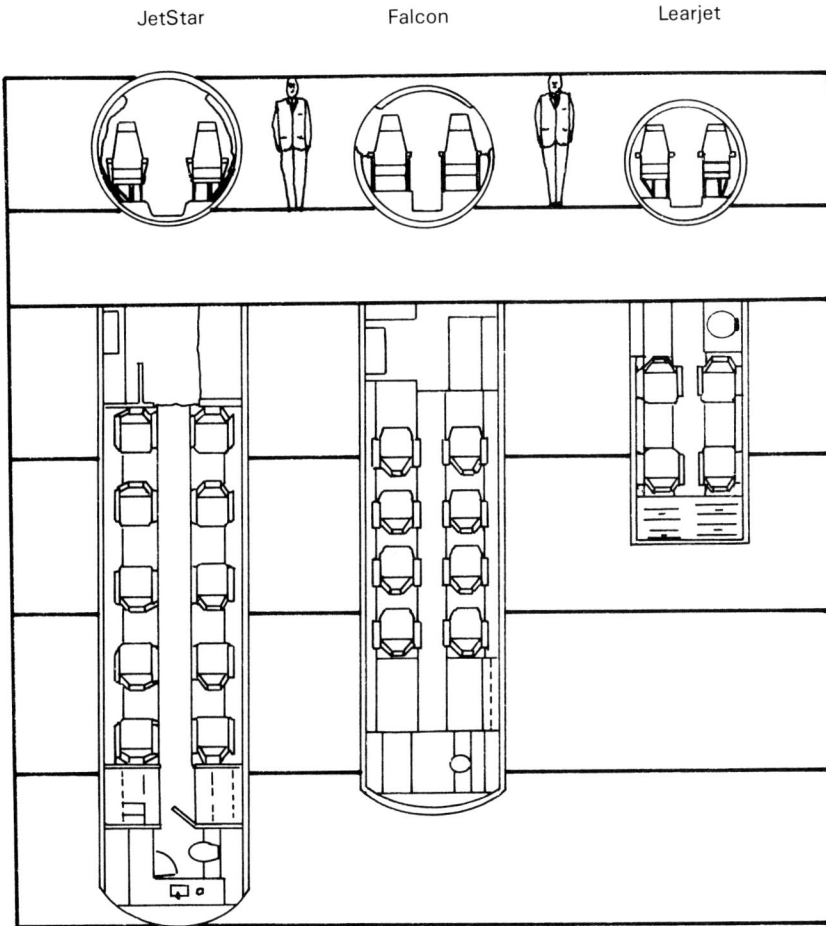

Figure 14.1 — Cabin interiors of three business jet aircraft.

stooped posture. A cabin floor free of obstructions is a desirable feature intended to reduce the possibility of a passenger tripping or falling. Such a floor design requires that the wing carry-through structure
be either beneath or behind the cabin. There are disadvantages to both
arrangements. An increase in fuselage diameter results from passing
the wing structure entirely beneath the floor; whereas, placing the wing
behind the cabin may result in a center of gravity that is farther forward than desired. Placement of the wing carry-through structure
behind the cabin combined with the use of a sweptforward wing offers
a means for overcoming the disadvantages of the other two methods of

465

achieving an unobstructed cabin floor. The German Hansa jet described below utilized this design concept.

Two other size-related design factors are worth mentioning. The short distance between the ground and the bottom of the wing precludes the use of the under-wing-engine mounting and is largely responsible for the aft-engine location employed on all current business jet aircraft. Two alternative arrangements suggest themselves: (1) a high wing location with engines mounted beneath the wing or (2) a low wing configuration in which the engines are mounted on top of the wing. So far, neither of these arrangements has been utilized on a business jet, although one small transport aircraft (the VFW Fokker 614) has been produced that employs the over-wing-engine arrangement. In most cases, the aft-engine arrangement used on business jets forces the horizontal tail to the tip or part way up the vertical tail. Possible problems associated with a high horizontal-tail location are discussed in chapter 10. Finally, the small size of the business jet results in a Reynolds number[1] that is much lower than the Reynolds number characteristic of transport aircraft. That portion of the drag coefficient attributable to skin friction is accordingly higher for the small aircraft. For example, if all the dimensions of a small business jet are assumed to be one-fifth those of a large jumbo jet, the skin-friction drag coefficient of the small aircraft will be about 30 percent higher than that of the jumbo aircraft. For this reason and because the ratio of wetted area to wing area may be higher than that of many larger aircraft, the maximum lift-drag ratios characteristic of business jet aircraft tend to be lower than those of the large transports.

Representative Aircraft Types

Eight representative business jet aircraft are briefly described below and are illustrated in figures 14.2 to 14.10. Information on the many different models of business jet aircraft now available may be found in references such as reference 144 and the various issues of *Jane's All The World's Aircraft*.

Lockheed JetStar

The first of the dedicated business jets, the Lockheed JetStar, completed its maiden flight in September 1957. Initial development of the

---

[1] The Reynolds number is a nondimensional quantity expressing the ratio of inertia to viscous forces in the fluid flow. Reductions in aircraft size and speed as well as increases in flight altitude cause a reduction in Reynolds number. In most practical cases, a reduction in Reynolds number causes an increase in skin-friction drag.

Figure 14.2 — Four-engine Lockheed JetStar. [Peter C. Boisseau]

aircraft was undertaken as a private venture. The first two prototypes were equipped with two Bristol Siddeley Orpheus turbojet engines. The aircraft was later entered in an Air Force competition for a small four-engine utility and personal transport, and in this version was equipped with four Pratt & Whitney JT–12–8 turbojet engines of 3300 pounds thrust each. The JetStar won the Air Force competition and in that service is known as the C–140. The aircraft is shown in figure 14.2. Production of the original JetStar ended in 1973; however, an improved version known as the JetStar II, powered with four Garrett TFE 731 turbofan engines of 3700 pounds thrust each, was offered by Lockheed in 1976. Production of the type ended late in 1978, at which time a total of 160 JetStar aircraft had been built.

The JetStar, with a gross weight of 42 500 pounds, is one of the heaviest of the business jets. A typical cabin configuration accommodates 8 to 10 passengers; a range of 2415 miles is possible with a payload of 3500 pounds. Takeoff and landing field lengths are 4700 and 3550 feet, respectively. These field lengths are based on climb and descent over a 50-foot obstacle, however, and are not to be compared with the FAR field lengths given in table VII for transport aircraft. Maximum cruising speed is 567 miles per hour at 21 000 feet, which corresponds to a Mach number of 0.80.

Wing of the JetStar is characterized by a 30° sweepback angle, an aspect ratio of 5.3, and airfoil section thickness ratios that vary from 12 percent at the root to 9 percent at the tip. An instant recognition feature of the aircraft is provided by the large external fuel tank located at the midspan position of each wing. Unlike most business jet aircraft, the high-lift system of the JetStar is relatively complicated and consists

467

of a double-slotted trailing-edge flap and a leading-edge flap. Lateral control is provided by ailerons without the assistance of spoilers, and a speed brake is located on the underside of the fuselage. The longitudinal trim system is unusual in that the stabilizer is fixed to the fin, which pivots to change the stabilizer angle. An indication of this pivoting action is provided in figure 14.2 by the apparently unpainted portion of the lower part of the fin. All controls are power operated.

Gates Learjet 24B and 55

The prototype Learjet model 23 made its first flight in October 1963 and may be considered as the progenitor of a whole family of Gates Learjet business aircraft of different gross weight, passenger capacity, and range. All the aircraft, however, are of the same basic configuration. The data in table VIII are for the Gates Learjet model 24B, shown in figure 14.3. Deliveries of model 24 began in 1966, and model 24B was certified in December 1968. Over 1000 aircraft of all versions had been built by the end of 1980, and several models are in production at this time.

The Learjet model 24B is one of the smaller business jets with a gross weight of 13 300 pounds and a cabin configured to accommodate a maximum of six passengers. The aircraft has a range of 1271 miles with a maximum payload of 1910 pounds; and with full fuel tanks and a reduced payload, the maximum range achievable is 2041 miles. The maximum cruising speed is 534 miles per hour, and the cost-economical speed is 508 miles per hour. Both of these speeds are at 41 000 feet; the corresponding Mach numbers are 0.81 and 0.77. The Learjet model 24B is equipped with two General Electric CJ610–4 turbojet en-

Figure 14.3 — Gates Learjet 24B. [Peter C. Boisseau]

gines of 2850 pounds thrust each. These engines, together with the low gross weight, give a high takeoff thrust-to-weight ratio of 0.43. This value of the thrust-to-weight ratio is much higher than any of those given in table VII for transport aircraft and is about the same as that of the well-known North American F–86D fighter of the 1950's. (See chapter 11.) As can be seen from the table, the high thrust-to-weight ratio, coupled with a wing loading of only 57.4 pounds per square foot, gives an outstanding short takeoff capability.

Wing-planform shape of all Gates Learjet aircraft is characterized by a small sweepback angle of 13°, together with a straight trailing edge. Shape of the wing can be seen in the view of a Gates Learjet 25C shown in figure 14.4. Wing airfoil-section thickness ratio is 10.9 percent. The high-lift system employed on the wing is simple and consists only of a single-slotted trailing-edge flap; no leading-edge devices are used. Ailerons, rudder, and elevators are manually actuated; spoilers for increasing drag and reducing lift are located ahead of the flaps and are power actuated. Longitudinal trim is achieved by varying the incidence of the stabilizer. Possible deep-stall problems (see chapter 10) associated with the T-tail are avoided by the use of a combined stick

Figure 14.4 — Gates Learjet 25C showing wing-planform shape. [mfr]

469

shaker/pusher. As in the case of the JetStar, part of the fuel load of the Gates Learjet 24B is carried in external fuel tanks; the tanks on the Gates Learjet, however, are located at the wingtip instead of the mid-span position employed on the JetStar.

Latest version of the Gates Learjet to be offered is the model 55, which is depicted in figure 14.5. Comparison of the data in table VIII between this model and model 24B shows that model 55 is larger, heavier, more commodious, and has a much longer range. Not shown by the data in table VIII is the cabin size of the Gates Learjet, which for model 55 is about a foot larger in both width and height than for earlier versions of the aircraft. Power in the Gates Learjet 55 is supplied by two AiResearch TFE 731–3 turbofan engines of bypass ratio 2.79 and thrust of 3650 pounds each. The lower specific fuel consumption of these engines as compared with that of the turbojets employed on model 24B is no doubt partly responsible for the increased range capability of the new aircraft. The large nacelles required to accommodate the turbofan engines are clearly evident in figure 14.5.

Perhaps the most noteworthy recognition feature of the Gates Learjet 55 is the small winglike vertical surfaces located at each wingtip. These tip devices are a modern development (by Dr. Richard T.

Figure 14.5 — Gates Learjet model 55. [mfr]

Whitcomb of the NASA Langley Research Center) of an old concept that is intended to trick the flow over the wing into behaving as though the wing span, and thus aspect ratio, is greater than is actually the case. "Winglet" is the popular name for one of these tip devices. The use of winglets causes a reduction in induced drag and a consequent increase of a few percent in maximum lift-drag ratio; some improvement in climb performance is also attributed to their use. At least two other new aircraft employ winglets.

Not evident in figure 14.5 is the increased wing span of model 55 as compared with earlier models of the Gates Learjet. The corresponding aspect ratio of the new aircraft is 7.3, as compared with 5.4 of model 24B. Improved airfoil sections are incorporated in the wing of model 55, as are fences and other flow-control devices designed to improve stalling characteristics. Control and high-lift systems are essentially the same as described for model 24B.

The Gates Learjet 56 is similar to the 55 but has a larger fuel capacity and longer range, coupled with a somewhat reduced passenger capacity. Detailed descriptions of the models 55 and 56 as well as others in the Gates Learjet series of aircraft may be found in reference 130.

Dassault-Breguet Falcon 20

The Falcon 20 is one of a series of business jets manufactured by the French firm of Dassault-Breguet. The aircraft, with a gross weight of 28 660 pounds, lies in a weight class about midway between the JetStar and the Gates Learjet 24B. Power is supplied by two General Electric CF700 aft fan engines of 4315 pounds thrust each and bypass ratio 1.9. The Falcon 20 is used extensively in the United States and is frequently referred to as the Fan-Jet Falcon in this country. First flight of the aircraft equipped with the General Electric engines took place in July 1964. A Falcon 20 is shown in figure 14.6.

The aircraft has a maximum payload capability of 3320 pounds and features a cabin that can accommodate 8 to 10 passengers. With a reduced payload of 1600 pounds, the aircraft has a range of 2220 miles. Maximum cruising speed is 535 miles per hour at 25 000 feet, and cost-economical speed is 466 miles per hour at 40 000 feet. The corresponding Mach numbers are 0.77 and 0.70, respectively. The data in table VIII indicate about the same landing and takeoff field lengths for the Falcon 20 as for the JetStar.

Configuration of the Falcon 20 is characterized by a wing of 30° sweepback angle, an aspect ratio of 6.5, and airfoil-section thickness

471

Figure 14.6 — Dassault-Breguet Falcon 20 business jet with aft-fan General Electric engines. [Peter C. Boisseau]

ratios that vary from 10 percent at the root to 8 percent at the tip. Figure 14.6 shows a large flow-control fence on top of the wing part way between the root and tip. A leading-edge flap, similar to an unslotted slat, is employed inboard of the fence and a conventional slat is utilized outboard. A single-slotted trailing-edge flap completes the high-lift system. Lateral control is provided by ailerons alone. Spoilers located ahead of the flaps are deployed symmetrically to increase the drag for braking and rapid descent and are not part of the lateral control system. Longitudinal control is provided by elevators, and trim is maintained with an electrically driven stabilizer. With the exception of the stabilizer, all the movable surfaces are hydraulically actuated.

The Falcon 20 and its derivatives continue in production. In addition to use as an executive transport, the aircraft is also available in a cargo version. The latest in the Falcon series, the Falcon 50, is equipped with three engines located in a manner similar to that of the Boeing 727.

Gulfstream Aerospace Gulfstream II

An examination of the data in table VIII indicates that the Gulfstream II,[2] shown in figure 14.7, is heavier in weight, larger in size, faster in speed, and longer in range than any of the other business aircraft. For example, the gross weight of the Gulfstream II is 62 500

---

[2] The original Gulfstream II was developed by a division of the Grumman Aerospace Corporation. For several years, however, this division has been owned by what is now known as the Gulfstream Aerospace Corporation.

Figure 14.7 — Gulfstream Aerospace Gulfstream II. [Peter C. Boisseau]

pounds, nearly five times that of the Gates Learjet 24B, and the wing area is about three-and-a-half times that of the smaller aircraft. The Gulfstream II has an intercontinental range capability and a maximum cruising speed of 588 miles per hour, or Mach number of 0.85, at an altitude of 25 000 feet. The aircraft, frequently referred to as the G–II, was developed as a jet-powered successor to the highly successful turboprop-powered Gulfstream I. First flight of the G–II took place in October 1966, and a total of 256 units were manufactured before production ended in 1979. The more advanced Gulfstream III became available in late 1980.

The Gulfstream II is a low-wing configuration incorporating a T-tail and a wing of aspect ratio 6.0, 25° sweepback, and airfoil sections varying in thickness ratio from 12 to 8.5 percent. Power is supplied by two Rolls-Royce Spey MK 511–8 turbofan engines of 11 400 pounds thrust each. These engines are equipped with a five-stage fan and have a bypass ratio of 0.64; target-type thrust reversers are employed. The high-lift system consists of single-slotted trailing-edge flaps. Lateral control is provided by a combination of ailerons and spoilers. The spoilers may also be deployed symmetrically to increase drag and reduce lift. Elevators are used for longitudinal control, and trim is ac-

473

complished with a variable incidence stabilizer. All controls are hydraulically actuated.

The passenger cabin of the Gulfstream II is usually configured for 10 to 14 passengers (maximum capacity of 19 passengers). The range-payload data given in the references are incomplete but indicate a range of 3881 miles with maximum fuel. Takeoff and landing distances are in the same class as those of the Lockheed JetStar.

As compared with the Gulfstream II, the Gulfstream III is slightly larger and heavier and has a greater range. The appearance of the new aircraft, however, differs little from that of the Gulfstream II. Winglets similar to those employed on the Gates Learjet 55 provide the primary identification feature of the Gulfstream III.

Cessna Citation

The Cessna Citation I and II are small business jet transports in the same weight class as the Gates Learjet. Low first costs, economy of operation, safety, and viceless handling characteristics were among the design objectives. In order to provide wide operational flexibility, the aircraft was designed to take off and land from most fields used by light and medium twin-engine propeller-driven aircraft, and from unpaved runways. First flight took place in September 1969, and the aircraft was certified in September 1971. That the Citation I and II have been widely accepted is clearly demonstrated by the more than 1000 aircraft that have been produced; the type is still in production and will likely continue to find a significant share of the business jet market for a number of years. Although the Citation I and II are similar in appearance, the Citation II is somewhat larger and heavier than the Citation I and has a longer range capability. A Citation I in flight is shown in figure 14.8, and data are given in table VIII for the Citation II.

The Citation II has an unswept wing, an aspect ratio of 8.3, and airfoil-section thickness ratios that vary from 14 percent at the root to 12 percent at the tip. The horizontal tail is located near the root of the vertical fin and incorporates a small amount of dihedral to reduce immersion in the jet exhaust. To improve directional stability, the vertical tail has a relatively large dorsal fin together with a small ventral fin. Power is supplied by two Pratt & Whitney JT15D-4 turbofan engines of 2500 pounds thrust each and bypass ratio of 3.3.

The high-lift system on both versions of the Citation consists of a single-slotted trailing-edge flap; no leading-edge devices are employed. Spoilers located on the upper wing surface ahead of the flap are used as air brakes and are not part of the lateral control system, which uti-

Figure 14.8 — Cessna Citation I. [mfr]

lizes only ailerons. Longitudinal control is by elevators, and trim is obtained by an electrically operated trim tab on the elevator. All controls are manually operated.

The Citation II has a gross weight of 13 300 pounds and a cabin that is usually configured to carry from 6 to 10 passengers. With six passengers, the aircraft has a range of 1969 miles. Normal cruising speed is 443 miles per hour, which corresponds to a Mach number of 0.64 at 25 000 feet; maximum operating speed is 485 miles per hour at 25 000 feet, which gives a Mach number of 0.70. The stalling speed of 94 miles per hour is the lowest of any of the aircraft listed in table VIII. This low stalling speed is obtained with a relatively simple high-lift system because the wing loading is only about 41 pounds per square foot. This low wing loading together with the high thrust-to-weight ratio of 0.38 are responsible for the short takeoff distance given in the table.

To complement the highly successful Citation I and II line of business jets, Cessna is now producing an entirely new aircraft of higher performance, the Citation III. First flight of this aircraft took place in May 1979, and first deliveries were scheduled for 1983. As can be seen from figure 14.9, the Citation III bears no resemblance to the earlier Citation I or Citation II. Instead of a straight wing, the new aircraft has a 25° sweptback wing of 9.11 aspect ratio. Incorporated in the wing are

475

Figure 14.9 — Cessna Citation III. [mfr]

NASA supercritical-type airfoil sections that vary in thickness ratio from 16 percent at the root to 12 percent at the tip. The high-lift system consists of trailing-edge slotted flaps; lateral control is provided by spoilers and small ailerons. In contrast to earlier Citations, the Citation III employs a T-tail. The aircraft is powered by two AiResearch TFE 731–3 turbofan engines of 3650 pounds thrust each and 2.79 bypass ratio. To assist in braking on landing rollout, the engines are equipped with hydraulically actuated thrust reversers.

An examination of the data in table VIII shows that the gross weight of the Citation III is in the same class as that of the Gates Learjet 55. The aircraft has a maximum passenger capacity of 13 and is capable of carrying 6 passengers (plus 2 pilots) over a nonstop United States coast-to-coast range of 2875 miles. Maximum cruising speed is 539 miles per hour at 33 000 feet (M=0.81), and maximum certified cruising altitude is 51 000 feet. Stalling speed is a relatively low 104 miles per hour and results from a combination of low wing loading, good high-lift flaps, and high maximum-lift characteristics of the blunt leading-edge supercritical airfoil sections.

Indeed, the Citation III appears to be a worthy stablemate to the highly successful Citation I and II aircraft.

476

MBB HFB 320 *Hansa*

The German MBB HFB 320 Hansa is included in this brief overview of business jet aircraft because of its interesting and unique configuration. It features a sweptforward wing, as shown in figure 14.10. Design of this unusual aircraft was begun in March 1961, and first flight took place in April 1964. Production of the aircraft began in 1966 and continued until approximately 50 units were manufactured.

The desirability of an unobstructed cabin floor and some of the means for achieving this objective are discussed at the beginning of this chapter. The wing of the Hansa is mounted near the middle of the fuselage (in the vertical sense), and the wing carry-through structure is located behind the passenger cabin. In order to place the wing aerodynamic center in the desired position relative to the aircraft center of gravity, 15° of forward sweep is incorporated in the wing. Fuel tanks are mounted at each wingtip; the small horizontal surfaces seen at the rear end of the tanks help to stabilize the wing-tank system against divergence. (See the section on swept wings in chapter 10.) The landing gear retracts into blisters located on the fuselage at the wing root, and the empennage incorporates a horizontal tail mounted at the top of the vertical surface in the T position. Power is supplied by two General Electric CJ610–1 turbojet engines of 2850 pounds of thrust each.

In contrast to a sweptback wing, which stalls initially at the tip, a wing with forward sweep stalls first at the root. Initial stall at the wing root can produce pitch-up just as does tip stall on a sweptback wing.

Figure 14.10 — View of MBB HFB 320 Hansa showing unusual sweptforward wings.
[Flt. Intl.]

477

To alleviate this problem, an inboard leading-edge slat and a large upper surface fence located at about mid semispan are used for stall control on the Hansa. The high-lift system utilizes these devices as well as a trailing-edge double-slotted flap. Upper and lower surface spoilers are deployed symmetrically for the purpose of increasing drag and decreasing lift, and ailerons are used for lateral control. Trim about all three axes is provided by tabs on the ailerons, elevators, and rudder; the horizontal stabilizer is not adjustable.

Gross weight of the Hansa is 18 740 pounds, and the aircraft can carry a maximum payload of 2650 pounds for a distance of 949 miles; with full fuel tanks and a reduced payload of 1760 pounds, the range is 1668 miles. The cabin is usually configured for nine passengers. Maximum cruising speed is 509 miles per hour at 26 000 feet, which corresponds to a Mach number of 0.74. Landing and takeoff field lengths are comparable with those of the Falcon 20.

A configuration layout incorporating a sweptforward wing would seem to offer interesting possibilities for the business jet aircraft. The reason for the short production life of the Hansa is not known. Perhaps the configuration concepts employed in this aircraft will be examined again at some time in the future. The divergence problem of the sweptforward wing may be alleviated without a significant weight penalty by the use of composite materials that permit a degree of control over wing torsional stiffness not possible with conventional metal structures.

Appendix A
Physical and Performance Data

Table 1.—Characteristics of Illustrative Aircraft, 1914–18

Aircraft; engine; and references	Physical characteristics								Performance characteristics					
	P_0	W_g	W_e	b	ι	S	W_g/S	W_g/P_0	V_{max}[a]	V_s	$C_{D,0}$	f	A	$(L/D)_{max}$
Fokker E-III; Oberursel U.I; 29, 82, 119	100	1 342	878	31.3	23.5	172	7.8	13.4	87	h 55	0.0771	12.61	5.70	6.4
DeHavilland DH-2; Gnome Monosoupape; 32, 82	100	1 441	943	28.3	25.2	249	5.8	14.4	93	h 45	0.0430	10.71	3.88	7.0
Nieuport 17; Le Rhône 9J; 82, 118	110	1 233	825	26.9	19.0	159	7.8	11.2	d 107	h 53	0.0491	7.81	5.51	7.9
Albatros D-III; Mercedes DII; 82, 119	160	1 949	1 454	29.8	24.0	231	8.5	12.2	e 109	h 55	0.0465	10.74	4.65	7.5
Fokker triplane, Dr.-1; Oberursel Ur II; 69, 82, 119	110	1 290	894	23.7	18.9	207	6.2	11.7	f 103	h 45	0.0323	6.69	4.04	8.0
Sopwith F.1 Camel; Clerget 9B; 33, 82, 30	130	1 482	962	28.0	18.8	231	6.4	11.4	g 105	48	0.0378	8.73	4.11	7.7
SPAD XIII C.1; Hispano-Suiza 8BA; 22, 82, 118	220	1 807	1 245	26.3	20.3	227	8.0	8.2	d 134	56	0.0367	8.33	3.69	7.4
Fokker D-VII; BMW IIIA; 82, 119	185	2 112	1 474	29.3	22.8	221	9.6	11.4	124	54	0.0404	8.93	4.70	8.1
Sopwith 5F.1 Dolphin; Hispano-Suiza; 31, 34, 82	200	1 911	1 406	32.5	22.3	263	7.3	9.6	g 128	h 51	0.0317	8.35	4.85	9.2
Fokker D-VIII; Oberursel Ur II; 82, 119	110	1 238	848	27.5	19.3	115	10.8	11.3	d 114	h 57	0.0552	6.34	6.58	8.1

Junkers D-I; BMW IIIA; 82, 112, 119	185	1 920	1 439	29.5	23.8	159	12.1	10.4	119	h 56	0.0612	9.75	5.46	7.0
Handley Page 0/400; Liberty 12-N; 94, 112, 119	b 350	14 425	8 721	100.0	63.0	1655	8.7	20.5	94	h 52	0.0427	70.67	7.31	9.7
Gotha G.V; Mercedes DIVa; 65, 94, 112, 119	b 260	8 558	5 654	77.8	40.0	963	8.9	16.5	87	h 56	0.0711	68.45	7.61	7.7
Caproni CA.42; Liberty; 1, 69, 94	c 400	17 700	11 ?00	96.4	42.9	2223	8.0	14.8	d 98	h 53	0.0444	98.7	5.43	8.2
B.E.2c; R.A.F.Ia; 32, 94, 112	90	2 142		37.0	27.3	371	5.8	23.8	d 72	h 45	0.0368	13.66	4.47	8.2
Junkers J-I; Benz Bz.IV; 112, 119	200	4 787	3 885	52.5	29.8	522	9.2	23.9	96	h 51	0.0335	17.5	6.4	10.3
DeHavilland DH-4; Liberty; 28, 112, 118	100	4 595		42.5	30.6	440	10.4	11.5	124	h 61	0.0422	21.82	4.97	8.1

[a] All speeds are for sea level unless otherwise noted.
[b] For each of two engines.
[c] For each of three engines.
[d] At 6500 feet.
[e] At 3280 feet.
[f] At 13 120 feet.
[g] At 10 000 feet.
[h] Estimated.

Table II.—Characteristics of Illustrative Aircraft, 1918–39

Aircraft; engine; and references	Physical characteristics								Performance characteristics						
	P_0	W_g	W_e	b	l	S	W_g/S	W_g/P_0	V_{max}^a	V_c^a	V_s	$C_{D,0}$	f	A	$(L/D)_{max}$
Curtiss JN-4H; Wright-Hispano; 109	150	2 017	1 467	43.6	27.3	352.6	5.72	13.45	93		f 47	0.0500	17.64	7.76	9.24
Handley Page W8F; Rolls-Royce Eagle IX, 360 hp (nose), Sideley Puma, 240 hp (each side); 75	840	13 000	8 600	75.2	60.1	1456	8.9	15.5	103	85		0.0549	79.93	4.67	7.1
Fokker F-2; BMW; 2, 71	185	4 180	2 640	56.6	33.8	452	9.3	22.6	93			0.0466	21.10	7.1	9.4
Curtiss R2C-1; Curtiss D-12 (modified); 51, 114	500	2 071		22.0	19.7	140	14.8	4.2	267		74	0.0206	2.88	4.18	10.9
Dayton Wright RB; Hall Scott L-62; 51, 114, 117	250	1 850	1 400	21.2	22.7	102	18.1	7.4	200		64	0.0316	3.22	4.38	9.0
Supermarine S-4; Napier Lion; 51, 114, 117	450	3 150		30.5	27.0	136	23.1	7.0	239		90	0.0274	3.73	6.84	12.1
Ryan NYP; Wright J-5C Whirlwind; 86	220	5 135	2 150	46.0	27.7	319	16.4	23.3	120	95	71	0.0379	12.10	6.63	10.1
Ford 5-AT; Pratt & Whitney R-1340 Wasp; 19, 84	b 420	13 500		77.8	50.3	835	16.2	10.7	150		64	0.0471	39.33	7.26	9.5
Lockheed Vega 5C; Pratt & Whitney R-1340 Wasp; 5, 21	450	4 033	2 465	41.0	27.5	275	14.7	9.0	190	150	58	0.0278	7.65	6.11	11.4
Curtiss Robin; Curtiss Challenger; 19, 78	185	2 600	1 648	41.0	25.1	223	11.7	14.1	115	102	47	0.0585	13.10	7.54	8.7
Travelair 4000; Wright J-5 Whirlwind; 3	220	2 450		34.7	24.2	297	8.3	11.1	135	110	46			4.80	
Curtiss Hawk P-6E; Curtiss V-1570; 6, 118	650	3 392	2 699	31.5	23.2	252	13.5	5.2	198	175	61	0.0371	9.35	4.76	8.7
Boeing P-26A; Pratt & Whitney R-1340 Wasp; 6, 118	600 (h = 6000)	3 012	2 271	27.9	23.6	149	20.2	5.0	234 (h = 7 500)	211	74	0.0448	6.68	5.24	8.3

Aircraft; Engine; Number														
Lockheed Orion 9D; Pratt & Whitney R–1340 Wasp; 5, 21	550	5 400	3 325	47.8	27.8	262	20.6	9.8	226	200	63	0.0210	5.502	7.01	14.1
Northrop Alpha; Pratt & Whitney R–1340 Wasp; 19	420	4 856		43.8	28.3	312	15.6	11.6	177	150	62	0.0274	8.55	5.93	11.3
Boeing 247D; Pratt & Whitney R–1340 Wasp; 5, 6	c525	13 650	8 940	74.0	51.3	836	16.3	13.0	202 (h=7 500)	185 (h=7 500)	61	0.0212	17.72	6.55	13.5
Douglas DC–3; Pratt & Whitney R–1830; 12	c1200	25 000	17 720	95.0	64.5	987	25.3	10.4	229 (h=7 500)	185 (h=10000)	67	0.0249	25.58	9.14	14.7
Boeing B–17G; Wright R–1820 Cyclone; 12, 118	d1200	55 000	36 135	103.8	74.3	1420	38.7	11.5	287 (h=25 000)	e182	90	0.0302	42.83	7.58	12.7
Seversky P–35; Pratt & Whitney R–1830; 8, 118	850 (h=8 000)	5 599	4 315	36.0	26.8	220	25.5	6.6	282 (h=10 000)	e260	79	0.0251	5.52	5.89	11.8
Piper J–3 Cub; Continental A–65; 12, 20	55	1 220	730	32.2	22.4	178	6.9	18.8	100	87		0.0373	6.64	5.81	9.6
Stinson SR–8B; Lycoming R–680; 7	245	3 650	2 310	41.8	27.5	256	14.3	14.9		140 (h=8 000)		0.0348	8.91	6.84	10.8
Beechcraft D17S; Pratt & Whitney R–985 Wasp Jr.; 10, 24	450	4 200	2 460	32.0	26.0	296	14.2	9.3		202 (h=9 700)	50	0.0182	5.39	4.18	11.7

a All speeds for sea level unless otherwise noted.
b For each of three engines.
c For each of two engines.
d For each of four engines.
e Altitude unknown.
f Estimated.

Table III.—Characteristics of Illustrative Aircraft, 1939–80

Aircraft; engine; and references	Physical characteristics								Performance characteristics						
	P_0	W_g	W_e	b	ι	S	W_g/S	W_g/P_0	V_{max}[a]	V_c[a]	V_s	$C_{D,0}$	f	A	$(L/D)_{max}$
Consolidated B-24J; Pratt & Whitney R-1830-65; 58, 118	[d]1200	56 000	38 000	110.0	67.2	1048	53.4	11.7	290 (h=25 000)	[f]215	95	0.0406	42.54	11.55	12.9
Boeing B-29;[b] Wright 3350-57; 58, 118	[d]2200	120 000	74 500	141.3	99	1736	69.1	13.6	357 (h=25 000)	[f]253	105	0.0241	41.16	11.50	16.8
Martin B-26F; Pratt & Whitney R-2800; 58, 118	[e]2000	37 000	23 700	71.0	56.0	658	56.2	9.3	274 (h=15 000)	[f]225	122	0.0314	20.66	7.66	12.0
North American P-51D; Rolls-Royce V-1650; 63, 66, 118	1490	10 100	7 125	37.0	32.3	233	43.4	6.8	437 (h=25 000)	[f]362	100	0.0163	3.80	5.86	14.6
Lockheed P-38L; Allison V-1710-111; 63, 118	[e]1470	17 500	12 800	52.0	37.9	327.5	53.4	6.9	414 (h=25 000)		105	0.0268	8.78	8.26	13.5
Grumman F6F-3; Pratt & Whitney R-2800; 63, 118	2000	12 441	9 101	42.8	33.6	334	37.3	6.2	375 (h=17 300)	[f]160	84	0.0211	7.05	5.34	12.2
Curtiss SB2C-1; Wright R-2600-8; 109, 118	1750	14 730	10 114	49.8	36.7	422	34.9	10.2	281 (h=12 400)	[f]158	79	0.0225	9.52	5.88	12.4
Lockheed L.1049G; Wright R-3350; 14, 67	[d]3250	133 000		123.0	113.5	1650	80.6	10.2	352 (h=10 500)	331 (h=23 000)	100	0.0211	34.82	9.17	16.0
Vickers Viscount[c] (700 series); Rolls-Royce Dart 506; 14, 67	[d]1600	60 000	36 776	93.8	81.2	963	62.3	9.4		334 (h=25 000)				9.14	

Aircraft; engine; ref															
Lockheed C-130; c Allison T-56; 16	d 4910	155 000	75 331	132.6	97.7	1745	88.8	7.9		386 (h = 20 000)	115				10.08
Piper Cherokee; Lycoming O-360; 15	180	2 450	1 386	32.0	24.0	170	14.4	13.6	148	141 (h = 7 000)	61	0.0358	6.09	6.02	10.0
Cessna Skyhawk; Lycoming O-320; 16	150	2 300	1 350	35.0	26.9	175	13.1	15.3	144	138 (h = 8 000)	49	0.0319	5.58	7.32	11.6
Beech Bonanza V-35; Continental IO-520; 16	285	3 400	2 051	33.5	26.4	181	18.8	11.9	210	203 (h = 6 500)	63	0.0192	3.48	6.20	13.8
Cessna Cardinal RG II; Lycoming O-360; 16	200	2 800	1 750	36.5	27.3	174	16.1	14.0	180	171 (h = 7 000)	57	0.0223	3.88	7.66	14.2
Cessna 310 II; Continental IO-520; 16	e 285	5 500	3 417	36.9	29.3	179	30.7	9.7	238	223 (h = 7 500)	77	0.0267	4.78	7.61	13.0
Beech Super King Air 200; Pratt & Whitney (Canada) PT6A-41; 16	e 850	12 500	7 315	54.5	43.8	303	41.3	6.9	333 (h = 15 000)	320 (h = 25 000)	92			9.80	

a All speeds for sea level unless otherwise noted.
b Aerodynamic parameters based on data in E-29 Cruise Control Manual.
c Uncertainties about power variation with altitude prevented estimation of aerodynamic parameters.
d For each of four engines.
e For each of two engines.
f Altitude unknown.

Table IV.—Characteristics of Illustrative Flying Boats

Aircraft; engine; and references	Physical characteristics								Performance characteristics						
	P_0	W_g	W_e	b	ι	S	W_g/S	W_g/P_0	V_{max}^a	V_c^a	V_s	$C_{D,0}$	f	A	$(L/D)_{max}$
Curtiss H-16; Liberty; 93, 118	b 400	10 900	7 400	95.1	46.1	1164	9.4	13.6	95	e 86	e 60	0.0738	85.92	9.40	8.4
Curtiss HS-2L; Liberty; 93, 118, 109	350	6 432	4 300	74.0	39.0	803	8.0	18.4	83	e 76	e 56	0.0676	54.24	8.24	8.2
Curtiss F-5L; Liberty; 93, 118, 109	b 400	13 600	8 720	103.0	49.3	1397	9.7	17.0	90	e 82	e 61	0.0694	96.95	9.33	8.6
Navy-Curtiss NC-4; Liberty; 93, 118, 109	c 400	27 386	15 874	125.0	68.3	2380	11.5	17.1	85	e 77	e 67	0.0899	213.96	8.07	7.0
Martin PM-1; Wright R-1820-64; 93, 118, 109	b 575	16 117	8 970	72.8	49.2	1236	13.1	14.0	119	e 108	61	0.0478	59.08	5.19	7.7
Hall XP2H-1; Curtiss V-1570-54; 6, 118	c 600	35 393	20 856	112.0	70.2	2742	12.9	14.8	139	120	59	0.0291	79.76	5.54	10.2
Loening OA-1C; Packard 1A-2500; 88, 89, 109	475	5 316	3 673	45.0	35.1	504	10.5	11.2	122	e 111	e 60	0.0458	23.08	4.86	7.64
Sikorsky S-38B; Pratt & Whitney R-1340; 5, 67	b 420	10 480	6 500	7_.7	40.3	720	14.6	12.5	125	110	55	0.0543	39.10	7.14	8.5
Consolidated Commodore; Pratt & Whitney R-1690 Series B; 67	b 575	17 600	11 500	100.1	68.0	1110	15.9	15.3	e 120	108	e 66	0.0562	62.38	9.00	9.4
Dornier Do X; Curtiss V-1570; 67, 114, 93	d 640	105 820	76 764	157.5	131.3	4844	21.9	13.8	134	e 122	e 75	0.0472	228.64	5.12	7.7
Sikorsky S-42; Pratt & Whitney R-1690–T1C1; 67, 114, 93	c 700 (h=5000)	38 000	24 000	114.2	64.2	1340	28.4	13.6	182 (h=5 000)	170 (h=12 000)	e 70	0.0362	47.51	9.73	12.2
Martin 130; Pratt & Whitney R-1830-G9; 9, 24, 67, 93	c 950	52 252	24 611	130.0	90.9	2170	24.1	13.8	180 (h=7 000)	163 (h=7 000)	e 80	0.0303	65.75	7.88	11.9

Aircraft; engine; propeller														
Boeing 314; Wright GR-2600; 67, 11, 93, 99	c 1 600	84 000	48 400	152.0	106.0	2867	29.3	13.1	201 (h=6 200)	184 (h=11 000)	70	0.0274	78.56	8.06	13.0
Douglas Dolphin; Pratt & Whitney R-1340-96; 5, 93, 109	b 450	9 337	6 377	60.0	45.1	592	15.9	10.4	153	e 139	e 64	0.0430	25.46	6.08	8.82
Grumman G-21; Pratt & Whitney R-985-AN-6; 9, 23	b 450	8 030	5 425	49.0	38.5	375	21.3	8.9	201 (h=5 000)	191 (h=5 000)	e 61	0.0325	12.19	6.40	10.5
Fleetwings F-5; Jacobs L-5; 9	285	3 750	2 450	40.5	32.0	235	16.0	13.2	150	135	e 53	0.0345	8.11	7.28	10.6
Consolidated PBY-5A; Pratt & Whitney R-1830-92; 24, 64, 93, 109, 118	b 1200	33 975	20 910	104.0	63.8	1400	24.3	14.2	179 (h=7 000)	117	e 79	0.0309	43.26	7.73	11.9
Consolidated PB2Y-3; Pratt & Whitney R-1830-88; 109, 118, 93, 64	c 1200	68 000	41 031	115.0	79.3	1780	38.2	14.2	224 (h=19 500)	140	e 76	0.0281	50.02	7.43	12.3
Martin PBM-3D; Wright R-2600-22; 109, 118, 93, 64	b 1 900	51 608	32 848	118.0	79.8	1408	36.7	13.6	202 (h=15 900)	135	e 76	0.0327	46.04	9.89	13.2
Martin JRM-1; Wright R-3350-B; 13, 109, 118	c 2200	145 000	78 805	200.0	123.2	3683	39.4	16.5	222	153	e 88	0.0233	84.34	10.86	16.4
Martin P5M-2; Wright R-3350-32W; 14, 109, 118	b 3450	76 595	49 218	118.1	100.2	1406	54.5	10.4	251	159	112	0.0275	38.67	9.92	14.4

a All speeds for sea level unless otherwise noted.
b For each of two engines.
c For each of four engines.
d For each of 12 engines
e Estimated.

Table V.—Characteristics of Illustrative Jet Fighter Aircraft

Aircraft; engine; and references	Physical characteristics									
	b	ι	S	A	Λ	W_{max}	W_g	W_e	T/W_g	W_g/S
Messerschmitt Me 262A; two Junkers Jumo turbojets of 1984 lb thrust each; 141, 162, 163	41.1	34.8	233.6	7.23	[c]18.5	15 720	14 101	8 378	0.28	60.4
Gloster Meteor F.Mk.4; two Rolls-Royce Derwent 5 turbojets of 3500 lb thrust each; 162, 163, 188	37.1	41.0	350.0	3.93	0	18 000	15 000	10 050	0.47	43.0
Bell P-59A; two General Electric J31-GE-5 turbojets of 2000 lb thrust each; 163, 171, 200	45.5	38.9	385.0	5.38	0	13 000	10 822	7 950	0.37	28.1
Lockheed P-80A; one Allison J33-A-11 turbojet of 4000 lb thrust; 162, 163, 200, 206	38.9	34.5	237.6	6.37	0	14 000	11 700	7 920	0.34	49.2
McDonnell FH-1; two Westinghouse J30-WE-20 turbojets of 1560 lb thrust each; 162, 163, 191, 200	40.8	38.8	274.0	6.08	0	12 500	9 974	6 699	0.31	36.4
North American F-86E; one General Electric J47-GE-13 turbojet of 5200 lb thrust; 162, 163, 171, 200	37.1	37.5	287.9	4.78	35.0	17 806	14 856	10 845	0.35	51.6
Grumman F9F-8; one Pratt & Whitney J48-P-8 turbojet of 7250 lb thrust; 162, 171, 191, 200	34.5	42.1	337.0	3.53	35.0	24 763	20 098	11 866	0.36	59.6
North American F-100D; one Pratt & Whitney J57-P-21 turbojet of 16 000/10 000 lb thrust; [a] 162, 163, 171, 200	38.8	49.3	400.2	3.76	45.0		34 050	20 638	0.47	85.1
Convair F-106A; one Pratt & Whitney J75-P-17 turbojet of 24 000/16 100 lb thrust; [a] 163, 171, 200	38.3	70.7	697.8	2.10	[c]60.0		34 510	24 038	0.70	49.5
Lockheed F-104G; one General Electric J79-GE-11A turbojet of 15 600/10 000 lb thrust; [a] 162, 163, 171, 200	21.9	54.8	196.1	2.45	0	29 083	27 300	13 996	0.57	139.2
Republic F-105D; one Pratt & Whitney J75-P-19W turbojet of 24 500/10 000 lb thrust; [a] 162, 171, 200	34.9	64.3	385.0	3.16	45.0	52 838	48 976	26 855	0.50	127.2

Aircraft									
Vought F-8H; one Pratt & Whitney J57-P-420 turbojet of 16 600/12 400 lb thrust; [a] 162, 163, 200	35.8	54.2	375.0	3.42	35.0	34 200	29 200	18 700	0.57	77.8
McDonnell F-4E; two General Electric J79-GE-17 turbojets of 17 900/11 1·0 lb thrust each; [a] 129, 162, 163, 200	38.3	63.0	530.0	2.77	[c] 45.0	61 651	53 848	29 535	0.66	101.6
Northrop F-5E; two General Electric J85-GE-21 turbojets of 5000/3500 lb thrust each; [a] 129, 162, 163, 200	26.8	48.2	186.0	3.86	24.0	20 486	15 745	9 588	0.64	84.7
General Dynamics F-111D two Pratt & Whitney TF30-P-9 turbofans of 20 840/12 430 lb thrust each; [a] 162, 171, 200	[b] 63/32	73.5	525.0	[b] 7.56/1.95	[b] 16/72.5	98 850	82 819	46 172	0.50	157.8
Grumman F-14A; two Pratt & Whitney TF30-P-412A turbofans of 20 000/12 500 lb thrust each; [a] 162, 163, 171, 200	[b] 64.1/37.6	62.0	565.0	[b] 7.3/2.5	[b] 20/68	74 348	70 345	39 930	0.57	124.5
McDonnell Douglas F-15C; two Pratt & Whitney F100-PW-100 turbofans of 23 904/14 780 lb thrust each; [a] 130, 162, 163, 171, 200	42.8	63.8	608.0	3.01	[c] 45.0	68 000	44 500	28 700	1.07	73.2
General Dynamics F-16A; one Pratt & Whitney F100-PW-200 turbofan of 23 830/14 800 lb thrust; [a] 162, 163, 200	35.0	47.6	300.0	4.08	[c] 40.0	34 500	23 357	14 567	1.02	77.9
British Aerospace Harrier AV-8A; one Rolls-Royce Pegasus 103 turbofan of 21 500 lb thrust; 130, 162	25.3	47.6	201.1	3.18	34.0	26 000	18 000	12 140	1.19	89.5

See footnotes at end of table.

Table V.—Characteristics of Illustrative Jet Fighter Aircraft—Continued

Aircraft; engine; and references	Performance characteristics										
	V_{max}		V_c	h_{SL}	T	h_{ce}	Ferry range, miles	f	$C_{D, 0}$	$(L/D)_{max}$	First flight [d]
	High altitude	Low altitude									
Messerschmitt Me 262A; two Junkers Jumo turbojets of 1984 lb thrust each; 141, 162, 163	540 (M=0.76) at h=19 685	514 (M=0.67) at h=0		3 939			528				3/25/42
Gloster Meteor F.Mk.4; two Rolls-Royce Derwent 5 turbojets of 3500 lb thrust each; 162, 163, 188	570 (M=0.81) at h=20 000	585 (M=0.77) at h=0	520	7 500	5.0 (h=30 000)		1000				3/5/43
Bell P-59A; two General Electric J31-GE-5 turbojets of 2000 lb thrust each; 163, 171, 200	413 (M=0.61) at h=30 000	380 (M=0.51) at h=5000	375	3 200	15.5 (h=30 000)	46 200	375				10/1/42
Lockheed P-80A; one Allison J33-A-11 turbojet of 4000 lb thrust; 162, 163, 200, 206	508 (M=0.75) at h=30 000	558 (M=0.73) at h=0	410	4 580	5.5 (h=20 000)	45 000	540	3.2	0.0134	17.7	1/8/44
McDonnell FH-1; two Westinghouse J30-WE-20 turbojets of 1560 lb thrust each; 162, 163, 191, 200	485 (M=0.67) at h=15 000	472 (M=0.62) at h=0	307	4 000	11.0 (h=30 000)	34 500	910				1/26/45
North American F-86E; one General Electric J47-GE-13 turbojet of 5200 lb thrust; 162, 163, 171, 200	601 (M=0.91) at h=35 000	679 (M=0.89) at h=0	537	7 250	6.3 (h=30 000)	47 200	1022	3.8	0.0132	15.1	10/1/47

Aircraft										
Grumman F9F-8; one Pratt & Whitney J48-P-8 turbo et of 7250 lb thrust; 162, 171, 191, 200	593 (M=0.89) at h=35 000	647 (M=0.86) at h=2000	516	4 800	8.3 (h=30 000)	42 000	1312			9/20/51
North American F-100D: one Pratt & Whitney J57-P-21 turbojet of 16 000/10 C00 lb thrust; [a] 162, 163, 171, 200	927 (M=1.39) at h=35 000	639 (M=0.97) at h=0	587	22 400		51 300	1971	5.0	0.0130	13.9	5/25/53
Convair F-106A; one Pratt & Whitney J75-P-17 turbojet of 24 000/16 100 lb thrust; [a] 163, 171, 200	1 525 (M=2.31) at h=40 000				6.9 (h=51 800)	52 700	1809	5.8	0.0083	12.1	12/26/56
Lockhead F-104G; one General Electric J79-GE-11A turbojet of 15 600/10 000 lb thrust; [a] 162, 163, 171, 200	1 328 (M=2.0) at h=35 000	860 (M=1.13) at h=0		48 000		50 000	1875	3.37	0.0172	9.2	2/7/54
Republic F-105D; one Pratt & Whitney J75-P-19W turbojet of 24 500/10 000 lb thrust; [a] 162, 171, 200	1 372 (M=2.08) at h=36 090	836 (M=1.1) at h=0	584	38 500	1.7 (h=35 000)	49 600	2207	6.65	0.0173	10.4	10/22/55
Vought F-8H; one Pratt & Whitney J57-P-420 turbojet of 16 600/12 400 lb thrust; [a] 162, 163, 200	1 156 (M=1.75) at h=36 100	762 (M=1.0) at h=0	556	23 300		51 000	1427	5.0	0.0133	12.8	3/25/55
McDonnell F-4E; two General Electric J79-GE-17 turbojets of 17 900/11 110 lb thrust each; [a] 129, 162, 163, 230	1 485 (M=2.25) at h=40 000	914 (M=1.2) at h=0	586	54 200		59 200	1885	11.87	0.0224	8.58	5/27/58

491

Table V.—Characteristics of Illustrative Jet Fighter Aircraft—Continued

Aircraft; engine; and references	Performance characteristics										
	V_{max}		V_c	h_{SL}	T	h_{ce}	Ferry range, miles	f	$C_{D,0}$	$(L/D)_{max}$	First flight [d]
	High altitude	Low altitude									
Northrop F-5E; two General Electric J85-GE-21 turbojets of 5000/3500 lb thrust each;[a] 129, 162, 163, 200	997 (M=1.51) at h=36 090	845 (M=1.17) at h=0		28 536		53 800	1353	3.4	0.0200	10.0	7/30/59
General Dynamics F-111D; two Pratt & Whitney TF30-P-9 turbofans of 20 840/12 430 lb thrust each;[a] 162, 171, 200	1453 (M=2.2) at h=50 100	914 (M=1.2) at h=0	500	25 800		53 400	3298	9.36	0.0186	15.8	12/21/64
Grumman F-14A; two Pratt & Whitney TF30-P-412A turbofans of 20 000/12 500 lb thrust each;[a] 162, 163, 171, 200	1 584 (M=2.4) at h=49 000	913 (M=1.2) at h=0			2.1 (h=60 000)						12/21/70
McDonnell Douglas F-15C; two Pratt & Whitney F100-PW-100 turbofans of 23 904/14 780 lb thrust each;[a] 130, 162, 163, 171, 200	1 676 (M=2.54) at h=40 000	922 (M=1.21) at h=0				63 000	3570				7/27/72
General Dynamics F-16A; one Pratt & Whitney F100-PW-200 turbofan of 23 830/14 800 lb thrust;[a] 162, 163, 200	1 333 (M=2.02) at h=40 000						2535				1/20/74
British Aerospace Harrier AV-8A; one Rolls-Royce Pegasus 103 turbofan at 21 500 lb thrust; 130, 162		720 (M=0.95) at h=1000			2.38 (h=40 000)	48 000	2070				10/21/60

[a] First value is maximum thrust with afterburning; second value is maximum thrust without afterburning.
[b] First value corresponds to minimum sweepback angle.
[c] Leading edge.
[d] Date for first prototype of series.

Table VI.—Characteristics of Illustrative Jet Bombers and Attack Aircraft

Aircraft; engine; and references	Physical characteristics									
	b	ι	S	A	Λ	W_g	W_p	W_e	T/W_g	W_g/S
North American B-45C; four General Electric J47-GE-13 turbojets of 5200 lb thrust each; 126, 200	89.0	75.5	1175	6.74	0	110 050	10 000	48 969	0.19	93.7
Boeing B-47E; six General Electric J47-GE-25 turbojets of 7200/5970 lb thrust each; [a] 125, 126, 170, 200	116.0	107.1	1428	9.42	35	198 180	10 845	80 756	0.22	138.8
Boeing B-52H; eight Pratt & Whitney TF-33-P-3 turbofans of 17 000 lb thrust each; 126, 200	185.0	156.0	4000	8.56	35	488 000	10 000	169 822	0.28	112.5
Convair B-58A; four General Electric J79-GE-5B turbojets of 15 500/10 300 lb thrust each; [b] 127, 200	56.8	96.8	1542	2.09	[d] 60	163 000		55 560	0.38	105.7
Martin YP6M-1; four Allison J71-A-6 turbojets of 13 000/9 500 lb thrust each; [b] 200	102.5	134.3	1900	5.53	40	167 011	30 000	84 685	0.31	87.9
Rockwell International B-1A; four General Electric F101-GE-100 turbofans of 30 030/16 975 lb thrust each; [b] 130, 170, 200	[c] 136.8/78.1	150.1	1950	[c] 9.85/3.13	[c] 15/67.5	389 000			0.30	202.6
Martin B-57B; two Wright J65-W-5 turbojets of 7200 lb thrust each 126, 135, 170, 200	64.0	65.5	960	4.27	0	53 721	5 240	27 091	0.27	56.0
Douglas A-4E; one Pratt & Whitney J52-P-6A turbojet of 8500 lb thrust; 127, 164, 200	27.5	41.3	260	2.91	33	18 311	2 040	9 624	0.46	70.4
Grumman A-6E; two Pratt & Whitney J52-P-8A turbojets of 9300 lb thrust each; 129, 200	53.0	54.8	529	5.31	25	54 393	2 080	25 980	0.34	102.8
Vought A-7D; one Allison TF41-A-1 turbofan of 14 250 lb thrust; 136, 200	38.8	46.1	375	4.00	35	38 008	6 560	19 733	0.38	101.4
Fairchild-Republic A-10A; two General Electric TF34-GE-100 turbofans of 9065 lb thrust each; 200	57.5	53.3	506	6.53	0	40 269	9 540	19 856	0.45	79.6

See footnotes at end of table.

Table VI.—Characteristics of Illustrative Jet Bombers and Attack Aircraft—Continued

Aircraft; engine; and references	V_{max} High altitude	V_{max} Low altitude	V_c	V_s	h_{SL}	h_{ce}	R_D	R_F	f	$C_{D,0}$	$(L/D)_{max}$	First flight
North American B-45C: four General Electric J47-GE-13 turbojets of 5200 lb thrust each; 126, 200	509 (M=0.76) at h=32 500	573 (M=0.75) at h=0	466	153			1008	2 426	18.80	[f]0.0160	[f]16.3	3/17/47
Boeing B-47E; six General Electric J47-GE-25 turbojets of 7200/5970 lb thrust each; [a] 125, 126, 170, 200	557 (M=0.84) at h=38 550	607 (M=0.85) at h=16 300	498	175	4 660	40 500	2013	4 035	21.13	[f]0.0148	[f]20.0	12/17/47
Boeing B-52H; eight Pratt & Whitney TF-33-P-3 turbofans of 17 000 lb thrust each; 126, 200	639 (M=0.91) at h=20 700		525	169	6 990	47 200	4480	10 145	47.60	[f]0.0119	[f,g]21.5	4/15/52
Convair B-58A; four General Electric J79-GE-5B turbojets of 15 500/10 300 lb thrust each; [b] 127, 200	1 321 (M=2.0) at h=63 150	700 (M=0.92) at h=0	610		17 830	64 800	1500	4 025	10.49	0.0068	[h]11.3	11/11/56
Martin YP6M-1; four Allison J71-A-6 turbojets of 13 000/9 500 lb thrust each; [b] 200	646 (M=0.86) at h=5 000		540	145	3 550	35 000	800	[f]3 500				7/14/55
Rockwell International B-1A; four General Electric F101-GE-100 turbofans of 30 000/16 975 lb thrust each; [b] 130, 170, 200	1 452 (M=2.2) at h=50 000	648 (M=0.85) at h=50 000										12/23/74

Aircraft and engines	Max. speed (altitude)	Max. speed (h=0)										First flight
Martin B-57B; two Wright J65-W-5 turbojets of 7200 lb thrust each; 126, 135, 170, 200	598 (M=0.79) at h=2500		476	124	6 180	45 100	948	2 722	11.45	0.0119	15.0	7/20/53
Douglas A-4E; one Pratt & Whitney J52-P-6A turbojet of 8500 lb thrust; 127, 164, 200	673 (M=0.88) at h=0		498	139		40 050	680	2 130				6/22/54
Grumman A-6E; two Pratt & Whitney J52-P-8A turbojets of 9300 lb thrust each; 129, 200	653 (M=0.86) at h=0		390	142		40 000	890	3 300	7.64	0.0144	15.2	4/19/60
Vought A-7D; one Allison TF41-A-1 turbofan of 14 250 lb thrust; 136, 200	663 (M=0.89) at h=7 000	654 (M=0.86) at h=0	507	174		38 800	556	3 045				9/27/65
Fairchild-Republic A-10A two General Electric TF34-GE-100 turbofans of 9065 lb thrust each; 200	460 (M=0.63) at h=10 000	448 (M=0.59) at h=0	329	120	6 200	37 800	e 288	3 510				5/10/72

a First value, with water injection; second value, dry.
b First value, with afterburning; second value, without afterburning.
c First value corresponds to minimum sweepback angle; second value corresponds to maximum sweepback angle.
d Leading edge.
e Loiter time of 2 hours on station.
f Author's estimate.
g For B-52G.
h Without pod.

495

Table VII.—Characteristics of Illustrative Jet Transport Aircraft

Aircraft; engine; and references	Physical characteristics									
	b	ℓ	S	A	Λ	W_g	W_L	W_e	T/W_g	W_g/S
DeHavilland Comet 1A; 4 DH Ghost turbojets, each 5000-lb thrust; 125, 126, 169	115	93	2015	6.6	20	115 000			0.17	57.1
Tupolev Tu-104B; 2 Mikulin turbojets, each 21 385-lb thrust; 127, 131, 190	113.3	131.5	1975	6.5	40/37.5	167 551	141 096	93 696	0.26	84.8
Boeing 367-80; 4 Pratt & Whitney JT3C turbojets, each 10 000-lb thrust; 126	129.8	127.8	2400	7.0	35	190 000		92 120	0.21	79.2
Boeing 707-320B; 4 Pratt & Whitney JT3D-7 turbofans, each 19 000-lb thrust; 129, 130, 147	145.8	152.8	3010	7.1	35	336 000	247 000	147 000	0.23	111.6
McDonnell Douglas DC-8 Super 63; 4 Pratt & Whitney JT3D-7 turbofans, each 19 000-lb thrust; 128, 131, 147	148.4	187.5	2926.8	7.5	30.6	358 000	245 000	158 300	0.21	122.3
Sud-Aviation Caravelle VI-R; 2 Rolls-Royce Avon turbojets, each 12 000-lb thrust; 127, 131	112.5	105	1579	8.0	20	114 640	104 990	59 985	0.21	72.6
Boeing 727-200; 3 Pratt & Whitney JT8D-17 turbofans, each 16 000-lb thrust; 129, 131, 148	108	153.2	1650	7.1	32	210 000	160 000	103 000	0.23	127.3
McDonnell Douglas DC-9-30; 2 Pratt & Whitney JT8D-15 turbofans, each 15 500-lb thrust; 129, 131, 148	93.3	119.3	1001	8.7	24.5	109 000	99 000	56 000	0.28	108.9
Boeing 737-200; 2 Pratt & Whitney JT8D-17 turbofans, each 16 000-lb thrust; 129, 131, 148	93	100	980	8.8	25	117 500	105 000	60 980	0.27	119.9
British Aircraft Corporation VC-10; 4 Rolls-Royce Conway RC042 turbofans, each 21 000-lb thrust; 127, 131	142.2	158.8	2932	6.9	32.5	314 000	216 000	146 979	0.27	107.1
Boeing 747-200B; 4 Pratt & Whitney JT9D-7R4G2 turbofans, each 54 750-lb thrust; 129, 131, 150	195.8	231	5500	7.0	37.5	836 000	564 000	382 130	0.26	152
Lockheed L-1011-200; 3 Rolls-Royce RB.211-524 turbofans, each 48 000-lb thrust; 129, 148	155.3	177.7	3456	7.0	35	468 000	368 000	245 800	0.31	135.4
McDonnell Douglas DC-10-30; 3 General Electric CF6-50C1 turbofans, each 52 500-lb thrust; 129, 148	165.3	181.6	3647	7.5	35	575 000	403 000	261 459	0.27	158

Boeing 767–200; 2 Pratt & Whitney JT9D–7R4E turbofans, each 50 000-lb thrust; 130, 150	156.1	159.2	3050	8.0	31.5	337 000	278 000	180 230	0.30	111
Boeing 757–200; 2 Pratt & Whitney PW2037 turbofans, each 38 200-lb thrust; 130, 150	124.5	155.3	1951	7.9	25	241 000	198 000	128 050	0.32	123.5
Lockheed C–5A; 4 General Electric TF–39 turbofans, each 41 000-lb thrust; 129	222.8	247.8	6200	8.0	25	769 000	635 850		0.21	124

See footnotes at end of table.

Table VII.—Characteristics of Illustrative Jet Transport Aircraft—Continued

Aircraft; engine; and references	Performance characteristics								
	V_c	V_{ce}	V_s	Maximum payload range [a]	Full fuel tanks range [a]	l_T [b]	l_L [b]	Number of passengers [c]	First flight [d]
DeHavilland Comet 1A; 4 DH Ghost turbojets, each 5000-lb thrust; 125, 126, 169	490 (M=0.74) at h=35 000			1 750				44	7/27/49
Tupolev Tu-104B; 2 Mikulin turbojets, each 21 385-lb thrust; 127, 131, 190	590 (M=0.85) at h=25 000	497 (M=0.75) at h=35 000	127	[e] 1 500 (W_p=26 455)	2 214 (W_p=13 225)	[f] 7 220	[f] 6070	100	6/17/55
Boeing 367-80; 4 Pratt & Whitney JT3C turbojets, each 10 000-lb thrust; 126	550			(W_p=25 000)					7/15/54
Boeing 707-320B; 4 Pratt & Whitney JT3D-7 turbofans, each 19 000-lb thrust; 129, 130, 147	593 (M=0.87) at h=30 000	550 (M=0.83) at h=35 000	121	6240 (W_p=53 900)	7 975 (W_p=33 350)	10 000	6250	189	1959
McDonnell Douglas DC-8 Super 63; 4 Pratt & Whitney JT3D-7 turbofans, each 19 000-lb thrust; 128, 131, 147	596 (M=0.87) at h=29 000	544 (M=0.82) at h=35 000	123	4 882 (W_p=67 735)	6 997 (W_p=37 101)	10 440	5900	259	1958
Sud-Aviation Caravelle VI-R; 2 Rolls-Royce Avon turbojets, each 12 000-lb thrust; 127, 131	526 (M=0.76) at h=25 000	488 (M=0.74) at h=35 000		1 829 (W_p=16 800)		6 750	3650	80	5/27/55

Aircraft								
Boeing 727-200; 3 Pratt & Whitney JT8D-17 turbofans, each 16 000-lb thrust; 129, 131, 148	610 (M=0.88) at h=25 000	349 (M=0.82) at h=33 000	121	3 335 (W_p=41 000)	3 738 (W_p=36 000)	9 950	4900	189	1963
McDonnell Douglas DC-9-30; 2 Pratt & Whitney JT8D-15 turbofans, each 15 500-lb thrust; 129, 131, 148	578 (M=0.84) at h=26 000	522 (M=0.78) at h=33 000	120	1812 (W_p=31 000)	2210 (W_p=27 527)	6 200	4700	115	1965
Boeing 737-200; 2 Pratt & Whitney JT8D-17 turbofans, each 16 000-lb thrust; 129, 131, 148	564 (M=0.81) at h=25 000	501 (M=0.75) at h=33 000	116	1 748 (W_p=34 000)	3 082 (W_p=21 750)	6 475	4430	130	1967
British Aircraft Corporation VC-10; 4 Rolls-Royce Conway RC042 turbofans, each 21 000-lb thrust; 127, 131	538	550 (M=0.83) at h=38 000	138	5 040 (W_p=39 769)		8 280	6380	151	6/29/62
Boeing 747-200B; 4 Pratt & Whitney JT9D-7R4G2 turbofans, each 54 750-lb thrust; 129, 131, 150	533	564 (M=0.85) at h=35 000	125	6 854 (W_p=144 520)	8 706 (W_p=87 800)	10 450	6150	550	2/9/69
Lockheed L-1011-200; 3 Rolls-Royce RB.211-524 turbofans, each 48 000-lb thrust; 129, 148	607 (M=0.90) at h=31 000	567 (M=0.84) at h=31 000	125	4 884 (W_p=74 200)	6 204 (W_p=42 827)	8 070	5820	400	11/16/70
McDonnell Douglas DC-10-30; 3 General Electric CF6-50C1 turbofans, each 52 500-lb thrust; 129, 148	593 (M=0.88) at h=31 000	574 (M=0.85) at h=31 000	125	4 853 (W_p=106 541)	6 296 (W_p=65 175)	10 370	5830	386	8/70

499

Table VII.—Characteristics of Illustrative Jet Transport Aircraft —Continued

Aircraft; engine; and references	Performance characteristics								
	V_c	V_{ce}	V_s	Maximum payload range [a]	Full fuel tanks range [a]	l_T [b]	l_L [b]	Number of passengers [c]	First flight [d]
Boeing 767-200; 2 Pratt & Whitney JT9D-7R4E turbofans, each 50 000-lb thrust; 130, 150	557 (M=0.84) at h=39 000	528 (M=0.80) at h=39 000	122	4 111 (W_p=72 770)	5 992 (W_p=42 545)	7 000	4850	290	9/81
Boeing 757-200; 2 Pratt & Whitney PW2037 turbofans, each 38 200-lb thrust; 130, 150	561 (M=0.83) at h=30 000	528 (M=0.80) at h=30 000	117	3 749 (W_p=56 050)	5 290 (W_p=36 900)	7 370	4600	239	2/82
Lockheed C-5A; 4 General Electric TF-39 turbofans, each 41 000-lb thrust; 129	541 (M=0.78) at h=25 000		120	3 744 (W_p=220 967)	6 521 (W_p=112 600)	[f] 8 400	[f] 3600		6/30/68

[a] With no allowance for reserve fuel.
[b] FAR field lengths.
[c] All-tourist seating arrangement.
[d] Date for first prototype of series.
[e] With allowance for reserve fuel.
[f] Not FAR field length.

Table VIII.—Characteristics of Illustrative Business Jet Aircraft

Aircraft; engine; and references	b	ι	S	A	Λ	W_g	W_L	W_e	$\frac{T}{W_g}$	W_g/S
						Performance characteristics				
Lockheed JetStar; 4 Pratt & Whitney JT–12–8 turbojets, each 3300-lb thrust; 127, 129, 167	54.5	60.5	542.5	5.3	30	42 500	35 000	21 676	0.31	78.3
Gates Learjet 24B; 2 General Electric CJ610–4 turbojets, each 2850-lb thrust; 127	35.5	43.3	231.8	5.4	13	13 300	11 880	6 700	0.43	57.4
Gates Learjet 55; 2 AiResearch TFE 731–3 turbofans, each 3650-lb thrust; 130,144	43.8	55.1	264.5	7.3	13	19 500	17 000	12 130	0.37	73.7
Dassault-Breguet Falcon 20; 2 General Electric CF700 turbofans, each 4315-lb thrust; 129,144,167	53.5	56.3	440	6.5	30	28 660		15 970	0.30	65.1
Gulfstream Aerospace Gulfstream II; 2 Rolls-Royce Spey Mk 511–8 turbofans, each 11 400-lb thrust; 129, 144, 167	68.8	79.9	793.5	6.0	25	62 500	58 500	37 186	0.56	79
Cessna Citation II; 2 Pratt & Whitney JT15D–4 turbofans, each 2500-lb thrust; 129, 130, 144	51.8	47.2	323	8.3	0	13 300	12 700	7 181	0.38	41.2
Cessna Citation III; 2 AiResearch TFE 731–3 turbofans, each 3650-lb thrust; 129, 130, 144	53.3	55.5	312	9.11	25	20 000	16 500	10 951	0.37	64.1
MBB HFB Hansa; 2 General Electric CJ610–1 turbojets, each 2850-lb thrust; 127, 131	47.5	54.5	324.4	7.0	–15	18 740	17 860	10 670	0.31	57.8

501

Table VIII.—Characteristics of Illustrative Business Jet Aircraft—Continued

Aircraft; engine; and references	Performance characteristics							Number of passengers	First flight
	V_c	V_{ce}	V_s	Maximum payload range [a]	Full fuel tanks range [a]	l_T [b]	l_L [b]		
Lockheed JetStar; 4 Pratt & Whitney JT-12-8 turbojets, each 3300-lb thrust; 127, 129, 167	567 (M=0.80) at h=21 000	520	122	2415 (W_p=3500)		c 47 00	c 3550	8 to 10	9/9/57
Gates Learjet 24B; 2 General Electric CJ610-4 turbojets, each 2850-lb thrust; 127	534 (M=0.81) at h=41 000	508 (M=0.77) at h=41 000	104	1271 (W_p=1910)	2041	3 100	3350	6	10/7/63
Gates Learjet 55; 2 AiResearch TFE 731-3 turbofans, each 3650-lb thrust; 130, 144	505 (M=0.76) at h=45 000	461 (M=0.70) at h=49 000	113		2489 (4 passengers)	4 950	3109	6 to 10	4/19/79
Dassault-Breguet Falcon 20; 2 General Electric CF700 turbofans, each 4315-lb thrust; 129, 144, 167	535 (M=0.77) at h=25 000	466 (M=0.70) at h=40 000	94		2220 (W_p=1600)	4 750 (W_g=27 130)	3220	8 to 10	7/10/64
Gulfstream Aerospace Gulfstream II; 2 Rolls-Royce Spey Mk 511-8 turbofans, each 11 400-lb thrust; 129, 144, 167	588 (M=0.85) at h=25 000	503 (M=0.76) at h=43 000	128		3881	5 000	3190	10 to 14	10/2/66
Cessna Citation II; 2 Pratt & Whitney JT15D-4 turbofans, each 2500-lb thrust; 129, 130, 144	443 (M=0.64) at h=25 000		94		1969 (6 passengers)	2 990	2270	6 to 10	9/16/69

Cessna Citation III; 2 AiResearch TFE 731-3 turbofans, each 3650-lb thrust, 129, 130, 144	539 (M=0.81) at h=33 000	104	2875	(6 passengers)	4 510	2770	Maximum of 13	5/30/79
MBB HFB Hansa; 2 General Electric CJ610-1 turbojets, each 2850-lb thrust, 127, 131	509 (M=0.74) at h=26 000	449 (M=0.68) at h=39 000	101	949 (W_p=2650)	1668 (W_p=1760)	4 650	2900	9 or 10	4/64

[a] With 45 minutes of reserve fuel.
[b] FAR field lengths.
[c] Not FAR field lengths.

Appendix B

Symbols and Abbreviations

Symbols

A	wing aspect ratio, b^2/S for monoplanes and $(Kb)^2/S$ for multiplanes (see app. C for values of K, Munk's span factor)
b	wing span (span of upper wing is given for biplane configurations), feet
c	wing chord, feet
c_d	section drag coefficient
c_p	specific fuel consumption, pounds of fuel per brake horsepower per hour
c_r	wing root chord, feet
c_t	wing tip chord, feet
c_l	section lift coefficient
$c_{l,max}$	section maximum lift coefficient
$c_l c/C_L \bar{c}$	span-loading parameter
$\bar{c}$	mean aerodynamic chord, feet
C_D	drag coefficient
$C_{D,0}$	zero-lift drag coefficient
$C_{D,min}$	minimum drag coefficient
C_L	lift coefficient
$C_{L,max}$	maximum lift coefficient
C_m	pitching-moment coefficient
$\bar{C}_F$	skin friction parameter (drag coefficient based on total wetted area)
D	drag, pounds

505

f	drag area, $C_{D,0}S$
g	acceleration due to gravity
h	altitude, feet
h_{ce}	service ceiling, feet
h_{SL}	sea-level rate of climb, feet per minute
$\overline{H}$	power parameter,

$$\sqrt[3]{\frac{P_0\lambda}{f\sigma}}$$

ι	aircraft length, feet
l_L	landing field length, feet
l_T	takeoff field length, feet
$(L/D)_{max}$	maximum lift-drag ratio
M	Mach number
P	engine power, horsepower
P_0	maximum power available at sea level, horsepower
R	aircraft range, statute miles
R_D	mission radius, statute miles
R_F	ferry range, statute miles
R_h	hypothetical range, statute miles
S	wing area (includes both wings for biplanes), square feet
T	time required to climb to specified altitude, minutes; or thrust, pounds
T/W	thrust-to-weight ratio or thrust loading
t/c	airfoil-section thickness ratio, percent
$\overline{U}$	useful load fraction, $1-(W_e/W_g)$
V	speed, miles per hour (statute miles)
V_c	cruising speed, miles per hour (statute miles)
V_{ce}	cost-economical cruising speed, miles per hour (statute miles)
V_{max}	maximum speed, miles per hour (statute miles)
V_S	stalling speed, miles per hour (statute miles)
W	aircraft weight, pounds

W_e	aircraft empty weight, pounds
W_g	aircraft design gross weight, pounds
W_g/S	wing loading for design gross weight, pounds per square foot
W_g/P_0	power loading for design gross weight, pounds per horsepower
W_L	maximum aircraft landing weight, pounds
W_{max}	aircraft maximum gross weight, pounds
W_p	payload weight, pounds
W_t	propulsion-system weight, pounds
W_t/W_g	engine weight fraction
W/P	power loading, pounds per horsepower
W/S	wing loading, pounds per square foot
y	distance along wing span measured from wing centerline, feet
α	angle of attack, degrees
α_0	section angle of attack (fig. 5.6), degrees
γ	percentage of maximum sea-level power
η	semispan wing position, $2y/b$; or overall propulsion-system efficiency, percent
η_c	engine cycle efficiency, percent
η_p	propulsive efficiency, percent
Λ	wing sweepback angle, measured at wing quarter-chord line unless otherwise noted, degrees
λ	wing taper ratio, Tip chord/Root chord
ρ	atmospheric density
ρ_0	atmospheric density at sea level
σ	atmospheric density ratio ρ/ρ_0

Abbreviations

AAHS	American Aviation Historical Society
AIAA	American Institute of Aeronautics and Astronautics
AIRCO	Aircraft Manufacturing Company
ALCM	air-launched cruise missile
ALDCS	active load distribution control system
ATA	Air Transport Association

AWACS	airborne warning and control system
BOAC	British Overseas Airways Corporation
CAP	combat air patrol
FAA	Federal Aviation Administration
FAR	Federal Air Regulations
Flt. Intl.	*Flight International Magazine*
FOD	foreign object damage
JATO	jet-assisted takeoff
LABS	low-altitude bombing system
LaRC	Langley Research Center
LMAL	Langley Memorial Aeronautical Laboratory
MAP	Military Assistance Program
mfr	manufacturer
NACA	National Advisory Committee for Aeronautics
NASA	National Aeronautics and Space Administration
NASM	National Air and Space Museum
NBAA	National Business Aircraft Association
RAF	Royal Air Force
RPM	revenue passenger mile
SAC	Strategic Air Command
SCRAM	short-range attack missile
STOL	short takeoff and landing
STOVL	short takeoff and vertical landing
ukn	unknown
USAF	United States Air Force
USAAF	United States Army Air Force
USN	United States Navy
VIFF	vectoring in forward flight
VSTOL	vertical/short takeoff and landing
VTOL	vertical takeoff and landing
WW	World War

Appendix C
Estimated Aerodynamic Parameters

Appendix C presents the methods employed for estimating the aerodynamic parameters given in tables I to IV in appendix A. The parameters were estimated from published performance data for the various aircraft. In most cases, the performance data in the tables formed the basis for the calculations. The methods are briefly described in the following paragraphs.

The zero-lift drag coefficient was determined from the equation

$$C_{D,0} = C_D - C_{D,i} \tag{C1}$$

where

$C_{D,0}$ zero-lift drag coefficient

C_D total drag coefficient for given combination of power, speed, and altitude

$C_{D,i}$ induced drag coefficient corresponding to same flight conditions as total drag coefficient

The total drag coefficient can be estimated from the following relationship:

$$C_D = \frac{550\eta P}{\frac{1}{2}\rho_0[\sigma S(1.47V)^3]} \tag{C2}$$

where

η propulsive efficiency
P engine power, horsepower
ρ_0 sea-level density, slugs per cubic foot
σ atmospheric density ratio for some altitude other than sea level

S   wing area, square feet
V   speed, statute miles per hour

Equation (C2) can be put in the form

$$C_D = 1.456 \times 10^5 \left(\frac{\eta P}{\sigma S V^3} \right) \qquad \text{(C3)}$$

by substituting a value of 0.002378 for the standard atmospheric density at sea level. Equation (C3) was used for estimating the value of the drag coefficient C_D. The values of propulsive efficiency η employed in equation (C3) varied between 0.70 and 0.85, depending on the aircraft, and were chosen on the basis of information contained in references 95 and 120.

The induced drag coefficient $C_{D,i}$ was obtained from

$$C_{D,i} = \frac{C_L{}^2}{\pi A \epsilon}$$

and

$$C_L = \frac{W}{\frac{1}{2} \rho_0 [\sigma S (1.47V)^2]}$$

which can be combined to give

$$C_{D,i} = \frac{4.822 \times 10^4}{A \epsilon \sigma^2 V^4} (W/S)^2 \qquad \text{(C4)}$$

where

W   weight, pounds
W/S   wing loading, pounds per square foot
ϵ airplane efficiency factor
A   aspect ratio, $K^2 b^2 / S$
b   wing span (upper wing span for biplanes and triplanes), feet
S   wing area (includes all wings for biplanes and triplanes), square feet
K   Munk's span factor (for biplanes and triplanes)

510

Munk's span factor is a function of the geometry of the multiplane wing arrangement and can be either less or greater than 1.0. On the basis of information given in references 46 and 103, an average value of the span factor of 1.1 was used for all biplane configurations, and values of K of 1.22 and 1.16, respectively, were used in computing the aspect ratios of the Fokker and Caproni triplanes discussed in chapter 2. Values of the airplane efficiency factor in the range of 0.70 to 0.75 were used, with the exact value dictated by the configuration and refinement of the aircraft.

The value of the maximum lift-drag ratio $(L/D)_{max}$ was computed by equation (3.20) given in chapter 3 of reference 90 as

$$(L/D)_{max} = \frac{1}{2} \sqrt{\frac{\pi A \epsilon}{C_{D,0}}} \tag{C5}$$

In addition to the assumptions described in the preceding paragraphs, the accuracy of the calculated aerodynamic parameters depends on two other important assumptions. First, the accuracy of the calculated results obviously depends upon the accuracy of the published information on the various aircraft; and, second, the accuracy depends on the completeness of the performance information. For example, can the power be determined for a given combination of speed and altitude. No general assessment of either of these possible sources of error can be made. Aerodynamic parameters for those cases in which the performance data were incomplete or could not be estimated with reasonable confidence were not included in the tables; and if comparative performance data for different aircraft showed unexplained anomalies, aerodynamic data were not presented for the aircraft whose published performance characteristics seemed questionable.

Appendix D
Biplane Terminology

The terminology used to describe the major features of a typical double-bay biplane of the World War I time period is illustrated in figure D.1. The number and arrangement of struts and wires employed in biplane design have varied greatly over the years; however, the terms indicated in the figure have survived and are still in use today in any discussion of modern-day sport or agricultural biplanes. A single-bay biplane, in contrast to the two-bay arrangement shown in figure D.1, has only one set of interplane struts between the wings on either side of the fuselage, and a triple-bay design has three sets of such struts on either side of the fuselage. In contrast to the incidence wires shown in the figure, many biplane designs have utilized a single strut, in an "N" arrangement, connecting the front and rear interplane struts (see the Travelair 4000 in figure 4.5, for example). This configuration eases the task of rigging, or aligning, the wings in the correct relation to each other and the fuselage. The proper rigging of wire-braced aircraft once formed an extremely important part of any aircraft erection, maintenance, or repair operation. Today, the experienced rigger is almost extinct, and the art is all but lost except for a few dedicated enthusiasts engaged in the restoration of antique aircraft or in the building and flying of sport biplanes. Decalage is a term, not illustrated in the figure, that is sometimes encountered in discussions of biplanes. It refers to the difference in angle of incidence at which the upper and lower wings are mounted on the aircraft.

More may be found on biplane terminology, construction, and assembly in references 26 and 79.

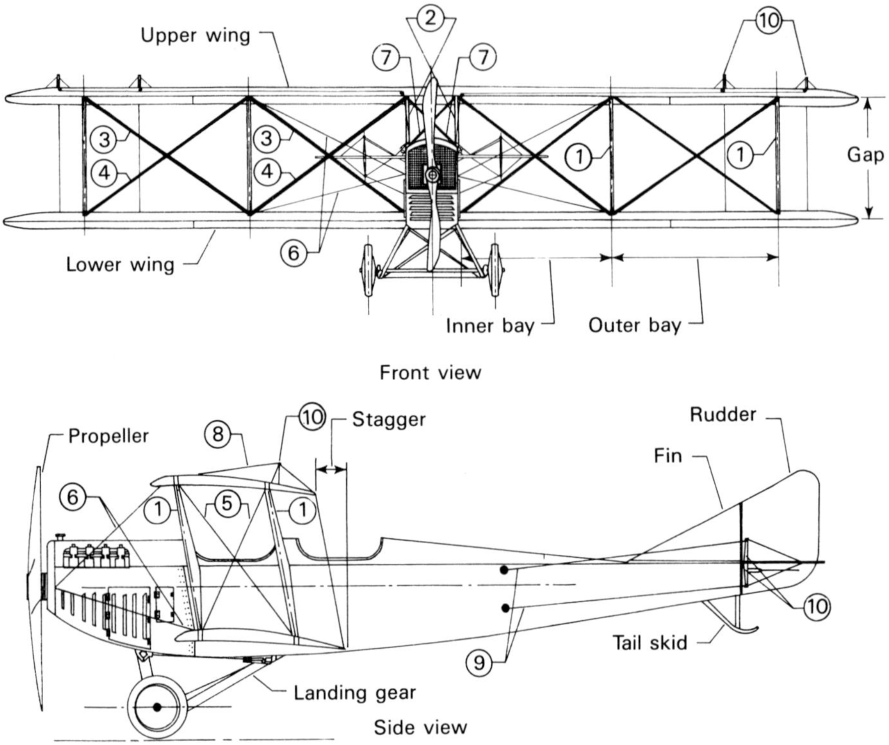
Upper wing
2
7
7
10
3
4
3
4
1
1
Gap
Lower wing
6
Inner bay
Outer bay
Front view
Propeller
8
10
Stagger
Rudder
Fin
6
1
5
1
10
Tail skid
9
Landing gear
Side view

1. Interplane struts
2. Cabane or center-section struts
3. Flying wires
4. Landing wires
5. Incidence or stagger wires
6. Drag wires
7. Center-section cross bracing
8. Aileron control wires
9. Elevator control wires
10. Control horn

Figure D.1 — Terminology of a double-bay biplane; World War I time period.

Appendix E

Mass-Flow Rate, Thrust, and Propulsive Efficiency

Among the advantages of the turbofan are that, for a given energy addition per unit time (fuel-flow rate), the turbofan will produce more thrust and have a higher propulsive efficiency than will a turbojet with a gas generator of the same size and level of technical sophistication as the turbofan. These advantages can be explained by the following highly simplified analysis of an idealized turbofan engine. Assume the air that enters the inlet of the engine to have a free-stream velocity of V_i and a uniform exhaust velocity from the fan and gas generator of V_e. The mass flow entering the inlet per unit time is $\dot{m}$. The thrust produced by the engine can then be expressed by the following simple relationship if the static pressure in the exhaust is assumed to have the free-stream static value where the exhaust velocity is measured and the momentum of the fuel itself is neglected:

$$T = \dot{m} (V_e - V_i) = \dot{m} \, \Delta V \qquad (E1)$$

where T is the thrust.

The amount of energy added to the flow by the fuel may be expressed as the difference between the kinetic energy per unit time entering and exhausting from the engine and is given as follows:

$$\dot{E} = \frac{\dot{m}}{2} \left[(V_i + \Delta V)^2 - V_i^2 \right] = \dot{m} \, \Delta V V_i \left(1 + \frac{1}{2} \frac{\Delta V}{V_i} \right) \qquad (E2)$$

or with the use of equation (E1),

$$= \dot{E} = T V_i \left(1 + \frac{1}{2} \frac{\Delta V}{V_i} \right) \qquad (E3)$$

515

The propulsive efficiency is defined as that fraction of the kinetic energy added to the mass flow $\dot{m}$ that is usefully employed in propelling the aircraft. The propulsive efficiency η_p can be expressed in the following form:

$$\eta_p = \frac{TV_i}{\dot{E}} \qquad \text{(E4)}$$

Substitution of equations (E1) and (E3) for the thrust and kinetic energy gives

$$\eta_p = \frac{2}{2 + \dfrac{\Delta V}{V_i}} \qquad \text{(E5)}$$

Equation (E3) clearly shows that for a given thrust level, the required rate of energy input is reduced as the value of $\Delta V/V_i$ is decreased. For a given thrust level, equation (E1) shows that as the value of ΔV is decreased, the mass-flow rate $\dot{m}$ must increase correspondingly. The most thrust is therefore obtained for a given energy input rate from the addition of a small velocity increment to a large mass-flow rate; and the propulsive efficiency, given by equation (E5), is increased as the value of ΔV is reduced. The turbofan engine therefore provides higher efficiency and more thrust than a turbojet engine with the same rate of energy input and having the same component (compressor, burner, and turbine) efficiencies.

Appendix F
Estimation of Overall Propulsion-System Efficiency

The overall propulsion-system efficiency discussed in chapter 10 is the ratio of the power usefully expended in propelling the aircraft to the heating value of the fuel consumed per unit time. The overall propulsion-system efficiency η is the product of the cycle efficiency η_c and the propulsive efficiency η_p. A simple method for estimating the overall propulsion-system efficiency is developed in the following for aircraft powered with either jet, turboprop, or reciprocating engines. The symbols used in appendix F are defined as follows:

c_P	specific fuel consumption, pounds of fuel per brake horsepower per hour
c_T	specific fuel consumption, pounds of fuel per pound of thrust per hour
H	heating value of fuel, British thermal units per pound
h	fuel-flow rate, pounds per hour
J	Joule's constant, 778 foot-pounds per British thermal unit
M	Mach number
P	power usefully expended in propelling the aircraft, foot-pounds per second
P_e	power developed by engine, horsepower
Q	heat added by fuel per unit time, British thermal units per second
T	thrust, pounds
V	velocity, feet per second

The jet propulsion system is considered first. In such a system the heat added per unit time is given by the following expression:

$$Q = \frac{HhJ}{3600} \qquad (F1)$$

and the power usefully expended in propelling the aircraft is

$$P = TV \tag{F2}$$

The overall propulsion-system efficiency is then given by

$$\eta = \frac{3600TV}{HhJ} \tag{F3}$$

If the heating value of the fuel is taken as 18 500 British thermal units per pound, the overall propulsion-system efficiency is given by the following simple expression:

$$\eta = \frac{0.00025V}{c_T} \tag{F4}$$

since

$$c_T = \frac{h}{T} \tag{F5}$$

Expressed as a percentage, equation (F4) becomes

$$\eta = \frac{0.025V}{c_T} \tag{F6}$$

Equation (F6) may also be expressed in terms of the Mach number as

$$\eta = \frac{24.3M}{c_T} \tag{F7}$$

where the speed of sound has been taken as 971 feet per second (this value being for altitudes above the tropopause).

An expression for the overall propulsion-system efficiency of propeller-driven aircraft, powered with either reciprocating or turboprop engines, will now be developed. The capability of these types of engines is usually expressed in terms of the power that they develop rather than their thrust. Consequently, the expression for the overall propulsion-system efficiency is developed in a slightly different way than that used for jet-propelled aircraft. The amount of power developed by the engine will first be related to the engine cycle efficiency η_c. The amount of heat added to the engine per unit time, given by equation (F1), is also applicable to propeller-driven aircraft and is used in forming the following relationship:

$$550P_e = \frac{\eta_c HhJ}{3600} \qquad (F8)$$

where the constant 550 converts the power P_e from horsepower to foot-pounds per second. If the specific fuel consumption c_P is defined as the amount of fuel used per brake horsepower per hour, the cycle efficiency may then be expressed as follows:

$$\eta_c = \frac{550(3600)}{18\ 500(778)c_P} \qquad (F9)$$

or

$$\eta_c = \frac{0.14}{c_P} \qquad (F10)$$

Expressed as a percentage, equation (F10) for the cycle efficiency becomes

$$\eta_c = \frac{14}{c_P} \qquad (F11)$$

If the propulsive efficiency η_p is taken as 86 percent, a reasonable average value, the overall propulsion-system efficiency becomes

$$\eta = \frac{12}{c_P} \qquad (F12)$$

Equations (F7) and (F12) were used in the construction of figure 10.2.

Appendix G

Reserve-Fuel Requirements for Transport Aircraft

Reserve-fuel requirements are discussed at some length in part 121 of the Federal Air Regulations.[G1] Specific rules for calculating the amount of reserve fuel are given by the Air Transport Association.[G2] The amount of reserve fuel given by these rules is in excess of minimum FAR requirements but is representative of current airline operational practices. The amount of reserve fuel specified by reference G2 depends upon the type of aircraft and the nature of its operation. For example, aircraft in domestic and international operations carry different amounts of reserve fuel, as do supersonic and subsonic transport aircraft. The reserve-fuel rules are also different for propeller-driven aircraft equipped with reciprocating engines and for turbine-powered aircraft.

The reserve-fuel requirements specified by reference G2 for subsonic turbine-powered aircraft employed in domestic and international operations are given as follows:

Domestic Operations

(1) Fly for 1 hour at normal cruise altitude at a fuel flow for end of cruise weight at the speed for 99 percent maximum range.

(2) Exercise a missed approach and climbout at the destination airport; fly to and land at an alternate airport 200 nautical miles distant.

[G1] "Certification and Operations: Domestic, Flag, and Supplemental Air Carriers and Commercial Operators of Large Aircraft," FAR Pt. 121, paragraph 121.195 (FAA, June 1974).

[G2] *Standard Method of Estimating Comparative Direct Operating Costs of Turbine Powered Transport Airplanes.* (Air Transportation Association of America, December 1967).

521

International Operations

(1) Fly for 10 percent of trip air time at normal cruise altitude at a fuel flow for end of cruise weight at the speed for 99 percent maximum range.

(2) Exercise a missed approach and climbout at the destination airport; fly to an alternate airport 200 nautical miles distant.

(3) Hold for 30 minutes at alternate airport at 1500 feet altitude.

(4) Descend and land at alternate airport.

Flight to Alternate Airport (All Airplanes)

(1) Power or thrust setting shall be for 99 percent of maximum subsonic range.

(2) Power setting for holding shall be for maximum endurance or the minimum speed for comfortable handling, whichever is greater.

(3) Cruise altitude shall be the optimum for best range except that it shall not exceed the altitude where cruise distance equals climb plus descent distance.

Appendix H
FAR Landing And Takeoff Field Lengths

The FAR landing and takeoff field lengths given in table VII contain certain built-in safety margins to allow for unanticipated situations. Brief and somewhat oversimplified descriptions of these distances for dry, hard-surface, level runways in zero-wind conditions are given below.

Landing Field Length

The landing field length is defined by the Federal Air Regulations for transport-category aircraft. Briefly, the landing distance is measured, horizontally, from the point at which the aircraft is 50 feet above the surface, in steady gliding flight at an approach speed not less than 1.3 times the stalling speed, to the point at which the aircraft is brought to a complete stop on a hard, dry, smooth runway surface.[H1] The FAR landing field length is obtained by dividing the measured landing distance by 0.6 in order to account for the possibility of variations in approach speed, touchdown point, and other deviations from standard procedures.[H2] A sketch depicting the FAR landing field length is shown in figure H.1. The landing field length as defined in figure H.1 usually appears in specifications for transport aircraft designed to the criteria of FAR part 25 and is the distance employed in table VII.

Takeoff Field Length

The FAR takeoff field length, often called the FAR balanced field length, contains certain inherent safety features to account for engine failure situations. This takeoff field length is defined in several slightly

---

[H1] "Airworthiness Standards: Transport Category Airplanes," FAR Pt. 25 (FAA, February 1, 1965).

[H2] "Certification and Operation: Domestic Flag, and Supplemental Air Carriers and Commercial Operators of Large Aircraft," FAR Pt. 121, paragraph 121.195 (FAA, June 1974).

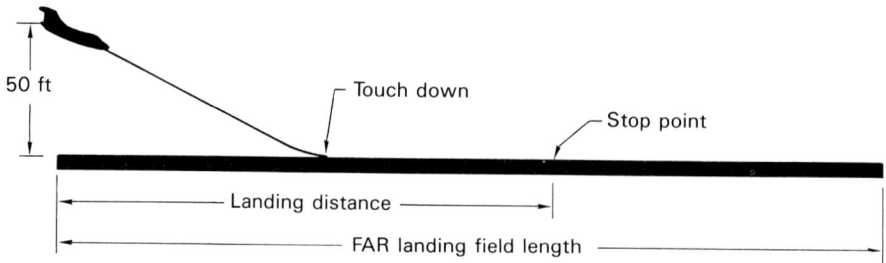

Figure H.1 — Landing field length.

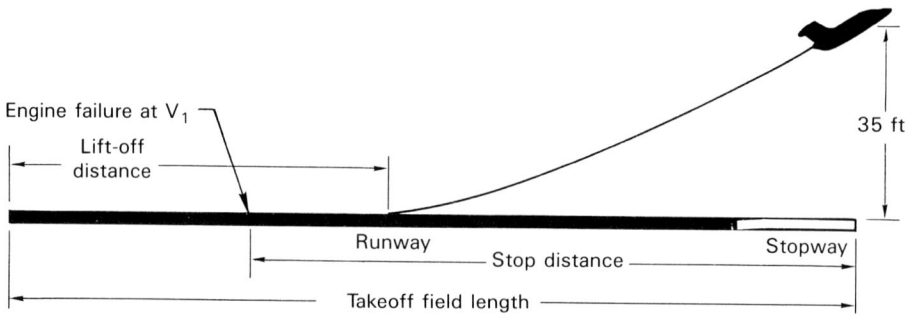

Figure H.2 — FAR balanced takeoff field length.

different ways and is described fully in reference H1. Briefly, if an engine should fail during the takeoff roll at a critical speed, called the decision speed V_1, the pilot is offered the option of two safe courses of action. He may elect to continue the takeoff on the remaining engines, in which case, the takeoff distance is defined as the distance from the point at which the takeoff run is initiated to the point where the aircraft has reached an altitude of 35 feet. In the second alternative, the pilot may elect to shut down all engines and apply full braking. The decision speed V_1 is chosen in such a way that the sum of the distance required to accelerate to V_1 and then decelerate to a stop is the same as the total distance for the case in which the takeoff is continued following engine failure. If an engine should fail before V_1 is reached, the aircraft is usually brought to a stop on the runway; whereas, if an engine fails at a speed greater than V_1, the takeoff is continued. The distances are based on smooth, hard, dry runway surfaces. A somewhat idealized sketch of the FAR takeoff field length is shown in figure H.2.

524

References

Part I

1. Grey, C. G., ed.: *All the World's Aircraft* (London: Sampson Low, Marston & Co., 1919).

2. Grey, C. G., ed.: *All the World's Aircraft* (London: Sampson Low, Marston & Co., 1922).

3. Grey, C. G.; and Bridgman, Leonard, eds.: *All the World's Aircraft* (London: Sampson Low, Marston & Co., 1928).

4. Grey, C. G.; and Bridgman, Leonard, eds.: *Jane's All the World's Aircraft* (London: Sampson Low, Marston & Co., 1931).

5. Grey, C. G.; and Bridgman, Leonard, eds.: *Jane's All the World's Aircraft* (London: Sampson Low, Marston & Co., 1933).

6. Grey, C. G.; and Bridgman, Leonard, eds.: *Jane's All the World's Aircraft* (London: Sampson Low, Marston & Co., 1934).

7. Grey, C. G.; and Bridgman, Leonard, eds.: *Jane's All the World's Aircraft* (London: Sampson Low, Marston & Co., 1936).

8. Grey, C. G.; and Bridgman, Leonard, eds.: *Jane's All the World's Aircraft* (London: Sampson Low, Marston & Co., 1937).

9. Grey, C. G.; and Bridgman, Leonard, eds.: *Jane's All the World's Aircraft* (London: Sampson Low, Marston & Co., 1938).

10. Grey, C. G.; and Bridgman, Leonard, eds.: *Jane's All the World's Aircraft* (London: Sampson Low, Marston & Co., 1939).

11. Bridgman, Leonard, ed.: *Jane's All the World's Aircraft, 1941* (Macmillan Co., c.1942).

12. Bridgman, Leonard, ed.: *Jane's All the World's Aircraft, 1945–46* (Macmillan Co., c.1946).

13. Bridgman, Leonard, ed.: *Jane's All the World's Aircraft, 1949–50* (McGraw-Hill).

14. Bridgman, Leonard, ed.: *Jane's All the World's Aircraft, 1955–56* (McGraw-Hill).

15. Taylor, John W. R., ed.: *Jane's All the World's Aircraft, 1973–74* (McGraw-Hill, c.1973).

16. Taylor, John W. R., ed.: *Jane's All the World's Aircraft, 1975–76* (Franklin Watts, c.1975).

17. Abbott, Ira H.; and Von Doenhoff, Albert E.: *Theory of Wing Sections* (Dover, c.1959).

18. Abbott, Ira H.; Von Doenhoff, Albert E.; and Stivers, Louis S., Jr.: *Summary of Airfoil Data,* NACA Rep. 824 (1945). (Supersedes NACA WR L–560.)

19. Aeronautical Chamber of Commerce of America, Inc.: *The Aircraft Year Book – For 1932,* vol. 14 (D. Van Nostrand Co., c.1932).

20. *The Aircraft of the World* (Doubleday & Co., 1965).

21. Allen, Richard Sanders: *Revolution in the Sky – Those Fabulous Lockheeds, the Pilots Who Flew Them* (Stephen Green Press, 1964).

22. Andrews, C. F.: *The SPAD XIII C.I,* no. 17 (Surrey, England: Profile Publishers, c.1965).

23. Angelucci, Enzo; and Matricardi, Paolo: *World Aircraft Origins – World War I* (Rand McNally & Co., 1975).

24. Angle, Glenn D., ed.: *Aerosphere – 1939* (Aircraft Publishers, c.1940).

25. Babington-Smith, Constance: *Testing Time: The Story of British Test Pilots and Their Aircraft* (Harper & Bro., 1961).

26. Bailey, C. G.: *The Complete Airman* (London: Methuen & Co., 1920).

27. Barnwell, F. S.; and Sayers, W. H.: *Airplane Design and a Simple Explanation of Inherent Stability* (Robert M. McBride & Co., 1917).

28. Bruce, J. M.: *The DeHavilland D.H.4,* no. 26 (Surrey, England: Profile Publishers, c.1965).

29. Bruce, J. M.: *The Fokker Monoplanes,* no. 38 (Surrey, England: Profile Publishers, c.1965).

30. Bruce, J. M.: *The Sopwith Camel F.I,* no. 31 (Surrey, England: Profile Publishers, c.1965).

31. Bruce, J. M.: *The Sopwith Dolphin,* no. 169 (Surrey, England: Profile Publishers, 1967).

32. Bruce, J. M.: *War Planes of the First World War, Fighters,* vol. I (Doubleday & Co., c.1965).

33. Bruce, J. M.: *War Planes of the First World War, Fighters,* vol. II (Doubleday & Co., c.1968).

34. Bruce, J. M.: *War Planes of the First World War, Fighters,* vol. III (Doubleday & Co., c.1969).

35. Bruce, J. M.: *War Planes of the First World War, Fighters,* vol. V (Doubleday & Co., c.1972).

36. Carter, Arthur W.: *Effect of Hull Length-Beam Ratio On the Hydrodynamic Characteristics of Flying Boats In Waves,* NACA TN 1782 (1949).

37. Carter, Arthur W.; and Haar, Marvin I.: *Hydrodynamic Qualities of a Hypothetical Flying Boat With a Low-Drag Hull Having a Length-Beam Ratio of 15.* NACA TN 1570 (1948).

38. Casey, Louis S.: "The First Non-Stop Coast-to-Coast Flight and the Historic T-2 Airplane," *Smithsonian Annals of Flight,* vol. I, no. 1 (Washington: Smithsonian Institution. 1964).

39. Child, S.; and Counter, C. F.: *A Historical Summary of the Royal Aircraft Factory and its Antecedents: 1878-1918,* rep. no. Aero. 2150 (British R.A.E., March 1947).

40. Christy, Joe: *Racing Planes Guide* (Sports Car Press, 1963).

41. Clark, D. H.: *What Were They Like to Fly?* (London: Ian Allen, 1964).

42. Coe, Paul L., Jr.: *Review of Drag Cleanup Tests in Langley Full-Scale Tunnel (From 1935 to 1945) Applicable to Current General Aviation Airplanes,* NASA TN D-8206 (1976).

43. Courtney, Frank T.: *The Eighth Sea* (Doubleday & Co., 1972).

44. Davies, R. E. G.: *Airlines of the United States – Since 1914* (London: Putnam & Co., 1972).

45. Dickey, Philip S.: "The Liberty Engine, 1918-1942," *Smithsonian Annals of Flight,* vol. I, no. 3 (Washington: Smithsonian Institution, 1968).

46. Diehl, Walter Stuart: *Engineering Aerodynamics,* rev. ed. (Ronald Press Co., c.1936).

47. Duval, G. R.: *British Flying-Boats and Amphibians – 1909–1952* (Aero Publishers, c.1966).

48. Ferri, Antonio: *Completed Tabulation in the United States of Tests of 24 Airfoils at High Mach Numbers (Derived From Interrupted Work at Guidonia, Italy, in the 1.31- by 1.74-Foot High-Speed Tunnel)*, NACA WR L–143 (1945). (Formerly NACA ACR L5E21.)

49. *Fifty Years of Aeronautical Research*, NASA EP–45 (1967).

50. Fokker, Anthony H. G.; and Gould, Bruce: *Flying Dutchman – The Life of Anthony Fokker* (Henry Holt & Co., c.1931).

51. Foxworth, Thomas G.: *The Speed Seakers* (Doubleday & Co., 1974).

52. Gibbs-Smith, Charles H.: *The Aeroplane – An Historical Survey of Its Origins and Development* (London: HMSO, 1960).

53. Gilruth, R. R.: *Requirements for Satisfactory Flying Qualities of Airplanes*, NACA Rep. 755 (1943). (Supersedes NACA ACR, Apr. 1941.)

54. *A Glimpse of Scientific Research on Fundamental Problems of Military and Civil Aircraft*, NACA (1936).

55. Gouge, A.: "Flying Boats and Their Possible Developments," *Journal of the Royal Aeronautical Society*, vol. XXXIX, no. 296 (August 1935).

56. Gray, George W.: *Frontiers of Flight – The Story of NACA Research* (Alfred A. Knopf, 1948).

57. Gray, Peter; and Thetford, Owen: *German Aircraft of the First World War* (London: Putman & Co., 1962).

58. Green, William: *Famous Bombers of the Second World War*, vol. I (Doubleday & Co., 1959).

59. Green, William: *Famous Bombers of the Second World War*, vol. II (Hanover House, 1960).

60. Green, William: *War Planes of the Second World War, Fighters*, vol. I (Hanover House, 1960).

61. Green, William: *War Planes of the Second World War, Fighters*, vol. II (Hanover House, 1961).

62. Green, William: *War Planes of the Second World War, Fighters*, vol. III (Doubleday & Co., 1962).

63. Green, William: *War Planes of the Second World War, Fighters*, vol. IV (Doubleday & Co., 1960).

64. Green, William: *War Planes of the Second World War, Flying Boats,* vol. V (Doubleday & Co., 1962).

65. Grosz, Peter M.: *The Gotha GI – GV,* no. 115 (Surrey, England: Profile Publishers, c.1966).

66. Gruenhagen, Robert W.: *Mustang – The Story of the P–51 Fighter,* rev. ed. (Arco Pub. Co., c.1976).

67. Gunston, Bill, ed.: *The Illustrated Encyclopedia of Propeller Airliners* (Exeter Books, 1980).

68. Haddow, G. W.; and Grosz, Peter M.: *The German Giants – The Story of the R-Planes, 1914–1918,* second ed. (Funk and Wagnalls, 1969).

69. Hadingham, Evan: *The Fighting Triplanes* (Macmillan Co., 1969).

70. Hallion, Richard P.: *Legacy of Flight – The Guggenheim Contribution to American Aviation* (University of Washington Press, c.1977).

71. Hegener, Henri: *Fokker – The Man and the Aircraft* (Letchworth, Herts, England: Harleyford Publishers, 1961).

72. Hoerner, Sighard F.: *Fluid-Dynamic Drag* (Brick Town, New Jersey: Hoerner Fluid Dynamics, c.1965).

73. Hunsaker, J. C.: *Forty Years of Aeronautical Research,* publ. 4237 (Washington: Smithsonian Institution, 1956).

74. *Index of NACA Technical Publications – 1915–1949,* NACA (1949).

75. Jackson, A. J.: *British Civil Aircraft – 1919–1959,* vol. II (London: Putnam & Co., 1960).

76. Jacobs, Eastman, N.: *Preliminary Report on Laminar-Flow Airfoils and New Methods Adopted for Airfoil and Boundary-Layer Investigations,* NACA WR L-345 (1939).

77. Jones, Robert T.: *Wing Plan Forms for High Speed Flight,* NACA Rep. 863 (1947). (Supersedes NACA TN 1033.)

78. Juptner, Joseph P.: *U.S. Civil Aircraft,* vol. II (ATC 101–ATC 200) (Aero Publishers, c.1964).

79. Klemin, Alexander: *Aeronautical Engineering and Airplane Design* (Gardner Moffat Co., 1918).

80. Knott, Captain Richard C.: *The American Flying Boat, an Illustrated History* (Annapolis, Maryland: Naval Institute Press, 1979).

81. Kurt, Franklin T.: *Water Flying* (Macmillan Co., 1974).

82. Lamberton, W. M., comp.: *Fighter Aircraft of the 1914–1918 War* (Letchworth, Herts, England: Harleyford Publishers, 1960).

83. Lamberton, W. M.: *Reconnaissance and Bomber Aircraft of the 1914–1918 War* (Letchworth, Herts, England: Harleyford Publishers, 1962).

84. Larkins, William T.: *The Ford Tri-Motor*, no. 156 (Surrey, England: Profile Publishers, c.1967).

85. Lewis, Cecil: *Farewell to Wings* (London: Temple Press Books, 1964).

86. Lindbergh, Charles A.: *The Spirit of St. Louis* (Charles Scribner's Sons, 1953).

87. Lippincott, Harvey: "The Navy Gets an Engine," *Journal of the American Aviation Historical Society*, vol. 6, no. 4 (1961).

88. Loening, Grover: *Amphibian, The Story of the Loening Biplane* (Greenwich, Connecticut: New York Graphic Society, 1973).

89. Loening, Grover: *Our Wings Grow Faster* (Doubleday, Doran & Co., 1935).

90. Loftin, Laurence K., Jr.: *Subsonic Aircraft: Evolution and the Matching of Size to Performance*, NASA RP–1060 (1980).

91. Mikesh, Robert C.: *Albatros D.Va German Fighter of World War I* (Washington: Smithsonian Institution Press, 1980).

92. Miller, Ronald; and Sawers, David: *The Technical Development of Modern Aviation* (Praeger, c.1968).

93. Munson, Kenneth: *Flying Boats and Seaplanes Since 1910* (Macmillan Co., 1971).

94. Munson, Kenneth: *The Pocket Encyclopedia of Aircraft in Color. Bomber, Patrol and Reconnaissance Aircraft, 1914–1918* (Macmillan Co., 1968).

95. Nelson, Wilbur C.: *Airplane Propeller Principles* (John Wiley & Sons, 1944).

96. Nowarra, H. J.; and Brown, Kimbrough S.: *Von Richtofen and the Flying Circus* (Letchworth, Herts, England: Harleyford Publishers, 1964).

97. Parkinson, John B.: *Appreciation and Determination of the Hydrodynamic Qualities of Seaplanes*, NACA TN 1290 (1947).

98. Paterson, J. H.: "Recent Developments in the Hydrodynamic Design of Seaplanes," *Journal of the Royal Aeronautical Society*, vol. 59, no. 533 (May 1955) pp. 349–355.

99. *Pedigree of Champions – Boeing Since 1916,* doc. no. D4889, fourth ed. (Boeing Co., 1977).

100. Penrose, Harold: *British Aviation. The Great War and Armistice – 1915–1919* (London: Putnam & Co., 1969).

101. Perkins, Courtland D.: *The Development of Airplane Stability and Control Technology – 1969 Von Karman Lecture,* AIAA Paper No. 69–1137 (October 1969).

102. Phillips, William H.: *Appreciation and Prediction of Flying Qualities,* NACA Rep. 927 (1949). (Supersedes NACA TN 1670.)

103. Reid, Elliott G.: *Applied Wing Theory,* first ed. (McGraw-Hill, 1932).

104. *Research and Development Contributions to Aviation Progress (RADCAP) – Executive Summary,* U.S. Air Force (August 1972). (Available as NASA CR–129574.)

105. Stack, John: *Compressibility Effects in Aeronautical Engineering,* NACA ACR (August 1941).

106. Stack, John: "Compressible Flows in Aeronautics," *Journal of Aeronautical Science,* vol. 12, no. 2 (April 1945) pp. 127–143.

107. Stack, John; Lindsey, W. F.; and Littell, Robert E.: *The Compressibility Burble and the Effect of Compressibility on Pressures and Forces Acting on an Airfoil,* NACA Rep. 646 (1938).

108. Stack, John; Draley, Eugene C.; Delano, James B.; and Feldman, Lewis: *Investigation of the NACA 4–(3)(08)–03 and NACA 4–(3)(08)–045 Two-Blade Propellers at Forward Mach Numbers to 0.725 To Determine the Effects of Compressibility and Solidity on Performance,* NACA Rep. 999 (1950).

109. Swanborough, Gordon; and Bowers, Peter M.: *United States Navy Aircraft Since 1911* (Funk & Wagnalls, c.1968).

110. Tallman, Frank: *Flying the Old Planes* (Doubleday & Co., 1973).

111. Taylor, C. Fayette: *Aircraft Propulsion, a Review of the Evolution of Aircraft Piston Engines* (Washington: Smithsonian Institution, 1971).

112. Taylor, John W. R., ed.: *Combat Aircraft of the World – From 1909 to the Present* (G. P. Putnam's Sons, c.1969).

113. Taylor, John W. R.: *Flight – A Pictorial History From the Wright Brothers to Supersonic* (Peebles Press International, 1974).

114. Taylor, John W. R., ed.: *Jane's 100 Significant Aircraft, 1909–1969* (McGraw-Hill, 1969).

115. Taylor, John W. R., ed.: *The Lore of Flight* (Crescent Books, 1976).

116. Truscott, Starr: *The NACA Tank – A High-Speed Towing Basin for Testing Models of Seaplane Floats*, NACA Rep. 470 (1933).

117. Vorderman, Don: *The Great Air Races* (Doubleday & Co., 1969).

118. Wagner, Ray: *American Combat Planes* (Hanover House, 1960).

119. Wagner, Ray; and Nowarra, Heinz: *German Combat Planes* (Doubleday & Co., 1971).

120. Weick, Fred E.: *Aircraft Propeller Design* (McGraw-Hill, 1930).

121. Wigton, Don, comp.: *From Jenny to Jet – Pictorial Histories of the World's Great Airlines* (Bonanza Books, c.1963).

122. Wilson, R. C.: *Preliminary Airplane Design* (Pitman Publishing Co., 1942).

123. Wright, T. P.; and Luburg, G. A.: "Seaplane Design," *Transactions of the American Society of Mechanical Engineering*, vol. 52, part I (1930), pp. 57–60.

124. Yates, Campbell C.; and Riebe, John M.: *Effect Of Length-Beam Ratio on the Aerodynamic Characteristics of Flying Boat Hulls*, NACA TN 1305 (1947).

Part II

125. Bridgman, Leonard, ed.: *Jane's All the World's Aircraft, 1952–53* (McGraw-Hill Book Co.).

126. Bridgman, Leonard, ed.: *Jane's All the World's Aircraft, 1954–55* (McGraw-Hill Book Co.).

127. Taylor, John W. R., ed.: *Jane's All the World's Aircraft, 1966–67* (McGraw-Hill Book Co., c.1966).

128. Taylor, John W. R., ed.: *Jane's All the World's Aircraft, 1970–71* (McGraw-Hill Book Co., c.1970).

129. Taylor, John W. R., ed.: *Jane's All the World's Aircraft, 1974–75* (Franklin Watts, c.1974).

130. Taylor, John W. R., ed.: *Jane's All the World's Aircraft, 1980–81* (Jane's Publishing Co., c.1980).

131. Taylor, John W. R., ed.: *Jane's Pocketbook of Commercial Transport Aircraft* (Macmillan Co., c. 1973).

132. Abbott, Ira H.; Von Doenhoff, Albert E.; and Stivers, Louis S., Jr.: *Summary of Airfoil Data*, NACA Rep. 824 (1945). (Supersedes NACA WR L–560.)

133. *The Aircraft Gas Turbine Engine and Its Operation*, Part No. PWA 182408, PWA Oper. Instr. 200 (Pratt & Whitney Aircraft, June 1952). (Reprinted with revisions May 1974.)

134. Anderson, Fred: *Northrop, An Aeronautical History* (Northrop Corp., 1976).

135. Anderton, David A.: *The Martin B–57 Night Intruders & General Dynamics RB–57F* (Windsor, Berkshire, England: Profile Publishers, 1973).

136. Anderton, David A.: *LTV(Vought) A–7A/E Corsair II* (Windsor, Berkshire, England: Profile Publishers, 1972).

137. Andrews, C. F.: *Vickers Aircraft Since 1908* (Funk & Wagnalls, 1969).

138. Baals, Donald D.; and Corliss, William R.: *Wind Tunnels of NASA*, NASA SP–440 (1981).

139. Becker, John V.: *The High-Speed Frontier, 1920–1950*, NASA SP–445 (1980).

140. Boyne, Walter J.; and Lopez, Donald S., eds.: *The Jet Age, Forty Years of Jet Aviation* (Washington: Smithsonian Institution, 1979).

141. Boyne, Walter J.: *Messerschmitt Me 262, Arrow to the Future* (Washington: Smithsonian Institution Press, 1980).

142. Busemann, A.: *Aerodynamic Lift at Supersonic Speeds*, Ae. Techl. 1201, Rep. No. 2844 (British A.R.C., February 3, 1937). (From Luftfahrtsforschung, Bd. 12, Nr. 6, October 3, 1935, pp. 210–220.)

143. Busemann, A.: *Swept-Back Wings at High Speeds* (Dayton, Ohio: Headquarters Air Materiel Command, 1946).

144. "Business Jet and Turbofan Directory," *Flight International*, vol. 120, no. 3784 (Nov. 14, 1981).

145. *Case Study in Aircraft Design—The Boeing 727* (AIAA Professional Study Series, September 14, 1978).

146. *The Commercial Air Transport Market—1976–1991*, Rep. C1–804–4022A (Douglas Aircraft Co., October 1976).

147. "Commercial Aircraft of the World," *Flight International*, vol. 104, no. 3370 (October 18, 1973).

148. "Commercial Aircraft of the World," *Flight International*, vol. 112, no. 3578 (October 8, 1977).

149. "Commercial Aircraft of the World," *Flight International*, vol. 114, no. 3634 (November 11, 1978).

150. "Commercial Aircraft of the World," *Flight International*, vol. 122, no. 3833 (October 23, 1982).

151. Constant, Edward W., II: *The Origins of the Turbojet Revolution* (The John Hopkins University Press, 1980).

152. Davies, R. E. G.: *Airlines of the United States — Since 1914* (London: Putnam & Co., c.1972).

153. Donlan, Charles J.: *An Assessment of the Airplane Drag Problem at Transonic and Supersonic Speeds*, NACA RM L54F16 (1954).

154. Donlan, Charles J.; and Weil, Joseph: *Characteristics of Swept Wings at High Speeds*, NACA RM L52A15 (1952).

155. *The Evolution of Aircraft Wing Design* (AIAA, 1980).

156. *FAA Statistical Handbook of Aviation* (U.S. Department of Transportation, 1968).

157. Fabri, J., ed.: *Air Intake Problems in Supersonic Propulsion* (Pergaman Press, 1958).

158. Garrard, Wilfred C.: *The Lockheed C–5 Case Study in Aircraft Design* (AIAA Professional Study Series).

159. Gray, George W.: *Frontiers of Flight – The Story of NACA Research* (Alfred A. Knopf, 1948).

160. Green, William: *War Planes of the Second World War – Fighters*, vol. I (Hanover House, 1960).

161. Green, William; and Swanborough, Gordon: *The Illustrated Encyclopedia of the World's Commercial Aircraft* (London: Salamander Books, 1978).

162. Green, William; and Swanborough, Gordon: *The World's Great Fighter Aircraft* (Crescent Books, 1981).

163. Gunston, Bill, ed.: *The Illustrated History of Fighters* (London: Phoebus Publishing Co., 1981).

164. Heinemann, Edward H.; and Rausa, Rosario: *Ed Heinemann, Combat Aircraft Designer* (Annapolis, Maryland: Naval Institute Press, 1980).

165. Heinkel, Ernst: *He 1000* (London: Hutchinson & Co., 1956).

166. Hertz, Terrence J.; Shirk, Michael H.; Ricketts, Rodney H.; and Weisshar, Terrence A.: "On the Track of Practical Forward-Swept Wings," *Astronautics and Aeronautics*, vol. 20, no. 1 (January 1982).

167. "International Business Jet and Turboprop Directory," *Flight International,* vol. 113, no. 3591 (January 14, 1978).

168. "International Turbine Engine Directory," *Flight International,* vol. 113, no. 3590 (January 7, 1978).

169. Jackson, A. J.: *De Havilland Aircraft – Since 1915* (London: Putnam & Co., c.1962).

170. Jones, Lloyd S.: *U.S. Bombers* (Aero Publishers, 1974).

171. Jones, Lloyd S.: *U.S. Fighters* (Aero Publishers, 1975).

172. Jones, Robert T.: *Wing Plan Forms for High-Speed Flight,* NACA Rep. 863 (1947). (Supersedes NACA TN 1033.)

173. Kinnaman, E. Berkeley: "Flutter Analysis of Complex Airplanes by Experimental Methods," *Journal of Aeronautical Science,* vol. 19, no. 9 (September 1952) pp. 577–584.

174. Knott, Captain Richard C.: *The American Flying Boat, an Illustrated History* (Annapolis, Maryland: Naval Institute Press, 1979).

175. Lippisch, Alexander: *The Delta Wing, History and Development* (The Iowa State University Press, 1981).

176. Loftin, Laurence K., Jr.: *Subsonic Aircraft: Evolution and the Matching of Size to Performance,* NASA RP–1060 (1980).

177. "Military Aircraft Census," *Flight International,* vol. 118, no. 3722 (September 6, 1980).

178. Miller, Ronald; and Sawers, David: *The Technical Development of Modern Aviation* (Praeger, c.1968).

179. Nicolai, Leland M.: *Fundamentals of Aircraft Design* (University of Dayton Press, 1975).

180. Nichols, Mark R.: *Aerodynamics of Airframe-Engine Integration of Supersonic Aircraft,* NASA TN D–3390 (1966).

181. *1973/74 Aerospace Facts and Figures* (Aero-Space Industries Assoc. of America, c.1973).

182. *Pedigree of Champions—Boeing Since 1916,* doc. no. D4889, fourth ed. (Boeing Co., 1977).

183. Polhamus, Edward C.; and Hallissy, Joseph M., Jr.: *Effect of Airplane Configuration on Static Stability at Subsonic and Transonic Speeds,* NACA RM L56A09a (1956).

184. Polhamus, Edward C.; and Toll, Thomas A.: *Research Related to Variable Sweep Aircraft Developments,* NASA TM 83121 (1981).

185. *Progress of NASA Research Relating to Noise Alleviation of Large Subsonic Jet Aircraft,* NASA SP–189 (1968).

186. Reed, Arthur: *F–104 Starfighter* (Charles Scribner's Sons, 1981).

187. *Research and Development Contributions to Aviation Progress (RADCAP) – Executive Summary*, U.S. Air Force (August 1972). (Available as NASA CR–129574.)

188. Shacklady, Edward: *The Gloster Meteor* (MacDonald Aircraft Monographs, Doubleday & Co., 1963).

189. Spreeman, Kenneth P.: *Design Guide for Pitch-Up Evaluation and Investigation at High Subsonic Speeds of Possible Limitations Due to Wing-Aspect-Ratio Variations*, NASA TM X–26 (1959).

190. Stroud, John: *Soviet Transport Aircraft Since 1945* (Funk & Wagnalls, 1968).

191. Swanborough, Gordon; and Bowers, Peter M.: *United States Navy Aircraft Since 1911* (Funk & Wagnalls, 1968).

192. Taylor, John W. R., ed.: *Combat Aircraft of the World – From 1909 to the Present* (G. P. Putnam's Sons, c.1969).

193. Taylor, John W. R.; and Swanborough, Gordon: *Military Aircraft of the World* (Charles Scribner's Sons, 1971).

194. Taylor, John W. R., ed.: *Jane's 100 Significant Aircraft – 1909–1969* (McGraw-Hill, c.1969).

195. Taylor, Robert T.; and Ray, Edward J.: "Factors Affecting the Stability of T-Tail Transports," *Journal of Aircraft*, vol. 3, no. 4 (July–August 1966) pp. 359–364.

196. Thoren, R. L.: *Recent Engineering Advances on the Lockheed L–1011*, AIAA Paper No. 69–828 (July 1969).

197. Torenbeek, Egbert: *Synthesis of Subsonic Airplane Design* (The Netherlands: Delft University Press, c.1976).

198. Truelsen, Richard: *The Grumman Story* (Praeger, 1976).

199. "Turbine Aero-Engines of the World," *Flight International*, vol. 119, no. 3741 (January 17, 1981).

200. Wagner, Ray: *American Combat Planes*, third enlarged ed. (Doubleday & Co., 1982).

201. Wagner, Ray; and Nowarra, Heinz: *German Combat Planes* (Doubleday & Co., 1971).

202. Whitcomb, Richard T.: *A Study of the Zero-Lift Drag-Rise Characteristics Of Wing-Body Combinations Near the Speed of Sound*, NACA RM L52H08 (1952).

203. Whitcomb, Richard T.; and Fischetti, Thomas L.: *Development of a Supersonic Area Rule and an Application to the Design of a Wing-Body Combination Having High Lift-To-Drag Ratios*, NACA RM L53H31a (1953).

204. Wigton, Don, comp.: *From Jenny to Jet – Pictorial Histories of the World's Great Airlines* (Bonanza Books, c.1963).

205. Wilkinson, Paul H.: *Aircraft Engines of the World – 1966/67,* rev. ed. (publ. by author (5900 Kingswood Road, N.W., Washington, D.C. 20014), c.1967).

206. Wooldridge, E. T., Jr.: *The P–80 Shooting Star – Evolution of a Jet Fighter* (Washington: Smithsonian Institution Press, 1979).

207. "World's Air Forces," *Flight International,* vol. 120, no. 3769 (August 1, 1981).

208. "World Airline Directory," *Flight International,* vol. 119, no. 3758 (May 16, 1981).

209. "World's Airliner Census," *Flight International,* vol. 120, no. 3789 (December 19, 1981).

210. "World Light Turbine Engine Directory," *Flight International,* vol. 117, no. 3696 (January 19, 1980).

Index

546

About the Author

Laurence K. Loftin, Jr. was born in Lynchburg, Virginia, and was graduated from the University of Virginia with a B.S. degree in Mechanical Engineering in 1943. He joined the staff of the Langley Research Center in 1944. In a variety of positions, he engaged in and supervised research in aerodynamics and aeroelasticity, and in 1958 was chosen to be Technical Assistant to the Langley Director. In 1961 he was named Assistant Director of the Langley Research Center with responsibility for all aeronautical research; and in 1970 was named Director for Aeronautics. Mr. Loftin, on assignment from NASA, served as Assistant for Aeronautics in the office of the Assistant Secretary of the Air Force for Research and Development from July 1971 to July 1972. He was chief Aeronautical Engineer at Langley from July 1972 until his retirement from NASA in December 1973. Mr. Loftin is now actively engaged in teaching, writing, consulting, and research studies.

Mr. Loftin is the author of numerous technical papers dealing with various aspects of aeronautics, and has published a highly regarded textbook dealing with aircraft design and development.

He is a member of the American Aviation Historical Society, and the Experimental Aircraft Association, and is an Associate Fellow of the American Institute of Aeronautics and Astronautics. He has received the Langley Research Center Special Achievement Award for Outstanding Leadership and the NASA Exceptional Service Medal for his significant contributions to aeronautical development. He has also been cited by the Air Force and the FAA for contributions to aeronautics.

Mr. Loftin resides in Newport News, Virginia.

☆ U.S. GOVERNMENT PRINTING OFFICE: 1985 — 474-144